# BANNOCKBURN
# 1314

# CHRIS BROWN

# BANNOCKBURN
# 1314

## *A New History*

First published 2008

The History Press Ltd
The Mill, Brimscombe Port
Stroud, Gloucestershire, GL5 2QG
www.thehistorypress.co.uk

British Library Cataloguing in Publication Data.
A catalogue record for this book is available from the British Library.

ISBN 978 0 7524 4600 4

Typesetting and origination by The History Press Ltd.
Printed and bound in Great Britain

# Contents

# Preface

Why write a book on Bannockburn at all? We can never hope to achieve a complete and undisputed understanding of any historical event, let alone a battle.

Bannockburn was only one battle in a very long war, or rather, a long series of wars, though all of them have the same issue at stake – the conquest or independence of Scotland as a political entity. The rarity of major battles of manoeuvre is such that none of the larger battles of the Wars of Independence can be considered 'typical', so Bannockburn is not really 'representative' of the general course or nature of the conflicts. Bannockburn was far from being typical in scale; in the half century between 1296 and 1346 there were only a handful of general engagements that involved more than a few thousand men – Stirling Bridge, Falkirk, Halidon Hill and Neville's Cross – and the latter is, arguably, not really a battle about the survival or otherwise of the Scottish kingdom, so much as a facet of the Hundred Years War. Even the capture of King David did not really pose a threat to the independence of his realm. Despite their defeat, the Scots seem to have had no shortage of confidence in their ability to withstand Edward III, and Edward himself seems to have taken little or no interest in restoring the short-lived administration which had held much of southern Scotland in the 1330s for the English crown.

Operationally, Bannockburn was far from being typical of the general conduct of the war. There are examples of a similar tactical policy in action at the battle of Loudon and elsewhere. Myton[1] and Culblean,[2] on the other hand, are battles in which mounted cavalry played no part at all. The majority of the actions that took place in Scotland between 1296 and 1314 – most of which are unknown outside the academic community – were encounters between rather modest bodies of heavy cavalry[3] or sieges of the towns and castles[4] which formed the focal points of local political, commercial, social and judicial activity.[5]

The battle occurred nearly seven hundred years ago, and so it should come as no surprise that the evidence tends to be limited, both in terms of quantity and quality. Even when studied in relation to the terrain, the material is often less informative than we might hope, indeed, study of the site may actually bring other factors into mind which might otherwise have escaped us. Relating written accounts to modern maps can be a frustrating – and not necessarily a rewarding – exercise. We may be confident that the burn we find on a map is the one referred to by this or that writer, but is it still in the same place? Has its course, width or current been affected by the construction of roads, railways or housing? Were its banks more treacherous in the past than they are today? Crucially, even if we are utterly certain that 'this' is the burn that a given force crossed on a given day, we cannot be so certain that it did so at any particular point in the water's course.

Maps or diagrams of battles often present difficulties of their own. The symbols used to denote formations on the battlefield seldom bear any in-scale resemblance to the size or shape of those formations. To some extent this is obviously a matter of ensuring that the reader can identify the formations; a product of showing the course of the battle in a map that is too small to allow the unit symbols to be depicted in the same scale as the geographical features. This is not a problem unique to battle diagrams; the symbol used to denote churches by the Ordnance Survey is not related to the physical size of the church in question. The combat elements of medieval armies were little more than specks on the landscape; they were not large and the majority of the men fought in very close order – something approaching one square metre per man for close-combat infantry, and perhaps six to eight square metres for every man-at-arms. It is quite possible that the entirety of Edward II's army at Bannockburn could have been seated in Wimbledon's Centre Court, which has a capacity of 16,000 and that all of King Robert's spearmen could – at a pinch – have stood on one full-size rugby pitch.

Further, we cannot rely on maps to show all of the features which might affect manoeuvre. A low mound or long ditch might have a dramatic influence on the course of a fight, but be too insignificant to appear on a map.[6] More importantly, few people spend enough time reading maps to really appreciate the extent to which visibility is limited by terrain. This is a matter of considerable importance. In an age when the fastest mode of transport was the horse, the advantage conferred on the army with the upper hand in reconnaissance was considerable. The commander who could obtain a position that allowed him to observe the approach of the enemy, whilst keeping his own forces hidden from view, could deploy his troops to their greatest advantage in the light of observations and deductions made from the enemy's order of march. If he could keep his own troops out of sight until the last moment, he could be reasonably confident that his enemy would not be able to redeploy his units in the most appropriate manner without considerable time and trouble.

The conduct and progress of medieval engagements once battle was joined is often, though not always, a good deal easier to follow if one has a reasonable understanding of the nature of the troops – their equipment, their approach to combat and, in many cases, some understanding of that crucial tool of medieval life, the horse. Without that knowledge it is easy to make deductions that do not stand the test of rational examination. There is, for example, a widely accepted mental picture of Sir William Wallace as a large man, clad in plaid and wielding a two-handed sword from the saddle. Putting aside the fact that two-handed swords were not the weapon of the day in the late thirteenth century, a moment's thought about the practicalities of using such a weapon on horseback, should be enough to dispel the suggestion instantly. Nonetheless, the image persists.

The purpose of this study is to relate the information contained in the contemporary sources to what we know of the military practice of the day and, so far as is possible, to the nature of the terrain. An obvious problem lies in the fact that we cannot precisely identify the sites of the different actions that took place on the 23rd/24th June 1314, but this is not so much of an issue as one might expect. Whether an engagement occurred a thousand metres to the west or east of a specific spot is only significant if aspects of the terrain would conflict with the existing body of evidence. The action that occurred in the vicinity of St Ninians would, for example, have been radically different had it occurred at a particular distance to the east, south or north of the chapel, due to the nature of the location. All of the relevant source material puts the action on flat, hard ground, therefore it clearly was not fought two miles to the northeast of Kirkton of St Ninians – unless it was fought in the waters of the fast and powerful River Forth. Moreover, battles are not, as a general rule, static events.

Armies manoeuvre for position; they advance to contact, they retire or advance during combat. This in turn presents problems for archaeological interpretation, particularly in instances where 'finds' are few and far between.[7] The discovery of a weapon fragment – even if the fragment can be indisputably attributed to the action in question – tells us no more than the fact that at some point the weapon was lost or abandoned. It need not even have been lost at the location in which it is found, and even if it was, the fragment is not evidence that a formation of either army passed that way; it may have been lost by a man escaping from a fight that was actually taking place at some considerable distance. Even the most assiduous study of the sources, the terrain and the archaeological material cannot, therefore, give us a complete and incontrovertible account of all the different aspects of this battle, nor for most others of the period.

On the other hand, the general sequence of events and the nature of the engagements can be readily understood from the source material if we relate that information to the practices of the day. It is certainly true that the sources contradict each other to some extent; indeed, if they did not do so, we should be suspicious that they all stemmed from one common account. However the degree of inconsistency is not great and, as we shall see, the discrepancies between sources are – to a considerable extent anyway – matters of perspective in the sense that the deployment for battle and the progress of the fight may have looked very different from the points of view of the Lanercost chronicler's witness and that of Sir Thomas Grey – both of whose accounts of the battle are reproduced in this volume.

Contemporary accounts, however carefully written, are of limited value unless we make a real effort to understand the nature of the armies and their nature of approach to battle. Failure to do so can lead to very serious misconceptions which, in turn, can lead us to very questionable conclusions. This is, perhaps, less of an issue for the army of Edward II than for that of Robert I. There are two reasons for this. One is that English armies of the fourteenth century have been studied in far more detail than Scottish ones, which is itself a matter of source material. Not only is there a great deal more in the way of record evidence – payrolls and horse valuations records, for example – but the material has been thoroughly examined by many very talented historians for the better part of one hundred years – particularly, though not exclusively, J.E. Morris, Professor G.W.S. Barrow and Doctors Michael Prestwich, Andrew Ayton and Andy King.[8]

Study of the armies and actions of a particular time and place is, of course, somewhat redundant without gaining some understanding of the political, social, economic and cultural conditions which brought about war between the nations concerned. Many fine scholars have devoted themselves to these aspects of medieval England and Scotland, and there are a number of volumes which are simply indispensable to the student who wishes to get to grips with the societies from which the political and military leaders of the day were drawn – those which provided the manpower, finance and political will to wage war. Professors Barrow and Prestwich have already been mentioned, but there are many others worthy of praise: Professors Nicholson, Keen and Duncan, and Drs Fiona Watson, Michael Brown, Norman Reid, David Ditchburn, Alexander Grant, Michael Penman and Colm McNamee, to name but a few.

There is no particular shortage of 'Bannockburn' books on the market, and one might question the value of writing another. No new source material has come to light, so perhaps it could be argued that there is nothing new to say. In a sense, this is true. There *is* nothing new to add to the existing body of evidence; however, there are a great many issues to be considered in relation to the interpretation of that evidence. To that end, I have chosen to cite and discuss all of the significant narrative sources, both in relation to one another and in the light of what we know of the military realities of the early fourteenth century as practiced in Scotland. I have endeavoured to keep endnotes to a minimum; the bulk of the significant material is contained in the chronicle accounts. I have devoted no space whatsoever to the authorship of those accounts; in this context it is the writing that is significant, not the writer. The one exception is Sir Thomas Grey, whose personal experience as a career soldier cannot be ignored.

No medieval battle can be perfectly understood; there is no-one alive today who has experienced the terror of an arrow-storm or the ferocity of a full-blooded charge by armoured cavalry, but I hope that the material contained in this book will give the reader a reasonable practical understanding of this remarkable battle which, despite modern claims to the contrary, was very much more than a clash between medieval gangsters. For Scottish people at least, it was an expression of the political preference of the majority of the community for independence.

Without the active support of a very wide segment of Scottish society, from labourers to lords, King Robert would never have been able to restore the sovereignty of his nation. The war was not, however, a simple matter of allegiance to a king, but a subtle and complex combination of issues of national and regional identities, traditions of support for, or opposition to, local leaders, perceptions of the political realities of the day, resentment of domination by a foreign power, personal ambition and ties of familial and social relationships. All of these factors, and probably many others which defy identification at a distance of seven hundred years, were instrumental in persuading many thousands of men to risk their lives at Stirling in the summer of 1314.

# The Story So Far:
# The War of Independence,
# 1296–1313

An extensive body of books, articles and essays on the wars of King John, Robert I, Edward I and Edward II has been published over the last hundred years or so, but the extent to which many of these works has contributed to our understanding of the 1314 campaign is questionable. Even the most cursory survey of the secondary material currently most accessible to the public – entries in encyclopaedias, general histories, Internet sites and dictionaries of battles – shows the enormous influence of the works of S.R. Gardiner[1] and C.W.C. Oman.[2] Both of these men still enjoy very positive reputations for their efforts in different fields; Oman's account of the Peninsula campaigns against Napoleon is still an invaluable piece of work after a century.[3] For Oman and Gardiner the battle took the form of an opposed crossing, one of the most hazardous approaches to battle. The challenge of forcing a passage over the deep muddy-banked stream that divided the armies was further complicated by the fact that the Scots had dug innumerable pits along the bank of the Bannock Burn. These inflicted many casualties on the English cavalry, who exhausted themselves in repeated attacks on the serried ranks of the Scots before eventually giving up the contest and abandoning the field to the enemy. None of this bears very much resemblance to any of the contemporary or near-contemporary accounts, but the fame of the writers has ensured that their interpretations and maps have gained a very real currency – so much so that they still have an influence on academic understanding of the events of June 1314 today.

Undermining the Gardiner/Oman interpretation is not a modernist 'debunking' exercise. In 1913 Rev. MacKenzie published his study of the battle – still one of the better works on the topic. MacKenzie's volume was not simply a counterblast to Oman and Gardiner; it was an attempt to consider all of the sources in relation to one another and in relation to examinations of the terrain. One might make a number of criticisms of MacKenzie's conclusions and of his preference for some medieval writers over others, but he certainly examined all of the significant material from the relevant contemporary accounts – Barbour's *Bruce*, Thomas Grey's *Scalacronica*, Fordoun's *Chronicle*, the *Lanercost Chronicle*, Bower's *Scotichronicon*, and *Vita Edwardi Secundi*.[4]

MacKenzie was not the only Scottish historian of his time to examine Bannockburn in some detail. Evan MacLeod Barron's work, *The Scottish War of Independence*,[5] still exerts an influence on Scottish medieval history nearly a century after its first publication. There are numerous weaknesses to Barron's understanding of Bannockburn that have been explored in detail by Professor Barrow.[6] Barron's contribution to the topic largely revolved around his conviction that the contribution of Highland communities to the cause of independence had been obscured by a concentration on Lowland magnate politics, and that the viability of the patriotic cause had been continually undermined by the capacity of lowland nobles and gentry to defect to the English. Barron could certainly provide many examples of serial defections among the Scottish magnates – Robert Bruce, for example, changed sides in 1297, 1301–2 and again in 1306. In the view of Barron, the southern nobility were less committed than their northern counterparts, a reflection of differing values between what he saw as two distinct Scottish cultural, social and political entities, the 'Teutonic' (southern/lowland) and the Celtic (Gaelic/northern). This aspect of Barron's interpretation has been thoroughly discredited by Professor Barrow, but continues to exert a considerable influence on the popular perception of the Battle of Bannockburn and of the war in general. Barron's intention was to redress what he saw as a tendency on the part of historians to focus on the activities of the southern magnates. His view was not without validity, but he exaggerated some pieces of evidence and marginalised others to make his case. He was not the first writer to draw attention to this perceived north–south imbalance. In 1909, John Shearer, in his *Fact and fiction in the Story of Bannockburn*,[7] wrote:

... there is nothing in Barbour that even gives a hint that the chiefs, with their men, from the hills and glens of Loch Lomond, Loch Katrine, Loch Tay, Loch Ness and Loch Shin, were fighting at the Battle Bannockburn. This is surely a great omission on the part of Barbour, and a terrible injustice to the Celts of Scotland.

Popular perception is one of the barriers to understanding the battle at all. Scottish romantic tradition tends to see the action as a struggle between impoverished Scottish peasants — unarmoured and ill-equipped — against endless hordes of armoured English knights, a triumph of the peasants over the nobility — a myth greatly enhanced by the popularity of the film *Braveheart*. There is also the question of the extent to which the Wars of Independence can be seen as a 'civil war' between Scottish factions rather than a war of aggression and conquest inaugurated by Edward I.[8] There was certainly an element of domestic political strife before 1291 which revolved around the question of whether Robert Bruce or John Balliol should have inherited the crown — an issue that led to the presence of the Bruces and others in the English camp. The objective of the Bruces was to acquire Scottish kingship, not to subject themselves to the authority of Edward I.

The 'civil war' theory, however, does have some validity in the sense that many Scots, for a variety of reasons and at different times, did align themselves with the Plantagenet cause, but that in itself is a long way short of proving that the War of Independence was a 'civil' war as such. There was no sense in the entirety of a series of conflicts — which lasted intermittently from 1296 to 1328 (and resumed in 1332) — when the war was exclusively, or even primarily, a conflict between Scottish political factions. Even Edward Balliol's invasion depended on the resources of English lords with Scottish ambitions. The presence of English garrisons[9] and field armies was always the most significant aspect of the military dimension of the struggle and, with the exception of the period between the death of Wallace and the inauguration of Robert I, there was always a part of Scottish society, from the labourers to the great lords, which was prepared to unite across barriers of class and culture in defence of the independence of their country. As the chronicler Guisborough wrote of the Scottish aristocracy, their bodies might be with the King of England, but 'their hearts were always with their own people.'

Despite assertions such as —

the misery and bloodshed in the wars between England and Scotland lies at the door of those rebellious Scots who adhered neither to their King, nor to their oaths of fealty to their supreme overlord, Edward[10]

– the basic cause of the Wars of Independence was the ambition of Edward I. It is of course true that without Edward's involvement in the period after the death of the young Queen Margaret on her voyage from Norway,[11] there would almost certainly have been a genuine civil war in Scotland between the Bruce and Balliol parties. It is worth bearing in mind, however, that both Robert Bruce and John Comyn were prepared to join forces against Edward in a joint Guardianship despite their very real political differences.[12]

Although the two men were far from being happy allies, it was not the prospect of military defeat at the hands of the English that made Robert Bruce defect to Edward I, but the increasingly strong possibility that King John might be restored to his throne, thus compromising any possibility that Robert might eventually become king himself. Again, this was a matter of domestic Scottish politics, but the key issue which had united Bruce and Comyn in the first place was that of political independence.

It is also true that Robert had to wage campaigns against powerful Scottish interests in the early part of his reign, primarily against the Comyn and MacDougal families, but it is misleading to see these campaigns simply as aspects of 'civil' war. After 1304 each of these groups had been drawn into an English administration of Scotland;[13] they were not assets of an alternative Scottish government acting in opposition to the Bruce party.

This, however, does not mean that either the MacDougals or the Comyns would necessarily have remained in English allegiance regardless of political developments. King Philip of France had been forced to abandon the Scots in the wake of the Battle of Courtrai,[14] but circumstances do change. If Philip had felt that it was in his interests (and within his capabilities) to deploy a significant force to Scotland in an attempt to restore King John after the collapse of the Balliol party in 1304, it is quite possible, even probable, that the Comyns would have reverted to their traditional role of supporters to the Scottish crown, a role from which they – and the crown – had profited greatly over a period of more than one hundred years. In practice, of course, this was not an option that the French could pursue; they had problems enough already. Diplomatically it suited Edward I and Edward II to depict their Scottish campaigns as a purely domestic matter; lawful kings exercising their right to discipline recalcitrant subjects in rebellion against their liege-lord. That they enjoyed some success is apparent from the tendency for English – and sometimes Scottish – historians to describe men like Comyn and Bruce as 'rebels.'

Naturally, the commitment of the Comyns to the Plantagenet cause was enhanced by their opposition to the Bruce party – hardly surprising given Robert's murder of John Comyn of Badenoch in February 1306.[15] But it was also encouraged by their defeat at Robert's hands in his Buchan campaign of 1308.[16] Once they had been driven out of the northeast, their only hope of recovering their property and, with it, their position of political power, was the hope that Edward II might defeat and destroy the Bruce party. By the close of 1313, this must have seemed increasingly unlikely, unless Bruce could be brought to battle on a grand scale. In terms of territorial control, King Robert was close to winning his war. He had gained control of all Scotland north of the Forth and Clyde, his armies were able to pass through those areas which were still in Plantagenet hands in order to mount operations in England, and the remaining assets of Edward II's administration were increasingly isolated and vulnerable – even Berwick had nearly fallen in 1312.[17] The commitment of a field army does not seem to have brought much progress. The campaign of 1310–11 had achieved little in the way of recovered ground for the expenditure of a very considerable sum – essentially a failure for the English and therefore a major propaganda coup for King Robert. The position of the Comyn family, and others who had remained in Plantagenet allegiance, became precarious throughout the military successes of a Scottish rival – Robert Bruce – however the Comyns were fighting not for an alternative Scottish kingship, but for the King of England. This is also true of Robert's western enemies, the MacDougalls and McCans. Their rivalry with the MacDonalds gave Robert an ally, but the MacDougalls – like the Comyns – were fighting to preserve Plantagenet kingship, not to bring back King John. Their conflict with the Bruce party had a 'civil' element, but was still the operational expression of a war between English and Scottish kings.

As a conflict between nations, it is hardly a surprise that nationalism – in all its guises – is a factor in itself. As we shall see, both Scottish and English people were perfectly aware of their nationality, but nationalism is also an issue within some of the source material. We need only compare the Lanercost chronicler's generally hostile views of the Scots with those of Sir Thomas Grey, who spent the greater part of his professional life in Scotland.

Nationalism and concepts of national destiny were already an important part of English historiography by the time of the Wars of Independence. To a great degree, this was bound up with a view that the King of England was the rightful and acknowledged superior of the whole of the British Isles. One need look no further than Geoffrey of Monmouth's assertion that Scotland was a dependency of England, which Professor Mason calls the 'Brut tradition'.[18] The 'evidence' on which Monmouth's case depended was that Brutus the Trojan, having escaped from the fall of Troy, had travelled to Britain and divided the British Isles between his sons, with the eldest, Locrinus, enjoying the kingship of England and superiority over his brother-kings, Albanactus of Scotland and Kamber of Wales.

The Trojan legend was supported in more recent times (by medieval standards) by the 'fact' that Arthur had been king of all Britain and, more cogently perhaps, the fact that at different times a number of Scottish kings had accepted the superiority of their English counterparts, the most recent being William the Lion in December 1174. In practice, William's acceptance of Henry II's feudal superiority was given under duress and was, in any case, soon traded away by Richard I of England for ready money under the terms of the Quitclaim of Canterbury in 1189.[19] It has been suggested that the terms of the Quitclaim were sufficiently vague to mean anything to anyone, however the key cause is very straightforward:

> …We (Richard of England) have freed him (William of Scotland) from all compacts which our good father, Henry, king of the English, extorted from him by new charters and by his capture.

More generally, the popular view of the society and economy of the northern kingdom has been shaped by what Dr Fergusson[20] called:

> the peculiarly English Victorian Gothic version of early medieval Scotland in which Gaels and Norse and Anglians and even Britons live in different parts of the country, separated by geography, culture, language and pretty much tribal kingdoms in themselves…not to mention Northumbrians and Galwegians.

There has also been something of a tendency for English historians to view any action contrary to English interests as being a threat to good practice and desirable outcomes. May McKisack[21] saw the development of a strong political alliance between Scotland and France in 1294–7 as being 'among the most sinister developments of the war of independence,' rather than being the only practical response to the ambitions of an aggressive and predatory neighbour. Few reputable English medievalists of recent times would choose to see Edward's behaviour in Scotland as the reasonable and lawful actions of a well-intentioned and benign neighbour, however the prevalence of that attitude in the past still exerts an influence on 'popular' history. One need look no further than John Harvey's book *The Plantagenets*, which clearly makes the Scots the villains of the piece. According to Harvey, the judicial murder of Sir William Wallace was a fate he brought upon himself:

> Had his offences been merely political he would have found the same mercy that Edward's other opponents never sought in vain; but Wallace was not the hero of romantic legend, but a leader of well-organised criminals in an assault upon society. For three hundred years the Borders suffered cruelly for this one man's misdeeds.[22]

In reality, Wallace was executed because his death suited Edward's own political purposes on a number of levels. The high-profile public execution and dismemberment of Wallace did more than provide a spectacle for Londoners, it gave a superficial veneer of 'closure' in the wake of the Strathord armistice. The execution was popular at home and, to some extent anyway, politically practical in Scotland. Edward could not afford to execute any of the men who had until recently been the leaders of the Balliol party since he needed their influence and military power if he was to make his conquest effective. If Wallace had been a great and powerful magnate, Edward would probably not have had him killed, but, since his defeat at Falkirk and his resignation from the Guardianship in 1298, Wallace had ceased to be a figure of any real importance in the Scottish political community. He was, however, very famous, so his capture and execution could be presented – in England at least – as a triumph.

In fact, Wallace's murder was probably a serious mistake on the part of Edward and for the future of his Scottish administration, since it 'raised the political temperature in Scotland.'[23] Wallace may not have been a great favourite of the senior aristocracy in Scotland, but he was still a popular figure in wider society. Wallace is a heroic figure to Scots – and others – and hero-worship can get in the way of a realistic appraisal of his career; the same applies to King Robert and Edward I as a hero to the English. To cite

Harvey again:

> ... it is impossible not to regret that the peace-lover, the arbitrator, the fountain-head of his country's prosperity and justice, should have exhausted himself in constant war.[24]

But in reality Edward's wars in Scotland and in Wales were problems that he brought upon himself, and the various financial and political crises faced by the English crown at the end of the thirteenth century were in fact products of Edward's military ventures. Edward's reputation as an outstanding soldier is something of a barrier in itself; had he lost the battle of Falkirk it is hard to see how that reputation could ever have flourished. Edward cannot have assumed that his 1296 campaign had really finished the Balliol cause, but presumably he did expect that the manpower and money he committed to the project would be adequate to the task of quickly overcoming any residual resistance and erecting an occupation administration. His strategic and tactical expertise failed him on both counts.

Traditionally Scottish historians have shied clear of describing Edward's rule as an 'occupation', partly perhaps for fear of giving offence, but chiefly because of the number of Scots who were involved in Edward's government, particularly in the period after the Strathord armistice of 1304. This is something of an over-simplification. There were certainly a great many Scottish men and women who accepted Edward as their king, some through conviction, some through duress. No doubt there were quite a few who were not really terribly concerned about who was king, so long as they could maintain their own position in society and either felt that Edward was too strong to resist or that he offered the best chance of stability.[25] There would probably have been some who felt that the country had been failed by the Bailiol monarchy and who were prepared to accept Edward – at least temporarily – for want of any other source of political leadership. To assume that Plantagenet kingship was the preferred option for all of these people is to do them a considerable injustice, comparable to assuming that men and women who retained their posts under the Germans or the Japanese during World War Two had embraced Nazi or Japanese imperial ideologies. Accepting authority for the sake of keeping one's job or one's business is not tantamount to being a collaborator.

On one level there was the question of avoiding forfeiture, imprisonment or even death for failing to accept Plantagenet rule, but there were also many internal Scottish political issues. Just because someone did not accept the Bruce party does not mean that they wholeheartedly endorsed the Plantagenets. Aryeh Nusbacher,[26] referring to the example of the Earl of Angus who responded to the summons to fight for Edward II in 1314, points out that, with him,

> …were a number of Scottish knights who had decided that their allegiance to their English sovereign was more important than their allegiance to the claimant of the Scottish throne.

Though typical of the conventional English view of the wars of independence articulated by Oman and others, there is an implication here that cannot go unchallenged. Scottish 'knights' might choose to support Edward II because they believed that his cause was legally sound or because they believed that the Plantagenet administration offered the best prospect of peace. They might, alternatively, choose Edward II's lordship for no better reason than that they rejected the Bruce party. Robert's conduct over the previous two decades had not been consistent in the sense of supporting the 'patriotic cause'; he had murdered his chief political rival and he was most certainly a usurper so long as there was a legitimate heir of the Balliol family. Further, many of the Scots who served as men-at-arms in the English army of 1314 were the tenants, relatives and associates of men who had firmly rejected the Bruce party and had lost their estates as King Robert extended his rule.

Some, no doubt, served Edward II (as they had served Edward I) for fear of losing their estates in England, though in reality these are likely to have been few in number since only a handful of Scots held estates of any great significance outside Scotland. The converse is true as well; some of the gentry and nobility who joined the Bruce cause, particularly after the defeat of the Comyns in 1308, surely did so because their properties, or at least their most significant estates, lay in areas dominated by the Bruces. As the Bruce party gained ground the chances of retaining those properties without accepting Robert's kingship must have seemed increasingly remote. This applied equally to great lords and minor gentry. The Earl of Ross, a Balliol supporter in 1291–2,[27] was firmly in the Plantagenet camp in 1306 when he captured King Robert's queen, Elizabeth de Burgh[28] and dispatched her to Edward I as a prisoner, but by 1308 his earldom had become very isolated and he was obliged to accept a truce with the Bruce party until June and then entered King Robert's peace on 31 October. Without the armed support of Edward II's forces to help him resist the Bruce party, the Earl was doomed to defeat and forfeiture unless he accepted Robert's kingship and authority. William of Ross's circumstances were, perhaps, particularly difficult. His earldom was vulnerable, not only to Robert's land-based forces, but also to raids mounted from the Hebrides by Robert's allies. The Earl of Angus, on the other hand, presumably felt that he was more likely to retain his earldom through giving his allegiance to Edward II. As it turned out he was mistaken and by the time of Bannockburn had already been an émigré for some time.

Individual Scots aligned themselves with the Bruce party for a wide variety of reasons, some political, some personal. Many people believed – rightly – that the legitimate King of Scotland was John Balliol or, after John's death in 1313, his son, Edward. The collapse of the Balliol cause in 1304 did not mean that all of the Balliol supporters defected to the Plantagenet cause, merely that the leaders of the Balliol party had come to the conclusion that, abandoned by the French[29] and by John himself,[30] their cause was no longer militarily viable. It does not, of itself, imply a preference either for the Plantagenets over the Bruces or a general preference for the occupation government. Clausewitz's observation that a nation might see defeat – even overwhelming defeat – as a 'temporary misfortune' that might, in due course, be reversed through a resumption of hostilities, is most appropriate here.[31]

Acceptance of the rule of the government of day did not imply political sympathy so much as a matter of keeping one's job and one's head; accepting that this or that party offered the best hope of stability and security and that it could provide 'good lordship.'[32] Similarly, people might be dissuaded from giving overt support to their favoured party because they doubted the ability of that party to impose its will on the country as a whole. As Barrow has shown, King Robert enjoyed support from nobles across the country from his inauguration as king.[33] Some of Robert's early supporters fell away through Plantagenet pressure in 1306–7, but many more joined as he began to look more credible, particularly after his campaigns of 1308.

Naturally, some Scottish landholders would have been deterred from joining the Bruce cause by the military power of the occupation government. Other than those periods in which Edward I and Edward II lead or despatched major filed armies to Scotland the power of their administration depended on the resources of Scottish lords in English allegiance and the garrisons. A good many Scots served in these garrisons; some through the attractions of wages and the potential for career advancement, others for political reasons. Recruiting Scottish men-at-arms and archers was an attractive proposition for the Plantagenet government; partly because it was often difficult to recruit adequate numbers from elsewhere, but also – particularly after 1308 – because there were increasing numbers of men whose properties lay in territory dominated by the Bruce party. Having been disadvantaged for their loyalty, these men could hardly be abandoned; they needed to be supported financially until such time as their heritage could be recovered. This was all well and good as long as the prospect of an English recovery in Scotland seemed a viable proposition. By mid-1314 this must have seemed an increasingly unlikely prospect unless the decay of Plantagenet government could be reversed by a major military initiative, however there were, by this point, relatively few Scots in English allegiance other than associates of the Comyn and MacDougal families. Although there were still several garrisons at the close of 1313, they had largely lost the capacity to impose lordship in their localities. Increasingly, the surviving garrisons were becoming – if they had not already become – assets of an 'outpost' policy rather than a genuine attempt to provide secure government.

This had come about through the increasing ability of the Bruce party to deploy greater numbers of men-at-arms at critical locations at given moments. In order to contain the garrisons the Scots did not necessarily have to find a general superiority in heavy cavalry, just local superiority of an order that would prevent the garrisons from venturing too far from their stations. This is a matter of some importance, since the purpose of the garrisons was not, at least until 1313, to guard the castles themselves, but to impose the will of Edward II, ensure the collection of rents and other issues, to be a visible political presence in the community and, of course, to prevent the Scots from extending their area of influence.

That the ability of Robert to attract the support of the people without necessarily having the support – overt or otherwise – of the aristocracy added to the problems of the administration, is clear from this letter from the commander of the Plantagenet garrison at Forfar Castle to an English courtier at Carlisle. It is dated May 1307 and relates recent events and current situations:

I hear that Bruce never had the good will of his own followers or of the people generally so much with him as now. It appears that God is with him, for he has destroyed King Edward's power both among the English and Scots. The people believe that Bruce will carry all before him, exhorted by 'false preachers' from Bruce's army, men who have previously been charged before the justices for advocating war and have been released on bail, but are now behaving worse than ever. I fully believe, as I have heard from Duncan of Frendraught and Gilbert of Glencairnie, who keep the peace beyond the Mounth and on this side, that if Bruce can get away in this direction or towards the parts of Ross he will find the people all ready at his will more entirely than ever, unless King Edward can send more troops; for there are many people living loyally in his peace so long as the English are in power.

May it please God to prolong King Edward's life, for men say openly that when he is gone the victory will go to Bruce. For these preachers have told the people that they have found a prophecy of Merlin, that after the death of 'le roy coveytous' the people of Scotland and the Welsh shall band together and have full lordship and live in peace together to the end of the world.

*This is Professor Barrow's translation, published in 'Robert the Bruce and the Community of the realm of Scotland', p.245. The letter is listed and described in CDS ii, No. 1926.*

This letter, probably from Sir Alexander Abernethy, a staunch officer and supporter of the Plantagenet government, is worth examining in some detail. It is clear that the writer was convinced that Robert enjoyed a good deal of popular support in both the northeast and the northwest – neither of them regions with a strong tradition of Bruce lordship. Moreover there were strong, well-established local political leaders who were adamantly opposed to the Bruce party; Duncan of Frendraught and Gilbert of Glencairnie were men of some prominence, and the Earl of Ross, the most significant mainland magnate in the northwest, was definitely still a member of the Plantagenet camp. Clearly the author of the letter hoped to encourage the deployment of more English troops (Bain's presentation of this letter refers to men-at-arms in particular), which is in itself an indication that the leaders of the local administration were feeling the strain of confronting Bruce sentiment. The most significant assertion, however, is that Bruce would find the people 'ready at his will more entirely than ever.' The letter dates from May 1307, while Edward was still alive and at a time when Bruce's kingship, though more than a year old, had largely been passed in exile or in hiding. Robert had had little opportunity to show himself in the far north, so it is surprising that he should have had the support of any significant proportion of the common people. This is quite at odds with traditional views of local political leadership in the later Middle Ages, which tends to be heavily focused on the behaviour of the nobility and gentry to the exclusion of the balance of the community. Kings were certainly only too well aware of the power of the magnate classes, and of their capacity to defy the crown if pushed, but they could also demonstrate an awareness of the importance of popular political opinion. Edward I issued at least one document in which he attempted to enlist the support of the wider community for his kingship by accepting that his government had been too harsh. He hoped to secure their support, but also to deny that support to the enemy. It would seem that Robert was convinced of the importance of popular support, since he clearly went to some effort to ensure that the people were informed of his actions. The prophecies of Merlin, among other aspects of Arthurian legend, were widely held to be significant, and were evidently sufficiently well-known to provide a propaganda vehicle for the Bruce cause. Identifying Edward I as the *Roy Coveytous* (greedy king) would have been a reasonably easy prospect to 'sell' to the people given Edward's general behaviour in Scotland. The prospect that the Scots and the Welsh would enjoy 'full lordship' (political independence) after Edward's death would also make an attractive and credible ambition, given that Edward was now an old man (by the standards of the fourteenth century) and was not in the best of health.

Had there been an accommodation between the Comyns, traditional leaders in the northeast, and the Bruce party, we might expect that Comyn political alignment would find an expression among the people at large, but of course the opposite was the case; the Comyns were utterly opposed to Robert's kingship – the murder of John Comyn had made sure of that. It is possible, though there is no evidence to support such a possibility, that the Comyns had lost the support of the wider community of the northeast through their support of the Plantagenet cause, or through their abandonment of King John in 1304. This would still be a demonstration of popular political sentiment. If the men and women of Buchan, Aberdeenshire and Kincardineshire rejected the leadership of the Comyns because the Comyns no longer represented the interests of Scottish kingship, then the people were making a political choice between independence and integration into the domain of English kingship. It is difficult to see any motivation other than national sentiment for the assertion that the people would be willing, even eager, to adopt the Bruce cause in 1307, particularly when we bear in mind that Robert could not yet impose his authority effectively in areas of strongly established Bruce lordship.

Accepting Bruce kingship did not necessarily mean that an individual was utterly convinced of the merits of Robert's claim to the throne. In 1306–7 Robert's campaign cannot have looked very promising, so one might assume that early commitment to the Bruce cause was a product of a conscious political decision. This was no longer the case by the close of 1308. By that time, Robert had brought a considerable swathe of territory under his sway so, in much the same way as Plantagenet lordship continued to be acceptable in the far south, acceptance of Bruce lordship in the far north was probably – to some extent at least – a matter of accepting the *de facto* government of the day regardless of personal preference. Once again, there may be an element of national consciousness underlying the growth of the Bruce party in the north of Scotland after 1307–8. Alignment with Bruce may, for some, have been no more than the product of rejecting Plantagenet rule. Men and women who had given their support to King John between 1292 and 1296 may have accepted the settlement negotiated by the magnates in 1304, but they were not obliged to like it. They may not have needed any great sympathy with the ambitions of King Robert, but still accepted him on the basis that any 'home grown' king was preferable to any foreigner.

The existence of the garrisons may have been a factor in encouraging support for the Bruces in the northeast. Between 1297 and 1304 the north had been little affected by the activities of English field armies and most of the garrisons installed by Edward I after the campaign of 1296 had fallen to the Balliol party within a matter of a year or so. There is no reason to suppose that the garrisons installed after 1304 were particularly harsh or even obtrusive, but they were still a visible demonstration of the will of a foreign power. Even if the men in the garrisons were largely Scots, a garrison as an institution was an instrument of an alien king, and therefore may well have been an irritant to the communities of the region. The same is true of the rest of Scotland inasmuch as there were garrisons scattered throughout the realm. About forty castles were held by Plantagenet garrisons in the later years of Edward I's reign, but there were also several baronial castles held by men in Edward's employ or sympathetic to his cause. By 1306, many of these, particularly in the south and east, had been in place for a decade. The local communities may not have liked the garrisons, but they must surely have become accustomed to them over the preceding ten years.

National sentiment is one of the factors that continue to make Bannockburn so prominent in Scottish opinions of the War of Independence to the present day; another is class sentiment. There is a rather romantic view that the Scots at Bannockburn represent the people in arms whereas the English army represents the power of kingship. Neither of these propositions bears examination. King Robert was well aware of the importance of attracting and retaining the support of the noble class as a political tool and as the source of military power. The men who served in his army of 1314 were far from being the 'common husbandmen and tribesmen' beloved of Scottish romance – and, unfortunately, of several historians. The popular mental picture of plaid-clad peasants armed with sharpened logs – and possibly blue face paint – prepared to risk their lives in a perilous, desperate trow of the dice against the rich and finely-mounted English, cannot be taken seriously. The rank and file of Robert's army consisted primarily of the more prosperous farm tenants (as opposed to farm labourers), burgesses and other townspeople[34] and he had access to men from the West Highlands and Western Isles for whom soldiering was a normal part of life. The rest – possibly as much as 10–15% of the total – were men-at-arms who, almost without exception, were drawn from the nobility. In terms of class representation, there would have been little social difference between the English and Scottish armies other than the contingents from the Western Isles and the northwest Highlands.

Another reason for the prominence of Bannockburn is of course the scale of the victory. In Scottish romance Bannockburn tends to figure as one of only two Scottish victories, the other being Stirling Bridge in 1297. This tradition steadfastly ignores several very important engagements – Roslin, Myton and Culblean, to name but a few. Similarly, this view tends to inflate the importance of various English victories, primarily Falkirk and Halidon Hill. In practice, Edward I derived very little benefit from his victory at Falkirk and in the long term his grandson gained nothing from his 1333 victory at Halidon, since his administration in Scotland had dwindled to a handful of increasingly isolated fortresses by 1338. To a certain extent, the same applies to Bannockburn. Victory allowed Robert to confirm his hold on the southeast and gave him a very enviable martial reputation but, contrary to popular perception, Bannockburn did not give him the political victory he sought. Edward II may have been roundly defeated, but he was not prepared to have peace on the basis of accepting Robert as King of Scotland. He did not even accept that he had actually lost his war irrevocably, but mounted fresh invasions. He did not do so simply in the hope that he would destroy Bruce, though that would have been highly appreciated;

he did so to recover what he saw as part of his heritage from his father. Edward II was not the brightest man ever to wear the English crown, but he was not an imbecile. If he was prepared to make the financial and political effort to raise an army for service in Scotland he clearly believed that conquest was not beyond his means. His army had been destroyed in 1314, but his will – and that of many English magnates – to bring Scotland under his rule was still strong and would remain so until his death. It was not Edward II who eventually acknowledged Robert's kingship in 1328, but the government of Edward III.

In the century and more that has passed since Gardiner, Oman, MacKenzie and several others have made their contributions to the study of Bannockburn, most historians have followed the template provided by one or the other. The actual process of any battle is not really that important in relation to the general march of events. Whether the outcome of the battle was decided by this or that incident, by this or that practice, by this or that feature in the terrain is, arguably, a trivial question in comparison to the effects of that outcome. Had Edward II been victorious at Bannockburn, the political consequences might have been far more interesting to historians than the means by which he achieved that victory, unless he had done so through a dramatically innovative approach to battle.

It would be rash to assume that victory at Bannockburn would have brought the War of Independence to a conclusion. Had Robert I and his brother Edward both been killed in action, the Bruce party would probably have come to an end since there was no legitimate male heir to pursue the Bruce claim to kingship, but that does not mean that the cause of independence would not have been taken up by another candidate, specifically Edward Balliol, son of King John, who had been deposed in 1296, and who would mount a serious challenge to the Bruce party a generation after Bannockburn.

# The Nature and Extent of the Evidence

The body of contemporary and near-contemporary documentary evidence relating to the battle of Bannockburn is not extensive, and none of what there is can really be considered as a full account of the action.

More positively, none of them really contradicts any of the others in any material sense, though Barbour pretty certainly 'invented' an extra Scottish formation for the main battle in order to provide a role for Sir James Douglas and for Walter the Stewart, the father of Barbour's patron, Robert II. This can serve as an example of the sort of thing that could influence medieval writers to include material that causes confusion for generations. Barbour wrote his epic poem half a century or more after the events that he described. This was close enough to prevent wholesale invention if the narrative was to have credibility. The account was written to entertain members of the noble class, men who saw themselves as the inheritors of a great military tradition. On a practical level, they were well aware of the nature of battle and well aware of the physical and emotional stresses of active service, but they were also aware of the tales of their fathers and grandfathers – men who had served in the Wars of Independence and who had known Douglas, Randolph and King Robert himself. If Barbour strayed too far from the realities of fighting, his audience would be unimpressed; on the other hand, he had every incentive to raise the profiles of his heroes and, indirectly, the prestige of Robert II.

Further, from Barbour's perspective in the 1360s/70s it would have been unthinkable that so great a figure as Douglas had had no prominent role in the greatest battle of the age. In 1314, Douglas had yet to attain great political stature. He was, no doubt, already the possessor of a serious reputation as a man-at-arms, but was still only a baron, and a fairly minor one at that. This does not imply that barons were not men of some substance, but they were not a homogeneous group in terms of influence and wealth. John Comyn, Lord of Badenoch, was a baron of the very highest order, a man of enormous power – so much so that he was acceptable to the political community as a national leader, serving as Guardian of the Realm from the aftermath of Falkirk to the appointment of Sir John de Soulis as sole lieutenant of King John. However the barons were not, as a rule, the class of society that provided the most senior political level of leadership. The sheriffdom of Lothian, for example, had at least thirty baronies within its bounds in the early fourteenth century. Obviously none of these Lothian barons enjoyed the status of John Comyn, whose wealth and power were sufficient to make him a major player on the national political stage, but their leadership and influence at a more local level was a vital part of the administrative, judicial and military structures that enabled kings to pursue their objectives.

In the years after Bannockburn Douglas became one of Robert I's principal lieutenants, and acquired vast estates across Scotland, while Walter the Stewart married the King's daughter, Marjorie. This is the Douglas that Barbour knew of – a great lord and military leader so, although every other source clearly describes the Scottish army as having three divisions, Barbour provides a fourth one for Douglas. His audience would be unconcerned about such an invention so long as there were plenty of passages about the fighting itself. Barbour's instinct told him that Douglas should have a narrative of his own within the wider description of the battle. To an extent, he was applying a rationale from his own experience, judgement and the literary needs of the narrative to produce a condition that was what he *wanted* to have been the case. This can also affect historians. In the same way that Barbour's addition of a fourth Scottish formation has conditioned the generally accepted picture of the battle, historians have shaped our perception through the presentation of the process of the action in such a way as to 'fit' their view of the nature of medieval combat. The account of Bannockburn presented by S.R. Gardiner and developed by Sir Charles Oman a century ago still dominates the popular view of the battle. Even a very cursory examination of the modern accounts available in popular histories or on the Internet will show that many of them are no more than paraphrases of Oman's work. Like Barbour, Oman was lead by his experience and instinct. He reasoned that since English arms enjoyed such great success throughout the medieval period – Falkirk, Crecy, Neville's Cross, Poitiers – there must have been curious factors in play for the Scots to defeat the English. How, after all, could the Scots win against the mighty longbow?

Since the conclusion of the fight was inescapable – the English lost and the Scots won – Oman sought to develop a scenario and sequence of events that could explain defeat without compromising the view of English martial ability that he had already adopted. In doing so he rejected the conclusions of the contemporary evidence, all of which clearly indicates a Scottish attack, in favour of his own interpretation in which the English attacked and exhausted themselves by repeated charges against unflinching Scottish spearmen. Not content with that, he placed the Scots and the English on opposing sides of the Bannock burn itself, thus turning the action into an opposed river crossing, unquestionably a very difficult and challenging manoeuvre to effect, but not one that came to the notice of any of the contemporary writers.

One can make the same observation about issues that seem rather minor. Oman may have been the first historian to declare that Scottish archers carried a short bow, unlike their English and Welsh counterparts, who wielded the famous longbow. This is a distinction that eluded medieval writers, though it is exactly the sort of observation that a professional soldier like Sir Thomas Grey (author of *Scalacronica*) would be likely to make. Grey and his contemporaries were clearly unaware of any great difference between Scottish and English archers as individuals, indeed many of the archers recorded as serving in English garrisons during the occupations of Edward I, Edward II (between 1296 and 1314) and Edward III (in the 1330s), were in fact Scotsmen.[35] The same applies, perhaps to a greater degree, to men-at-arms. There is a romantic view that the armies raised by William Wallace, Andrew Murray, John Comyn and Robert Bruce consisted almost entirely of spearmen with very modest contingents of archers and heavy cavalry. It would be easy to form the impression that knights and men-at-arms were almost an anomaly among Scottish troops of the Middle Ages. This is an impression that is sustained, superficially, when we consider the nature of the great battles of the age – Stirling Bridge, Falkirk, Bannockburn, Dupplin Muir, Halidon Hill and Neville's Cross. At each of these actions, the majority of the Scottish troops were spearmen, however we might reasonably consider that the battles themselves were anomalies since general engagements were so few and far between, and in any case, many of the spearmen at Bannockburn, Dupplin, Halidon and Neville's Cross (at least) were actually dismounted men-at-arms.

The usual practice of war between the English and the Scots throughout the fourteenth century was not a matter of bringing about general engagements, but of achieving local supremacy in order to maintain or extend political control over the community; to impose the lordship of one side at the expense of the other. The overwhelming majority of military action between the Scots and the English throughout the Wars of Independence consisted of clashes between rather small bodies of men-at-arms and the sieges of castles and towns. The bulk of the men who served King John or Robert I or David II at sieges were unquestionably infantrymen discharging their military obligations to lord, community and king. Even in that context there is some doubt about the amount of combat that these men might expect to experience. Most sieges conducted for the Balliol and Bruce parties seem to have been sieges of containment aimed at starving the garrison into surrender, though despondency seems likely to have been as significant a factor as starvation. Several castles and towns fell to coup-de-main operations, though some of these instances occurred during the process of a close siege and should be seen as part and parcel of the wider operation.

It would be unnatural if the primary combatants in such an attack were anything other than men-at-arms. They were, obviously, the best equipped and – as a general rule at least – the most comprehensively trained element of the army, but they also had greater personal motivations. A great feat of arms, even if committed in the context of a siege rather than the better-regarded arena of the open battlefield, could have profound career implications for an ambitious fourteenth-century noble; acquiring a good martial reputation almost invariably enhanced an individual's social and political standing. When we read of the Earl of Moray's successful attack on Edinburgh Castle during the siege of 1314, we should be in no doubt that the picked men who clambered up the Castle Rock in the middle of the night were – for the most part anyway – members of the gentry and aristocracy giving service as men-at-arms for properties held in exchange for a mixture of cash, administrative, social and military obligations. They were emphatically *not* the common peasantry in arms.

# What Did the Combatants Fight For?

Although Edward II carries the weight of blame for the defeats in Scotland generally and at Bannockburn in particular, he is something of a scapegoat. The martial reputation of his father and the defeat of the Scots at Falkirk have rather obscured the fact that the Scottish war which undermined Edward II's authority was, in every sense, the fault of Edward I. His ambition to annex Scotland by force of arms led to three hundred years of cross-border antipathy, so it is worth giving a little thought to his reasons for doing so. In part Edward simply wanted achieve primacy throughout the British Isles, but he surely did not want to do so at the cost of landing himself and his successors with a long-term drain on the resources of the English state. It would seem likely that Edward did not fully understand the scale of the project. This is not to imply that he had no knowledge of Scotland, but rather that he was misled by the nature of his experience. He was aware that Scotland was worth having for economic reasons. He spent time there in 1291–2,[1] but his visits were limited to southern and eastern parts of the country – the areas that were most prosperous and most vulnerable to the sort of military pressure that his resources could most easily provide. Having manipulated the Scottish political class to temporarily cede him a very considerable degree of administrative authority for the duration of the 'great cause,'[2] Edward was well aware of the income and liabilities of the Scottish crown.[3] He could see that there was potential for raising his own income and, perhaps, furnishing himself with an additional source of manpower. When he chose to push King John into armed resistance he was familiar with many of the leading figures of the Scottish political establishment, some of whom, notably the Bruce family, hoped to advance their own

careers by supporting Edward or, at the very least, by failing to support King
John. Even if John had been able to depend on having the military resources
of all of the political community for the campaign of 1296, he would have
toiled to raise a force capable of resisting Edward's army. Without that level
of support, he was facing almost inevitable defeat.

The rout of the Scottish nobility at Dunbar and the rapid and unopposed
progress as far north as Elgin led Edward to believe that he had conquered
Scotland to such an extent that he could resume his projects on the con-
tinent, leaving his lieutenants to finish the job of installing an occupation
government. The success of the 1296 campaign was remarkable, but decep-
tive. Edward failed to grasp two important factors. He did not appreciate the
importance of national sentiment and he would seem to have failed to grasp
that his progress to Elgin[4] had not really given him, or his lieutenants, a valid
understanding of the resources his enemy. The greater part of the northern and western parts of Scotland remained virtually untouched by English
forces by the end of 1296. Additionally, he may have assumed that since so
many Scottish nobles had fallen prisoner at Dunbar or had been obliged to
give him their allegiance by appending their seals to the Ragman Roll,[5] that
there was no realistic prospect of a Scottish recovery. Confident that he had
dealt with Scotland, and with several other military commitments, Edward
failed to ensure that his Scottish government had the necessary resources to
impose his rule in the face of opposition. Although he installed garrisons in
castles and towns throughout the country, the numbers involved were very
small and his lieutenants were not provided with a standing force of any
stature that could be quickly brought into action against a 'revolt' among
the Scots. In part, the size of the garrisons may have been a political, rather
than military, decision. Edward would have liked the Scots to accept his
kingship with equanimity, and may have felt that installing garrisons on a
similar scale to the forces which had been available to Scottish sheriffs in the
reigns of Alexander III and his predecessors would be sufficient to maintain
law and order without giving offence to the populace. Essentially, Edward
seems to have preferred to adopt a 'business as usual' ethos in both local and
national government functions.

Clearly he was very much mistaken, as Hugh Cressingham, Edward's
treasurer for Scotland, had discovered before the end July of 1297,[6]
when he wrote to inform Edward that only two Scottish counties
– Roxburghshire and Berwickshire – were fully under English control
and properly provided with Plantagenet officials. Edward's government

had possession of the castles, but had failed to gain power over the rest of the country. Furthermore, the Plantagenet cause was not prospering; in fact, the Balliol party was gaining ground steadily, appointing baillies and other officials to gather issues and recruit troops. They worked to make it clear that even though John was a prisoner, government in his name was not yet dead. Clearly a good many Scots were still willing to fight, but what did they hope to achieve, and what did they risk by resistance?

It is almost axiomatic that Scottish nobles were lukewarm in their support for independence in order to protect their estates in England. A number of Scottish nobles – some of them very obscure men and women – did hold land in England, either from more substantial persons than themselves or from the king himself. Very few of them were landholders of any great significance. The Bruce family held a variety of valuable properties in the south of England, but were not sufficiently important to be figures of any real significance in the local political community, let alone on the national stage. In Scotland, on the other hand, they held a major lordship (Annandale) and an earldom (Carrick), a heritage that ensured a place at the very highest level of Scottish society. Like most cross-border landholders, their Scottish property was the focus of their life and the source of their wealth and influence. Their English properties were well worth having, but not at the risk of losing their position in Scotland. Bruce's defection to the Scots in the wake of the battle of Falkirk risked the forfeiture of his heritage in England, but failure to support the Balliol party might have eventually excluded him from the entire political process in Scotland, possibly leading to the loss of Carrick and Annandale.

The challenges of cross-border landholding were not limited to the upper ranks of the nobility. A very minor landholder in Midlothian, Hugh de Penicuik, was forfeited of two small properties in Northumberland for his adherence to the Balliol party in 1298.[7] Hugh was precisely the sort of man who might be expected to give his allegiance to the Plantagenet party. He had appended his seal to the Ragman Roll in 1296 and he lived in an area which was – at least nominally – securely held by Edward I's administration. He stood to lose valuable property rights by opposing that administration, but he nonetheless chose to do so.

No doubt his decision to resist was influenced by the same factors that affected the rest of the community, and it is worth giving a little thought to what those factors might have been. Resistance to Edward I grew from several issues: a fear that taxation might rise; that new laws and procedures would be imposed; that men might be conscripted to serve in Edward's armies in France and Flanders and, in all probability, a degree of resentment at the presence of English garrisons in Scottish towns and castles. There is no reason to believe that any of the material burdens would have been heavier in Scotland than in England, but they would have been heavier than those to which the community were already accustomed.

In part this was a product of the lighter demands of Scottish kingship. The medieval belief that a king 'should live of his own' – that is, from the proceeds of the crown estates – was not a realistic proposition given the responsibilities of the crown, but the financial demands on Scottish kings were certainly much lighter than those on their English counterparts. Consequently, Scottish kings had not had any great need to impose regular taxation on their subjects and were, as a general rule, able to live from the rents of their properties and the export duty on wool.

Scots might also have to face a considerable extension of military obligation as subjects of Edward I. A good deal of Edward's career had been taken up with warfare, indeed he had issued demands for military service to several Scottish magnates and King John himself for a campaign against France.[8] If Edward could secure Scotland he would undoubtedly make full use of the military obligations of the political class, and probably of the wider community as well.

The appointment of English sheriffs, constables and other officials to posts in Scotland, not to mention the installation of garrisons, surely provoked some degree of resentment as the visible evidence of defeat and conquest, but it had another aspect in terms of local political life. Posts that were filled by Englishmen could not be filled by Scots. The installation of English candidates disrupted the existing patterns of custom. The patronage of English kings might therefore lead to a diminution in the status of the existing political community. Perhaps more significantly the erection of English kingship in Scotland would unquestionably move the focus of political life. Like their counterparts in England or France, the kings of Scotland lived a fairly mobile life, passing through the kingdom from one royal castle to the next. The economic value of sojourns at different locations was considerable. Moving the court to another location was frequently more cost-effective than bringing the produce of crown estates to wherever the king happened to be at a particular moment, however there were also significant political benefits to be gained from travelling through the country.

Moving between communities gave the king the opportunity to monitor his officers and to be seen by his subjects, but it also provided members of the political community with an opportunity to seek favour or justice from the monarch. If the king of England became king of Scotland he would inevitably spend most of his time in other domains; not just England, but a substantial portion of France as well. Access to a king based in Edinburgh, Perth and Aberdeen might be difficult for Scottish lords from Dumfries or Skye, but still very much easier than gaining access to a king based in London. For the magnates of Scotland, there was also the question of personal political status. The earls and great lords of Scotland were very big fish in a rather small pond. Few of them could command the sort of wealth that would accord them similar status in the much larger 'pond' in which the magnates and baronage of Edward I operated.

Loss of political independence at a national level had, potentially, implications for the more senior members of the Scottish political community. Scottish earls enjoyed a considerable degree of political, judicial and military authority within the boundaries of their lordships. Although neither Edward I nor Edward II made any concerted effort to reduce the powers of the earls and barons of Scotland, the men and women who held these positions could not be sure that integration into the dominions of the Plantagenets would not in due course lead to a reduction in their authority. Any candidate for the Scottish throne would have to acquire the support of the senior nobility, support that was hardly likely to be forthcoming if the nobility had any doubt that their privileges might be compromised under Bruce or Balliol rule.

There has been a tendency to assume that Edward I entertained an ambition to annexe Scotland from an early date, perhaps even from the time of the death of Alexander III. In the widest sense this is not impossible. Edward and Alexander had certainly planned to bring about a wedding between Alexander's granddaughter, Margaret, and Edward's eldest son, Edward of Carnarvon.[9] This attempt to secure a dynastic union of the two countries might well have been successful had it not been for Margaret's premature death in 1290. Edward was willing to commit himself to the preservation of Scottish laws and procedures and the Scottish aristocracy do not seem to have felt unduly threatened by the prospect of a joint monarchy, however this was in the context of the later thirteenth century. England and Scotland had developed strong cultural, economic and political bonds over a lengthy period of peace. The events of the tail end of the thirteenth century and of the fourteenth century would render such a proposition utterly unacceptable for the next three hundred years. Margaret's death did more than change Edward's hopes for a union through marriage; Margaret had no clear heir. The issue of the Scottish succession became a thorny and dangerous problem for the Scots, but it was also an event that Edward could not afford to ignore. Any problem that might bring about instability in Scotland might have difficult repercussions for English kings in the future. Edward may not have taken very much interest in the northern sheriffdoms of his country, but he would not be prepared to ignore their plight in the event of a Scottish civil war that could spill over the border or dislocate the local economy. Additionally, the death of Margaret gave Edward an opportunity to become directly involved in Scottish affairs, possibly with a view to resurrecting the claims of English kings to be the feudal superiors of Scottish monarchs. This was not a new gambit on Edward's part. In 1278 he had attempted to extract homage for Scotland from Alexander III, only to be informed that Alexander owed homage 'to God alone' for his kingdom.[10]

Edward had not abandoned all hope of procuring feudal superiority; his actions in relation to the 'competition' of 1291–2 make it perfectly clear that he was willing to conduct the court which would eventually decide the issue, but only if all of the candidates were willing to accept his superiority.

On the death of Alexander, a regency council had been entrusted with the government of the country on behalf of the young queen,[11] but they could not rule forever. Even if there had been no ambitious nobles with a desire for kingship, the credibility of a regency rests of the premise that – in due course – the monarch will come of age and take the reins of power into his own hands. There were, however, several men who did harbour ambitions for the throne, primarily John Balliol and Robert Bruce of Annandale (grandfather of Robert I). Neither of these men had any interest in standing aside in favour of the other, and both had sufficiently strong cases that neither could be dismissed out of hand. Furthermore, both men had considerable military resources of their own or powerful allies to support their ambitions.

The possibility of a civil war was very real and clearly some action would have to be taken to avert it. The council of Guardians (regents) faced a problem that they did not have the resources to resolve. Robert Bruce of Annandale was, seemingly, prepared to go to war to make good his claim to the throne – a claim which, according to himself anyway, had been endorsed by Alexander II as long ago as 1238. If his resources had been limited to the lordship of Annandale and the various lesser properties in his hands, the guardians might have been able to suppress any attempt to bring about a Bruce kingship through force of arms. However, Robert's son – also Robert – had married the great Celtic heiress, Marjorie, Countess of Carrick,[12] whose earldom greatly extended the power and influence of the Bruce family. He too enjoyed the support of a number of Scottish magnates who, collectively, might be able to secure military victory.

His chief competitor, John Balliol, could not deploy the same degree of military strength from his own resources as the Bruce family, but he did enjoy the support of Scotland's foremost noble family, the Comyns. The Comyns had come to prominence through a long tradition of support for the crown[13] and held several great lordships and important offices of state, as well as the support of numerous noble families across the length and breadth of the country. With the prospect of a major national war and no internal means of preventing it, the guardians had little choice but to seek the intervention of an outside party. To all practical intents and purposes, the only candidate worthy of consideration was Edward I. The guardians had been the target of a great deal of criticism, not to say vilification, for their actions in this regard, but in reality they had very little choice. Only Edward could apply the level of military force sufficient to cow the Bruce and Balliol parties, and even if the matter came to blows, Edward would obviously only have to fight one of the two candidates. As the king of Scotland's only neighbour, Edward could hardly be ignored.

Over a period of more than a year (1291–2)[14] Edward served as the administrator of a court which gave consideration to the claims of all the declared claimants, though in practice only Robert Bruce and John Balliol were considered viable choices. Out of 104 'auditors' appointed to hear the case, forty were chosen from the Bruce party and forty from the Balliol party.[15] The eventual outcome of the hearing gave the throne to John Balliol, though the decision of the court was not accepted by Robert Bruce, who transferred his claim to his eldest son. It has often been claimed that Edward chose to favour the Balliol party because he believed that John would be a more malleable figure than Robert, and because John was willing to accept Edward as his feudal superior, however there is no evidence to support that contention. In practice, all of the candidates had been obliged to accept Edward's lordship as a condition for consideration, and there is no reason to believe that Edward feared Robert Bruce any more than he feared John Balliol.

Claims of feudal superiority of English kings over their northern counterparts had been accepted under duress by several Scottish kings in the past, but they had never been an important aspect of the general pattern of Anglo-Scottish relations. Unlike his predecessors, Edward was determined to put such claims into practice. Again, it has been suggested that Edward chose John because he believed that it would be easier to impose his will as the superior of John than of Robert. Obviously it is impossible to put such an assertion to the test, but it is difficult to believe that Edward would have treated a Bruce monarch any differently to a Balliol monarch. Even if Edward had been more accommodating to Robert – perhaps for personal reasons, since they had known one another for decades – it is worth bearing in mind that Robert was now more than eighty years old and could not be expected to live for very much longer. Robert's son does not seem to have been either a very ambitious or a particularly strong-willed person; undoubtedly Edward would have undermined him in the same way as he undermined John Balliol.

As it turned out, King John's rule was compromised by Edward in several ways. Within a matter of months, Edward was hearing appeals from John's courts, claiming much the same rights over the Scottish king that he enjoyed over English barons. The sequence of events of 1292–95 have been examined at length by several scholars[16] and do not bear repeating here, but the final issue that drove John – or possibly a council of nobles acting on his behalf – was military service. In 1295 Edward issued writs to several Scottish earls and barons and to John himself, demanding troops for his war with France.[17] This was too much to be borne, and the Scots turned to the only quarter from which they could reasonably hope for succour – Philip, King of France.

The decision to enter into a formal alliance against England gave Edward an excuse to take up arms against the Scots, but since he was already on campaign himself, he could not react to this development immediately, and so was obliged to wait until the spring of 1296 before he could take direct action. In theory, the Scots precipitated events inasmuch as they were the first to mount operations by raiding into England, including an abortive attack on Carlisle.

In short, the Scots simply had no real plan for victory and were therefore almost bound to experience defeat. It had been so long since the Scots had been involved in a major war that there was no reservoir of experience in conducting operations. Edward, on the other hand, may not have been an especially accomplished soldier, but he was certainly an experienced one. Moreover he was the undisputed ruler of a much larger realm. The Scots were far from united as well as being inexperienced. The Bruce and Dunbar families may have been the most prominent of the Scottish nobles who elected to either fight for Edward or to not fight at all, but they were not alone. In practice, the absence of the Bruces and the Earl of Dunbar probably had no effect whatsoever on the campaign. On 30th March 1296 Edward's troops stormed the town of Berwick and slaughtered the inhabitants in their thousands.

Criticism of his behaviour is justified in moral terms, but it was an effective strategic gambit. The horrors of the sack of Berwick would have lost nothing in the telling, and any intention to fight entertained by other Scottish towns must have evaporated very swiftly indeed. Four weeks after this the Scots suffered another signal reverse at the battle of Dunbar. Despite the claims of one contemporary writer that the Scottish casualties at Dunbar amounted to more than 11,000,[18] it seems likely that the action was not in fact a particularly large one. There is no evidence to suggest that a great battle of manoeuvre took place at all, rather that the Scottish cavalry – or a portion of it – met a division of Edward's cavalry in the vicinity of Dunbar Castle and were roundly beaten in short order. At least one hundred Scottish nobles were taken prisoner and dispatched to various castles in England, but only one fatal casualty – Patrick Graham – is mentioned and there is no evidence to indicate that the Scottish infantry were engaged at all.

Over the next five months Edward was able to make his way through Scotland as far as Elgin, accepting the surrender of Scottish towns, castles and eventually of King John himself. The complete collapse of the Scottish military and political establishment in the summer of 1296 is rather misleading – it may have misled Edward himself. Quite simply, given the defeat of the nobles and the apparent disintegration of the balance of the army, there was no incentive for garrisons to resist the English army. Edward clearly had a considerable train of siege equipment – his troops bombarded Edinburgh Castle for five days before it surrendered – but there would have been no point in forcing the English to mount a lengthy siege since there was no Scottish army to provide a relief force, nor was there any member of the senior nobility available to raise and lead such a force since virtually all of the magnates were either in the peace of Edward I or were prisoners of war in England – a factor which must have encouraged Edward to believe that had achieved the conquest of Scotland.

The assumption was, however, very seriously flawed in several ways. First and foremost, a shortage of Scottish political and military leadership between the summer of 1296 and the spring of 1297 did not mean that there was no will to resist, merely that there was no stable structure to guide that resistance. The absence of a Scottish force under arms did not mean that there was an absence of men willing to continue the fight given the opportunity to do so. Little more than a year after Edward's return to England, the Scots had found new leaders in the shape of William Wallace and Andrew Murray, who restored Scottish government through most of the country and won a significant battle at Stirling Bridge.[19] Over the following seven years, Edward invested vast sums in his Scottish project, but despite a resounding victory at Falkirk, which propelled Wallace from the post of Guardian, the capture of towns and castles, and the construction of several peels at Linlithgow, Selkirk and Livingstone, Edward was unable to impose his rule through force of arms alone. In February 1304 he came to terms with the Scots. A number of individuals, including William Wallace and the garrison of Stirling Castle – captured by the Scots in 1299 – were specifically excluded from the agreement. Wallace and his small band of men-at-arms continued to mount operations until his capture in August 1305 but, superficially at least, Edward had achieved his objective.

Even at this point, the extent to which he actually believed that the business of conquering Scotland was really concluded is open to question. The relatively easy terms allowed to the Scots are probably a reflection of Edward's urgent need to bring the war to a close for reasons of cost and personal prestige. He was an old man, not in the best of health, and eager to leave a clear legacy of success. By bringing the Balliol party into his peace he achieved his objective of unifying the British Isles under one central authority – that of English kingship – but his achievement was more apparent than real. The Strathord agreement was short-lived and by the spring of 1306, a new threat to Plantagenet rule in Scotland emerged as Robert Bruce declared himself King of Scotland. For the next year and more his prospects were not exactly promising, but by 1308 he had established himself as a serious threat to the occupation.

Continued success brought Robert new supporters and undermined the authority of the Plantagenet administration in Scotland. Edward hardly needed a war to add to his difficulties, but he could hardly have abandoned his father's

Scottish project even if he had wanted to. Withdrawing his troops and administrators from Scotland would have undermined his prestige and authority, not just in England and Wales, but in the great lordships that he held from the king of France. Furthermore, there was a degree of pressure from those members of the political community of England who had received grants of land in Scotland from Edward I, and from those Scots who continued to support the provisions of the Strathord agreement of 1304.

As the Bruce party gained ground over the years after 1307, the plight of English nobles with claims to Scottish titles and from those Scottish nobles who had been displaced by Robert's campaigns increased the pressure on Edward to restore Plantagenet administration in Scotland. Edward mounted several campaigns against the Bruce party, none of which helped to improve his prospects, but they all cost him money and political credibility and may have helped to push some Scots into the Bruce camp. Finally, there was the issue of the credibility of England as a military power and the practicalities of national security. Defeat at the hands of the Scots would undermine the reputation of the English as a nation in arms, but it would also compromise one of the attractions in conquering Scotland in the first place. So long as Scotland was under English control, Edward had a secure northern border. Without that control there was always the prospect that the Scots would ally themselves with the French, which was of course one of the issues that had brought about the campaign of 1296. Edward was caught between a rock and the proverbial hard place. He could not afford to abandon the war in Scotland for political reasons, nor could he achieve the military success necessary to put the Bruce party out of business.

By late 1313 the problem of Scotland had reached crisis proportions. When Edward came to the throne in July 1307 the English administration had covered most of the country, but by the close of 1313 it had been reduced to a mere rump in the southern counties. Even in the counties of the southeast, where a strong chain of castles and fortresses had been developed to prevent the Bruce party from seizing complete control, the ability of the Plantagenet administration to impose Edward's rule had become very isolated. The garrisons may have been able to preserve a veneer of power, but were unable to mount effective operations against the Scots. On the other hand the Scots were increasingly inclined to carry the war to the enemy by mounting operations into England demanding ransoms in cash and produce, which damaged the morale of the communities concerned and undermined Edward's credibility. Just as importantly, the funds raised were a godsend to King Robert. The

operations allowed him to develop a considerable resource in the way of men
with some experience of war and enabled him to pay his men well enough to
prevent them raiding and pillaging at will. This was vital to the success of his
policy. If the people of northern England were to pay Robert's blackmail they
needed to have confidence that they would not suffer from indiscriminate
robbery, rape and murder.

It must have been obvious in the winter of 1313–14 that failure to take
positive action against Robert would eventually result in the loss of all that
remained of the English administration in Scotland, but there was an even
greater threat. One of the most important factors in medieval government
was the ability – or otherwise – to provide 'good lordship'. Clearly Edward
was failing to provide this for his adherents in Scotland, but he was also failing
to provide it for his subjects in Northumberland, Westmorland and Cumbria.
Regardless of whether or not Robert ever harboured ambitions to extend his
borders southwards, there was always the possibility that the political communities of northern England might eventually seek his lordship – as indeed was
the case in the years after Bannockburn. If Edward was to restore his credibility
at home and in Scotland, he desperately needed to defeat Bruce.

The political pressures on Edward to seek battle with the Scots are fairly
self-evident, however we should not assume that there were no political considerations for Robert. His military initiatives in the period between 1307
and 1314 are generally characterised as 'guerrilla' campaigns. In fact, Robert's
general war policy was quite conventional by the standards of the time.
Throughout the medieval period the practice of destroying an enemy's willingness and ability to continue the fight through what we might of think of
as economic warfare was a perfectly normal approach to campaigning. There
was certainly plenty of warfare across Europe throughout the thirteenth and
fourteenth centuries, on the other hand many campaigns, even those involving
large forces, failed to result in a general engagement, and even fewer brought
about more than one major battle. In Scotland there had been more or less
continual warfare from 1296–1304, but the number of actual battles was very
small and only two of these involved more than a couple of thousand combatants in total – Stirling Bridge and Falkirk. This does not mean that battle
was necessarily regarded as undesirable or unimportant, merely that a large
engagement was not something to be undertaken lightly. It must surely have
been apparent to King Robert – and to King Edward for that matter – that
the removal of English garrisons from Scottish town and castles and repeated
raids into England, however profitable, would not be sufficient to bring about

a political settlement of the issue of Scottish independence. Robert needed more than military success if his dynasty was to sit securely on the throne. He also needed more than domestic acceptance of his rule; he needed to achieve the recognition of his right to the throne both at home and abroad. Military success would not be enough to provide him with long-term political credibility and security. If his kingship rested on military means alone then it could also be disrupted, even destroyed, by military means.

Above all, he needed to achieve recognition of his kingship from England. It is not impossible that he might have brought this about through continued success in war, though it is difficult to see quite how that could have come about. Arguably, it might have been achieved through the annexation of large tracts of northern England which could have been returned to England in exchange for a permanent peace agreement, but there are two major flaws to such a possibility. Firstly, it assumes that Edward II would have been prepared to surrender his claims to Robert in exchange for counties of very limited economic value to the crown of England, and secondly, the long-term military occupation of Northumberland, Westmorland and Cumbria would unquestionably have been an insupportable drain on his resources. Even if such an occupation could have been achieved, it would have done nothing more than give Robert the same problems that Edward faced in Scotland – the challenge of maintaining a military occupation in the face of a hostile population. More importantly perhaps, Scottish occupation of English counties might well have inspired the wider political community of England to redouble their efforts in support of Edward's Scottish ambitions, serving to unite the magnates of England behind a king who was somewhat less than popular.

Assuming that Robert's English campaigns were intended to bring Edward to the negotiating table, it was a policy that had clearly failed by the spring of 1314. Edward had been willing to allow his representatives to enter into truces with the Bruce party,[20] but only on the understanding that they were acting – at least in theory – on their own initiative, not on the orders of, or even with the acquiescence of, the English crown. Clearly Robert needed to develop another dimension to his strategy. It would be rash to assume that he had come to the conclusion that victory in battle was the only means of achieving his aims, but equally it would be unrealistic to assume that he did not have it in mind as an option. Another option would have been to continue with his existing policy in the hope that Edward's domestic political difficulties would eventually cause revolution and civil war in England. This was certainly possible given Edward's relationship with some of his nobles. In the recent past,

Edward had been obliged to accept the banishment of his closest friend, Piers Gaveston, and the constraints of a set of conditions imposed by a coalition of magnates known as the 'Ordainers.'[21]

Edward may not have been either popular or particularly secure at the end of 1313, but the worst of the crisis was past and so was any immediate chance that political instability in England might provide an opportunity for Robert to gain recognition as King of Scotland.

Another avenue for a non-military political settlement was diplomacy. Robert may have entertained hopes that recognition by the King of France and the Pope might be a precursor to inclusion in a wider political settlement of outstanding issues between Edward and Philip relating to French lordships held by the king of England. However, there were significant barriers to anything of that nature, not least the fact that Robert was an excommunicate on account of the murder of John Comyn at the Greyfriars church in Dumfries. More to the point, Edward would have had little to gain and a great deal to lose by reaching an accommodation with Robert. Any attempt to discard what was seen as the 'right' of his father – and himself of course – to lordship over Scotland would have been seen as a betrayal of the nation and the vast sums that he had expended on his Scottish campaigns and garrisons would have been thrown away for the sake of bringing an end to a war that most English magnates had yet to see as a lost cause.

Given the very limited prospects for a political settlement that would bring recognition of his kingship abroad, it would be unreasonable to assume that Robert did not give serious consideration to the possibilities that might arise from a major victory on the battlefield. It is certainly true that a repeat of his strategy of avoiding combat might yet bear fruit. If Edward were to lead another great army into Scotland but fail to force battle on the Scots, the damage to his political prestige might be enough to reopen the question of his political authority in England. The expense of a major expedition which did not bring the restoration of Plantagenet rule in Scotland would have been a blow to Edward's prestige and might have led to widespread resentment at the increased burden of taxation that would have been necessary to pay for the troops and munitions committed to the operation. On the other hand, both Edward and his father had been through this process before and neither had felt obliged to give up on the conquest of Scotland. Indeed, even a relatively successful invasion that did result in a major victory for English arms might not produce any tangible benefits. In 1298 Edward I had destroyed the army of Sir William Wallace at Falkirk, but all that had been achieved was the removal of

Wallace from the office of Guardian. That victory had not brought about the collapse of the Balliol party, but had provided the opportunity for the traditional political leadership of Scottish society to assert itself.

An English victory in 1314 therefore, might or might not have a positive effect on Edward's prospects, but a defeat would certainly have had very real benefits for Robert. If the Scots scored a victory, even a marginal one, Edward's credibility would have been seriously impaired at home and also in Scotland. Failure to defeat Robert in the field would unquestionably jeopardise the remaining garrisons, but it would also undermine the loyalty of those Scots who still adhered to the Plantagenet cause. This was an issue of some importance to King Robert in the winter of 1313 – English garrisons and administrators still retained a measure of control in some southern counties.

As it turned out, by the summer of 1314 the crucial strongholds of Edinburgh and Roxburgh had already been recovered and the English administration in Lothian, Roxburghshire and Berwickshire had virtually ceased to exist. Mr Nusbacher is quite wrong in his assertion that:

> The Lothian fortresses were firmly in English hands, making it difficult indeed for King Robert to muster his army in Lauderdale.[22]

Edinburgh fell in March 1314[23] and there is no English record material to indicate that any of the other Lothian castles still contained English garrisons or any material to indicate that Robert ever had any intention of mustering his army in Lauderdale.

There were still some Scots in the southern and eastern counties who were prepared to turn out to support the Plantagenet cause and probably rather more who, though no longer active for King Edward, were not yet prepared to turn out for King Robert, but the few remaining garrisons, such as Bothwell and Berwick, were no longer able to impose Edward's lordship in the surrounding communities. The failing strength of the English garrisons did not, in itself, mean that Robert's kingship had been fully established in Lothian, Lanarkshire, Roxburghshire, Berwickshire and Dumfriesshire, so even in the spring of 1314 the southern counties must still have represented something of a challenge to the Bruce cause. If an English invasion could be defeated without battle then these communities would, in all probability, have fallen into King Robert's hands, but the process would surely be hastened if he could inflict a defeat on his rival.

There was also the wider question of Robert's credibility throughout the country as a whole. Bluntly, most of the political community must have been aware that, even with the best will in the world, Robert was not the legitimate king. Victory on the battlefield would not in itself give him political legitimacy, but it would certainly enhance his prestige and damage the prospects of any movement to restore the Balliol monarchy. This was not such a far-fetched prospect bearing in mind that despite his victories – military and political – King Robert was threatened by a coup in 1320.[24] Although it is known to history as the De Soulis Conspiracy, the real objective of the conspirators was to replace Robert with Edward Balliol. If there was still a strong sympathy for the Balliol party in 1320 it would be unreasonable to assume that there was none at all in 1314 or that Robert was unaware that there were people in his allegiance who would be willing to transfer their loyalty to the man who was, after all, the legitimate heir to the throne.

If victory on the battlefield held potential benefits in the military, diplomatic and political spheres there was also, arguably, a religious dimension; victory could be construed as an endorsement by God. It is quite possible that some people would have seen defeat of the English as an indication that God favoured the Bruce cause, or that defeat of the Scots would have been an indication that he favoured the Plantagenets; however there is very little evidence to support such a view. Neither the Scots nor the English could claim to have enjoyed continual success in their campaigns at different times, which would rather undermine the idea that divine intervention was a major factor in warfare. Naturally, both sides claimed to have God on their side; the bishop of Moray[25] going so far as to claim that taking up arms against the English was as worthy as going on crusade. No doubt there was a limited degree of propaganda value among the more credulous, but given the severity of the defeat at Falkirk in 1298, it is hard to imagine that many people were deeply affected by the theological considerations or by whether or not the conflict could be categorised as a 'just war' for either the Scots or the English. In practice, most people probably saw the conflict for what it was – a political struggle between kings and nations, and not a demonstration of God's will.

# Lions and Leopards: The Careers of Robert I and Edward II

## The Leopard: Edward II

In many respects Edward II was a very similar man to his father. He was strong, handsome and personally courageous; he was fond of the outdoor life and strenuous exercise including swimming and wrestling. He was a literate man, partial to romances and drama. His hobbies and passions have led to him being seen as a man who was not in sympathy with the members of his court. To a great extent he was not, but not because of the pleasure he took in literature – there was nothing 'unmanly' or 'anti-aristocratic' or even unusual about a man of his class owning books or enjoying plays. He also had some of his father's faults. He was partial to gambling and prone to promoting men because he liked them, not because of their abilities. Both father and son were ambitious men, though not perhaps in quite the same sense. Edward I was eager to conquer Scotland; Edward II was eager to retain her, but not perhaps so much as a demonstration of his will and ability, as a sheer reluctance to give up any part of what he viewed as his 'heritage'.

He was not a very successful soldier, but he was not devoid of military experience either. In 1301[1] he was in command of a substantial force at Carlisle that had been tasked with operations against the Scots in the south west in the

hope, according to his father, that he would acquire 'the chief honour of tam-
ing the pride of the Scots.' The campaign that ensued was not a great success,
but it was not a complete failure either. By September, the Bruce stronghold of
Turnberry had fallen to the Prince Edward's troops.[2]

Shortly after he came to the throne, Edward married Isabella, daughter of
King Philip of France. It was not a very happy union, though it did produce
four children and Edward had at least one other child out of wedlock.[3] By
the time of his marriage, Edward had already formed a close relationship
with Piers Gaveston and before the end of 1308 there was already a rumour
that Edward was rather more partial to the company of his friend than of
his queen. She was described as a 'most elegant lady and beautiful woman,'[4]
but it is worth noting that she was also just twelve years old. She would
have to have been a most precocious teenager to be capable of offering better company than the witty, elegant and entertaining Gaveston, even if he
and Edward were not lovers, and if they *were* lovers – as seems most likely
– she would have had no chance at all of ousting Gaveston from the king's
favour.

Edward did not spend much time with his queen, and seems to have
made no great effort to involve her in either his political or social life. At
the time of Bannockburn, Isabella would only have been about eighteen
years old and therefore still unlikely to be a stimulating companion for any
grown man, let alone one who was homosexual. On the other hand he
did not neglect her entirely. He showed considerable interest in her physical comfort and well-being and he seems to have been very fond of his
children. Even after she elected to remain in France, Edward seems to have
been genuinely upset and not a little confused at her reluctance to return
to England.

The blame for the failure of Edward and Isabella's marriage has often
been laid at the feet of Piers Gaveston or, more reasonably, attributed to
Edward's preference for, and generosity to, his close friend. Gaveston himself is generally seen as a 'nobody' plucked from obscurity by the king's
friendship. Gaveston certainly benefited from Edward's largesse; he did not
stem from an especially humble background, but from a prominent Gascon
noble family. He was widely resented among the English magnates, not least
for his practice of giving uncomplimentary nicknames to prominent members of Edward's court. Gloucester was 'whoreson', Pembroke was 'Joseph
the Jew' and Warwick – who would eventually kill Gaveston – was 'The
Black Dog of Arden.' As well as his fierce wit, Gaveston was resented for his

remarkable rise in status and wealth, particularly after Edward made him Earl of Cornwall. A more circumspect and tactful person might have found a way of smoothing ruffled magnatial feathers and integrating themselves into the community of earls and great lords, but Gaveston seems to have had a real talent for offending the mighty.

Gaveston served Edward in Scotland during the abortive campaign of 1310–11, and appears to have discharged his duties in a reasonably effective manner, however the army raised was not adequate to the task of carrying the war to the Scots. Indeed, the main purpose of mounting the campaign at all seems to have had much more to do with Edward's desire to avoid his domestic political problems and protecting his favourite than it did with pursuing the recovery of the Plantagenet government. If Edward thought that a Scottish campaign would defuse opposition he was sadly mistaken; few English magnates heeded his call to arms, and by the summer of 1312 matters had come to a head, with several English magnates taking up arms against the king's government. It was at this point that the Ordainers, who had forced Edward to accept the existence of a committee of twenty-one magnates charged with producing a blueprint for government reforms, over-reached themselves. Gaveston, besieged in Scarborough Castle, surrendered to Aymer De Valence, Earl of Pembroke, but was snatched from De Valence's custody by Warwick, who promptly had him executed. This was a gross insult to De Valence and to John de Warenne, Earl of Surrey, who had given their word to Gaveston that he would not be harmed in their hands. Warwick's actions pushed Pembroke and Surrey into the king's party, and Gaveston's death eased Edward's domestic situation to some degree. His queen, Isabella, had resented Gaveston's prominence, which, she felt, diminished her own position. This in turn helped Edward's relationship with his father-in-law, the King of France, despite that fact that Philip had, effectively, though not formally, recognised Robert's kingship. While Edward tried to deal with his domestic and political problems, the Scots continued to apply military pressure, but not just in Scotland. As early as 1309, the community of Northumberland was incapable of contributing to a crown subsidy due to the impact of raids by Robert's troops.[5]

The opposition of the English magnates prevented Edward from raging war in Scotland and a truce was arranged early in 1309 which would run to the summer of 1310, at which point Edward was able to renew the conflict.[6] However, the increasingly strong position of Robert and the slender force that Edward could commit to the campaign meant that little was achieved.

He returned to England and entered into negotiations with his opposition – the Lords Ordainers – to bring matters relating to taxation and the royal prerogative to a mutually acceptable conclusion. It seems to have been a tortuous business, but an agreement was reached at Edward's Parliament of October 1313.

The range of events that transpired at this time – King Robert's declared intention to forfeit Scottish lords who failed to come to his peace over the next twelve months,[7] a petition of Sir Adam Gordon and the Earl of Dunbar seeking protection against both the Bruce party and the troops of the Plantagenet garrisons[8] and the increasing isolation of his remaining Scottish assets – suggest, perhaps, that Edward was prepared to make more concessions to the Ordainers than he would have liked. But he was obliged to go some way toward meeting their demands in the interests of raising troops for a campaign in 1314, a matter eased by a grant of taxation from his 1313 Parliament.

It would be unfair to suggest that Edward's need to mount an offensive in 1314 was simply the product of his failure to address the situation earlier in his reign. It is true that he abandoned the campaign that his father had mounted in 1307, but he did have pressing problems, not least the enormous debt which Edward I had incurred over the previous twenty years and more. This amounted to something in the region of £200,000 – a massive sum, even for government debt, and well beyond Edward's immediate resources. That he managed to discharge his obligations and even put away a substantial sum by the time of his deposition and death was a remarkable achievement, but it could not have been done in the short-term, and the pursuit of a 1307 campaign against Robert would only have made matters worse. In addition to his immediate financial difficulties, Edward faced a good deal of political opposition from the very first days of his reign. Some of these – particularly his determination to shower lands, wealth and power on Gaveston – were of his own making, but others were inherited from his father's reign. Edward I had also had to deal with a lot of opposition from his magnates, but he had always been able to face them down before anger turned into defiance. Edward II was not so astute a politician as his father, and certainly did not have such a weight of experience. It would not be surprising if some part of the opposition to Edward II had its roots in the resentment of men who had been out-manoeuvred by his father.

Edward II's reign was hardly an example of English kingship at its best; his reputation as an incompetent and ill-advised monarch is, by and large, justified. On the other hand, he was not the only English king to experience serial misfortunes, nor the only one to bring many of his problems on himself. Henry II faced opposition from his sons, let alone his barons; Richard I managed to become a prisoner; Henry III had to deal with an extensive civil war and Edward I's ambitions had brought on a financial crisis – but none of them carries the weight of censure and opprobrium heaped onto Edward II. Defeat in Scotland was not Edward's only problem by a long way, but it is the issue with which he is most closely associated. National leaders – until modern times at least – have often had to bear the responsibility for national disasters, and Edward has had to carry the blame for Bannockburn. To an extent, this is neither surprising nor unrealistic, but it is not altogether fair. War with Scotland was not Edward's project, it was a situation that had been engendered by his father. He was not responsible for the dire financial situation of 1307, nor was he entirely responsible for the difficult relationship between the crown and the senior nobility, but he is widely held to be entirely responsible for the defeat at Bannockburn and the depredations of the Scots in northern England.

The latter was a product of the inability of the English crown to impose a settlement on the Scots through force of arms, and is a rather wider issue than victory or defeat in one battle. The former was certainly Edward's problem, but the extent to which he was personally responsible for losing the battle can be exaggerated. Edward was not alone at Bannockburn; he was surrounded by several very experienced and competent soldiers – Aymer de Valence, Sir Robert Clifford and Henry Beaumont to name but a few. None of these men seem to have been dismayed at the prospect of bringing the Scots to battle and none seem to have been responsible for the location chosen for the English camp on the night of 23/24th June 1314 – probably the single most significant factor in the Scots' victory.

Edward's most crucial failure in relation to Scotland was his decision to carry on the fight at all. Edward I had failed to impose Plantagenet rule despite a decade of massive political, military and financial effort. However, even if he had wanted to do so, Edward could not have abandoned his father's project. Accepting Robert as King of Scotland and disbanding the garrisons in 1307 would have been seen as an admission of defeat and weakness. Furthermore, the military situation at the time of Edward I's death did not indicate massive support for the Bruce cause, so withdrawal would have had an adverse impact on Edward's prestige. Additionally, in the period since 1296, a number of prominent English lords had developed interests in Scottish properties. Some of these were men of great status who had provided the English crown with troops in 1296 with a view to receiving grants of land at the expense of Scottish lords who resisted Edward's invasion. Some were men who had made their careers in Scotland, men like Pier de Lubaud[9] and the Hastangs family,[10] whose service as soldiers and administrators in the occupation had been rewarded with substantial landholdings. Both of these groups had a vested interest in maintaining English rule, since they stood to lose their acquisitions if the Bruce party (or the Balliol party between 1296 and 1304) were to restore Scottish kingship. These were not the only factors that put pressure on Edward to continue the war. By the close of 1308 several Scots who had aligned themselves with the Plantagenet cause had been driven off their estates and had become pensioners of the English crown pending the recovery of English fortunes in Scotland. Defections to the Bruce party from this group would have a deleterious effect on Edward's credibility; if he were to retain their loyalty, he would have to take steps to restore them to their former prominence.

The repeated incursions of the Bruce party into the northern counties of England must have diminished Edward's standing at home.[11] The economic burden of these raids was marginal in terms of the damage to Edward's income, though highly significant to King Robert. Failure to protect his subjects in the far north may not have had a great impact on the magnates of the far south, but Edward could not afford to ignore Scottish operations indefinitely; if Robert's campaigns were not stopped, the political communities of Northumberland and Cumbria might eventually turn to Robert for 'good lordship.' There were no signs of this in 1314, despite the huge sums levied by Robert's lieutenants and the ability of the Scots to demand free passage through the most northern English counties in order to pursue campaigns further south, but the risk of disaffection and defection among the landholders and burghal communities of northern England must surely have been apparent to Edward and his counsellors.

Finally, there was the question of Edward's personal prestige. As the king of a major European power, he could not afford to be defeated by a relatively minor nation like Scotland. Moreover, if he could bring the Scots to battle and defeat them, his political stock would rise at home since he would have been following in the footsteps of his father, a man more popular in death than he had been in life. A successful campaign would do more than damage the Bruce party – it would provide an opportunity to bring the political community of England together in defence of the 'right' of their king at a time when Edward was in sore need of a unifying influence among his nobles.

Whether the conquest of Scotland was really a viable project given the resources of late medieval English kings is another matter. Edward's father's achievements in Scotland had probably already become inflated in the perception of the English, and any reduction in Edward's power in Scotland may have been seen as a betrayal of the late king. With hindsight it is easy to see that Edward I's Scottish ventures had not brought a real victory, just transitory gains in periods when he could maintain a large force north of the border. At best he had procured a peace of sorts in February 1304, but was not able to put an end to Balliol resistance until the summer of 1305 when Wallace was captured. Edward I may have wished to believe that he had finally achieved his goal with Wallace's death, but it was hardly a 'final' peace. Little more than six months after Wallace's death, Robert Bruce renewed the struggle for Scottish independence.

The rise of the Bruce party and the diminution of the occupation through 1308–1313 had not been marked by any large-scale battles; there had been no large-scale general engagements since Falkirk in 1298. The experience of the English during that period was that it was exceptionally difficult to force battle on the Scots, but if a battle could be brought about, the superior numbers of the English army in general and of the heavy cavalry element in particular, would be more than sufficient to ensure victory. The experience of Falkirk had demonstrated the effectiveness of a 'combined arms' approach to battle. The cavalry had proved incapable of crushing the Scottish schiltroms without archer support, but the Scots had no effective answer to massed archery.

We should not assume that the English command was utterly complacent about combat. On the contrary, we should be safer to assume that Edward and his lieutenants – some of whom, like Clifford, Beaumont and De Valence, had served in 1298 – had analysed what they knew about Falkirk and had developed policies and plans to make the best use of English assets when attacking an army in a strong defensive position. We should not doubt that Edward intended to take the initiative and force the Scots to fight and that he – or his subordinates – had adopted a plan for victory based on their knowledge and experience. They may of course have hoped, even expected, to score a victory without actually coming to blows at all. The Scots had avoided combat during the 1303–4 and 1310–11 campaigns and might well attempt to do so again. Failure to bring the Scots to battle would not reflect well on Edward's abilities, but both he and his lieutenants seem to have been perfectly confident that the Scots could be defeated if they could be forced to fight. Without a battle, Edward could only hope that Robert's credibility might be fatally undermined if, having raised a large army, he did not take the field, but instead returned to his usual policy of evasion.

Edward was eager to fight, and the composition of his army illustrates that. Aware of the likely nature of a campaign in Scotland, Edward had called for large number of infantry, but he had also ensured that a very powerful cavalry army was mustered. Essentially he hoped to have an overwhelming superiority in foot should the Scots give battle and an equally impressive superiority in men-at-arms to pursue them if they did not. None of this proves that Edward really expected to have to fight. The sheer size of his army might be enough to persuade the Scots to decline battle and retire to less accessible terrain, but if the Scots were to accept battle, Edward had an army suitable for the purpose. Further, Edward and his lieutenants had a healthy knowledge and understanding of Robert's military resources. They knew that Scottish men-at-arms, spearmen and archers were no different to English ones, but that the numbers available to Robert were very much inferior. In the campaigns of small actions and sieges that had characterised the preceding years, this superiority had not been too significant; English troops could not be everywhere at once, so the Scots only needed to achieve local superiority. It would be a different matter if they could be manoeuvred into a major action; the Scots might even be so demoralised by the scale of the English army that 'shock and awe' might drive them into total flight.

# The Lion: Robert I

When King John's army assembled at Caddonlea to resist Edward I in March 1296 there were a number of notable absences in its ranks. Three of Scotland's most prominent magnates – Gilbert D'Umfraville, Earl of Angus (an Englishman with extensive properties south of the border), Patrick, Earl of Dunbar and Robert Bruce, Earl of Carrick – had chosen to give their allegiance and their military resources to Edward I. It is more likely that none of them actually saw any combat during the 1296 campaign, but they were certainly in the peace of the King of England and were therefore in a state of rebellion against the King of Scotland. Each had his own reasons for failing to support their monarch. For Dunbar, there was the risk to his property. Virtually all of his landholdings lay in the counties of Roxburghshire, Berwickshire and Lothian and were therefore extremely vulnerable to an English invasion. Dunbar evidently did not feel confident that the Scots would be able to offer the kind of resistance to Edward that would protect his property, but was in the curious position of not having possession of his chief residence, Dunbar Castle, which was being held for the Balliol cause by his own wife.[12]

Like Dunbar, the Bruce family was no longer in possession of its heritage. Failure to endorse the recent treaty made with France and to respond to the summons for military service had resulted in the family estates of the Lordship of Annandale and the Earldom of Carrick being seized and put into the hands of John Comyn, but Bruce ambitions were probably more significant than the loss of property. Robert's grandfather had never accepted his rejection for the throne, and had passed his claim to his heirs. His eldest son, also Robert, does not seem to have entertained any regal ambitions and remained steadfast in Plantagenet allegiance until his death in 1304. His grandson – another Robert – was rather more ambitious. By supporting Edward I against King John he hoped to do more than achieve the restoration of his lands and titles, he apparently still harboured hope of a resurrection of the Bruce family's claim to the throne. If so he was to be sorely disappointed. Edward swept Robert's ambitions aside and then set about forming a new administration that would govern Scotland in his name.

By the summer of 1297 the Balliol cause had made a remarkable recovery under the leadership of the heir of a senior northeast baron, Andrew Murray and the younger son of a minor gentry family, William Wallace. The uprising of Wallace and Andrew Murray is the most well-known act of resistance to Edward, but the fame of these young men and the battle they won at Stirling Bridge has rather obscured another significant attack on Edward's rule. The bishop of Glasgow, James the Stewart of Scotland and Sir William Douglas (father of King Robert's lieutenant, Sir James) gathered troops and conducted some minor operations against the occupation in the southwest while William Wallace and Andrew Murray did the same in central and northeast Scotland respectively. It is by no means certain that all three of these insurrections were planned as a concerted effort, though it is difficult to imagine that the bishop and the Stewart thought they would be capable of defying Edward's government on their own. They were both men of considerable wealth and influence, but their resources were very limited in comparison to those of the English crown.

They did, however, have the backing of one other great lord, Robert Bruce. As Professor Barrow has pointed out,[13] Bruce had '...everything to gain by loyalty to Edward, everything to lose by supporting the hopeless and reckless enterprise of Wishart and the Stewart,' but join them he did. What is most remarkable about Bruce's defection is that he was supporting King John, the very cause that he had refused to espouse in 1295–6. His motivation for doing so is not at all clear. There were rumours that he had the crown in his sights, but no real evidence to support this. By the end of June, the forces of this 'noble revolt' were at Irvine, where they were approached by a major English force under Sir Robert Clifford and Sir Henry Percy. The troops assembled by the Scottish lords were no match for the army, and no sooner had Percy and Clifford arrived at Irvine than the Scots were seeking terms for surrender. Percy and Clifford do not seem to have been anxious to force battle and negotiations continued for a month and more before a settlement was reached.[14] In the meantime, Wallace and Murray were able to gather more men, conduct more operations and, most importantly, start to erect a Balliol administration in competition with Edward's government. Robert himself managed to avoid surrendering and was still at liberty and probably active in the Balliol cause until at least November 1297, but the noble revolt had fizzled out by September, when Wallace and Murray led their troops to victory at Stirling Bridge.

By November Murray was dead, possibly from wounds incurred at Stirling and Wallace, now a knight, had become the sole leader of the Balliol party. For the next ten months Wallace carried on the process of restoring government in the name of King John,[15] but was utterly defeated by Edward at the Battle of Falkirk in July 1298. Wallace's political power had been a product of his military success rather than the more traditional basis for political influence, landed wealth. Before the end of the year he had either resigned or been removed from the post of Guardian of the Realm[16] and returned to the role that had brought him to prominence in the first place – leader of a company of men-at-arms.

Before the end of the year he had been replaced by two magnates, men whose leadership of major family and geographical affiliations gave then a degree of political weight that Wallace could not aspire to – John Comyn of Badenoch and Robert Bruce of Carrick and Annandale. Comyn's participation is hardly surprising; his family had been strong supporters of the Scottish crown for generations. But the continuing presence of Robert Bruce in the Balliol party makes less sense. Why should Bruce, a candidate for Scottish kingship himself (at least in his own opinion), act in support of a king that he had opposed in arms as recently as the spring of 1296, and a cause that had recently suffered a major defeat at the hands of King Edward? Politically, if Robert was ever to acquire the crown, it was vital that he be seen in a favourable light in regard to the struggle for independence. He could hardly claim to be active in the patriotic cause if he was in the service of Edward I. His alignment with the Balliol party does not necessarily imply that he was confident of King John's reinstatement, merely that he saw the Balliol cause as the best avenue for political independence in current circumstances. Militarily, the situation of the Balliol party was not so precarious as we might at first expect. Edward had scored a victory at Falkirk, but had made little real progress in bringing the country under his control. Wallace and Murray's efforts had led to the recovery of Balliol administration throughout most of Scotland north of the River Forth, and the Plantagenet garrisons, though powerful, were failing to extend Edward's rule. Further, though Bruce and Comyn must have been all too well aware of the relative weakness of the Scottish military establishment compared to that in England, they will also have been aware that Edward already had other military objectives to pursue and that he was facing increasing antipathy from his own lords.

The Bruce-Comyn alliance was not an easy one; there was political rivalry and a personal animosity that resulted in violence on at least one occasion, but they did manage to keep the war going and even to extend the scope of Balliol rule. Hugh and Margaret de Penicuik were active in the Balliol interest in Lothian,[17] Stirling Castle fell to a force under Sir Herbert Morham before the end of 1299[18] and the Balliol party were able to hold two Parliaments in 1300,[19] but it had already become necessary to redefine the Guardianship. In August, a fight broke out at a meeting of the Scottish leadership at Peebles, in the course of which Comyn had taken Bruce by the throat.[20] Clearly there needed to be a calming influence in the upper echelons of the Balliol party, and William Lamberton, the Bishop of St Andrews, was elected as the chief guardian with Bruce and Comyn as his lieutenants. This arrangement was short-lived. At some point before the spring of 1302 Bruce defected to Edward I. He may have done so because of the actions of King Edward, who led a large army into southwest Scotland in that summer. Apart from lifting the Scottish siege at Lochmaben, laying siege to Caerlaverock and scattering a force of Scottish in a modest action on the River Cree,[21] the English army – the first really significant force to be committed to Scotland since the Falkirk campaign – achieved very little. Edward, obliged to attend to his other pressing concerns, agreed a truce with the Scots which was to last from the end of October to 21st May 1301. Although Edward continued to pursue his campaign, the Scots were able to hold their own and on 26th January 1302 he was obliged to make another truce with them, this time for a duration of nine months.

Since Edward was making little, if any, progress against the Balliol party it should seem curious that Robert should defect to the English before the middle of February 1302, but there had been a considerable change in the Scottish political arena. In place of the joint guardianships, Sir John Soulis had been appointed as sole Guardian, probably with direct authority from King John.[22] The issue that prompted Robert's defection was probably the news that John, who had been entrusted to Papal custody, had now been given into the custody of the King of France. The prospect of a Balliol restoration was now a very real threat to Robert's position, for although he had been active in the Balliol cause between 1297 and late 1301 or early 1302, he had been one of the most significant absentees from John's army in 1296 and was of course a potential threat to John's kingship.

Naturally, if he was to defect, Robert needed to reach an accommodation with King Edward. The terms of the agreement have been discussed by historians at great length and there are two particular items which have been the occasion of comment. The first refers to Edward's promise that he would do his utmost to ensure that Robert would not be disinherited of his heritage lands, whether in England or Scotland; the second is his acceptance that Robert should be free to 'pursue his right' in the event of King John returning to Scotland.[23] The precise nature of 'his right' is not stated, but it has been suggested that the only 'right' Robert might wish to pursue in 1302 would have been his claim to the throne. This raises the possibility that Edward was prepared to consider acceptance of Robert as the Scottish king, presumably on the basis of the feudal superiority that he had demanded of John in 1292. This might have led to a schism among the Scots which would, obviously, be in Edward's interests, but it is difficult to imagine that Edward would have been prepared to promote the interests of a man who had but recently been a sore thorn in his flesh.

Bruce's defection was only one of a number of blows that the Balliol party suffered over the next two years. The defeat of the French at Courtrai weakened King Philip's negotiating position with Edward, and the Scots were excluded from the terms of a peace agreement between England and France. The Balliol cause was not yet dead, but it had been fatally wounded. Edward led another army into Scotland, and this time stayed there for the whole winter, driving the Scots to surrender on terms at Strathord in February 1304. There were still minor elements of resistance – Fraser and Wallace were still in the field and the garrison of Stirling continued to defy Edward until July, but the Balliol cause had ceased to be a viable one.

The siege of Stirling was a major event. Edward even built a special viewing platform so that his queen and her courtiers could observe its progress.[24] A number of Scottish magnates were present, but the most significant among them were Robert Bruce and Bishop Lamberton. The two men made a pact that bound them not to undertake any hazardous ventures without the consent of the other.[25] The document does not state explicitly the nature of what such ventures might be, but the only logical possibility is that they were referring to Robert's claim to the throne; a major change in the position of Lamberton who had, until this point, been a faithful and constant prop to John's kingship. For the next year or so, Robert seems to have largely devoted himself to the business of lordship, but at Edward's Parliament of 1305 he, along with Bishop Wishart of Glasgow and Sir John Moubray – a prominent baron – was called upon to advise Edward on the future of Scotland.[26] In due course this led to the appointment of a lieutenant for Scotland who, with the aid of a chancellor and chamberlain and the advice of a number of Scottish and English nobles, would appoint a council to help draw up an ordinance for the future government of Scotland – a council that would include arch-rivals Robert Bruce and John Comyn.

E.M.Barron has suggested that Bruce had already fallen from favour by the time the Ordinance was finalised in September 1305, in part because of one of the entries, which reads:

> Also, it is agreed that the Earl of Carrick shall be commanded to put Kildrummy Castle in the keeping of such a man as he himself will be willing to answer for.[27]

The wording conveys – as Professor Barrow has pointed out – a 'tone of mistrust,' however exactly the same phrase appears in another document, requiring the same commitment from Aymer de Valence,[28] who can hardly have been considered suspect. He was, after all, a senior and trusted aide, advisor and friend of King Edward.

Robert's attempt to restore independent Scottish kingship was probably premature, but his hand was forced by his own actions. In February 1306 he met with his chief rival on the Scottish political scene, John Comyn. In Barbour's narrative, Robert offered Comyn a deal which would allow the Comyn and Bruce parties to co-operate against Edward's administration. In a meeting at the Greyfriars Church in Dumfries, Bruce offered to cede his lordships to Comyn if Comyn would give him unequivocal support as king, or, alternatively, Comyn would transfer his lordships to Bruce and take the throne himself. However Professor Duncan suggests that it was 'unlikely' the meeting was arranged to discuss Scottish kingship, accepting the Guisborough interpretation that the Earl of Carrick was accusing John of undermining his position with Edward I.[29]

The chief problem with Barbour's story is that neither Bruce nor Comyn really had a legitimate claim to the throne as long as King John or his heir, Edward Balliol, was still alive. Moreover, if the Bruce claim were invalid, any Comyn claim would be even less credible. It is difficult to see how either Bruce or Comyn could commit themselves to the pact described by Barbour. Whichever stood aside to allow the other the throne would be in a very vulnerable position. Had Robert passed his lordships to John Comyn he would have been giving up his family's heritage lands in exchange for the properties of the crown, but only if he could make his kingship a reality; the Comyn family on the other hand would have gained an enormous addition to what was already a vast range of properties. In addition to being the most significant magnates in the northeast, they would become the most powerful political force in the southwest and therefore potentially too strong a force to be contained should they decide to desert the Bruce cause. On the other hand, who could they look to for aid if they were persecuted by King Robert and were unable to defeat him from their own resources? By helping Robert to become king they would have forsaken any chance of appealing for aid from the King of England. The reverse would also hold true if the Comyn heritage passed to the Bruces.

Any chance of future co-operation between the Bruce and Comyn parties was, in any case, made impossible by Robert's actions since the Greyfriars meeting was concluded by Robert – or possibly one of his adherents – stabbing John Comyn to death at the altar of the church. Comyn's murder pushed Robert into premature action. He could either attempt to defend himself against criminal charges in court, take to the hills and hope to negotiate a pardon from King Edward, or attempt to put himself on the Scottish throne. The first of these possible courses of action would have had to depend on principles of law – possibly a claim that he had acted in self-defence. The second would have depended on acquiring the favour of King Edward. Neither of these courses seems to have held out much hope for Robert, and he immediately set about gathering support for his kingship. On Lady Day, 25 March, 1306 he had himself installed as King of Scotland in a ceremony conducted by three of the twelve Scottish bishops– Glasgow, St Andrews and Moray – and the Abbot of Scone. This was followed by a second ceremony on Palm Sunday, 27 March.[30] By tradition the Earls of Fife played a major part in the inauguration of Scottish kings. The current Earl, Duncan, was still under age, and was, in any case, effectively in the custody of Edward I. It would seem that his role was taken by his sister, Isabel.

Her participation is interesting on two accounts. It is generally accepted that women had no position in the political life of the Middle Ages, yet here is an example of a woman performing a significant political act and nobody at the time seems to have regarded this as an unnatural or even very innovative event. Additionally, Isabel was more than the sister of the Earl of Fife, she was the wife of John Comyn, Earl of Buchan, a sworn enemy of Robert Bruce.

Robert threw himself into the business of enlisting political and military support, but his future did not look bright, even his great ally Bishop Lamberton was sufficiently dubious about the outcome that he opened negotiations to rejoin Edward's peace sometime before 9 June.[31] Before the end of that month Aymer de Valence had assembled a strong force and captured Perth, an action which attracted the attention of the newly-inaugurated king, who moved to recover the town. Robert may have been misinformed about the scale of De Valence's force or simply over-confident about the capacities of his own army. Far from containing the enemy in the town and laying siege to it, Robert's army was attacked and scattered by De Valence.[32] Robert led the remainder of his force westward, only to be defeated again, this time by John MacDougall.[33]

His primary objective for the next six months and more was survival, and he spent the winter of 1306–7 in hiding – possibly in the West Highlands, possibly on the island of Rathlin off the northeast coast of Ireland, or possibly in Norway, at the home of his sister, queen of the late King Eric. He had not given up the fight, and around the beginning of February mounted two operations against the English, one in Galloway led by his brothers Thomas and Alexander, and the other under his own leadership, to Carrick.[34] Neither of these operations was successful. Thomas and Alexander were captured and executed and, although Robert's force inflicted a minor defeat on men of the Turnberry castle garrison, the weakness of his following and the strength of the occupation forced him to take to the hills of Carrick and Galloway. By May, however, he had gathered enough men to meet and defeat an English party at Glen Trool[35] and, on 10 May, to confront a more significant force under De Valence at Loudon[36] and another led by the Earl of Gloucester just three days later.[37]

The Bruce cause seems to have started to gain real political momentum after these actions, but Robert's war was still little more than a localised problem for the occupation, and a major invasion was in hand for the summer of 1307. The operation was delayed by the long-expected death of Edward I in July, but it was not abandoned. The new king led his troops northwards, but only as far as Cumnock, Ayrshire, before returning to England. This, rather than the death of Edward I, was a turning point for Bruce's fortunes. Edward II has borne a great deal of criticism for not pursuing the objective of destroying the Bruce cause, but he did have several pressing concerns to deal with. Bruce had scored a few minor victories, but Edward had no reason to presume that the forces of the occupation government were not adequate to the task of defeating Bruce, or at least containing him until such time as Edward could raise another army. In the meantime, Edward had to attend to the issues that confronted any new king: asserting his authority; entering negotiations about giving homage for his lordships in France; and seeking a bride who would provide him with an heir.

Bruce's actions over the next few years have been examined and analysed in great detail by several scholars – most notably Professor Barrow and Dr McNamee. They do not need to be rehearsed here, suffice to say that by the spring of 1314, Robert had brought virtually the whole country under his control, restoring the forms of administration that had existed under Alexander III, King John and the Guardians. Although he was a very successful soldier in the years after 1307, he was not committed to war as the only means of achieving recognition of his kingship. He was prepared to negotiate truces with Edward's officers and with specific communities, but would only consider a final peace on the basis of acceptance of kingship free from any suggestion of English superiority – a condition that was utterly unacceptable to Edward II. Robert may not have been committed to offering battle in the summer of 1314, but his only tool of any consequence was war.

# Sources and Interpretation

The shortcomings of medieval chroniclers are all too familiar to historians – chronicle accounts of battles are particularly prone to exaggeration of numbers and to political and national prejudices. Even so, they provide narrative accounts of events that can be very revealing when they are analysed in relation to the record material and, in the case of campaigns and actions, to the terrain and to and our understanding of military practice. The compilers of medieval chronicles did not, as a rule, set out to wilfully mislead their readership, but they did endeavour to portray their favoured figures in a very sympathetic light. Prejudices, exaggeration and the considerations of literature, patronage and patriotism should not, however, lead us to dismiss chroniclers as ignorant. It is true that almost all of the chronicles of England and Scotland were written by churchmen, but their occupation should not be construed as a barrier to any understanding of military affairs. Most of the chroniclers – and Barbour is a very clear example – were men with an extensive classical education, much of which was focused on the martial qualities and activities of heroes from antiquity. Additionally, almost all of them were the children of noble families and as such training with arms and horses would have been part of their cultural and social background.

One of the common observations about Bannockburn is that there is very little 'of what an historian calls primary source material.'[1] It is certainly true that the contemporary record and narrative source material is very limited; the only account by an indisputable eye-witness is that of Friar Baston, who was captured at the battle. Sadly, Baston's poem gives very little information of any value for the purposes of strategic or tactical analysis. Of the other contemporary or near contemporary material, two accounts demand to be taken seriously: Thomas Grey's *Scalacronica* and *The Lanercost Chronicle*.

Neither of these were written by an eye-witness, however the *Lanercost Chronicle* is, in general, quite well-informed about Scottish issues and the chronicler specifically tells us that his information was provided by a 'reliable' person who was present.

Grey's *Scalacronica* was compiled some forty years after the battle from a variety of Scottish verse and narrative chronicles while the author was a prisoner of war in Stirling and Edinburgh castles. Grey's father, taken prisoner during the first day's fighting at St Ninians can reasonably be assumed to have had a rather better understanding of the sequence of events than most. There is no reason to assume that Grey's captors would have prevented him from watching the main engagement, but even if they did, he must have discussed the action with some of the men who had the misfortune to join him in captivity at the end of the battle. As a professional soldier of considerable practical experience his understanding of the sequence and significance of the events of 23rd/24th June 1314 must command some respect.

Chronicle accounts are not, however, the only source of information. Surviving Scottish crown records of the early fourteenth century are somewhat thin on the ground, though not, perhaps, quite as sparse as one might expect. But there is a great quantity of English record material that applies to Scotland, so much in fact that three extensive collections of English documents with Scottish subject matter were published in the second half of the nineteenth century – McPherson's *Rotuli Scotiae*,[2] Stevenson's *Documents Illustrative of Scottish History*[3] and Bain's *Calendar of Documents Relating to Scotland*.[4] Of these, Bain's work contains by far the largest body of material relevant to the nature and practice of the English occupation government of Scotland between 1296 and 1314. Naturally only a very tiny proportion of the many thousands of documents calendared by Bain relate specifically to the battle at Stirling in June 1314, but a great many of them pertain to the business of raising troops, money and provisions to the English garrisons and armies that operated in Scotland under Edward I and Edward II. The documents cover a vast range of subjects including petitions for financial aid, demands for supplies, valuations of horses, pardons granted in exchange for military service, the forfeiture of Scots defecting to the Bruce party, the restoration of other Scots defecting to the Plantagenet party and notes of indentures. Indentures were contracts by which an individual contracted to supply the crown of England with a given number of troops, usually men-at-arms, for a given period and for an agreed fee. Indentures became an important means of raising troops, particularly – in Scotland at least – for garrison service in the widest sense, that is to say, the provision of men-at-arms to mount active operations against the Scots rather than for the defence of a castle, town or pele.

Some of the documents in Bain and McPherson's compilations do refer specifically to Bannockburn or 'the battle at Stirling.' Many of these relate to the heirs of men killed at the battle, rather than to the fighting; some are appeals for help with ransoms or 'protections' for men travelling abroad in search of financial aid from other quarters. Collectively, the English record material gives us some insight into the military practices of the day relating to garrison work and, occasionally, to operations against the Scots. They do not provide us with a detailed guide to the tactical practices of field armies, but they do give us some idea of the policies, actions and intentions of the occupation government.

The amount of English government record specifically relating to the army of 1314 is rather more limited than we might usually expect for a major army of this period. To a considerable degree this is a product of defeat. The records of the 1314 army would have included a great deal of information that historians would dearly love to have, in particular those records that deal with enlistment. It is all well and good that we have records of the number of infantrymen demanded from English counties, but without pay records we have no way of estimating the number of men who actually served. It does not help that the various summonses issued by Edward II are either contradictory or ambiguous or both. Equally, though we can identify a very large number of men seeking and obtaining 'protections' for the duration of their service, we have no way of knowing what proportion of the total complement of men-at-arms sought such protections.[5] The complete absence of pay records and 'restauro' (horse valuation) rolls prevents us from making any detailed assessment of the army of 1314 compared to the armies of 1296 and 1298. There is of course a simple explanation for the paucity of army records for 1314. The destruction of Edward's army as a viable force was accompanied by the loss of the army's administrative documents. In the main, information relating specifically to the actions at Bannockburn is to be found in chronicle accounts rather than from record sources, and they are worth examining in some detail.

# English Narrative Sources

## *The Scalacronica* of Sir Thomas Grey

Of the various accounts of Bannockburn, that of Sir Thomas Grey, though brief, is in some senses the most valuable. Grey was not an eye-witness himself, but his father was, having been made prisoner during the first day of the action. It would be reasonable to assume that Grey was aware of his father's view of the battle, but he also had access – so he tells us – to verse and narrative chronicles, possibly including a 'life' of Robert I and perhaps a 'life' of Sir James Douglas, while he was himself a prisoner of war a generation later. These accounts no longer exist, but there is no reason to suppose that Grey invented them. Barbour, writing half a century later, seems to have had access to accounts of both King Robert and Sir James that have since disappeared and it is by no means impossible that he worked from at least some of the same sources that were available to Sir Thomas. Additionally, Grey was himself a professional soldier who spent most of his career serving against the Scots and was therefore a better judge of what Colonel Burne called 'inherent military probability' than many of his contemporaries (his fellow-chroniclers, were, without exception, clerics) or for that matter, modern historians. As a member of the nobility he was chiefly concerned with the deeds of other nobles, but this should not be taken as an indication that he was not aware of the wider picture.

The said King Edward planned an expedition to these parts, where, in attempting the relief of the castle of Stirling, he was defeated, and a great number of his people were slain [including] the Earl of Gloucester and other right noble persons; and the Earl of Hereford was taken at Bothwell, whither he had beaten retreat, where he was betrayed by the governor [of the castle]. He was released [in exchange for] the wife of Robert de Brus and the Bishop of St Andrews.

As to the manner in which this discomfiture befell, the chronicles explain that after the Earl of Atholl had captured the town of St John [Perth] for the use of Robert de Brus from William Oliphant, captain [of the town] for the King of England, being at that time an adherent of his, although shortly after he deserted him, the said Robert marched in force before the castle of Stirling, where Philip de Moubray, knight, having command of the said castle for the King of England, made terms with the said Robert de Bruce to surrender the said castle, which he had besieged, unless he should be relieved; that is, unless the English army came within three leagues of the said castle within eight days of St John's day in the summer next to come, he would surrender the said castle. The said King of England came thither for that reason, where the said constable Philip mat him at three leagues from the castle, on Sunday, the vigil of St John, and told him there was no occasion for him to approach any nearer, for he considered himself as relieved. Then he told him how the enemy had blocked the narrow roads in the forest.

The traditional view that the Earl of Carrick agreed a pact for the surrender of Stirling, and that his brother, King Robert, was dismayed and angered, is seriously undermined by Grey's account. In Grey's view, the pact was made between Moubray and the king; Edward Bruce is not mentioned at all. In the absence of powerful evidence to the contrary it would be unreasonable to assume that the king was not involved in this operation. The other major operations of Spring 1314 consisted of the capture of Edinburgh Castle by a force under the Earl of Moray and the capture of Roxburgh by a force under James Douglas. The king must have been somewhere, and where better than at the very centre of his country, conducting operations against a strategically vital installation. Compacts of this nature were not in any sense extraordinary; it seems likely that Dundee[6] had fallen to the Scots under a similar arrangement. By agreeing to the compact the Scottish leadership was able to remove a large force from the tedious business of conducting a siege and either redeploy them elsewhere or send them home on leave.

Philip Moubray was technically correct to point out that his garrison had been relieved within the terms of the agreement, but politically and militarily Edward was still obliged to force battle on the Scots if it were at all possible. The political, administrative and financial effort to raise a large army for foreign service was considerably more than could be justified by the bloodless relief of one castle, however significant. Once the army was brought to Stirling, failure to bring the Scots to battle – and defeat them – would do little or nothing to restore Edward's government in Scotland. This was, of course, the real object of the exercise. The loss of Perth and Dundee had reduced the area of English administration in eastern Scotland to Lothian, Roxburghshire and Berwickshire; the loss of Roxburgh and Edinburgh castles had reduced it to a little more than a toe-hold in the southern corner of Berwickshire. If Edward could defeat King Robert – preferably resulting in Robert's death or capture – he would be in a good position to recover the towns and castles that had fallen to the Scots since 1307 and to reimpose his administration. If, however, he failed to do so, he could not maintain a large field army in Scotland for very long, and would, sooner rather than later, have to withdraw his army. This in itself would represent a major victory for the Bruce party and further diminish any prestige and authority that Edward's rule might retain north of the border.

Edward was not alone in his determination to bring about a general engagement, as Grey reports:

The young troops would by no means stop, but held their way. The advanced guard, whereof the Earl of Gloucester had command, entered the road within the Park, where they were immediately received roughly by the Scots who had occupied the passage. Here Peris de Mountforth, [Grey is referring to Henry de Bohun] knight, was slain with an axe by the hand of Robert de Brus, as was reported.

While the said advanced guard were following this road, Lord Robert de Clifford and Henry dew Beaumont, with three hundred men-at-arms, made a circuit upon the other side of the wood towards the castle, keeping to the open ground. Thomas Randolph, Earl of Moray, Robert de Brus's nephew, who was leader of the Scottish advanced guard, hearing that his uncle had repulsed the advanced guard of the English on the other side of the wood, thought that he must have his share, and issuing from the wood with his division marched across the open ground towards the two afore-named lords.

Sir Henry Beaumont called to his men 'Let us wait a little; let them come on; give them room!'

'Sir', said Sir Thomas Grey [father of the author], 'I doubt that whatever you give them now they will have all too soon.'

'Very well!' exclaimed the said Henry, 'If you are afraid be off!'

'Sir,' answered the said Thomas, 'it is not from fear that I shall fly this day.' So saying he spurred in between him [Beaumont] and Sir William Deyncourt, and charged into the thick of the enemy. William was killed, Thomas was taken prisoner, his horse being killed on the pikes, and he himself being carried of with them on foot when they marched off, having utterly routed the squadron of the two said lords, some of whom fled to the castle, others to the king's army. Which having already left the road through the wood had debouched on a plain near the water of Forth beyond Bannockburn, an evil, deep, wet marsh, where the said English army unharnessed and remained all night, having sadly lost confidence and being too much disaffected by the events of the day.

Although it is generally accepted that medieval spearmen could not stand against men-at-arms without the support of archers and/or the benefit of terrain that would present a challenge to mounted troops, Sir Thomas (junior) does not seem to be surprised by the ability of Moray's force to defeat the English cavalry, indeed, his father seems to have expected no other result. Clearly it was perfectly possible for well-drilled spearmen to dominate the field as long as they were not subjected to the attention of archers. This had in fact been amply demonstrated at the Battle of Falkirk in 1298. Although Wallace's army was roundly defeated in that action, his schiltroms proved impenetrable to Edward I's cavalry until their formations had been disrupted by the shooting of the English and Welsh archers. Having described the state of affairs in the English camp, Grey goes on to relate the deliberations at King Robert's headquarters.

> The Scots in the wood thought they had done well enough for the day, and were on the point of decamping and marching through the night into the Lennox, a stronger country, when Sir Alexander de Seton, who was in the service of England, and had come thither with the King, secretly left the English army, went to Robert de Brus in the wood. And said to him 'Sir, this is the time if you ever intend to undertake the reconquest of Scotland. The English have lost heart and are discouraged, and expect nothing but a sudden, open attack.
>
> Then he described their condition, and pledged his head, on pain of being hanged and drawn, that if he would attack them on the morrow he would defeat them easily without loss. At whose [Seton's] instigation they resolved to fight, and at sunrise on the morrow marched out of the woods in three divisions of infantry. They directed their course boldly on the English, which had been under arms all night with their horses bitted.

According to Grey, then, the English army had not rested properly through the night. This is less remarkable than it seems if, as Seton allegedly told King Robert, they expected to be attacked. Alternatively, if the English expected the Scots to withdraw during the night, there might be an opportunity to attack them as they marched away from the field, but only if the English army, and the cavalry in particular, were ready to give chase at first light. There can be little doubt that the English command were eager to bring the Scots to battle and equally little doubt that they considered it unlikely that the Scots would choose to stand and fight, let alone attempt to force battle on the English. The experience of both Edward I and Edward II and of their senior lieutenants – Aymer de Valence, Robert Clifford and others – was that campaigning in Scotland tended to be a matter of pursuing an elusive enemy who would avoid a major engagement if at all possible. Edward I had failed to bring the Scots to battle between 1298 and 1304 and Edward II had experienced the same problem in his campaign of 1310. Edward senior had managed to bring his Scottish war to a conclusion of sorts in 1304, but the 1310 campaign had not only failed in its objective of forcing battle on the Scots, it undermined Edward's credibility in England and among his supporters in Scotland, while simultaneously enhancing the prestige of King Robert.

They [the English] mounted in great alarm, for they were not accustomed to fight on foot; whereas the Scots had taken a lesson from the Flemings, who before that, had, at Courtrai, defeated on foot the power of France. The aforesaid Scots came in line of 'scholtroms' and attacked the English columns, which were jammed together and could not operate against them, so direfully were their horses impaled upon the pikes. The troops in the English rear fell back upon the ditch of Bannockburn, tumbling one over the other.

The English squadrons, being thrown into confusion by the thrust of the pikes upon the horses, began to fly. Those who were appointed to the King's rein, perceiving the disaster, led the King by the rein off the field towards the castle, and off he went, though much against the grain. As the Scottish knights, who were on foot, laid hold of the King's charger in order to stop him, he struck out so vigorously behind him with a mace there was none whom he touched that he did not fell to the ground.

As those who had the King's rein were thus drawing him always forward, one of them, Giles de Argentine, a famous knight who had lately come over the sea from the wars of the Emperor Henry of Luxembourg, said to the King; 'Sire, your rein was committed to me, you are now in safety; there is your castle where your person may be safe. I am not accustomed to fly, nor am I going to begin now. I commend you to God.' Then, setting spurs to his horse, he returned to the melee, where he was slain.

The King's charger, having been piked, could go no further, so he mounted on a courser and was taken around the Torwood, and so came to the plains of Lothian. Those who were with him were saved; all the rest came to grief. The King escaped with great difficulty, travelling thence to Dunbar, where Patrick, Earl of March, received him honourably, and put his castle at his disposal. And even evacuated the place, removing all his people, that there might be neither doubt nor suspicion that he would do nothing short of his devoir [duty] to his Lord, for at that time he [Patrick] was his liegeman. Thence the King went by sea to Berwick and afterwards to the south.

As far as Sir Thomas Grey was concerned, neither the course of the main action, nor its outcome, was in any sense mysterious. The Scots were simply the better army on the day of the battle. Unlike Barbour he does not seem to have thought that the fighting was a drawn-out affair, but rather that the English army, caught against the 'ditch of Bannockburn' were unable to deploy properly for the fight or derive any benefit from their numerical superiority. Interestingly, in common with the Lanercost chronicler and the author of *Vita Edwardi Secundi*, Grey makes no mention of Scottish cavalry, asserting that the entirety of the Scottish army, including the nobles, fought on foot. Nor does he mention any attempt by the English commanders to bring the archers into the action. This is remarkable insofar as the importance of archery had been amply demonstrated at Falkirk in 1298, which was the last major tactical success for English arms in Scotland. Edward I had been able to force the Scots to an accommodation in 1304, but he had done so through strategic and political pressure, not by success on the battlefield. The archers were not the only arm of service to fail to get a mention in Grey's account. The majority of the English army were undoubtedly spearmen, as we might expect of any major western European army of the day, but Grey makes no reference to them at all. To a certain extent this might be explained by Grey's social background and the literary demands upon a narrative aimed at an aristocratic readership, however both the chronicler and his father were professional soldiers, and were surely well aware of the power of close combat infantry; indeed Grey specifically refers to the defeat inflicted on French men-at-arms by the Flemings at Courtrai more than a decade before Bannockburn.

## Vita Edwardi Secundi

*Vita Edwardi Secundi* (The Life of Edward II) was written some years after the events he describes. Although somewhat dramatic in style, the *Vita* is one of the best narrative sources for Edward's reign. The following extract follows the course of the campaign from the spring of 1314 to the flight of King Edward and his immediate entourage to Berwick:

About the beginning of Lent messengers came to the King with news of the destruction of Scottish cities, the capture of castles and the breaching of the surrounding walls. The constable of Stirling came too, and pointed out to the King how he had been compelled by necessity to enter upon the truce. He persuaded the King to lead an army into Scotland, to defend his castle and the country. When the King heard the news, he was very much grieved, and for the capture of his castles could scarcely restrain his tears. He therefore summoned the earls and barons to come to his aid and overcome the traitor who called himself King. The earls replied that it would be better for all to meet in Parliament and unanimously decide what ought to be done in this matter rather than to proceed so inadvisedly; this moreover would be in accord with the ordinances. But the King said that the present business was very urgent and he could not therefore wait for the Parliament. The earls said that they would not fight without Parliament, lest it should happen that they infringed the Ordinances. Some counsellors and household officials therefore advised the King to demand their due service from all, and set out boldly for Scotland. It was certain that neither Robert Bruce nor the Scots would resist. What of the Earl of Gloucester, the Earl of Hereford, Robert de Clifford, Hugh Despenser and the King's household and the other barons in England? All these would come with their knights; there was no need to worry about the other earls. The King therefore demanded due service from all, and ordered the necessary stores to be provided. The Earl of Pembroke he sent ahead with a force of knights, to seek out the ambushes of the Scots and prepare the King's route into Scotland.

As far as the writer of the *Vita* was concerned, the stimulus for the invasion of 1314 was the threat to Stirling Castle, which the constable, Sir Philip Moubray, had promised to surrender to King Robert unless his garrison was relieved by Midsummer, though in fact Edward had been under pressure from his Scottish supporters since November 1313 if not before. The growing success of the Bruce party and the depredations of the English garrisons, particularly that of Berwick, had seriously undermined the prestige of Plantagenet lordship. Edward's kingship was not entirely secure at home either. The Ordinances that the writer refers to were a series of conditions imposed on Edward by the magnates of England in the hope of procuring a better standard of government. Edward, naturally enough, resented both the implication of poor governance and the restrictions placed on royal authority. Equally, the earls and barons who had forced him to accept the Ordinances in the first place were determined to keep their king within the bounds of the agreement, hence their request that the project of invading Scotland should be considered in Parliament. Most of the magnates of England could be depended upon to follow the king to war at the head of their retinues. The Earl of Pembroke had been instrumental in imposing the Ordinances on Edward II, but had parted company with the other chief instigators over the execution of Piers Gaveston. Gaveston had surrendered to Pembroke on assurance of his personal safety, but had been executed by the Earl of Lancaster (see above) thus tarnishing Pembroke's word of honour – a serious breach of aristocratic protocol. The writer puts a brave face on the absence of several leading English magnates from the army, but there can be little doubt that Edward was weakened both militarily and politically by the failure of such important men as Thomas, Earl of Lancaster to take part in the campaign.

When all of the necessaries had been collected, the king and the other magnates of the land with a great multitude of carts and baggage-wagons set out for Scotland. When the lord king had reached Berwick, he made a short halt there to await the arrival of the rest of the army. But the Earl of Lancaster, the Earl Warenne, the Earl of Arundel and the Earl of Warwick did not come, but sent knights equipped to do their service for them in the army. On the sixth and seventh days of the feast of St John the Baptist, our king with all his army left Berwick and took his way toward Scotland. The cavalry numbered more than two thousand, without counting a numerous crowd of infantry. There were, in that company, quite sufficient to penetrate the whole of Scotland, and some thought that if the whole of Scotland had been gathered together, they would not have strayed to face the king's army. Indeed, all who were present agreed that never in our time has such an army gone forth from England. The multitude of wagons, if they had been placed end to end, would have taken up a space of twenty leagues.

The king therefore took confidence and courage from so great and so distinguished a multitude and hastened to the appointed place, not as if he were leading an army to battle, but as if he were going to St James's. Brief were halts for sleep, briefer still for food; hence horses, horsemen and infantry were worn out with toil and hunger, and if they did not bear themselves well it was hardly their fault.

The *Vita* writer was eager to convince his readers of the strength and magnificence of Edward's army in general, and the cavalry force in particular. A body of 2,000 men-at-arms was indeed a powerful force, but not really an exceptional one by the standards of other major English armies of the period. The army that Edward I led to victory at Falkirk in 1298 had included at least that number of men-at-arms and the invasion force of 1296 had probably been even stronger. The writer may have relied on the estimates of men who had taken part in the 1314 campaign, or may have simply plucked a figure from the air. Alternatively he may have been aware that more than 2,000 men-at-arms had had their horses valued for *restauro* or that the number had been in receipt of crown wages. This would not, however, have given him an accurate reckoning of the armoured cavalry force, since not all of the men serving in the cavalry would have been entitled to pay. Great lords might refuse wages for both themselves and their retinues as a matter of personal prestige and men who served in exchange for pardons – a common practice in thirteenth- and fourteenth-century England – served at their own expense and risk. If they lost a horse in action they would not be recompensed by the crown, nor could they expect any help with ransoms if they were taken prisoner. Although the writer stressed the power of the army, he also prepared his readers for the actual outcome of the fight by mentioning the speed with which the army moved north, highlighting the 'brief' breaks in the march for eating and sleeping which resulted in the army arriving at Stirling in a tired and hungry condition through no fault of their own.

Interestingly, he writes only of a 'numerous crowd' of infantry, aware, no doubt that the men and women who might read his work would be of the noble class, and would be chiefly interested in the deeds and fortunes of the men-at-arms. However Edward was well aware of the significance of the infantry and had been careful to demand large quotas of men from English communities since the army would probably have to fight the Scots in terrain that would be difficult for cavalry operations.

> The Earl of Gloucester and the Earl of Hereford commanded the first line. On Sunday, which was the vigil of St John's day, as they passed by a certain wood and were approaching Stirling Castle, the Scots were seen straggling under the trees as if in flight, and a certain knight, Henry de Boun [Bohun] pursued them with the Welsh to the entrance of the wood. For he had in mind that if he found Robert Bruce there he would either kill him or carry

him off captive. But when he had come thither, Robert himself came suddenly out of his hiding place in the wood and the said Henry, seeing that he could not resist the multitude of Scots, turned his horse with the intention of returning to his companions; but Robert opposed him and struck him on the head with an axe that he carried in his hand. His squire, trying to protect his lord, was overwhelmed by the Scots.

The fight between Bruce and de Bohun is one of the great tales of King Robert's martial prowess, and is sufficiently well-recorded that there is no doubt that the incident took place. The *Vita* account differs somewhat from that of Grey and Barbour in that de Bohun is depicted as leading a body of Welsh troops – presumably infantry – and that he was attacked by the King, rather than vice versa. This is the only account of the battle that involves any action on the part of Edward's infantry on the first day of the battle, however it would be rash to dismiss the writer's assertion out of hand. While it is clear that the approach to the Entry was made by a force of men-at-arms, it would have been an example of 'good practice' if they had been accompanied by an infantry force which could take to the woods in pursuit of the Scots should they be broken by the cavalry. The writer does, perhaps, undermine his inference that de Bohun was the leader of the Welsh infantry by telling us that de Bohun was trying to make his way back to his 'companions' – surely his fellow men-at-arms – when he was set upon by King Robert. Moreover, it seems very likely, both from other accounts and from the *Vita* writer's own words, that de Bohun was actively seeking a confrontation with the King. Evidently the writer saw the demise of de Bohun and the repulse of the English at the Entry as a pointer to the course of the rest of the action:

> This was the beginning of their troubles! On the same day a sharp action was fought, in which the Earl of Gloucester was unhorsed and Robert de Clifford disgracefully routed and, though our men pursued the Scots, many were killed on either side.

Here the writer describes the action between a body of Scots under the Earl of Moray and a party of English men-at-arms under the Earl of Gloucester. His statement that 'our men pursued the Scots, many were killed on either side' rather contradicts the balance of the source material. Grey and Barbour have no doubt that the Scots enjoyed the upper hand in this engagement, Barbour even claiming that the Scots suffered very few casualties at all.

That would seem unlikely, since there was obviously a hard fight, but it is clear that the English force was completely routed. This does not necessarily mean that many deaths, or even injuries, were inflicted on Gloucester's force, merely that they were driven from the field. None of the contemporary writers name many men killed in this part of the battle, though at least one relatively prominent English soldier, Sir Thomas Grey (father of the chronicler) was taken prisoner. Whether or not casualties were significant, the outcome of this action must have had a damaging effect on English morale. Not only had the cavalry failed to overcome a rather modest force of spearmen, they had been roundly defeated and had failed to accomplish either of the two most likely objectives of their mission. The intention of the operation was probably either to effect a technical relief of Stirling castle or to perform a major reconnaissance in force to locate the main body of the Scottish army or both. By this point the day was too far gone for any other initiatives, and the English army made camp.

> The day being spent, the whole army met at the place where it was to bivouac that night. But there was no rest; for they spent it sleepless, expecting the Scots rather to attack by night than to await battle by day. When day came it was abundantly clear that the Scots were prepared for the conflict with a great force of armed men. Wherefore our men, the veterans that is, and the more experienced, advised that we should not fight , but rather await the morrow, both on account of the importance of the feast and the toil that they had already undergone. This practical advice was rejected by the younger men as idle and cowardly.

The *Vita* author clearly believed that Edward's army concentrated in the bivouac area through the later part of the day on the 23rd June, and that the army 'stood to' throughout the few hours of darkness. The fear of a night attack was not unreasonable. It would be entirely realistic for the English command to assume that the Scots were numerically weaker in general and very much weaker in terms of men-at-arms and archers. Equally, it would have been reasonable to expect the Scots to withdraw through the night. King Robert had, after all, achieved two rather dramatic successes on the previous day, and could therefore withdraw with his military prestige intact. He would have failed to force the surrender of Stirling Castle, but Edward's failure to force battle on the Scots and achieve a major victory would have been damaging to English morale and to Edward's political credibility. He would have spent a vast sum of money and good deal of political capital in gathering a large and powerful army but have gained nothing tangible in the process. Stirling Castle, one of only two first-class royal fortresses still in English hands (the other being Berwick; Bothwell was a baronial castle, held by the Earl of Hereford from Edward II and commanded by Sir Walter FitzGilbert), would have been saved, but only so long as Edward's army remained in Scotland. The financial strain of maintaining a force of such magnitude for an extended period would have been beyond his resources, but even if it had been possible his army would inevitably have melted away through desertion and illness, potentially putting his in a very high-risk situation. He might have chosen to pursue the Scots into the more arduous terrain to the north and west of Stirling, but there would have been little prospect of forcing battle on them, save under conditions that put the English at a great disadvantage. Robert would most certainly have been aware that a major victory on the battlefield would enhance his prestige, but he would have been equally aware that he was not obliged to offer or accept battle in order to achieve a success in the campaign; he merely needed to avoid defeat.

The prospect of having a day of rest before moving against the Scots seems, superficially at least, to have been a reasonable and pragmatic suggestion, which, according to the writer, was proposed by the 'veterans and the more experienced.' The problems with such a policy were, however, quite valid. If the English made no effort to force battle on the Scots, Robert would be able to withdraw his troops to more advantageous terrain unimpeded, which would in itself add to his credibility as a wise and effective leader in war while Edward would be made to look indecisive. The enormous expense of mounting the operations of 1314 would have been a complete waste and might well have compromised Edward's ability to mount another invasion in the future. Whatever the rationale behind the decision to accept or force battle, Edward was not open to persuasion:

> The Earl of Gloucester counselled the King not to go forth to battle that day, but to rest on account of the feast, and let his army recuperate as much as possible. But the king spurned the earl's advice, and, growing very heated with him, charged him with treachery and deceit. 'Today' said the Earl 'it will be clear that I am neither a traitor nor a liar,' and at once prepared himself for the battle.
>
> Meanwhile Robert Bruce marshalled and equipped his allies, gave them bread and wine and cheered them as best he could. When he learned that

the English line had occupied the field he led his whole army out of the
wood, About forty thousand men he brought with him and split them into
three divisions; and not one of them was on horseback, but each was furnished with light armour, not easily penetrable by a sword. They had axes at
their sides and carried lances in their hands. They advanced like a thick-set
hedge, and such a phalanx could not easily be broken. When the situation
was such that the two sides must meet, James Douglas, who commanded the
first phalanx of the Scots, vigorously attacked the Earl of Gloucester's line.
The Earl withstood him manfully, once and again penetrated their wedge,
and would have been victorious if he had had faithful companions. But look!
At a sudden rush of the Scots, the earl's horse is killed and the earl rolls to
the ground. Lacking defenders, and borne down by the weight of his body
armour he could not easily arise, and of the five hundred cavalry whom he
had led to the battle at his own expense, he almost alone was killed. For
they saw their lord unhorsed, they stood astonished and brought him no aid.
Accursed be the chivalry whose courage fails in the hour of greatest need!
Alas! Twenty armed knights could have saved the earl, but among some five
hundred men, there was not one found.

Interestingly, the author of the *Vita* agrees with Barbour in according a
major command position to James Douglas. Unlike Barbour, but in agreement with all of the other sources, he has the Scots deploy in three divisions
rather than four. This has certain implications for the author's view of
the Scottish command structure. If we are to assume that King Robert
commanded the central division of his army, how was command of the
others allocated without disparaging at least one of his senior officers? With
Douglas leading one division and the king another, there would have only
been one major command position left to be allocated either to the king's
brother, Edward, Earl of Carrick, or to Sir Thomas Randolph, Earl of Moray.
The author may have been misled by his knowledge of the campaigns of the
latter years of Edward's reign. By the time of the Battle of Myton or Byland
Edward Bruce was dead and Douglas had become one of King Robert's
chief lieutenants. He had also achieved a spectacular military reputation,
both as a commander and as an individual paladin.

Regardless of who was in command of the first division of the Scots, the
author is in no doubt that the Scots mounted forward to attack the English
and not vice versa. In this he is in complete agreement with all of the contemporary sources, though not, it must be said, with a considerable number

of historians. It would have been unthinkable for the English cavalry to stand fast in the face of advance by enemy infantry, so a counter charge was inevitable, but there may have been a delay in deploying properly for such a manoeuvre due to a disagreement about command responsibilities.

The reported argument between Gloucester and Hereford was not simply a matter of aristocratic precedence and posturing, significant as that may have been. Medieval armies were not simply mobs of armed men; the importance of cohesion on the battlefield was thoroughly understood. There are many examples from record evidence of men being disciplined for failure to follow orders, particularly the serious offence of moving in front of the chief banner of the formation. Again, this was not an issue of precedence and manners, but one of vital operational importance. To derive the greatest benefit from a charge – whether mounted or on foot – it was crucial that the front ranks of the formation arrived 'on target' at the same moment, thus it was important that men should not scatter in search of personal glory, but adhere to the most effective formation. In the opinion of the writer of the *Vita* failure to co-ordinate the attack properly led to Gloucester's force advancing in disorder, resulting in a piecemeal descent on the Scots rather than a concerted blow. Additionally, the lack of cohesion meant that Gloucester was not adequately supported by his own formation and so, when unhorsed, was vulnerable to the Scots. The failure of Gloucester's charge drew other men into that part of the conflict:

Giles de Argentine, a fighting soldier and very expert in the art of war, while in command of the king's rein, watched the fate of the earl, hurried up in eager anxiety to help him, but could not. Yet he did what he could, and fell together with the earl, thinking it more honourable to perish with so great a man than to escape death by flight; for those who fall in battle for their country are known to live in everlasting glory. On the same day Robert de Clifford, Payn Tibetot, William Marshal, famous, powerful and active knights were overcome by the Scots and died in the field.

When those who were with our king saw that the earl's line had been broken and his men ready to run, they said that it would be dangerous to tarry longer and safer for the king to retreat. At these remarks the king quitted the field and hastened to the castle. Moreover when the royal standard was seen to depart, the whole army quickly dispersed. Two hundred knights and more, who had not drawn their swords nor even struck a blow, were reduced to flight.

The *Vita* author seems to have reduced the scope and duration of the action compared to the other sources. It seems improbable that Edward would be prepared to abandon the fight because one formation of one branch of service had been defeated. He makes no reference at all to the other Scottish formations closing on the English lines and no reference to the rest of the English army other than to relate their flight and subsequent entrapment.

Thus while our people fled, following the king's footsteps, lo! A certain ditch entrapped many of them and a great part of our army perished in it. The king, coming to the castle and thinking to find refuge there, was repulsed as if he were the enemy; the drawbridge was raised and the gate closed. Wherefore the castellan was thought by many to be not innocent of treason, and yet that very day he was seen in armour arrayed for battle as if to fight for the king. I neither absolve the castellan nor accuse him of treachery, but I think that it was God's doing that the king of England did not enter the castle, for if the had been admitted he would never have escaped capture.

When the king saw that he was thus repulsed and that no other refuge now remained to him, he turned his steps toward Dunbar, and coming there, took ship. He landed with his following at the port of Berwick. Others having no ship came by land. The knights shed their armour and fled without it; the Scots continually harassed their rear; the pursuit lasted fifty miles. Many of our men perished and many, too, were taken prisoner. For the inhabitants of the countryside, who had previously feigned peace, now slaughtered our men indiscriminately, wherefore it was proclaimed by Sir Robert Bruce that they should take prisoners and hold them to ransom. So the Scots busied themselves with taking prisoner the magnates in order to extort large sums from them. There were captured the Earl of Hereford, John Giffard, John de Wylyntone, John de Segrave, Maurice de Berkely, undoubtedly barons of great power, and many others whom it is not necessary to specify, of whom many agreed their ransoms and paying the money were set free. Cognizances were no advantage there, because ransom was then more difficult. Five hundred and more were thought to be dead who had been taken captive and were later ransomed. Indeed, amidst all their misfortunes, this at least turned to the advantage of our army, that, while our people sought safety in flight, a great part of the Scottish army was occupied in plunder, because, if all the Scots alike had been attending to the pursuit of our men, few would have escaped. So while Robert Bruce with his men attacked our baggage train, the greater part of the English came back safe to Berwick.

This account suggests that the battle was a short-lived affair, and that the English army was so disrupted and demoralised by the first clash of arms that it descended into disorder and rout extremely quickly.

For the writer of the *Vita*, the blow to the English at Bannockburn was one very much of their own making, and an exceptional event. He goes on to suggest that:

> ...someone will ask why the Lord smote us on this day, why we succumbed to the Scots, when for the last twenty years we have always had the better of them.

This was some way from being a valid description of the ebb and flow of the preceding two decades. The English had certainly enjoyed major battlefield success at Falkirk and, on a smaller scale, Methven. Equally, they had suffered significant reverses at Stirling Bridge, Roslin and Loudon Hill. More importantly, they had been steadily losing their war with the Scots for several years. With the exceptions of Stirling and Berwick the castles and town which formed the backbone of Plantagenet administration had all fallen to the Scots by the spring of 1314. This capture was much more than a matter of military success and failure. Without the support of a well-found network of garrisons the officers of Edward II's Scottish administration could not maintain their position in the face of competition from the Bruce party.

## The Lanercost Chronicle

*The Lanercost Chronicle* is one of the most useful sources for Anglo-Scottish affairs in the fourteenth century. The compiler of the chronicle was, by and large, well informed about events north of the border. This does not mean that the chronicle is always accurate, or that the information is necessarily presented in a non-partisan manner. The Abbey did, after all, suffer from time to time from Scottish invasions of the north of England. King Robert availed himself of the Abbey's hospitality on at least one occasion, using it as the headquarters for his raiding operations. To the Lanercost chronicler, Edward's campaign of 1314 was an attempt to restore the situation of 1304 in the face of treacherous and recalcitrant Scots led by the turncoat and sacrilegious murderer Robert Bruce. To some extent he had a point. The settlement of 1304 had been accepted by the Scottish political community and in England that was seen as a reasonable conclusion to the matter of Scottish political independence as a nation. Edward's intention of recovering Scotland for the English crown was, therefore, a matter of administering royal discipline to vassals acting in defiance of their rightful lord and not a question of war between kingdoms.

> Thus before the feast of the Nativity of St John the Baptist, the King having massed his army, advanced with the aforesaid pomp towards Stirling Castle, to relieve it from siege and to engage the Scots, who were assembled there in all their strength. On the vigil of the aforesaid Nativity, the King's army arrived after dinner near Torwood; and upon information that there were Scots in the wood, the King's advanced guard, commanded by Robert de Clifford, began to make a circuit of the wood to prevent the Scots escaping by flight. The Scots did not interfere until they [The English] were far ahead of the main body, when they showed themselves, and, cutting off the King's advanced guard from the middle and rear columns, they charged and killed some of them and put the rest to flight. From that moment began a panic among the English and the Scots grew bolder.

The chronicler's description of the activity on the first day of the battle is clearly at odds with the material from the *Vita* and *Scalacronica*. There is no mention of the action at the Entry, nor of the duel between King Robert and de Bohun. Instead of two reconnaissance operations that go awry, the chronicler's informant – 'a trustworthy person who was an eye-witness' – believed the Scots deliberately positioned themselves to separate one division of the English from the rest of the army, and defeated it in isolation. The informant, evidently serving in Edward's army, was also of the opinion that the English army comprised three divisions in total. If that was the case, it would be most likely that each of these divisions had contingents of all of the branches of service – archers, spearmen and men-at-arms – which could be construed as supporting evidence for the *Vita's* description of the action at the Entry. In the *Vita* account the unfortunate de Bohun was a leader of Welsh infantry.

Barbour does not mention a close-combat infantry fight at the Entry, but that should not be construed as evidence against the Lanercost interpretation. If the English army really was arrayed in three divisions it would be realistic to see each of these formations as a body of troops fighting as an independent formation, operationally identical in concept to the use of the term 'Division' in military terminology since the Napoleonic wars if not before. This still does not contradict Barbour. Merely because a 'Division' is in contact with the enemy does not mean that all of the elements of the division are engaged. It is therefore possible that the 'Division' as a whole had approached the Scots, but that only the cavalry element of that 'Division' actually made contact with the enemy. This does not contradict the assertion that de Bohun was a leader (or even the leader of a contingent of infantry), since he was also a man-at-arms. It is not impossible that he chose to leave his command at some distance from the fighting in order to pursue personal glory or, more charitably perhaps, to reconnoitre the area.

Obviously, the Lanercost chronicler's 'eye-witness' account only describes one of the actions of the first day's operations, however it is important to remember that the account reflects the experience of one individual. Since he refers to Robert Clifford as the commander of the division in question and does not mention the de Bohun incident it is reasonable to conclude that he is referring to the action between Moray's force below St Ninians chapel, rather than the fight at the Entry.

> On the morrow – an evil, miserable and calamitous day for the English – when both sides had made themselves ready for battle, the English archers were thrown forward before the line, and the Scottish archers engaged them, a few being killed and wounded on either side; but the King of England's archers quickly put the others to flight.

This segment of the Lanercost account does seem very credible; a Scottish 'skirmish line' quickly dispersed by English archers. This is the only record of such a manoeuvre, but it dose make very good sense. The Scottish archers, probably very much weaker than their English counterparts in number, would be very unlikely to inflict much in the way of casualties, but would serve to screen the main Scottish formations from the sort of massed archery which disrupted Wallace's schiltroms at Falkirk. It does, however, raise the question of what became of the English archers. It is possible that by the time the Scottish archers had been dispersed the schiltroms were close enough to the English archers that they were obliged to retire swiftly for fear of being over-run, on the other hand there is no record of the English archers impeding the advance of either the Scots or the major formations of the English army, despite that fact that the battle was joined very quickly after this exchange of arrows. Nonetheless, it would be rash to discard the Lanercost account out of hand. If, for example, the archers were only deployed on that part of the English front that was not confronted by the first Scottish formation to engage, it might easily have appeared to the 'eye-witness' that archers were deployed by both sides and across the whole of the front. Assuming that the 'eye-witness' was stationed in the main body of the English army it is most unlikely that he would have had a clear view of the whole of the battlefield.

> Now when the two armies had approached very near to each other, all the Scots fell on their knees to repeat Pater Noster [the Lord's Prayer], commending themselves to God and seeking help from heaven; after which they advanced boldly against the English. They had so arranged their army that two columns were abreast in advance of the third, so that neither should be in advance of the other; and the third followed, in which was Robert. Of a truth, when both armies engaged each other, and the great horses of the English charged the pikes of the Scots, as it were into a great forest, there arose a great and terrible crash of spears broken and destriers wounded to the death; and so they remained without movement for a while. Now the English in the rear could not reach the Scots because the leading division was in the way, nor could they do anything to help themselves, wherefore there was nothing for it but to take to flight. This account I heard from a trustworthy person who was an eye-witness.

Here the Lanercost account fits perfectly with the other contemporary and near-contemporary descriptions of the fight. Although the Scots were heavily outnumbered, the constricted nature of the battlefield meant that only a portion of the English army was able to take part in the fighting, allowing the Scots to achieve numerical superiority at what modern military terminology calls 'the forward edge of the battle area.'

> In the leading division were killed the Earl of Gloucester, Sir John Comyn, Sir Edmund de Mauley and many other nobles besides foot soldiers, who fell in great numbers.

The chronicler's 'eye-witness' offers a suggestion that is not repeated in other chronicle accounts. In this version of events, the division which was first to come into contact with the Scots consisted of both infantry and cavalry. This would be well within the scope of the normal operational practices of the early fourteenth century; indeed any other arrangement could be seen as atypical. The 'battles' or divisions of the English armies that fought at Halidon Hill, Poitiers and Crecy consisted of archers, spear-men and men-at-arms and thus consisted of both horse and foot. The fact that the men-at-arms deployed on foot does not indicate that they were infantrymen, but that they were dismounted cavalry. Similarly the mounted archers of Edward III's reign should not be considered cavalry, but mounted infantry; they were never deployed with the intention that they should fight from the saddle. Assuming that the chronicler's informant had observed this part of the engagement accurately it would seem that a major portion of the English army, a formation large enough to conduct independent manoeu-vres and operations, fell on the leading Scottish formation but were unable to bring their advance to a halt.

Another calamity which befell the English was that, whereas they had shortly before crossed a great ditch called Bannockburn, into which the tide flows, and now wanted to re-cross it in confusion, many nobles and others fell into it with their horses in the crush, while others escaped with much dif-ficulty, and many were never able to extricate themselves from the ditch; thus Bannockburn was spoken about for many years in English throats.

The King and Sir Hugh Despenser (who, after Piers Gaveston, was as his right eye) and Sir Henry Beaumont (whom he [Edward] had promoted to an earldom in Scotland), with many others mounted and on foot, to their perpetual shame fled like miserable wretches to Dunbar Castle, guided by a certain knight of Scotland who knew through what districts they could escape. Some who were not so speedy were killed by the Scots, who pursued them hotly; but these, holding bravely together, came safe and sound through the ambushes to England. At Dunbar the King embarked with some of his chosen followers in an open boat for Berwick, leaving all others to their fate.

In like manner as the King and his following fled in one direction to Berwick, so the Earl of Hereford, the Earl of Angus, Sir John Segrave, Sir Anthony Lucy and Sir Ingleram de Umfraville, with a great crowd of knights, six hundred other mounted men and one thousand foot fled in another direction to Carlisle. The Earl of Pembroke left the army on foot and saved himself with the fugitive Welsh; but the aforesaid earls and others, who had fled towards Carlisle were captured on the way at Bothwell Castle, for the sheriff, the warden of the castle, who had held the castle down to that time for the King of England, perceiving that his countrymen had won the battle, allowed the chief men who came thither to enter the castle in the belief that they would find a safe refuge, and when they had entered the castle, took them prisoners, thereby treacherously deceiving them. Many also were taken wandering around then castle and hither and thither in the country, and many were killed; it was said also that certain knights were captured by women, nor did any if them get back to England, save in abject confusion.

Again, Lanercost is in agreement with the other accounts of the battle. It is not absolutely clear what the writer means when he tells us that the English had crossed the ditch of the Bannockburn 'shortly before.' It could be construed as an indication that the army had only crossed the Bannockburn that very morning, however it is surely safer to assume that the writer means that the army had crossed on the previous evening, given that the Scots started to advance early in the morning. An attempt to move the army across the Bannock burn during the night would have been a very difficult task indeed, and one fraught with danger. It is apparent that the English commanders were concerned that the Scots would make a night attack, in which case attempting a river crossing in the dark in the close vicinity of the enemy would have been a rash undertaking, and one that might well have given rise to comment among contemporaries. Alternatively, had the English army made their crossing of the Bannock burn early on the morning of the 24th the Scots would have had a tremendous opportunity to mount their attack at a point when the English were in an extremely vulnerable situation. The Lanercost description of the confused retreat of the English army raises an interesting, and perhaps very significant issue, and one that gives some credence to the claim that the account was based on the perceptions of one who took part in the campaign. The Bannock burn is indeed tidal throughout its lower course, a piece of information unlikely to have been available, or to have seemed significant, to a monk at Lanercost.

# Friar Baston

Friar Baston is unique among the contemporary and near-contemporary writers who gave accounts of the battle in that he was the only indisputable eye-witness. A Carmelite and a noted poet of the day, he had travelled north with the English army for the specific purpose of recording what was expected to be a great victory. He was denied the opportunity of composing a paean of praise for English arms and Edward II by the outcome of the battle, but he did get to write about a Scottish victory; indeed he had little choice in the matter, since he was taken prisoner and was obliged to write his account as part or all of the price of his liberty. Baston really has nothing to say of any value in terms of helping us to reconstruct the action, and the fragment printed here is no more than an indication of the style and content of Baston's work:

> The dry ground of Stirling sustains the first conflicts,
> Splendid is the attacking host, but it soon takes a downward turn,
> Great is the grief, grief enhancing grief…

It is of course a great shame that Baston did not choose to give a blow-by-blow account of the course of he action, focusing instead on the fortunes, or rather the misfortunes, of the leading men of the day, but we should not assume that the nature of his presentation would have been radically different had the Scots been defeated. It was not his intention to analyse the fight, but to provide a glowing recognition of victory along the lines of Andrew Marvel's *'Ode to Cromwell on his Return from Ireland'* rather than the construction of a realistic account of the action.

# Geoffrey Baker of Swinbroke

To Stirling the King brought his forces with all the pomp usual at that date when the chivalry of England still fought on horseback, with curvetting chargers and flashing armours, and when men, in their arrogant rashness were so confident that in addition to the necessary equipment of horses, arms and provisions, they brought gold and silver vessels such as are used at the banquets of the mighty of the earth in days of peace. Men of that day had never seen such an overweening array of chivalry, as that poor Carmelite, friar Baston, in his poem on the campaign, at which he was present and was taken prisoner by the Scots, bewailed bitterly. That night you might have seen the English – not angels – drenching themselves with wine and drinking healths; while the Scots kept watch and fasted. Next morning the Scots chose a fine position, and dug ditches three feet deep and three feet wide along the whole of their front from left to right, covering them over with intertwined branches, that is to say, hurdles, screened by grass, across which indeed infantry might pass if they knew the trick, but which could not bear the weight of cavalry.

Baker's account is the first to ascribe any tactical value to Scottish preparation of the battle site. Although his description of trenches covering the
front of the Scottish army is highly detailed, it is also highly questionable.
The construction of coverings that would bear the weight of a man, but not
of a horse, would be both difficult and of doubtful effectiveness and it is very
questionable that they could be concealed adequately. If true, it would indicate that Robert was so confident of the location the English would choose
for their camp that he was prepared to devote a great deal of time and effort
to the project. Despite the fact that his assertions about the trenches are a
rather obvious attempt to explain (or perhaps excuse) a major defeat, several
writers have chosen to give them credence. There are two very clear arguments against the existence of the trenches; one is that such a project would
have been difficult, if not impossible to hide from the garrison of Stirling
Castle, who would surely have passed that information to the English army
on 23rd June if not before. The other problem is that Baker's account very
clearly implies that the Scots stood on the defensive behind these trenches.
Although this might have stood the Scots in good stead from the point of
view of bringing an English advance to a halt, merely denying the English
the opportunity to advance would not have brought victory. Since it is clear
from all of the other accounts that the Scots advanced against the English
and drove them back into the Bannock Burn and the River Forth one has
to wonder how they could have maintained their good order – crucial to
the success of bodies of spearmen – as they passed over the trenches.

> None of the Scots was allowed to mount their horses, and arrayed in brigades
> as usual they stood in a closely formed line behind the aforesaid cannily, I will
> not say deceitfully, constructed ditch. As the English moved from the west the
> rising sun shone on their gilded shields and helmets.

Baker's informant, assuming that he had one, would seem either to have
misled the chronicler or was badly misunderstood by him. The route followed by the English army very clearly led to their deployment to the *east*
of the Scots, not to the west. It is possible however that Baker misconstrued
his information. As the Scots descended to the plain from the woods early
on the 24th they would have had the sun in their faces, but their arms and
armour would have reflected the sun back at the English lines. If Baker's
informant complained about the glare of the sun it would not be unreasonable for the chronicler – in the absence of more detailed information – to

assume that the English army had indeed been drawn up facing to the east, rather than the west.

> Such a general as Alexander would have preferred to try conclusions on some other ground or other day, or at least would have waited till midday when the sun would have been on their right. But the impetuous and headstrong obstinacy of the English preferred death to delay. In the front line were the cavalry with their heavy chargers, unaware of the concealed ditch; in the second were the infantry, including the archers, who were kept ready for the enemy's flight; in the rear the King with the bishops and other clerics, amongst them that foolish knight, Hugh the Spenser.
>
> The front line of the cavalry charged, and as the horses' legs were caught in the ditch through the hurdles, down fell the men and died before the enemy could strike; and at their fall on came the enemy, slaughtering and taking prisoners, and sparing only the rich for ransom. There died Gilbert, Earl of Gloucester, whom the Scots would willingly have saved for ransom, if they had recognised him, but he was not wearing his coat-armour. Many were killed by the archers of their own army, who were not placed in a suitable position, but stood behind the man-at-arms, whereas at the present day the custom is to post them on the flanks. When they saw the Scots charging fiercely on the horsemen who had fallen at the ditch, some of them shot their arrows high in the air to fall feebly on the enemy's helmets, some shot ahead and hit a few Scots in the chest, and many English in the back. So all yesterday's pomp came to naught.

Here Baker is on rather firmer ground. At least some portion of the English cavalry – Gloucester's formation – were deployed in front of the main body of the army and they did indeed charge the leading formation of Scots, however the absence of any description of Gloucester's men falling into concealed ditches from other sources strengthens the suggestion that there were no ditches to fall into. The issue of the trenches should not lead us to dismiss the rest of Baker's account, though there is very little else that he adds to the story, however his description of English archers having their view of the enemy obscured by the cavalry may be of value and has a certain ring of credibility. The sort of speculative shooting that he relates would be very likely to bring about as many casualties among the English as among the Scots. Placing archers in the second line of English formations does not invalidate either Lanercost's description of a brief exchange of archery prior to the advance of King Robert's army or Barbour's account of Sir Edward Keith's charge against English archers on the flank of the main battle. There is no reason to assume that all of the archers in King Edward's army were concentrated in one unit; indeed that would be contrary to the general practice of English armies of the later Middle Ages, and is simply inconceivable in terms of common sense.

# Trokelowe

Trokelowe's account, though very brief, is broadly in agreement with Lanercost, Barbour and the *Vita*, save on the question of the initial deployment of the English infantry.

Trokelowe obviously had access to some source material and was aware of King Robert's decision to fight on foot. He sees this as the morale-building gesture that it was, telling us that Robert and his lords dismounted to ensure that the danger of battle would be shared equally by nobility and commoners alike.

> The next day each army made ready for battle, and about the third hour they were drawn up in formidable array…The English leaders put in their first line their infantry, archers and spearmen; their cavalry, centre and wings, they drew up behind…
>
> …the Scots, inspired by the speeches of their leaders, resolutely awaited the attack; they were all on foot; picked men they were, enthusiastic, armed with keen axes, and other weapons, and with their shields closely locked in front of them, they formed an impenetrable phalanx… The cause of the disaster I do not know, unless it was that the English were too impetuous and disorderly; they were tired and weak, both men and horses, because of their excessive haste, and they were hungry and had had no sleep. Also the Scots, knowing the ground, which the English did not, attacked sooner than expected in dense battle array.

It might be tempting to reject Trokelowe's account simply on the basis of his assertion that the English infantry were deployed in front of, not behind, the cavalry, which is the reverse of every other account, however this may be a matter of perception. If his information was gleaned from an eye-witness – even if it only reached Trokelowe by hearsay – we should consider the possibility that this was how the situation looked to that witness. If he was stationed to the rear of the main body of the army and was unaware of Gloucester's formation then his observation may have some validity. The assumption that *all* of the English cavalry were positioned to the front of the army is not substantiated by any of the contemporary material, indeed the accounts of Lanercost, Barbour and the *Vita* clearly have only one English cavalry formation to the fore – that of the Earl of Gloucester. Assuming that the English were divided into four formations – as they were for the Dunbar and Falkirk campaigns – an eye-witness might well see the English deployment as a great body of infantry to the fore and three cavalry formations, 'centre and wings,' to the rear. This would make good tactical sense and would conform to Edward's declaration before the campaign that the Scots were going to be found in rough terrain where the cavalry would find it difficult to come to blows. Neither Edward nor his subordinates seem to have given any consideration to the possibility that the Scots might actually force battle; they expected to have to attack, and attack uphill into wooded terrain. Given the experience of Falkirk it would not be at all unreasonable if Edward had decided to put his infantry to the fore with a view to 'pinning' the Scots before the cavalry came into action. This would not of itself compromise those accounts that have Gloucester's formation in apposition in front of the rest of the army. The English command clearly thought it possible that the Scots might not offer or accept battle, but attempt to withdraw from the field; they had already done enough on the night of the 23rd to give Robert a major propaganda victory. It would have been prudent to have a strong mobile force to the fore which could either take advantage of any opportunity to disrupt the withdrawal of the Scots or to screen the main body of the army from a sudden advance if the Scots chose to attack.

In common with the other commentators of the period, Trokelowe is in no doubt that the Scots forced the pace of the battle by advancing to contact, telling us that they had formed an 'impenetrable phalanx' and that they advanced in 'dense battle array.' The English army was also deployed ready for battle, however the Scots advanced 'sooner than expected,' and the general tenor of all the other accounts is that the English had expected that they, not the Scots, would take the offensive. This, and the fact that the English were tired and hungry after their rapid marches to Stirling, were the salient issues in Trokelowe's opinion.

Interestingly – and this is shared by all of the other medieval accounts – Trokelowe's interpretation gives no indication of the effect of pools or swamps

on the course of the action, though clearly there might be practical difficulties in digging ditches in a morass. For Trokelowe the most significant issues
would seem to have been the nature of the Scottish formations – that they
advanced with their 'shields locked together' – and possibly that the English
were undermined by their own impetuosity and lack of good order. A plausible interpretation of these factors is that the English army, though deployed
for battle, was arrayed for an advance, not to receive an attack, and that they
either failed to adjust their deployment quickly enough to withstand the Scots
and were caught in the midst of reorganisation, or that they made no effort to
redeploy and were forced to fight in an inappropriate formation.

Trokelowe points to one other factor of significance that has seldom attracted
the attention of historians – that the Scots 'knew the ground' and made the
best use of the terrain. It is difficult to know exactly what Trokelowe means by
this assertion in the sense that once the armies were face-to-face on the plain
there would be little advantage to be gained from knowledge of the ground.
According to all of the contemporary material the main action took place on
a dry, flat field. The English had been camped right next to the field since the
previous evening and would have had ample opportunity to examine it. On
the other hand, the Scots had the advantage of local knowledge in a rather
wider sense and may have been able to move down to the plain, deploy for
battle and commence their advance before the English command could complete steps to reorganise the army appropriately.

Trokelowe tells us that the battle started 'about the third hour,' though one
might wonder who would have been sufficiently detached to keep an eye
on the time. The medieval day, like that of the Romans, was divided, nominally, into twelve equal portions regardless of the time of year. In Scotland
at midsummer the nights are very short indeed, so an 'hour' of daylight for
the medieval observer would equate – conservatively – to ninety minutes.
This would imply that the battle commenced about four and a half hours
after dawn or in the region of eight or nine o'clock. If this is correct then
there had been plenty of time for Robert to make a detailed observation of
the English army before leading his army to the battlefield, but there would
also have been plenty of time for the English army to prepare for battle. It is
possible, therefore, that instead of attacking at first light, Robert waited until
the English army had formed up for an advance toward the Torwood and
beyond and were therefore vulnerable to attack.

Failure to redeploy to more suitable formations may not have been a
practical proposition for Edward's commanders in the time available once

they had become aware that the Scots were going to force battle. If they were in columns for the march rather than lines for combat the business of reforming the units accordingly would be more than just a matter of moving individual formations from column to line. Each unit would require a great deal more 'frontage' space, and if they were to present an organised and continuous front to the enemy units on the flanks of the army would very probably have to move some distance to the left or right to accommodate those in the centre. This would be a time-consuming business at the best of times, and the risk of serious disorganisation would be high even if the enemy were not present. Attempting to achieve a major redeployment as the enemy approached would be a very great gamble even if the troops were well trained, disciplined and in good heart, none of which applied to Edward's army. It is possible, therefore, that Edward and his subordinates saw the Scots descend to the field and assumed, initially, that they would halt and wait for the English attack. When they saw that the Scots were intent on advancing to contact they decided that the risk of joining battle in less-than suitable formations was outweighed by the risks involved in attempting to redeploy in great haste. The maxim that 'order and counter-order leads to disorder' is, like most military clichés, based on sound observation and deduction and one that would have been well-known to Edward and his lieutenants. It is important to bear in mind that neither Edward nor his senior officers were lacking in military experience and knowledge. Edward, admittedly, had not taken part in a battle of manoeuvre on this scale (nor had Robert), but several of his senior officers had been present at Falkirk or other large actions. We would be doing these men a great injustice if we were to presume that when they saw the Scots advance they failed to consider any steps to counter the attack, but it is a realistic possibility that their experience of battle led them to conclude that there was no time to make radical changes to the arrangement of the army.

# The Meaux Chronicle

So the English and the Scots met on the plain of Bannock near Stirling, the English very confident in their strength and numbers, the Scots after confession and communion calling on God alone as their protector. The armies being arrayed against each other, the Scots put their foot in the front line, and the English their horse, and at the first onset gave victory to the Scots, and

the English turned their backs and were slain....because iron spikes had been
placed in hollows under the ground so that both horse and foot might trip.

Abbot Burton, the author of the Meaux chronicle, is as clear as all of the
other writers about the time of the main action taking place on the 'plain.'
He, too, agrees that the English army was quite confident that their superior numbers would be enough to ensure victory and that the English had
deployed with their cavalry in front of the infantry whereas the Scots had
deployed with the infantry to the fore. Unlike some of the other commentators he does not suggest that the entire Scottish army fought on foot,
though he obviously understood that the majority did so, since he makes no
reference to Scottish cavalry being engaged at all. Clearly, in Burton's view,
the English cavalry had failed to make any great impression on the Scots and
were forced to retire. His assertion that the Scots had placed iron spikes in
'hollows under the ground' is less than convincing. If the English retreated
and were pursued by the enemy – which would have been absolutely vital
if the Scots were to secure a major victory – then the Scots would have had
to negotiate these traps during their advance. If iron spikes caused English
troops 'both horse and foot to slip' they would have inflicted the same problems on the Scots. Burton stresses the importance of intercession by God,
hardly surprising given that he was a cleric and would have put great value
on the fact that the Scots had made confession, taken communion and put
their faith in 'God alone as their protector.'

# The Scottish Sources

## John Barbour

Of all the medieval sources for Bannockburn, John Barbour's 'life' of
Robert I, *The Bruce*, is by far the longest and most detailed. It is also the
only account that contains anything much in the way of useful information about the Scottish army, and is therefore indispensable to medievalists
with an interest in the subject. Barbour is not always completely reliable;
there are many errors of date and some of location, but the sheer scale of

his work probably makes this inevitable. Many of these errors are really quite insignificant. So long as the order of events is not compromised it is generally of little importance whether some incident occurred on the eve or feast day of a particular saint or festival. This does not mean that Barbour was always above putting the needs of his narrative above the demands of accuracy. For example, he asserts that Edward Bruce agreed to a pact that would allow a period of a full year for the relief of Stirling Castle by an English army. He may of course have been misinformed, or he may have misread his sources inadvertently, but there is every possibility that the year-long pact was a device to show the rash and impetuous nature of Edward Bruce and/or to enhance the achievement of victory.

Like any writer he was conditioned by the customs of his times. There were literary, political, social and theological implications to be considered. The first of these is also the easiest to recognise. Since the poem was probably intended – at least to some extent – as a performance piece it was important to maintain the rhythm of the words, and various phrases are used to 'fill up' space to avoid interrupting the flow of the narrative. Accordingly we find, for example, that individuals and groups are often described as moving from one place to another 'in hy' – at great speed – but generally the phrase has no real significance; we should not assume that medieval Scotsmen and Englishmen spent their lives in frantic haste.

We should also bear in mind the nature of Barbour's audience. Like Barbour himself they were, for the most part, members of the noble class and they were chiefly interested in the deeds of other nobles. We must also remember that there were significant political themes to be addressed or, in some cases, wilfully ignored. Barbour hoped to inspire his audience with the martial ardour of their forbears and to justify the actions of King Robert and his adherents, but he was also careful not to ascribe any value to King John or to the Balliol party generally. Naturally, Barbour devoted a good deal of space to relating the efforts of King Robert to heroic figures from scripture. The same approach to figures from antiquity gave him the opportunity to demonstrate the remarkable breadth and depth of his classical education.

Even so, *The Bruce* is a very valuable source; many incidents which get little or no attention in other accounts are more thoroughly aired by Barbour. David de Strathbogie's raid on King Robert's stores at Cambuskenneth and Keith's charge against the English archers are two such examples, with neither incident being described by any other author. Barbour wrote for an audience that was deeply immersed in war with England as an historical tradition. He could certainly afford to inflate or reduce the importance of specific events since there would have been very few, if any, who actually lived through the campaign of 1314 by the time Barbour wrote his poem. On the other hand, most of his audience would have grown up on a diet of hero-worship for King Robert, Moray and Douglas and on tales of the experiences of their fathers or grandfathers.

Since Barbour put pen to paper so long after the events but still maintains a remarkably sound chronology of the war years it is clear that Barbour did not compile his account from popular folk tales of the day, but from works that have not survived to the present day. Professor Duncan has examined the likely nature of Barbour's source material in his masterful presentation of *The Bruce*, which cannot be too highly recommended, not simply for the 'translation' of the work into modern English but for the invaluable introduction and exceptionally fine footnotes.

Barbour's Bannockburn account starts with Edward Bruce laying siege to the castle of Stirling, which was commanded by Sir Philip Moubray:

> Thartill a siege they set stythly,
> Thai bykyrrit oftsys sturdily,
> Bot gret chivalry done wes nane.

> [*They set close siege, and fought many skirmishes, but there were no great deeds of chivalry.*]

Barbour immediately shows his preoccupation with the actions of the noble classes. He does not suggest that the fighting itself was unproductive or ineffectual, but that the combat was not 'graced' by noble deeds performed by noble men. Naturally, since he was writing for an aristocratic audience, one imbued with romantic concepts of chivalry, he quickly passes on to the arrangements for the pact under which Moubray promised to surrender his charge unless relieved by an English army by midsummer. Barbour dates this arrangement to the summer of 1313, though it is clear from record evidence and other chronicle accounts that Edward Bruce laid siege to Stirling around the beginning of Lent, 1314. Barbour may have been influenced by a text that no longer exists, but which was available to Sir Thomas Grey, whose dating of the events leading to Bannockburn is, as Professor Duncan has pointed out, slightly ambiguous. Barbour goes on to criticise Edward Bruce for giving 'so outrageous a day' – such a long period – for the pact, emphasising the length of time that Edward II would have for the mustering of a great army and gives King Robert a speech in which he takes his brother to task.

> The king said quhen he hard the day,
> 'That wes unwysly doyn, perfay.
> Ik hard never quhar sa lang warning
> Wes gevyn to sa mychty a king.'

[*The king said, when he heard the day* [agreed date], *'That was unwisely done, I never heard of such a long warning given to so mighty a king.'*]

The precise date of the agreement has not survived, though it was clearly made shortly after the fall of Edinburgh and Roxburgh castles in the spring of 1314. Although Stirling could, in theory, be supplied by water, in practice the loss of the other occupation strongholds in Lothian and Fife must have given Robert effective control of the River Forth. It would, perhaps, have been possible to force a passage as far as Stirling, but that would hardly constitute a reliable means of re-supply, so Moubray's command was in a perilous situation. Professor Duncan has suggested that the siege was set toward the end of March and that Edward Bruce – Barbour does not refer to him as the Earl of Carrick – and Moubray made their pact around the middle of May, thus reducing the period of the pact from one year to six weeks. This is certainly a realistic and plausible analysis. Regardless of when the siege commenced, Edward Bruce was certainly absent from Stirling in the middle of April when he conducted a major raid through Cumbria, returning to Scotland about 18 April. Edward had, according to Lanercost, invaded England 'contrary to agreement' – that is to say in contravention of a truce. However the chronicle goes on to say that the Scots attacked because the community of Cumbria 'had not paid them the tribute that they had pledged themselves to pay on certain days.'

Although Barbour is often eager to portray Edward Bruce as a rash and intemperate man, the military situation at Stirling must be taken into account. If the surrender pact had not yet been made by the time Edward left to travel to Cumbria the garrison of Stirling would have had an opportunity to gather supplies from the vicinity unless Edward had left enough of a force to keep them contained. This would obviously have forced Edward to divide his force in order to provide a presence at Stirling and a mobile force

to lead into England, a risky undertaking since the numbers of men available to him would not have been particularly large. Any foray into England
was a risky business, so Edward would surely have endeavoured to have as
large a force of men-at-arms as he could gather. This would compromise
the size of force that he could afford to leave behind, a force that would
have to include a strong heavy cavalry element to counter the men-at-arms
element of the Stirling garrison. Despite Barbour's assertions, it is not clear
that Edward Bruce was a rash commander, (though his death at the battle
of Faughart may have been a consequence of over-confidence) and he had
been entrusted by his brother with a number of independent commands
which he had led with conspicuous success. It is therefore very possible that
the pact had been concluded before Edward departed Stirling for Cumbria.
Edward certainly took a force of some scale on his expedition, enough
to make an attempt on Carlisle, possibly, as Professor Duncan suggests, to
'equal the chivalry of Moray and Douglas,' whose successes at Edinburgh
and Roxburgh had already contributed to the situation at Stirling.

Having set the scene with Edward Bruce's compact and the reaction of the
king, Barbour goes on to describe the mustering of troops for the campaign:

> Than all that worthi war to fycht
> Off Scotland set all hale that mycht
> To purvey tham agane that day,
> Wapynnys and armouris purvayit thai
> And all that afferis to fechting.
> And in Ingland the mychty king
> Purvayit him in a gret array
> That certis hard I never say
> That Inglis men mar aparaile
> Maid than did than for bataill,
> For quhen the tyme wes cummyn ner
> He assemblit all his power
> And but his awne chivalry
> That wes sa gret it wes ferly
> He had of mony ser counter
> With him gud men of gret bounte
> Of France, worthi chevalry

He had intill his company,
The erle of Henaud als wes thar,
And with him men that worthi war,
Off Gascoynne and of Almany,
And off the duche of Bretayngny
He had wycht men and wel farand
Armyt clenly bath fute and hand.

[*Then all the men of Scotland who were capable of fighting set themselves to the purchase of arms and armour and all that is needed for war. And in England, the mighty king made preparations for war on a grand scale. I am certain that the English never made a greater effort than for this battle. When the time* [for the campaign] *drew near he gathered all his power, and apart from his own chivalry* [in the sense of cavalry] *who were so numerous that it was terrifying, he had men of great ability from many other countries. He had great paladins from France in his army and the Earl* [Count] *of Hainault also was there, and with him worthy men of Gascony and Almayne and from the Duchy of Britanny he had strong men, well armed* [armoured] *on hand and foot.*]

Barbour's objective was to show the extensive resources of Edward II when compared to Robert I, however he was not above gilding lilies. It would be remarkable if no one from Edward's extensive French possessions served at Bannockburn, but there is no reason to expect that any large body of foreign troops took part in the campaign. Barbour is certainly mistaken in his assertion that the 'Earl' (Count) of Hainault joined Edward's force, though the count did join Edward III for the disastrous Weardale campaign of 1327. Barbour adds further contingents:

All Wals als wiuth him had he
And off Irland a gret mengne,
Off Pouty Aquitane and Bayoun
He had gret mony of renoune,
And off Scotland he had yeit then
A gret menye of worthy men.

[*He* [Edward] *also had with him all of Wales and a large company from Ireland. He had many man of great prowess from Poitou, Aquitane and Bayonne and also from Scotland he still had a great company of worthy men.*]

Like any chronicler worthy of the name, Barbour is at pains to 'talk up' the
scale of the armies, particularly – for obvious dramatic and patriotic reasons
– the Englsih host:

> Quhen all thir sammyn assemblit war
> He had of fechtaris with him thar
> Ane hunder thousand men and ma
> And fourty thousand war of tha
> Armyt on horse bath heid and hand,
> And of thai teit war thre thousand
> With helyt horsing plate and mailye
> To mak the front of the batailye,
> And fifty thousand of archeris
> He had foroutyn hobelar,
> And men of fute and small rangale
> That yemyt harnays and vittaile
> He had sa fele it wes ferly.

[*When all of these were gathered together he had with him 100,000 and more fighting
men, and forty thousand of these were on horseback, armoured on head and hand, and
of these three thousand were on horses armoured with plate and mail to form the front
of the battle. And he had fifty thousand archers apart from hobelars and so many foot-
men and men to carry harness and rations that it was terrifying.*]

Clearly Barbour's estimates of the English army can only be accepted as
literary, not literal, figures. No European medieval army ever amounted to
anything like 100,000 men, on the other hand, the figure of 3,000 men
of 'covered' horses may not be too far from the mark, though it is almost
certainly something of an exaggeration. Bernard de Linton, who, unlike
Barbour, was around at the time and may even have been present at the
battle, tells us that Edward's army included 3,100 men on covered horses
and was very probably one the sources of Barbour's information. Barbour
has the entire English army muster at Berwick – though some proportion
of it actually gathered at Wark – where, on the advice of his chief officers,
Edward divided his army into ten divisions:

> In alkane war weile ten thousand
> That lete thai stalwartly suld stand

In the bataile and stythly fycht
And leve nocht for that fayis mycht.
He set ledaris til ilk bataile
That knawn war of gud governaile,
And til renownyt erls twa
Of Gloysster and Herfurd war tha
He gaf the vaward in leding
With mony men at thar bidding
Ordaynit into full gud array
Thai war sa chivalrous that thai
Trowyt giff thai come to fycht
Thar suld na strength withstand thar mycht.
And the king quhen his mengne
Divisit intill batallis ser
His awne bataill ordanyt he
And quha suld at his bridle be,
Schir Gillis Argente he set
Apon a half his reyngye to get,
And of Valence Schir Amery
On other half that wes worthy

[*In each battle* [division] *there were at least* 10,000 *men who would stand and fight fiercely in battle, and not flee from the enemy's power. He set leaders to each battle that were known as good leaders and to two famous earls, Gloucester and Hereford he gave leadership of the vanguard, with many well-armed and drilled men under their command. They were so chivalrous that they believed that if they had to fight no power could withstand them. And the king, when his army was divided into separate commands, organized his own battle, and who should be at his bridle. He set Sir Giles d'Argentan on one side to hold his reins and on the other he set Sir Aymer de Valence, a worthy* [knight].]

Barbour's assertion that the English army was divided into ten formations has, perhaps, been taken too literally by scholars. Like the gross inflation of the army sizes (both English and Scots) this is probably more a matter of the demands of literature than any realistic appraisal; of the order of battle adopted by Edward and his officers, however, there is a possibility that Barbour is conflating different pieces of information. The divisions (battles) of a medieval army frequently consisted of both horse and foot. The infantry were enlisted for one of two functions, spearmen or archers, and we should expect – unless there is pressing evidence to the contrary – that each 'battle' would contain both. It is very rare to find a description of a medieval army that consisted of more than three battles, but the cavalry element of English armies often comprised four formations, the largest of which would normally include the royal household arrayed for war and be commanded – nominally at least – by the king himself. If we consider that each of three 'battles' was divided into a body of spearmen and one of archers it might well seem to an observer that there were in fact six formations, not three formations with two subdivisions in each. These, with the addition of four cavalry formations might well present the appearance of ten separate formations, though in fact they might be only three 'battles', each with contingents of spearmen, archers and cavalry and a 'tenth' unit comprising the king's cavalry formation.

Barbour leaves the English as they depart from Berwick and turns to the Scottish army, listing Robert's senior officers – Edward Bruce, Douglas, Randolph and Walter Steward – as well as:

> Outakyn other mony barounys
> And knychtis that of gret renowne is
> Come with thar men full stalwartly.
> Quhen thai war assemblyt halely
> Off fechtand men I trow thai war
> Thretty thousand and sumdele mar,
> Foroutyn carriage and petaill
> That yemyt harnays and vitaill.
> Our all the ost than yeid the king
> And beheld to thar contenyng
> And saw thaim of full fayr affer.
> Off hardy countenance thai wer,
> Be liklynes the mast cowart
> Semyt full weill to do his part.
> The king has sene all thar having
> Thai knew him weile into sic thing,
> And saw thaim all commouinall
> Off sic contenance and sa hardy
> Forout effray or abaysing.
> In his hart had he gret liking
> And thoucht that men of sa gret will

Gif they wlad set thar will thartill
Suld be full hard to wyn perfay.

[*...many other barons and knights of great renown [who] stalwartly brought their own men. When they were all gathered together I swear there must have been thirty thousand fighting men and more as well as carriage-men and lesser people that carried harness and rations. The king inspected the whole army, and saw that they bore themselves well. They were of stern countenance and even the most cowardly-looking seemed like he would play his part very well. In his heart he had great joy, thinking that men of such great will, if they should set their will to it* [combat] *would be very hard to defeat.*]

Again, Barbour's figure of 30,000 (and somewhat more) combatants is not to be taken seriously. His intention is to show the reader – or listener, since the poem was probably written with performance in mind – that King Robert had gathered a very powerful force, though clearly very much smaller than that of Edward. Barbour tells us that Robert was happy about his situation, and then moves on to a discussion between the king and his senior officers:

...And callyt his consaile preve
And said tham, 'Lords, now ye se
That Inglismen with mekill mycht
Has all disponyt thaim for the fycht
For thai yone castel wald reskew.
Tharfor is gud we ordane now
How we may let tham of thar purpose
And sua to thaim the wayis clos
That thai pas nocht but gret letting.
We haf here with us at bidding
Weill thretty thousand men and ma,
Mak we four bataillis of tha
And ordane us on sic maner
And quhen our fayis cummys ner
We to the New Park hald our way,
For that behovys thain need away
Bot gi that thai will beneath us ga
And our the merrais pass, and sua
We sall be at avantage thar
And me think that rycht spedfull war

To gang on fute to this fechting
Armyt bot in litill arming,
For schup we us on hors to fycht
Sen our fayis ar mar of mycht
And better horsyt than ar we
We suld into gret perell be
An gyff we fecht on fute perfay
at avantage we sall be ay,
For in the park amang the treys
The horsmen alwayis cummerit beis,
And the sykis alssua that ar thar-doun
Sall put thaim to confusione.

[*He called his privy council and said to them, 'Lords, now you see that the English seek battle with great strength, and want to relieve that castle. Therefore it is wise that we should decide now how we are to deny them their objective, closing the roads so that they cannot get through without great loss. We have here thirty thousand men and more under our command. We will divide them into four divisions and deploy in such a way that when our enemy approaches we hold our position in the New Park, for they will probably have to come that way, but if they go below us and cross over the morass we shall be at an advantage. Also, I think that it would be best to go to battle on foot, and with little armour, for if we mount our horses for the fight, when our enemy is stringer and better-horsed than we, we should be in a lot of trouble. And if we fight on foot, we shall always have an advantage, for in the Park, among the trees, the horsemen will be less manoeuvrable, and the streams down below [on the plain] will disrupt them.*]

Evidently Barbour believed that King Robert, though not necessarily committing himself to a major engagement, was prepared to fight if the circumstances seemed promising. The relief of Stirling Castle is presented as the chief objective of the English army, but Robert's decision to station his own forces in the strong position of the New Park – where it would be very difficult for the English cavalry to make an effective attack but where he would still be able to intervene should the English try to approach Stirling 'below' the high ground on which the Park was situated – does rather indicate that he believed the 'real' objective to be to force battle. Presumably this was actually self-evident, not only to the king, but to the army generally. Whatever the strategic and political significance of Stirling Castle, Edward cannot have believed that the retention of one fortress was so important that it was worth the expense of raising a large army. Realistically, unless he could bring the Scots to battle – and defeat them – the relief of the castle would be of little value. He could not keep an army in being for very long due to the enormous expense and the high rate of desertion typical of armies of the day. As soon as the army disbanded, the Scots would be able to renew the siege. The streams across the plain were obviously expected to cause problems for the English, but it is not certain that the streams in question ran across the English position. Barbour may simply mean that the courses of the Bannock and the Pelstream would prevent the English army from adopting the optimum formation for battle or would prevent them from moving to out-flank a Scottish advance.

King Robert's instruction to his men to be 'armyt bot in littil armyng,' though an important piece of information, does not imply that the Scots went to battle without armour, just that they should dispense with some of the heaviest pieces, perhaps exchanging great barrel helms – which were in any case going out of use – for the lighter, and much more fashionable, bacinet. In practice this would only really apply to the men-at-arms. The rank and file would, in the main, wear armour of cloth and leather. With the leaders appointed and the army divided into four formations of infantry, Barbour goes on to describe the planned deployment, with the King taking the rearguard:

He said the rerward he wuld ma
And evyn forrouth him wald ga
The vaward, and on ather hand
The tother bataillis suld be gangand
Besid on sid a litill space,
And the king that behind thaim was
Suld se quhar thar war mast myster
And releve thar with his baner.

[*He said he would take the rearguard, and straight in front of him would be the vanguard, and on either side, a little distance apart, would go the other two divisions, and the king, who was behind them should see where there was the greatest threat and relieve them with his banner.*]

The deployment of the four main formations – for there were also archers and cavalry present – was planned well before the arrival of the English army. Barbour's description could mean that the Scots adopted a 'diamond' formation, however the term *vaward* (vanguard) should not be interpreted strictly and simply to mean that that formation should always form the leading edge of the battle on their own. Barbour does not actually say that the vanguard was ranged in front of the other units, only that two other formations were deployed a little distance on either side with the king's formation directly to the rear of the vanguard, so that he could see what was going on and commit his force where it would do the most good. This may indicate a little wishful thinking on Barbour's part. If we are to assume that each of these formations was something in the region of two hundred metres wide – and they can hardly have been very much less – it would be extremely difficult for the king to identify the most pressing need unless one or other of the formations to his front was utterly overwhelmed. Further, should that occur, the only really practical option would be to move his own formation to the left or right to face the enemy, unless of course it was the *vaward* that was defeated, in which case preventing his own formation from panicking and taking to their heels would surely present an insuperable challenge, even for a leader of King Robert's calibre.

Training a large body of men to move forward in unison is not that great a challenge, but changing the direction of their advance by inclining on the march is very difficult to achieve without losing the uniformity of 'dressing' (the intervals between the men) which would be vital to the success of a force of spearmen.

Having decided on his order of battle, Robert set his men to the task of preparing the 'pots' that figure so prominently in accounts of the action. The army spent the whole of the Saturday night digging and heard mass early on Sunday morning, at which point the combatants were ordered to arm themselves for battle, while the carters, farriers, lorimers, blacksmiths, cooks and other ancillaries were ordered to move away from the main body of the army:

> Syne all the smale folk and pitail
> He send with harnays and vitaill
> Intil the park weill fer him fra
> And fra the bataillis gert them ga
> And als he bad went thar way
> Twenty thousand weile ner war thai.
> Thai held thar way til a vale

[*Then all the ancillaries, with stocks of equipment and food, were sent some distance into the Park, well away from the fighting formations. They obeyed his* [the King's] *orders. Ther were nearly twenty thousand of them, and they made their way to a valley.*]

These, of course, were the 'small folk' – the porters, craftsmen, cooks, grooms and servants – that were a vital component of any medieval army, and who, so Barbour tells us, joined the battle at a crucial juncture to help secure Robert's victory on the Monday morning. It is easy to dismiss their involvement, particularly since they do not appear in any of the other contemporary or near-contemporary accounts, however this may be a matter of the perception of those whose observations formed the basis of the other depictions of the battle. Lanercost's 'reliable eye-witness' may not have been in a position to see the advance of the 'small folk' since at that point he was, presumably, either in the thick of the fighting or attempting to escape with his life. He would, in any case, have the main body of the Scottish army between himself and the 'small folk'. Their absence from the *Scalacronica* account is, perhaps, more telling. Sir Thomas Grey senior was certainly present, but that does not mean that he had an unobstructed view of the action, though, if the intervention of the 'small folk' were of any significance, he would surely have become aware of it in the aftermath of the fight. Alternatively, he – or Thomas junior, who wrote the account – may have known of the intervention but considered that it was either unimportant or that it would not be of interest to an audience. Given his preoccupation with the deeds of 'noble knights', it may just have held no interest for him personally. Having disposed of the ancillaries, Barbour turns his attention back to the king and the army:

The king gert thaim all buskit be
For he wyst in certante
That his fayis all nycht lay
At the Fawkyrk, and syne that thai
Held towart him the way all straucht
With mony men of mekill maucht.
Tharfor til his nevo bad he
The erle of Murreff with his menye
Besid the kyrk to kepe the way
That na man pas that gat away
For to debat the castel,
And he said himself suld weill

Kepe the entre with his batail
Giff that ony wald assale,
And syne his broder Schyr Edward
And young Walter Steward
And the lord of Douglas alsua
With thar mengne gud tent suld ta
Quhilk off thaim had of help myster
And help with thaim that with him wer.

*[The king ordered them all to prepare themselves, for he knew that his enemies had*
*camped at Falkirk for the night, and were moving against him with many men of great*
*might. Therefore he ordered his nephew, the Earl of Moray, with his troops, to guard*
*the road that passed beside the church to ensure that no man could pass that way to*
*the castle, and he said that he would guard the entry with his own division in case the*
*enemy advanced by that direction. And his brother, Sir Edward, and young Walter the*
*Steward and the lord of Douglas should pay close attention as to which of them [the*
*king or Moray] should be most in need of support.]*

There were only two approaches to the castle that were practical propositions for the English army; the road through the New Park or across the low
ground to the east of the Park. The location of the Park is beyond dispute,
though the exact course of the road, and therefore the location of the Entry,
cannot be identified precisely. In general, historians have assumed that the
'kyrk' beside the road that Moray was to guard was St Ninians. Professor
Duncan has pointed out that the only possible alternative to St Ninians
would be the chapel of Larbert, which lay to the east of the Falkirk–Stirling
road and a little to the southeast of the Torwood. This would place Moray's
action against Clifford and Beaumont several kilometres away from the
New Park. This is not impossible, but it would mean that elements of
Robert's were widely separated, surely too far apart to allow Robert to
observe the advance of the English and instruct Moray to take the field to
prevent them reaching the castle. The distances involved would have made
it virtually impossible for Edward Bruce, Douglas and the Stewart to bring
their troops into action in support of either the king or Moray. If they were
close enough to support one formation, they would be far too far away to
intervene in support of the other. The conclusion must be that Barbour had
St Ninians in mind.

The king send than James of Douglas
And Schyr Robert the Keyth that was
Marschell off the ost of fe
The Inglismennys come to se,
And thai lap on and furth thai raid
Weile horsyt men with thaim thai haid,
And sone the gret ost haf thai sene
Quhar scheldis schynand was sa schene
And basynetis burnyst brycht
That gave agayne the sone gret lycht.

[*The king then sent Sir James Douglas and Sir Robert Keith, who was the marchal of the army by heritable right, to observe the English. They mounted and rode off with well-mounted men and soon saw the great army, whose shiny shields and burnished bacinets reflected the sun brightly.*]

Robert's decision to send men to observe the approach of the English army was unremarkable, failure to do so would have been positively negligent, however this passage gives us two scraps of useful information about the nature of the Scottish army. Sir Robert 'the' Keith – 'the' is inserted to meet the demands of the meter of the poem – held the post of Marshal of the king's army, which was a hereditary office, a normal practice of the time. The precise nature and extent of his responsibilities cannot be ascertained, but obviously he was the most senior officer in a formal and customary command structure of some antiquity in the cavalry element of Scottish armies. The other significant point relates to the nature of Scottish noble cavalry. Barbour tells us that the party that Keith and Douglas led was 'well-horsed', an expression which appears from time to time in a variety of contemporary documents. One of the first references to William Wallace refers to him as a leader of men who were all 'well-horsed', a clear indication that his party consisted of men-at-arms. A minor point is Barbour's reference to 'bacinets'. This might be construed as an example of a writer using observations of the military practice of his own time when describing events of an earlier period, such as Bower's description of the English army (see below) being equipped with cannon. Although generally assumed to be a development of the 1340s, there are many references to bacinets dating from the early years of the fourteenth century. In 1316 Edward obtained a grant of one infantry-man from every villa in England that stipulated that each man should have a bacinet as part of their equipment; an indication that the bacinet was no longer the preserve of fashionable gentlemen. Antiquarians and historians may have been misled by what we night call 'artistic' evidence, primarily funeral brasses and statuary. Bacinets do not become common in effigies before the 1340s, but we should bear in mind that most of these effigies are of men who died of natural causes. The armour depicted may have involved a deal of 'artistic license', but the wide variety of styles surely indicated that some at least were in fact taken 'from life' – that they were genuine depictions of the armour owned by that particular individual in their soldiering days, and may therefore be representative of the style of armour worn in their youth, not at the time of their death.

Keith and Douglas observed the English army, and returned to the king:

Towart the king thai tuk thair way,
And tauld him intil prevete
The multitude and beaute
Off thair fayis that come sa braid
And off the gret mycht that thai haid.
Than the king bad thaim thai suld ma
Na contenance that it war sua
Bot lat thaim into commouine say
That thai cum intil evyll array
To confort his on that wys,
For oftrsys thou a word may rys
Disconford and tynsail with–all
And throu a word als weill may fall
Conford may rys and hardyment
May get men to do thar intent.

[*They returned to the king and told him privately of the great strength and power of the enemy. The king told them that they should not spread that information, but rather to let in be known that the enemy was approaching in very poor order, which would be a comfort to the troops, for often defeat can come from one word, but confidence and determination can be enhanced by another, inspiring the men to do their duty.*]

Control of the 'news agenda' is not, apparently, a modern phenomenon. Robert manipulated the information that would pass through the army with the clear intention of bolstering the morale of the troops as the English approached.

And quhen thai cummyn war sa ner
That bit twa myle betwixt thaim wer
They chesyt a joly company
Off men that wicht war and hardy
On fayr coureris armyt at rycht
Four banrentis off mekill mycht
War capitaynis of that route,
The Syr the Clifford that wes stout
Wes of thaim all soverane leidar
Aucht hunder armyt I trow thai war.
Thai war all young men and joly
Yarnand to do chivalry,
Off best of all the ost war thai
Off contenance and off array.
Thai war he fairest company
That men mycht find of sa mony,
To the castell thai thocht to far
For gif that thai weill mycht cum thar
Thai thocht it suld reskewit be.
Forth on thar way held this menye
And towart Streviine held thar way,
The New Park all eschewit thai
For thai wist weill the king wes thar
And newth the New Park ghan thai far
Weill newth the kyrk intill a rout.

[...*and when they [the English] had come so close that there was only two miles between the armies, they chose a brave company of men that were strong and brave, whose chargers were string and well armoured. Four bannerets of great prowess led this force, and Clifford was the officer in command. I believe that there were eight hundred of them. They were all brave young men, eager to perform acts of chivalry. They were the finest troops that could be found in the whole army in skill and equipment. They intended to pass to the castle, for if they could get to it, it would be relieved. This company made their way toward Stirling. They kept away from the New Park because they were aware that the king was there so they passed well below the New Park and below the church in one body.*]

Evidently Barbour believed that the objective of Clifford's command was to effect a formal or technical relief of the castle. This would indeed be a chivalrous deed, since it would involve passing the entirety of the Scottish army. Even if Clifford's force amounted to eight hundred – Grey, whose father served in that formation, gives a figure of three hundred – this would still be the sort of achievement that brought honour to the participants.

Strictly speaking the castle would have been technically relieved if the English army came within three miles, but that would not have the social cachet of a relief by a 'joly' company of men-at-arms. Barbour does not name the four bannerets whose commands made up Clifford's force, though presumably one of them was Sir Henry Beaumont. The force may have consisted of brave men, but Clifford was not a rash commander. Aware that Robert – with the main body of the army – was in a strong position in the New Park, he kept to the open fields below the Park and toward St Ninians Church. Their progress was observed by the king, a clear indication that the ensuing action occurred within a relatively modest distance of the king's position at the Entry, since it was Robert who brought their advance to the attention of Moray, who promptly led his men to bar their way.

> The Erle Thomas that wes sa stout
> Quhen he saw thaim sa ta the plane
> Ingret hy went he thaim agane
> With five hunder foroutyn ma
> Anoyit in his hart and wa
> That thai sa fer wer passit by,
> For the king haid said him rudly
> That a rose of his chaplete
> Was fallyn, for quhar he wes set
> To kep the way thai men were passit
> And tharfor he hastyt him sa fast
> That cummynin schot tyme wes he
> TRo the plane filed with his menye,
> For he thocht that he suld amend
> That he trespassit had or than end
> And quhen the Inglismen him saw
> Cum on foroutyn dyn or aw
> And tak sa hardely the plane
> In hy thai spoed thaim him agane

And strak with spurs the stedis stith
That bar thaim evyn hard and swith.
And quhen the erle sa that menye
Cum sa stoutly, til his said he
Be nocht abaysit for that schor
Bot settis speris you befor
And bak to bak set all your rout
And all the speris poyntis out
Suagate us best defend may we
Enveronyt with thaim gif we be.

[*When Earl Thomas, who was so staunch, saw them take the plain he moved against them in great haste with no more than five hundred men, angered in his heart that they had gone as far, for the king had rebuked him, saying that a rose had fallen from his chaplet, for the enemy was passing the place where he had been stationed. He quickly led his men to the plain filed for he felt that he must make amends for his negligence, and when the English saw him coming on without fear and so bravely take the plain they quickly moved against him, using their spurs on the chargers that bore them. And when the Earl saw them advancing bravely he spoke to his men 'Do not be afraid of their appearance, but put your spears before you, and arrange yourselves so that all your spears point outwards, that we may defend ourselves if we are surrounded by them.'*]

Moray, then, had failed to fulfil his orders. Clifford's force had been able to cross most of the low ground to the east of the Torwood and was well on its way to effecting a relief of the castle. The fact that the king was able to observe Clifford and rebuke his nephew, but that there was still time for Moray to gather his troops and lead them out to obstruct the enemy, is a strong indication that the Scottish army did not have a very extensive front, but was relatively concentrated. Moray's speech to his troops is almost certainly a product of Barbour's pen – his troops should have needed no instruction about the value of their formation as they had, after all, been at Stirling for some weeks, training for exactly this sort of situation. Barbour continues with a stirring and graphic account of the ensuing action, describing the inability of the English cavalry to break into the Scottish formation, until, frustrated and desperate, they began to throw their weapons at the Scots in the hope of disrupting their ranks. The struggle continued for some time, prompting Douglas to ask permission from the king to go to Moray's aid. Initially this was refused; in part, because the king was not prepared to have his plans disrupted, and in part to allow Moray to have the undiluted honour of scoring a significant victory with only his own command. However, the king eventually relented, and Douglas led his men down onto the plain, where he drew to a halt to observe the progress of the fight. While all this was going on, the king was faced with another problem – the earls of Gloucester and Hereford, at the head of a strong company of men-at-arms, were attempting to fore a passage into the New Park:

> The vaward, that wist na thing
> Off this arrest na his dwelling
> Raif to the Park all straucht thar way
> Foroutyn stinting in gud array,
> And quhen the king wist that thai wer
> In hale bataill cummand sa ner
> His bataill gert he weill array.
> He raid apon a littil palfrey
> Laucht and joly arayand
> His bataill with ane ax in hand
> And on his bassynet he bar
> Ane hat of quyrbolle ay-quhar,
> And thar-upon into taknyng
> Ane hey croune that he wes he king

[*The English vanguard, who knew nothing of this reverse, made their way straight to the Park in good order and when the king became aware of them, he put his division into good order. He was mounted on a small palfrey, directing the troops, axe in hand. On his bacinet he wore a cap of boiled leather and on top of that a crown to show that he was the king.*]

Robert's choice of mount – a palfrey – has been construed as evidence that the Scots did not have access to the more muscular destrier, but is really a matter of having the most appropriate mount. He clearly did not expect to be taking part in the action himself. This was nearly his undoing as Sir Henry de Bohun, riding somewhat in advance of Gloucester and Hereford's force, saw the king and saw an opportunity to perform a great act of chivalry. Barbour describes the encounter in some detail and relates how the king's success gave heart to his troops. The English, on the other hand, were seriously demoralised.

And quhen the kingis men thaim saw
Sua in hale bataill thaim withdraw
A gret schout til thaim gan thai mak
And they in hy tuk all the bak,
And thai that folowit thaim ha slane
Sum off thaim that they hat ourtane
Bot thai war few forsuth to say
Thar hors fete had ner all away
Bot how-sa quhoyne deyt thar
Rebutyt foulily thai war

[*When the king's men saw them withdraw in a single body, they gave a great shout and they* [the English] *retreated quickly, and those* [Scots] *who pursued them killed some that they had overtaken. Those killed were few in number, and the rest were taken away speedily by their horses, heavily defeated.*]

The number of casualties incurred by Gloucester and Hereford's force must have been quite small. Barbour would not miss an opportunity to regale his audience with talk of large numbers of English dead, but the action was a significant boost to the confidence of the Scots. This was a superstitious age, and the troops would be likely to take the king's successful duel as a good omen.

The attack at The Entry had been repulsed, but Moray's men were still in action near St Ninians when Douglas's formation approached:

The Erle Thomas wes yet fechtand
With fayis apon athyr hand
And slew of thaim a quantite
Bot wery war his men and he
The-quhether with wappynnys strurdely
Thai thaim defendyt manlely
Quhil that the Douglas come ner
That sped him on gret maner,
And Inglismen that war fechtand
Quhen thai the Douglas saw ner-hand
Thai wandyst and maid ane opynnyng.
James of Douglas be thar relying

Knew that thai discumfyt wer
Than bad thaim that with him wer
Stand still and pres na forthyrmar.
'For thai that yonder fechtand ar,'
He said 'ar off sa gret bounte
That thar fayis weill sone sone be
Discumfyt throu that awne mycht
Thocht na man help thaim for to fycht
And cum we now to the fechting
Quhen thai ar at discumfyting
Men suld say we thaim fruschit had,
And sua suld thai that caus has mad
With gret travail and hard fechting
Los a part of thar loving,
And it wer syn to les that prys
That of sa soverane bounte is.
And he throu plane and hard fechting
Has her eschevyt unlikly thing

[*Earl Thomas was still fighting foes on either side, and killed many, both he and his men were very tired, but still wielded their weapons manfully, until Douglas approached with speed and power, and the English that were fighting, when they saw Douglas close by, they hesitated and drew back. Douglas could tell from their retreat that they were close to defeat and told his men to halt and not to press any further forward. He said, 'those that are fighting over there are so brave that they will shortly overcome the enemy through their own efforts, though no man aids them in their fight. And if we join the fighting now, when they [the English] are already being defeated, men should say that we had beaten them, and those who have achieved this with hard work and fighting would be robbed of the honour they deserve.*]

After a hard fight the English troops, realising that they could do no more, withdrew, leaving the field to the earl's force, and having incurred – according to Barbour – only one fatal casualty, an unnamed yeoman.

At his juncture Barbour has the army gather together to hear a rousing speech from the king in which he leaves the decision of whether or not to fight on the following day to his troops. This is unlikely to say the least, but there is evidence to suggest that Robert was not yet fully committed to giving battle against the whole English army. His troops had acquitted themselves well and he could, perhaps, have avoided battle without serious political consequences. True, the castle would be relieved, but so long as Robert kept his army intact, Edward would not be able to take the risk of splitting his troops to carry out operations to impose his lordship, and the retention of one castle would be a poor prize for the effort and expense of leading a large army into Scotland. Naturally, Barbour has the army react in a positive way, cheering the king and declaring their willingness to fight. Although Barbour's main narrative of the first day's action limits participation to the 'battle' of the king and five hundred men under Moray, when he comes to sum up the events of the day, he introduces another element, informing us that Edward Bruce – and presumably at least some proportion of his command – joined the action at The Entry in the pursuit of Gloucester and Hereford. This might be dismissed as a product of Barbour's imagination, since none of the other accounts mentions Edward Bruce's intervention, but it is hard to see what motive he could have for inventing an episode to show Edward Bruce in a good light, and it is perfectly possible that he could have joined the fight without anyone in the English army being aware that he had done so. The English were making a hasty retreat by that time, and probably had more pressing matters in mind than questions about who was or was not involved in the action. In a sense, it is not an important issue – the Scots had defeated the English in the action at the Entry. However it may have been a matter of some importance to the men involved. If Edward Bruce's division took any part in the fighting it would mean that at least half of the Scottish army had been engaged in successful actions on the Sunday evening. Furthermore, Douglas's command may not have actually been in action, but his men had witnessed Moray's fight at St Ninians. Both of the engagements had demonstrated the power of confident infantry when attacked by unsupported cavalry and there must have been a morale dividend for Robert's troops equal to or greater than the damage to the confidence of the English.

Important as they undoubtedly were, the two actions on Sunday night were hardly such significant defeats as to persuade Edward II to abandon his plan to bring the Scots to battle, so the English army made camp for the night and Edward consulted his staff officers:

The king with his consaill preve
Has tane to rede that he wald nocht
Fecht or the morne bot war he socht,
Tharfor thai herberyd thaim that nycht

Doune in the Kers, and gert all dycht
And maid redsy thar aparaill
Agayne the morne for the bataill,
And for in the Kers pulis war
Housis thai brak and thak bar
To mak briggis quhar thaim mycht pas,
And sum sayis that yeit the folk that was
In the castell quhen nycht gan fall
For thai that knew the myscheiff all
Thai went full ner all that thai was
And duris and wyndowys with tham bar,
Swa that thai had before the day
Briggyt the pulis swa that thai
War passit our everilkane,
And the hard feld on hors has tane

[*The king* [Edward]*, with his privy council, has taken advice that he would not fight before morning unless forced to, therefore they camped that night down in the Carse and prepared their arms for battle the following morning, and, because there were streams in the Carse they demolished houses and took the thatch to make bridges where they might pass* [over the streams]. *And there are those who say that after dusk almost all of the men in the castle, knowing the problems* [of the terrain] *carried doors and windows, so that before daybreak they had bridged the streams and moved onto the hard field on horseback.*]

This passage has led historians to reach an untenable conclusion that has bedevilled the study of this battle. There are two specific issues. Firstly, a misunderstanding of the word 'Carse', frequently misinterpreted as 'swamp' or 'marsh' and secondly the word 'pulis', often translated as 'pools' for obvious, if incorrect, reasons. A carse is not a marsh, but an area which, though wet and difficult in the winter, is hard ground in summer. We might take note of the work of another Scottish poet, Samuel Colville who tells us that in spring the ground is like '…..toasted breid /and through the Carse a man may reid (ride).' The term 'pulis', far from indicating stagnant water, actually means streams or burns. Covering these 'pulis' with thatch from houses in the vicinity and with doors and windows from the castle is therefore a more practical proposition than one might expect. The object of the exercise was to make bridges that would allow the English army to cross on to the 'hard feld' where they would spend the night. They would be 'All reddy for till gif batale/Arayit intill thar apparaill' (all ready to give battle/arrayed in their equipment), an observation which accords perfectly with the *Scalacronica* account, in which Grey tells us that the English cavalry 'stood to' all night with their horses 'bitted'.

It would seem, then, that the English army passed an uncomfortable night on the 'hard feld', while the Scots were able to rest in whatever bivouac arrangements they had had over the preceding weeks. These were hardly likely to be sophisticated tents and pavilions – other than for the wealthy – but they surely enjoyed much better conditions than the English. This is a matter of some significance, especially when we remember that the English army had performed two hard marches on the Saturday and Sunday. Having brought the English to the battlefield, Barbour turns his attention back to the Scots.

> The Scottismen quhen it wes day
> Thar mes devoutly gert thai say
> Syne tuk a sop and maid thaim yar
> An quhen thai all assemblit was
> And in thair battaillis all purvayit
> With thar braid baners all displayit
> Thai maid knychts, as it afferis
> To men that usit thai mysteries,
> The king made Walter Stewart knycht,
> And James of Douglas that wes wycht
> And other als of gret bounte
> He maid ilkane in thar degree.
> Quhen this wes donyne that I you say
> Thai went all furth in gud array
> And tak the plane ful apertly,
> Mony gud man wicht and hardy
> That war full of gret bounte
> Intill thai routis men mycht se.

[*When it was day, the Scots devoutly heard mass and took food and prepared and when all their divisions were arrayed with banners unfurled, knights were made, as is proper for men to such men. The king made Walter Stewart a knight, and the valiant James Douglas and others of great prowess. He knighted each in appropriate degree. When what I tell you was completed, they set out in good order and quite openly took the plain.*]

The most significant piece of information from this passage is that the Scots 'full apertly' left the higher, wooded ground of the New Park, a clear indication that Robert had decided, not to accept battle, but to force it. The act of 'making knights' was something of a tradition on the eve of battle, and what is interesting is that James Douglas was one of the recipients of the accolade. Barbour's assertion that the recipients were knighted 'in thar degre' had led to the assumption that Douglas was in fact being promoted to a banneret, however that puts a lot of weight on a slender piece of evidence. Douglas was not, apparently, a knight in the spring of 1307, when he approached an unnamed officer of the occupation government and 'begged to be received' into King Edward's peace, though he quickly changed his mind and plumped for the Bruce party. It would not be surprising if Robert had knighted him at some point over the next seven years, though he was definitely not yet a knight at the time of his earliest appearance as a witness to a royal charter in April 1308 (*RRS*, v, pp.295–6). It is not clear that King Robert had made many knights before Bannockburn, though there is a strong possibility that he was the unnamed Scottish magnate who knighted William Wallace in 1297/8. The King, or Douglas, may have felt it appropriate to wait for a suitably dramatic occasion.

The Scots, then, were carefully deployed for the flight, but Barbour contradicts himself when describing the English. Having already declared that they had made themselves ready for battle, he now tells us that Edward's army:

War nocht arayit on sic maner
For all thar bataillis samyn war
In a schiltrum, but quhether it was
Throu the gret straitens of the place
That thai war in to bid fechting
Or that it was for abaysing
I wat nocht, but in a schiltrom
It semyt thai war all and sum,
Outane the vaward anerly
That rycht with a gret company
Be thaimselvyn arayit war.

[*...were not arrayed in that manner, for all their divisions were in one schiltrom, but whether that was due to the narrow space in which they were ordered to fight or* *whether it was to make a daunting appearance I do not know, but it seems that they were all in one body, save for the vanguard alone, which was arrayed in a great body by themselves.*]

From the perspective of the Scots, then, the English army appeared to be divided into two bodies of troops, including the vanguard, which was separate from the rest of the force and – presumably – to their front. Barbour has set the stage for the battle, but before the action can commence, he relates a conversation between King Edward and Sir Ingram de Umfraville. Umfraville suggests that the English withdraw their camp in good order, confident that the discipline of the Scots would not withstand the temptation to break ranks and loot the tents and wagons of the English army. They would therefore be vulnerable to an attack by the cavalry. Edward, however, rejects the proposal, since he feels a victory over 'sic rangale' (such rabble) through a stratagem would not be so honourable as a straight fight. Ever keen to show the importance of piety, Barbour describes the Scots kneeling for a brief prayer, which Edward interprets as a plea for mercy and an overture to surrender, but which Umfraville tells him is simply the Scots putting their trust in God.

This whole episode might be dismissed as Barbour's desire to attribute victory to God's help were it not supported by the Lanercost account. However inspiring the power of prayer, there may have been a very sound practical military value to the business of having the army kneel. The business of marching large linear formations down to the plain would have led inevitably to some loss of order. If the rank and file of the formations were to kneel down, even for just a couple of minutes, the formation commanders and their subordinates would have an excellent opportunity to identify and rectify any irregularities that had developed during the descent from the Park. If what we would nowadays call the 'junior leaders' remained standing while the rest of the troops prayed they would be able to see, and therefore remedy, any gaps or deficiencies in the dressing of the formation. Both armies were now committed to battle:

Thuis war thai boune on ather sid,
And Inglismen with mekill prid
That war intill thar avaward
To the Bataill that Schyr Edward
Governyt and led held straucht thar way
The hors with speris hardnyt thai
And prikyt apon thaim strudely,

And thai met thaim rycht hardely
Sua that at thar assemble thar
Sic a fruschyng of speris war
That fer away men mycht it her.
At that meting foroutyn wer
War stedis stekyt mony ane
And mony gude man borne doun and slayne,
And mony ane hardyment douchtely
Was thar eschevyt, for hardely
Thai dang on other with wapnys ser.
Sum of the hors that stekyt wer
Ruschyt and rely rycht rudlye,
Bot the remanand nocht-forthi
That mycht cum to the assembling
For that led main na stinting
Bit assemblyt full hardely,
And thai met them ful sturdily
With speris that were scharp to scher
And axys that weile groundyn wer.
Quhar-with was roucht mony a rout.
The fechting wes thar sa fell and stout
That mony a worthi man and swicht
Throu fors wes fellyt in that fycht
That had na mycht to rys agane.

[*So on both sides they were ready, and very proud English men in their vanguard made straight for the division of Sir Edward Bruce. They put their spurs to their horses fiercely and they met them [the Scots] with such vigour that there was such a breaking of spears that men might hear it from a great distance. At this clash many horses were undoubtedly killed, and many men were brought down and killed, and many brave deeds were performed, for they attacked one another fiercely with various weapons. Some of the horses that were stabbed fell down hard where they were, but the others pressed on into the fight. And they [the Scots] met them in a determined manner with spears sharp enough to cut and well-ground axes. That fight was hard and fierce, and many worthy and brave men were killed that had no strength to get up.*]

This, then, was the first major clash of the battle. The Scots advanced toward the English lines and were counter-attacked by cavalry, but were able to maintain the integrity of their formation.

As the fight developed, Moray brought his formation into action; not, apparently, just the five hundred men who had fought the previous evening, but one of the four divisions which Barbour allots to the Scottish army for the main battle.

And Quhen the erle of Murref swa
Thar vaward saw sa stoutly ga
The way to Schyr Edward all straucht
That met thaim with full mekill maucht,
He held hys way with his baner
To the gret rout quhar samyn wer
The nyne battailllis that war sa braid.
That sa fele banereis with thaim hald
And of men sa gret quantite
That it war wonder for to se.
The gud erle thidder tuk the way
With his battail in gud array
And assemblit sa hardily
That man mycht her that had bene by
A gret frusch of the speris that brast,
For that fayis assmblyt fat
That on stedis with mekill prid
Come prikand as thai wald our-rid
The erle and all his company,
Bot thai met thaim sa sturdily
That mony of thaim sa till erd thai bar,
For mony a sted was stekyt that
And mony gud man fellyt under fet
That had na hap to rys up yete.
Thar mycht se a hard bataill
And sum defend and sum assaile
And mony a reale romble rid
Be roucht thar apon ather sid
Quhill throu the byrnys bryst the blud
That til the erd doune stremand yhude.

[...*and when the Earl of Moray saw their* [the English] *vanguard advance on Sir Edward who met them with such strength, he made his way with his banner toward the great force of the nine formations which, with their many banners and great force of men, were a wonder to see. The good Earl made his way there with his formation in good order, and attacked so fiercely that men who might be near at hand could hear a great breaking of spears, for their enemies attacked very quickly on horseback with great confidence, spurring* [their horses] *as though they would ride over the Earl and his company. But he met them so fiercely that many of them were dashed to the ground, for many a horse was stabbed there and many good men who fell under their feet had no hope of rising up again. Men could see a great battle there, with some attacking and some defending, and many great combats were performed by each side until blood burst through their armour and streamed down to the ground.*]

Here Barbour repeats his assertion that the English army was divided into ten formations, one of which had already engaged with Edward Bruce's formation. Although he refers only to the English cavalry, it is by no means clear that he wants the reader to believe that all of the ten formations consisted of mounted men, but that the cavalry were to the fore of the rest of the army – a credible possibility in the light of the other accounts of the battle. It is perfectly possible that the English commanders were confident that the cavalry would be able to deal with the Scots, or that with the cavalry occupying all or most of the English front line, it was not possible to bring the infantry into action. It cannot be over-emphasised that the battle had developed quite contrary to English expectations, and that Edward II and his subordinates had assumed, on the basis of their lengthy experience of fighting the Scots, that they would be mounting an attack, not coping with one. Once again, the English cavalry proved unequal to the task of breaking into the Scottish formations and were soon in difficulties.

> The erle of Murreff and his men
> Sa soutely thaim contenyt then
> That thai wan place ay mar and mar
> On thar fayis the-quhether thai war
> Ay ten far ane or may perfay
> Sua that it semyt weill that thai
> War tynt amang sa gret menye
> As thai war plungyt in the se.

[*The Earl of Moray and his men then contained them* [the English] *so fiercely that they pushed their enemies back more and more though I am sure that they were outnumbered ten to one or perhaps more until it seemed that they were immersed among that great crowd just as if they were plunged into an ocean* [of their enemies].]

Many historians have interpreted the last two lines of this section as an indication that the Scots stood still, surrounded by their opponents like rocks in the sea, however Barbour tells his readers that the Scots pressed forward 'more and more', forcing the English backwards. There are several problems with that proposition. The first is the undoubted difficulty of achieving a steady advance to the plain with a body of perhaps 2,000 men in a circular formation; not impossible, but certainly very challenging. The second, and perhaps more crucial question, would be why the English cavalry commanders, having failed to break the Scots at the first onset, made no effort to lead their men westward, past the Scots. This would have allowed them to regroup behind the Scots and allowed the English infantry to engage. If we accept the interpretation of Barbour to the effect that the four Scottish formations were deployed in one line, once the cavalry had passed around Moray's formation – and the same applies to Edward Bruce's troops – they would be in no immediate danger.

Given Barbour's careful description of Moray's troops in action on the Sunday evening, it would be a curious thing if he neglected to mention that the Scots had formed circular schiltroms on the Monday morning. The third question, inevitably, must be 'how could the Scots achieve victory without advancing?' If they were motionless, Edward II and his officers would have been able to redeploy their troops, but, more importantly, they would only need to draw back a matter of a couple of yards to be safe from the Scottish spearmen. We cannot seriously consider that the Scots stood firm and that the English simply threw themselves onto Scottish spear points until the sheer weight of their casualties drove them to despair and flight. It is reasonable to assume that peer pressure and the physical courage and martial enthusiasm of men imbued with the chivalric values of the fourteenth century could spill over into recklessness, but not into mass suicide.

Barbour's description of the clash, that it was as if the Scots had been plunged into a 'sea' of their enemies, may lie at the root of a popular image of the battle – a great round mass of Scottish spearmen surrounded by waves of English cavalry, however neither Barbour nor any of the other accounts of the battle suggest that the Scots deployed in ring formations.

Barbour concludes this segment of the poem with a dramatic relation of the exploits of Edward Bruce and Moray's formations then passes to the next Scottish formation, that of the Stewart and Sir James Douglas.

Quhen they twa first bataillis wer
Assemblyt as I said you er,
The Stewart Walter that than was
And the gud lord als of Douglas
In a bataill in gud array,
And assemblyt sa hardely
Besid the erle a litill by
That thar feyis feld that cummyn wele,
For with wapynnys stalwart of stele
They dang upon with all thar mycht.

[*When those two formations were engaged as I said before, Walter, who was then the Stewart, and also Sir James Douglas, when they saw how the Earl and his formation attacked so stoutly, led their men in one formation and in good order, and met the enemy a little way from the earl, and made their presence felt, for with strong steel weapons they struck them with all their might.*]

Although Barbour believed that the Scottish army had been divided into four formations arrayed in a lozenge or diamond, he clearly shows the Scottish army advancing 'en echelon', bringing one formation into action at a time – Edward Bruce, then Moray, then the Stewart and Douglas, each joining the fight to the flank of the preceding formation:

That tyme thar thre bataillis wer
All syd be sid fechtand weill ner.

[*By that time the three formations were fighting nearly side by side.*]

Barbour's description is clear: as each formation came into action, the Scottish line was effectively lengthened by the width of each one, thus denying the English the opportunity to envelope the open flank of each formation as it approached. Any attempt to mount an attack around the Scots would have to be mounted while another Scottish formation was approaching the exposed flank of the would-be attackers. This description is less incompatible with that of Lanercost's 'eye-witness' than one might at first think. *The Lanercost Chronicle*, in common with the other contemporary accounts of the action, has the Sots divided into three formations rather than four; even if we assume that Barbour is correct we cannot assume that the Lanercost witness was wrong – he may not have been able to see a fourth Scottish division. Furthermore, it might not have been apparent to the Lanercost witness that the Scots were, in fact, 'en echelon,' as Barbour describes it, rather than deployed with two formations abreast in advance and a third in the rear.

With three of the formations engaged, Barbour turns to the English archers, who were now starting to make an impression on the Scots.

The Inglis archeris schot sa fast
That mycht schot haff ony last
It had bene hard to Scottismen
Bot King Robert that wele gan ken
That thar archeris war perilous
And thar schot rycht hard and greous
Ordanyt forouth the assemble
Hys marschell with a gret menye,
Five hunder armyt into stele
That on licht hors war horsyt welle,
For prik amang the archeris
And sua assaile thaim with thar speris
That thai na layser haiff to schut
This marscell that Ik off mute
That Schyr Robert of Keyth was cauld
As Ik befor her has you tauld
Quhen he saw the bataillis sua
Assembill and togidder ga
And saw the archeris schoyt stoutly,
With all thaim off his company
In hy apon thaim gan he rid
And ourtuk tham at a sid,
And ruschyt amang thaim sa rudly
Stikand thaim sa dispitously
Ands in sic fusoun berand doun
And slayasnd tham foroutyn ransoun

That trhai thaim scaylit everilkane,
And fra that tyme furth thar wes nane
That assemblyt schot to ma.

[*The English archers shot very quickly, and if they had continued it would have been hard on the Scots, but King Robert was well aware of how dangerous their archers were; that the wounds they inflicted were hard and grievous, so he sent out a party from the main army; namely his marshal with a great force, five hundred men, well-armoured in steel, and well-mounted on chargers, to attack the archers strenuously with their spears to prevent them from shooting. This marshal was Sir Robert Keith, as I have told you before. When he saw the formations go into action and saw the archers shoot stoutly, he rode steadfastly toward them with all his men and attacked them from the flank, breaking among them so fiercely and striking them pitilessly, slaying them without quarter, that he whole body took to their heels, and from then on no-one tried to gather men for more shooting.*]

It has been suggested that this entire episode is a product of Barbour's imagination, largely because it is not an incident that figures in any of the other accounts of the battle, and perhaps because British medievalists struggle to accept the possibility that archers might be defeated by unsupported cavalry in light of the great longbow victories – Dupplin Muir, Halidon Hill, Crecy, Poitiers and Agincourt. There are, however, several problems with that analysis. At Dupplin and Halidon, the English archers were faced by attacks from infantry, not cavalry. The target threatening them was a slow one. More significantly perhaps, each of the longbow victories mentioned above consisted of attacks made on carefully-deployed troops facing their opponents, not an attack on archers who were already engaged in a different direction. Finally, in all of these examples the archers were deployed uphill of their opponents. There was a world of difference between marching steadily uphill under a rain of arrows and galloping across flat ground into the flank of a body of archers with no close-combat troops in support.

Despite the promise at the start of his work that he would put in 'suthfast wryt' (accurate writing) the career of King Robert, Barbour was not above embroidering his account for the sake of providing the audience with an exciting tale, and, given the experiences of the Scots with English archery, tales of English archers being swept away would have gone down well with his leadership, however this would probably have been too significant an incident to invent if he wanted to remain credible in the eyes of his readers. Barbour could relate or inflate or just plainly invent noble deeds of King Robert – especially those claimed to have occurred when he was 'in the hills' – with impunity, but would need to have taken some care over the depiction of events that were close to people's hearts. If Keith rode down the English archers and was not accorded his place in Barbour's narrative, we can be confident that Keith's descendants would be less than pleased. If, on the other hand, Keith's attack was an invention, we can be sure that the descendants of other men would be concerned that their ancestor's worth was not receiving due attention.

A question raised by this passage is 'where did Keith's force come from?' Barbour is quite emphatic about the Scots being divided into four formations, and that all those formations fought on foot. He makes no reference to an independent command for Keith until he is ordered to lead an attack against the English archers. There are several possible explanations. Keith may have had command of a distinct element within one of the Scottish formations – presumably that of the king, since the other three were already engaged. This would imply that either Keith's men were mounted or that their grooms were nearby, ready to bring the chargers to the troops as required. Alternatively, Keith's troops may have formed a small unit, quite separate from any of the main formations, charged with intervention in the wake of either victory or disaster. King Robert may have decided to fight on foot for reasons of policy and morale, but we should not assume that he was absolutely determined to conquer or die. If the battle was going badly, Robert might well be glad of a body of men-at-arms. None of this really compromises the assertion in the other accounts that the Scottish army fought on foot. There can be no real doubt that almost all of them did, and that it is what the witnesses recalled about the nature of the fighting, but we should bear in mind that the witnesses – the Lanercost source and Friar Baston – were rather probably more pre-occupied with the business of staying alive than of recording their experience of the battle. Other writers, after the way of time, focus almost exclusively on the deeds – or deaths – of the aristocracy, and perhaps had little mind for the thousands of common infantry.

In addition to giving us the only account of Keith's attack, this passage probably lies at the root of the tradition that Scottish armies fielded 'light' cavalry throughout the wars of the Middle Ages. Barbour tells us that Keith's men were 'on licht hors', but we should not ask one word – 'lycht' – to bear too much weight. Barbour tells us, in the same line, that they were 'horsyt weille'; or that they were 'well-horsed', a term exclusively used at the time to describe men-at-arms with good quality mounts suitable for war. A reasonable interpretation would be that Barbour only means to tell us the

Scots, or most of them anyway, did not have destriers of the first order, or at least did not use them for his engagement. The riders are described as 'armyt into stele' and were clearly men-at-arms.

Keith's attack was a resounding success, and Barbour returns to the Scottish archers.

Quhen Scottis archeris saw that this sua
War rebutyt thai woux hardy
And with all thar mycht schot egrely
Amang the horsmen that thar raid
And woundis wid to thaim thai maid
And slew of tham a full gret dele
Thai bar tham hardely and wele
For, fra thar fayis archeris war
Scaylit as I said till you are
That ma na thai war be gret thing
Sua that thai dred nocht thar schoting.

[*When the Scottish archers saw that they* [the English archers] *had been defeated, they became bolder, and shot eagerly and with all their might against the* [English] *horsemen that were riding there, giving them wide wounds and killing many of them. They were confident and bold, for since the other archers, who were much more numerous, had all run away as I told before, they* [the Scots] *did not fear their shooting.*]

All this seems to have occurred before the King took his own formation into battle, which would certainly facilitate drawing a portion of troops from his own direct command and entrusting them to Keith. In Barbour's account, then, at this juncture there were three Scottish formations in the fight, with King Robert's formation in the rear. Again, this does not really clash with the other accounts very significantly. To the Lanercost witness the horizon must have been seemed with wide bodies of hostile approaching Scots with another great body of more Scots in the rear – whether the front line of the Scottish army consisted of two units or three was probably not an immediate concern. What is not clear from Barbour's account is the location of the Scottish archers. The English archers would seem to have been drawn together on a flank where they could enfilade the Scottish spearmen, and we might reasonably assume that King Robert might station his archers to the flanks of his army to provide a degree of cover to his close-combat troops, however Barbour does not give us that information. The Lanercost account however describes an exchange of archery before the first contact between Edward Bruce and Gloucester's formations in which the Scottish are defeated by what we can reasonably assume to be a greater force of English archers. Given that the main body of the Scottish army closed quickly on their opponents it is quite possible that the exchange took place as Lanercost describes it, and that both English and Scottish archers were forced out of the way by the advance of Edward Bruce and of Gloucester's cavalry, and then by Moray, forcing a confused concentration of English archers to the extreme flank of the Scottish army. Most historians have chosen to locate Keith's action on the left of the Scottish army, based on the assumption, perhaps, that Edward Bruce led the right-hand formation and was first into action, followed by Moray on his left, however Barbour does not make this absolutely clear. If the Scottish advance started from the left flank rather than the right, the archers of both sides might find themselves pushed toward Bannockburn rather than the Pelstream. If the Scots advanced with two formations abreast, as Sir Thomas Grey tells us, the effect need not be any different. Even if the two Scottish formations were in perfect alignment, there is no reason to assume that the English army had a flat front line. Other accounts suggest that Gloucester's formation was detached from the rest of the army even before his advance to contact. He evidently attacked, and with no support on his flank there would have been, however briefly, a space between the other Scottish formation(s) and the main body of the English army. Edward Bruce's formation seems to have marched with the Bannock burn (or possibly the Pelstream, if he was on the left flank of the army) protecting their flank, so the easiest apparent route to safety – or at least away from the current melee – would be to move away from the burn and Edward Bruce's Scots.

The dispersal of the English archers greatly encouraged their Scottish counterparts but did nothing to help the morale of the rest of the army. 'Nakyt' (unarmoured), they fled from the 'armyt' Scottish cavalry:

> Thai scaylit thaim on sic maner
> That sum to that gret bataill wer
> Withdrawyn thaim in full gret hy
> And sum wer fled all trely,
> Bot the folk that behind thaim was,
> That for thar awne folk had na space

Yheyt to cum to the assembling
In again smartly gan thai ding
The archeris that thai met fleand
That then war maid sa recreand
That thar hartis war tynt clenely.

[*They fled in such a way that some escaped into the great body* [of the English
army] *and some fled utterly, but the men who were behind them, who had no space
for manoeuvre and had yet to be engaged, came right up against the archers who were
running away, and were so discouraged that they, too, lost heart completely.*]

Keith's action, then, had had a major impact on the flow of the battle. The
English archers had been prevented from making any great impact on the fighting and had also been thrown back onto the main body of the English army,
causing confusion and demoralisation among those who had not yet fought.
Seeing that all is going well, Robert gives a short speech to the effect that if the
Scots press their advantage home, they will achieve a great victory. Barbour has
all four Scottish formations in line, pushing against an English army that has
lost its cohesion and any separation between commands since they had now
been pushed into one great heaving formation, 'Thai than war in a schiltrom
all.' Barbour gives us a lengthy description of the bravery of the Scots and of
the martial prowess of their leaders, and the battle is clearly won, but he has
other episodes to relate. The first of these is the story of the 'sma' folk'.

In this tyme that I tell of her
At that bataill on this maner
Wes strykyn quhar on ather party
Thai war fechtand enforcely,
Yomen and swanys and pitaill
That in the Park to yeme vittaill
Wart left, quhen thai wist but lessing
That thar lordis with fell fechting
On that fayis assembyt wer'
Ane of thaimselvyn that war thar
Capitane off thaim all thai maid,
And schetis that war sumdele braid
Thai festnyt in steid of baneris
Apon lang treys and speris,

And said that thai wald se the fycht;
And help thar lordis at thar mycht.
Quhen her-tilall assentyt wer
In a rout thai assemblyt er
Fyfteen thousand thai war or ma,
And than in gret hy gan they ga
With thar baneris all in a rout
As thai had men bene styth and stout.
Thai come with all that assemble
Rycht quhill thai mycht the bataill se,
Than all at abys thai gave a cry,
'Sla! Sla! Apon thaim hastily!'
And thar-withall cummand war thai,
Bot thai were wele fer yete away.
And Inglismen that ruschyt war
Thouch for of fycht as I said ar
Quhen they saw cummnad with sic a cry
Towart thaim sic a company
That thaim thocht wele als mony war
As thai wes fechtand with thaim thar
And thai before had nocht thaim sene,
That wit ye weill withoutyn wene
Thai war abaysit sa gretumly
That the best and the mast hardy
That was intil thar ost that day
Wald with thar mensk haf bene away.

[At this point in the battle, I tell you, just as the fight was being pursued furiously by both sides, men and boys who had been left in the Park to look after food, aware that their lords were heavily engaged with the enemy, chose one of their number to be their captain, and they fastened broad sheets to long poles and spears and said that they would see the battle and help their lords to the best of their ability. When they had all agreed to this they gathered together in one body, fifteen thousand of them or more with their banners, and then they went to a place where they could have a good view of the battle. Then all at once they gave a shout 'Kill! Kill! Attack them quickly!' And then they started to advance toward the fighting, though they were still a good distance away. The English, who were exhausted by the fighting as I said before, saw them coming on with a great cry and thought them to be an even greater company than those that they

*were already fighting, and one that they had not seen before. You can be sure that they*
*were so downcast that even the best and most hardy men that were in that army that*
*day wished they could be somewhere else and preserve their honour.*]

Once again, it is difficult to accept the possibility that this was an episode that
Barbour invented; the bones of the episode might be found in many other
medieval battles. Once it becomes clear that the enemy are beaten, the various
ancillaries of the army – grooms, porters, farriers, drivers, cooks and servants
– might gravitate to the locations of the fighting in search of plunder, or just
out of morbid curiosity. Although he was keen to give the camp followers their
due, Barbour's narrative does not indicate that they were crucial to victory;
the English are already exhausted, demoralised and disorganised and are being
pressed back steadily. King Edward sees that the day is lost, and leaves the field.

And quhen the king of Ingland
Saw his men fley in syndry palce,
And saw his fayis rout that was
Worthyn sa wycht and sa hardy
That all his folk war halyly
Sa stonayit that thai had na mycht
To stynt thar fayis in the fycht,
He was abaysit sa gretumly
That he and his company
Fyve hunder armyt all at rycht
Intill a frusch all tok the flycht
And to the castell held thar way.
And yeit haiff Ik hard som men say
That of Valence Schir Aymer
Quhen he in the feld saw vencsyt ner
Be the reyngye led awy the king
Agane his will fra the fechting.
And quhen Schyr Gylis the Argente
Saw the king thus and his menye
Schap thaim to fley as spedyly,
He copme rycht to the king in hy
And said, 'Schyr, sen it is sua
That ye thusgat your gat will ga
Havyn gud dayt for agayne will I,

Yeit fled I never sekyrly
And I cheys her to bid and dey.'

[*And when the King of England saw his men deserting in various places, and saw that his enemy's army was so stout that they had stunned his own people so much that they were unable to fight, he was so downcast that he, and his company of five hundred men-at-arms ran off in a mob and made their way to the castle. And I have heard men say that when he saw defeat was near Sir Aymer de Valence took the king's rein and led him away from the fighting against his will. And when Sir Giles D'Argentan saw the king and his followers prepare for flight he came right up to the king and said 'Sir, since you think to get away, have a good day, for I shall return [to the fight], indeed, I never fled, and I choose to stay here and die.'*]

Edward's exit was an acknowledgement of defeat, and an indication to the English army that any who could still do so should do their best to escape. For those who could see what was going on and who had the opportunity to do so, the best plan was to join the king's party if possible. A strong body of well-mounted men-at-arms would have a good chance of making their escape from the battlefield, and one could hardly be accused of desertion if one was in the company of the king. If the worst came to the worst and the Scots were able to force Edward's surrender, it would be no worse than falling prisoner in any other action, and one could hope that some help might be available in one's ransom negotiations. The Scots continued to press forward, continually reducing the space available to the English army, who, seeing the king disappear toward the castle, scattered before the enemy.

And fled sa fast rycht effrayitly
That of thaim a full gret party
Fled to the water of Forth and thar
The maist part of thaim drownyt war.
And Bannokburne betwixt the brays
Off men and hors sua stekyt wais
That apon drownyt hors and men
Men mycht pass dry out-our it then.

[*And fled in such terror that a great many fled to the waters of the Forth and most of a great party of them were drowned there. And the Bannock Burn was so stuffed between its banks with drowned men and horses that a man might cross over it dry.*]

Claims that men could have walked dry-shod over a stream or river because it was overflowing with bodies are not unknown in chronicle accounts; similarly streams that ran red with blood for three days after a battle. Literary flourishes should not be taken too literally, but there can be little doubt that English casualties were heavy. Interestingly, Barbour is very clear that the retreating English soldiers were pressed back toward the Forth as well as the Bannock Burn, an indication perhaps that the army scattered and fled in whatever directions seemed to offer a better prospect than the battlefield itself.

King Edward had escaped the field, but his situation was still bleak; his army had been destroyed and he had to seek shelter in the nearest haven, Stirling Castle. Any shelter there would have been most hazardous, as the governor, Sir Philip Moubray explained:

> The king with thaim he with him had
> In a rout till the castell rad
> And wald haiff bene tharin, for thai
> Wyst nocht quhat to get away,
> Bot Philip the Moubra said him till
> 'The castell, Schyr, is at your will,
> But cum ye in it ye sall se
> That ye sall sone asssegyt be
> And thar sall nane of Ingland
> To mak you rescours tak on hand
> And but rescours may na castell
> Be haldyn lang, ye wate this wele.
> Tharfor confort you and rely
> Your men about you rycht starkly
> And haldis about the Park your way
> Knyt als sadly as ye may,
> For I trow that nane sall haff mycht
> That chassys with sa fele to fycht.'
> And his consail they haff doyne
> And beneath the castell went thai sone
> Rycht be the Rond Table away
> And syne the Park enveround thai
> And towart Lythkow held in hy.

[*The king, and those with him, rode in a close formation to the castle, and would have entered, for they did not know what road to take to escape, however Sir Philip Moubray spoke [to the king] 'Sir, the castle is at your disposal, but if you enter you will see that you will soon be besieged. No-one from England can undertake your relief and you know that no castle can be held for long without relief. Take comfort; and rally your men close around you. Make your way round the Park, as close-knit as you can be, for I am sure that none who might pursue you will have the strength to attack [such a strong party].' They took his advice and shortly rode below the castle, past the Round Table and around the Park before making their way toward Linlithgow.*]

Edward was doubtless further demoralised by Moubray's advice, but the situation was clear. The English army was in no fit state to renew the fight and there was no realistic possibility of a new army being raised to come to Edward's rescue, certainly not within the period that the castle garrison might be expected to hold out. Technically, Sir Philip was not obliged to surrender the castle at all. An English army had arrived in the vicinity of the town within the period stipulated in the agreement that Moubray had made with Edward Bruce, but surrender was the only realistic option.

King Edward made his escape, pursued by Douglas at the head of a small body of men-at-arms, less than sixty in number according to Barbour. Not all of the English leadership was as fortunate. Gloucester, Clifford, Comyn and many others were dead on the field – Hereford escaped, apparently with a strong company, and sought safety behind the walls of Bothwell Castle, one of the few strongholds still in Plantagenet hands, only to be taken prisoner by its commander, Sir Walter Gilbertson (or FitzGilbert). Interestingly, Gilbertson was English by birth, but had lived in Scotland since before the invasion of 1296 and was one of a small number of English soldiers to decide that their career in Scotland was more important than allegiance to their king.

The English army left the field in several directions, but a large number of them, perhaps trying to follow King Edward's example, found their way up through the town to Stirling Castle, where, unable to gain entry, they congregated around the castle rock.

Bot to the castell that wes ner
Off Strevilline fled sic a mengye
That it war winder for to se,
For the craggis al helyit war
About the castell her and thar

Off thaim that for strenth of that sted
Thidderwart to warand fled,
And for thai sa fele that war
Fled under the castell war
The King Robert that wes witty
Held his gud men ner him by
For dred that ris agayne suld thai
This was the caus forsuth to say
Quharthouch the king of Ingland
Eschapyt hame intill his land
Quhen that the feld sa clene wes maid
Off Inglismen that nane abaid
The Scottismen sone tuk in hand
Off tharis all that ever thai fand,
As silver gold clathis and arming
With vescahll and all other thing
That ever mycht lay on thare hand.
So gret a riches thair thai fand
That mony man mychty wes maid
Off the riches that thai thar haid
Quhen this wes donyne that her I say
The king send a gret company
Up to the crag thaim til assaile
That war fled fra the gret battail,
And thai thaim yald foroutyn debate
And in hand has tane thaim fute-hate.

[*A great number, so many that it was a wonder to see, fled to the castle of Stirling which was nearby. The rocks around the castle were covered in men that had made their way there, trusting to the strength of the place. So many of them gathered at the castle that King Robert, who was aware* [of this] *kept his troops close at hand for fear that they* [the English] *would re-group. Truth to tell, this was the way that the King of England was able to escape home to his own land; once the field had been completely cleared of Englishmen, the Scots soon set themselves to looting every thing that they could, lay their hands on; silver, gold, clothing, armour, vessels and everything else. They found such great wealth that many a man was 'made for life' from the riches they seized there. When this was done, the king sent a large company to the Castle Rock to attack those who had fled there from the battle, and they surrendered immediately and were quickly taken into custody.*]

The men assembling on Stirling Castle rock, though evidently a large body of troops, probably did not really pose much of a threat to King Robert's army. They could hardly depend on the castle garrison for water, food and any necessary replenishment of arms or ammunition. They had endured a long march followed by two sharp defeats on Sunday evening and then another crushing defeat on the Monday morning. The majority of them were bound to be tired, demoralised and hungry as well as leaderless. Robert could have chosen to starve them off the rock or he could have let them make their own way home – either course would call for a continued deployment of troops. The English refugees could be bottled up on the heights of the castle or they could be pursued out of the country, but they could not be allowed to wander freely, foraging their way home.

Barbour turns back to the battlefield briefly, mentioning various prominent English lords who had been killed in action, and the only two prominent Scottish fatalities, Sir Walter Ross and William Vipont, before going on to discuss the only success of the day for King Edward's army. Ross was a dear friend of Edward Bruce, but not as dear as Ross's sister, the love of Edward's life. He loved her more than he did his own wife, Isabelle of Atholl. Isabelle's brother, David de Strathbogie, Earl of Atholl, had been a member of Edward II's occupation government until the spring or summer of 1312, when he defected to the Bruce party. He abandoned the Bruce cause when his sister was spurned by Edward in favour of his mistress. He may not have actually joined Edward II's forces so much as taken action for his own reasons, but he conducted a night-raid on Cambuskenneth Abbey on 23rd/24th June.

> ...apon Saynct Jhonys nycht
> Quhen bath the kingis war boun to fycht,
> In Cammyskynnell the kingis vitaill
> He tuk and sadly gert assaile
> Schyr Wilyam of Herth and him slew
> And with him men ma than ynew
> Tharfor syne intil Ingland
> He wes bannyst and all his land
> Wes seyst as forfaut to the king
> That did tharoff syne his liking

*[...on St John's night, when both the kings were prepared for battle, he* [Atholl] *cap-*
*tured the king's stores and fiercely attacked Sir William Aird, and killed him and many*
*others. Therefore he was banished to England and all of his land was forfeited to the*
*king, who used it as he saw fit.]*

Atholl's raid on the night dividing the two days of the battle had no significant effect at the time, either militarily or politically, however his fracture
with the Bruce leadership would become an issue in the 1330s, when Atholl
would be one of the mainstays of Edward Balliol's attempt on the kingship.
Residual local loyalty to the Strathbogie family would make him a power to
be reckoned with in the northeast between the battle of Dupplin Muir in
August 1332 and his death at the battle of Culblean in November 1335.

Professor Duncan has suggested that the stores kept at Cambuskenneth
consisted of foodstuffs for horses and that Atholl, recently appointed as King
Robert's constable, would be aware of this. That does not, however, explain
why stores of any kind should have been deposited at Cambuskenneth.
Elsewhere (see above) Barbour writes of the men who were sent to a valley
during the main action, and that they were responsible, among other things,
for food. King Robert's army was certainly a very impressive force by Scottish
standards, and would have needed enormous quantities of bread, meat, oats
and hay on a daily basis. It might well have been convenient to have supplies
delivered to a secure location and then carried to the army for consumption,
in which case the Abbey of Cambuskenneth was conveniently situated and
would probably have been enclosed with a precinct wall which would ease
security against thieves, though, clearly, not against a party of men-at-arms.

Barbour returns to the king once again, relating the tales of Sir
Marmaduke Twenge, who surrendered in person, and Sir Philip Moubray,
who came to surrender at the castle, before telling the reader of Douglas's
pursuit of King Edward.

> Than cum Sir Philip the Mowbra
> And to the king yauld the castell,
> His cunnand has he haldyn well,
> And with him tretyt sua the king
> That he belevyt of his dwelling
> And held him lely his fey
> Quhill the last end off his lyf-day
> Now will we of the lord of Douglas

Tell how that he folowit the chas.
He had to quhone in his company
But he sped him in full gret hy,
And as he throuch the Torwood fur
So met he ridand on the mur
Schyr Laurence off Abernethy
That with four scor in company
Come for till help the Inglismen
For he was Inglisman yet then,
Bot quhen he hard how that it wes
He left the Inglsi-mennys pes
And to the lord Douglas rycht that
For to be lele and tru he swar.
And or the king of Ingand was
Passyt Lythkow thai come sa ner
With all the folk that with him wer
That weill amang thaim schout thai mycht,
Bort thai thocht tham to few to fycht
With the gret rout that thai had that
For five hunder armyt thai war
Togidder sarraly raid thai
And held thaim apon bridill ay,
Thai wat governyt wittily
For it semyt ay thai war redy
For to defend tham at thar mycht
Gif thai assailyt war in fycht.

[*The Sir Philip Moubray came to yield the castle to the king, keeping his word. He and the king accorded so well that he joined the king's household and served him loyally to the end of his life. Now we tell of the Lord of Douglas, and how he followed the chase. He had very few in his company, but pursued in great haste, and, as he passed out of the Torwood he met Sir Laurence Abernethy riding on the Muir, who had come with a company of four score [80] to help the English, because he was then still an Englishman, but when he heard what had happened, he left the peace of the English and he swore to Douglas that he would be loyal and true. Then they both followed the chase, and, before the king of England reached as far as Linlithgow, they [Douglas' party] came near enough that they could shout at them, but they thought themselves too few to fight with the great crowd of them there, for there were five hundred men-at-arms riding in close order with their reins held short. They were well-led, for it seemed that they were always ready to defend themselves with all their might if they were forced to fight.*]

Moubray, of course, had little choice but to surrender the castle to King Robert, and the ease of his acceptance into the Bruce party perhaps indicated that this was part of the price for the surrender pact in the first place. Douglas, meanwhile, was still in pursuit of Edward II, but with too small a force to engage Edward's party. As he passed out of the Torwood he encountered Sir Laurence Abernethy at the head of a party of eighty men. Abernethy quickly embraced the Bruce cause and added his force to that of Douglas. Clearly Abernethy's troops were men-at-arms. Their number was far too few to make any sort of valuable contribution to Edward's army, so presumably they were not spearmen or archers. Equally clearly, they joined the pursuit and were able to keep up with the fleeing English, some five hundred men-at-arms mounted on sound, if tiring, chargers. Since Barbour has already told us that King Edward rode around the New Park to escape, we might reasonably conclude that he passed behind the main body of the Scottish army, that is on the west side of the New Park, and not between the high ground and the western end of the battlefield. In this case, Douglas may have been able to close the gap between him and his quarry by travelling through the New Park, possibly emerging in the vicinity of The Entry before heading for Linlithgow, having met – and recruited – Sir Laurence Abernethy 'riding on the muir'. Douglas did not feel his company was strong enough to force a fight, but he was determined to pursue Edward as far as possible.

> And the lord Douglas and his men,
> How that he wald nocht schaip him then
> For to fecht with thaim all planly,
> He convoyit thaim sa narrowly
> That of the henmaist ay tuk he,
> Mycht nane behin his falowis be
> A pennystane cast na he in hy
> Was dede, or tane deliverly
> That nane rescours wald till him ma
> All-thocht he luvyt him never sua.
> On this maner convoyit he
> Quhill that the king and his menye
> To Wenchburg all cummyn ar.

Than lychtit all that thai war
To bayt that hors that wer wery,
And Douglas and his cumpnay
Baytit alsua besid thaim ner.
Thai war sa fele withoutyn wer
And in armys sa clenely dycht
And sua arayit for to fycht,
And he sa quhone and but supleyng
That he wald nocht in plane fechting
Assale thaim, bot ay raid thaim by
Waytand hys point ay ythandly.
A litill quhill thai baytyt thar
And he was alwayis by thaim ner,
He leyt thaim nocht hhaff sic layser
As any water for to ma,
And giff ony stad war sa
That he behind left ony space
Seysyt alsone in hand he was.
Thai convoyit thaim on sic a wis
Quhill thai the king and his rout is
Cummyn to the castell of Dunbar
Quhar he and sum of his menye war
Resavyt rycht weill, for yete than
The Erle Patrik was Inglisman.

[*The lord Douglas and his men could not attack them openly, but he shadowed them so closely that he could take any who fell behind, so a man could not even be a stone's-throw from his companions but he would be killed or taken prisoner instantly, for none could help him, however beloved he might be. In this fashion, he* [Douglas] *pursued the king and his party as far as Winchburgh. Then they* [the English] *all dismounted to rest their horses, which were very weary, and Douglas and his company rested nearby. They were so strong in number, so well equipped and so well arrayed for battle, and he so few and without hope of reinforcements, that he could not attack them, but rode close to them, seeking a favourable opportunity. They rested there for a short while, then mounted and went on their way, but he was always close to them. He would not let them so much as halt to pass water, and if any were left behind, even a short distance, he was quickly taken prisoner. They accompanied them in this way until the king and his party came to the castle of Dunbar, where he and some of his party were made very welcome, for at that time Earl Patrick was an Englishman.*]

From the very outset of the pursuit of King Edward Barbour makes a point of the weakness of Douglas's force and the strength of the English; allegedly little more than one hundred Scots – including Abernethy's men – against five hundred English. Given that the pursuit was so aggressive, one might well ask why the English did not turn and fight. First and foremost, there was the presence of King Edward. His company were, doubtless, well-armed and brave, but if there was an engagement, anything might occur – the king might even be killed or captured, in which case the political situation would have plunged from bad to dreadful. The king would have to be ransomed at enormous financial and diplomatic cost; anything that remained of his royal prestige in the wake of the defeat at Bannockburn would be lost. There is also the question of fitness to fight. The men around King Edward had already witnessed or taken part in three separated defeats in less than twenty-four hours, been effectively refused entry to Stirling Castle, and then performed a long retreat under close pressure from the enemy, losing many comrades along the way as horses became exhausted. Their morale cannot have been in good condition, either physically or mentally, for combat. The two forces halted briefly at Winchburgh to let their horses rest before pressing on toward Dunbar. Major fortress as it was, Dunbar Castle could not possibly accommodate all of Edward's party, so the king, and a few of his party, entered the castle, where they were well received by Earl Patrick, an English adherent since the invasion of 1296 and a crucial prop to the occupation government in Roxburghshire, Berwickshire and East Lothian. As Barbour tells us, 'The Erle Patrik was Inglisman.'

The arrival of King Edward's party put Patrick in a difficult position. The occupation government had been failing for years, but the location of Patrick's estates – regardless of his political preferences – meant that he could not afford to entertain any sort of rapprochement with the Bruce party without exposing his property to retaliation from English forces, particularly the garrison of Berwick. It might seem that he now had a golden opportunity to out King Robert in his debt forever, since he could take King Edward prisoner, however this may not have been a practical proposition. Even if he entered the castle with just a handful of his closest associates, Edward would still probably have a couple of dozen men-at-arms at his back. It would be remarkable if the Earl had more than a modest handful of men able to fight at all. Additionally, the Earl had to take a long view of the situation. Robert was proving capable of defeating the English on the battlefield and might well prove capable of achieving the diplomatic and political victories he needed to put his kingship beyond doubt, but what of his successor? English kings were plainly capable of invading and destroying the southern counties of Scotland, even if the conquest of the whole nation was beyond them. At some point in the future, Earl Patrick – or his successors – might well have to find a way into the 'peace' of another English king, who might not be disposed to accept the allegiance of a man who had handed Edward II to the Scots.

# Fordoun

The most remarkable aspect of Fordoun's account of Bannockburn is that he has so little to say about it. The actual process of the campaign and the engagements themselves receive virtually no attention whatsoever, but the importance of divine intervention, or, more significantly perhaps, the trust that King Robert reposed in God, form the basis of Fordoun's few words on the topic. Beyond telling us that Edward II brought a large army of horse and foot to the battle and that the Earl of Gloucester and many other English nobles were killed or taken prisoner, Fordoun tells us that victory fell to the Scots through Robert's reliance on God rather than numbers. He then claims – quite wrongly, as he himself must have been all too aware – that from Bannockburn onwards the Scots enjoyed continual victories over the English and that the country 'overflowed with boundless wealth.' In fairness, there was probably some truth in this in the sense that a good number of Scots certainly benefited from the spoils of war on a number of levels. The ransacking of the English baggage train and the ransoms of English nobles certainly brought considerable wealth to some, and the campaigns that King Robert mounted in the northern counties of England over the next decade doubtless improved the financial status of a good many more.

Even so, Fordoun must have been aware of the military and economic blows suffered by the Scots in the 1330s and 1340s, indeed Fordoun's chronicle – though brief on any topic – is an important source for the wars of David II and Edward III. Fordoun's brevity on the subject of Bannockburn is something of a curiosity. Though much less partisan in his accounts than Bower, Fordoun's chronicle does have a rather nationalistic theme and one might have expected that such a great victory might have brought more from Fordoun's pen than assertions about the importance of divine endorsement to the Bruce cause. He might have avoided giving an account of the fighting for any one of a number of reasons. As a cleric, he may have felt that his lack of specialist knowledge and experience prevented him from giving a useful description of the action, though that does not seem to have been an issue to most ecclesiastical chroniclers. He may have considered that the story of the fighting had been so thoroughly taken to heart by the Scots that there was no value in going over it again. Alternatively, he may have been of the opinion that the nature of the armies, the terrain and the tactics were simply not as important as the decision of God to award victory to King Robert.

> Edward II, king of England, hearing of these Glorious doings of King Robert's and seeing the countless losses and endless evils brought upon him and his by that king, gathered together in revenge for the foregoing, a very strong army, both of well-armed horsemen and of foot – crossbowmen and archers, well-skilled in war-craft. At the head of this body of men, and trusting in the glory of man's might, he entered Scotland in hostile wise; and laying it waste on every side, he got as far as Bannockburn. But King Robert, putting his trust, not in a host of people but in the Lord God, came, with a few men against the aforesaid king of England, on the Blessed John the Baptist's day, in the year 1314, and fought against him, and put him and his to flight, through the help Him to whom it belongeth to give the victory. There the Earl of Gloucester and a great many other nobles were killed; a great many were drowned in the waters or slaughtered in the pitfalls; a great many, of divers ranks, were cut off by divers kinds of deaths; and many – a great many – nobles were taken, for whose ransom not only were the queen and other Scottish prisoners released from their dungeons, but even the Scots themselves were, all and sundry, enriched very much. Among these was also taken John of Brittany, for whom the Queen and Robert, bishop of Glasgow, were exchanged. From that day forward moreover, the whole land of Scotland not only always rejoiced in victory over the English, but also overflowed with boundless wealth.

The only military element to be considered here is Fordoun's assertion that many English soldiers were 'slaughtered in the pitfalls.' To what extent Fordoun relied on the work of other writers or on contemporary popular belief is open to question, but clearly he thought that 'pitfalls' were an important aspect of the battle; important enough to be the only tactical application that is mentioned at all in Fordoun's account. We should not, however, automatically accept that the pitfalls – assuming that these should be equated with the 'pots' of Barbour's epic – had a significant impact on any part of the action. Fordoun may mention them for no better reason than that they were not a normal part of the tradition of Scottish war. The other elements – spearmen, archers and men-at-arms – may not have struck Fordoun as being worthy of any description since these would all have been perfectly familiar to his readership. He may mention the pitfalls simply because he was aware that they had been dug, though the term itself surely suggests sizeable traps for man and horse rather than modest holes in the ground, as Barbour describes them. Naturally, the digging of traps does not guarantee that anyone will fall into them; there is no evidence to indicate that pots or pitfalls had any effect whatsoever on the main battle.

## Bower's *Scotichronicon*

Bower was more passionately nationalistic than the author of Fordoun's chronicle, but he, too, had remarkably little to say about the course of the battle, though he was certainly aware of Barbour's account, referring to 'The book which the archdeacon of Aberdeen composed in the mother tongue.' He may have felt that a full description of the fighting was not necessary since Barbour had already produced one, but he was, in any case, more interested in the trust that the Scots put in the power of God's intervention. Bower opens his account with a list of the countries from which Edward drew support:

> ...from every part of the kingdoms of England, Scotland, France and Germany, Wales and Ireland, Flanders and Gascony, Boulogne and Brittany, Gueldres and Bohemia, Holland, Zeeland and Brabant.

He then returns to the value of faith and divine intervention:

> Thus the King of England trusted in his military power; King Robert trusted only in the help of God alone. The first took his stand with excessive confidence: the other remained suitably fearful.

Bower's chronicle includes a poem by the Abbot of Arbroath, Bernard de Linton, one of King Robert's most trusted advisors and probably the man who framed much of the king's diplomatic correspondence, including the

Declaration of Arbroath. Sadly the abbot's lines offer nothing much beyond assertions of English arrogance and overconfidence, and the worthiness of the Scots for putting their trust in God, but does not forget Bruce propaganda needs:

> May the assembly of the Scots flourish, abounding in valour;
> And may the king rejoice, turning tears to joy,
> Now that the English have been cast down in all directions and routed
> And made prisoner
> 'May the king be praised for his goodness!'

Inasmuch as Bower discussed the fighting at all, there must be some suspicion that Bower is merely rehearsing his knowledge of the equipment kit needed for war in his own day, not that of King Robert. Accordingly he ascribes weapons to the English that had yet to be invented; his account Edward's army included:

> … petraries and mattocks, trebuchets and mangonels, ladders and engines, pavilions and awnings, slings and cannons, and other engines of war.

There is no evidence to suggest that Edward brought a siege train at all. He did not expect to have to attack Stirling or Bothwell and there were very few other castles of any significance that were still intact. Whatever else Edward may have brought to the battlefield he most certainly did not bring cannons of any description.

> After the king of Scotland had had them [the English army] reconnoitred, he caused pits to be made with sharp stakes fixed in them and covered over so that they could not be noticed: and he advised his men to make confession and hear masses devoutly, and that they should all take communion in the sacrament of the body of Christ, and to put their trust in God alone.

The influence of Barbour is clear; Robert makes preparations to the field, but his chief ally in the fight is to be God. Recognition of the importance of divine intervention is not limited to the Scots. In an episode lifted from Barbour's account, Bower describes the confidence of the English but shows the wisdom of an older head among their ranks:

[The English] began to shout 'Look! All those Scots have surrendered to us with trembling hearts.' An older English knight, Ingram de Umfraville, formed a sounder understanding and replied to them saying 'You are right, that they are surrendering, but to God, not to you.'

The battle rages, but Bower has nothing of significance to add to Barbour's depiction of the fighting, though he his keen to show the reader the extent to which God favoured the Scots.

On the English side two hundred knights were killed, besides the Earl of Gloucester and innumerable others. On the Scottish side two knights fell, namely William de Vieuxpont and Walter de Ross.

Bower does, however, cite Friar Baston's poem. Baston asserts the English 'spend the night in braggartry and revelry with Bacchus,' and clearly believes that arrogance and failure of religious observation lay at the heart of the defeat, but once again there is little information about the battle. Knights mount steeds, and esquires leap up 'to put the bridle ready to hand,' but we are offered little about the deployment for battle or the progress of the fighting.

The Scottish king ranges and arranges deadly battle-lines.
Cavalry and foot-soldiers are there: what a marvellous assemblage.

Baston's words here could be seen as a contradiction of the chronicle accounts in which all of the Scots fight on foot. Clearly there is evidence that some of the Scottish army served on horseback, but Baston's line is probably more a matter of the needs of the poem than an attempt to show the nature of the army.

Baston was at least present and it would be unreasonable to assume that he somehow managed to avoid seeing the battle unfold; quite the reverse. A good deal of the poem is focused on the deeds and reputations of the aristocracy and the deaths of famous men-at-arms, notably the fall of Sir Giles d'Argentan: 'I scarce retained my senses when I saw you drop.'

## The *Pluscarden Chronicle*

Compiled in 1461, the relevant material in the *Pluscarden Chronicle* is largely a condensed amalgam of Bower and Fordoun, and, like them, puts much more emphasis on the hand of God than the approach to, and conduct of, battle.

> Edward, the new King of England, burning with rage on seeing the count-
> less evils brought upon him and his by King Robert, and brooding over his
> glorious deeds and achievements, roused himself to avenge them; and having
> got his whole forces together, hastened to levy war afresh against Scotland.
> He collected troops from all sides, from England, Wales, Ireland, Cornwall,
> Normandy, Picardy, Flanders, Almayne, Gascony, Gueldres, Brabant and
> Holland, and from amongst the rest of those who favoured his cause, and,
> together with his Anglicised Scots, effected a hostile entrance into the coun-
> try, a brave show, with every appliance of settling in the country forever, and
> tilling it with his husbandmen.

Pluscarden puts the English army at 300,000 men-at-arms, with all the 'unarmed followers and traders and husbandmen and settlers on foot.' Obviously this is a huge exaggeration, even over Barbour's claims. Once again the failure to trust in God is presented as the most important factor in the defeat of the English, while simple faith is the most important factor in the Scottish victory.

> Accordingly, surrounded by this proud host and trusting in the glory of man's
> might, he got as far as a place called Bannockburn and pitched his tents. But
> trusting in the lord and making God his strength and asking the blessed apos-
> tle Andrew and Saint John the Baptist to help him to deliver the wretched
> people of Scotland from undue bondage, King Robert, with an army small in
> comparison with the multitude of the said King of England, fought a deadly
> battle with him and, by the help of the Most High, to whom it belongeth to
> give the victory, and in whose hands are all the ends of the Earth, put him to
> flight with all his pomp and countless forces. Here the Earl of Gloucester and
> many nobles of England fell slain; some were killed in the pitfalls which the
> Scots had made; some again, thinking to save themselves, were drowned in
> the Firth of Forth; some lost their lives in the confusion of the crowd while
> escaping, some fled, some were taken, some were slaughtered, overtaken by
> sundry kinds of death, and were destroyed without number with the edge of
> the sword.
>     Among these was captured John of Brittany, for whom the captured
> Queen of Scotland was exchanged, for it would have been absurd to hear of

a Queen being a prisoner. For him too was exchanged the Bishop of Glasgow, a venerable man of great age, who had been in like manner kept in prison by the tyrant. Note that this war began between Edward Bruce, the King's brother, and Philip Mowbray, commander at Stirling on behalf of the King of England, who the said Edward besieged, the former promising that, if that castle were not relieved by the King of England in one year's time from then, he would without further delay surrender it into his hand for behoof of the King of Scotland. But the King rebuked his brother for this, telling him that he had behaved most foolishly in having trysted with that most powerful King of England to fight at the aforesaid term of a year and a day.

The Pluscarden writer repeats what is surely Barbour's tale of a year's notice being allowed for the relief of Stirling Castle, and likewise King Robert's displeasure at Edward Bruce's contract with Sir Philip Moubray. However, Edward Bruce was a very experienced soldier and his 'rash' temperament may well be nothing more than a device used by Barbour to enhance the measured wisdom of the King. There is nothing in English record or narrative evidence to indicate that a pact of one year's duration had been made, though Moubray would surely have been dismissed for such dealings. The Bruce-Moubray compact strongly suggests that the strong garrison at Linlithgow pele had proved incapable of preventing the Scots from laying siege to Stirling, but the pele was still operational in August 1313. It is possible that the complement of men-at-arms at Linlithgow had dwindled to the extent that they were incapable of mounting operations against the Scots at all.

# Brave Companies:
# The Armies of the English
# and the Scots

The Scottish and English men-at-arms, spearmen and archers who served their kings in the thirteenth and fourteenth centuries were largely indistinguishable from one another. Field armies raised in either country consisted of the same troop types, though not necessarily in similar numbers or proportions. To a considerable degree this is a matter of scale rather than national capabilities. Scottish kings could not call on the numbers of men-at-arms available to the Kings of England simply because England was a very much larger state. On the other hand, although English kings could, if they chose, raise much larger numbers of infantry than their Scottish equivalents, they would struggle to keep them fed and paid for any length of time. If we are to have any understanding of medieval battle in general, and the Bannockburn action in particular, it is useful to form some idea of the strengths and weaknesses of the different arms of service – how they were recruited, trained, led, and their roles on the battlefield.

## The Cavalry: Knights and Men-at-arms

The term 'man-at-arms' is one that demands explanation. Any man serving in the heavy cavalry role was a 'man-at-arms' (the 'homines ad arma' of Plantagenet muster rolls and pay records), though several other terms – vallet, socius and esquire – appear frequently in contemporary records.[1]

The precise nature of the level of equipment required to serve as a man-at-arms is never really discussed in great detail by the writers of the late thirteenth and early fourteenth centuries, presumably because there was a broad – even universal – understanding of what was meant by the term. A man-at-arms would be expected to have adequate armour, sword, spear, shield and, most importantly, a horse suitable for cavalry service. Effectively this actually meant a minimum of two horses, since the loss, injury or illness of one's mount would, naturally, compromise one's ability to serve in the cavalry. There are examples of men who rose from obscurity to serve as men-at-arms, but the majority of the heavy cavalry were drawn from the nobility – the people who could afford to serve.

They were not all lords of great estates or knights of the royal household. The majority were men of rather humbler station, holding estates that consisted of a handful of farms or the brothers and sons of such men. These estates were not, as a rule, held in exchange for armed service alone, but rather for a range of services including administrative and court duties, and an obligation to provide advice and support for one's superior in political and social affairs. There might also be a cash element or an obligation to offer a token recognition of the fact that landholding was based on leases, not outright purchase. Some of the 'token' rents which appear to be trivial might actually be regarded as rentals protected against inflation. A burden of – for example – a pound of cumin[2] might be valued at 2*d* for the purposes of accounting, but that value need not bear any real relationship with the actual cost of a pound of cumin at a given moment in time. Whether by policy or accident, the burden of man-at-arms service falls into the category of rentals hedged against the changing value of money. A man undertaking to give forty days' knight service in exchange for land in the early twelfth century[3] would need to provide himself with suitable arms, armour and mount, undoubtedly an expensive business, but the level and quality of equipment and horseflesh required to qualify as a man-at-arms in 1300 was considerably better than the standards that had been expected a century and a half before.

To a great extent this increase in the demands placed on prospective men-at-arms was offset, or even outstripped, by the general economic improvement that Scotland – like the rest of western Europe – had experienced throughout the same period. It is even possible that economic growth had eclipsed the increasing cost of military service to such an extent that the increased burden passed unnoticed over the six or seven generations concerned.

The absence of any recorded resistance to the increasingly heavy burdens of military obligation on tenants should not, however, be interpreted as sure evidence that they were necessarily content with the situation. Very little in the way of personal writing has survived from the late Middle Ages, and only a tiny portion of that emanates from the lesser nobility, the people who would have been most seriously affected. Another major consideration is the experience of war among the Scots of the late thirteenth century. For three generations war had been virtually unknown in Scotland. There had been a handful of minor crises and a couple of rather modest expeditions to confirm the suzerainty of Alexander II and Alexander III in the West Highlands. There had even been an invasion. A Scottish army conquered the kingdom of Man in 1275[4] but there was no longer – if there ever had been – very much demand for regular active service from the political classes across the nation. It is possible, therefore, that the men who served King John in the early stages of the Wars of Independence were not, in fact, equipped to quite the standard that was expected of men-at-arms – their equipment was slightly old-fashioned and their horses of a slightly lesser quality.

Against this, we should bear in mind that the opening of hostilities in March 1296 had not been unexpected. Some proportion of the class who served as men-at-arms must surely have thought it wise to ensure that their kit was up-to-date and their horses adequate for the business of fighting. A number of men, such as Simon de Horsburgh and Richard de Siward served in Edward's army in 1296 and must surely have had suitable mounts and arms.[5] Furthermore, there had been a real risk of a general civil war between the Bruce and Balliol parties after the death of Alexander III and again after the death of Margaret, Maid of Norway. Even if many Scottish men-at-arms at Dunbar in 1296 were seriously under-equipped, it is abundantly clear that many of them were able to bring themselves up to the required standard in a very short space of time. By 1298 there were several Scots serving as men-at-arms in English garrisons such as Edinburgh, Stirling and Dundee on exactly the same basis as their colleagues from England, France and Ireland and some Scots were present in the army that defeated Wallace at Falkirk.[6] This does not appear, however, to be evidence that the Scots in question had necessarily acquired better kit very recently. The early appearances of William Wallace show him as the leader of a small band of men-at-arms, 'all well-mounted',[7] that is to say, with horses appropriate for cavalry action, not just beasts fit to transport the men from A to B. Wallace's men may have acquired suitable mounts in the recent past, but it is probably safer to assume that the men of his company were members of the gentry and minor aristocracy who had not served at all in the summer of 1296 and whose equipment and chargers were therefore still available.

In the years after Wallace's defeat at Falkirk, the Scots avoided general engagements with the armies of Edward I, but operations did not come to an end.[8] The general practice of war became one of local domination through mobile forces, rather than of confrontation between large field armies. There were certainly actions, but they were, almost without exception, cavalry affairs, though they have not all been seen in that context by chroniclers or historians. The battle of Roslin illustrates this perfectly. Of the contemporary and near-contemporary writers, Bower and Blind Harry alone describe a vast 'all-arms' battle of manoeuvre with thousands upon thousands of men committed to the fight and a great open-field victory for the forces of King John, but these men were writing more than a century after the event. The rest of the chroniclers and all of the record material points in a very different direction.

A cavalry force was assembled at Berwick to mount an operation into Scotland. Grey tells us that the intention was to raise a Scottish siege of Linlithgow.[9] There is no suggestion in English records that Linlithgow was under threat from the Scots at all, let alone under siege, though an entry in Bain's Calendar of Documents,[10] does show that two men were paid considerable sums to carry out a reconnaissance to locate the Scottish army in that vicinity, which suggests that there was a perceived threat of some magnitude.

Whatever the intended target, the English force – including a contingent of Scottish men-at-arms in the following of the Earl of Dunbar – was caught by surprise by a force of Scottish men-at-arms under the Guardian, John Comyn, and were roundly defeated. There is nothing to suggest that this was an engagement of more than a few hundred men on either side, but it was an important victory for the Scots. It was good for morale at home, but it was also good for the reputation of the Scots in the diplomatic arena. This is an important point about medieval battles in general, and perhaps particularly in the relatively small-scale context of the wars between England and Scotland. The size of the engagement is not always a useful guide to the political significance of the event. The fight at Roslin has probably received more attention from historians than the battle of Culblean in November 1335, though Culblean was almost certainly a much larger action, and unquestionably more significant.[11]

The primacy of the heavy cavalry in the thinking of Robert I is clear from the early days of his campaign for kingship. It was also very nearly his undoing. In the wake of his inauguration in March 1306 he attempted to gather an army to expel the English from Scotland. It is almost axiomatic that his intention was to bring about a battle at an early opportunity and wage a conventional war of manoeuvre against Edward I. This is further taken, very often, as evidence that Robert I was immature and unrealistic, which would certainly be the case had that been his plan. It does, however, rather fly in the face of what we know of Robert's experience before 1306. His knowledge of the events of the past ten years and his own roles in both the English and Scottish military structures must have made him aware that he could not hope to raise men-at-arms in anything like the quantity that Edward could. Even so, the striking arm of Robert's small army at Methven was definitely the men-at-arms element of his force. The same applies to his adversary. An English document of the time[12] indicates that there were over 70 knights and men-at-arms, nearly two thousand archers and 140 crossbowmen in De Valence's force, however Scottish men-at-arms from areas under English control would also have been called upon to discharge their military obligations.[13] This does not mean that Robert necessarily chose to rely exclusively on the heavy cavalry of the nobility, but that those were the men available to him. There are also social factors to be considered of course. If Robert was to make good his claim to the throne, he would need the support of the political community, and the sort of service that they could provide was chiefly that of men-at-arms. Additionally, his prestige as king would be impaired if he was not surrounded by men of substance, men with a stake in the country. In the eyes of his contemporaries Robert would have been little more than a successful brigand if he could not command the support of such men.

Equally, the Bruce cause could provide a vehicle for advancement for such men and also for men of more humble origins. If a man could acquire the relevant equipment and skills he could reasonably expect to be accepted into the comitiva of one or other of the greater lords. Gib Harper, an associate of Edward Bruce, Earl of Carrick, who was killed in action at Faughart, would appear to have been a man of 'low birth',[14] but he certainly served as a man-at-arms and had probably ascended the social order through military service.

Despite his close relationship with Edward Bruce, Harper does not appear to have become a knight, probably because of his social status, however we should not assume that knighthood was necessarily an impossible career ambition for men of his background, nor should we assume that men of greater status necessarily became knights at a given age or at a specific point in their career. According to Barbour (see 'sources' above), James Douglas was not knighted until the eve of Bannockburn, though he was certainly of the right class, had the right sort of experience and had even established a reputation as a paladin. It is widely assumed that Douglas was not knighted at Bannockburn, but that he was promoted to the status of banneret.[15] This may not have been the case since there are a number of factors which might have prevented him from becoming a knight at an earlier point of the war. In 1314 Douglas had yet to become a magnate; his career prospects rested on his fame as a soldier and he was not a person of any great political status. He may have felt that knighthood should be postponed to an auspicious moment and the eve of battle was a traditional juncture for making knights. Alternatively, it may have been a matter of royal policy. There is nothing to indicate that Robert had made many, if any, knights before 1314. He, too, may have been waiting for a dramatic moment.

The value of giving heavy cavalry service was not limited to development, retention or confirmation of political status. For some men the lure of adventure would probably have been sufficient motivation in itself, but for others there were the attractions of profit and of building a chivalrous reputation. As Dr MacDonald puts it,[16] 'There can be little doubt that financial gain through warfare was important to the Scottish magnate, as it was to his English and continental counterparts.' The most significant possibilities for financial gain lay in the possibility of gaining land grants or offices through successful military service or from the ransoms of prisoners. The social/military ethos of chivalry was also an important motivating factor, though not in isolation. To quote Dr MacDonald again, it was a crucial element in the 'mental world of the secular and clerical aristocracy.' Proving that nobles fought precisely because of the chivalric ethos is, however, a rather different matter.[17] Although it may have been the single most important issue for a few individuals, for most men it was only one part of a complicated set of social values, pressures and traditions.

Dr Michael Brown[18] has demonstrated that successful service and leadership in war could be a useful political career vehicle in the 1330s and 1340s. To some degree, the personal career aspect may have been less significant in 1314, when the most pressing issue was national political independence. This does not mean that the supporters of King Robert were any less ambitious than their successors, but if they – and their heirs – were to retain the gains they made under Robert, they would have to ensure that his kingship was established beyond doubt. This still applied in the early years of David II's reign. If Bruce kingship had been extinguished they would be in a very precarious position. However, once it became clear that Edward III and Edward Balliol were not capable of achieving their objectives, personal ambition come to fore. William Douglas of Lothian could afford to murder Alexander Ramsay of Dalhousie – a rival for local prominence – despite the fact that Ramsay enjoyed the support of King David. This was partly because Douglas was aware that David could not afford to lose Douglas's support, but also because Douglas was confident that the Bruce dynasty was no longer at risk of being destroyed through English intervention.

It is apparent that by 1314 the majority of the political and armigerous class of Scotland had come to see the Bruce party as the best prospect for career advancement, but this had not been the case in the early years of his kingship and he had to compete with the occupation government to gain the allegiance of such men. Initially he was at a considerable disadvantage. Men who opted to join the Bruce party in 1306 faced a very real risk of permanent forfeiture should Bruce fail to impose his rule. In addition to that risk there was also the attraction of serving in the occupation garrisons and English field armies for pay. Edward I and Edward II both faced cash-flow problems that made it difficult to ensure that wages were paid regularly and on time, but the men who served in the garrison could be reasonably confident that they would receive their money eventually.

Despite the prospect of pay and the fact that men who lived in areas under English rule were expected to discharge the military obligations attached to their properties, the occupation government often toiled to find the scale of cavalry service that was needed to counter Bruce expansion. As early as the summer of 1306 Henry Percy, Edward's lieutenant for Wigtonshire, Dumfriesshire and Ayrshire, informed James Dalilegh that he could not attract men to the king's service unless he could offer to pay them.[19]

Obviously landholders in these areas owed military service for their properties, but could not be persuaded to discharge that service – at least beyond their accustomed obligation – without compensation. Further, if they were not in receipt of pay the risks of being on campaign were substantially greater in that they would not have their horses valued for 'restauro,' and would therefore not be entitled to compensation for chargers lost in action. Percy went on to order Dalilegh to pay wages to the men who were serving in his company and to make similar provisions for men-at-arms in the companies of Sir Robert Clifford and Sir John de St John. It is clear from many other documents that there was a perennial shortage of men-at-arms for both field and garrison service in Scotland, but Percy's instructions would also suggest that local men-at-arms could be found if funds were forthcoming for their wages and expenses.

There is no record material relating to the retinues of Scottish lords and magnates in the service of Robert I, but this does not imply that such material did not exist. Fortunately, there are several instances of the retinues of Scottish lords in English service and some of these records relate to specific garrisons. Sir Archibald Livingstone, for example, served as the commander of Livingstone Peel and later of Linlithgow with a retinue of ten men-at-arms, all of whom were Scots and probably tenants of Sir Archibald.[20] Others relate to field service formations. In 1306–7 a force under Sir John de St John included the retinue of Sir Roger de Kirkpatrick with five chargers and Sir John de Campbell with two, along with Dougal and Fergus McDowal.[21] Clearly knight service was not limited to what some historians have described as 'Anglo-Norman' or Feudal Scotland. We find that Sir John de Moubray was paid 200 marks for 'keeping lands between the mountains and the Orkneys' with 30 men-at-arms between August 1307 and February 1308.[22] It is, of course, possible that some portion of these men were not Scots, though in the same period (and document) we find Sir Richard Siward serving with 20 men-at-arms in Dumfriesshire and Ingram de Umfraville leading a retinue in Galloway under the command of Sir John de St John. Evidently Umfraville's force was considerable and surely included English soldiers, but it is difficult to imagine that there was not a sizeable Scottish contingent in their ranks. Umfraville was an important Scottish landholder who would have been due a substantial quantity of service from his tenants.

In October 1313 the garrison of Lochmaben had several small retinues of Scottish men-at-arms, including Sir Roger de Kirkpatrick with another knight and four 'esquires' (in this period the terms esquire, vallet and man-at-arms all meant the same thing – an armoured cavalryman with a covered or barded/barbed charger) and William Herries and Sir Thomas Torthorald with one esquire each.[23] It would seem most likely that the esquires who served in these retinues were the tenants of Kirkpatrick, Herries and Torthorald, however the fact that a man held land from a lord in Plantagenet allegiance is not a secure guide to his allegiance. Some men surely favoured the Bruce (or, in 1296–1304, Balliol) cause to the extent that they were willing to risk all in the expectation that they would be restored at the close of the war. Many landholders, however, were tenants and vassals of more than one superior. A man who held his more important property from a Bruce adherent, or whose chief property lay in an area of Bruce dominance, might well join the Bruce party even though he also held land in occupied territory.

The military and political significance of the armigerous class is clear from both record and narrative sources, but not all soldiers who served with horses were men-at-arms. English and Scottish armies both contained a troop-type known as 'hobelars'. The hobelar was a mounted soldier, but hobelars did not normally fight in a mounted capacity. Less heavily armoured, and less well-mounted than a man-at-arms, the hobelar could not, as a rule, take a place in the cavalry force during a general engagement, but would serve as infantry in battle. However, general engagements were something of a rarity during the Wars of Independence, and the hobelar could carry out several different functions in the army. As light cavalry, they had an obvious reconnaissance role. They could generally expect to be able to take their horses into difficult terrain to evade opposing men-at-arms or to simply outrun opposing foot soldiers. They could be used to 'pad out' bodies of men-at-arms for raiding, foraging and interdiction of the enemy's reconnaissance.

By the second half of the fourteenth century the distinction between men-at-arms had become somewhat blurred, at least in the context of English garrisons. The commander of Berwick in the 1320s pointed out that it was unfair to pay the hobelars under his command half of the rate paid to men-at-arms when there was little, if any, difference in the quality of either their mounts or their armour. By that point the hobelar had become an established part of the military structure of England, but in 1314 they were rather few and far between. In 1313, the garrison at Lochmaben included fourteen men-at-arms and sixty-five archers, but only one hobelar, presumably retained as a scout or messenger rather than a one-man unit.[24]

There is no evidence to suggest that hobelars had a mounted role at Bannockburn or in the campaign generally, though Barbour and Bower both tell us that there were many mounted English soldiers present apart from the men-at-arms. They had certainly been employed in earlier English armies. In 1296 the Earl of Ulster, Richard de Burgh (father of Robert's queen, Elizabeth), brought 266 light cavalry to Scotland and supplied 391 for the campaign of 1301.[25]

There is a widely held belief that Scottish men-at-arms were substantially less well equipped and less well mounted than those of England or France, however contemporary material would indicate that there was no real disparity in overall effectiveness. Beyond the acquisition of a decent hauberk, helmet, shield and so forth, greater expenditure on armour gave only a marginal benefit to the wearer, but the investment was well worthwhile if that margin was potentially life-saving. The money invested in horseflesh varied enormously, but for practical purposes the performance parameters of a mount that cost £5 – which seems to have been the minimum acceptable value for the charger of a man-at-arms – was not that much inferior to a very expensive destrier. The additional benefit of a costly horse made more of a difference to the rider than to his opponent and was probably more a question of stamina and prestige than of battlefield effectiveness. From the point of view of the target there would have been very little difference between an adversary with a £5 horse and one with a £50 horse.

At least one writer has stated categorically that Scottish 'knights' rode lighter horses that could carry the same weight as destriers, but could not achieve the same speed, and that 'the reduction in speed meant that they did not ride with couched lances.' In the total absence of any medieval chronicle evidence or modern analysis to support this contention, and more particularly, the fact that the pay rolls and horse valuations of the occupation governments of Edward I, II and III make no distinction whatsoever between Scottish and English knights and men-at-arms, would suggest that this is purely an invention of Victorian and later historians.

This does not mean that Scottish armies, chiefly, if not exclusively, those operating in England, did not contain a large proportion of men who served with light horses, but it is important to bear in mind the distinction between cavalry and mounted infantry. The rank and file of the armies led by Douglas and Randolph into Northumberland, Cumberland, Westmorland, Yorkshire and Lancashire did indeed travel on 'hobins', but the wealthier strata of Scottish society, the earls, barons, knights and men-at-arms, were mounted and armed to much the same standard as the English or French nobility. The practice of ensuring that the entire force was mounted was a matter of strategic mobility, not of tactical practice. The men might ride to battle, but they dismounted to go into action. The battle of Myton is a case in point. Douglas and Randolph's men moved across the country on horseback, but when the opportunity arose to join battle, they dismounted and – according to the *Lanercost Chronicle*:

…came together in one schiltrom, and having done so, all together, they gave a mighty shout, terrifying the English, who, when they heard it, at once turned to flight.

# The Templars

Over recent years a good deal has been written about the intervention of the Templars at Bannockburn. Immediately after the suppression of the order in France, a Templar fleet disappeared from La Rochelle and shortly thereafter it turned up in Argyll, where they were offered sanctuary by Robert I, repaying his generosity by throwing themselves into the fight at a crucial juncture. There are several problems with this story. Naturally, the complete absence of any supporting contemporary material whatsoever is an issue. The tale seems to have originated in Paris at the beginning of the eighteenth century, but did not become popular until the later years of the twentieth century when several pseudo-historians incorporated it into conspiracy-theory novels. Many of these works included assertions about the connection between the Templars and Roslin Chapel, a collegiate church founded in the middle of the fifteenth century, more than one hundred years after the Templar order had been dissolved in Scotland.

Realistically, there is not the slightest speck of evidence to suggest that King Robert would have had any interest whatsoever in offering sanctuary to the Templars. The Templars were suppressed at the instigation of the King of France, Philip the Fair, and given that French recognition of his kingship was an important, even crucial, aspect of his foreign policy, it is quite unimaginable that Robert would have risked giving offence to King Philip for the sake of gaining the services of a handful of men-at-arms. Similarly, it is most unlikely that Robert would have chosen to do anything that might further complicate his relationship with the papacy. Although King Philip had been the prime instigator in suppressing the Templars, he could not have done so without the acquiescence of the Pope. In 1314 Robert had been an excommunicate for some time, and was eager, even desperate, to be readmitted to the church – an act that could not be brought about without papal sanction.

By the time of Bannockburn, the Templars had long lost their military *raison d'etre*. The last toe-hold of the Crusader kingdoms had been lost in

1291, and the Templars had become little more than an international land conglomerate. Far from being 'battle-hardened veterans' the Templars had largely become 'conference hardened property dealers.' It is of course quite possible that men who had, at one time, been Templars did serve on either side at Bannockburn, but there is nothing to suggest that there was any such thing as a formed body of Templars anywhere in 1314, let alone in Scotland. It is true that there were a great many Templar properties in Scotland, but we should not equate that with any great number of actual knights; most of these properties probably never saw a Templar from one year to the next. The granting of lands to the order did not signify that Templars took up residence in those locations, merely that the rents and other incomes generated passed to the order, ostensibly for the support of their operations in the Holy Land and elsewhere.

The imagined role of the Templars at Bannockburn has been fiercely defended by enthusiasts, however it is notable that not one of the many talented scholars who have studied the Wars of Independence in great detail – Professors Barrow, Nicholson, Duncan, Prestwich and Doctors Watson, M. Brown, Barrell, Ayton and King and many others – has made any reference to the intervention of the Templars. Various writers – particularly on websites – have claimed that the story is supported by contemporary material, though none, as yet, have actually produced any references to medieval record or narrative evidence, presumably because it does not exist. Absence of evidence is not the same thing as evidence of absence, but it is difficult to see where the rational for Templar involvement comes from given that there is no mention of their role in any of the contemporary accounts.

# The Infantry

Robert's return to the Scottish mainland in 1307 marked a change in his approach to warfare. Before 1306 his career as a soldier had been passed in a traditional 'knightly' environment, but for the first year and more of his campaign to impose his kingship he relied heavily on men recruited from the western seaboard and the Isles.

Securing the northeast gave him control of areas that could provide him with men-at-arms to complement his Hebridean infantry, and the capture of Inverness and Aberdeen gave him access to the European market. This was not simply a matter of access to arms and armour, but also of acquiring the means of exporting the most important Scottish cash crop, wool. In 1309–10 his campaigns were focused on extending his area of control within Scotland, but by 1311–12 he had begun to mount extensive raiding operations into the north of England. These had two useful aspects. The ability of northern English counties to make war against the Scots was severely compromised, but, more importantly, they provided Robert with very significant sums of money and allowed him to keep substantial forces under arms for rather longer than the traditional forty days of service.

It is not clear that West Highland troops continued to be the mainstay of Robert's armies after 1309–10. As Robert extended his rule into Tayside, Perthshire and Fife he was able to gather troops and income from some of the more densely populated and prosperous parts of the country. In practice, the Highland troops of Robert's early campaigns probably only comprised a few hundred men at any one time and could therefore be replaced relatively easily once he had established his rule north of the Rivers Forth and Clyde.

There is no specific record of Highland men serving in large numbers at Bannockburn, though equally, there is no reason to assume that they did not. Only Barbour offers any information about the geographical origins of Robert's army, and then only of the king's formation. Robert's immediate command consisted of men from Carrick, Argyll, Kintyre and a contingent of men from the Isles whose lord was Angus Og, though Barbour does not actually say that Angus was present himself. Professor Duncan[26] has pointed out that this is surely an anomaly, since the Earl of Carrick was not the King, but his brother Edward. The balance of the army consisted of men from the 'plane land' or Lowlands.[27] This virtual exclusion of Highland troops may be a reflection of Barbour's personal outlook – as a lowland man himself he may have had some prejudice against Highland people. Alternatively the army may have been drawn chiefly from those areas with most to lose from an invasion. However successful he might be in battle, Edward II was unlikely to be able to carry his campaign into the far north and west of Scotland in the near future.

Although English and Scottish troop-types were more or less interchangeable, an exception might be made for the followings of Angus Og MacDonald and the other West Highland lords who served in the Bruce cause. They certainly differed from their comrades and their enemy in language and, probably, dress, but there is no suggestion in any of the contemporary accounts that they were different to the close combat infantry of either the Scottish or English armies, or indeed those of any other west European country in terms of application. In the context of a field engagement, they were spearmen first and foremost and therefore were as much bound by the practical realities of spear tactics as anyone else. Such evidence as has survived of the military community of the medieval West Highlands – the Kilmartin stones for example – clearly indicates that the prevailing military fashions of the late thirteenth-century Argyll were not radically different from those of the rest of Europe. They depict men wearing chainmail and fabric armour bearing the same style of swords that we find in the art and archaeology of France, Belgium and England.

Where West Highland lords differed from their counterparts elsewhere in Scotland was in the obligation to provide military service at sea, or at least on water. For obvious geographical reasons the communities of the West Highlands were, inevitably, less focused on the horse than those of eastern Scotland. A severe limitation of pastureland made horse ownership more expensive and the shortage of good land routes meant that many journeys could be made more easily and more quickly by water. This should not be taken as an indication that the lords of the west coast were not capable of fighting on horseback, but rather that cavalry service was not a normal part of the lives of most of their tenants. It is unlikely, for example, that a man as prominent as Angus Og would not have learned the skills of mounted combat, and the same would apply to the men who would have formed his immediate military entourage. But the overwhelming majority of the men available to highland lords served as infantry and as crew for birlinns, the galleys that formed a mainstay of warfare on the western seaboard, and the Isles. Nusbacher's description of northern lords as the 'chiefs of highland tribes'[28] is somewhat patronising and misleading. They were the lords of a highly developed society.

We should not expect that there was very much operational distinction to be drawn between Highland and Lowland troops. According to their means, men would equip themselves with spear, sword, armour and helmet and fight in the same manner wherever they came from. The belief that Highland men armed, dressed and fought differently to their Lowland brothers is not founded in narrative or record evidence, but in Gothic literature and modern nationalist romance. It would be easy to assume that Highland warfare lagged behind the times, but the first curtain wall castle in Scotland was not built in the more prosperous east, but in Argyll.[29]

# Spearmen

It is a long-established maxim of medieval military history that the prime function of infantry in battle was to act as cannon-fodder (or arrow-fodder). There are several fairly obvious drawbacks to that view. First and foremost, there is the concept of 'cannon-fodder' itself. It is a concept widely understood amongst historians, journalists, novelists and the general public, but utterly unknown to military theory. There is no such thing as 'spare' soldiers in war any more than there is 'spare' money in accountancy. As a matter of common sense, it is evident that the infantry must have been seen as having a vital function or they would not have been recruited in the first place. As a general rule the major field armies of the later medieval period throughout Europe were 'infantry heavy'. This was more evident in Scottish armies than English ones, but not by a very great margin. If we accept that King Robert's army at Bannockburn was in the region of 7,000 men, of whom 500 served on horseback, we might conclude that the cavalry element of a late medieval Scottish army was likely to be no more than ten per cent of the whole force, however this would be very misleading.

It is possible that the men-at-arms who normally formed the *comitiva* of Douglas, Moray or the king's household all served under Sir Edward Keith during the main action, but it is not probable. When the king and the great lords fought on foot they surely did so in the company of their tenants and associates. There was nothing particularly innovative about men-at-arms dismounting to fight, though clearly the preferred option was to fight on horseback. Even so, the majority of King Robert's army, like that of his adversary, were most certainly infantrymen. If they were not considered a vital part of the business of battle, one has to ask why they were recruited at all. Admittedly Robert did not always have to pay his troops regular wages, but he did have to feed them, and that would have been a major burden. At the time of the battle, Robert's force – even excluding the non-combatants – would have been one of the largest concentrations of human beings in the country, larger than any town in Scotland, with the probable exception of Edinburgh.

In part, the idea that the infantry had no real battlefield function is a product of the social attitudes of chroniclers. The ethos of the day held that the most significant acts on the battlefield were those carried out by armoured cavalrymen, an element of the army largely drawn from the political community. It should be stressed that this was a literary and social convention, not an observation by the military thinkers of the day. The concentration on the martial deeds of the nobility was in part a product of the social prominence of the individuals concerned. This should come as no surprise to the celebrity-obsessed society of the 21st century. Our newspapers are filled with gossip relating to the actions of people who are already well known to the wider public, the misdemeanours of the obscure are of generally little or no interest compared to the crimes of the famous.

This was equally true in the Middle Ages. The defection of a minor landholder or burgess was not considered as crucial to the processes of politics or war as that of a senior lord or prelate. Also, the chronicles of the medieval period were not written for the general public. An ecclesiastical chronicle such as *Lanercost* might be complied for the edification of the members of the monastery or abbey, but other accounts – *Scalacronica* or Barbour's *Bruce*, were written for the entertainment and education of the noble class. It would be surprising if a noble audience was as concerned with the actions of men of the lower ranks of society as they were with those of their social equals. Further, medievalists do rather tend to focus on the significance of lordship and kingship to the exclusion of other factors. This is as much a feature of political history as of social history.

As an example of this we might look to a major development in Scottish society during the fourteenth century. At the close of the reign of King John servile status, though in decline, was still commonplace. Before the end of the reign of David II it seems to have disappeared.[30] It is certainly true that servile status was falling into desuetude across Europe generally, but there is no evidence to suggest that it was declining as rapidly as seems to have been the case in Scotland. There seems to be no clear rationale for the early disappearance of serfdom in Scotland, however the fact that the last act of manumission for a Scottish serf dates from the 1360s does indicate that it was no longer part of the normal fabric of Scottish society. There are a number of factors that we might consider relevant – a degree of social dislocation engendered by the wars, or the difficulty of preaching the cause of national political liberty to men who were not personally free – but none of these issues was unique to Scotland. Other nations suffered decades, even generations of war; other nations engaged in great campaigns to achieve or recover political independence.

What is not in doubt is that members of the non-noble portion of society could and did develop political views and that those views were of interest to the senior members of the political community. In May 1307 Edward I received a report from an officer at Forfar (possibly Sir Alexander Abernethy, see above) telling him that:

> ...if Robert Bruce comes over the mountains now he will find the common people more at his will than ever.

This report implies a number of things that may not be immediately apparent. First of all, Edward's officer was clearly of the opinion that his king would be interested in the climate of opinion amongst the lower orders. This in itself rather undermines the traditional view of medieval kingship. All men might be vassals of the king, but that evidently did not mean that the king assumed that all of the people necessarily shared his own political view. The report gives us some insight into the widest political issue of the day, or at least, one officer's view of how the wider population saw that same issue. Had the report come from an officer in the southwest, where the Bruce family had long-established traditions of lordship, it would be no surprise that popular opinion in that area favoured the kingship of Robert Bruce. However the report came from the northeast, an area in which the Bruce family held neither great estates nor senior office. Evidently the people of the northeast were more inclined to accept the kingship of Robert Bruce than of Edward Plantagenet. Quite why that should be the case is open to question. It may be that the Plantagenet occupation was seen – rightly or wrongly – to be intolerably harsh, or that the people of the northeast believed that they were not being governed effectively, but it is difficult to accept that simple nationalism (or xenophobia) was not a significant aspect. The relative novelty of the Plantagenet administration may also have been a factor. In Lothian or Roxburghshire, the occupation had been a reality for little more than a decade by the time Edward I received his report. There had been alarms and crises – such as William Wallace's march to Haddington in 1297, or the action at Roslin in 1303 – but the administration had not been eclipsed at any point.

This was not the case in the northeast. Edward I had marched as far north as Elgin in 1296, but for most of the period between then and the Strathord armistice of 1304, the northeast had been under the control of the Balliol party. The mere presence of Plantagenet garrisons in the castles and towns of Kincardineshire and Aberdeenshire may have been seen as provocative and burdensome regardless of whether or not they really made any difference to everyday life. The final point to make in relation to this report is that the writer tells Edward the Scots would be more 'at the will' of Robert than they had been in the past. This strongly indicates that Robert had enjoyed a deal of support in a 'past' which can only really refer to his brief kingship in the spring and early summer of 1306, since he spent the autumn and winter of 1306–7 in hiding.

Popular support for the Bruce cause in Carrick or Annandale might reasonably be attributed to a lengthy tradition of Bruce lordship, however the Bruces had no great tradition of lordship in the northeast. Clearly the inhabitants of the lands north of the Mounth were motivated by something more than considerations of the local political arena. Whether they were moved by the cause of Robert's claims to kingship or by the cause of Scottish kingship more generally is impossible to say, but evidently they were prepared to take a stand against the administration of Edward II, indeed, given that his reign was only a year old, it is probably more realistic to see the adoption of the Bruce cause as a reaction to Edward I, not to his son. Moreover, there is little evidence to suggest that the Plantagenet administration of the early 1300s was really very much different to that which Robert I put in place, or that which had existed under Alexander III or King John, in which case we must surely question the extent to which the nature of the administration was an issue for the political community beyond the question of its nationality.

Evidently some non-noble Scots had developed a degree of political awareness that was not simply a product of support for their lord. This is an important issue, since without wide support among the common people, Robert would have toiled to recruit the troops he needed to make good his claims to the throne. His campaigns of 1307–8 – and possibly beyond – may have depended on the services of troops raised in the Hebrides, but he could not hope to recover Scotland without very much greater resources than could be provided by Angus Og and other Highland magnates. Apart from the very obvious question of manpower – how many men could be provided for and for how long – there would also be a risk of alienating the very people to whom he would have to appeal to make his kingship a reality. There is no reason to assume that the inhabitants of the south and east of Scotland would have happily accepted a Bruce dynasty imposed at the point of Highland swords any more than a Plantagenet dynasty imposed with English ones.

Interestingly, neither Edward I nor Edward II seems to have made any serious attempt to exploit the military service due to the crown from the common populace in the regions which lay in their control. One draft writ survives from March 1304[31] in which Edward instructs the sheriff of Stirling to bring all of the forces, both horse and foot, of his bailiwick, including the baronies in it, but excluding those from 'any part of the earldom of Lennox.' Although this document was not, so far as we are aware, actually issued, there are a number of elements in it that give us some indication of the nature of service obligations and, perhaps, of the limitations of English administrative power in the region as perceived by Edward and his advisors. The call for both horse and foot indicates that Edward expected the sheriff to call out those men who owed cavalry service which, broadly speaking at least, we can equate with knight service due for landholding. This was not an innovation since individual landholders and burgesses in several counties – notably Lothian, Dumfriesshire, Roxburghshire, Berwickshire, Aberdeenshire and Lanarkshire – can be identified as serving in English garrisons and field armies throughout the period 1296–1304, however Edward's call for infantry service from Stirling would seem to be the only example of its kind.

Edward's writ makes it clear that he expected the sheriff to ensure that men were conscripted from the baronial franchises as well as from other properties in the county. This might be construed as an attempt to go over – or perhaps under – the heads of the barons by appealing directly to their tenants, thus gaining their service regardless of whether the barons themselves were in Plantagenet or Balliol allegiance. It is possible that, if the writ had actually been issued, it would have been more an exercise in 'testing the waters' than an attempt to swell the ranks of the army.

The writ was drafted on 20th March, less than two months after the Strathord agreement had brought hostilities to an end. One might question what Edward would actually have wanted these troops to do, given that the only current operations were the siege of Stirling Castle where the defending garrison was still holding out, and the hunt for William Wallace. Clearly Edward had sufficient forces to conduct the siege, and infantry would have been of little use in tracking down Wallace's small and highly mobile band of men-at-arms. Rather than a genuine attempt to raise troops, the writ may have been more an exercise in testing whether the acceptance of his lordship stretched beyond the nobility into the wider community. The specific exclusion of the earldom of Lennox from the call for men is worthy of note. On 11 March 1304 Edward sent instructions to the earls of Lennox, Strathearn and Menteith to ensure that the 'fords of Forth and country around be guarded with horse and foot' and thereafter to attend him in parliament. Clearly the writ excluded men from the Lennox because they were already called to service under the earl, but there is a possibility that Edward was confident that existing traditional leaders would be able to demand army service from their tenants and other men over whom they enjoyed customary military authority.

Quite why the writ was never issued – and it would seem that no efforts were made to conscript infantry from any other part of the country, other than through the agency of local lordship – is open to question. It is possible that Edward came to the conclusion that the writ would be widely ignored, in which case his prestige and lordship might be badly undermined or, more prosaically, he may have decided that he had no immediate need for more troops. The latter is certainly a strong possibility, given the military situation in the spring of 1304, but it is curious that neither Edward I nor Edward II, nor indeed Edward III in the 1330s, tried to make use of the military obligations of the common people in their campaigns to impose their kingship in Scotland. Apart from the obvious advantage of swelling their own forces, conscription would have helped to starve the armies of King John and King Robert of infantry. Shortage of foot soldiers does not seem to have been much of an issue for either the Balliol or the Bruce parties, even after the disaster at Falkirk in 1298.

Regardless of exactly why Scots embraced the Bruce cause is, naturally enough, less important that the fact that they did. They did not do so immediately, nor were there a vast number of supporters. The establishment of Robert's authority took many years of active campaigning and was still some way from completion in June 1314. His power was, however, sufficiently well established to allow him to recruit a major army to meet Edward II at Stirling and the bulk of the manpower certainly consisted of men of common origin. Almost all of these men served as either spearmen or archers, but we would be wrong to assume that they were ill-equipped, impoverished peasants. There is no surviving legislation defining the military liabilities of Scottish commoners as applied in the reigns of Alexander III or John or for the earlier part of the reign of Robert I, so it is impossible to give cast-iron declarations about the extent or nature of armament they carried. On the other hand, Barbour informs us that many of the men who volunteered for Robert's army in 1314 were turned away for want of adequate arms and armour. Also, we should consider King Robert's 1318 legislation on the subject.[32] All men with lands to a value of £10 or goods to a value of £40 per annum should acquire a spear, an iron cap, armoured gloves and a 'haubergeon'. This last was presumably a thick quilted coat or jacket, stuffed with raw wool at the very least or, more probably, a short chainmail hauberk. This was exactly the sort of level of equipment commonplace among the infantry of all European countries, but was clearly beyond the reach of the poorest members of society. These people – men with goods to the value of a cow – were obliged to equip themselves with a spear or a bow and arrows. It would be reasonable to conclude that the latter group were not expected to serve in war as a general rule, but were only called upon in times of great danger. Their more affluent colleagues – the £10/40 men – were not the lowest rung of the social ladder, but farm tenants, tradesmen and the majority of burgesses. The more successful burgesses were more likely to fall into the category of men-at-arms which, though it involved significant expense, could help to establish one as a member of the political community. The legislation of 1318 may have been an innovation on the part of Robert I's government, but it is equally, if not more likely, that it was more an exercise in defining responsibility more closely. It is unreasonable to assume that this prosperous class of men had, in the past, been ignored for the purposes of army service.

Scottish armies were not alone in being formed, chiefly, out of close-combat infantry. The army that Edward II led to Bannockburn probably consisted of at least 15,000 men. Of these, about 2,000 to 3,000 were men-at-arms and perhaps something in the region of 3,000 to 5,000 were archers. Rationally, therefore, we should conclude that somewhere in the region of 7,000 to 10,000 of the men who served did so as close-combat infantry. Some no doubt carried polearms and axes of different kinds, but the majority would most surely have carried spears. Victorian illustrators and writers were inclined to ascribe quite a variety of pole-arms to medieval Scottish and English infantry, but contemporary accounts uniformly refer to spears as the primary infantry weapon, not 'Jeddart' axes or bills.[33]

Clearly the spear was the normal weapon for close order infantry, but it was not the only weapon carried. The *Vita* author, among others, refers to the Scots as carrying sharp axes as a subsidiary arm. At least one modern author has suggested that the use of axes was forced on the Scots through their poverty; that swords were too expensive and too hard to come by, however swords were undoubtedly easily available in Scottish markets, even in the immediate aftermath of the campaign of 1296.[34] The Plea Rolls (court martial records) of Edward's 1296 army include a reference to the theft of seven swords from a shop in Perth. A more plausible explanation rests in the operational application of weapons. In a tightly-packed formation of spearmen, a sword would be a difficult weapon to wield effectively when compared to the humble axe.

The spear itself was more than a stick with a sharp piece of metal at one end. The shaft had to be strong enough to withstand the shock of contact, though clearly this was not always the case. Barbour is not alone in relating the noise of breaking spears. This would be more common in combat between infantry and cavalry formations. Most horses would come to a halt before contacting the front rows of the enemy's spearmen, but some – through the forcefulness of their riders, the pressure of other animals behind or through panic – would make contact, and the weight and impetus of the horse might well cause a breaking of spears. It would also undoubtedly cause severe wounds to the horse, which in turn would cause it to shy and attempt to escape.

If there was no real difference between Scottish spearmen and English ones, it is reasonable to ask why the Scots should have enjoyed such success at Bannockburn, since the majority of their enemies were armed and armoured to the same standard. There are several tactical factors that apply to the main action – exhaustion, hunger, low morale – and the distraction and dismay caused by seeing Gloucester's cavalry worsted by the infantry of the enemy. There is, however, one factor that is more crucial than any other – training. The English army had started to assemble in early June, and therefore elements of the army may have been embodied for as much as two weeks before marching on Scotland. The army had left Wark and Berwick in June and had spent virtually all of the period between leaving Northumberland and arriving at Stirling performing major marches. There can have been very little time for personal weapon training, and even less time for training in formation.

The Scots, on the other hand, had been mustering at Stirling since about the end of May. No doubt a large proportion of them did not arrive until nearer the date of battle, but it is very much easier to incorporate unskilled people into existing workplace routines and disciplines than to 'start from scratch' which, regardless of the number of men with some experience in Edward's infantry, would have been very much the case for his army as a whole. There must surely have been English men who had served in the army in previous campaigns and some who had served in a major battle, although only Stirling Bridge and Falkirk would qualify as 'major' engagements. They might have had very good personal skills, but the formations in which they served in 1314 cannot have been drilled to any great standard on the march from Northumberland.

Edward definitely believed that his infantry would have an important role to play in the battle that he hoped would ensue from his offensive, but he probably envisaged a rather wider role as well. If the Scots could be beaten – and both Edward and his troops seem to have been confident that this could be achieved – the infantry could then be used to re-impose English administration, partly through their assignment to garrisons, but also just by the act of marching them through the countryside to impress the locals with the power of English kingship.

The issue of training with the spear is not one that has received much attention from historians; understandably, given the shortage of medieval writing on the topic. We should not, however, assume that spear training was limited to the acts of stabbing and parrying. It would be useful to have a better understanding of the dynamic of the unit. It is easy, for example, to assume that when common spearmen and men-at-arms were arrayed in a single unit, the men-at-arms formed the front rank of the formation. This is superficially attractive in that the men-at-arms would, all in all, be better armoured than their comrades, but there are problems with such an analysis. If men of the noble class served alongside their tenants, we might expect that they would be entrusted with a 'junior leader' role, accepting responsibility for maintaining the dressing of the troops in their immediate vicinity. It is more than just a challenge to see how this role could have been discharged effectively whilst in the front rank of the action. Further, it is difficult to see how service in the front rank could be anything more than a death sentence if the combat lasted any length of time. One possibility is that well-trained units could apply 'introduction' – a process of having the rear ranks pass through to the front of the unit, thus rotating the men at the 'sharp end'. This was a normal practice for musketeers in the seventeenth century since it enabled the unit to maintain a steady, continuous fire. There is no obvious reason to assume that the required standard of drill could not be achieved in the fourteenth century.

It would also be very useful to have some idea about the preferred depth of formations. Classical observers disagreed about the value of excessively deep formations, some arguing that only the front ranks could be brought into combat, others arguing that the rear ranks bolstered the confidence of the men to their front, while simultaneously discouraging flight. No doubt the same arguments raged in the medieval period. In the absence of such information, historians are unable to make valid observations about the depth, and therefore the frontage, of a unit of a given size. We might reasonably assume that each man in the front rank would need about a metre to fight in, but even this cannot be clearly demonstrated. Observations of re-enactors in training would seem to suggest that a slightly greater allowance of frontage might allow more men of the supporting ranks to engage.

Manoeuvring these units was far from easy. Men can achieve much better march distances if they are arrayed in columns rather than lines, and can put more men into the fight if they are in line rather than column, so an army on the march faced with the prospect of battle would need to turn columns of march into lines of battle. The simplest way to achieve this is by wheeling the column to the left or right until the entire column has changed direction, then halting the unit and turning it to face the enemy. Unless the unit is arrayed on a flat field, this is a difficult thing to achieve without causing some degree of confusion in the ranks unless the troops have been trained to a reasonable standard of foot drill. The Scots had had several weeks to learn and perfect such evolutions, but the English had not. More crucially, whilst the English army cannot have had much time to rehearse these or any other manoeuvres at all, there is little chance that they had been rehearsed in anything like battlefield conditions; even if they had been trained, they had not been exercised. There is a very real possibility that the English army formed up on the morning of 24 June with the intention of marching toward the Scots and may therefore have been deployed in columns. If so, the advance of the Scots would not have been ideal circumstances for a change of formation. Converting from column to line would have been difficult enough, and more so when threatened, but it would also have been complicated by the fact that several other formations would have been trying to do the same thing in a very limited space, and all at the same time as Gloucester's cavalry were being repulsed by the Scots. We should not assume that the cavalry would have been prepared to collide with the infantry in their efforts to regroup for another charge, nor that the infantry would let themselves be brushed aside by their own horsemen, but the potential for accidental interference would have been very great.

If the arms and practice of Scottish and English close-combat infantry were effectively identical, can we say the same for their enlistment and terms of service? In both countries men were selected for service by agents of the crown – specific officers for the purpose in England, and sheriffs, earls and barons in Scotland. In both cases, we should expect to find a degree of dis-honesty, with men bribing officials to avoid enlistment. This may have been a more difficult thing to achieve in Scotland. The population was much smaller and more widely distributed, and the liability for military service probably less common for the sort of army raised for service in England than those mustered for home defence. In an emergency, all males between the ages of sixteen and sixty might be liable for service, but the majority of such men would have been poorly armed and poorly armoured, hence Robert's insistence that only properly equipped men should be accepted into the army. Description of Scottish army as 'simple labourers and ploughmen' or 'tribesmen and common husbandmen' cannot be taken at face value, the implication being that the Scottish army's rank and file was composed of the lowest orders of society.

While this is attractive to a certain Scottish sentimental tradition, it bears no real resemblance to the social composition of Robert's forces. The majority of the men who served were not impoverished farm labourers, but men of some substance in their immediate locality – burgesses and other town dwellers formed some part of the whole, but the bulk of Robert's spearmen and archers would have been the tenants of farms, not landless peasants. They were men who could afford the burden of purchasing arms and armour, but also men whose tenancy of a property obliged them to give military service at the behest of their landlord or sheriff.

# Archers

The adoption of the longbow as a crucial and integral part of English mili-tary practice had yet to occur in 1314. It is certainly true that English armies had included archers since time immemorial, but in the past there had been many crossbowmen, and the archers were still considered more an ancillary to the spearmen and the cavalry than a combat group in their own right.

The first battle in which the bow played an important part in the defeat of a Scottish army was Falkirk in 1298. Edward I managed to steal a march on the Scottish army, forcing Wallace to accept a defensive battle. Initially the fighting favoured the Scots, who were able to hold their own against Edward's knights and men-at-arms. Once it had become apparent that the English cavalry were not capable of bursting through the ranks of Wallace's spearmen, the archers were deployed to disrupt the schiltroms until they had been sufficiently disrupted to allow the men-at-arms to penetrate their formations. There was little change, if any, in the status of the archers over the next quarter of a century, though archers were recruited for service in Plantagenet garrisons in Scotland. Examination of muster rolls and pay-records shows that a significant portion of these archers were in fact Scots, indeed it seems much more likely than not that the entire garrison of Livingston Peel in the early 1300s comprised Scotsmen.[35] Since the military activity of the Plantagenet garrisons was largely confined to raids and patrols by the men-at-arms, and since none of the bowmen were either described or paid as 'mounted' archers, it is surely the case that the chief role of these men was the defence of the castle, peel or town in which they were stationed.

In addition to the widely-held notion that Scottish archers employed a short bow, there is a common belief that Scottish archers were recruited almost exclusively from the Forest of Ettrick. Quite why this belief has acquired such currency is hard to say, though the efforts of romantic novelists may have had a considerable influence. In practice, Robert I, and very possibly his predecessors, enlisted archers from wherever they might be found. Professor Duncan[36] suggests that Robert I may have issued charters which would have provided him with at least one hundred archers, and possibly many more. Of all the charters that demand archer service, the heaviest burden is that of Kilsyth, which required thirty archers from the property holder. King Robert seems to have valued archery highly in that he chose to convert several military tenures from knight service to archer service obligations.[37] As Professor Barrow has pointed out,[38] Robert did not ignore knight service; it was still a crucial component of the Scottish military system. He may, however, have been prevented form extending the conversion of knight service to archers by the conservative nature of medieval society. Most, if not all, of the conversions applied to properties whose characteristics were being changed in other ways – generally by division into two or more distinct entities, suggesting that the King found it difficult to change the existing burdens on properties that were re-granted as a single fief.

A conspicuous absence from the Scottish military scene is the crossbowman. Professor Duncan has identified one charter that may demand the service of a crossbowman,[39] but even this is not certain. This does not mean that Scottish kings and lords were unaware of the power of the crossbow, or that crossbows could not be purchased or constructed locally. The accounts of Scottish castles in the reign of Alexander III are not sufficiently detailed to allow a viable analysis of the weapons available to the minute garrisons they housed, but it would be unreasonable to assume that crossbows were not available. Crossbows were certainly in use in Plantagenet garrisons and Edward I would appear to have hired a company of mounted crossbowmen for his campaign in 1298.[40] The absence of such men in later English armies may be an indication that they were too expensive or that they were not seen as having fulfilled a useful role, though it is also possible that crossbowmen were recruited for field service in the armies of Edward I and Edward II, but that they were not recorded as specific units.

Another weapon that is seemingly absent from the Scottish medieval arsenal is the sling, though a number of authors have chosen to include slingers in their accounts of the battle of Bannockburn.[41] There is, however, no mention of slingers in any of the contemporary narrative or record material save in a recitation of equipment (including cannon) ascribed to the English army in Bower's *Scotichronicon*. It would be rash, however, to assume that nobody, on either side, used a sling. A staff sling is a remarkably powerful weapon, easily capable of projecting a two-ounce stone over a distance of two hundred yards and more at the sort of velocity that could easily inflict a major wound.

We might give some thought to the reasons behind the apparent lack of interest in archery in Scotland when compared with England, however it is easy to conflate rather different situations. The armies of Edward III generally included large numbers of archers compared to those of Edward I and Edward II. This would seem to have been the result of a deliberate policy of fostering archery in general and of preference recruiting, that is to say that recruiters in the middle of the fourteenth century were under more pressure to recruit archers than other types of soldier.

This does not mean that the shires of medieval England were filled with budding expert bowmen waiting to be enlisted, but rather that a larger proportion of men were issued with bows and arrows. The act of providing a man with archery equipment does not, of itself, produce an expert archer, but that may not have been as significant as one might at first expect. The power of the bow as a battlefield weapon – and the same is true of the spear – rested on the deployment of large numbers. If the body of archers was sufficiently large and could be persuaded that the safest course of action in battle was to confront the enemy with steady shooting rather than to take flight, heavy casualties could be inflicted, even if the quality of the shooting was poor.

The efficacy of concerted archery would be demonstrated at the battles of Dupplin Muir, Halidon Hill, Crecy and Poitiers in the 1330s and 1340s, but the power of the bow had not yet been demonstrated in 1314. In fact, the archers did not even have an accustomed line-of-battle role in the English army, since there was not yet a 'typical' or 'traditional' English infantry policy. The value of archery was not in doubt. Edward I was clearly well aware of the power of the infantry in general and the archers in particular; he did not recruit infantrymen by the thousand without good reason. However he did not formulate a general plan of action for their deployment, but instead committed them to the fight as and when required.

It is important to remember that even in the great longbow victories, archers were only ever part of an army destined for general engagements. Edward I and his contemporaries were well aware of the concept of 'combined arms' as the route to victory. Even when deployed in strength, the archers were still very vulnerable to attack unless well supported by men-at-arms and spearmen.

If they could not be deployed in good time they could be charged down by even a relatively modest force of men-at-arms – as happened at Bannockburn – but they were also vulnerable to the weather. Rain would be an obvious problem; indeed, at the battle of Agincourt, English archers unstrung their bows so that they could protect their strings from a shower of rain, but even a slight breeze – whether tailwind, crosswind or headwind – would compromise the value of archery severely by reducing accuracy and/or velocity. If the archers were deployed in sufficiently large numbers, impeding the accuracy of their shooting might not be a matter of great significance, but any reduction in velocity would have dire implications for the effectiveness of the force. Given the relatively low weight of an arrow compared to its surface area, any amount of headwind would reduce the impetus of the projectile considerably, and therefore its effectiveness against armoured men.

# Articulation

Little or nothing is known about the nature of practical articulation in the Scottish armies of the fourteenth century, but we can make some observations about the administrative structure of the English infantry. Under

Edward I – if not before – there was a system of major and minor con-
stituent units. The lowest level of articulation was based on junior leaders
described variously as vintenars – a title derived from the French word *vingt*
– corporals and Petty Officers. Each of these officers was responsible for
a body of twenty men. To what extent this was a tactical unit and to what
extent an administrative unit is unknown, but there were undoubtedly very
few occasions where a twenty man unit was deployed as a discrete formation on the battlefield. Certainly, none have been mentioned in chronicle
or record sources. The next level of command rested with the centenars
who presumably had charge of five vintenars. The centenars came under
the authority of the millenars who must have been men with responsibility
for ten of the companies led by the centenars. These units were certainly
entrusted with a degree of operational responsibility. The Plea Rolls of
Edward I's army of 1296[42] include a reference to an officer, Richard Tailleur,
being fined for failing to ensure that his company performed sentry duty
when it was their turn to do so, and so there was clearly an operational
function. Whether this was the case on the battlefield is another matter,
though it would seem peculiar if Edward had failed to make use of an existing tool of articulation. Even the relatively substantial formations of the
millenars were not deployed as discrete units on the battlefield, but were
brigaded to form larger units as required. It is not certain that these larger
units necessarily consisted of the same formations throughout a campaign,
though the advantages of maintaining an order having a consistent chain of
command would surely have been obvious to the commanders of armies
given that armies were, as a general rule, divided into major divisions for
tactical purposes.

The spear-armed element in each army must have functioned in broadly
similar ways, since the behaviour of such units in the field was largely dic-
tated by the nature of their equipment. One issue that might be construed
as a radical difference in the approach to battle between the English and
Scottish infantry is the question of the schiltrom. In the popular imagination, a schiltrom was a circular formation of spearmen, arrayed with their
spears pointing outwards, thus providing an all-round defence against cavalry. Modern descriptions and depictions of the battle of Bannockburn are
replete with such formations. There are, however, only two examples of
the Scots adopting circular schiltroms. The first was at the battle of Falkirk,
where Wallace's four large formations stood in circles to receive – and initially repulse – Edward I's cavalry. The second occurred on the first day of

Bannockburn, when the Earl of Moray's force adopted a circular, or perhaps oval, formation against Clifford and Beaumont's division of the English cavalry with rather more success. Other than these two examples, the Scots seem to have invariably deployed for battle in linear formations.

The problem of the circular formation – primarily lack of mobility and a reduction in the number of men who could be brought into combat without compromising the integrity of the circle – were not significant when standing against cavalry, but would have been paramount issues when committing to the attack. In particular, it would have been very difficult indeed to dominate the front ranks of the enemy. At the initial contact the leading men of the circular schiltrom would have been very heavily outnumbered by their opponents in a linear formation. By the time the weight of the schiltrom was really brought to bear on the enemy, those leading elements might well have been crushed, thus breaking the continuity of the formation and allowing an aggressive opponent to break into the centre. Additionally, though the evolutions required of a block of spearmen were not very demanding, it is not easy to keep men in regular formation on the move unless that formation has clear and simple ranks. Moving a circular formation can only be achieved with any degree of security if the men in the unit have been trained to exacting standards in the way of foot-drill. In an age when cadenced marching had yet to be invented the advance (or retreat) of a circular schiltrom would have been challenging to say the least.

This is not to imply that it was impossible to manoeuvre a circular or elliptical schiltrom. If we are to accept Barbour's description of Moray's action against English cavalry on the first day of the battle – and there is no reason why we should not – it is clear that Moray was able to manoeuvre his force with some confidence against a mounted enemy. However, there are at least three significant factors to be borne in mind. Barbour's account does not describe an action by a great body of Scots, but an action involving a portion of the men under Moray's command. These are referred to as Moray's 'mengne'.[43] We might debate what exactly Barbour meant by the term, though it is reasonable to assume that its meaning was clear enough to Barbour's audience. The most logical interpretation would be to assume that Moray's 'mengne' comprised the men who owed him military service, whether as his tenants or because they were members of communities over which Moray had rights of military leadership. Clearly this was not the formation that Moray commanded on the following day. Virtually all estimates of the Scottish army put the close-order element in the region of six to eight thousand including the archers and the cavalry, and all the contemporary accounts refer to either three (or in Barbour's case four) formations. We should therefore assume that the divisions committed to the fight on the second day of the battle were anything from fifteen hundred to more than two thousand strong, and that Moray's own 'mengne' was a formation within the division that he led on 24th June.

Mr Stuart Reid[44] has suggested that the major formations of Robert's army were, in turn, divided into three of four individual schiltroms. Although there is no evidence to support this, it is a plausible proposition to some extent. It would be extremely difficult to instil basic drill practices in very large formations of one thousand men or more. It would be rational to assume that the troops were taught their 'basic' skills in relatively small groups, before these groups were combined into larger formations for more advanced training. His suggestion that these sub-unit schiltroms would have been drawn up with a distance between them is less convincing. The gaps between the units would have greatly reduced the ability of the Scots to form an effective barrier across the stretch of land between the Bannock and Pelstream burns, and the collapse of just one sub-unit might seriously imperil those to the left and right. Mr Reid also suggests that Barbour's description of the Scottish deployment on the 24 June is 'consistent with the normal Scottish practice of deploying four divisions rather than the three common to most medieval armies,' however, the four schiltroms of Wallace's army at Falkirk would seem to be only one example and may be a reflection of the scale of Wallace's army. It would probably have been very difficult to control a single body of more than 2,000 men.

Even so, Barbour's description of the fighting at St Ninians may offer some support for the existence of articulation at a lower level than that of the three (or four) battlefield formations employed by the Scots. The Earl of Moray had been active in the Bruce cause for some years and had attained great rank and status as one of King Robert's most trusted commanders. It would be reasonable to assume that he had brought his troops to a high standard of efficiency. He could therefore depend on the quality of the training and experience of his troops and his subordinate commanders to maintain the cohesion of formation necessary for manoeuvres against a more mobile enemy. Barbour gives Moray's 'mengne' a strength of no more than 500 men. Interestingly, although Barbour tells us that Moray ordered his men:

...bak to bak set all your rout
And all the speris poyntis out

he does not use the term schiltrom, or indeed any other term, to describe
Moray's formation, though what significance – if any – can be attached to
this is unclear. He was certainly familiar with the term, since he used to
describe the appearance of the English army.[49]

Barbour's description of Moray's force as his own 'mengne' is possibly
of interest in an administrative context. There must surely have been some
form of articulation in the Scottish army, if only for the sake of organising
the distribution of rations and apportioning guard duties and work-parties.
Moray's five hundred men may be an indication that the major battlefield
formations of King Robert's army had a degree of internal sub-division and
that those sub-divisions could be allotted to specific operations as discrete
units. But the deployment of one body of men from a major formation is
not sufficient evidence to indicate that this was normal practice.

Articulation at the smallest scale is occasionally indicated by the wording of
charter evidence. A body of men required from the recipient of a charter
might comprise so many archers and an 'armed man' to lead them. An example from Formulary 'E'[46] indicates that a burgh might be expected to supply a
given number of troops and a man – or men – 'sufficiently' equipped to lead
them. These examples do, however, refer to very small groups. We know that
rights of military leadership over quite extensive areas might be granted to an
individual regardless of whether the men concerned were tenants of that individual. We also know that a lord – Sir James Douglas, for example[47] – might
be granted military leadership rights over all of his tenants throughout the
kingdom regardless of existing custom. An individual might also be granted
leadership rights over men who lived on properties that did not belong to
him.[48] This surely implies that as a general rule those men would fall under
the authority of a local officer of the crown – whether earl, baron or sheriff
– but that that authority might be passed on to another.

We might ask how that would be of benefit either to the person receiving this privilege or to the king, who obviously granted it in the first place.
For the beneficiary of such a grant there was an element of enhanced
prestige – he evidently enjoyed the confidence and favour of the king, but
there must surely have been some practical advantage as well. Such grants
may have simplified the business of getting men into the field. There was

obviously some potential for conflicts in the chain of command if, for example, a lord's tenant owed military obedience to both his superior and the local sheriff. It may have been a means of assisting lords to raise larger and/or discrete formations. The tenants of Sir Thomas Randolph in his capacity as Earl of Moray were, presumably, under his command when they took to the field, but his tenants in other parts of the country may have been the responsibility of the local sheriff or Earl with specified local military responsibilities. By granting someone the leadership 'of all his men throughout the realm' the king may have been able to obtain 'army units' with a common allegiance to one man, and thus achieve some degree of tactical articulation and cohesion at a more practical level. The administrative challenge of leading an army which consisted of a great many lordly retinues of varying sizes would be enormous, so it would be in the interests of the crown to encourage the development of larger formations for campaigning generally and for the battlefield in particular.

There is no extensive body of evidence to suggest that the Scots adopted a system of administrative articulation of any kind, though it is hard to see how the daily life of an army could be maintained without one. Wallace allegedly imposed a system of junior commanders of units down to the level of five men, though this is probably an example of the literary fancy of the writer rather than a valid description of the Scots at war in 1296–98. On the other hand, Bower describes two Scottish men-at-arms, John Stirling and Alan Boyd, as being commanders of the Scottish archers at the siege of Perth in 1339.[49] It would therefore seem that the archers at least were considered to be a distinct portion of the army, rather than consisting of men from the rank and file who just happened to be armed with bows. Neither Boyd nor Stirling were men of the first rank in the Scottish nobility, but they were certainly not commoners.

# Enlistment

The experiences of the three Edwards in Scotland brought about a number of changes in the English approach to mustering armies. Long before the end of Edward III's reign in 1377 the contracted soldier in receipt of government wages had become more the rule than the exception. His pay was poor – 2*d* to 4*d* a day – and we have little knowledge of the conditions of his employment. He might volunteer in search of adventure or perhaps to avoid problems at home, but most infantrymen were chosen by local authorities such as the sheriff or the borough council. They were not, therefore, always the best specimens, but rather the dregs of the community. Counties and towns were asked for contingents of men, and might be obliged to furnish those men with arms, armour and foodstuffs. In some instances they were also burdened with the provision of the men's wages for the duration of their march from their community to the muster point of the army, where the crown assumed responsibility for pay. The pay scale might be adjusted for service inside and outside England on the premise that the men would be able to supplement their wages through foraging and plunder – a rather short-sighted policy given that plundering would inevitably alienate residents in areas under Plantagenet control. Moreover the areas through which the army passed were likely to have been stripped bare before the army arrived, leaving very little for hungry soldiers to requisition.

Scottish soldiers, in theory, were seldom paid at all, though it is likely that the large sums collected by Robert I from the communities of northern England did in fact find their way into the pockets of his soldiers. As Professor Duncan has pointed out in reference to King Robert's campaigns of 1312–13,[50] 'such protracted campaigning cannot have been carried out with only the free service of the common army.' If Robert did not provide wages, it is difficult to see how he could keep such firm control of his troops as they marched through Northumberland, Westmorland, Cumbria, Durham and Yorkshire. Numerous medieval documents give us scraps of information about Scots in military service, but they are – largely – documents which describe personal liability. There are few that shed light on the wider issues of army enlistment. Broadly speaking, the rank and file of Scottish armies were recruited or conscripted under the authority of specific local potentates. For most people this probably meant the sheriff or a senior noble – an earl or baron. Naturally, the earls and barons had their own resources to call on, either as landholders with military obligations, or as local officers of the crown whose rights and responsibilities included mustering men for war in time of need. The right to call out men for service was not a simple matter of authority. While still Earl of Carrick, Robert Bruce was obliged to give an undertaking that he would not, in future, use his authority to call out the tenants of Melrose Abbey to fight in support of his personal career ambitions, but only when the whole community was called upon to serve in the national interest.[51] As Earl of Carrick or Lord of Annandale, Robert had a responsibility to conscript men to serve in defence of the realm, and the authority to do so, but men were not obliged to fight for the baronial interests of the Bruce family. Naturally the situation was somewhat different once Robert had made his kingship a reality; the desires of the king and the duties of community being – in the eyes of contemporaries – virtually one and the same.

An extract from 'formulary E' (see above), possibly detailing the military obligations of the Burgh of Ayr as an example, indicated that the town had to find a given number of properly equipped infantry and a man-at-arms to lead them. The same applies to the 1304 charter of the Earl of Fife relating to Kilsyth (see above), the recipient of the grant being obliged to provide ten archers. Clearly infantry service was considered important enough for it to figure in the charters of great lords, but there is insufficient evidence to allow us to formulate a rationale for the practical integration of such men into a large field army. To some extent this may have been offset by the extension of rights of military leadership. As we have already seen, men like Sir James Douglas and Sir Alexander Seton might be given charters which cut across the customary practices of the day, in that they were given the 'leadership' of all their tenants, regardless of which sheriffdom those tenants came from.

Although the bulk of Robert's army was certainly recruited on the basis of customary military duty, we should not assume that they were all men discharging obligations. Barbour tells us that the king turned away volunteers who did not have adequate arms and armour, but there is no reason to assume that properly equipped men were not acceptable wherever they came from. There may have been no prospect of regular wages, but there was the prospect of plunder if the Scots were triumphant or – as had happened in the past – the English had failed to force battle and were obliged to withdraw. Service in the army might also attract men who, for whatever reasons, had fallen into banditry. Pardons granted for army service were a normal part of the recruiting structure of English armies, and there is no reason to presume that a similar practice was not acceptable in Scotland just because we have no record of it.

Military obligations were not necessarily as simple as the supply of soldiers for the crown. Religious houses in Scotland (unlike their counterparts in England and France) were not obliged to provide knight service for the King's army, though their tenants certainly were. This does not mean that the convents, abbeys and monasteries of Scotland were automatically exempt from providing a contribution to the military, either in wartime or peacetime. An undated charter of Robert I relieved the community of Paisley Abbey from the annual burden of providing five chalders of oats to the garrison of Dumbarton Castle.[52] Robert's policy of slighting castles to render them useless to future English invasions may have made the existing obligation redundant. If there was no castle there would be no garrison to support, and the church might undertake other tasks connected with the finances of war. In 1339 Robert the Steward (later Robert II) relieved the Priory of St Andrews from an undertaking to collect funds from the 'community' (that is to say the lords, landholders and burgesses of the county) for the upkeep of the garrison of Loch Leven Castle.[58]

The burdens of Paisley Abbey or St Andrews Priory were probably not dissimilar in principle to those of other religious houses, and individual clerics certainly took up arms in pursuit of political aims. Bishops Lamberton and Wishart were certainly very active in the Bruce cause and, among the Edinburgh garrison of Edward III, we find the Parson of Pencaitland serving, not just as a man-at-arms, but as a knight.[54] Several other clerics appear in record and narrative sources in military roles – perhaps the most famous of these being Antony Bek, Bishop of Durham, who served Edward I on more than one campaign. Bek commanded an expeditionary force from the main body of the army of 1298 in a brief campaign to recover three castles in Lothian which had fallen (or whose garrisons had defected ) to Wallace's army in the year or so since the Battle of Stirling Bridge.

# The Logistic Effort

The large forces raised in 1314 required huge quantities of foodstuffs for both men and beasts, quantities that could not be achieved through foraging or through reliance on supplies provided by the troops themselves or by merchants following the army. Dr McNamee has examined the scale of provisions collected at Berwick and Newcastle[55] and has concluded that, if collection of material continued on the same scale, it would be sufficient to allow 'English garrisons to remain in Scotland indefinitely.' However, such a concentration of supplies would have been very hard to maintain for any length of time and was achieved only by buying huge shipments of produce from Italian merchants and bankers like Antonio Pessagno.[62] Maintaining garrisons would, naturally enough, depend on recovering towns and castles to house them, a practical proposition if Edward could secure a major victory on the battlefield, but not if the Scots were able to evade battle long enough to force Edward to abandon the campaign – a strong possibility given the campaign of 1310–11. However, maintaining garrisons was not simply a matter of providing food and funds. If the garrison could not impose Edward's lordship effectively they would be no more than an expensive way of keeping the Scots occupied.

Provisions were obviously a major issue for both armies, but there were other logistical requirements. Scottish commerce could supply any form of equipment and armourers and lorimers appear in many medieval Scottish documents long before the wars of independence. As early as the reign of William the Lion, a 'galeator' (a specialist helmet-maker) was operating in Perth, but local tradesmen could not provide arms in the quantities necessary for a long-term, large-scale war. War materials were certainly being imported for the Balliol party in 1302 when a Flemish ship carrying arms, probably bound for Aberdeen, was captured by the English.[57] In addition, in the autumn of 1309, Edward II complained to the count of Flanders that the Scots were receiving aid from German merchants operating through the ports of his province.[58] Edward even found that his own merchants could not be trusted to desist from selling arms to the Scots either directly or through Irish ports.

We can say very little indeed about the Scottish approach to supply. It is evident from charter material (see above) that institutions might carry a responsibility to provide foodstuffs for royal garrisons on a formal, regular basis, but there is no evidence of a government department with responsibility for providing arms, food or wages to Scottish troops. This does not mean that we should assume the Scottish armies were expected to live on supplies that they had brought to the army personally, nor that they lived by foraging, though that was unquestionably a major source of rations when communities in the north of England had failed to come up with ransoms.

The army that King Robert assembled at Stirling could not possibly have survived simply by requisitioning material from the local community. Apart from anything else the army of summer 1314 was probably of at least the same order of magnitude as the largest burghs in the realm. If non-combatants are included, the number of mouths to fed may have amounted to 10–12,000, conceivably more. Mr Nusbacher[66] categorically states that King Robert cannot have recruited more than five thousand men for service in 1314, but offers no supporting evidence or rationale. Even if the army itself was as small as 5,000 – and that would be a very low estimate indeed – we can be confident that the collection of metalworkers, cooks, servants, prostitutes and general 'hangers on' that were part and parcel of any army would have inflated that number very considerably. Strictly speaking, these people were not part of the army in the sense of being combat soldiers, but they still lived – or at least attempted to live – at the expense of the army.

By the time of the Bannockburn campaign, Robert had gained control of the majority of Scotland. In fact, Robert's army may have been very much greater, even twice the size of Nusbacher's estimate. There are a number of issues to be considered here. Obviously the size of the population as a whole cannot be adequately estimated, and figures extrapolated from estimates of fourteenth-century population figures should not be taken too seriously. We might more usefully consider the estimates of other Scottish armies. The army that David II led to defeat at Neville's Cross is generally believed to have been of the order of 10,000 troops, including one to two thousand men-at-arms. We might consider the possibility that David was able to raise a larger army than his father. It is quite possible that Robert had not been able to establish his lordship sufficiently in Berwickshire, Lothian and Roxburghshire to be able to fully exploit the manpower of those counties, but on the other hand, King Robert very obviously made more extensive use of men from the West Highlands and the Western Isles in 1314 than King David did in 1346. Estimates of the strength of Robert's army have, in essence, been arrived at by assuming that Barbour's numbers should be divided by four to give a reasonable 'working guide' to Robert's army, however Barbour's figure is a literary one and was therefore not intended to give an accurate account. A figure of 7,000 is not unreasonable, but neither is a figure of 10,000. Robert had, after all, been gathering troops and training them for several weeks before the battle and, since his army was not on the march, the potential for deserters to slip away unnoticed would have been very much reduced. We should not doubt that Robert's army included a detachment tasked with the security of the camp, and therefore, almost inevitably, with the apprehension of would-be deserters.

Whether the army comprised 5,000 or 10,000 – and we are probably safe in assuming that these are the upper and lower limits – it was still a very considerable body of men and would have demanded a sophisticated system of administration. The army would have had to have some form of articulation, if only for the sake of arranging training groups, work details and ration parties, and there would also have to have been a regulated system for the collection of provisions from the rest of the country.

A force of several thousand might be able to live 'off the land' if it was on the march, but King Robert's army was unquestionably static. This had the advantage that his lieutenants could concentrate on training and organisation, but there would be no prospect of gathering the sheer volume of foodstuffs necessary to feed several thousand people and horses from the immediate vicinity. Even if the community of Stirlingshire had been wealthy enough to provide the rations, the ill-will generated by wholesale requisition would have done nothing to enhance Robert's prestige as king – he would be failing to provide the 'good lordship' on which acceptance of medieval kingship rested. We do not know what measures were taken to feed the army, but clearly something was done or the army would either have stared to death or simply disintegrated.

If we do not know how supplies were collected, we do at least have some idea about where they were deposited. During the night of 23–24 June the Earl of Atholl – who had recently defected to the English after Edward Bruce's jilting of his sister – led an attack on the Scottish supply trains at Cambuskenneth Abbey. The attack seems to have had little or no effect on King Robert's plans, nor on his army, but clearly there was an established centre for supplies which could be identified and raided.

The administrative and logistical elements of the English army can be described with more confidence, though a good deal of material has not survived. No doubt some portion was lost on the battlefield. There are no muster rolls or horse valuation rolls for the army of 1314. These records would be of great benefit in estimating the strength of the army overall, but more importantly the proportions of different troops present. They would also provide us with some idea of the ancillary effort that was required to make and keep such an army ready for battle.

Horse valuation – restauro – was an important process in the enlistment of men-at-arms. In order to qualify for his 12d/day wage, each man-at-arms had to have his charger valued by a panel of officers. If the animal was lost on campaign, the owner would be reimbursed accordingly by the crown. Only one horse could be assessed for restauro, but if the animal was lost, or simply unfit for action, the man-at-arms could lose his day's wages.

*Left:* 30 A sixteenth-century English artwork, depicting a fictitious parliament of Edward I attended by Llewellyn, Prince of Wales and Alexander III. Artworks and forged documents were an important weapon in the propaganda arsenals of medieval kings: the 'Dodgy Dossier' is not a modern innovation.

*Below left:* 31 The coronation of Edward I. Edward only commanded one Scottish action in person, the Battle of Falkirk, 1298. His death in 1307 was a major blow to the fortunes of the English occupation forces, however the tide of the war had probably already started to turn in favour of the Scots.

*Below:* 32 John Balliol, from a Scottish amorial illuminated between 1581 and 1584. The king is surrounded by the broken symbols of his rule.

**CASTLES AND FORTRESSES OF THIRTEENTH CENTURY SCOTLAND**

33 Map of the more important castles and strongpoints of medieval Scotland. Most of these lie in the south and east of the country. There were of course a great many castles and fortresses in the far north, west and isles, however medieval conflict in Scotland was dominated by the Wars of Independence. The occupation of governments of Edward I, II and III failed to make much headway in the north and west. Even in the brief period of unchallenged English occupation in 1304–1306, Edward I was largely reliant on the power of indigenous lordship outwith the southern and eastern portions of the country.

34 Cities and significant towns of Scotland c.1300. The loss or retention of administrative and economic centres was a crucial indicator of success or failure in war throughout the medieval and early modern periods.

*Right:* 1 The last remaining building of Cambuskenneth Abbey. Scene of the only action of the battle which can be located with complete confidence.

*Below:* 2 View toward 'The Entry' into the New Park. The first action probably took place in the vicinity of the gentle ridge line slightly to the south of what is now the National Trust Visitor Centre.

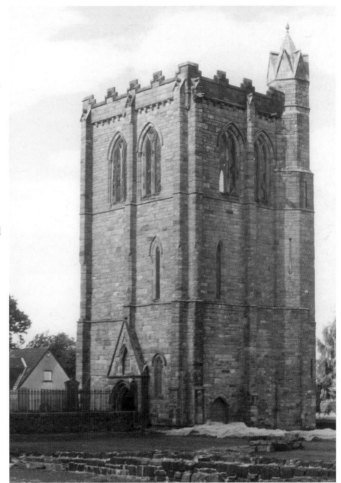

3 View south from the Visitor Centre. The Earls of Gloucester and Hereford led their troops into 'The Entry' and were defeated by Scottish spearmen and archers. King Robert's famous duel with De Bohun probably occurred close to this area.

4 View toward Stirling Castle. The medieval town did not extend far beyond the tail and eskar on which the castle stands.

5 Looking south from the centre of the level area now occupied by Bannockburn High School. All of the most reliable source material indicates that the Scots moved downhill from woods onto the 'carse'. This would have been an ideal 'forming up' area for Robert's army.

6 Looking north from the same location.

7 The slope down to the carse. King Robert's army would have had to negotiate this incline to advance to contact with the English army down on the carse.

8 The Bannock Burn from the Telford Bridge. The Scots, concentrated on the high ground to the west of the carse, would have been quite invisible to the English below, giving King Robert a tremendous reconnaissance advantage.

9 The Bannock Burn runs through the carse and formed the southern boundary of the English camp and deployment area.

10 The carse. Although primarily pasture today, this area was predominantly arable in the fourteenth century due to the high value of grain. Modern tradition would have us believe that the English army camped in a swamp among pools, but medieval writers are clear that the fighting took place on firm, flat terrain.

11 Medieval infantryman. English and Scottish troops were armed and armoured in much the same manner. The cap below this soldier's bacinet provides vital cushioning.

12 Heavy cavalry soldier. This man's flat-topped helmet would have been a little old-fashioned, but still serviceable.

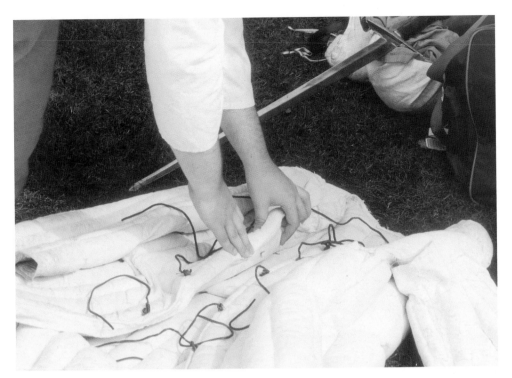

*Above:* 13 Padded jackets stuffed with raw wool would give good protection against impact weapons, but would become terribly hot on a summer day, leading to heat exhaustion.

*Right:* 14 This soldier's armour is, arguably, a little late in period for Bannockburn, but articulated plate armour for the arms and legs was becoming very fashionable. The picture was taken on the high ground overlooking the approximate area from which Gloucester and Hereford advanced on the first day of the battle.

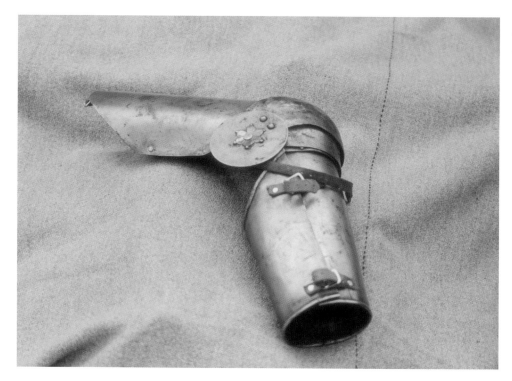

15 Articulated armour for the forearm and upper arm. A piece like this would have been the height of military fashion, worn by men-at-arms of both armies.

16 Medieval spearmen. Troops armed and armoured like these would have formed a large part of the army of Edward II and a very large proportion of that of Robert I, though we should expect the spears to have been rather longer than the 10 foot weapons shown here.

17 Close-up of spearmen. As long as spearmen maintained their formation they were virtually invulnerable to cavalry.

18 An archer. Contrary to a tradition that has developed over the past century, there is no evidence to suggest that Scottish and English archers used different types of bow.

19 Livery – the practice of dressing troops in particular colours – was only just becoming fashionable in the early fourteenth century.

20 An archer in padded coat 'nocking' his arrow.

21 The film *Braveheart* popularised myths about the nature of Scottish military equipment, in particular a belief that Scottish troops wore very distinctive leather tunics like this one.

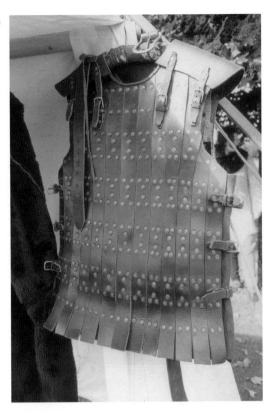

22 Arms of Scottish some of the Scottish Earls, barons and knights who served at at Bannockburn.

*Left:* 23 A well-equipped infantryman with three layers of protection – a thick padded coat worn over a chainmail hauberk over a thinner padded jacket.

*Below:* 24 A considerable proportion of the men-at-arms in the Scottish army – including the earls of Carrick and Moray and the King himself – served on foot with spear in hand.

25 Receiving cavalry. The strong modern tradition that Scottish spearmen knelt down to rest the butts of their spears on the ground is supported by medieval evidence.

26 Inchcolm Abbey, where Abbot Bower composed his *Scotichronicon*.

27 Torphichen, headquarters of the Hospitallers in Scotland. Contrary to modern tradition, there is no evidence to suggest that a body of Templars received sanctuary in Scotland and continued to exist as a branch of he Hospitallers or that they served under King Robert at Bannockburn.

28 A re-enactor in the role of Edward II. In reality, the king would have been rather better armoured, with plates for his arms and legs, plate gloves and a helmet, probably a bacinet.

29  Pilkington Jackson's statue of Robert I at the Bannockburn Visitor Centre.

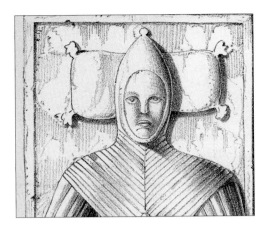

*Above left:* 35 Detail from a Scottish grave effigy. This soldier wears a bacinet helmet, the height of fashion in the early fourteenth century. Men like this were the backbone of the forces raised for service under Robert I from Glentrool 1307 to Bannockburn 1314 and beyond.

*Centre left:* 36 A page of the Scalacronica of Sir Thomas Grey of Heton. Here is his account of the removal of the Stone of Destiny from Scone.

*Above:* 37 The resting place of the Scottish coronation stone. The 'Stone of Destiny' was due to be returned to Scotland as part of the 'perpetual peace' treaty of Edinburgh–Northampton in 1328, but riotous crowns in London prevented it from being removed from Westminster Abbey.

*Left:* 38 Silver penny of Robert I. Ransoms, plunder and 'protection money' offered by the northern English counties brought a great influx of bullion to Scotland, especially after 1314.

*Top left:* 39 Seal of Robert Bruce as Earl of Carrick. Robert's inheritance of the earldom through his mother, Countess Majory, provided him with an entry into the Gaelic world of western Scotland from where he was to draw much of his military and naval support after 1306.

*Above:* 40 Patent letter of John Balliol, King of Scots, recording that he had sworn fealty to Edward I of England. This acknowledgement of Edward's overlordship was intended to provide evidence for the subjection of Scotland to England.

*Left:* 41 Great seal of Robert I (1306–29) showing the king crowned and enthroned in state. The seal is modelled deliberately on that of his predecessors.

*Bottom:* 42 Great seal of Robert I (1306–29) showing the king as a mounted and armoured knight. This symbolism is appropriate for a king who ruled at the head of a military regime.

*Clockwise from above:* 43 Nineteenth-century drawing showing bitter close-quarter fighting at Halidon Hill in 1333, where the Scottish army attacked on foot.

44 One of the many swords reputed to have been carried by Robert I, this example is much more likely to date from the fifteenth century.

45 The memorial of Angus Og, Lord of the Isles. His support was crucial to the early success of Robert I.

46 A weapon fragment from the battlefield of Bannockburn. Due to the nature of the soil very few such fragments have been recovered from the field.

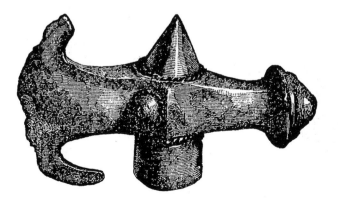

*Above:* 47 The seal of Edward I, showing him as a knight and as judge, demonstrating two of the chief duties of kingship. Edward commanded only one Scottish action in person, the Battle of Falkirk in 1298

*Left:* 48 Detail from a Scottish grave effigy. The assumption that soldiers from the Celtic areas of Scotland differed greatly from their counterparts elsewhere is widespread, but not well supported by the evidence. This soldier is equipped with a spear, chainmail armour, a bacinet helmet and carries his heraldic arms on a typical 'heater' shield, as would any English or French man-at-arms. Men like this served at Turnberry, 1307, Slioch, 1308 and throughout Robert I's campaigns.

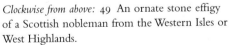

*Clockwise from above:* 49 An ornate stone effigy of a Scottish nobleman from the Western Isles or West Highlands.

50 & 51 Scottish foot soldiers of the late thirteenth centuries as depicted in an English manuscript.

52 Scots manning a catapult at the siege of Carlisle.

*Left:* 53 The grave effigy of Sir Roger de Trumpington, dated to 1280, this image depicts a typical knight or man-at-arms of the thirteenth century. Other than the guards on his knees, the armour consists entirely of chainmail.

*Below:* 54 The arms of the King of Scotland. At the Battle of Bannockburn Robert I carried a spear in a schiltrum, a gesture indicating he was prepared to fight and die like any common soldier. A similar stance on the part of James IV 200 years later led to disaster for the Scots at Flodden.

*Bottom:* 55 The arms of Gilbert de Clare, Earl of Gloucester. A cousin of Robert I, de Clare was a senior commander in the Engliash army at Bannockburn.

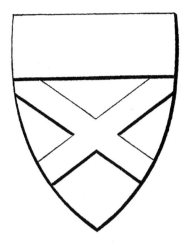

*Above:* 56 The arms of Edward Bruce, Earl of Carrick, who commanded one of the Scottish schiltrums at Bannockburn. An attempt to make himself King of Ireland came to an end when he was killed at the Battle of Faughart.

*Above right:* 57 The arms of Ingram d'Umfraville. Although he owned extensive properties in England, d'Umfraville was a noted leader of the Balliol party.

*Right:* 58 By the time of the Battle of Myton in 1319, plate armour was becoming a more common sight on the battlefield. This figure has a particularly well-articulated suit of armour, especially in the gauntlets and foot pieces.

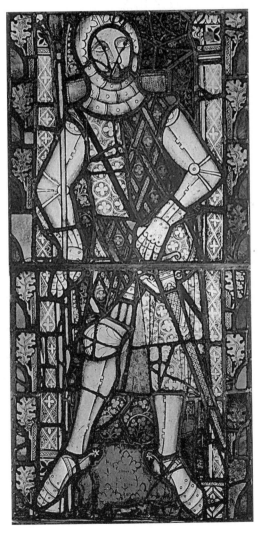

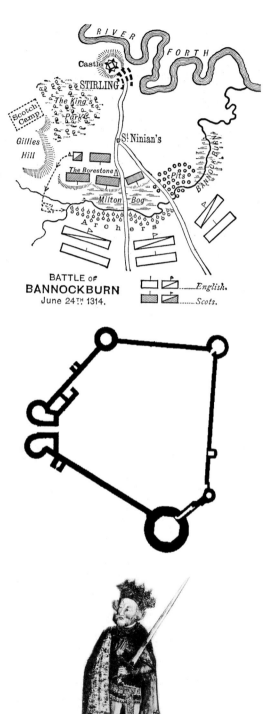

*Above:* 59 Illuminated letter depicting the defence of Carlisle.

*Top right:* 60 The battle of Bannockburn as envisaged by Sir Charles Oman (after S.R. Gardiner.) Gardiner and Oman's interpretations were for many years the 'recieved history' of the battle, although neither bears examination in the light of the documentary evidence.

*Centre right:* 61 Outline map of the walls of Bothwell Castle.

*Bottom right:* 62 Edward I. His aggressive interventions in Scotland destroyed the generally positive relationship between Scotland and England for a century. Despite his posthumous nickname 'Malleus Scottorum' (Hammer of the Scots) Edward failed miserably in his attempt to annex Scotland.

BATTLE of
**BANNOCKBURN**
June 24TH 1314.

........English.
........Scots.

*Above left:* 63 The arms of English kings until Edward III adopted the Fleur de Lys to indicate his claim to the throne of France.

*Above:* 64 The seal of John Balliol. Deposed by Edward I in 1296, the restoration of John was the target of the Scottish resistance to the Plantagenets which was demonstrated at the battles of Stirling Bridge, 1297, Falkirk, 1298 and Roslin, 1303.

*Left:* 65 A medieval highland fantasy. Great swords of this style did not come into use until long after Bannockburn and were never a common weapon.compared to the spear.

ANO EFTER KING ROBERT
YE BRVCE MARIIT YE
DVKE OF HVILLESTERIS DOCHTER

*Left:* 66 Robert I and his queen, Elizabeth. Elizabeth was captured in 1306 and held a prisoner in England until Scottish victory at Bannockburn forced Edward II to accept an extensive exchange of prisoners.

*Below left:* 67 The great seal of Edward Balliol as King of Scotland. Balliol's attempts to gain the Scottish crown were dependent on the military, financial and diplomatic support of Edward III. Despite the stunning victories of Dupplin Muir in 1332 and Halidon Hill in 1333, the Balliol cause was lost by the mid 1330s.

*Below:* 68 Brass of Robert Bruce, Dunfermline Abbey. Above his shoulders are, on the left, the lion rampant of Scotland and, on the right, the saltire of the Bruce family.

Therefore, the vast majority of the men concerned would actually take at least two mounts to war, and men of greater status might well take several. If we can realistically accept a contingent of roughly 2,000 men-at-arms in the army of Edward II from contemporary accounts, we can be reasonably confident that the his army's supply arrangements had to cater for an absolute minimum of 4,000 cavalry chargers and a vast number of grooms and farriers.

To some extent, issues of pay and supply could be the responsibility of the leaders of retinues. Men of great status might choose to serve without pay as a means of demonstrating personal independence, exceptional loyalty to the crown or simply to show off their wealth. For the majority of the army there were four principal sources of supply: foraging; carrying personal supplies; purchase from merchants travelling with the army and purchase from stores of food arranged by the crown. The first of these was, in a sense, the most attractive option. There was no need to pay for the materials collected and the requisition of foodstuffs by an English soldier obviously prevented them being consumed by a Scottish one, however there was little to be gained by foraging the same area twice. Foraging was therefore only really valuable as a supply source when the army was on the move. Moreover in the southern and eastern areas foraging was likely to push Scots who had accepted Plantagenet rule – in some cases more or less continuously since 1296 – into the arms of the Bruce party. Finally there was little chance of acquiring all of the materials necessary for war by foraging alone. A force which involved at least 4,000 horses as remounts would consume a vast number of hay, oats, barley, harness, horseshoes, nails and other items that would be scarce in an area that had already been scoured by the Scots. Carrying a good supply of one's own foodstuffs was an option, but only for men with the wealth to provide themselves with a wagon, a team, a driver and perhaps a guard for the wagon. Obviously the common infantryman would be capable of carrying some quantity of flour, and a cavalryman more, but neither was likely to be able to carry enough to feed himself, let alone a horse, for the duration of the campaign.

Commercial involvement in campaigning could help to ease supply problems so long as merchants could maintain stocks in the vicinity of the army. So long as the troops were receiving regular issues of pay, there was every incentive for merchants to tend to the military, though presumably the risk of theft from one's own army, let alone the actions of the enemy, must have discouraged some from participating in that market. Merchants might, in any case, have some difficulty in just keeping up with an army on the move, and might well experience problems in trying to maintain adequate stocks of the foodstuffs, weapons, harness and other items that the troops would want to buy.

The provision of foodstuffs through the efforts of the government was a long-established part of English campaigning in Scotland. Each campaign since 1296 had seen calls for shipping and crews from virtually every significant port in England. As a broad rule, ships from the north and west of England were requisitioned for the purposes of transporting troops from Ireland and to the replenishment of castles and formations operating in the west of Scotland. Those from the eastern seaboard were dedicated to the supply of English armies marching through eastern Scotland. Although very sound in principle, the logic of re-supply by sea was a complicated and unreliable business. The ships were dependent on favourable winds to carry them north from their home ports, so their arrival could hardly be guaranteed, let alone accurately predicted. When vessels did arrive at a convenient location and at a convenient time, there was no certainty that they would be carrying the stores most urgently required. A delivery of wine to Edward I's army in 1298 was one of the root causes of a dangerous riot which, had it not been strenuously suppressed, might have led to a major conflict within Edward's army at a point when the army of William Wallace was quite close at hand.

Crown supplies, whether delivered by sea or by land, were not necessarily distributed free to the troops, but could be sold by officers of the crown, thus recouping some portion of the money paid out in soldiers' wages. The range of products available through each of these sources was fairly limited. Supply contracts and inventories of stores in garrisons suggest a rather monotonous diet of wheat bread, beef, bacon, dried fish, ale and wine. The last of these was much prized, but was often in short supply. Each year's vintage was very fugitive compared to the 'shelf life' that we expect today. Little of the wine produced in the late summer and autumn would last beyond the late spring or early summer of the following year. The rations may have been predictable, and there were frequent failures of delivery for a variety of reasons. Shortages of shipping, wagons, draught animals, money and produce were compounded by failures of administration and by widespread dishonesty, but the sheer quantities of grain and meat demanded and delivered are staggering.[67]

Delivering supplies to English garrisons in Scotland was fraught with difficulty. In addition to the risks of sea and weather there was the prospect of piracy and the problem of transporting provisions from the point of delivery to the point of use. This was less of a problem for those fortresses and burghs which lay on the coast, but a landlocked installation – Linlithgow for example – had to depend on the ability of the surrounding garrisons to ensure that convoys could pass from Blackness Castle (where the supplies were landed) to Linlithgow, Livingstone and other garrisons. Providing foodstuffs for a major field army was an altogether more challenging proposition. Overland transport was slow, cumbersome and expensive. The fodder for the draught animals and the provisions for the men who drove and guarded the wagons must have represented a considerable drain on the victuals they were transporting. This could be offset to some extent by carrying the goods in ships. This practice was certainly cheaper in the sense of miles, tonnage and money, but it was not necessarily very effective. Adverse weather could prevent the landing of provisions, or even lead to the loss of ships, whose owners would need to be recompensed. To complicate the issue further, the demand for ships and mariners might not be met, with the result that the foodstuffs desperately needed by the army might be rotting in warehouses in ports up and down the length of England. Even if material was delivered to the right place at the right time, an imbalance of supplies could lead still to difficulties.

A substantial fleet amounting to at least sixty vessels[68] was requisitioned for the Bannockburn campaign, but a considerable part of the major effort depended on land transport – over 200 heavy wagons were ordered from English county authorities for service in Scotland. Even so, this major collection of vehicles cannot possibly have provided for the needs of the army and was probably only intended as the transport element of the royal household. The balance of the army's supplies would have to be transported at the expense of individuals and leaders of retinues, or would have to be acquired en route. Those acquisitions can be divided into two categories: supplies bought from merchants travelling with the army, and supplies bought or requisitioned from the communities through which the army passed. Both of these means of provisioning an army were well-established practices, but the latter presented Edward with a political problem. His adherents in southeast Scotland had already made at least one major representation to Edward concerning the behaviour of his garrisons. If he wanted to establish his rule effectively he had to be seen as a man who could provide 'good lordship' to the men in his allegiance. If his army plundered its way from

Berwick to Stirling it would inevitably be damaging to the very people whose loyalty Edward hoped to retain.

Edward seems to have made no effort to requisition transport until 6 June,[61] when thirteen sheriffs of English counties were ordered to send a total of more than 140 wagons of different types to arrive in Berwick for 6 July. Since the intention was that the army would have arrived at Stirling and either have fought an action against the Scots or have forced them to retire, the date seems something of a curiosity. However, it is possible that this considerable train of wagons, and many others ordered for 8, 15 and 22 July, plus a further draft of transport for 1st August, meant that Edward – or his staff – envisaged a campaign that would last well beyond the few weeks that Edward seems to have expected initially. It may even signify an intention to bring substantial forces into Scotland to supplement, or perhaps replace, the troops enlisted for the June campaign.

The lack of records relating to transport requirements before 6 June is not a clear indication that no effort had been made to form a baggage train for the campaign. Much has been made of Edward's general incompetence and of his lack of military skill, but he did have a certain level of war experience. It is unthinkable that he would have embarked on a major campaign without making transport arrangements, if only to provide for the needs of the royal household at war. It is all too easy to dismiss the defeat at Bannockburn as simply the consequence of Edward's incompetence. It is worth bearing in mind, however, that he did only lose *one* battle in a career that may not have seen much in the way of major engagements, but certainly involved a good deal of time in the field.

# Going to the War: October 1313–May 1314

The traditional view that the campaign of 1314 was prompted by the threat to Stirling Castle is well established, but not well founded. By late 1313 the occupation government was already in a perilous condition. Many of the great castles of the southern counties were still in English hands. Bothwell, Stirling, Edinburgh, Roxburgh, Berwick and perhaps some of the baronial castles – Dirleton, Yester and Hailes – continued to hold out against the Bruce party, but the ability of the Plantagenet administration to actually impose Edward's rule was very limited. In October or November 1313 Edward II received a petition for aid from 'the people of Scotland' (in practice this meant that part of the political community of the southeast which was still in English allegiance) pleading for help against the Scots. They claimed that the counties of the southeast had lost the sum of £20,000 over the preceding three years and had recently been forced to find 1000 quarters[1] of wheat for King Robert's armies in exchange for a truce until Martinmas (2 November).

The Bruce party was not the only problem faced by the people of Lothian, Berwickshire and Roxburghshire. The English garrison at Berwick, possibly for want of adequate and regular supplies from England, had taken to raiding the very people that they were there to protect. A foray into the lands of the Earl of Dunbar had resulted in the loss of 4,000 sheep and the kidnapping of thirty people who were held for ransom.[2] Naturally, this soured relations between the administration and the community, but it also undermined the credibility of King Edward's lordship. If he could not protect the community from his own troops, let alone from the activities of the enemy, there was little to recommend support for the Plantagenet cause. Even the senior officials of the administration were vulnerable to the depredations of the Berwick garrison. Sir Adam Gordon, a significant landowner and Edward II's justiciar for Lothian had been taken prisoner and had the humiliation of having to promise to appear before Edward for judgement, though no specific charges seem to have been levelled against him. Gordon had been a consistent supporter of the Plantagenet party for many years,[3] and obviously enjoyed King Edward's trust. If a man of his prominence and proven loyalty could be treated in such a manner, there was little prospect of good government for the rest of the community.

By the time Edward received the 'envoys' of the people of Scotland – Sir Adam Gordon and Patrick Earl of Dunbar – the truce was either close to expiry or had in fact already expired, and the community was clearly desperate for a resolution to their problems. On 28 November Edward issued a response in which he declared his intention to mount a major offensive in the summer of 1314. This may not have given very much encouragement to his remaining supporters in southern Scotland, but realistically it was probably as much as he could do. Raising an army – and finding the funds to keep it paid and fed – was a complicated business and could not be achieved on the spur of the moment. It is not impossible that Edward had already decided to lead an army to Scotland before this. It is also credible to assume that the presentation of the petition was a political device used in order to give Edward opportunity to announce his intentions appropriately. What cannot be seriously doubted is that Edward planned to march into Scotland long before Edward Bruce made his pact with Philip Moubray.

This would not be Edward's first attempt to restore his fortunes. His campaign of 1310–11 was not wholly ineffective and Edward was certainly active in the Roxburghshire/Selkirkshire/Peeblesshire area in September 1310.[4] He had taken an army north and had remained in Scotland until July 1311, but had achieved very little. In part, this was because he could not bring the Scots to battle. King Robert retired before him, stripping the countryside of livestock and crops, thus putting a considerable strain on Edward's logistical situation. Edward's withdrawal from Scotland was a great boost to Robert's reputation as well as a blow to the credibility of the occupation government and the prestige of English kingship. The 1310–11 campaign may have helped to bolster the occupation forces for a brief period, but Edward's withdrawal undermined confidence in his ability to push the Scots onto the defensive. A number of prominent lords, including the earls of Atholl and Strathearn, who had previously supported the Balliol or Plantagenet causes, defected to King Robert. For Edward, the return to England was a matter of 'out of the frying pan and into the fire,' since his own magnates were now plotting to restrict his authority.

By late 1313 there were a number of factors fuelling Edward's desire to seize the military initiative in Scotland: the growing power of the Bruce party; the increasing vulnerability of the remaining garrisons; the plight of his Scottish supporters and the need to restore his authority at home. There was also a pressing political dimension in Scotland. He had already lost the resources of several significant adherents among the Scottish nobility to military action and through disenchantment, but in October – probably at a Parliament held at Cambuskenneth Abbey or a meeting of the King's council at Dundee[5] – it would seem that King Robert had issued a proclamation to the effect that any Scottish landholders who were still in the peace of Edward II would have one year to join the Bruce party or be forfeited forever. The fact that Robert could safely hold a Parliament at Cambuskenneth at all was an indication both of his own confidence and of the weakness of the occupation forces. Cambuskenneth lies close to Stirling, so clearly the commanders of the garrisons at Stirling and Edinburgh did not believe that their forces were adequate to the task of preventing Robert from making what was both a political statement and a military challenge. Robert many have been emboldened by the fall of Linlithgow pele in the late summer of 1313. The loss of Linlithgow was a serious blow since it had held one of the largest of the occupation garrisons, but it was also a political loss of some magnitude. Before the war, Linlithgow had been one of the three constabularies of the sheriffdom of Edinburgh with little or nothing in the way of a standing garrison – there was no castle, but it was a fairly important centre of local government. In 1301[6] Edward I had chosen the town as the location for a major military base capable of housing a substantial body of men-at-arms. Its loss increased the isolation of Stirling, but could also be seen as a failure to protect the legacy of Edward I.

Robert's threat to forfeit men who remained in Plantagenet allegiance was obviously valueless if he could not secure the territory in question, but by late 1313 his progress against the occupation government had made that a real possibility. Edward had no choice but to take action in the light of Robert's declaration, but it would be unreasonable to assume that he had not planned to do so anyway. The threats to Stirling and to Edward's Scottish adherents may have put pressure on Edward to move more quickly and perhaps to choose Stirling as the primary objective, but he was surely intending to take action of some sort from October 1313 at the latest.

The fall of Roxburgh in February and Edinburgh in March increased the pressure on Edward further. As well as the blow to his prestige and political credibility there was the practical issue of the advantage that the capture of Lothian and Roxburghshire gave to King Robert. Obviously it was politically advantageous in that it enhanced Robert's standing, but it also extended his power base. Lothian was probably the most populous and wealthy sheriffdom in Scotland, and, though the county had suffered from having to pay large sums to avoid incursions by the Bruce party, the fact that they had been spared pillage and destruction meant that the local economy was largely undamaged. Robert could reasonably expect to acquire considerable amounts of money, provisions and manpower if he could impose his kingship over the Lothian communities.

All of these factors would have brought about an invasion sooner or later regardless of the situation at Stirling. However important Stirling castle might be, it was hardly likely to be worthwhile to mount a major offensive just to save one stronghold. It is, in any case, easy to exaggerate the significance of Stirling castle as a military installation. The castle is generally seen as the means of dominating the lowest crossing of the River Forth – 'the gateway to the Highlands' – and to central and north eastern Scotland generally. It was perfectly possible to cross the Forth lower in its course, but only by ferry – not really a practical route for a major army. However the castle could only control the crossing if the garrison could operate freely. The Bridge was far too far from the castle to allow the garrison to control the crossing with the missile weapons of the day. If the striking force of the garrison was contained within the walls and precincts of the castle they might as well not be there at all. Containment would, of course, require a considerable commitment of men, and Robert would probably have struggled to maintain such a force indefinitely. For military reasons as well as political ones, Robert would have been eager to capture it and release the troops for other operations.

The various turns of events in late 1313 – Gordon and Dunbar's petition, King Robert's proclamation about forfeiture, the general decay of the occupation government and the political situation of Edward II – were all factors that made an English offensive in 1314 a strong possibility. Had it not been for the challenge of Edward Bruce's pact, Edward could have chosen to make the recovery of Edinburgh. He could invade Scotland by the western route, pass over the Clyde and carry the war into Bruce-held territory with the intention of forcing Robert to abandon his position at Stirling and either meet Edward's army at a different location, or continue his policy of avoiding battle. Either of these options might have proved more effective than seeking battle at the earliest opportunity.

It would seem that no historian has considered the possibility that Robert, aware that Edward was preparing to make a move against him, deliberately chose to encourage Edward to make Stirling his target. The advantages in such a plan would have been considerable. If Robert could be confident that Edward would take his forces to Stirling, he would not have to commit extensive forces anywhere else and could therefore concentrate the largest possible force in a location central enough to make the mustering of troops and gathering of supplies relatively straightforward. The terrain offered good options for a defensive battle and possibilities for an offensive one, but it was also a place from which he could retire safely if necessary. It is not safe to assume that Robert always intended to fight a major action at all, but equally it would not be safe to assume that he did not deliberately exploit the political conditions to try to ensure that Edward's army would aim for Stirling. It is even conceivable that Robert's dismay on hearing of Edward Bruce's pact with Moubray was in itself a piece of deception.[7] If Robert was eager to induce Edward to march on Stirling, he can hardly have wanted Edward to know that this was the case.

Regardless of whether or not King Robert intended to offer or accept battle, there were several factors which might have encouraged him to gather an army. His own prestige might suffer considerable damage if he allowed Edward to enter Scotland without fear of serious opposition, and failure to prevent the English from crossing the Forth might well lead to the loss of much of what had been gained since 1307. In 1296, Edward I had been able to march as far north as Elgin without serious opposition. Of course, Edward had been aware that there was no Scottish army worthy of the name to obstruct his progress, whereas Robert had assembled a major army in 1314. Even so, if Edward was able to cross the Forth, Robert might not be able to find a suitable location in which he could offer battle on reasonable terms, and Edward's undoubted superiority in cavalry would give him a tremendous advantage in a mobile campaign. Just as significantly, Edward would not actually need to procure a victory on the battlefield to undermine Robert's kingship, nor did he necessarily need to gain and retain a great deal of territory. If he could march through eastern Scotland, perhaps as far as Aberdeen, destroying crops and towns, Robert's credibility as a source of good lordship would be seriously undermined and his reputation for military effectiveness might sustain a blow from which it would never recover. The political and military situation may not have made a confrontation absolutely unavoidable form Robert's perspective, but failure to make effective resistance certainly carried a high risk. The risk would have been greater if Robert had raised a large army and then not led it into battle. Mustering a major army called for a national effort in both manpower and produce. If men came to believe that they were deserting their homes, families and livelihoods to no apparent purpose it might well prove difficult to motivate them to serve in the future. Even if the army mustered at Stirling was not committed to battle, so long as the English were prevented from achieving their objective of destabilising the Bruce government and so long as the men in the army could see that their sacrifices were not in vain, then Robert's reputation was probably safe.

The risks of raising an army and then disbanding it without coming to blows with the enemy may have been significant, but there were potential gains to be had from doing so and successfully preventing Edward from achieving anything very positive from the campaign.

The act of raising a large army was a matter of some political importance. Demanding military service helped to make people accustomed to his kingship, and there had been a god deal of military activity over the past years. For the infantry who formed the majority of Robert's force, the bulk of that service had been discharged at sieges. The value of that experience was, perhaps, rather limited. Sieges were, by and large, more a matter of containment and isolation than of combat, but the fact that men were accustomed to life with the army – even if it was only for forty days a year at most – would have been of considerable benefit to King Robert. Such men were accustomed to following particular leaders, and they were accustomed to – and understood the importance of – obeying orders. More importantly, given the success of Robert and his lieutenants in capturing towns and castles – whether through failure of supply, surrender pacts, coup-de-main operations or stormings – the men were also accustomed to winning. This is not to say that all of the men in Robert's army of 1314 had seen action in the past, or that they had always been victorious, but that a large proportion of them had taken part in successful operations. Service at a siege may not have been very exciting, but it did provide opportunities for training and building confidence.

Robert started to muster his army around the end of May and thus had several weeks to develop the skills and esprit de corps that any army needs if it is to have confidence and strong morale. He would not have failed to ensure that his men were properly fed and we know, from Barbour's account, that he was careful to restrict recruitment to those who had proper equipment.

Additionally, Robert – and no doubt the army as a whole – would have been aware that their opponents were almost bound to arrive at the battlefield in a less than ideal condition.

The Scottish army, on the other hand, would be rested, well trained and well organised. Further, the experience of the Scots over the preceding eight years or so had largely been one of repeated success. The only major operation to have failed utterly was an attempt of Berwick in 1312 which had been foiled by the barking of a dog, alerting the garrison to the approach of the Scots. There can be little doubt that King Robert was prepared to avoid battle in the summer of 1314, but equally we cannot assume that he was unwilling to give battle if the circumstances were propitious. He had evidently raised a substantial army and brought it to a good standard of training. Quite how large that army was is open to question; chronicle estimates cannot be taken at face value. Barbour's assertion that Robert had thirty thousand men under arms as well as a great number of ancillaries is obviously a gross exaggeration, but we should not assume that he intended the reader to take the figure literally. Quite how strong that army may have been is open to question. The assumption that the Scots numbered somewhere in the region of five to ten thousand men is probably well founded in the sense that we might reasonably take these figures as the parameters of the army. We might assume that his strength would have been limited by the fact that some of the most populous and prosperous counties of Scotland had only come under his control since the capture of Edinburgh and Roxburgh castles. This would, however, depend on the assumption that the Edinburgh and Roxburgh garrisons were able to maintain Plantagenet administration in those areas right up to the moment when they fell to the Scots. Given the strong commitment of the political communities to the Bruce cause in the 1330s, despite the power of Edward III's occupation government – over one hundred men and women were forfeited for resistance in 1335–7[8] – it would be rash to assume that Robert did not enjoy a degree of support in 1314. Indeed, the men of Lothian and Roxburghshire faced a variety of pressures to turn out for the Bruce cause. If Robert stripped the counties to deny produce to the advancing English army, as he did in later campaigns, Lothian men would have had little choice other than to serve. Furthermore, there would be some pressure to join the army to show loyalty to the new regime, particularly if their families and goods had been evacuated north of the Forth.

Even so, what we know of Scottish armies in the later Middle Ages generally would suggest that an absolute outside limit of 10,000 combatants is a realistic estimate, though it is possible that Robert could only field 5000 men.

Equally, he may have brought as many as 10,000 men to the fight. There is no particularly good reason to assume otherwise, though it would surely have been very difficult to control three formations, each consisting of the better part of 3,000 men, if we assume that the balance of the army consisted of men-at-arms and archers.

There seems to be a general assumption that the archery element of a Scottish army would not exceed 10 per cent of the whole, though the army that served in France in the early 1400s seems to have consisted of about 4,000 archers and 2,000 men-at-arms and spearmen. The quantity of archer service stipulated in charters is no guide to availability of archers from the community as a whole. The latter would be trained, competent men – men for whom military service over and above universal obligation was a normal part of life. Of course, successful massed archery in large numbers did not depend on individual marksmanship, but in the effectiveness of a large number of arrows delivered in controlled concentrations.

The proportion of different troops within the close-combat element of the army is as hard to judge as the total strength. We might assume that the men-at-arms were concentrated in one body under the Earl Marischal, Sir Robert Keith, as a subtracted reserve to react to threats or to exploit opportunities, however it is evident that several senior magnates served on foot in the main formations of the army, including the king himself. It is unthinkable that he, or Edward Bruce, did not go into action in the company of their immediate military entourages, thus the man-at-arms element of the Scottish army as a whole is likely to have been considerably in excess of the 500 men-at-arms mentioned by Barbour. The army that David II led to defeat at Neville's Cross may have had as many as 2,000 men-at-arms in its ranks, which would certainly represent a really successful mobilisation, but not one beyond credibility. David may of course have been able to recruit more men-at-arms than his father thirty years before, since there was no real competition for authority in the southern counties. But even if we were to assume that Robert could not call on the men-at-arms of Lothian and Roxburghshire, it would be unrealistic to assume that the loss of two counties would deprive him of seventy-five per cent of the available men-at-arms. If pressed to give an estimate of the total number of men-at-arms under Robert's command at Bannockburn, it would not be unreasonable to suggest a total of somewhere in the region of 1,000.

The absence of English records relating to the army of 1314 means that estimating the numbers in Edward's army is fraught with difficulties. It is, for example, very easy to assume that of the 22,140 men called to service from

English and Welsh counties and a further 4,000 demanded from Ireland,[9] only a modest proportion turned up at all and that a very large number would have deserted by 23–24 June. To assume that the turnout was only in the region of fifty or sixty percent – the case in a previous campaign – is not altogether convincing.

We can certainly be confident that fewer served than were called and that desertion would have been a problem, but the rate of desertion in an army raised for service in winter would almost certainly be very much greater than in a force raised for a summer campaign. We should also be wary of assumptions that large numbers should never be taken seriously, simply because they refer to the strength of a medieval army. In February 1298, an army of about 21,000 had been assembled at Newcastle for service in Scotland. This may have been an exceptionally successful muster, however sizeable infantry forces were raised on this, and other occasions. Professor Barrow[10] has drawn attention to material which might suggest that Edward I had arranged for 60,000 to be in pay at Newcastle for March 1296, however there was a great difference between calling men to arms and actually having them turn up. Edward called for 16,000 men for his campaign in 1300,[11] but the force peaked at about 9,000. Similarly, we cannot assume that all of the demands for troops have actually survived. Edward II's writ of 27 May 1314 only sought to enlist 3,000 troops from Wales, which is in sharp contrast to the Falkirk campaign, where the majority of the infantry were Welshmen. Although he could count on the support of some Scottish lords, Edward cannot have gained much in the way of infantrymen from Scottish sources. Most of the Scots in English allegiance were men who had been driven from their estates and were not, therefore, in a position to demand the service due from their erstwhile tenants. Some men may have been forthcoming from the properties of lords in the border areas, assuming that the Bruce party had yet to establish its authority in those localities, but the contribution, if any at all, must surely have been insignificant.

Additionally, the writs issued in 1314 refer only to demands placed on specific communities. They take no account of men volunteering for service in search of plunder, adventure or pardons for criminal behaviour. There is no record material relating to Irish troops at Bannockburn, but considerable numbers had served in earlier Scottish campaigns and it is quite possible that records of their service did not survive defeat. Even so, it is unlikely (but not impossible) that the infantry component of Edward's army exceeded a figure in the region of 15,000 men. The same applies to the cavalry element, however here we can have a little more faith in the estimates of chroniclers. There is no obvious reason to assume that Edward II's army in 1314 was less well furnished with men-at-arms than that of Edward I in 1298, in which case we would probably be quite close to the mark in accepting a figure of something a little in excess of two thousand heavy cavalry, indeed it would be difficult to make a case for anything less given the chronicle estimates, what we know of English armies of the period generally and the fact that Edward's army was seen by contemporaries as an impressive force by the standards of the day.

It would be easy to dismiss estimates of the strength of both the Scottish and English armies as mere guesswork, which, to a considerable degree, they are. Barbour and the other chroniclers offer quite incredible numbers, but as Dr McKisack has pointed out, modern attempts to reduce Edward's army to 'Between 6,000 and 7,000 infantry with no more than 450–500 cavalry, are hardly less so.'[12]

Even if that estimate of infantry strength is a valid assessment – and there is no particular reason to assume that it is – the cavalry estimate does not bear examination. J. E. Morris[13] suggests that the heavy cavalry element of the 1298 army was in the region of 2,400, and has drawn attention to the fact that 830 protections were issued for the 1314 campaign, however these protections were issued for the members of the retinues of particular lords. The Earl of Gloucester's retinue alone received 132 protections and a large proportion of the balance of 698 were given for the retinues of just eight men: the Despensers (62), the Earl of Pembroke (96), the Earl of Hereford (45), Richard Grey (26), John Moubray (26), Henry Beaumont (29) and Robert Clifford (12). At least another sixty protections can be found in Bain's *Calendar of Documents Relating to Scotland*. Again, we must remember that not all of the men who served would have sought protections and that we have no way of estimating numbers of those who might have served voluntarily or of any Irish contingent. In 1296 Richard De Burgh, Earl of Ulster, supplied a body of 310 men-at-arms including seven bannerets, and in 1301 he provided 264 men-at-arms.[14] De Burgh may not have served at Bannockburn, but he was certainly with Edward at Newminster on 29 May and, as Professor Barrow has pointed out,[15] he is unlikely to have come empty-handed. Further, there is no record material to allow us to make an estimate of foreign volunteers (though they are likely to have been few in number) or of Scots in English service. Again, these men are not likely to have constituted a major contribution, but it is difficult to believe that the various major Scottish lords who had been driven from their estates did not bring parties of men-at-arms. Sir

Laurence Abernethy led a party of eighty men-at-arms, and it would be unrealistic to assume that he was the only Scot who was able and willing to provide a retinue for Edward's army.

There is no unequivocal evidence to prove the presence of either light cavalry or hobelars in the English army, though equally there is no evidence to indicate otherwise. J.E.Morris, making the point that light cavalry were a rarity in the armies of Edward I and Edward II, dismisses Walter of Hemingburgh's assertion that the army of the Falkirk campaign included 4,000 light cavalry in addition to 3,000 men-at-arms, but it is difficult to imagine that there was no light cavalry or hobelar element at all. In 1298 and again in 1310, the Earl of Ulster provided modest, but not negligible, numbers of light cavalry in addition to his contribution of men-at-arms, but there is no reason to suppose that there was a substantial body of such troops in the army as a whole, useful though they might have been. They certainly had no role in the battle as far as the chronicle records go, but there again, hobelars and perhaps other cavalry below the status of men-at-arms, would have dismounted for action and would therefore not be distinguished from the infantry.

Finally, there may have been contingents of troops who served, but whose presence was not recorded, or rather that no record of their service has survived. Edward I employed a company of mounted crossbowmen for the 1298 campaign, though there is no record of their presence in battle. We should also expect that there would have been modest units of specialists of one kind or another – pioneers, miners, etc. – whose normal role would not necessarily have excused them from combat.

On balance, though we must obviously reject the wilder claims of chroniclers, we must accept that the English army of 1314 was an imposing force, sufficiently so to give Edward and his lieutenants confidence that they could attack the Scots, even if they were deployed in a very strong defensive position, with every confidence of gaining a major victory.

There can be no doubt that Edward and his lieutenants did expect to defeat the Scots. Not only did they lead a larger force, but their experience indicated that the Scots were likely to avoid battle if they could, and that if they could have battle forced upon them, they would be very likely to lose. The English army was a versatile tool, and if victory could not be secured through the power of a cavalry attack, the deployment of the army could be adjusted to disrupt Scottish formations and allow the cavalry to break their ranks. There was nothing particularly innovative about fielding large bodies of spearmen. The Scots had done that at Falkirk and had been defeated by the application of combined arms tactics.

This had been achieved in the past. Like the Scots, the Welsh had depended on spearmen in their wars with Edward I. At Builth in 1282 the English archers had played a vital part in the fighting, and as Hemingburgh put it:

> ... through our archers, who were fighting by concert in between our cavalry, many of them fell.

Similarly at the battle of Maes Madoc, an attack by the English cavalry was initially unsuccessful, but then the archers and crossbowmen were deployed:

> ... and when many of the spearmen had been brought down by the bolts, the horse charged again and defeated them with greater slaughter, it is thought, than had ever been suffered by them in past times.

Some writers have taken this to mean that the English had developed a habitual posture for battle which placed bodies of archers between bodies of men-at-arms, but this takes no account of other battlefield experiences such as Falkirk. Here, the cavalry formations were very clearly separate bodies, and in smaller actions, such as Dunbar or Roslin, the cavalry fought without any infantry support at all. The practice of deploying archers on the wings of close-combat troops which would bring about the great longbow victories of Dupplin Muir, Halidon Hill, Crecy, Poitiers and Agincourt had yet to be invented.

One of the considerations which may have given the English commanders confidence of victory was the knowledge that the Scots had very little experience of large engagements, however there was very little experience of that kind in the English army either. The last great battle of manoeuvre for both sides was Falkirk. Given that the army of Robert I was little different in structure to that of William Wallace, Edward and his subordinates may well have felt that the tactical principles which had brought victory in 1298 would give them another victory in 1314. This might well have proved correct if the Scots had followed Wallace's example and stood on the defensive. If they withstood an initial attack – whether by foot or horse – the army could be reformed for another attempt. If, on the other hand, the Scots chose to attack, there would be neither space not time to achieve redeployment and mount a new attack.

Most of the more senior members of the national political and military elites
of England and Scotland were present at Bannockburn: the Earls of Moray and
Carrick; Lord Douglas and the Stewart for the Scots; the Earls of Pembroke,
Hereford, and Gloucester, and several prominent barons such as Beaumont and
Clifford for the English. Equally, several major figures were conspicuous by
their absence. The Earl of Lancaster's failure to attend his king is hardly surprising; the two men were hardly on good terms. On the other hand, the Earl of
Dunbar was a remarkable absentee. He was certainly in the peace of Edward
II in the summer of 1314 and was instrumental in helping Edward to make his
escape to Berwick after the battle. Earl Patrick – and his father before him –
had been steadfast in support of the Plantagenet cause for nearly twenty years.
Under normal circumstances, Edward would surely have expected his presence in the English army at the head of the men-at-arms of Roxburghshire
and other areas in which the Earl had extensive property and influence, however the circumstances were far from normal. The network of garrisons that
had imposed Plantagenet rule in the east of Scotland had fallen to the Scots
over the preceding year and more. By the spring of 1313 Patrick's position had
become precarious in the extreme. The only English garrison close enough
to give him any kind of support was Berwick, and he could not afford to rely
on the effectiveness or commitment of the troops there. Both Patrick and Sir
Adam Gordon had had cause to petition Edward on behalf of the communities
of Lothian, Roxburghshire and Berwickshire in late 1313 about the behaviour
of the Berwick garrison. They were inclined to help themselves to the property
of the locals, even kidnapping them for ransom, but worse than that, they were
prone to mounting operations that infringed the truces that the local people
had made with the Bruce party. These truces were expensive undertakings.
Since he enjoyed complete operational superiority, Robert could impose a
truce on terms that suited him. Generally, they involved very considerable sums
of money and very often a right for Robert's troops to pass freely through the
area in question. Evidently Edward's administration in Lothian and the south
east had more or less collapsed by the summer of 1314. Whether King Robert
was in a position to impose his rule effectively is a different matter. Clearly he
had not been able to exert the level of lordship necessary to force the Earl of
Dunbar to turn out for the Bruce cause.

The Earl was not the only notable Scottish absentee. Sir Alexander Seton, a
prominent baron with interests in the south eastern counties, had in fact been
one of the first men to commit himself to the Bruce cause in 1306,[16] but had
defected to the Plantagenet party by 1308. He had continued in the peace of

Edward II for the next six years, presumably fulfilling his duties and obligations as a senior member of the political community of Lothian. He joined Edward's army in 1314, but chose to return to the Bruce party during the night of 23–24 June.[17] The political choices of a man like Seton were not simply a matter of personal commitment. As a prominent baron, he would obviously have a strong influence on his tenants and relatives, but he would also have a more general leadership role in the wider community. Neighbouring landholders might well look to him for a lead in political matters, perhaps assuming that a man of his stature would have better sources of information, but certainly well aware of the power that he could wield in the vicinity. Seton's defection may have been one of the factors that persuaded Robert to carry the fight to the English. Seton was an experienced soldier and his change of heart would not have occurred if he had been confident that Edward II would achieve a victory on the 24 June. He can hardly have been unaware of the progress of the Bruce party and the nature and strength of the Scottish army, so we must assume that he was making an informed choice on the basis of the capabilities of Edward's and Robert's forces, and on their relative merits as commanders.

Seton was a useful addition to Robert's cause, but he was not yet a man of very great substance either politically or militarily. Failure to attract the support of the Earl of Dunbar and other senior figures in the political community was a more pressing problem for Robert I. The prestige of his kingship was undermined by the absence of any major noble, but failure to procure the support of men like Dunbar and, to a lesser extent, Adam Gordon, had a military dimension. Although men-at-arms could be, and were, recruited from all over Scotland, the availability of such service was very much smaller in the north and west than in the south and east. Although the cavalry service due to the crown from Gordon and Dunbar for their lands would not have provided a significant force in itself, the political influence of these men was very extensive, and undoubtedly discouraged support for the Bruce cause from other members of the landholding communities. As long as Bothwell castle was retained in Plantagenet control, there would be considerable pressure for the local landholders to continue in their allegiance to Edward II. This was a matter of some importance militarily, since failure to bring these areas under control would have had an adverse effect on the numbers of men-at-arms that Robert could call to his service.

Equally, the absence of the Earl of Dunbar and the defection of Seton can be seen as indications of the state of the English administration in Scotland. Both could claim – perhaps with some justice – that their resources were already fully committed in resisting the expansion of Bruce administration, but seemingly neither was very confident of Edward's ability to bring Bruce to battle and achieve victory. The former point was probably more of an issue than the latter in the minds of Dunbar, Seton and others. If, as had happened in the past, Edward failed to force battle on the Scots, he would almost certainly be forced to disband his army and return to England without having made any serious progress against the Bruce party. This would inevitably strengthen Robert's hand against those who remained in English allegiance.

Confidence in Edward to protect the interests of landholders had obviously diminished by 1314, but clearly not to the extent of a universal defection to the Bruce cause. By mounting an expedition to Scotland, Edward was declaring his intention to restore his administration through armed strength. He certainly had every intention of bringing the Scots to battle if at all possible, but was probably realistic enough to realize that the Scots would very probably choose to avoid a major engagement, as they had in the past. On the other hand, if he could force a battle – and he would have every confidence that he would win one – he might well be able to finish off the Bruce party once and for all. In the event of Robert and Edward Bruce being killed in action or taken prisoner, the Bruce cause would really have no future at all, in which case, Edward would almost certainly be able to establish his rule with little, if any, political opposition. Clearly a victory for Edward would have the potential to bring the Scottish war to a successful conclusion, an outcome that would greatly enhance his political prestige credibility at home and abroad. Even if the Bruce party survived a major battle in the sense that Robert or Edward escaped to fight another day, the credibility of the patriotic party would have been dealt a major blow. A significant battlefield defeat at Stirling would probably have led to wholesale defections from the Bruce party and the recovery of towns and territory across the country.

# Locating the Battle

In the late eighteenth century, the battle was believed to have been fought in the area around a feature known as the borestone. The stone itself has long disappeared, but it is believed to have lain in the vicinity of the Bannockburn Visitor Centre maintained by the National Trust for Scotland. Ascribing specific locations for the different actions that occurred on 23 and 24 June is a thankless and ultimately futile undertaking. Of the four separate fights – at 'The Entry', St Ninians, Cambuskenneth Abbey and the main engagement itself – only the raid that David de Strathbogie mounted on King Robert's trains at Cambuskenneth can be identified with any great degree of confidence; the remaining tower of the Abbey still stands.

In a sense, this is not really a problem of any great significance. For the purposes of tactical analysis it matters very little whether an action took place at 'this spot' or at another location in the vicinity, so long as the topography is compatible with what we know from the source material. The narrative sources do not give us sufficient information to allow absolute precision in locating the fighting, but the principles are absolutely clear. Again, whether the fighting was conducted at one given spot or another is not of great importance, though of course it would be very satisfying if the locations could be ascertained with more precision. It is not impossible that this may yet be settled by archaeology.

One of the very few finds which, on balance, can reasonably be attributed to the summer of 1314 is a bodkin arrow head which was uncovered in the vicinity of the National Trust for Scotland's Visitor Centre. It is of course possible that the arrowhead has no connection with Bannockburn at all, and that it was used – or even just mislaid – at an earlier or later date. It has been suggested that it may not even have any connection with military activity at all; the New Park was, after all, a hunting preserve. However, bodkin arrows were developed for warfare, and hunting arrows were generally much broader and more heavily barbed. Even so, though we can probably safely assume that the arrowhead was at one time in the hands of a Scottish archer, we cannot be sure that it was actually used in the fighting at The Entry. How can we be certain that it was not shot in an incident relating to the Scottish siege of Stirling Castle in 1299 or the English siege of 1304? It could even be argued that, since only one arrowhead has been recovered from the area, it is actually unlikely that the fighting occurred in the vicinity of the find at all, but this is hard to accept.

A medieval battlefield was likely to be picked clean after the event by local salvagers. More importantly, once the action was completed, the archers of the victorious side would surely search the field for arrows to replenish their quivers; arrows were not cheap. There is, however, more material to support the National Trust site as the location for the fight at 'The Entry'. We are aware that the southern boundary of the New Park lay in that general area and that a road ran through it, probably along much the same route as the modern A80. Further, the lie of the land immediately to the south of the Visitor Centre would have provided a good site for the Scots, since the English force would not have been able to see them until they reached the brow of the hill. It would seem, then, that neither the source material nor archaeology allows us to agree on a precise identification, but that the cumulative value of the sources and tactical analysis can give an *approximate* location and a reasonably clear picture of the *nature* of the action. The same problems apply to the other action of 23 June – Moray's engagement with Beaumont and Clifford.

Moray may have met Clifford and Beaumont at a distance of one hundred meters or one thousand metres from St Ninians chapel, indeed we cannot be certain that the location that we associate with the chapel was identical to the location of the chapel seven hundred years ago, though the only alternative, Dunipace, does not seem to be a realistic possibility.[1] If we cannot be certain of the precise location, we can at least identify the general area by the course of the action as described by Barbour and by Sir Thomas Grey, whose father was captured in the fighting.

An advance party of English cavalry passed across the low-lying ground to the east of the Torwood, keeping to the open ground to avoid ambush. They were then intercepted by a Scottish force which moved out of wooded terrain and on to the lower ground to the east of St Ninians chapel (see 'First Clash – St Ninians'). Beyond that, all we can be sure of is that the two forces met on the plain. Further, battles are not static events. Moray's men were stationary when the English cavalry came into contact, but once they had achieved supremacy they pushed the English away. Other than the fact that the English force seems to have split in two with one party making for Stirling castle and the other retiring on the main body of the army, we cannot even say in which direction the Scots advanced. Again, this is not terribly significant. Moray's force was able to push the English cavalry hard enough to split them into two parties, but they could hardly pursue either body. As Barbour tells us, they halted to catch their breath, having performed a considerable feat of arms. The nature and progress of both of these actions are quite clear from contemporary accounts, but unless more information comes to light, there is very little prospect of furthering our current level of knowledge.

The same is true of the main action on the morning of 24 June. We can be reasonably confident that the Scots made their way from higher ground to lower ground and advanced to contact on a stretch of relatively narrow but firm, flat terrain to the south and east of Stirling on the north side of the Bannock Burn, but no more can be said with any great degree of certainty. We can, however, make some valid observations about the nature of the terrain and of the nature of the fighting. All contemporary accounts agree on the nature of the ground, though a great many historians have chosen to reject that information.

Early references to the battle often do not mention the name Bannockburn at all, but realte to a battle at or near Stirling. This should not come as a surprise; few people outside of Stirlingshire would ever have heard of Bannockburn, but many people in England, let alone Scotland, would have heard of Stirling. As Professor Barrow has pointed out,[2] we should not think of Bannockburn as a village, but as a hamlet. It was certainly an identifiable community, long known as Bannock, and the Burn was named for the hamlet, not vice versa. The hamlet of Bannock was significant enough to have two subdivisions: Ochtirbannok and Skeoch. Skeoch at least was a fairly valuable property. In 1329, the 'ferm', that is the rental due to the crown, amounted to the not inconsiderable sum of £26, 13s, 4d. Superficially, this would seem to be a carefully calculated sum, but in fact the figure is an expression of a round sum of forty marks.[3] According to Trokelowe, the main action occurred on Bannokesmora. This should not be confused with the modern usage of Muir of Bannockburn, which lies to the south of the burn. The term 'muir' can itself lead to confusion; it is not necessarily synonymous with the English 'moor'. The latter may be interpreted as rough heathland of no real value, but 'muir' tends to indicate grazing in common use by a community such as the Burgh Muirs of Edinburgh or Peebles. Medieval battles were generally named for a settlement, not a geographical feature, and Professor Barrow[4] is surely correct to reject MacKenzie's belief that the fighting occurred on the fields of the farms of Upper Taylorton or Muirton. Alternatively, it is not impossible that Bannockburn was adopted as a name for the fight because it was the last settlement that the English army passed through on their way to the battlefield.

The biggest single barrier to understanding the nature of the physical combat of the main battle is the distribution of the bogs, pools, swamps and trenches which prevented the English from delivering effective attacks. Curiously, none of the contemporary writers seem to have been aware of the dramatic effect these various barriers had on the course of the main battle. Grey, admittedly, refers to the ditch of the Bannock Burn, but he also makes it very clear that the English army had already crossed over the Bannock before the fighting commenced, that the battle had already been decided and that the ditch became a problem for the English in retreat, not in attack.

The only source which makes any reference to trenches is Trokelowe, who tells us that the Scots dug extended ditches three feet deep and three feet wide from the right to the left flanks of the army, filling them with a brittle plait of twigs, reed and sticks, and covering them with grass and weeds. Infantry might be aware of a safe passage through these, but the heavy cavalry would not be able to pass over them.

The design and execution that would be required to make the coverings of the trenches effective should be enough to warn historians not to take their existence too seriously at all, but there are other problems to be considered. In order for these trenches to be effective in the sense of being in the right place, King Robert would have had to be extremely confident that the English army would camp in a very specific location, not simply 'down in the Carse.' Just as importantly, he would have to depend on the English army failing to make even the most rudimentary reconnaissance in the immediate vicinity of their camp, and to trust that no word of these trenches would reach the ears of the Stirling garrison. Despite being contained in a tactical sense, they were clearly capable of making contact with the English army, as Sir Philip Moubray was able to meet with King Edward on the evening of 23 June.

If the trenches were located between the Scottish and English armies it is difficult, if not impossible, to see how they could have failed to be an impediment to the advance of the Scots. Dr De Vries[5] sets much store by these trenches in his account of the battle. He gets around the issue of whether the trenches would have affected the Scottish formations by asserting that Trokelowe missed the essential point, that is, that the Scots were on the defensive and the English attacked. All contemporary material, however, points in exactly the opposite direction. Source material points to a Scottish attack, indeed it is a challenge to see how the Scots could possibly have won the battle unless they attacked. Had they remained static, the English army would have been able to reform and adopt a different form of attack with impunity. Finally, we might expect that the trenches would have left some archaeological trace in the way of parch-marks, but none have been identified.

We can make similar observations about the pools, bogs and swamps which litter modern plans of the battle. The 'pools' originate in a misunderstanding of the word 'pows' – small slow streams which crossed the lower areas of the Carse. There is nothing in the contemporary evidence to indicate that they had any affect whatsoever on the course of the battle. The same applies to marshes and bogs. Edward II believed that his enemies were gathering:

> … in strong and marshy places, where access for horses will be difficult, between us and our castle of Stirling.[6]

but this communication was written well in advance of the campaign and is not in any sense a description of the battlefield. Edward clearly expected the Scots to adopt a defensive posture in a location which would be a challenge to cavalry, but he still expected to fight on horseback; access to the Scots might be difficult, but he did not expect it to be impossible. Furthermore, it is not as if the terrain around Stirling would have been *terra incognita* to his lieutenants, or even perhaps to himself. Several of the senior officers of Edward's army had visited Stirling at some point in their career; Edward himself may have been present at his father's siege of Stirling Castle in 1304. Sir Philip Moubray can hardly have been unaware of the nature of the terrain and was certainly in contact with Edward on the night of 23/24th June. Surely he would have brought any treacherous swampland to Edward's attention.

Not only do bogs and marshes fail to appear in any of the contemporary material, but what we know of the terrain as it stood in the later Middle Ages does not fit well with any suggestion of a battle in the mire. There were several mills in the immediate vicinity, including Milton of Bannock, Park Mill, Skeoch, Ochtirbannock and very possibly another mill at the Kirkton of St Ninians. We know from earlier record material that the corn teinds of the area were worth having,[7] that it is extremely difficult to grow wheat, barley or oats in a swamp, and that it is, in any case, difficult to believe that anyone would build mills if there was no grain to grind. Additionally, as Professor Barrow has pointed out, the name Balquiderock – a Gaelic place-name in what was most certainly an English-speaking area long before 1314 – 'would hardly have survived continually as a farm name had this area been out of cultivation for a long time.'

There is also the matter of the choice of a suitable battlefield for large bodies of spearmen and cavalry. If the major action took place in a swamp, it would have been very difficult indeed for Gloucester's force to make their charge on Carrick's formation. Just as importantly, it would have been very difficult indeed for the Scots to make an effective advance. Large bodies of men in close order cannot be expected to drill efficiently on anything other than firm ground, and if they could not keep very good dressing they would almost inevitably be overcome by a cavalry charge. Maintaining control over a body of troops which might easily be 200 metres across and five or ten metres deep would be virtually impossible if the men did not have secure footing.

Despite the absence of marshes from contemporary accounts of the main action, we cannot utterly dismiss soft ground as an issue, only as an issue in the decisive phase of the fighting. Mr Sadler[8] suggests that 'the English were pushed back toward the morass around the Pelstream,' which is certainly a possibility, though it is hardly a proven fact that the Pelstream – at least in the immediate vicinity of the action – was surrounded by morasses at all. More significantly, Sir Thomas Grey was of the opinion that the English were forced back on the Bannock Burn, not the Pelstream. Given that the English army had crossed the Bannock during the night of the 23 and that armies in precipitate retreat are inclined to retire in the direction from which they have advanced, it is difficult to see why they might move northward rather than southward.

Evidently the ground on which the battle was decided was quite firm, but the area of deployment was evidently quite narrow, since the English were unable to mount effective flanking attacks despite a very considerable superiority in cavalry. We can be reasonably sure, therefore, that the main action took place in an area bounded by serious obstacles and that these obstacles were the ditches of burns.

This does not, unfortunately, allow us to locate the battle with any great precision, other than to conclude that it occurred on firm ground and probably between the Bannock and the Pelstream. Even if we assume that the courses of these two burns today are identical to their courses in 1314, the fighting could have taken place at any point over a distance of more than a mile. There is, of course, a remote possibility that Gardiner and Oman were correct in their analysis and that far from facing the Scots across firm terrain between the Bannock and the Pelstream, the English camped on the south side of the Bannock, the Scots deployed in the north bank, and the battle took the form of an opposed river crossing. There are two insurmountable problems with that analysis which cannot be ignored. The primary problem is that none of the contemporary evidence suggests that the English had to advance across a burn on the morning of 24 June in order to attack the Scots. On the contrary, the overwhelming weight of evidence from the narrative records clearly indicates that the Scots advanced on the English and that a portion of the English cavalry under the Earl of Gloucester made a hasty counter-attack on the leading Scottish formation under the Earl of Carrick.

The other problem is one of tactical analysis. Edward II had no experience of command in a large-scale battle, but he was not a complete novice at soldiering. It is hard to see why he might chose to make an attack over terrain that would put his force at a severe disadvantage unless there was a pressing need to mount his attack immediately. The argument that he needed to move rapidly to prevent the Stirling garrison from having to surrender under the terms of the pact does not bear examination. The English army was already close enough to the castle to have effected a technical relief, and it is in any case extremely unlikely that the garrison commander would have chosen to surrender his charge as long as there was a strong and undefeated English army close at hand.

Although he was not thought of as a particularly wise or intelligent man – and with good reason – there is no reason to assume that Edward II was completely witless, but he has certainly come in for a good deal of criticism for his decision to make camp in the vicinity of the River Forth. There is no way of knowing the precise time of Edward's arrival on the scene, but

it is clear that the day was well-advanced. His army had made a considerable march on a hot day and must have been tired, so Edward's primary
requirements were security and water. The first of these could, perhaps, have
been achieved simply by making camp at some distance from the Scots
somewhere south and east of the Bannock. Concentrating the army for the
night two or three miles from the Bannock might well have been enough
to discourage the Scots from mounting a night attack, which seems to have
been regarded as a real possibility. The drawback to such a plan was that the
Scots might take advantage of the distance between the armies to effect a
withdrawal through the night. Since the destruction of Robert's army was a
primary objective of the whole invasion project, Edward could hardly afford
to let his enemy slip away, so establishing his force in the vicinity of the Scots
was, if not necessarily crucial, certainly desirable. Regardless of the exact
location chosen, it is clear that Edward's army crossed over the Bannock
on the evening, or through the night of 23–24 June, and therefore lay in
an area bounded by the Bannock burn to the south, the Pelstream burn to
the north, and with the River Forth in his rear. This afforded the English
army a degree of protection against a sudden night attack by the Scots on
three out of four possible approaches. It also meant that the English were
well-provided with water points. It is difficult to exaggerate the importance
of access to water to any classical, medieval or early modern army. The army
did not consist of men alone; there were several thousand animals to consider. A dehydrated horse is a skittish and unpredictable creature and will
very quickly run out of stamina, a matter of some importance if there is
the prospect of a major battle and possibly a lengthy pursuit. It is possible
to explain to a man that there is no prospect of water and that he will have
to make do until tomorrow, but there is little value in trying to explain that
to a horse. Further, it is important to remember that we are talking about a
great many horses.

If we accept that the heavy cavalry element of Edward's army amounted
to two or three thousand men, we must assume that between them they had
at least four to six thousand horses, probably more. In fact, the whole tally of
beasts would probably have been rather greater than that. Even a relatively
obscure knight or baron with a handful of animals would inevitable need at
least one groom who in turn would need a horse of their own if they were
to lead two or three beasts for their master. In addition there were draught
animals – some horses, some oxen – and probably meat 'on the hoof,' all of
which would need to be watered. Finally, if Edward camped his army to the

east of Broomridge, as Professor Barrow suggests,[9] he would have a relatively level and firm area to the front (west) of his army between his forces and the Scots on which he could deploy his troops for the attack that he intended to mount the following morning. To the modern observer, the site seems to be rather constricted which, for an army whose main striking arm was mounted, would be something of a risk, as mobility might be impaired in the event of a general attack by the Scots. However, we should also consider the possibility that the two operations conducted on the evening of the 23 June – at St Ninians and at The Entry – were part of a plan, as opposed to accidental engagements.

If Hereford and Gloucester had been able to establish themselves to the south of the Scots and Clifford and Beaumont to the north, any advance by the Scots could easily result in their flanks and rear being left open to English cavalry attacks, in which case the English would have been able to defeat the Scots. Alternatively, if the Scots had been discouraged from making such an attack but had been unable to withdraw through the night, the entirety of the English army could have been brought into the fight much more effectively since Edward would have had plenty of space to form up his troops for an advance into the New Park. In this case, an ensuing victory would be regarded as a stroke of genius by historians. Indeed, Edward may even have had the battle of Falkirk in mind as a model. Wallace's army was not very different from that of King Robert. Robert may have had a rather larger number of men-at-arms under his command, and the average quality of the armour of his rank and file may have been rather higher given that he apparently turned away men whose equipment was not up to the mark, but the vast majority of both armies were spearmen. Like William Wallace, Robert chose to deploy his army initially on high ground, from which he could observe the enemy. It would not have seemed unreasonable to Edward or his lieutenants to assume that Robert intended to fight a defensive battle if, indeed, he chose to fight at all. Professor Duncan finds Barrow's site unacceptable because it includes a steep incline which is not mentioned by any of the contemporary accounts, however this rather misses the point. The Scots advanced on the English and therefore deployed from the higher ground down to the plain, leaving the wooded New Park to array themselves on flat ground in front of the English position. This would rather undermine the proposition that the main action took place in the area now covered by Bannockburn High School. The school is of relatively recent construction and the ground had been levelled for the buildings and also for the extensive playing fields, but seems to have been a relatively flat expanse before that. The site would not, however, fit with the 'flat' terrain which all of the contemporary sources agree was the location of the fighting. It would, however, form a good place for King Robert to marshal his troops before their advance down to the plain, in which case it is surely a strong possibility that the initial clash between Carrick and Gloucester may have taken place in the vicinity of the railway line which cuts across the flat ground to the east of Bannockburn High School. The school grounds would also have provided a suitable location for King Robert to meet the English if he had chosen to fight a defensive action. Edward's cavalry could not have negotiated the slope to the south of the school grounds, nor could it have made a good charge pace up the slopes to the east and north. Further, although he could have marched his archers up the slope to engage the Scots, they would have been very close to the enemy and vulnerable to an advance by their infantry or a charge from their cavalry.

Edward's deployment on the 24 June is open to criticism because he lost his battle, but in fairness, he did not get to fight the sort of battle that he would have envisaged. On balance, both commanders chose their concentration and deployment areas for rational reasons; Edward's position gave him water, night protection and a clearly defined bivouac area which his officers could control reasonably easily, and Robert's move to the New Park had similar advantages. Several burns pass through the boundaries of the Park, so there was no shortage of water and the Park itself would have been defined by fences and/or ditches to control the movement of game, thus providing his officers with a clear definition of boundaries which could be monitored to prevent, or at least impede, desertion.

# Muster and March to Battle: June 1314–22 June 1314

## The March to Stirling

The English army left its muster areas at Wark and Berwick on 17–18 June[1] and marched through Lauderdale and Tweeddale to Edinburgh, arriving on or before the 22nd.[2] Here they may have collected provisions from shipping[3] before marching on to Falkirk, where they spent the night of the 22–23rd. They had made reasonably good time, but had hardly been setting speed records, even by the rather slow rates of march common to medieval armies. There is no reason to assume that the troops arrived at Falkirk in a state of exhaustion. The final leg, form Falkirk to Stirling, may have well been the longest single day's march performed by the army but, again, it was not so great a distance as to cause excessive fatigue. A similar march in mid-winter would have been a far greater achievement given the very short period of daylight. At midsummer, dawn would break before four o'clock . and there would still be enough light to march by at ten o'clock Obviously the army could not march continuously for eighteen hours, save, perhaps in a dire emergency. It would take some time to get the army on the road and there would need to be an allowance for making camp and an opportunity for men and beasts to be fed and watered. Medieval estimates of the time of day cannot be taken too seriously, but is clear that the day was well advanced by the time the leading elements of Edward's force came within sight of Stirling. Even so, the army appears to have been able to cross the Bannock Burn and make camp by dusk on 23 June. There is nothing in the contemporary material to indicate that the army had suffered a heavy loss from men or horses dropping by the wayside. Any degree of exhaustion would be as much a product of heat as anything else. Scottish summer days can be very warm, but the issue would have been more the effort of carrying arms and armour than the physical temperature. Assuming that the army had commenced its march from Falkirk within two hours of dawn and made an average of about two miles per hour, the forward elements of the infantry would probably have arrived at the Bannock burn by late afternoon. The wagons and carts of the supply train may have taken a little longer to arrive, but there is no reason to assume that they had not crossed the Bannock before the end of the day. The forward elements under the Earls of Hereford and Gloucester and Lords Clifford and Beaumont may have arrived rather earlier in the day. Sir Philip Moubray met with King Edward a few miles from Stirling 'after dinner,' which Mackenzie interpreted as meaning around midday, though perhaps mid to late afternoon would be a more realistic assessment.[4]

The army had made reasonably good time and there is no reason to assume that they arrived at Bannockburn in anything other than good order. Barbour had King Robert spread word that the English were in disarray due to the length of their journey and poor march-discipline, but this was clearly a matter of propaganda. Robert took the precaution of moving his men into the woods of the New Park, thus ensuring that his force could not be observed by the advancing English or by the Stirling garrison, but by doing so he also ensured that his troops could not see the enemy as they made their way across the Bannock and into their bivouac area. This allowed him to control information within his own army, and anything the troops knew about the enemy was only what Robert chose for them to know.

This was not the case in Edward's camp. The defeats at The Entry and St Ninians prevented any adequate reconnaissance of the Scottish position and the acquisition of detailed intelligence relating to the Scottish army. The latter, though it would obviously have been desirable, was not, perhaps, as significant as all that. The English cannot have waged war in Scotland for more than eighteen years without gaining a reasonable working knowledge of Scottish military practice and of the scale of army that a Scottish government could raise. This does not mean that any conclusions the English command might come to would necessarily be valid. It is perfectly possible, even probable, that the force under Robert's command was substantially larger than any that he had gathered in the past. He had certainly mustered an army in 1310–11 in the face of invasion, but the force had not been large enough to challenge the English in open battle. In effect, Edward and his lieutenants would have had a good understanding of the nature of Robert's army, but perhaps little idea of its strength.

# Preparing for Battle

The Scots of course were already on-site. They had no need to make camp, their victualling arrangements had been in place for a month or more, and King Robert was able to observe the English army as it arrived. Robert started to muster his army several weeks before the battle, but we should not assume that he achieved his full strength in short order; medieval musters were notoriously slow. He may not, in any case have wanted to bring all of his men together at once. There would be a lot to be said for bringing a relatively modest number of men together initially, so that they could be intensively trained and form a cadre to facilitate the training of others as the army grew, rather than trying to instil all of the necessary drill and weapon training to a very large body of troops.

His army was certainly not idle in the weeks before the battle. Sir Philip Moubray informed Edward II that the Scots were gathering at Stirling and that they were blocking up the paths that passed through the New Park. There were several reasons why he might do this. Robert would have been very rash indeed had he assumed that no-one in the English army would have been familiar with the area. Since the army was mustering in or around a hunting reserve and since hunting was such an important and popular entertainment for the noble classes, it would be very unlikely indeed that there were no English gentlemen who had, at one time or another, hunted in the New Park. They would therefore be familiar with the paths, tracks and views that would have traversed the woods and thickets of the Park. By rendering these paths impassable, Robert would obviously have reduced the possibility that a body of English troops might make their way into the rear of his army unnoticed.

He may have undertaken a more ambitious project at the same time. If he could block paths to impede the English, he could also make new paths which would allow him to move troops quickly and unobtrusively to react to developments. We might consider this as a possible factor of some importance to the opening phase of the main action on 24 June. It is clear that the Scots moved down to the plain from the higher wooded terrain of the Park in order to engage the English. This would not have been easy to accomplish either quickly or in good order if the troops had had to make their way down the slope through the trees in line abreast. If, on the other hand, they could march down the hill in column along paths which led directly to the plain, there would be a very good chance that they could move from column to line at the edge of the wooded area out of sight of the enemy before advancing into view and kneeling to pray.

In addition to training his men and ensuring that they were adequately armed, Robert put some effort into preparing the field. If we can reject Trokelowe's trenches we cannot reject the 'pots' which Barbour tells us were dug in a field near 'The Entry'. Barbour tells us that the king stationed his army in the New Park and ordered the construction of these pots to channel the route of the English advance:

> Tharfor withoutyn mar delay
> He til the New park held his way
> With all that in his leding war
> And in the New park herberyt thar
> And in a plane field by the way,
> Quhar he thocht ned behovyd away
> The Inglismen gif that thai wald
> Thou the park to the castel hald
> He gret men mony pottis ma
> Off a fute-breid round , and all tha
> War dep up til a mannys kne,
> Sa thyk that thai may liknyt be
> Til a wax cayme that beis mais.

[*Therefore the king immediately made his way to the new park with all the men under his command, and made camp in the Park, then, in a clear field beside the road, which he thought the English would need to take if they were to pass to the castle, he had his men dig many holes a foot wide and as deep as a man's knee, so thickly that they might be likened to a wax comb, such as bees make.*]

The pits have been an important fixture of secondary accounts of the battle, but have yet to be reliably identified by archaeology. Even if they were

deliberately filled in after the fighting, one might have expected that they
would still show up as parch-marks in aerial photography. Although they
appear in many plans of the battle, they have never been reliably identified
by observers. J.E. Morris[5] cites a Lieutenant Campbell who, visiting the
generally accepted site of the time (prior to 1845), claimed to have observed
marshes bordering the Bannock being drained and to have seen:

> … many circular holes about eighteen inches deep, very close to one another,
> with a sharp pointed stake in the centre of each. The stakes were in a state of
> decomposition… There were some swords and spearheads, horseshoes…

Campbell asserted that these pots were at the western end of Halbert Marsh,
which Morris takes to mean that they were distributed along the western
foot of Coxet Hill. Campbell's description does not appear in later editions of
Tytler; and, as Morris says, no-one corroborates him. It is surely very unlikely
that these pits could have been exposed without more investigation. Further,
medieval swords and spearheads were already considered to be desirable arte-
facts by antiquarians and collectors and would therefore have a good potential
cash value to the men working on the drainage project. If Campbell's claims
were true, one would have expected that some of the swords and spearheads
would have survived in local collections. More to the point perhaps, one must
question why the Scots would chose to arm the pots with expensive items
such as swords and spearheads, indeed one must wonder why Lt Campbell
did not help himself to a few examples as curiosities or souvenirs.

   This does not mean that we can arbitrarily discount the existence of the
pots. On the contrary, we should assume that the pots were dug and that they
fulfilled their purpose in forcing the English cavalry to advance on a very
narrow front and into an area where they would be vulnerable to Scottish
archery attacks to their flanks and spearmen attacks to their front. But we
have, as yet, no evidence to show exactly where they were situated. In the
absence of further evidence, we should accept that they lay close to the course
of the road that ran through the New Park to the town and castle of Stirling
and that they were distributed on either side of the road to deny space to the
English and to protect the flanks of the Scots from significant infiltration. It
is, of course, quite possible that individual English men-at-arms could have
made their way to the rear of the Scots by gingerly picking a path through the
pots and woodland to the left and right of the Scottish position, but we can
be confident that there was no viable route for a formed body of any strength.

Any intrepid souls who did try to pass around the flanks of the main body of the Scots would also have had to brave the shooting of King Robert's archers, who were stationed among the trees and shrubs of the Park.

Clearly, at least in Barbour's view, the 'pots' were dug in one location: a flat field aside the road near to where it passed into the New Park. Neither he, nor any of the chroniclers, suggests that they played any part in the main action. Interestingly, Barbour was sure that the pots were dug in the course of one night, Saturday 22 June. Robert's army had been gathered at Stirling for some weeks by this point, so one might assume that any preparation of the field would have been made well before this juncture. Digging a vast number of holes would, after all, be a very labour-intensive business, and since Robert was, by this point, very familiar with the terrain, it can hardly have been news to him that the English army would very probably attempt to force a passage to Stirling through the New Park. With a force of several thousand combatants and a considerable number of non-combatants on hand, Robert was not short of labour, but there may also have been a security aspect. The earlier the pots were constructed, the more chance there would be of their location coming to the attention of the Stirling garrison and of that information being passed to the English army, which would rather compromise their value. Setting the army to a lengthy physical task through the Saturday night may have had another advantage, in that it gave the troops something to keep them occupied rather than allowing them to dwell on the prospect of combat. It would also have made the army rather easier to observe, reducing the opportunities for desertion.

Blocking paths in the New Park and digging posts may possibly have been supplemented by the distribution of caltrops. A number of these wicked instruments are alleged to have been recovered from the battlefield. If used at all they must have been limited to the areas around The Entry and St Ninians. If they had been scattered between the armies prior to the main battle they would have been more of a problem for the Scots than the English. Had they been used at St Ninians, we should certainly expect that Grey would have mentioned them since they would have been an instrumental part in the defeat of Clifford and Beaumont's command – this was where Sir Thomas Grey senior was taken prisoner after all. Caltrops are also conspicuous by their absence in Lanercost or the other accounts. Mr Shearer, citing Oman's 'History of the Art of War', offers a useful comment, one which we should take seriously since there are several caltrops in private collections which are claimed to have been recovered from various locations in the Bannockburn area:

> It is whispered that caltrops for tourists are occasionally manufactured by modern enterprise.[6]

It is of course impossible to prove definitively that no caltrops were used at Bannockburn, though they do not seem to have been a part of the normal equipment and tactical practice of the Scots of the Middle Ages, but it would seem very unlikely that they played any part in the battle. Even so, Shearer was quite wrong to assert that those caltrops which are alleged to have been recovered from the area would have been ineffective due to their small size, being only 'two or three inches' in height and of rather flimsy construction. It is true that they might be crushed by the hoof of a horse, but the 'frog' enclosed by the hoof is quite delicate and easily damaged by a lodged stone, let alone a sharp spike and anyone who has stood on a drawing pin in their stocking soles will be aware that even a very small object can cause a remarkable degree of discomfort.

There seems little doubt that regardless of when Robert decided that he would offer battle, his troops were well prepared for the business of fighting. Professor Duncan makes the observation that the battle was a huge gamble '…which perhaps a wise general would have refused.'[7] This opinion is echoed by several other historians, including Dr McNamee,[8] however observation and experience led Robert to believe that he could achieve a major victory, and his experience of battle, his knowledge of the capacities of his troops – and those of the English army – cannot be discounted. He was clearly confident, and this is an important consideration. Competent generals do not choose to fight lightly; they do so either because they have no real choice or because they believe that they will win.

The same is true of Edward II. He was very confident that his army had the power and expertise to deliver a decisive victory. One might make the observation that the previous great victory over the Scots – Falkirk – had been a tactical success, but brought the English no closer to victory in war, but that is a different matter. On the morning of 24 June, Edward clearly believed that he was on the cusp of a major military success. Victory might not bring the end of the war, but it would certainly help to restore his political credibility and prestige at the expense of Robert Bruce, and might well allow the recovery of towns and castles in central and southern Scotland at least.

Offering or accepting battle is always something of a gamble regardless of the strength or equipment of the armies involved, but the risks must have seemed rather less serious to Robert than they do to us. There are several reasons why this should have been the case. The disparity of numbers may not have been as apparent to Robert and his lieutenants as we might expect. James Douglas and Sir Edward Keith had made a reconnaissance of the English army and had been impressed by its scale, but it is notoriously difficult to gauge numbers, as we can see from the wildly varying estimates of attendance at demonstration marches. Also, our view of the situation is heavily coloured by questionable perceptions about the nature of Anglo-Scottish battles. It is important to remember that no-one at Bannockburn had witnessed more than one really large-scale confrontation between Scottish and English armies for the simple reason that there had only been one such action – Falkirk – since the battle of the Standard in 1138. Wallace's great victory at Stirling Bridge was far from being a conventional general engagement.

There is also the matter of the confidence of the army. If the troops were in good heart, well-fed, well-armed, well-trained and well-rested, they were likely to be confident about their own abilities, but they were also likely to have confidence in their leaders. The army was, by Scottish standards, very large, and there would have been a high level of combat experience among the rank and file.

Men would have been aware of the 1310 campaign which had not resulted in a general engagement and would have had confidence in the king's abilities as a commander. If he chose not to fight, it would be for good reasons, and if he chose to give battle, it would be because he believed in his men. The morale of the army was likely to be very high. Not only was the army strong, but all of the heroes of the age were present – Douglas, the Earl of Moray, the Earl of Carrick and, of course, the king himself. The lack of 'big battle' experience may not have been as significant as we might expect. It is not at all clear that there was very much difference between being in the front rank of a formation of 200 and a formation of 2,000; the business of fighting or of being wounded or killed would surely be much the same however many men were engaged. Nor is it certain that past defeat necessarily had very much influence on the morale of the troops. Men who had survived Falkirk and were under arms at Bannockburn may have believed that the quality of the army – and of the commanders – was very much better in 1314 than it had been in 1298.

Evidently Robert was able to persuade his troops that a battle at Bannockburn could be won and that a repeat of the Falkirk debacle was not inevitable. The situations were certainly different in one sense. Unlike Wallace, Bruce had a plan for victory rather than a plan to avoid defeat.

The successful of actions at The Entry and St Ninians on 23rd June obviously had a positive affect on the army as a whole. The men involved would have been pleased with themselves and the men who had not fought on the Sunday would probably be all the more eager to prove themselves in the greater engagement on the Monday. Familiarity with the ground, confidence in their arms and training and a clear understanding of what was expected of them were all factors that would breed confidence. On top of this there was the inspirational figure of the king. His duel with De Bohun at The Entry cannot have failed to encourage confidence in the king and his cause, but his presence probably had a greater value. The speeches put in the mouths of medieval commanders by chroniclers do have a theatrical unreality about them, but we should not doubt that the king did spend some time on the evening of the 23rd talking to his men, encouraging their self-confidence. This would probably be more effective for those men – and there must have been a good many of them – who had never been in battle before. The veteran soldiers would know the score already, but even the most hardened of them would be likely to draw confidence from the presence of a leader with whom they had shared previous fights and the hardships of life in the field.

The proportion of veterans to novices would have been relatively high for a medieval army since there had been intermittent war with the English for the best part of twenty years; a whole generation of men would have grown up with war as the background of their lives. This would not be an unmixed blessing. Men who have seen a lot of combat are not easily moved to undertake dangerous operations and their experience would tell them whether a particular approach to battle was inherently unsafe. The fact that Robert's army was clearly ready and willing to carry the fight to the enemy, despite the high level of experience among the more experienced troops, is an indication that they saw the movement to the plain from the woods and high ground overlooking the carse as a viable proposition. The implications of this are greater than the matter of abandoning high ground for low ground. An advance against Edward's army would inevitably mean a confrontation with the English horse on terrain that was eminently suitable for mounted combat. Clearly the rank and file of the Scottish army were not intimidated by this prospect. To some extent they would have been encouraged by the successes of Moray and the King's formations on the evening of the 23rd, but those successes could not have happened unless the Scots were already confident of their ability to meet and defeat cavalry with spears. There was nothing terribly revolutionary about this. The initial English cavalry attacks at Falkirk had been repulsed, the Flemings had defeated the French at Courtrai, King Robert's troops had been victorious at Loudon and elsewhere, but the strength of disciplined infantry was well known from theoretical treatises. Many, perhaps most, of the senior commanders would have been familiar with the works of Vegetius, who was very aware of the weaknesses of heavy cavalry:

> [who] are safe from being wounded on account of the armour they wear, but because they are hampered by the weight of their arms, are easily taken prisoner.[9]

In the right circumstances and if the opposing infantry failed to keep good order, heavy cavalry could be devastating, but their vulnerability to well-ordered infantry who would keep their formation when attacked, unsupported cavalry had grave weaknesses. To fight at all is always a risk, but for Robert, his commanders and his troops, the risks were outweighed by the advantages. The potential for victory was, in their eyes at least, rather better that the potential for defeat. There were, of course, several political pressures on Robert which made battle an attractive option, but none of these was so great as to make battle a vital step in the process of gaining recognition for his kingship. A great defeat would undo the achievements of the preceding eight years, and it is impossible to believe that he would have led his men into the field if he was not confident that victory would be his.

Robert was not alone in having confidence that he could secure a victory; the English army does not seem to have lacked self-belief. Edward had raised a large and well-found army, probably at least as large as the one that his father had led to victory at Falkirk. The vital man-at-arms component was very much larger than its Scottish counterpart and possibly – though this is not supported by the evidence[10] – equipped and mounted to a higher standard.

Until 23rd June, Edward and his lieutenants were at least as confident of victory as King Robert. The army was large and there is no reason to suppose that the troops were not well-equipped. The senior commanders included several men with extensive experience of war generally and of campaigning against the Scots in particular. Robert Clifford and Aymer de Valence had been involved in several operations against the Bruce party, and De Valence had even inflicted a defeat on King Robert at Methven in

1306. There were many veterans and at least one internationally-acclaimed paladin, Sir Giles D'Argentan. Edward himself had spent a good deal of time campaigning in Scotland during his father's reign and his own; he cannot simply be dismissed as being militarily ignorant. The confidence of the troops may have started to break down because of the two actions on the evening of 23 June, but neither of those engagements was large enough to inflict serious damage on the strength of the English army as a whole. There certainly seems to have been no reluctance to accept or seek battle on 24 June; on the contrary, it would seem that there was a strong belief that the Scots would not be able to withstand a general engagement.

Some of the English chroniclers, such as Baker and the author of the *Vita* in particualr, saw over-confidence as a major issue, identifying the impetuous and arrogant behaviour of the commanders as the chief cause of defeat. For others – and this includes the Scottish chronicler, Bower – there was a theological element. In their view, the Scots had put their faith in God and had been suitably rewarded with victory. For these writers, the defeat at Bannockburn was more the product of God's punishment for English arrogance and impetuosity than his endorsement of the Scots.

English confidence was not altogether ill-founded. They had secured a major victory in the only other really grand-scale battle that the war had produced. There had been other victories and defeats. The Scots had won at Stirling Bridge, but that could be dismissed as an anomaly and the cause of defeat was fairly obvious. Roslin had been a fight of some significance politically, and a considerable boost to Scottish morale, but it was not a really major engagement. Similarly, the defeat of De Valence at Loudon had given Robert some domestic military credibility, but the forces engaged were not large and the circumstances unusual. On the other hand, Falkirk was a very large battle of a fairly conventional nature, and the English had unquestionably scored a great victory. Given the nature of their experience to date, the English had every reason to believe that they could and would defeat the Scots in 1314.

# Arma Virumque Canto

Whatever planning and preparation took place before the fighting, the action itself came down to the business of men fighting one another with swords, spears and bows. A great deal of effort has been devoted to the study of horseflesh[11] and the construction of armour,[12] but remarkably little attention has been paid to the experience of combat beyond references to spears breaking or men (and horses where appropriate) being mown down by hailstorms of arrows. It is important to remember that one of the reasons – perhaps the chief reason – that the great longbow victories made such an impression on contemporary writers was that they were rare events. On the other hand, the experience of defeat at the hands of longbowmen was not sufficient to prevent the Scots or the French from accepting or even seeking battle. Despite the effect of massed archery, none of the great battles of the Middle Ages was decided by missile combat alone; they all culminated in close combat. No English commander took to the field with an army which consisted of archers alone. Furthermore, all of the longbow battles were essentially defensive actions. Henry V may have advanced on the French at Agincourt, but he did so in order to force the French to attack; his troops did not advance to contact. Archery could not be sustained indefinitely. Even the most practiced archer will start to tire after loosing a relatively small number of shafts in quick succession and a man can only carry a relatively slender supply of arrows. Exhaustion of ammunition does not seem to have been a regular problem for medieval archers, but that is, in part at least, because the enemy would come to contact before the archers ran out of arrows, at which point the archer would have to rely on close combat weapons such as swords and axes or on the protection of their spear-armed colleagues.

Our perception of the effect of archery is heavily influenced by the progress of particular battles and, perhaps, a certain amount of 'Robin Hood' romanticism. Our understanding of the experience of close combat at unit level is little better, and numerous questionable perceptions arise from that. It is almost axiomatic that infantry could not withstand cavalry save in very favourable circumstances, though there are few, if any, examples of cavalry defeating disciplined infantry without the support of archers or other missile-armed troops. There is also a risk of conflating the infantry experience of different eras. It is possible, for example, that Oman assumed that the Scots must have adopted a static defensive posture because that was his (correct) observation of successful infantry actions against cavalry in the Napoleonic wars. For example, he would have been well aware that Marshal Ney's cavalry failed to penetrate the Allied squares at Waterloo despite mounting several courageous attacks. The situations were, however, very different. Wellington's infantry were not spearmen, but musketeers with bayonets. Having the front rank of the infantry kneel and place the butts of their weapons on the ground to present a uniform row of bayonet points to the enemy was viable with a five foot musket. The second and third ranks of the formation were not required to engage the enemy with their bayonets; their contribution was to maintain a steady volleys of musket balls. This was obviously not an option for medieval spearmen. If they were to inflict casualties on the enemy at all then they had to make physical contact with the points of their spears.

The assumption that infantry must inevitably take a defensive posture against cavalry is well-established. Morris[13] suggests that Robert:

> ... must have trained his men to halt to receive cavalry a few moments before the impact came.

A justification of 'must have' is hardly firm evidence, and we must surely question *why* they 'must have' done anything of the sort. A major element in repulsing cavalry is the fact that a horse, being a reasonably intelligent creature with a well-developed sense of self-preservation, will not throw itself into an apparently solid structure. However well-schooled the beast might be, it would be more than difficult to persuade it to crash onto a great immobile hedge of spear points, but it would be even more of a challenge to persuade it to crash into a hedge that was moving steadily toward it in a threatening manner. We must also give some thought to the infantrymen. How would the men know when to halt? If they did not do so in absolute unison, the integrity of the formation would be compromised by some men coming to a halt before others, and the fact that they were allowed to halt in combat under any circumstances would be an encouragement for the less-committed to halt as far away from the enemy as they possibly could. Additionally, any apparent hesitation on the part of one formation might well have an adverse effect on their comrades in formations not yet engaged, which would not help to maintain the confidence required to commit to the fight.

The assumption that sheer impetus would be enough to carry cavalry men into the heart of an infantry formation cannot be accepted at face value. It is absolutely clear from accounts of early modern warfare that horses would balk and shy rather than plunge into the ranks of the enemy. The 'scrum' effect which many historians have attributed to cavalry formations is simply not credible. The chief effect of one horse cannoning into the hindquarters of another would be to incapacitate both animals. Simplistic mechanics-based assumptions about the weight and speed of a horse against the weight and strength of a man with a spear are similarly unacceptable for a number of reasons. A good charger could probably attain a speed of around twenty miles per hour at a hard gallop, but the strength of a cavalry charge rests primarily in the ability of the leading rank of the formation to make contact with the enemy as a formed body. The speed of the charge is therefore limited by the speed of the slowest animal, not the fastest. Even the most aggressive of animals will slow down as it approaches any sort of threat however competent the rider may be. Additionally, each charging horse was not facing one man with a spear, but several men. Even if we were to accept the mechanistic approach of assuming that a man and horse weighing the better part of a tonne and travelling at twenty miles an hour would simply brush aside or trample a 70kg soldier, we must take account of the fact that for every cavalryman in the leading rank, there would be six or eight infantrymen – possibly more – wielding sharp and heavy spears. To some extent, the speed of the horse would actually increase the effectiveness of the spear at the point of contact and, if the spear formation was deep, penetration into that formation might actually allow more spearmen to join the fight.

Two further points about spearmen and our perceptions of spear combat should be considered. There is a medieval sketch[14] which shows a Welsh soldier with only one shoe. The assumption is that removing one shoe would somehow give the man better purchase on the ground. Extensive experiments on differing surfaces, from bare sun-baked soil to grass to wet ground and thick mud, have not given this author any confidence that this would be the case. It is quite possible that there is an aspect to this that has eluded me. Equally, it is possible that the artist happened to observe a soldier who had lost a shoe.

The other issue is the use of shields. Extensive experiments suggest that a shield is more of an encumbrance that it is worth unless the bearer is using a weapon that can be usefully wielded with one hand. Chronicle references to shields are, with one exception, related to the men-at-arms, not the infantry. The one exception is Trokelowe, who describes the Scots as advancing with their shields closely locked together. The assumption that Scottish spearmen went into battle with shields strapped to their fore-arms, though widespread, cannot be taken as a certainty since it would greatly impede the use of the primary weapon, the spear. The lack of shields would help to explain the very real fear of archery among the rank and file of Scottish armies.

# The First Clash:
# The Entry,
# Evening of 23 June 1314

As the main body of Edward's army approached the Scots, two detachments of heavy cavalry made separate advances toward Stirling. A variety of objectives have been attributed to these forces by historians, so it is worth giving some thought to what the English command may have hoped to achieve in mounting these operations. Traditionally, the technical relief of the castle has been offered as the rationale behind the manoeuvres. Affecting that relief would certainly have been an acceptable gambit in itself, but the offensive of 1314 was intended to do more than just secure one castle, however significant. Edward hoped to bring the Scots to a general engagement where his superior numbers, particularly in men-at-arms could be brought into play. Previous invasions of Scotland had failed to force battle on the Scots, with the result that the huge expense of keeping a major force under arms had obliged Edward to disband his troops and return home without having achieved anything very much. These abortive campaigns had done nothing to enhance Edward's popularity or his credibility as king. Additionally, another failed campaign would probably make it more difficult to raise a respectable force in the future. Edward was unquestionably committed to a combat policy, but if he was to pin the Scots down and force battle on Robert, he had to gather all the intelligence he could about the strength and location of the Scottish army. Edward was certainly aware that the Scots had gathered in the area of the New Park, and he and his lieutenants must have had a good working knowledge of the general nature of Scottish armies and of the general military policies of Robert I.

Given that the Scots were lying in wooded ground and uphill from the perspective of the advancing English forces, they were effectively out of sight. Edward decided to carry out two operations that are probably best thought of as reconnaissance in strength – fighting patrols on a grand scale. Alternatively, there may have been a rather more ambitious rationale to these operations. Since failure to bring the Scots to battle would inevitably compromise the general objectives of the campaign – the destruction of the Bruce party and the restoration of Plantagenet rule – discovering the current location of the Scots would only be part of the solution. If Robert was able to extricate his army without loss and continue to evade the English, little or nothing would have been achieved despite an enormous commitment of manpower and money. Robert's prestige might be damaged if he avoided battle, but Edward's prestige would suffer much more if he had nothing to show for his efforts in mounting the invasion. It is possible, therefore, that the intention of committing the force led by the earls of Gloucester and Hereford to The Entry was to 'pin' the Scots in their current position. If the English could establish a strong mobile force at the south end of the Scottish position and possibly another at the north end, it might prove difficult for Robert to lead his troops into the Lennox. It was late in the day by the time the action took place at The Entry, so if the Scots were trapped on the high ground to the south of Stirling they would be accessible to the main body of the English army the following morning. In Barbour's account, it is clear that Robert was not committed to continuing the action, even after the two successful engagements at the Entry and at St Ninians church. He saw that withdrawal to terrain that would be difficult for a pursuing English force to negotiate safely would be a viable option.

'The Entry' lay at the point where the road from Falkirk via Denny – roughly the same route as the A80 today – passed into one of the more densely-wooded parts of the Park.

The precise location of the Entry, or at least of the scene of the fighting, cannot be ascertained with any great degree of accuracy, though the recent discovery of an armour-piercing arrowhead in the vicinity of the modern Visitor Centre is perhaps an indication that at least some part of the action occurred there. It would seem that the Scots had deployed a considerable force at the top of a rise and across the road at a point where the distribution of trees formed a sort of tunnel with the road at its centre.

As long as the Scots held this point it was effectively impossible for the English to enter the Park, either to make a reconnaissance of the Scottish positions or to pass through to the castle.

This seems, on balance, to be the most likely location for the 'pots' or 'pitfalls' which have figured in virtually every description of Bannockburn ever written. As others have pointed out,[1] the pots can be seen as a form of medieval minefield, but it is worth bearing in mind the practical function of a minefield. The purpose of laying tracts of mines is not to inflict casualties, but to deny a stretch of terrain to the enemy. Inflicting casualties is a secondary, and generally rather minor, consideration. This is not to suggest that the pots did not cause casualties among the English troops as they tried to approach the Scots, in fact it was probably the means by which the pots were discovered in the first place. However, as soon as a couple of horses had tripped over, knowledge that there were pots and that they were to be avoided would have spread very quickly through the rest of the force. Assuming that the pots were dug in the area of The Entry, it is difficult to see what function they could have had other than to direct the English troops in a particular direction and prevent them from getting around the flanks of the Scottish force stationed there.

The defensive value of the pots would have been considerable as a means of forcing the English either to attack the Scots head-on or to abandon their operation and return to the main body of the army, but we should not automatically assume that they covered a very extensive area. Evidence from the World Wars of the twentieth century clearly shows that awareness – even suspicion – of mine-laying could lead to an assumption that a particular area was thickly covered in mines when in fact only a small number had been deployed. The psychological impact of just one or two mine detonations might be enough to persuade advancing troops that they were at great risk. The same might well apply to medieval cavalry encountering pots. At the very least, the knowledge that one or two comrades had fallen into traps would discourage an all-out charge on the enemy's position.

Forcing the enemy to attack on a particular axis was not a new gambit for King Robert; he had employed a similar stratagem against the army of Aymer de Valence, Earl of Pembroke, at the battle of Loudon in 1307.[2] On that occasion, Robert had arranged to have a series of ditches dug at right angles to the road along which de Valence's troops advanced, forcing them to attack the Scots on a very narrow front. Given that Robert had used this stratagem successfully in the past, one might wonder how he managed to use it a second time, indeed, superficially, the outcome of the fight reflects very badly on Hereford and Gloucester. It is, however, important to remember that although two combat situations might have many similarities, they are never absolutely identical; further, the experiences of two commanders might lead them to make utterly different decisions in the light of the same information.

It is possible that De Valence, had he been present, might have refused combat or have endeavoured to find an alternative route around the Scots with a view to preventing them from retreating into the Lennox or to disrupting their deployment from the rear. De Valence was not present, however, and even if he had been, he might not assume that the outcome of an action at The Entry would necessarily be the same as that which had occurred at Glentrool six years earlier. He might, for example, have believed that his defeat at Glentrool was not due to the general weakness of unsupported cavalry against formed infantry, but to a lack of 'moral fibre' among the men-at-arms he had led in 1307.

It is, of course, perfectly possible that Hereford and Gloucester did not either expect or intend to come to blows at all, but that he followed the road into The Entry hoping or expecting that the Scots would not attempt to obstruct his passage. There is no good evidence to indicate the strength of his column, though it was undoubtedly a powerful force. It is certainly most unlikely that he intended to engage with the entire Scottish army with only the men under his command, but he may well have felt that his formation was strong enough to deter the Scots from giving battle. Although it is generally assumed that Hereford and Gloucester's party was a force of men-at-arms operating in isolation, there is one piece of evidence to indicate that he led a combined force of horse and foot. Thomas Grey tells us that Henry de Bohun (identified incorrectly by Grey as Piers de Mountforth) who was certainly present – he had the misfortune to be killed by King Robert – was the commander of a body of Welsh infantry. Given that Edward himself had identified the importance of infantry for the campaign of 1314, it would not be surprising if infantry formations were deployed to support cavalry operations. De Bohun seems to have left his command to make a personal reconnaissance when he saw King Robert riding alone some distance from his troops. The famous duel took place after which De Bohun was in no condition to return to his command and bring them into action.

Regardless of the presence or absence of the infantry, the English cavalry formation advanced on the Scots only to find that they could not penetrate the serried ranks of spears. Having been brought to a halt, they were also vulnerable to the Scottish archers in the woods to left and right, and so, after some ferocious fighting in which the Earl of Gloucester was unhorsed, were obliged to retire. The Scots, excited by their own efforts and, no doubt, by the king's duel with De Bohun, pursued for a short distance but were quickly recalled, an indication of the level of control that King Robert had been able to establish over his soldiers. Hereford and Gloucester now retired across the Bannock and made their way toward the main body of the army which was now crossing the Bannock and making camp somewhere in the low-lying area to the west of the River Forth.

The success at The Entry gave Robert a range of choices of action. He could still retire into the Lennox and avoid a major battle. Leaving the field to the English would have some effect on his own prestige and on the morale and confidence of his troops. It would probably give King Edward an opportunity to restore his rule in much of the south of Scotland, but it is unlikely that he would be able to bring about a wave of defections from the Bruce cause among the political community. Without their support, he would struggle to impose, let alone maintain, a stable and secure administration. Even if he could attract support from landholders in the south and east, he could hardly hope to retain their loyalty unless he could dislodge the Bruce party from the rest of the country.

Any political profit from the campaign was likely to be very short-lived if the Bruce party could simply return to their campaigns as soon as Edward's army marched back to England. Alternatively, he could await developments in a position of some strength. Preventing the English from penetrating into the New Park meant that he still had the upper hand in the intelligence and reconnaissance aspects of the battle. Edward was aware of the general location of the Scots, as he had been for some weeks, but was not wiser as to their deployment or strength than he had been before the action. If the Scots were hidden to the English, the reverse was not true. The English were on lower ground and could be kept under observation from the Scottish position. Since Gloucester and Hereford had not managed to establish themselves on the flank or in the rear of the Scottish army, Robert was still able to retire if he chose to do so, but the possibility of offering, or rather forcing, battle must have been in his mind.

The defeat of Gloucester and Hereford would surely have caused some degree of doubt and dismay among the English troops and it certainly had a positive effect on the morale of the Scots. The action at the Entry could hardly have been better for Robert. By the time the fighting was over, it was late in the day, too late for a general advance and attack by the English, many of whom were still filing across the Bannock to their camp area. The

English were tired from the march and some of them from the fighting, but only a portion of the Scottish army had been engaged at all. The majority were therefore comparatively well-rested, though given the length of the marches executed since the army left Berwick and Wark, none of the English army can really have been considered 'fresh' for the fight.

Additionally, Robert's duel with De Bohun and the action at The Entry would, inevitably, have had a positive effect on the morale of his troops. No doubt many of them would have been more than happy to follow the king into the Lennox with a view to conducting the sort of evasion campaign that had been so successful in the past but, as events the next day would demonstrate, there was surely some appetite for a fight.

# The Second Clash: St Ninians and Cambuskenneth Abbey, Evening of 23 June 1314

The action at The Entry was not the only engagement of the day. A second body of men-at-arms marched across the low-lying area to the west and south of the Forth under the command of Sir Robert Clifford and Sir Henry Beaumont. Their most likely approach would have been to take the road past Snabhead, passing to the east of the New Park and St Ninians and on to Stirling. The relief of the castle was surely one of their objectives, possibly the most important one, but it is clear that the commanders were more than happy to fight if an opportunity arose. Dr McKisack[1] has suggested that there was an intention to reinforce the castle garrison, but it is difficult to see what would have been achieved by this. The chief objective of Edward II was to draw the Scots into battle. If the English were victorious the castle would be perfectly secure. In the unlikely event of a defeat Moubray would most certainly have to surrender his charge regardless of whether or not he had been technically relieved. The Scots would simply renew the siege and any reinforcement of the garrison would do nothing more than increase the number of men who would fall prisoner when the castle was eventually forced to surrender. Adding to the complement of men-at-arms under Moubray's command would do little to help his situation and would reduce the cavalry arm of Edward's army.

The size of the party is open to debate. Grey, whose father was a member of the force, gives a strength of 300, but Barbour suggests a strength of eight hundred. If we are to assume that the English army of 1314 was similar in structure and articulation to that of earlier forces, such as the army of 1296 or the army of 1298, it would be a fair guess that the heavy cavalry element was divided into four bodies. Several historians have described these bodies as 'brigades', which is a rather misleading term since the word 'brigade' indicates a group of permanent formations brought together to form a long-term operational formation within the army. The term 'regiment' might therefore be more appropriate. The major formations of cavalry could be considered 'brigades' in the sense that many of the members of the formations did belong to discrete groups, the retinues of more prominent men than themselves. This is not, however, an adequate description of the nature of these 'brigades.' Retinues came in all sorts of shapes and sizes, and the retinue of one earl might be very much larger than that of another. Some minor barons might bring only one or two men-at-arms to the campaign, but they were still leaders of retinues. A good many men were enlisted as individuals, whether through landholding obligations, in exchange for pardons, for pay, or just men who volunteered in search of adventure. No doubt the smaller retinues and individual men-at-arms were apportioned to the formations of the greater magnates at the head of formations based on the core of their own comitiva to achieve a degree of similarity in strength between one formation and another. But there was not, so far as is known, a regular system to define the size of cavalry formations to equal the millenars and centenars of the infantry. There were formation commanders, and the formations consisted of the retinues of bannerets and great lords, but the retinues were not of a uniform size.

Assuming that the total of men-at-arms available to Edward came to something in the region of 2,000–3,000, it would be convenient to assume that each of the cavalry formations was of a similar strength, however this was not the normal practice of the day. The king would almost certainly have personal command of one formation which, unsurprisingly, might well be double the strength of the other cavalry formations of the army. Without a good deal of the material that exists for other English armies of the period, it is quite impossible to make more than a guess at the sizes of the cavalry formations of 1314.

At least one writer has dismissed the possibility that Clifford and Beaumont led a formation as small as 300 men-at-arms. The idea has been dismissed on the grounds that a major formation of cavalry within an English army of such magnitude would surely be a quarter of the total force

of men-at-arms and that that total would be at least 2,000 men, thus the
formation in question would have some 500 men in its ranks. Another has
dismissed Barbour's figure of 800 as being unreasonably large. Neither of
these assertions can be supported from the source material relating to the
1314 campaign, nor from material relating to other armies of the period.

Clifford's and Beaumont's command could easily be as small as 300 or as
large as 800, though it is probably safe to accept these as the outside parameters, since a force led by two such prominent men would unquestionably
be a powerful one. Working from Barbour's description of King Edward's
army, Professor Barrow[2] accepts Barbour's assertion that the English cavalry
were divided into ten formations, and assumes that each of these formations
was of equal size. In this case, the combined total of their command would
have been something in the region of 500–600 men-at-arms – a credible
figure. One might even suggest that Thomas Grey junior was mistaken in
his estimate. If each of the formations consisted of approximately 300 men,
it is conceivable that Grey misinterpreted information from his father.

This may have been the case, but if so, it was something of a departure
from the usual practice of the period. The heavy cavalry elements of the
English armies of 1296 and 1298, both of which had at least 2,000 men-
at-arms, were divided into four formations, but they were not of equal
strength. The king's own formation being substantially greater than the
others.

Regardless of the strength of the Clifford/Beaumont party, the commanders were evidently prepared to fight, but it would be rash to assume that the
objective of the operation was to come to blows with the enemy. Naturally,
the relief of Stirling Castle was an objective for the whole army, but grasp-
ing opportunities to discomfit the Scots would be 'fair game' for a strong
armoured column. On the other hand, the nature of Anglo-Scottish war had
changed since 1296 when one formation of English men-at-arms had utterly
routed the heavy cavalry element of the Scottish army near Dunbar. The lack
of infantry support clearly indicated that mobility was an important aspect of
the operation, and to some extent that supports the belief that the primary
objective was the technical relief of the castle. On the other hand, it is clear
that the commanders of the operation did not feel obliged to avoid a fight
if the opportunity came their way, and if they felt confident that they could
inflict a defeat on the Scots without compromising their orders.

Whether or not their orders really gave them the discretion to engage as
they saw fit, Clifford and Beaumont certainly chose to do so. Their march

on Stirling was identified and reported to King Robert who promptly sent the Earl of Moray to prevent them entering the town. The only reference to the strength of Moray's force is Barbour, who tells us that this body of troops comprised 500 men. At least one writer has rejected this on the basis of the fact that Moray commanded a very large portion – perhaps a quarter or even a third – of the Scottish army in the main battle, however that is a very misleading contention. It is true that Moray did command a much larger body of troops when the whole army was deployed for battle on the morning of the 24th, however these men were the retainers, tenants and associates of a number of prominent men, whereas the troops that Moray led against Clifford and Beaumont comprised – according to Barbour – his own 'mengne', that is to say, men who lay under Moray's authority for military purposes. Naturally, one would expect that Moray's tenants would fall into that category, but other men would have been encompassed in Moray's military responsibility. As Earl of Moray, he would have authority over men called out from the earldom, many of whom would, of course, be Moray's tenants. Additionally, the Earl of Moray had been at war for several years, during which he would have attracted other men to his banner, members of Moray's comitiva on the basis of their personal relationship. This does not conflict in any sense with Moray's leadership of a larger formation during the fighting on the 24 June, indeed it is probably reasonable to assume that Moray's 'mengne' formed part of that larger formation. It was not extraordinary for one individual to have concurrent command responsibilities at more than one level. Clifford and Beaumont were the appointed leaders of a major body of troops, but they were also leaders of personal retinues.[3]

Apparently Clifford and Beaumont's progress took the Scots by surprise to some extent since –according to Barbour – the king had to draw Moray's attention to the threat they posed. That threat may have been considerable. If Clifford's and Beaumont's force was only three hundred strong, it is unlikely that they were expected to establish themselves at the northern end of the Scottish position with the intention of forcing a general engagement. They might, however, be considered strong enough to inflict a lot of damage on the Scots if they tried to effect a withdrawal, enough, at least, to cause some disruption in the ranks of Robert's army. This would seem to corroborate the Lanercost account, which asserts that Clifford and Beaumont chose to march around the northern end of the New Park to 'prevent the Scots escaping by flight.' It seems to be generally assumed that Clifford's actions were not in any way coordinated with those of Gloucester and Hereford. This is certainly true to an extent, since there was no means of effective communication between the two forces. It is crucial to bear in mind that the English command had no reason to believe that the Scots would accept battle unless forced to do so. Alternatively, Clifford may have been tasked with the relief of the castle and with establishing the exact location of the Scots with view to an attack on the following day. Equally, it is quite conceivable that neither of the engagements were really part of a plan at all, and that the commanders of the two columns were acting on their own initiative, eager to build themselves martial reputations. This does not mean that either Gloucester and Hereford or Clifford and Beaumont were exceeding their orders, or that they were incompetent leaders. Senior field commanders are expected to use their initiative and to seek opportunities to damage the enemy.

Had both of these reconnaissance-in-strength operations – Clifford and Beaumont to the north of the Scots, and Gloucester and Hereford to the south – been successful, the Scots would have been in great difficulty. Even if there had been no combat, the inability of the Scots to prevent English troops from reconnoitring their lines would surely have destabilised Scottish morale while simultaneously encouraging the English. More importantly, Robert would have lost the initiative which allowed him to mount his attack on the morning of the 24 June.

As it turned out, the Scots intervened successfully and prevented Clifford and Beaumont from attaining their objectives whatever they might have been. The story of the action is quite straightforward and the only sources to describe it – Grey and Barbour – accord well with one another. Each has Moray lead his men out of the woods on the high ground and down to the open plain. The English commanders, sure of the offensive capabilities of their troops, actually retired a space to allow the Scots room to deploy, and then executed a charge which failed to penetrate Moray's schiltrom. Eventually the Scots turned to the offensive and split the English force into two parts, one of which made its way to the castle while the other retired to the main body of the army.

This engagement is one of only two in which the popular understanding of a Scottish schiltrom – a circular formation of men with spears turned outward – can be clearly demonstrated. Barbour tells us that Moray had his men stand back to back and that as the action progressed the English became increasingly frustrated, so much so that they eventually stopped trying to charge into the formation and started to throw weapons at the Scots instead.

The fight continued for some time, and the outcome may have been in doubt. In Barbour's account Douglas, concerned that Moray might be overcome, sought permission form the King to intervene. This was only given reluctantly,[4] since Robert was eager to preserve his deployment. Although Douglas moved to support Moray, he did not actually engage the enemy, but halted his command some distance from the action. This was presumably to avoid encroaching on Moray's moment of glory, since the English were, by this time, losing the fight. His arrival may in fact have been the factor that decided the result. Clifford and Beaumont were heavily engaged, and the threat of another Scottish force joining the fight may have been enough to persuade them to abandon their objective. If, as Professor Duncan suggests,[5] Douglas's force consisted of cavalry, there would be a real risk that the English, tired and disorganised, could be pursued and destroyed. Alternatively, the English commanders may have already come to the conclusion that nothing more could be achieved by continuing the action. The arrival of Douglas encouraged them to accept that they could do no more, and suggested that they should therefore retire to avoid pointless loss of life. Grey does not mention Douglas's presence at St Ninians at all. He may not have considered it significant if, in the opinion of his father, the matter had already been decided by the time Douglas arrived. Alternatively, Grey senior may have been completely unaware of this development; he was, after all, a prisoner in the midst of the Scottish formation and may not have been able to see anything beyond their ranks.

Douglas's decision not to engage may, of course, have been no more than a matter of following his orders. It is quite possible that he was under strict instructions not to intervene unless Moray was in danger of being overrun by the English cavalry, but the decision to hold back from the fight may well have been intentional. On a more practical level, leaving Moray to conclude the business unaided may well have been seen as a valuable boost to the morale and confidence of the army as a whole. If Moray could inflict a defeat on the English with just 500 men, what could be achieved if and when the whole army was committed to battle?

The nature of this action tells us a number of things about medieval infantry operations against cavalry. Since Moray seems to have had no difficulty in bringing his men to the fight, it is clear that they were confident in holding their own against mounted opposition. There were examples of successful actions by foot against horse that may have been known to the Scots, such as the victory of the Flemings over the French at Courtrai in 1302, but there is a good deal of difference between occupying a position of strength against a mounted enemy and marching onto flat terrain to confront him. Evidently Moray's men were sure that they could hold their own, but that confidence may have been encouraged by the nature of the English force. Without the close support of infantry, particularly archers, the English force was actually very vulnerable. If they could not break into the schiltrom, they could achieve nothing beyond providing targets for Scots. If they chose to retire, the Scots could not pursue them very effectively since a man on a horse is a good deal more mobile than a man on foot. On the other hand, any withdrawal would be an admission of defeat.

Equally, the willingness of Clifford and Beaumont to give the Scots space to 'come on' before launching their attack is also an indication of the confidence of English men-at-arms and their leaders. They too will have been aware of Courtrai and of Stirling Bridge and, perhaps most significantly, of Falkirk. Students of history who are steeped in the narratives and records of the time will be aware that the defeat of the Scottish schiltroms at Falkirk was a product of 'combined arms' tactics, though these were not employed until the cavalry had already failed to achieve a breakthrough. The men who served under Clifford and Beaumont were probably rather more conscious of the eventual victorious charges of the men-at-arms at Falkirk than of the archery that disrupted the Scottish formations and made those charges possible.

Assuming that Barbour is correct in his assertion that Moray's force consisted of only 500 men, it is quite possible that Clifford and Beaumont believed that their own force was more than capable of scattering their opponents. Assuming that they were aware of the nature of the action at Falkirk — and they surely must have been, seeing as they had both taken part in the battle — they were obviously also aware that Wallace's schiltroms had been able to hold off the English cavalry. But the situations were not the same. Wallace's schiltroms were probably something of the order of 2,000 men strong, not 500, and they had been deployed at the top of a fairly steep rise. On top of that, the English men-at-arms had had to negotiate soft ground and muddy burns in order to engage and had had to endure shooting form Scottish archers positioned around and between the schiltroms. At St Ninians, the schiltrom was only 500 strong and, most significantly, the engagement took place on flat, hard ground where the advantages of speed and impetus should have lain with the English.

The inability of Clifford and Beaumont's troops to force their way into the Scottish ranks should not be regarded as a mystery. As a general rule throughout history, cavalry have struggled to impose themselves against formed and confident infantry, particularly in circumstances where the infantry carried spears or other pole arms. This was not merely a medieval phenomenon; there are several examples from the Napoleonic wars of infantry squares maintaining their formations against cavalry charges even when they themselves had run out of ammunition. The explanation for this must surely lie in the psychology of the horse. An inspiring leader might be able to persuade a body of men to throw themselves onto a thicket of spears, but it is very difficult to persuade a horse to do anything so rash. It is true that training and the herd instinct might be sufficient to bring a mounted formation close to a body of infantry, but as long as the infantry stood fast, the majority of horses would pull up, rather like show-jumpers 'refusing' a fence. The horses in the rear ranks of the cavalry formation would obviously have rather less of a view of the enemy and might well press on, but only into the backs of the foremost ranks. Some historians seem to believe that this would bring about a scrummaging effect which would push the leading ranks of the cavalry in to the front ranks of the infantry. It is perfectly credible that this might occur in a few isolated instances within a formation, but it is difficult to imagine that anything of that nature could be adopted as a tactical practice. In general, if a horse really does not want to proceed, it can always stop. Far from pushing into the midst of a schiltrom, a cavalry formation forcing a close attack on infantry would be much more likely to dissolve into a great mass of collisions and fallen chargers.

This was not, of course, the intention of cavalry commanders. What they hoped to achieve was the collapse of order among the opposing infantry as terrified soldiers cast away their weapons and fled. When this occurred, the cavalry would be in their element, pursuing the hapless infantry to their hearts content. Given the nature of the terrain at St Ninians, the absence of Scottish archers and boggy streams, and the strength of their formation, it would be unreasonable to accuse Clifford and Beaumont of rash behaviour. They were both experienced and competent soldiers with, presumably, a good understanding of what cavalry could or could not achieve on the battlefield. Like any commanders worthy of the name, they chose to engage the enemy because they were confident that they could defeat them, not because they were an available target.

The two actions of 23 June are well known, but it would seem that there was a third engagement. Barbour is the only source for a raid on King

Robert's stores at Cambuskenneth. The Earl of Atholl, David de Strathbogie, had been active on behalf of Edward II since his defection from the Bruce party before May 1307. He had been entrusted with truce negotiations in 1311–12, but had entered the peace of King Robert before the end of the year. In 1314 he left the Bruce party again, this time because his sister Isabella had been jilted by Edward Bruce. To what extent this action was a matter of defecting to the English or of defying the Bruces is unclear, but he did not return to Robert's peace. Professor Duncan[6] has suggested that the stores at Cambuskenneth may have been the fodder for the royal horses, and that Strathbogie, who was the King's constable, would have been aware of this. It is possible, however, that the Abbey was the chief supply head for the Scottish army. It would have been a well-known institution, well-served for roads and situated beside the Forth at a point where the river is reasonably navigable. Robert could not be absolutely certain of Edward's intentions until the English army came into view on its march toward Stirling. By concentrating the supply effort at Cambuskenneth, Robert would be able to control the distribution of provisions to the army and reduce the incidence of pilfering. Strathbogie's raid, though apparently very successful, had no real impact on the campaign. But it did, perhaps, ease his return to Plantagenet allegiance.

# The Night of 23 June 1314

Defeat in the actions at The Entry and at St Ninians prevented Edward's forces from making an adequate reconnaissance of the Scottish positions. It was probably far too late in the day to concentrate the army and array it for an immediate full-scale attack. His forces had covered a considerable distance on 23 June and would surely benefit from a night's rest. Virtually all of the chronicle accounts agree that the English army crossed the Bannock on the Sunday night and must therefore have made camp on low ground to the east of the New Park. There is no reason to suppose that the great train of wagons and carts carrying provisions, tentage, tools and other supplies were not brought into the camp before the end of the day and that rations were distributed to the troops.

On the morning of the 24th the English army was drawn up in front of their camp, which would indicate that the supply trains and the pavilions of the wealthy were concentrated toward the eastern end of the camp site, as far from the Scots as was practical. In Barbour's account, D'Umfraville[1] suggests that Edward should withdraw his army through the camp so that the Scottish attack might be disrupted by the attraction of looting the English baggage, in which case there would need to have been a considerable space of firm, flat terrain behind the camp on which the English could deploy. It is, of course, quite possible that Barbour was misinformed or that he misinterpreted the available data, or even that he invented the episode for the sake of his story.

The camp certainly seems to have been reasonably well established and the supplies brought up in good time, since there are indications that some of the English troops spent the evening drinking and socialising. We should not assume that they all did so. Grey tells us that at least some of the English cavalry spent the night beside their chargers ready for battle. The practical business of campaigning – more a matter of marches and supplies than of combat – was not virgin territory to the English; they had mounted many campaigns in Wales, France, Flanders and Scotland over the preceding thirty years and must have accumulated a wealth of experience in arranging and administering temporary camps. We should not assume that the troops were especially comfortable, but they were probably as well found as they could reasonably hope to be, given that they were in a field in Scotland and in fairly close proximity to the enemy.

The Scots had been on site for some weeks and we can safely assume that they had made themselves reasonably comfortable with tents for the wealthy and shelters for the many. It is possible that there were effectively two Scottish camps; one for the fighting troops and another, which would be quite substantial in itself, for the various craftsmen, merchants, servants and the rest of the hangers-on that were part and parcel of the medieval army. The infantry of either army could at least expect to sleep in relative warmth by wrapping themselves in padded jackets. These garments were *de riguer* for the close-combat men, but there is no reason to assume that archers could not acquire them if they wanted to. The drawback to sleeping in a jack is the weather. If the Jack is soaked, it can become too heavy to wear. It is not difficult, however, to make a crude personal shelter out of a piece of cloth and a couple of sticks. Such a 'bivvy' would not keep the jack dry exactly, but it would keep off the worst of the wet. No doubt the medieval armies were aware of such a technique.

The troops could bed down for the night, but the commanders had to make plans for the battle or withdrawal and pursuit that they expected to take place the following day.

With hindsight, it is far too easy to criticise Edward's approach to a battle which he had actively sought. His own experience, and that of the men around him, had led him to believe that there was no prospect of the Scots making a conventional attack, and he would therefore have to carry the fight to the enemy. This was not an unreasonable analysis, but it was a mistaken one, and Edward's army paid a heavy price for it.

On the night of the 23rd, the Scots were stationed on higher ground than Edward's troops, and were out of sight. He had no means of gauging their strength beyond the estimates that his own experience and that of his subordinates might generate, plus any information that he may have received from Sir Philip Moubray. If the Scots were to be engaged, then Edward's army was going to have to advance from the plain, find the enemy and then engage. The manner and order in which he was to commit his men to the fight would have to depend on the nature of the Scottish deployment. If they intended to fight a purely defensive action, they might well have constructed trenches and barriers which would present too much of a challenge for a simple cavalry attack. In this case, the English would need to use archers in the initial phases of the action in order to disrupt the Scots and possibly drive them from their positions. The cavalry could then make effective attacks on the Scots once they were in motion.

The events of the evening of the 23rd may have caused him some concern. The outcome of the action at the Entry was easily understood. The cavalry had attacked a force of disciplined infantry who had taken up a strong position in an area where the cavalry could not deploy freely. Their repulse was not, in all probability, too much of a surprise. The vulnerability of armoured cavalry against heavy infantry would have been well known to any student of Vegetius. The fact that Gloucester had attacked at all would have been open to criticism, but not incomprehensible. The English had a poor opinion of the capacity of the Scots to fight large engagements, and Gloucester may have thought there was a real possibility that the Scots at The Entry would break and run if threatened by a powerful mounted force. They did not do so, and Gloucester's men were defeated, but there is no evidence to indicate that they had suffered heavy casualties and been driven from the field. It is more likely that Gloucester, realising that there was nothing to be gained from pressing the attack, withdrew his force to rejoin the main body of the army with a view to renewing the action in the morning with infantry support.

The action at St Ninians may have been harder to take. The Scots had met Clifford and Beaumont's force on the open field with no trenches, woods, streams or pots to disrupt the cavalry and, so far as we are aware, no archers either, but had still won the day. There were no mitigating factors to explain or excuse the failure of the cavalry to penetrate the Scottish ranks. This was not the case at the Entry. The Scots had prepared the ground with pots and had archer support on hand. Edward may have been dismayed by the defeat at St Ninians, but equally he may have identified factors – unknown to us –which put a very different complexion on the fight. Neither Edward nor his subordinates seem to have taken the view that the success of the Scots at St Ninians could be repeated on a larger scale.

The English command did not, apparently, make any contingency plans to meet a Scottish attack, but that does not mean that they had not given careful thought to the manner in which they were going to mount their own offensive. They had every reason to believe that the Scots, if they accepted battle at all, would retain their position on the high ground and wait for the English to attack them. Ordering and re-ordering great bodies of men and horses was not an easy thing to achieve. Given that the English commanders were eager to bring the Scots to battle before they could escape, it is reasonable to assume that Edward and his officers made a conscious and deliberate effort to ensure that the deployment adopted by the army for the morning of the 24th would be consistent with their intention to move toward the high ground to attack. It would also have to be flexible enough to be adjusted once a clearer picture of the Scottish position and strength had been acquired, but this does not mean that they had necessarily chosen to array the army in the optimum deployment for an immediate attack. The Scots were some distance away and the army would have to march, possibly for as much as an hour, before they could come into contact if the Scots maintained their position on the New Park.

The English position was strong in the sense that the Scots could not hope to approach on the flanks of the English without being noticed, and so Edward's staff could be confident that there would be ample opportunity to pout the army into the posture that they felt most appropriate without interference from the Scots. The maxim that 'plans do not survive contact with the enemy' was demonstrated by the Scottish attack; it was a contingency that had not been seriously considered. We should not assume that the English deployment was unwise for the purpose for which it was designed, just that it was not suitable for a defensive battle on a plain. On the other hand, if the Scots did not move to the attack until four or five hours after first light (see below) it is perfectly feasible that Robert did not make a final decision about his own movements until the English had completed their deployment, or at least until their intentions were obvious. Nor should we assume that he saw attack or withdrawal as his only options. His position in the New Park was a strong one. He had made some preparation of the field at the Entry and may well have made similar arrangements at other locations.

Robert had probably blocked up paths in the Park to channel the English advance as much as to deny them access to the Park, so it would be no surprise if he had constructed pots and trenches at the points where he expected to confront them. He could not be sure that the English would not mount their attack at the first opportunity, nor that they would take a careful and measured approach. If they could position elements of their army in such a way as to prevent the Scots from making a safe withdrawal, Robert might well find himself obliged to fight a defensive battle in the New Park rather than mounting an attack on the plain. It is simply inconceivable that he did not have a plan for a defensive battle as well as one for attack; indeed, the attack option may not even have been his first choice, but the one that made most sense in the light of the English choices of bivouac and deployment areas. Had Edward become aware of the risks facing his army, he might well have chosen to deploy his army in such a way as to make a Scottish attack impractical, in which case we should expect that Robert would have adopted a different policy – either retreat to the hills or stand his ground and fight on the defensive.

Attack was clearly Edward's preference, but it is by no means certain that he would have committed his troops to a simple frontal assault on Robert's positions. He could have attempted to move his entire force across the Pelstream burn and endeavoured to force battle on the Scots from the north rather than the east. Alternatively, he could have divided his army, committing a substantial force to pin the right flank formations of the Scottish army while the rest of the troops advanced westwards from the camp area. He may even have considered avoiding battle in the short term and moving across the plain to seize the bridge at Stirling to pursue a campaign north of the Forth.

If so, the action at St Ninians may have persuaded him that the risks were too great. The Scots were clearly capable of putting a force between the bridge and the main body of the army which would be capable of preventing a body of men-at-arms from capturing the bridge. The bridge itself might be very difficult to take 'at a run'. It was quite narrow – wide enough for a wagon to cross, but not for two wagons to pass one another and might therefore be held for some time by the modest force of archers and spearmen, even in the face of a very much larger force.

Edward may even have planned on keeping the bulk of his army in camp rather than making an attack on the 24th. According to the *Vita*, Gloucester suggested he should wait another day in order to rest the troops. Edward's rejection of his advice may be no more than the assumption of the writer. The Scots had obviously developed a reliable supply system, but Edward had a much larger cavalry arm than Robert. There was every chance that he could destroy the Scottish logistical chain with columns of heavy cavalry that would be more than equal to the task of countering their Scottish counterparts. Edward could not await developments indefinitely. His wagon train could not sustain his army for long and the livestock – horses, draught oxen, meat on the hoof – would need fresh grazing, but there is no suggestion from contemporary evidence that the army was facing serious shortages. The advance of the Scots on the morning of the 24th meant that Edward had no choice but to accept battle on Robert's terms. This does not imply, though, that Edward had not considered a number of options, any of which might have brought him victory or at least saved him from total defeat.

# XII

# The Great Battle at Stirling: 24 June 1314

Given the need for security and water and a 'forming up' area, it is difficult to see a better location for the English army on the night of the 23rd than the one that was chosen. We should also bear in mind that Edward was not alone. He was surrounded by men with considerable professional experience of war in general and of war against the Scots in particular, including Aymer de Valence, Robert Clifford, Henry de Beaumont, John Comyn and Ingram D'Umfraville. As far as one can judge from the contemporary material, none of Edward's officers took issue with the choice of camp site. Indeed, it is by no means certain that Edward chose the site at all. We might assume that Edward was at the head of the main body of his army as it followed the forward formations under Gloucester, Hereford, Clifford and Beaumont.

It cannot be too heavily stressed that the English expected to have to force battle on the Scots. The experience of Edward, and of his lieutenants, was that the Scots would do their utmost to avoid a major confrontation with a large field army. Previous expeditions had foundered for that very reason. A great force could only be maintained for a matter of weeks before desertion, illness and financial stress reduced the ration strength dramatically, so if the opportunity arose to commit that force to battle on reasonable terms, it was best to get on with it before the army dwindled away to nothing. Furthermore, Edward had raised his army with every intention of bringing the Scots to battle if he possibly could; his credibility would be undermined if the armies passed a night in close proximity but did not come to blows.

The onus, then, was on Edward to force battle, and both his troops and his lieutenants seem, in the main, to have been confident of victory, but the condition of the army was not good. The marches from Edinburgh to Falkirk and then to Stirling had been made at some speed, and though they were hardly remarkable feats, both men and horses were less than completely fresh. Two substantial formations had already been in action and been defeated. In all probability, neither had suffered very heavy casualties, but they can hardly have been encouraged by their repulse. Even if the chroniclers did not tell us that the troops were tired and hungry, common sense would tell us that, since the supply wagons were at the tail of the column and had not crossed the Bannock burn until late in the day, there may have been very little time for the preparation and distribution of food. It is, of course, quite possible that the army completed its concentration early enough on the evening of the 23rd to allow a reasonable period for feeding the troops, watering the horses and pitching tents. If, however, this was not the case, any rations ready for consumption that were carried by individuals – bread, cooked meat, cheese, wine and ale – would almost certainly have been consumed during the march from Edinburgh. Additionally, waiting for rations to be distributed would have meant less time for sleep, so it would not be surprising if men chose to forgo food in favour of rest.

The poor condition of the horses can be exaggerated. The majority of the cavalry would not have ridden their primary charger on the march, but would have saved the stamina of their mount for battle. According to Grey, the English cavalry spent the night beside their mounts with the beasts bitted and, perhaps, saddled ready for battle in the morning. This in itself would have involved a good deal of activity in the camp. Men-at-arms who had travelled to the field on 'riding' horses rather than their chargers would have had to retrieve their mounts from the grooms as well as ensuring that their animals were watered and, if possible, fed. It would be unrealistic to assume that the English camp was inefficiently organised; there were plenty of men in the army with extensive campaign experience, but forming the camp would still have taken some time and midsummer nights are short.

Edward's army had suffered two significant rebuffs during the later afternoon or early evening of the 23rd, but they were far from defeated. Only a relatively small portion of one element of army, the cavalry, had been engaged at all and it is probable that casualties had not been particularly heavy. It is easy to assume that the army did not achieve concentration for the night until very late in the day, but it is impossible to give a definitive timing for the actions at The Entry and St Ninians. It is perfectly possible that both of these fights had been concluded by late afternoon and that the army as a whole had established its bivouac long before dusk. We cannot even be certain that the day was too far advanced to force a major action. Edward and his lieutenants may have decided that it would be better to let the army have time to eat and rest rather than to press for an immediate battle. This would be the wiser course, since it would allow time to consider their options and would allow for a more careful deployment.

There can be no doubt that the army crossed the Bannock burn before making camp and that the leading formations which had already fought the Scots re-joined the army. The Bannock did not present a great obstacle to the troops, but it would appear that it was something of a challenge for the wagons. In Barbour's account, the roofs and doors of neighbouring houses were stripped to provide materials for making ramps and bridges to ease their transit. The sources are not unanimous in their description of the condition of the army. According to Trokelowe the English were:

> ... bitter because of their repulse and vowed to be revenged on the morrow or die... they were hungry and had had no sleep.

On the other hand, Baker tells of drinking and revelry, as does Friar Baston, who was of course in the camp on the Sunday night:

> ... while they thus boast with wine in the night revelling, they kill thee Scotland, with vain words upbraidng. They sleep, they snore.

Grey, whose father was not present since being taken prisoner at St Ninians, tells us that the English cavalry spent the night beside their bitted horses, ready to repulse a surprise attack by the Scots. We should not assume that these views are mutually exclusive. It is perfectly possible that the more experienced commanders of formations or of individual retinues ensured that their men and horses rested, while the less competent allowed their men to indulge in premature celebration. Regardless of their behaviour through the night, it is clear that the army was 'arrayed' early on the morning of the 24th, but we cannot assume that they were deployed for immediate action. The bivouac area must surely have lain some distance from the Scottish position. If the commanders felt there was any chance at all that the Scots would mount a night assault they would hardly have chosen to site their camp within easy striking distance of the New Park, since they were well aware that King Robert's army lay on the high ground overlooking the plain.

Beyond the possibility of a night attack, there was no reason for Edward or his subordinates to believe that the Scots would offer battle; their experience of war against King Robert and against William Wallace before him, would have led them to expect that the Scots would keep to high ground and fight on the defensive. This being the case, it is much more likely than not that the English army was deployed for an advance and might have to march for more than a mile before coming within striking range.

The sources disagree about the nature of the English deployment, but the bulk of the material indicates that at least one body of English cavalry – Gloucester's command – lay to the front of the army, possibly behind a light screen of archers. Mr Nusbacher[1] takes the view that:

> When Edward II deployed his troops for battle on Stirling Carse, he set up a line of units abreast. On his left and right flanks were his archers, in the centre was his horse.

This takes no account of the English close-combat infantry who would undoubtedly have been present in large numbers and is not, in any case, supported by any of the contemporary accounts. Lanercost gives Gloucester a command of cavalry and infantry which advanced to counter the Scots, Trokelowe has the English deployed with the cavalry in the rear of the infantry. Grey does not discuss the deployment of the army as a whole, but certainly indicates that the initial counter-attack was delivered by cavalry, as does the author of the *Vita*, while the Lanercost account tells us that the battle proper commenced with a vigorous attack on Gloucester's command by the leading Scottish formation. There can be little doubt, then, that the forward element of the English army, with the possible exception of Lanercost's body of archers, was a cavalry formation under Gloucester, which, with or without attached infantry, made a counter-attack against the Earl of Carrick's formation.

This would make good tactical sense if Edward expected to move in on the Scots. A screen of archers would provide a degree of night protection against an approach from the west, and the Pelstream and Bannock burns would form a barrier to approaches from the south and the north. Edward may have positioned Gloucester to the front of the main body of the army to prevent the Scots escaping or to pin them in one position should they choose to fight. If the Scots chose to attack – and this was clearly thought highly improbable – Edward would have a strong force that he could commit immediately with a view to disrupting their plans. Edward, of course, expected that he would be moving against the Scots and not vice versa. His father had adopted a similar plan at Falkirk, where the Earl of Surrey had been tasked with attacking Wallace's right flank while the other cavalry formations under the Bishop of Durham, the Earl of Lincoln and the King's own formation assaulted the centre and the left flank of the Scottish army. Those attacks had failed, but they did prevent Wallace from adjusting his deployment while the English infantry moved up to support the cavalry.

Edward II may have adopted a more sophisticated plan than his father. Trokelowe describes the English army as having the infantry to the fore with three bodies of cavalry – the 'centre and wings' – in their rear.[2] This does not necessarily contradict other sources which have Gloucester in front of the main body of the army. It seems to have been common practice for English cavalry to be divided into four formations. If this was the case at Bannockburn, then it is quite possible that there were indeed three formations to the rear of the infantry, with Gloucester deployed in front of the army as a whole. This would give him a mounted striking force which would prevent the Scots from redeploying if they were arrayed in static schiltroms. The infantry could then advance to the bulk of the cavalry in reserve ready to break into the Scottish formations or to mount a really effective pursuit if they were to break and run.

Whatever Edward's intentions may have been, his plans were thrown into confusion by the advance of the Scots. Once again, we cannot be sure of the time of day. Dawn would have broken at about half past three and it would have been full light shortly after four o'clock at the latest, but it is not at all certain that the Scots attacked in the early dawn. None of the source material suggests that the English were still abed when the Scots moved out of the woods and into the open field. Whatever arrangements Robert made for moving his troops from the New Park to the lower ground, he can hardly have chosen to march his men down a relatively steep incline and through woodland while it was still dark. He may of course have brought his men to field late on the evening of the 23 June, trusting to darkness to keep his movements and intentions secret from the enemy, but this would be a grave risk. Manoeuvring several thousand men in complete silence would have been a considerable challenge, and there was always the risk that an English patrol would alert the English army to his presence. Assuming that the Scots did not start their move down to the plain until first light, it is difficult to see how they could have been in position until at least an hour after dawn.

In Trokelowe's account, the battle commenced at 'about the third hour' which we might expect to mean about nine o'clock. Quite who was monitoring the time – and how – is not clear, and the timing may be no more than a guess, but it is by no means impossible. King Robert was in a good position to observe the behaviour of the English army and may well have been waiting to see what sort of approach they would adopt before making his own move. Robert had very extensive experience of war and had spent the preceding month or more training large infantry formations. He very obviously had a good understanding of what infantry could and could not do. It is therefore a possibility that he decided to keep his troops concealed until the English army had completed deployment for a march on the New Park. He would then advance, confident that Edward would not be able to rearrange his army into formations suitable for receiving an attack while they were in the process of changing their positions.

The move to battle certainly began with the emergence of the Scottish army from the woods. The Lanercost account – based on the experience of a 'reliable' eye witness – states that both armies were 'arrayed' and that each had a screen of archers in front of the main concentration of troops. It is reasonable to assume that the body of English archers was not particularly large; they were able to drive off their immediate adversaries – the Scottish archers – with little difficulty, but were not prepared to attempt to force the spear formations to halt through shooting.

Famously, the main bodies of Scots knelt, either to hear mass or to say the Lord's Prayer. It is quite possible that this remarkable act was not performed by the whole army, but only by the forward elements to divert attention while the balance of the army entered the field.[2] It is also possible that the real purpose of this exercise was to give the junior officers an opportunity to ensure that the ranks and files of the units were correctly aligned (see above). It certainly made an impression on the English. Edward is alleged to have assumed that the Scots were kneeling to beg for mercy, which is surely not a credible claim, but this religious act may have had a significant effect on the morale of both sides since it was an indication of confidence that God would reward the pious.

The English commanders seem to have failed to grasp, even at this late stage, that they were about to be attacked, and watched the proceedings with interest, perhaps incredulity, instead of concentrating on the business of preparing for the fight. Prayers over, the Scots resumed their advance. The weight of evidence suggests that the Scots came on in three bodies, with the commands of the Earls of Carrick and Moray to the fore and that of the King stationed centrally and to the rear. Neither the numerical strength nor the breadth of these units can be ascertained, but it is clear that the extreme flanks of the first two formations were protected by the ditches of burns, presumably the Pelstream and the Bannock. They were arrayed in line abreast and were presumably separated by enough of a distance to allow the third formation to come into action between the first two.

As the Scots advanced, Gloucester – whether on his own initiative or under orders from King Edward – took the only rational course of action and led his men in a charge. No doubt he expected this action to stop the Scots in their tracks.

The time between the first appearance of Scots and clear identification of their intentions would have been quite short, and so there would have been very little time for analysis or reaction. The analysis aspect was straightforward; the Scots were advancing and would soon be in contact unless they decided to halt and wait for the English to come to them. This would not have been a credible proposition. Every moment lost would give the English more time to adjust their deployment. Some English archers had been driven away from the schwerpunkt[3] of the battle, but there were many more available. If they could be brought into action against stationary Scottish spearmen, Robert would have lost the tactical initiative and his men would have lost impetus, and with it the morale advantage of advancing to combat. Gloucester's counter-attack might provide a little time for adjustment, but what would be the best policy? If the English troops were in marching columns, would it be better for Edward to accept battle in the current deployment or to attempt to change formation in the hope that the troops would have re-formed before the Scots made contact?

If the entirety of the English front line consisted of *cavalry*, it would be very difficult to bring the archers into action. If the first line of battle behind Gloucester's men consisted of *infantry*, it would be very difficult to bring the cavalry into battle against the flanks of the Scots because of the burns to the left and right. Gloucester's counter-attack could not achieve much more than a brief delay unless the Scottish formation collapsed at the first onset. If repulsed – which he clearly was – his troops could outrun the Scots and reform, but that would not present a very encouraging example to the formations in the rear, whether mounted or on foot. Additionally, if Gloucester's men retired, the Scots would naturally follow up, thus rapidly reducing the amount of space available for regrouping, reforming or manoeuvring.

Contemporary accounts are very clear about the constricted nature of the battlefield from north to south – that is, the distance between the Pelstream and the Bannock – but the east-west axis was not terribly extensive either. The English had drawn up in front of their camp, which presumably stretched most of the way back to the River Forth. Sir Ingram D'Umfraville is alleged to have advised Edward to draw his troops back through the camp when the Scots first came into view, but there would have been great problems in doing so. The area would have been littered with hundreds of wagons, tents, remounts and draught animals which would have been a severe impediment to an orderly withdrawal. Even if such a retreat could have been performed safely, there may not have been sufficient room between the camp and the Forth to deploy the army at all, and even if there *was*, there would probably not have been time to array the troops in an effective manner before the Scots were upon them.

Time was not the only problem; Edward's army was short of space. Gloucester's attack on the leading Scottish formation under Carrick (the *Vita* author ascribes this formation to Douglas, but is alone in this) had not achieved anything. Gloucester himself was dead, either because he had neglected to put on his surcoat or because he was deserted by his comrades. Having failed to break through Carrick's spearmen, Gloucester's troops were pushed back in disarray and, having had little opportunity to regroup, were probably driven into the main body of the English army. On the other side of the field, Moray's formation advanced to contact and a stiff fight ensued in which the Scots quickly gained the upper hand.

Even so, all was not yet lost. The English army still outnumbered the Scots by a respectable margin and it would seem that there was still an appetite for the fight. There was now a development which only Barbour relates. A body of English archers started to concentrate on one particular flank of the engagement. Their shooting was effective and the battle might have turned in favour of the English, however this was an eventuality that King Robert had foreseen. He had retained a body of mounted men-at-arms as a subtracted reserve, and this formation, 500 strong and under the command of the Earl Marischal, Sir Edward Keith, made a charge and scattered them. It has been suggested that Keith's charge is no more than a figment of

Barbour's imagination. This is possible, though it is unlikely that he would have been able to persuade his audience to suspend their disbelief to such an extent.

It is certainly in conflict with other sources which tell us that the entire Scottish army fought on foot, but this may be no more than a conflict of physical perspective. Just because none of the English witnesses saw this part of the action taking place does not mean that it did not happen. At least one English commentator – Baker – tells us that the English archers were unable to come into the fight since they were in the second tier of units and were therefore screened by their own men. This does not compromise Barbour's interpretation. Accepting that there were archers in the rearmost portions of the English army does not mean that there were no archers in other areas. There is no reason to assume that the men who had faced the Scots archers in the Lanercost account of the initial phase of the battle had been destroyed; they had, apparently, seen off their opposition, but there is no compelling reason to assume that they had left the battlefield. It is perfectly plausible that they might move out of the way of Carrick and Moray's formations and await an opportunity to rejoin the fight. Further, we cannot simply assume that no-one in the English army attempted to gain the initiative by leading a body of archers away from the main body of the army and commit them elsewhere. Edward was not bereft of competent experienced officers with courage and determination.

We might question Barbour's narrative in terms of the relative effectiveness of cavalry and archers, however the various defeats inflicted on men-at-arms by archers were not simply dependent on the effectiveness of the longbow against men and horses. If archers were to defeat horses they needed to be carefully deployed, preferably behind a barrier of some description. They also required an ample supply of ammunition. None of these conditions could be met at Bannockburn. The attention of the archers was focused on the Scottish infantry, relatively few in number and short of ammunition. Whether these factors were relevant or not, the archers can hardly have been expected to withstand a charge unless they had the support of close combat troops, which they clearly did not. Worse still, as they fled from the Scottish cavalry, many of them collided with other English formations who in turn were pushed back onto their neighbours, increasing the crush and confusion.

In Barbour's view this was a crucial moment in the battle. Freed from the attentions of the English archers, the Scottish spearmen could devote their attentions to the enemy in front of them, who were now disorganised and under great pressure. Since the Scottish formations stretched across the field from the Pelstream to the Bannock, there was nowhere to go but backwards.

A controlled withdrawal is a very challenging manoeuvre for any army, but all the more so when it has to be performed in close combat. Moreover the issue for the Scottish formations was really quite straightforward; they just had to press on in the direction in which they had started the battle. For the English formations, the situation was much more complex. When King Robert's troops joined the fight, all of the Scottish units were roughly in a single straight line and they could be sure that anyone to their front was the enemy. If an English commander attempted to extricate his formation from the great heaving mass of cavalry and infantry around him, he could not be sure that he was not exposing his flank to a Scottish force that he had not previously identified, and would in any case have to find a route around other English units. To complicate matters further, his men would have to contend with broken cavalry and panicking riderless horses while trying to retire through the tents, wagons and livestock of the camp, as well as keeping a tight formation against the Scots.

Things now went from bad to worse. In Barbour's account, though not in any other, the camp followers, servants, carriage men and grooms of the Scottish army had been watching the spectacle of battle and now decided to make a contribution. Grabbing whatever weapons they could find, they chose a leader and, improvising banners from sheets, they advanced to join the fight. The absence of this episode from English accounts does dot invalidate it. To Barbour, it was an event of some significance, but it may have passed unnoticed by the witnesses who provided information to English writers. Assuming that the attack of these 'small folk' actually happened – and there is no good reason to discount it – it was probably not an important part of the action in the sense that the battle was already won. Whether the involvement of these grooms, carriage men and camp followers was a matter of planning by King Robert or was a 'group initiative' is open to question. Mr Sadler,[4] citing General Christison, takes the view that the King had stationed them on the rim of high ground overlooking the battlefield to exploit any opportunity that might arise. Barbour, however, indicates that they had been tasked with guarding the provisions and that they were led by a 'captain' of their own choosing. Whether the intervention of the 'small folk' was part of Robert's plan or not, they were obviously close enough to the action to be able to see the progress of the battle and move down to the plain in time to make their own contribution to the fight. Whether they could be seen from the English lines is another matter, but the absence of the small folk from English accounts does not prove their absence from the battle.

No doubt English commanders did their level best to rally their troops and turn the tide, but it was too much to ask of men who had, just a short while before, been looking forward to victory and plunder. The army lost any semblance of good order as the Scots pressed forward and, as it became clear that the day was lost, the men charged with King Edward's personal security decided that it was time to take him away from the battlefield. He does not seem to have been eager to leave, and there should be no question that he lacked personal valour. He had been active in the fighting and though his death might have reflected well upon his character, his capture would be a political disaster of huge proportions. His reins were seized by De Valence and Giles d'Argentan and, accompanied by the knights and men-at-arms of the royal household, they lead him toward Stirling Castle.

This was a great blow to the morale of those who were still in the thick of the fighting, and a complete collapse was now inevitable. There was no possibility of an orderly withdrawal and no-one to take control of the large numbers of men still milling about on the battlefield. Additionally, Edward's exit would have provided a justification for others to leave the field. If the King was in danger – and he very clearly was – men might decide that their primary duty was to do whatever they could to help protect him. Furthermore, men fleeing the field might be accused of dereliction of duty if they simply made their way home. Finally, when Edward quitted the field there would have been no clear chain of command. Many of the surviving senior officers left with him, and why should those still engaged continue the struggle in his absence? If they could do no more in his cause and were not able to join his company, then their primary duty was to survive, not to add to the horrendous toll of casualties.

Escape was now the only priority, but it was not easy to accomplish. With the Forth in their rear, the only course open to the majority of the army was to head south across the Bannock:

That sua cumbyrsum was
For slyk and depnes for to pas

[*That was difficult to pass over, being deep and slippery.*]

Barbour's claim that men could walk across the burn dry-shod because it was filled to the banks with dead men and horses is undoubtedly an exaggeration, but it was unquestionably a major obstacle in itself and the clamour to escape the advancing did nothing to ease matters.

It would seem that there was an alternative path which some men took; they followed King Edward's party and made for Stirling. To do this, they would have had to pass around the left flank of the Scottish army. This perhaps suggests that the front lines of the army, the men in contact, had swung around to the right so that the Scots no longer occupied the whole of the stretch of land between the Pelstream and the Bannock. A gap would have opened up to their left, through which King Edward had already passed with a portion of his army following behind. Such an account would tally well with Grey's description of the remainder of the English army, who were pressed back into the Bannock rather than forced into the River Forth.

Edward's company reached the castle safely, and although the governor, Moubray, was willing to admit him, he also pointed out that he could not offer a secure haven. Recommending him to make his way through the King's Park, pass around the rear of the Scots and then on to Linlithgow. In the strictest sense, Moubray had been relieved within the terms of his pact with the Earl of Carrick, but realistically there was no point in trying to retain the castle. King Edward would not be able to raise another force for some time, and the castle would certainly fall within a short period. In any case, as a senior Scottish nobleman with little or no property elsewhere, Moubray had his own future to consider. Even if he had been tempted to refuse to surrender his charge, Moubray could hardly have admitted the great crowd of men who, according to Barbour, now ensconced themselves on the castle rock.

For the men still stuck in the Carse it was a different matter. Hemmed in by the Scots and the Bannock, those who could not force their way across the burn could only surrender or fight on to their death.

Of the men who did manage to escape the battle itself, few returned home safely. The Earl of Hereford led a large party of men away from the field and sought shelter at Bothwell – a baronial castle still held for the Plantagenet cause – only to be taken prisoner by its commander, Sir Walter Gilbertson.[5] The Earl of Pembroke, ever the true military professional, having discharged his duty to King Edward by guiding him from the battlefield, collected a considerable number of Welsh troops who had escaped the fight, and led them back to safety in Carlisle.[6] It would not be far-fetched to suppose that these were the men who had made their way to the castle rock, having formed a large enough party to discourage interference from the Scots. Pembroke appears to have left the battlefield with King Edward, but was not in the party that Douglas pursued to Winchburgh and then on to Dunbar. Barbour may have confused Pembroke with Sir Maurice Berkely, who he credits with leading a party of Welsh soldiers away from the battle. However, he also tells us that a great many of them were killed before reaching England.

They were not alone. Other than the party who accompanied Edward and Pembroke, the disintegration of the English army seems to have been more or less complete, and the prospects for individuals or small groups making their way home on their own initiative were very bleak. For many, surrender was the only option. In the words of the *Lanercost Chronicle*:

> Many were taken wandering around outside the castle and in the country-side and many were killed; it was said also that certain knights were taken by women. None of them got back to England unless in a miserable state.

For the chronicler, surrender to women was particularly shameful, but for a shocked and lost knight or man-at-arms, possibly wounded and horseless, it was a sensible course of action. If one was a prisoner, there was at least someone who had an interest in keeping you alive for the sake of a ransom.

Of the great swathe of English soldiers who were captured, the vast majority were either ransomed or exchanged for Scottish prisoners including the Queen, Princess Marjorie, and the Bishop of Glasgow. One notable exception was Sir Marmaduke Twenge, who managed to hide himself in the aftermath of the fighting until he saw an opportunity to surrender to King Robert in person. Quite why he should have done so is not clear, but he may well have been known to the King personally, having been a prisoner of the Scots in 1299 when Robert was acting as one of the Guardians of the Realm on behalf of King John.

English casualties were simply horrendous. If we were to assume that Edward's army amounted to 15,000 combatants - and it unlikely to have been much less — we cannot take that as the grand total of the number of men he led into Scotland. There would also have been a considerable number of grooms, servants, craftsmen and camp-followers of every description. There may well have been at least as many as 17,000 or 18,000 of Edward's subjects present at Bannockburn, possibly as many as 20,000.

There is nothing to indicate that any great number of them survived to tell the tale. This does not mean that they all died or fell prisoner; it is more likely than not that herd instinct brought men together in bodies large enough to dissuade attacks as they passed through the southern counties en route to the border.

Further, pursuit is unlikely to have been very effective; the majority of the Scots were preoccupied with plundering the English camp and the dead and wounded who lay scattered across the battlefield. Even so, it is quite possible that at least a third of Edward's army died on or around the field of Bannockburn or of wounds suffered there. The losses were on a par, perhaps greater than any medieval battle fought between England and a foreign power.[7] In relation to size of population, it was at least as heavy a blow to English society as the first day of the battle of the Somme in 1916. The majority of the infantry were recruited from northern and central England, and very few from south of the River Trent.

Scottish losses were probably considerable, but – as is usually the case for the victor – they were very much lighter than those of the English. Barbour records just two Scottish knights killed in action, William Vipond and Walter Ross, and had nothing whatsoever to say about the men of the rank and file of the army. The fighting had been intense and many Scots must have fallen in battle or died of wounds. Post-combat surgery was rather better than we might expect; men could and did endure the most dreadful injuries and still survive, but there was no effective remedy for infection, gangrene and septicaemia, and peritonitis must have carried off a considerable portion of the non-fatal casualties.

The battle may have been fierce and bloody, but it may have been a fairly brief affair. It was not unknown for a battle to continue for some hours, but there is nothing to suggest that this was the case at Bannockburn. If the Scots took to the field at 'the third hour' and we take that to mean somewhere around nine o'clock, the outcome of the battle may have been decided within little more than an hour. King Edward left the action, rode to the castle, met with the commander and then made a journey from Stirling to Winchburgh. Here he halted his party to rest their horses, before travelling on to reach Dunbar before the end of the day. Dunbar and Stirling are separated by a distance of almost fifty miles as the crow flies, and rather more as the road lies. When his ride to the castle and his journey around the western edge of he New Park are taken into account, it is clear that Edward covered rather more than sixty miles and, to avoid having his men's chargers collapse of exhaustion, he can hardly have averaged more than about six miles per hour. Even if the halt at Winchburgh lasted only an hour or so, Edward must surely have left the battlefield at least eleven or twelve hours before reaching Dunbar. Assuming that he did not arrive there until nightfall, he must have left the battlefield before midday at the very latest.

Understanding defeat or victory is seldom a simple matter of identifying one specific area of superiority or weakness, but there are several factors that we might consider crucial to the outcome of Bannockburn. There is no reason to assume that the English commanders were wilfully negligent or painfully ignorant, but they were over-confident. To some extent, this was the confidence of a larger army faced by a weaker one, but the assumption that the Scots would fight a defensive battle along the lines of Falkirk and the success that Edward I had achieved there led the English commanders to believe that they were invincible. The Scots, on the other hand, were confident because of their faith in King Robert and his subordinates, and they had been intensively trained. The English army fought because they owed service to their King, as did the Scots; but, crucially, they did not feel that their national sovereignty was at stake.

# XIII

# After the Fight

## Outcomes of the Battle of Bannockburn

For those men who died in the battle or who had escaped unscathed, the business was finished; but for the principals – Robert and Edward – the struggle was far from over. Well over a hundred of the English nobles who fell can be identified by name,[1] a vast number for a battle this period and an indication of the price paid by the political community. In 1318, Robert de Blakebourne petitioned Edward II for aid in recongnition of his twenty-two years' service in Berwick Castle garrison and against the Scots in other locations. As it was generally known in English record, he had lost his brother and no fewer than ten of his friends at the battle of Stirling.[2] Many more became prisoners of war. They did not expect to remain prisoners until a permanent peace could be negotiated, but they might have to wait many years. Instead, they had to set about agreeing ransoms with their captors. The sums involved could be huge. The younger son of Sir Walter de Fauconberg was freed for 500 marks (a little over £330), Robert Neville of Raby had to find 200 marks for his liberty and William D'Umfraville had to seek permission from Edward II to travel to France to raise the finance for the ransom of Sir Ingram.

Many of those who had escaped had still incurred serious financial damage. The loss of wagons, stores and weapons had to be borne by the individuals, but they could expect at least some degree of compensation for lost chargers, though they might have to wait some time for the money. Roger Heiron[3] claimed £148 for chargers lost at Bannockburn and Sir Richard Lovell was granted the issues of the manor of Eylesham until he had recovered the sum of £96 16s 8d for his eleven mounts lost in the fighting. It is all too easy to assume that the reputation of English armies was ruined by Bannockburn, but it is not clear that they had very much of a reputation in the first place. There had been war with the Scots since 1296, but there had only been one great battle. Edward I had campaigned in Wales, but he had not had to fight against Wales as a united country, as a great deal of the principality had already been under English control for some time. Furthermore, neither Wales nor Scotland was seen as a great military power. Failure to overcome a smaller and – broadly speaking – poorer country in a war of nearly twenty years intermittent duration can hardly have established England as one of the great military powers of the day. On the other hand, while the political damage to Edward II – and to the cause of bringing Scotland under Plantagenet rule – was considerable, neither he, nor his lieutenants, considered the war lost. There would be more campaigns – and defeats – before that became evident.

If the war was not yet lost from the English point of view, it was not yet won for the Scots, however great the victory at Stirling. The assumption that King Robert's kingship was now unchallenged is very misleading. John Balliol was dead, but his son Edward was alive and therefore still the legitimate King of Scotland. Some Scots who would have preferred the Balliol dynasty chose to accept Bruce kingship through *force-majeur* and through fear of forfeiture. Other Scots accepted his rule for lack of another credible Scottish candidate for the throne. No doubt there were those who could not have cared less for any party, but were obliged to accept the government of the day. They may have felt that the Bruces offered the best prospect of peace, security and stability.

Bannockburn empowered Robert as King; it also empowered the Scots militarily. For the rest of Robert's reign, the Scots enjoyed a remarkable level of military superiority which even the failure of the Bruce campaigns in Ireland could not erase. Bannockburn did not, however, end the war with England. In 1316 or 1317[5] an English force which made a landing in Fife was destroyed by a force under the Bishop of Dunkeld, William Sinclair. In 1322 Edward led an army into Lothian, but could not bring King Robert to battle and had to withdraw because of desertion and for want of supplies.[6] The Scots were not idle either. If he was to have peace and establish his family on the throne, Robert needed to force recongnition of his kingship from Edward I. This was not going to be achieved easily. Edward was hardly likely to accept the restoration of Scottish independence and kingship at all, let alone at the behest of a man whose political authority was derived from military force and who was not even the legitimate claimant to the Scottish throne. Of course, pots and kettles are both black; Edward II, like his father before him, had no right whatsoever to try to impose his government on Scotland.

Although Robert was more than willing to have a negotiated settlement, he was not willing to compromise on sovereignty, and the only tool he could wield to force Edward to accept defeat was military action. The policy of raiding into northern England was stepped up; the forces were greater and more daring. English counter-measures were ineffective and led to further defeats at Myton, Byland and Scawton. Edward himself was lucky not to be captured at Rievaulx,[7] and communities as far south as Beverly in Yorkshire found themselves obliged to fork out large sums to avoid being sacked by Scottish forces. Despairing of the capacity of their own king to provide adequate lordship, men in Northumberland, Cumbria and Westmorland started to approach Robert for justice, protection and even for confirmation of their charters.

The war would continue until the disastrous Weardale campaign of 1327, which very nearly resulted in the capture of the young Edward III.[8] The terms of the Treaty of Edinburgh–Northampton of 1328[9] at last gave Robert what he sought – recognition and peace. But he did not have long to enjoy it. On 7 June he died at his country home of Cardross on the River Clyde.[10]

Superficially, his dynasty was secure. He had frustrated an attempted coup in 1320[11] which had been mounted to put Edward Balliol on the throne. He had also restored order and encouraged economic recovery, and had secured a formal peace with England which recognised his kingship and the rights of his heirs. He hoped to ensure his son's safety from English aggression by marrying him to Joan of the Tower, sister of the new English King, Edward III. None of these things prevented Edward III from renewing the war, in the first instance by proxy. In 1332, despite his treaty obligations, he allowed Henry de Beaumont to raise a force of English, French and Low Country adventurers and Scots who had lost their estates through opposition to the Bruce party.[12] Beaumont was the real leader of this army, which mustered on the Humber before taking ship to land in Fife. The titular commander, however, was Edward Balliol, son of the late King John. The army won a great victory over the Scots at Dupplin Muir in August, but by the end of the year, Balliol had already been ejected. The following year, Edward III gave Balliol his overt support; they won another great victory – Halidon

Hill – and Edward III was able to impose an occupation government in the south and east of Scotland. There is something of an assumption that only the outbreak of the Hundred Years War prevented Edward II from succeeding where his father and grandfather had failed, but in fact, the occupation government was already failing by the beginning of 1335 when the Earl of Dunbar – who had defected to the English after the disastrous battle of Halidon Hill in 1333 – returned to Scottish allegiance.[13] Given that virtually all of his property lay within a day's hard ride of the border, he can hardly have chosen to change sides unless he believed that the Scots were going to win this war as they had the last. Success at Stirling was not the only action to have given them confidence in their ability to defeat the English in war. Battles at Myton, Byland, Scawton, Culblean, Crichtondene and many others contributed to a sense of self-belief, but none were as dramatic, or indeed as significant, as that at Bannockburn.

# Illustrations

16. Medieval spearmen. Troops armed and armoured like these would have formed a large part of the army of Edward II and a very large proportion of that of Robert I, though we should expect the spears to have been rather longer than the 10 foot weapons shown here.

17. Close-up of spearmen. As long as spearmen maintained their formation they were virtually invulnerable to cavalry.

18. An archer. Contrary to a tradition that has developed over the past century, there is no evidence to suggest that Scottish and English archers used different types of bow.

19. Livery – the practice of dressing troops in particular colours – was only just becoming fashionable in the early fourteenth century.

20. An archer in padded coat 'nocking' his arrow.

21. The film *Braveheart* popularised myths about the nature of Scottish military equipment, in particular a belief that Scottish troops wore very distinctive leather tunics like this one.

22. Arms of Scottish some of the Scottish Earls, barons and knights who served at Bannockburn, courtesy of Mr Peter Armstrong.

23. A well-equipped infantryman with three layers of protection – a thick padded coat worn over a chainmail hauberk over a thinner padded jacket.

24. A considerable proportion of the men-at-arms in the Scottish army – including the earls of Carrick and Moray and the King himself – served on foot with spear in hand.

25. Receiving cavalry. The strong modern tradition that Scottish spearmen knelt down to rest the butts of their spears on the ground is supported by medieval evidence.

26. Inchcolm Abbey, where Abbot Bower composed his *Scotichronicon*.

27. Torphichen, headquarters of the Hospitallers in Scotland. Contrary to modern tradition, there is no evidence to suggest that a body of Templars received sanctuary in Scotland and continued to exist as a branch of the Hospitallers or that they served under King Robert at Bannockburn.

28. A re-enactor in the role of Edward II. In reality, the king would have been rather better armoured, with plates for his arms and legs, plate gloves and a helmet, probably a bacinet.

29. Pilkington Jackson's statue of Robert I at the Bannockburn Visitor Centre.

30. Art and propaganda. This purports be a thirteenth-century illustration showing Alexander III appearing at an English parliament as a subordinate of Edward I, but is a much later work. (Courtesy of Jonathan Reeve)

31. The coronation of Edward I. Edward's ambitions would plunge England into a series of wars with England that would last for centuries. (Courtesy of Jonathan Reeve)

32. The deposition of King John at the hands of Edward I. (Courtesy of Jonathan Reeve)

33. Castles and fortresses of medieval Scotland. In the early 1300s Edward I held about forty castles across the country. Robert I adopted a policy of slighting castles as he captured them to prevent the restoration of a Plantagenet government.

34. The more significant towns of medieval Scotland.

35. A West Highland soldier's grave effigy showing a fashionable combination of bacinet helmet and chainmail protection for the neck and shoulders. (Courtesy of Jonathan Reeve)

36. A page from Sir Thomas Grey's *Scalacronica*. Grey's extensive personal experience of war in medieval Scotland makes his account one of the most valuable sources. (Courtesy of Jonathan Reeve)

37. The Coronation Stone of Scottish kings, taken from Scone by Edward I, it remained at Westminster for seven centuries and is now at Edinburgh Castle. There is considerable doubt as to whether Edward's prize was in fact the genuine article or just a piece of

local rock passed off as the real thing. (Courtesy of Jonathan Reeve)

38. Coins of Robert I. Silver pennies like these were minted throughout western Europe and circulated freely since they were of a similar weight and fineness of silver. (Courtesy of Jonathan Reeve)

39. Seal of Robert Bruce, Earl of Carrick. (Courtesy of Jonathan Reeve)

40. A Letter Patent of King John. (Courtesy of Jonathan Reeve)

41. Seal of Robert I, depicting him in one of the crucial roles of the medieval king; the soldier. (Courtesy of Jonathan Reeve)

42. Great seal of Robert I, showing him in another vital role of kingship, as Judge and law-giver. (Courtesy of Jonathan Reeve)

43. A dramatic and romantic Victorian depiction of medieval battle. The armour is, perhaps, a little fanciful, but it gives an impression of the crowded nature of the battlefield. (Courtesy of Jonathan Reeve)

44. One of several swords associated with Robert I. Although this one is of rather later date, great swords of state were made for processions and ceremonies, but the swords of the early fourteenth century were light, strong and well-balanced. (Courtesy of Jonathan Reeve)

45. The memorial stone of Robert I's ally Angus Og. There is no clear evidence that he served at Bannockburn, though his long association with the Bruces would point in that direction. Angus died in battle against the English during Edward Bruce's campaign to make himself King of Ireland. (Courtesy of Jonathan Reeve)

46. A hammerhead, apparently recovered from the area of the battle. (Courtesy of Jonathan Reeve)

47. Seal of Edward I, showing him as warrior and law-giver. Although he is known to history as the 'Hammer of the Scots', that epithet was not accorded him until he had been dead for 200 years; he only ever won one battle in Scotland – Falkirk in 1298. Edward II's seal was lost at the battle of Bannockburn. (Courtesy of Jonathan Reeve)

48. Detail of a west of Scotland grave effigy, showing the warrior with all the trappings of the medieval gentleman at war – bacinet, chainmail, padded jacket and a formal heraldic device on his shield. (Courtesy of Jonathan Reeve)

49. An ornate stone effigy of a Scottish nobleman from the Western Isles or West Highlands.

50 & 51. Scottish foot soldiers of the late thirteenth centuries as depicted in an English manuscript.

52. Scottish troops besieging Carlisle. Robert I was bedevilled by a lack of effective artillery.

53. Grave effigy of a typical man-at-arms of the late thirteenth century. (Courtesy of Jonathan Reeve)

54. Arms of the King of Scotland. (Courtesy of Jonathan Reeve)

55. The arms of Gilbert de Clare, Earl of Gloucester. A cousin of Robert I, de Clare was a senior commander in the Engliash army at Bannockburn. (Courtesy of Jonathan Reeve)

56. The arms of Edward Bruce, Earl of Carrick, who commanded one of the Scottish schiltrums at Bannockburn. An attempt to make himself King of Ireland came to an end when he was killed at the Battle of Faughart. (Courtesy of Jonathan Reeve)

57. Arms of Ingram d'Umfraville. An important supporter of the Balliol kingship, d'Umfraville fought for Edward II at Bannockburn. (Courtesy of Jonathan Reeve)

58. Depiction of a man-at-arms in the very height of military fashion as worn in 1314. (Courtesy of Jonathan Reeve)

59. Illuminated capital from the charter of Carlisle, showing Andrew de Harcla's pivotal role in the defence of he town against King Robert. Harcla would later come to believe that peace with the Scots was the only realistic option and entered negotiations with Robert I, to the fury of Edward II who had Harcla executed for treason.

60. Plan of the main action at Bannockburn as presented by Gardiner, Oman and many others since. This interpretation has the English perform an opposed river crossing then moving across a swamp to attack the Scots, utterly contradicting all of the contemporary source material.

61. Outline drawing of Bothwell Castle. It is likely that the castle had not been fully constructed in stone by 1314, though there was an extensive English garrison. The Earl of Hereford escaped to Bothwell after the battle, only to be taken prisoner by the commander, Fitz Gilbert, an Englishman long–resident in Scotland, who decided that his best career prospects now lay with King Robert rather than King Edward.

62. Edward I. It was his ambition that started the war in 1296. (Courtesy of Jonathan Reeve)

63. Arms of the King of England. (Courtesy of Jonathan Reeve)

64. The seal of John Balliol. (Courtesy of Jonathan Reeve)

65. A medieval highland fantasy. Great swords of this style did not come into use until long after Bannockburn and were never a common weapon compared to the spear.

66. Depiction of King Robert and his Queen, Elizabeth. (Courtesy of Jonathan Reeve)

67. Seal of Edward Balliol. The death of his deposed father made Edward Balliol the legitimate King of Scotland. The objective of the De Soulis conspiracy of 1320 was to restore the Balliol dynasty. (Courtesy of Jonathan Reeve)

68. Brass of Robert Bruce, Dunfermline Abbey. Above his shoulders are, on the left, the lion rampant of Scotland and, on the right, the saltire of the Bruce family. (Courtesy of Jonathan Reeve)

# Notes

Preface

1. Myton, 20th September, 1319.
2. Culblean, 30th November, 1335.
3. Burghmuir, 30th July, 1335, Crichtondene, November/December, 1337.
4. Stirling castle fell to Edward I in 1296, to the Scots in 1299, to Edward again in 1304 and to the Scots in 1314.
5. See Dr Fiona Watson's essay, 'The Expression of Power in a Medieval Kingdom; Thirteenth Century Castles.' S. Foster, A. McInnes, R. McInnes, (ed.), *Scottish Power Centres* (Edinburgh, 1998).
6. The feature known as the 'Ripple' near Gettysburg, Pennsylvania only appears on maps because it was feature which had some effect on the course of the fighting. It is too low to be recorded on a conventional map.
7. Two stirrups (not a pair), one bodkin arrowhead and one hammerhead fragment are the sum total of Bannockburn 'finds' to date.

I. The Story So Far

1. S.R. Gardiner. *Outline of English History*, (1896), C.W.C. Oman, History of England (1910).
2. C.W.C. Oman, *History of the Peninsular War*, (5 volumes), (1902–30)
3. W.M. MacKenzie, *The Battle of Bannockburn*, (Glasgow, 1913).
4. *Scalacronica, Fordoun, Lanercost, Scotichronicon, Vita Edwardi Secundi*, see 'abbreviations'.
5. E.M. Barron, *The Scottish War of Independence*, (Inverness, 1912).
6. G.W.S Barrow, 'Lothian in the War of Independence' (SHR 55, 1976).
7. J. Shearer, *Fact and Fiction in the Story of Bannockburn*, (Stirling, 1909)
8. M. Penman, *The Scottish Civil War*, (Stroud, 2002)
9. The garrisons of Coull castle, (possibly Aboyne) were relatively large at only 53. A.A.M. Duncan, 'The War of the Scots', p.144, (TRHS, 1991).
10. J. Harvey, *The Plantagenets* (London, 1967), p.121.
11. A.D.M.Barrell, *Medieval Scotland* p.96, (Cambridge, 2000), hereafter Barrell, *Scotland*.
12. See F. Watson, *Under the Hammer* for a detailed examination of the Balliol resistance to the administration of Edward.
13. See A. Young, The *Comyns. Robert the Bruce's Rivals*. Hereafter 'The Comyns' for a detailed examination of the rise and fall of the Comyn family.
14. R. Nicholson, *Scotland. The Later Middle Ages*, p.64 (Edinburgh, 1974), hereafter, SLMA
15. G.W.S Barrow, *Robert the Bruce and the Community of the Realm of Scotland* (London, 1965 and subsequent editions) for a detailed examination of the career of Robert I; hereafter Barrow, *Bruce*.

16. *The Comyns*, p.208.
17. C. McNamee, *The Wars of the Bruces*, p. 59, (East Lothian, 1997), hereafter McNamee, *Wars*.
18. R. Mason, 'Scotching the Brut' in *Scotland Revisited* (Ed) J. Wormald, (London, 1991).
19. G. Donaldson, *Scottish Historical Documents* p.29, (Edinburgh, 1975), hereafter SHD.
20. W. Fergusson, *Scotland's Relations with England. A Survey to 1707*, p.27. (Edinburgh, 1977).
21. M. McKisack, *England in the Fourteenth Century*, p.35 (Oxford 1959).
22. J. Harvey, *The Plantagenets*, p.122.
23. *The Comyns*, p.197.
24. J. Harvey, *The Plantagenets*, p.122.
25. *War of the Scots*, p.127.
26. A. Nusbacher, *Bannockburn, 1314*, p.110 (Stroud, 2000).
27. Barrow, *Bruce*, p.62.
28. *Fordoun*, I, 342.
29. SLMA, p.65.
30. Stevenson, *Documents*, DCXXIV.
31. C. Von Clausewitz, *On War*. (Ed). A. Rapoport, (London, 1971)
32. *War of the Scots*, p.127
33. Barrow, *Bruce*, p.447–52 lists many southern Scots who supported Robert I in 1306. The list shows only those Scots whose properties were sought by supporters of Edward I, not all of those who accepted Robert's kingship.
34. Only a very modest proportion of town dwellers enjoyed the status of 'burgess', see E. Ewan, *Town Life in Fourteenth Century Scotland* (Edinburgh, 1990).
35. See Barrow's 'Lothian in the War of Independence' for a detailed examination of Scots in Plantagenet garrisons.

II. What Did the Combatants Fight For?

1. Edward took his responsibilities as 'locum' ruler of Scotland pending the outcome of the Great Cause of 1291–2 quite seriously, as indicated by the many surviving documents relating to Scottish affairs calendared by Bain and Stevenson.
2. Barrell, *Scotland*, pp.95–103.
3. The first volume of Stevenson, *Documents*, lists many examples of the fees of sheriffs and household knights who had served Alexander III which were paid under the authority of Edward I for the duration of the Great Cause.
4. 'Itinerary of King Edward I Throughout his Reign', H. Gough, *English Historical Review* vol. 16. (July 1901).
5. CDS, ii, p.194–208.
6. Stevenson, *Documents*, ii, p.455.
7. Hugh de Penicuik was forfeited of his chief property at Penicuik, Midlothian and various properties in England for 'rebellion' and had his estates restored under the terms of the Strathord agreement of February 1304. He seems to have been active for the Balliol party throughout the years after 1287/8. CDS, ii, Nos. 1481, 1594.
8. SLMA, p.47.
9. SLMA, p.27
10. A.A.M. Duncan, *Scotland. The Making of the Kingdom*, pp.590–1, (Edinburgh, 1975).
11. Barrow, *Bruce*, pp.21–2.

12. Ibid, pp.25–7.

13. See *The Comyns*, Chapters 2 and 3 for a detailed examination of the rise of the Comyn family through their service to the crown.

14. M.Prestwich, *The Three Edwards*, pp.44–7, (London, 1980), hereafter *Three Edwards*

15. SLMA, pp.38–41.

16. Barrell, *Scotland*, pp.95–103 for a brief and lucid discussion of the issues of the Great Cause.

17. Barrow, *Bruce*, p.87.

18. The toll of casualties may well have been confused with an estimate of the number of people killed during the sack of Berwick four weeks earlier.

19. 11th September, 1297.

20. Sir Alexander Seton was involved in arranging a truce with the Bruce party in 1308.

21. *Three Edwards*, pp.100–106.

22. Nusbacher, *Bannockburn, 1314*, p.115.

23. SLMA, p.85.

24. Penman, *The Scottish Civil War* pp.85–6.

25. Barrow, *Bruce*, p.62.

## III. Lions and Leopards

1. CDS, ii, 1244.

2. CDS, v, 448.

3. *Three Edwards*, p.80

4. Ibid.

5. J.Willard, 'The Scottish Raids and the Taxation of Northern England' Colorado, 1908, cited in McKisack, *England in the Fourteenth Century.*

6. *War of the Scots*, p. 144.

7. RRS, v, 41.

8. TNA, C47/22/10/11. Sir Adam had served as Chancellor for Scotland under Edward I.

9. Pierre de Lubaud served as a man-at-arms in Edward I's Lothian garrisons, rising to the post of constable of Linlithgow by September 1305 (CDS, ii, No. 1691). He became a major Lothian landholder under Edward I and Edward II. He defected to the Scots to preserve his position as the Plantagenet administration crumbled, gaining, among other properties, the Barony of Dalkeith, of which he was forfeited in 1316 (RMS, I, 62).

10. Robert de Hastang received temporary grants of the properties of a number of Lothian Scots who were in Bruce allegiance in 1312 (CDS, iii, Nos. 230, 244). Some of these men had been with King Robert for several years before forfeiture, suggesting that Edward II, unlike his heir who forfeited over 100 Lothian men and women in 1335–7, felt that forfeiture was a weapon of last resort.

11. See McNamee, *Wars*, chapter 3 for a detailed examination of Robert I's operations in northern England.

12. Marjorie Comyn, *The Comyns*, p.179.

13. Barrow, *Bruce*, p. 118.

14. SLMA, pp.53–4.

15. Ibid, 556–6.

16. Barrell, *Scotland*, pp.108–9.

17. Barrow, *Bruce*, 151, 188.

18. SLMA, p.59.
19. *The Comyns*, p.174.
20. TNA, C47/22/8.
21. SLMA, p.60.
22. SLMA, p.61.
23. Barrow, *Bruce*, pp.172–5.
24. SLMA, p.67.
25. Barrow, *Bruce*, p.184.
26. Bruce was to be disappointed by his eventual exclusion from senior office. Barrell, *Scotland*, pp.112–3.
27. Barrow, *Bruce,* p.196.
28. C. Brown, *Robert the Bruce. A Life Chronicled.* p.116. (Stroud, 2004)
29. *War of the Scots*, p. 135.
30. Barrow, pp.210–13. Robert's coronation or inauguration was witnessed by a surprisingly large section of the senior political community of Scotland including at least three earls – Atholl, Lennox and Menteith – and probably by the young Earl of Mar. According to Guisborough there were five earls, four bishops and 'the people of the land.' The absence of the Comyn family is hardly surprising.
31. Bishop Lamberton, though a strong supporter of Scottish independence, could see the way the wind blew and entered into negotiations to return to the peace of Edward I, claiming that he had been forced to support Bruce, SLMA, 72.
32. McNamee, *Wars*, pp.31–2.
33. Ibid, 31.
34. SLMA, 74–5.
35. C. McNamee, *Wars*, p.40.
36. Ibid, 40–1.
37. Barrow, *Bruce*, p.244.

IV. Sources and Interpretation

1. Nusbacher, *Bannockburn* 1314, p.11.
2. See abbreviations for full title.
3. See abbreviations for full title.
4. See abbreviations for full title.
5. Protections were, as the name applies, documents issued by the crown to give 'protection' from court actions to men who were on active service.
6. *Rot. Scot.* I, p.106.

V. Brave Companies

1. The terms Vallet (or vadlet), Socius, esquire (or escuyer) homines ad arma and occasionally companion are all used interchangeably in many documents calendared by Bain and indicate men-at-arms.
2. CDS 3, pp.376–91, accounts of Sir John de Strivelin, sheriff of Edinburgh for Edward III.
3. SHD, p.54.
4. A.A.M. Duncan, Scotland. *The Making of the Kingdom* pp.582–3. (Edinburgh, 1975).

5. CDS, ii, Nos .952, 1011
6. CDS, ii, 1011.
7. In a description of one of his early operations, Wallace's force was said to be 'all well mounted'; a term used exclusively of men-at-arms to indicate that they had mounts suitable for war.
8. See Watson's *Under the Hammer* for a detailed and accessible account of the efforts of John Balliol's supporters against Edward I's administration.
9. *Scalacronica*, 25.
10. CDS, v, No.472.
11. R. Nicholson, *Edward III and the Scots. The Formative Years of a Military Career,* pp.232–6 (Oxford, 1965)
12. TNA, E101/13/15.
13. *War of the Scots*, p.138.
14. A.A.M. Duncan, *The Bruce*, p.670, 674, 676. (Edinburgh, 1997) Hereafter *Barbour*.
15. Barrow, *Bruce*, p.300.
16. 'War and the Later Medieval Scottish Nobility' in (Ed) T. Brotherstone & D. Ditchburn, *Freedom and Authority*, p.120. (East Lothian, 2000).
17. Ibid, p.121.
18. M. Brown. 'The Development of Border Lordship' 1332–58. (*Historical review*, LXXV, February 1997).
19. CDS, v, No. 434.
20. CDS iii, pp.408–11.
21. CDS, v, No. 514,
22. Ibid, No. 515.
23. CDS, iii, No. 336.
24. CDS iii, No. 682.
25. J.E.Morris, *Bannockburn*, p.51.
26. *Barbour*, p.420.
27. Ibid, p.423.
28. Nusbacher, *Bannockburn, 1314*, p.116.
29. F. Watson, 'Expressions of Power', p.71.
30. F. Watson, 'The Enigmatic Lion' in (ed.) D. Broun, R. Finlay and M.Lynch, *Image and Identity*, (East Lothian, 1998).
31. CDS, v, 353.
32. RRS, v, 414.
33. J. Sadler, Scottish Battles, pp.45–53, (Edinburgh, 1996).
34. 'Plea Rolls of the Army of Edward I, 1296.' *Scottish History Society Miscellany* ix, 1990.
35. C. Brown, 'We are Cummand of Gentilmen' (PhD thesis, St. Andrews, 2006), p.51. Forthcoming as *Knights of the Scottish Wars of Independence*, (Stroud, 2008).
36. *War of the Scots*, p.145.
37. Barrow, *Bruce*, p.403.
38. Ibid, p.405.
39. RRS, v, pp.48–9.
40. TNA, C47/22/2/57.
41. J. Sadler, *Scottish Battles*, pp.45–53.
42. 'Plea Rolls of the Army of Edward I, 1296.' *Scottish History Society Miscellany* ix, 1990.
43. *Barbour*, p.437.
44. S. Reid, 'Bloody Bannockburn', *Military Illustrated*, No. 224.
45. *Barbour*, p.471.

46. RRS, v, p.261.
47. Ibid, p.453.
48. Ibid, p.459.
49. *Scotichronicon*, viii, p.140.
50. *War of the Scots*, p.148.
51. *Liber Melrose*, I, pp.313–4.
52. RRS, v, p.679.
53. RRS, vi, p.63.
54. CDS, iii, No. 653.
55. McNamee, *Wars*, 66.
56. Ibid, p.126.
57. CDS , ii, No. 1479.
58. *Rot. Scot*, i, p.78
59. McNamee, *Wars*, p.126.
60. Barrow, Bruce, p.291.
61. *Rot. Scot*, i, p.127

## VI. Going to the War

1. TNA C47/22/10/11
2. CDS, iii, No.337
3. TNA, SC8/70/3470.
4. *War of the Scots*, p.141.
5. M. Penman, *The Scottish Civil War*, p. 76 (Stroud, 2002), however Professor Duncan suggests that the declaration was issued at the same time as a series of documents issued at a council in Dundee, RRS, v, 35–7.
6. C47/3/51/5, PRO 30/26/37.
7. S. Reid, 'Bloody Bannockburn', *Military Illustrated*, No. 224.
8. CDS, iii, p. 376-91.
9. McNamee, *Wars,* p.62.
10. Barrow, *Bruce*, p.94, n.1, citing TNA E159/69 m.11d.
11. Morris, *Bannockburn*, p.39.
12. McKisack, *England in the Fourteenth Century*, p.35.
13. Morris, *Bannockburn*, P.32.
14. Ibid, p.31.
15. Barrow, *Bruce*, p.293.
16. *Barbour*, p.102. Alexander Seton became a prisoner of war. He probably taken at the battle of Methven and was sent to York.
17. Barrow, *Bruce*, p.319.

## VII. Locating the Battle

1. *Barbour*, p.444.
2. Barrow, *Bruce*, 306.
3. A Merk or Mark was a unit of account; the only coin of this period being the sterling, a silver coin of a given weight and purity, common to what we would now call Germany, The Netherlands and Belgium as well as to Scotland and England. Pennies

of all nationalities circulated freely throughout western Europe. A merk was eight score (160) sterlings. Pennies were also accounted in shillings (12) and pounds (240). The fact that a merk was 2/3 of one pound was pure coincidence.

4. Barrow, *Bruce*, p.309.
5. K. De Vries, *Infantry Warfare in the Fourteenth Century. Discipline, Tactics and Technology.* (Woodbridge, 1996).
6. CDS, iii, pp.126–7
7. Barrow, *Bruce*, p.304.
8. J. Sadler, *Scottish Battles*, pp.45–53.
9. Barrow, *Bruce*, p.305

## VIII. Muster and March to Battle

1. SLMA, p.87.
2. Ibid.
3. MacKenzie, *The Battle of Bannockburn*, p.41, (Glasgow, 1913)
4. Ibid, p.53.
5. J.E. Morris, *Bannockburn*, p.62.
6. Shearer, *Fact and Fiction in the Story of Bannockburn*, p.75.
7. *War of the Scots*, p.170.
8. McNamee, *Wars*, p.63.
9. N.P. Milner, *Vegetius; Epitome of Military Science*, p.111 (Liverpool, 1993).
10. See Dr Andrew Ayton, *Knights and Warhorses* (Woodbridge, 1994) and Andy King's paper 'Military Service of Northumbrian Knights' (Durham University medieval Conference, 2001) for a detailed analysis of northern English cavalry service in the later Middle Ages.
11. See R. Davies, *The Medieval Warhorse*, (London 1989) and R. Oakeshott, *A Knight and his Horse*, (London, 1995) for a detailed examination of chargers in the later Middle Ages.
12. G. Cameron Stone, *A Glossary of the Construction, Decoration and Use of Arms and Armour* (New York, 1961).
13. J.E. Morris, *Bannockburn*, p.87.
14. See C. Brown, *The Second Scottish War of Independence*, p.13 (Stroud, 2002).

## IX. The First Clash

1. Barrow, *Bruce*, p.311.
2. *Barbour*, pp.296–8, 304–8.

## X. The Second Clash

1. McKisack, *England in the Fourteenth Century*, p.36.
2. Barrow, *Bruce*, p.314.
3. The retinue of Sir Robert Clifford included a minimum of twelve men-at-arms, see p.152 above.
4. *Barbour*, p.438.

5. *Barbour*, p.445.
6. *Barbour*, p.505.

XI. The Night of 23–24 June, 1314

1. *Barbour*, p.471.

XII. The Great Battle at Stirling

1. Nusbacher, *Bannockburn* 1314, p.108.
2. Dr De Vries interprets this as meaning that the English cavalry were in two formations behind the infantry, however the words 'wings and centre' surely indicate three separate formations, presumably with King Edward's division in the centre.
3. The focus of the action.
4. J. Sadler, *Scottish Battles* p.51.
5. *Barbour*, p.500.
6. Barrow, *Bruce*, p.331.
7. Towton, for example, though probably a large battle in terms of numbers, was a purely domestic conflict.

XIII. After the Fight

1. Walsingham gives a figure of 154 Earls, barons, knights and gentry killed at Bannockburn. Barbour's implied figure of 700 cannot be taken as a careful estimate, but if losses among the men-at-arms were of the order of twenty-five per cent, he might not be so very far from the mark. A song of the time ran 'Maidens of England sore may you mourn/For you have lost your men at Bannockburn.'
2. CDS, iii, no. 627.
3. CDS, iii, no. 624.
4. G. Donaldson, *Scottish Kings*, p.25 (New York, 1967).
5. McNamee, p.214. The expedition was mounted by the Earl of Arundel from the Humber estuary.
6. SLMA, p.104.
7. McNamee, *Wars,* pp.100–1.
8. R. Nicholson, *Edward III and the Scots*, p.35.
9. SHD, p.61-3.
10. Barrow, *Bruce*, pp.444–5.
11. M. Penman, 'A Fell Coniuracioun Agayn King Robert the Doughty King: the Soules Conspiracy of 1318–20', *Innes review*, 50, 1999 is the best examination and analysis of this remarkable event.
12. R. Nicholson, *Edward III and the Scots*, pp.76–84.
13. Ibid, pp.190–1.

# Bibliography

## Printed Primary Source Material

*Acts of the Parliaments of Scotland*, C. Innes & T. Thomson (London, 1844).

*Anglo-Scottish Relations*, 1174–1328, Some Selected Documents. E.L.G. Stones (London, 1965).

*Calendar of Chancery Rolls Miscellaneous* (London, 1916).

*Calendar of Close Rolls*. HMSO (London, 1892-1907).

*Calendar of Documents Relating to Scotland*, vol.i-iv. J. Bain. (Edinburgh, 1881-88).

*Calendar of Documents Relating to Scotland*, vol.v. G. Simpson and J.Galbraith. (Edinburgh, 1988).

*Calendar of Inquisitions* (Miscellaneous) (London, 1916).

*Calendar of Inquisitions Post Mortem* (London, 1908–10).

*Carte Monialium de Northberwic* Bannatyne Club (Edinburgh, 1847).

*Chronicle of Holyrood*. (Ed) O. Anderson. SHS (Edinburgh, 1938).

*Chronicle of Melrose* (Trans) J. Stevenson (Llanerch reprint, 1991).

*Chronicles (of Jean Froissart)*. (Tr.&Ed.) G.Brereton. (London, 1968).

*Chronicles of the Reigns of Edward I and Edward II* (Ed) W. Stubbs (London, 1882).

*Chronicon de Lanercost*. Bannatyne Club. (Edinburgh, 1839).

*Chronique de Jean Le Bel* (Ed) J.Viard & E.Deprez. Societe de l'Histoire de France (Paris, 1904).

*Documents and Records Illustrating the History of Scotland*. Sir F. Palgrave. Treasury and Exchequer (London, 1837).

*Documents Illustrative of the History of Scotland*. J.Stevenson. (Edinburgh, 1870).

*Early Sources of Scottish History* A.O. Anderson (Stamford, 1990).

*Edward I and the Throne of Scotland*, 1290–96. E.L.G. Stones and G.Simpson. (Oxford, 1978).

*Exchequer Rolls of Scotland*. vol i, (Ed) J. Stuart and G. Burnett. (Edinburgh, 1876).

*Foedera, Conventiones, Litterae et Cuiuscunque Generis Acta Publica* (Ed) T. Rymer (London, 1816–69).

*Gascon Rolls*, 1307–17 (Ed.) Y. Renouard (London, 1962).

*Liber Cartarum Prioratus Sancti Andree in Scotia* Bannatyne Club (Edinburgh, 1841).

*Liber de Sancte Marie de Calchou*. Bannatyne Club. (Edinburgh, 1846).

*Liber Sancte Marie de Melros*. Bannatyne Club. (Edinburgh, 1887).

*Memoranda Rolls* 1326–1327 (London, 1968)

*Orygenale Cronykil of Scotland*. Andrew Wyntoun (Ed) D. Laing (Edinburgh, 1872–9).

*Parliamentary Writs and Writs of Military Summons*. (Ed) F. Palgrave (London, 1827–33).

*Records of the Wardrobe and Household*. (Ed) F. and C. Byerley (London, 1985).

*Regesta Regum Scottorum*. vol. vi. (Ed) .B. Webster Edinburgh University Press (Edinburgh, 1982).

*Regesta Regum Scottorum*. vol.v. (Ed) A.A.M. Duncan Edinburgh University Press (Edinburgh, 1988).

*Registrum de Sancte Marie de Neubotle*. (Ed) C. Innes (Edinburgh, 1849).

*Registrum Honoris de Morton* Bannatyne Club (Edinburgh, 1853).

*Registrum Monasterii de Cambuskenneth* (Ed) W. Fraser, Grampian Club (1872).

*Rotuli Scotiae*. J. MacPherson. Record Commission (London, 1814–19).

*Scalacronica of Sir Thomas Grey*, (Ed.&Trans) Sir H. Maxwell, Maclehose. (Edinburgh, 1907).

*Scotichronicon of Walter Bower* (Ed) D. Watt. (Aberdeen, 1991).

*Scotland in 1298: Documents relating to the campaign of Edward I in that year and especially to the battle of Falkirk* H. Gough (Paisley, 1888).

*Scottish Historical Documents*. G. Donaldson. (Edinburgh, 1974).

*Source book of Scottish History* (Ed) W. Croft Dickinson, G. Donaldson and I. Milne. Nelson (Edinburgh, 1952).

*The Bannatyne Miscellany* (Edinburgh 1836).

*The Book of Fayttes of Armes and of Chivalry* (Ed. A. Byles) OUP (Oxford 1932)

*The Bruce*. J.Barbour (Ed.) A.A.M. Duncan Canongate (Edinburgh, 1997).

*The Charters of Holyrood* Bannatyne Club (Edinburgh, 1840).

*The Chartulary of Newbattle* Bannatyne Club (Edinburgh, 1849).

*The Chartulary of Coldstream* (Ed) C. Rogers. (London, 1879).

*The Chronicle of Lanercost*. (Tr.) H. Maxwell (Glasgow, 1913).

*The Chronicle of Walter of Guisborough* (Ed.) J.Rothwell (Camden, 1957).

*The Laing Charters* (Ed.) J. Anderson. James Thin (Edinburgh, 1899).

*The Original Chronicle of Andrew of Wyntoun*. S.T.S. (Ed.) J. Amours (Edinburgh, 1903–14).

*The Register of the Great Seal of Scotland*. (Ed.) J.Thomson (Edinburgh, 1984).

*The Roll of Caerlaverock* (Ed) T. Wright (London, 1864).

*Treaty Rolls* (Ed.) P. Chaplais (London, 1955)

*The Scottish King's Household* (Ed) M. Bateson, SHS Miscellany (Edinburgh, 1904).

*Vita Edwardi Secundi* (Ed.) N. Denholm-Young (London, 1957)

# The National Archives, Kew

The majority of these documents refer to stores, casualties, ransoms and horse valuations. They do not refer specifically to the Battle of Bannockburn, but collectively they make an important contribution to our understanding of the general approach to military service and conditions in the Scottish administrations of Edward I and Edward II.

E101/13/15
E/39/2/21
E101/7/5
E101/7/1
E101/531/7
E101/531/8
E39/99/19
E39/99/18
E101/7/24
E/39/15/3
E101/7/9
E101/7/17
E101/7/28
E39/15/1
E101/10/5
E101/11/14
E101/12/11
E101/531/13
E101/13/37
E101/17/29
E101/14/21
E101/68/1/2
E101/68/1/3
E101/428/25
E101/331/5
C47/22/2/33
C143/27/10
SC8/88/4369
SC8/88/4375
SC13/A57
SC8/46/2255
SC8/43/7141
SC13/A102
SC13/E6
SC13/E9
SC13/S746
SC13/S476
C47/22/3/24
C47/22/4/2
C47/22/5/57
C47/22/9/59

E101/11/9
E101/12/38
E101/17/25
E101/68/20
E101/482/20
E135/10/1
E101/16/11
E39/3/47
C47/22/2/12
C47/22/2/32
E39/100/138
C47/3/32/25
C47/22/9/109
C47/22/6/18
SC13/S150
SC13/A88
SC1/39/19
SC32/67
SC33/3
SC33/31
SC34/179
SC8/51/2504
SC8/9/432
C47/22/9/65
E101/12/12
E101/11/14
C47/22/2/57
C47/3/51/5
C47/22/8

# National Archives of Scotland

The RH5 series consists of documents transferred to the Scottish Record Office from the Public records Office in London, most of which also have TNA code references which have been included here. Virtually none of these documents refer specifically to Bannockburn, but they are relevant to our general understanding of military obligation and the political process of late medieval Scotland.

RH5, 39 C47/22/6(43)
RH5, 20 C47/22/5(1)
RH5, 22 C47/22/5(3)
RH5, 31 C47/22/5(16)
RH5, 32 C47/22/5(15)
RH5, 41 C47/22/9(2)
RH5, 53 C47/22/12(5)
RH5, 56 E93/94/5(1)
RH5, 66 E39/94/5(11)
RH5, 86 E39/94/8(1)
RH5, 90 E39/84/8(5)
RH5, 98 E39/94/8(14)
RH5, 114 E99/100/146(2)
RH5, 115 E39/100/147(1)
RH5, 120 E39/100/150(1)
RH5, 205 E39/100/188(8)
RH5, 220 E39/100/189/5
RH5, 227
RH5, 230
RH6, 67
RH6, 68
RH6, 70
RH6, 80
RH6, 83
RH6, 98

RH6, 99
RH6, 100
RH6, 104
RH6, 105
RH6, 106
RH6, 112
RH6, 118
RH6, 119
RH6, 120

# Secondary Material

Alger, J., *The Quest for Victory: The History of the Principles of War* (Connecticut, 1982).

Allmand, C., *Society at War. The Experience of England and France during the Hundred Years War* (Edinburgh, 1973).

Allmand, C., *Power, Culture and Religion in France* (Woodbridge, 1989).

Allmand, C., *The Hundred Years War* (Cambridge, 1998).

Anderson, M., *A History of Scottish Forestry*, ed. Taylor, C.(London, 1967).

Ayton, A. *Knights and Warhorses* (Woodbridge, 1994).

Bain, J. *The Edwards in Scotland 1296–1377* (Edinburgh, 1901).

Balfour Paul, Sir John. The Scots Peerage (Edinburgh, 1904–14).

Barrell, A. *Medieval Scotland* (Cambridge, 2000).

Barrne, J., *War in Medieval Society* (London, 1974).

Barron, E.M., *The Scottish War of Independence* (Inverness, 1934).

Barrow, G.W.S., *Feudal Britain* (London, 1956).

Barrow G.W.S., *The Kingdom of the Scots* (London, 1973).

Barrow G.W.S., *Robert the Bruce and the Community of the Realm of Scotland* (London, 1965)

Barrow, G.W.S., *Kingship and Unity* (London, 1981).

Barrow, G.W.S., *Scotland and its Neighbours in the Middle Ages* (London, 1992).

Barrow, G.W.S., *Scotland and her Neighbours in the Later Middle Ages* (London, 1992).

Barrow, G.W.S., *The Anglo-Norman Era in Scottish History* (Oxford, 1980).

Bingham, C., *The Life and Times of Edward II* (London, 1973).

Blair, C., *European Armour 1066–1700,* (New York, 1972).

Boardman, S. & Ross, A. (Ed.) *The Exercise of Power in Medieval Scotland* (Chippenham, 2003).

Bothwell, J. *The Age of Edward III* (Woodbridge, 2001).

Bradbury, J. *The Medieval Siege* (Woodbridge, 1992).

Brotherstone, T, & Ditchburn, D. (Ed.) *Freedom and Authority* (East Lothian, 2000).

Broun, Finlay and Lynch (Ed.) *Image and Identity* (Edinburgh, 1998).

Brown, C., *Encyclopaedia of Scottish Battles* (Stroud, 2008).

Brown, C., *Robert the Bruce. A Life Chronicled* (Stroud, 2003).

Brown, C., *William Wallace* (Stroud, 2005).

Brown, C., *Knights of the Scottish Wars of Independence* (Stroud, 2008)

Brown, M., *The Black Douglases* (East Linton, 1998).

Brown, M., *The Wars of Scotland 1214–1371* (East Linton, 2005).

Brown, R.A., Colvin, H.M. & Taylor, A.J. *The History of the King's Works* vol.i (London, 1963).

Burns, W., *The Scottish War of Independence* (Glasgow, 1874).

Bush, M., *Rich Noble, Poor Noble* (Manchester, 1988).

Clark, J. (Ed.), *The Medieval Horse and its Equipment c.*1150–1450 (Woodbridge, 2004).

Clausewitz, C., *On War* (Harmondsworth, 1968).

Contamine, P., (trans) M. Jones, *War in the Middle Ages* (Oxford, 1987).

Coss, P., Lordship, *Knighthood and Locality: A study in English Society* (Cambridge, 1991).

Coss, P., *The Knight in Medieval England* (Stroud, 1993).

Costain, T., *The Three Edwards* (New York, 1958).

Croft Dickinson, W. *Scotland from the Earliest Times to 1603* (Oxford, 1977).

Curry, A. & Hughes, M. (Eds), *Arms, Armies and Fortifications in the Hundred Years War* (Woodbridge, 1994).

Davies, R., *The Medieval Warhorse* (London, 1989).

Davies, R., *Conquest, Co-existence and Change; Wales 1063–1415* (Oxford, 1987).

De Vries, K., *Infantry Warfare in the Early Fourteenth Century: Discipline, Tactics and Technology* (Woodbridge, 1996).

Dickinson, J., *The Battle of Neville's Cross* (Durham, 1991).

Dickinson, W., Croft, *Scotland from the Earliest Times to 1603* (Edinburgh, 1965).

Ditchburn, D., *Scotland and Europe* (East Linton, 2001).

Dixon, P. *Puir Labourers and Busy Husbandmen* (Edinburgh, 2003)

Dodghson, R.A. *Land and Society in Early Scotland* (Oxford, 1981).

Donaldson, G., *Scottish Kings* (New York, 1992).

Dowden, J., *The Medieval Church in Scotland* (Glasgow, 1910).

Duncan A.A.M., *Scotland. The Making of the Kingdom* (Edinburgh, 1975).

Du Picq, Col. A., *Battle Studies. Ancient and Modern Battle*. (Trans. J. Greeley & R. Cotton) (New York, 1921).

Dunne, D. (Ed), *War and Society in Early Medieval Britain* (Liverpool, 2000).

Dupuy, R.& T., *Numbers, Prediction and War* (Indianapolis, 1979).

Dupuy, T., *Understanding Defeat* (New York, 1990).

Easson, E., *Medieval Religious Houses in Scotland* (London, 1957).

Ewan, E., *Townlife in Fourteenth Century Scotland* (Edinburgh, 1990).

Fergusson. W., *Scotland's Relations with England. A Survey to 1701* (Edinburgh, 1977).

Fergusson, W., *The Identity of the Scottish Nation: An Historic Quest* (Edinburgh, 1998).

Fowler, K. (Ed), *The Hundred Years War* (London, 1971).

Frame, R., *The Political Development of the British Isles, 1100–1500* (Oxford 1995).

Fryde, E., *Peasants and Landlords in Later Medieval England* (Stroud, 1986).

Fryde, N., *The Tyranny and Fall of Edward II, 1321–26* (Cambridge, 1979).

Funcken, L. & F., *Le Costume, L'armure et les Armes au Temps de Chevalerie,* (France, 1977).

Gilbert, J.M., *Hunting and Hunting Reserves in Medieval Scotland* (Edinburgh, 1979).

Gillingham, J & Holt, J. (Ed.), *War and Government in the Middle Ages* (Woodbridge, 1984).

Grant, A. & Stringer, K. (Eds.), *Medieval Scotland, Crown, Lordship and Community* (Edinburgh, 1993).

Grant, A., *Independence and Nationhood* (London, 1984).

Grant, I.F., *The Social and Economic Development of Scotland before 1603* (Edinburgh, 1930).

Gravett, C., *Medieval Siege Warfare* (Oxford, 1991).

Griffiths, R., *The Fourteenth and Fifteenth Centuries* (Oxford, 2003).

Haines, R., *King Edward II. Edward of Caernarfon. His Life, His Reign and its Aftermath,* (Dublin, 2006).

Hale, J. (Ed.), *Europe in the Late Middle Ages* (London, 1965).

Hall, D., *Burgess, Merchant and Priest. Burgh life in the Scottish Medieval Town* (Edinburgh, 2002).

Hamilton, G., *Piers Gaveston, Earl of Cornwall, 1307–1312* (London, 1988).

Handel, M., *Masters of War. Classical Strategic Thought,* (London, 2004).

Hanawalt, B., *The Ties that Bound; Peasant Families in Medieval England* (Oxford, 1986).

Harding, A., *England in the Thirteenth Century* (Cambridge, 1993).

Hardy, R., *The Longbow, a Social and Military History* (London, 1992).

Harvey, J., *The Plantagenets* (London, 1959).

Herbert, T. and Jones, G.E., *Edward I and Wales* (Cardiff, 1988).

Hewitt, H., *The Black Prince's Expedition 1355–5* (Manchester 1958).

Hilton, R., *The English Peasantry in the Later Middle Ages* (Oxford, 1975).

Howard, M., *War in European History* (Oxford, 1976).

Jones, A., *The Art of War in Western Civilization* (Chicago, 1987).

Jones, M. (Ed), *Gentry and Lesser Nobility in Later Medieval England* (Gloucester, 1986).

Kaeuper, R., *Chivalry and Violence in Medieval Europe* (Oxford, 2001)

Kagay, D. & Villalon, L., *The Circle of War in the Middle Ages* (Woodbridge, 1999).

Keen. M., *Chivalry* (New Haven, 1984).

Keen, M., *England in the Later Middle Ages* (London, 1973).

Latimer, J., *Deception in War* (London, 2004).

Leyser, H., *Medieval Women. A Social History of England 450–1500* (London, 1995).

Lomas, R., *North-East England in the Middle Ages* (Edinburgh, 1992)

Lord, E., *The Knights Templar in Britain* (London, 2002).

Lucas, H., *The Low Countries and the Hundred Years War* (Michigan, 1929).

Lynch, M., *Scotland: a New History* (London, 1991).

Lynch, M., Spearman, M., & Stell, G. (Eds.) *The Scottish Medieval Town* (Edinburgh, 1988)

MacDonald, A., *Border Bloodshed* (East Linton, 2000).

MacDougall, N. (Ed), *Scotland and War* (Edinburgh, 1991).

MacDougall, N. *An Antidote to the English* (East Lothian, 2001).

MacFarlane, K.B., *The Nobility of Later Medieval England* (Oxford, 1973).

McKenzie, W.M., *The Battle of Bannockburn* (Glasgow, 1913).

McKisack, M., *The Fourteenth Century* (Oxford, 1959).

McLeod, W., *Divided Gaels* (Oxford, 2004).

MacNamee, C., *The Wars of the Bruces* (East Linton, 1997).

McNeill, P. and Nicholson, R., *An Atlas of Scottish History to 1707* (Edinburgh, 1996).

MacQuarrie, A., *Scotland and the Crusades* (Edinburgh, 1997).

McQueen, H.L., *Common Law and Feudal Society in Medieval Scotland* (Edinburgh, 1993).

Mapstone S. & Wood. J. (Ed.), *The Rose and the Thistle* (East Lothian 1998).

Mason, R. (Ed)., *Scotland and England, 1286–1817* (Edinburgh, 1987).

Mason, R. & MacDougall, N. (Eds), *People and Power in Scotland* (Edinburgh, 1992).

Mayhew, N. and Gemmill, E., *The Changing Value of Money in Medieval Scotland* (Cambridge, 1996).

Mertes, K., *The English Noble Household 1250–1600* (Oxford, 1988).

Miller, E., *War in the North. The Anglo-Scottish Wars of the Middle Ages* (Hull, 1960).

Miller, E. & Hatcher, J., *Medieval England – Rural Society and Economic Change, 1086–1348* (London, 1978).

Morgan, P., *War and Society in Medieval Cheshire 1277–1403* (Manchester, 1977).

Morris, J., *Bannockburn* (Cambridge, 1914).

Milner, N., *Vegetius: Epitome of Military Science* (Liverpool ,1993).

Nicholson R., *Scotland. The Later Middle Ages* (Edinburgh, 1974).

Nicholson, R., *Edward III and the Scots. The Formative Years of a Military Career* (Oxford, 1965).

Nusbacher, A., *The Battle of Bannockburn* (Stroud, 2000).

Oakeshott, R., *A Knight and His Horse* (London, 1995).

Oman, Sir Charles, *A History of England* (London, 1910).

Oman, Sir Charles, *A History of the Art of War* (London, 1898).

Parry, M.L. & Slater, T, *The Making of the Scottish Countryside* (London, 1980).

Penman, M., *David II* (East Linton, 2002).

Penman, M., *The Scottish Civil War* (Stroud, 2003).

Pillar, P., *Negotiating Peace: War Termination as a Bargaining Process* (New Jersey, 1983).

Phillips J.R.S., *Aymer de Valence* (Oxford, 1972).

Postan, M., *The Medieval Economy and Society* (Harmondsworth, 1972)

Powicke F. M., *The Thirteenth Century* (Oxford, 1953).

Powicke, F.M., *Military Obligation in England* (Connecticut, 1975).

Prestwich, M., *Armies and Warfare in the Middle Ages* (New Haven, 1996).

Prestwich, M., *Edward I,* (London, 1988).

Prestwich, M., *The Place of War in English History* (Woodbridge, 2004).

Prestwich, M., *The Three Edwards; War and State in England, 1272–1377* (London, 1980).

Prestwich, M., *War, Politics and Finance Under Edward I* (London, 1972).

Rait, R., *The Parliaments of Scotland* (Glasgow, 1924).

Rayner, M., *English Battlefields* (Stroud, 2004).

Reid. N. (Ed)., *Scotland in the Reign of Alexander III* (Edinburgh, 1990).

Ridpath, P., *Border History of England and Scotland* (Berwick, 1848).

Ritchie, R., *The Normans in Scotland* (Edinburgh, 1954).

Rogers C., War Cruel and Sharp (Woodbridge, 2000).

Rollason, D. & Prestwich, M. (Ed.), *The Battle of Neville's Cross* (Stamford, 1998).

Ross, A., *In the Footsteps of Robert Bruce Sutton* (Gloucester, 1999).

Saul, N. (Ed.), *Fourteenth Century England* (Woodbridge, 2000).

Sadler, J., *Scottish Battles* (Edinburgh, 1996)

Scott, J., *History of Berwick-upon-Tweed* (London, 1888).

Seynour, W., *Battles in Britain 1066–1745* (Chatham, 1997).

Simpson G., (Ed.) *Scotland and the Low Countries,* (East Linton, 1996).

Simpson, G., *Scottish Handwriting 1150–1650* (Aberdeen, 1977).

Simpson, G., (Ed) *The Scottish Soldier Abroad* (Edinburgh, 1992).

Snell, F., *The Fourteenth Century* (Edinburgh, 1999).

Smurthwaite, D., *Battlefields of Britain* (London, 1984).

Stevenson, J. and Wood, M., *Scottish Heraldic Seals* (Glasgow, 1940).

Stenton, D., *English Society in the Early Middle Ages (1066–1307)* (Harmondsworth, 1965)

Stone, G., *Cameron Glossary of the Construction of Arms and Armour* (London, 1978).

Strickland, M., *Armies, Chivalry and Warfare in Medieval Britain and France* (Stamford, 1998).

Stringer, K. (Ed.) *Essays on the Scottish Nobility* (Edinburgh, 1985).

Sumption, J., *The Hundred Years War* (London, 1990).

Taylor, J. & Childs, W., (Ed.) *Politics and Crisis in Fourteenth Century England* (Gloucester, 1990).

Tuck, A., *Crown and Nobility, 1272–1461; Political Conflict in Late Medieval England* (London, 1985).

Tytler P.F., *A History of Scotland* (Edinburgh 1828, 1845).

Vale, M., *Edward III and Chivalry* (Woodbridge, 1983).

Vale, M., *War and Chivalry* (London, 1981)

Watson, F., *Under the Hammer* (East Linton, 1998).

Whittington G. and Whyte I. (Ed.), *A Historical Geography of Scotland* (London, 1983).

Young, A., *Robert the Bruce's Rivals; The Comyns.* (East Linton, 1997).

# Unpublished Theses and Papers

*Military Service of Northumbrian Knights.* A. King. Durham University Medieval Conference (2001)

*Technology and Military Technology in Medieval England.* Randall Storey, University of Reading, (2003)

# Articles

'A Medieval Scots Merchant's Handbook,' A. Hanham, *SHR* l, (1971)

'An Unpublished Early Account of Bruce's Murder of Comyn', T.M. Smallwood. *SHR*, liv. (1975)

'The Battle of Bannockburn. A Report for Stirling Council', F. Watson and M. Anderson, (2004)

'Battle of Bannockburn Report.' The Battlefield Trust.

'Chronicle Propaganda in Fourteenth Century Scotland', S.Boardman, *SHR* 76 (1977).

'Clausewitz, Nonlinearity and the Unpredictability of War', A. Beyerchen. *International Security* 17.3 (1992)

'Edinburgh Castle, Iron Age fort to Garrison Fortress.' P.Yeoman, *Fortress Magazine,* 4 (1990)

'Lothian in the First War of Independence.' G.W.S. Barrow. *SHR* 55 (1976)

'The Aftermath of War.' G.W.S. Barrow, *TRHS*, 28 (1978)

'The Community of the Realm of Scotland and Robert Bruce.' A.A.M. Duncan, *SHR* xlv.

'The Development of Scottish Border Lordship, 1332–58.' M. Brown, *Historical Research* lxxv, No.171. (February 1997)

'The Guardians of Scotland and a Parliament at Rutherglen in 1300', G. Sayles, *SHR* xxiv (1945)

'The Use of Money in Scotland, 1124–1230.' W. Scott, *SHR* lviii (1979)

'The War of the Scots, 1306–23' A.A.M. Duncan, Prothero Lecture, *TRHS* (1992)

'War, Allegiance and Community in the Anglo-Scottish Marches; Teviotdale in the Fourteenth Century.' Dr M. Brown, *Northern History,* xli (2004)

# Abbreviations

*APS*    *The Acts of the Parliaments of Scotland* (Ed.) T.Thomson and C. Innes (Edinburgh, 1814–75).

Barbour, *The Bruce*   *The Bruce*, J. Barbour (Ed.) A.A.M. Duncan. Canongate. (Edinburgh, 1997).

Barrow, *Bruce*    G.W.S. Barrow, *Robert Bruce and the Community of the Realm of Scotland* (London, 1965).

*CDS*    *Calendar of Documents Relating to Scotland*.Volumes i–iv, (Ed.) J. Bain, (Edinburgh, 1881–88), volume v, G. Simpson & J. Galbraith.

*Chron.Fordun*    *Johannes de Fordun, Chronica Gentis Scottorum*. (Ed.) W.F. Skene (Edinburgh, 1871–2).

*Chron.Lanercost* (Maxwell)    *The Chronicle of Lanercost, 1272–1346*. (Ed. &Trans) H. Maxwell, (Glasgow, 1913).

*ER*    *The Exchequer Rolls of Scotland* (Ed.) J.Stuart. (Edinburgh, 1878–1908).

*PSAS*    *Proceedings of the Society of Antiquarians of Scotland*.

*St. Andrews Liber*    *Liber Cartorum Prioratus Sancti Andree in* Scotia, Bannatyne Club, (Edinburgh, 1841).

*Melrose Liber*    *Liber Sancte Marie de Melros*, Bannatyne Club (Edinburgh, 1837).

*RMS vol. i*    *Regesta Magni Sigilii Regum Scottorum* (Ed.) M. Livingstone (Edinburgh, 1882–1914).

*Rot.Scot i Rotuli Scotiae in Turri Londiniensi et in Domo Capitulari Westmonasteriensi Asservati.* (Ed.) D. MacPherson. (London, 1837).

*RRS vol. vi.*    *Regesta Regum Scottorum vol. vi*, (Ed.) B.Webster (Edinburgh, 1982).

*RRS.vol. v*    *Regesta Regum Scottorum. vol. v*, (Ed.) A.A.M. Duncan (Edinburgh, 1988).

*Scalacronica* (Maxwell)    *Scalacronica, the Reigns of Edward I, Edward II and Edward III.* H.Maxwell. (Glasgow, 1907).

*Scotichronicon*    *Scotichronicon of Walter Bower* (Ed.) D.E.R.Watt (Aberdeen, 1996).

*SHR*    *Scottish Historical Review*.

*Stevenson, Documents*    *Documents Illustrative of the History of Scotland, 1286–1306.* (Ed.) J.Stevenson. (Edinburgh, 1870).

*TRHS*    *Transactions of the Royal Historical Society*.

# Acknowledgements

As ever, there are several individuals whose interest, information and encouragement demand recognition. In the academic sphere, these include Professor Mason and Dr Reid of the Scottish History Department at St Andrews University, who brought a much needed degree of 'raddure' to my PhD studies, repairing the damage and demoralisation caused by a long period of desultory and incompetent supervision. I cannot thank them enough for reawakening a passion for medieval Scottish history that had come very close to being utterly extinguished. I am also indebted to the unfailingly helpful – and cheerful – archival staff at East Register House and Kew. I also owe a great debt to the many scholars who have written about Scotland, England and France during the fourteenth century, and in particular to the small group of scholars who, since the 1960s, have brought the study of medieval Scotland out of the murk of romance and myth and into the mainstream of medieval historiography – Professors Barrow, Duncan and Nicholson.

I am also grateful for the patience and understanding of my wife, Pat, and my children and their partners – Robert, Colin, Christopher, Charis, Alex and Juliet. They have all had to put up with endless ramblings about the nature of medieval society and war. I have no idea how they have coped, but they have.

I would like to point out that my understanding of the battle is a product of how I see the source material, the terrain and the practice of war at the time of writing. It is perfectly possible that developments in archaeological techniques, a spate of new 'finds', or even a previously unknown piece of source material may yet emerge which might compromise or confirm the evidence on which all of the existing studies of this battle have depended.

Chris Brown, Kennoway, 2008

# Index

Robert I, Edward I and Edward II have not been included in this index; their index entries would have a reference to virtually every page. For the same reason I have not included 'Bannockburn' or 'St. Ninians'.

## The Forgotten Battle of 1066, Fulford
CHARLES JONES
£25
0 7524 3810 7

## The Roman Conquest of Scotland
The Battle of Mons Graupius AD 84
JAMES E. FRASER
'Challenges a long held view'
*The Sunday Express*
£17.99
0 7524 3325 3

## Harold II

The Doomed Saxon King
PETER REX
'Rex's powerful defence of Harold is refreshing'
*The Daily Mail*
£25
0 7524 3529 9

## The Foul Death of the English
Scotland's Black Death
KAREN JILLINGS
'So incongruously enjoyable a read, and so attractively presented by the publishers'
*The Scotsman*
£14.99
0 7524 2314 2

## Edward III
W.M. ORMROD
'Compelling and eloquently written'
*History Today*
£12.99
0 7524 3320 2

## King John
England's Evil King?
RALPH V. TURNER
'A most valuable introduction to the general reader' *American Historical Review*
£17.99
0 7524 3385 7

## Cnut
England's Viking King
M.K. LAWSON
'Excellent' *English Historical Review*
£17.99
0 7524 2964 7

## Anne Neville
Queen To Richard III
MICHAEL HICKS
'A masterful and poignant story' *Alison Weir*
'Does little for Richard III's tattered reputation'
*BBC History Magazine*
£9.99
0 7524 4129 0

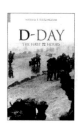

## D-Day The First 72 Hours
WILLIAM F. BUCKINGHAM

'A compelling narrative' *The Observer*
A *BBC History Magazine* Book of the Year 2004
£9.99   0 7524 2842 X

## The London Monster
Terror on the Streets in 1790
JAN BONDESON

'Gripping' *The Guardian*
'Excellent... monster-mania brought a reign of
terror to the ill-lit streets of the capital'
*The Independent*

£9.99   0 7524 3327 X

## London
A Historical Companion
KENNETH PANTON

'A readable and reliable work of reference that
deserves a place on every Londoner's bookshelf'
*Stephen Inwood*

£20   0 7524 3434 9

## M: MI5's First Spymaster
ANDREW COOK

'Serious spook history' *Andrew Roberts*
'Groundbreaking' *The Sunday Telegraph*
'Brilliantly researched' *Dame Stella Rimington*

£9.99   978 07524 3949 9

## Agincourt
A New History
ANNE CURRY

'A highly distinguished and convincing account'
*Christopher Hibbert*
'A *tour de force*' *Alison Weir*
'*The* book on the battle' *Richard Holmes*
A *BBC History Magazine* Book of the Year 2005
£12.99   0 7524 3813 1

## Battle of the Atlantic
MARC MILNER

'The most comprehensive short survey of the
U-boat battles' *Sir John Keegan*
'Some events are fortunate in their historian, none
more so than the Battle of the Atlantic. Marc
Milner is *the* historian of the Atlantic campaign... a
compelling narrative' *Andrew Lambert*

£12.99   0 7524 3332 6

## The English Resistance
The Underground War Against the Normans
PETER REX

'An invaluable rehabilitation of an ignored
resistance movement' *The Sunday Times*
'Peter Rex's scholarship is remarkable'
*The Sunday Express*

£12.99   0 7524 3733 X

## Elizabeth Wydeville: England's Slandered Queen
ARLENE OKERLUND

'A penetrating, thorough and wholly convincing
vindication of this unlucky queen'
*Sarah Gristwood*
'A gripping tale of lust, loss and tragedy'
*Alison Weir*
A *BBC History Magazine* Book of the Year 2005
£9.99   978 07524 3807 8

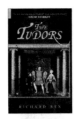

## Quacks Fakers and Charlatans in Medicine
ROY PORTER

'A delightful book' *The Daily Telegraph*
'Hugely entertaining' *BBC History Magazine*

£12.99    0 7524 2590 0

## The Tudors
RICHARD REX

'Up-to-date, readable and reliable. The best introduction to England's most important dynasty' *David Starkey*
'Vivid, entertaining... quite simply the best short introduction' *Eamon Duffy*
'Told with enviable narrative skill... a delight for any reader' *THES*

£9.99    0 7524 3333 4

## The Kings & Queens of England
MARK ORMROD

'Of the numerous books on the kings and queens of England, this is the best'
*Alison Weir*

£9.99    0 7524 2598 6

## The Covent Garden Ladies
Pimp General Jack & the Extraordinary Story of Harris's List
HALLIE RUBENHOLD

'Sex toys, porn... forget Ann Summers, Miss Love was at it 250 years ago' *The Times*
'Compelling' *The Independent on Sunday*
'Marvellous' *Leonie Frieda*
'Filthy' *The Guardian*

£9.99    0 7524 3739 9

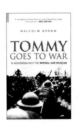
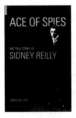

## Okinawa 1945
GEORGE FEIFER

'A great book... Feifer's account of the three sides and their experiences far surpasses most books about war'
**Stephen Ambrose**

£17.99    0 7524 3324 5

## Tommy Goes To War
MALCOLM BROWN

'A remarkably vivid and frank account of the British soldier in the trenches'
**Max Arthur**
'The fury, fear, mud, blood, boredom and bravery that made up life on the Western Front are vividly presented and illustrated'
*The Sunday Telegraph*

£12.99    0 7524 2980 4

## Ace of Spies The True Story of Sidney Reilly
ANDREW COOK

'The most definitive biography of the spying ace yet written... both a compelling narrative and a myth-shattering *tour de force*'
**Simon Sebag Montefiore**
'The absolute last word on the subject' *Nigel West*
'Makes poor 007 look like a bit of a wuss'
*The Mail on Sunday*

£12.99    0 7524 2959 0

## Sex Crimes
From Renaissance to Enlightenment
W.M. NAPHY

'Wonderfully scandalous' *Diarmaid MacCulloch*
'A model of pin-sharp scholarship' *The Guardian*

£10.99    0 7524 2977 9

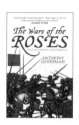

## The Wars of the Roses
The Soldiers' Experience
ANTHONY GOODMAN
'Fascinating... a meticulous work' *TLS*
'Sheds light on the lot of the common soldier as never before' *Alison Weir*
'Fascinating reading' *BBC History Magazine*
£12.99

0 7524 3731 3

## Byazntium: A History
JOHN HALDON
'A triumph of synthesis'
*Speculum: A Journal of Medieval Studies*
£12.99

0 7524 3472 1

## The Great Dying
The Black Death in Dublin
MARIA KELLY
'An infectious chronicle... pacy popular history'
*The Irish Sunday Times*
£14.99

0 7524 2338 X

## A History of the Black Death in Ireland
MARIA KELLY
'A fine example of how history can be made interesting to the layman as well as the scholar'
*The Irish Times*
'A remarkably vivid and perceptive account. Written with verve, it makes a compelling read'
*Maurice Keen*
£12.99

0 7524 3185 4

## The Crusades
MALCOLM BILLINGS
'Demonstrates that one can write in the light of the most recent research without losing excitement and colour' *Jonathan Riley-Smith*
£12.99

0 7524 2974 4

## The Welsh Kings
Warriors, Warlords & Princes
KARI MAUND
£12.99

0 7524 2973 6

## The Return of the Vikings
The Battle of Maldon 991
DONALD SCRAGG
'An accessible, well illustrated study... a lively historical introduction' *BBC History Magazine*
£17.99

0 7524 2833 0

## The Byzantine Wars
JOHN HALDON
A *BBC History Magazine* Book of the Year 2001
£9.99

0 7524 1795 9

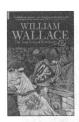

## William Wallace
The True Story of Braveheart
CHRIS BROWN
'The truth about Braveheart'
*The Scottish Daily Mail*
£17.99
0 7524 3432 2

## An Abundance of Witches
The Great Scottish Witch-Hunt
P.G. MAXWELL-STUART
'An amazing account of Scots women in league with the Devil' *The Sunday Post*
£17.99
0 7524 3329 6

## The Roman Conquest of Scotland
The Battle of Mons Graupius AD 84
JAMES E. FRASER
'Challenges a long held view'
*The Scottish Sunday Express*
£17.99
0 7524 3325 3

## Scottish Voices from the Great War
DEREK YOUNG
'A treasure trove of personal letters and diaries from the archives' *Trevor Royle*
£17.99
0 7524 3326 1

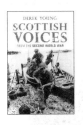

## Culloden
The Last Charge of the Highland Clans
JOHN SADLER
'Drawing extensively on first-hand accounts, paints a vivid picture of the campaign and battle' *Scotland in Trust: The Magazine of the National Trust for Scotland*
£25
0 7524 3955 3

## The Scottish Civil War
The Bruces & the Balliols & the War for the Control of Scotland
MICHAEL PENMAN
'A highly informative and engaging account' *Historic Scotland*
£16.99
0 7524 2319 3

## The Pictish Conquest
The Battle of Dunnichen 685 & the Birth of Scotland
'A well-researched account… a must'
*The Scots Magazine*
'Informatively illustrated and well-written'
*War in History*
JAMES E. FRASER
£12.99

## Scottish Voices from the Second World War
DEREK YOUNG
'Poignant memories of a lost generation… heart-rending' *The Sunday Post*
£17.99
0 7524 3710 0

## Scotland
From Prehistory to the Present
FIONA WATSON
*The Scotsman* **Bestseller**
£9.99
0 7524 2591 9

## 1314 Bannockburn
ARYEH NUSBACHER
'Written with good-humoured verve as befits a rattling "yarn of sex, violence and terror"'
*History Scotland*
£9.99
0 7524 2982 5

## Flodden
NIALL BARR
'Tells the story brilliantly'
*The Sunday Post*
£9.99
0 7524 2593 5

## Scotland's Black Death
The Foul Death of the English
KAREN JILLINGS
'So incongruously enjoyable a read, and so attractively presented by the publishers'
*The Scotsman*
£12.99
978 07524 3732 3

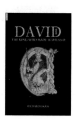

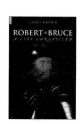

## David I The King Who Made Scotland
RICHARD ORAM
'Enthralling... sets just the right tone as the launch-volume of an important new series of royal biographies' *Magnus Magnusson*
£17.99
0 7524 2825 X

## The Kings & Queens of Scotland
RICHARD ORAM
'A serious, readable work that sweeps across a vast historical landscape' *The Daily Mail*
£12.99
0 7524 3814 X

## The Second Scottish Wars of Independence 1332–1363
CHRIS BROWN
'Explodes the myth of the invincible Bruces... lucid and highly readable' *History Scotland*
£12.99
0 7524 3812 3

## Robert the Bruce: A Life Chronicled
CHRIS BROWN
'A masterpiece of research'
*The Scots Magazine*
£30
0 7524 2575 7

# A NOTE ON THE TITLE

In October 1987, a twenty-one-year-old Mike Tyson was due to fight Tyrell Biggs to become the Undisputed Heavyweight Champion of the World. In the build-up, Tyrell Biggs had been talking a lot about how he had a plan to beat his opponent. When this was put to Tyson, he replied 'they all have a plan, until they get hit.'

Mike Tyson was a massive inspiration to me growing up. I watched his fights until the videotapes faded away to nothing. When I knew I wanted to write a book about boxing, I knew I wanted to pay homage to Tyson and that iconic moment.

To me it captures the essence of what I think boxing can teach us all. You don't learn what's important when things are going well. It's about how you deal with the punches.

And, man, Tyson could punch.

# EVERYBODY HAS A PLAN UNTIL THEY GET PUNCHED IN THE FACE

## 12 THINGS BOXING TEACHES YOU ABOUT LIFE

## TONY BELLEW

SEVEN DIALS

First published in Great Britain in 2021 by Seven Dials
an imprint of The Orion Publishing Group Ltd
Carmelite House, 50 Victoria Embankment
London EC4Y 0DZ

An Hachette UK Company

1 3 5 7 9 10 8 6 4 2

A CIP catalogue record for this book is
available from the British Library.

ISBN (Hardback) 978 1 8418 8470 7
ISBN (eBook) 978 1 8418 8472 1

Typeset by Input Data Services Ltd, Somerset

Printed in Great Britain by Clays Ltd, Elcograf S.p.A.

MIX
Paper from
responsible sources
FSC® C104740
FSC
www.fsc.org

www.orionbooks.co.uk

*To my wife Rachael. You're the best of me and the reason
I saw all of my dreams.*

# CONTENTS

# INTRODUCTION

## GOODISON PARK, 29 MAY 2016

*My nose is the first thing his hand smashes into. The force crunches sickeningly into the cartilage and bone. Then he follows through. Some fighters only punch to score, maybe knock your head back again. Fighters like that are happy to stop at breaking your nose. But Ilunga Makabu punches to hurt you. He knows that when you want to do real damage, you punch right through the target.*

*The impact of the punch travels down through my face and pushes my jaw back. My legs collapse completely underneath me and I fold down like a deckchair. For a couple of seconds, my thoughts are a jumble of surprise and pain. This is bad. This is very fucking bad. Everything I've dreamed of, everything I've worked for, right out of the window. If I don't get to my feet quickly, the night will be over before it's begun. I'll have been retired by Makabu's left hand. I'm thirty-three years old in the most important fight of my career. My arse hits the floor. The referee starts counting.*

*'One . . .'*

1

# FOUR HOURS EARLIER

Goodison is still quiet when we arrive. There are a few stewards and ticket sellers, a few punters queuing. Its stillness and calm are starkly different to the intensity I feel. The thing that for years I'd predicted would happen is happening. It's happening *now*. Everything rests on whether or not I can beat Ilunga Makabu and seize the vacant WBC Cruiserweight title. What happens in the next few hours will shape the rest of my life. And yet the venue where my future will be decided looks as if it's winding down for the night. We drive past, into the special car park that's normally used by Bill Kenwright, Everton's chairman.

Some fighters are prima donnas – they'll pay other men to carry the stupid collection of Louis Vuitton bags that for them are somehow essential. They start off at the beginning of their careers with a couple of mates helping them and end up with an entourage of twenty-five guys in their dressing room, all claiming they're doing something and all taking a fat wage for doing fucking nothing.

I'm not like that. I've always just turned up with a big, heavy rucksack and then walked into the venue with my boxing kit in my left hand.

Then it happens. I can feel the difference in me as soon as I step onto the tarmac. I've been calm all the way in.

Even while I've been thinking of nothing but the fight, with rap pounding through the car at an unbelievable volume. Aggressive songs. Stuff that I know will provoke me: 50 Cent, Puff Daddy, Wretch 32, Kano. We don't talk, just listen as the bass shakes the car. I try to think as little about my family as I can; they can't have any place in my mind on a night where I know blood is going to be spilled.

Now, I want to hurt everyone. Even the people around me, the people on my side. I want to kill everyone. Nobody's my friend. If anyone gets in my way, I want to damage them, take their head clean off. I don't even want to think about what I'd do if anybody on my team stepped in front of me by mistake. *Mate. You're going to fucking get it.*

I carry on through the stadium I know so well, into the dressing room that means so much to me. It's the place where the first team change and it was the one thing I insisted on. And yet nothing is really sinking in yet. When I'd dreamed about this moment years before, I thought I'd be savouring it all, drinking in the moment, but I'm too angry. Too wired. It isn't about football today, it's about me. It's my face on the posters that are plastered all over the ground.

For a moment my aggression is interrupted by a brief surge of sadness, because I know that if I lose tonight, I won't ever come back here. It's an idea that's been going round and round my head for weeks. I love Everton Football Club. After my wife and kids, it's the most important thing in my life. I've been going to Goodison Park every other

Saturday since I was ten. But if I'm defeated, there's just no way I'll be able to face coming here again. It would hurt too much.

When I enter the dressing room, I spot the man who wraps my hands, Jay Sheldon, laying things out, making sure everything's in order. I look around more and see my coach, Dave Coldwell, who's been at my side for the last three years, and the other members of my tight-knit team: Kerry Kayes, Mick Williamson, my mates Gary and Fran, and my dad. There's just eight of us here in a huge room that's designed for twenty to thirty men. Any noise we make echoes loudly back at us.

I turn to Dave. 'I'm just going to go upstairs and have a look.'

I want to familiarise myself with the surroundings so that when I come out, I'll know what to expect. I don't want any surprises in the crucial seconds before I step into the ring. I also want to have a moment to take in what I've achieved in just getting here.

I've only been nervous before two fights in my life. My first amateur bout, against a lad called Rob Beech. And this one, here. If I lose, I know it's over. I won't get another chance. And there's no way you'll ever see me in the ring again. Since I was fifteen, I've been telling people I'm going to win a world title *here*, at this ground that means so much to me. Even when I was a nobody, a cocky kid in baggy rappers' clothes who'd won nothing, had done nothing, I'd be telling anybody who'd listen what I planned to do. Lots of them laughed in my face. *I'm going to win at Goodison Park.*

We go through the usual pre-match routines – I get my hands wrapped, I fix my low blow – then we reach the moment when normally I'd turn the music up to an obscenely high level. But I've noticed something. I look across to Fran, who's been with me in these moments more times than I can count. I tell him to turn the music off. He looks at me as if to say: *What the fuck? You've never done this before.*

'Trust me,' I say, 'just turn it off.'

There's no way of describing what it's like to hear thousands of people calling your name. But the Everton fans in the Gladwys Street End are singing my name. My fucking name. They're shouting 'Tony, Tony Tony, Tony Tony, Tony, Tony Bellew' – to the tune of 2Unlimited's 'No Limit' – so loud that it makes the dressing room shake.

I turn to Fran, who's standing by the door. We look at each other again.

'I've dreamed of this,' I say. 'I've dreamed of this for so long.'

'Come on, lad. Fucking get on it!'

This is it.

The last twenty minutes fly by so quickly that afterwards, I'll have no memory of any of it until we get the knock on the door from the Sky runner, Ralph.

'Tony, you've got sixty seconds.'

I tell everyone to get out of the room. Then I find the

picture of Rachael and the kids that I've brought with me. The boxer and former footballer Leon McKenzie gave it to me a while ago. Ever since, I've kept it in my gym bag ahead of fights. I stare at the picture for a few seconds, kiss it, then get on my knees.

The room is empty now. I can hear the constant chant of my name and then the swell of excitement as Makabu enters the ring. I'm not a religious person. I don't believe in any divine power; I've seen too much shit to have that sort of faith. But before every fight, I speak to the people I've been close to that I've lost. First, I tell my nan and my grandad not to worry, that I'll get home safe. Then I talk to an ever longer list of people I still care for, even if I can't see them any more.

Last of all, I say a few words to Jimmy Albertina, the coach who changed my life. He's been dead for over ten years, but I've never stopped thinking about him. Not ever. He was a mad Everton fan, too; maybe more than me. I wish more than anything he could be here. Except, of course, in my mind he is.

'Please let me perform,' I say to him. 'You know how hard I've worked. You know what I've done to get here. Just let me perform to the best of my abilities.'

I don't want to be handed the victory. I don't want intervention. All I want is to be able to do everything that I'm capable of. If I'm good enough, I'll win. If I'm not, well, I'll soon find out.'

Then I get up. Time to go to work. I let out one big primal

scream, so loud and fierce that it tears at my throat. 'Come ooooooooooon.'

The hairs are standing up on the back of my neck now. Goodison Park is bathed in an eerie blue light. And even over the insane noise that's filling every corner of the stadium, it's possible to pick out Russell Crowe's voice bellowing his character's famous speech from *Gladiator*: 'Are you not entertained? Are you not entertained? Is this not why you are here?' It's followed by the manic screech of an air-raid siren.

I've always known that the public want a bit of entertainment. And I've always been willing to serve it up, whether that's at a press conference or the weigh-in or just before the fight. But I ultimately know that when all that is over, it's time to go to war.

I need that air-raid siren because I want the audience to understand what's about to happen. More importantly, I want Makabu to know what's coming.

Then comes 'Z-Cars', the song that Everton always come out to, which is greeted by an enormous roar. As I walk through the seething crowd, I break into a huge fucking grin. It's like I can't believe that this is happening. I'm so close to achieving everything I've ever dreamed of. It's the best chance I'll get, I know this. Everybody has big moments in their life. Usually you don't realise how significant they are until it's way too late. But I know. I'll never live through a more important night. The song's cymbals are crashing through the stadium's PA system and yet my heart's beating so loudly, I'm surprised that people can't hear it over the music.

All I'm thinking as I approach the ring is: *he cannot hurt me; he cannot hurt me.*

The excited disbelief has worn off now and my body is a mass of nerves. I can feel my heart hammering as if it's trying to escape from my chest. It's up to 160 beats, then 170, rising higher and higher. Nausea slides around my belly and adrenaline rushes around every other part of me. Every couple of seconds I look up and it's almost a shock to remember where I am. I'm scared all over again because I'm at Goodison Park.

I can see the Gladwys Street End. It's completely full. At some point, every single person sitting there lifts their phone to video me as I walk past lights glittering in the air above me. I stop.

'Look at that,' I say, 'that's fucking unbelievable.'

I stand there for two or three seconds, staring. Then I turn my head and see Makabu, already in the ring. He's laughing and smiling. He's cocky. Which is unsurprising, since he's the overwhelming favourite. Most people inside the boxing world think he's going to win and he seems to think so, too. What they've all forgotten is that I've made a career out of upsetting the odds. Proving people wrong has been my speciality.

We touch gloves. I'm watching Makabu, studying all of his body movements. Is he doing anything out of character?

There's no sign of nerves beneath the grin. For a moment I'm disappointed. I want there to be a crack in his armour, something I can exploit. He's in a foreign country with a different climate, I've stuck him in a tiny postbox of a dressing room. He *should* be nervous. He *should* be unsettled, but he's still calm. I can see the sweat beading off him that shows he's warmed up properly. And then I realise that there is something. He believes his own hype. He doesn't think I'm a threat.

Makabu starts the fight slowly, as he always does. Like he's warming up, feeling his way into the contest. Even as my nerves are still firing, my arse twitching, he gives no sign that he's feeling any sort of pressure. There's part of me still telling myself, *he can't hurt you, he can't touch you.* But there's another part that's rubbing up against reality. *This guy knocks other men out cold. Heavyweights, dangerous cruiserweights, former world champions, it doesn't matter – he sends them all to sleep. Over ninety per cent of his victories have been by knockout –* ninety per cent. *He's a wrecking ball.*

I know he's dangerous, I know I'll have to be so switched on, but I don't ever, not for a second, think: *shit, I could lose this.* I have to keep any negative thoughts about defeat out of my mind. If I start to believe I could lose, then it'll make it so much harder to win. That's been another feature of my career: no matter how exhausted I am, or how much punishment I've taken, I'll always think to myself that I've still got that punch that could turn it all round.

I realise that I need to hit him quickly, hard enough that

he starts to respect me and understands that he's in a fight. So I cruise the first round. I'm pinging him with jabs. He's still a slow-moving easy target, so it's boom, boom, boom. Every punch is fast. They're all catching and yet none of them are gaining his respect. Then I hit him on the nose with a straight right hand down the pipe. Fuck off. I can see he's felt it and although it hasn't hurt him, I notice that he's looking at me differently now, like he's thinking, *oh, you've got a bit of a pop on you.*

He gives me a little nod that mixes pain and approval, then smiles at me and plods away. I get him against the ropes again. Another big right hand and then I whack a left hook into his body. He sags. For a second, I even think he's going to go down. Then he makes a noise that only I, in this stadium full of 20,000 fans, can hear. A guttural moan that seems to come from inside his torso.

That's when I think, *I've fucking got ya.* I follow up with a right hand down the pipe and another left hook to the side of his head. A couple of others miss him, going right over his head. But I look in his eyes, which are big and staring, and I can see his mood has changed again. He's thinking, *what the fuck!*

For the first time, he backs up urgently. I've studied him for so long and so closely that I recognise this as an unmistakable sign that I've hurt him. I touch him a few more times and edge him towards the ropes. It's still the first round, but already I'm looking for the finish.

What a fucking stupid thing to do. There's no way you

should ever be looking for the finish so early against a man like Ilunga Makabu.

As I back out of the corner after throwing a few more, I make another stupid mistake. I show him my face. He's crouched down in a defensive pose. But then he explodes upwards, throwing a jab that hits me on the chin and knocks my head right back. I should take the punch then slip, staying in range with my hands still up. Instead, like a big dope, I back up with my chin in the air. It's a big easy target. I might as well have wrapped it up and put a label on saying 'open this'. He catches me with his left hand. Just seconds ago I'd been looking forward to victory, now I've just been hit with one of the hardest punches I've ever experienced. Four, maybe five times through my career I've been hurt really badly by punches. This is one of them.

'One.'

My arse hits the floor.

This is bad. This is very fucking bad.

'Two.'

I roll backwards and time seems to freeze.

## THE TEN COUNT

Everything that mattered in my life rested on that ten count. My reputation, my financial security, my family's whole future. Literally everything I'd ever done, all the sacrifices I'd made, those horrible long fucking days training

11

so hard that I spewed. All of it came down to one moment on a warm May evening in May 2016. The most dangerous opponent I'd ever faced had caught me with one of the hardest punches I'd ever taken. I'd gone in that ring with a very good plan. In a matter of seconds, Ilunga Makabu had smashed it to pieces.

When you're on your back and all you can hear is the referee counting, you're faced with a decision that only you can make. Nobody can help you. The responsibility sits entirely upon your shoulders. You can sit there, let the referee reach ten and accept that you've lost. That's the easy route. Or you can haul yourself to your feet, put your gloves up and get ready to fight. This way is harder. It means more work, more effort, more pain. But, here's the thing: nobody ever became a world champion by taking the easy way out.

Nothing rips the layers off like boxing. It's the purest test there is. Most sports are team games. In a boxing match it's just you and him. You're on your own. There's no equipment that can improve or hinder your performance: it's a completely level playing field. No teammate to lift you up or drag you down. The only thing that matters is who's worked the hardest. Who's sacrificed more. And, very quickly, the one who's given less gets found out.

That's the first thing I learned about boxing. Everything is up to you. You need the right people around you and you need to listen to people who know more than you do. Whether you aim high or are willing just to be blown this way or that by the wind. Whether you listen to good advice or hang out with fucking clowns. Whether you work hard or waste your talent. Whether you push on, no matter what the circumstances, or quit. Whether you choose to project confidence or give up. Whether you treat learning as a lifelong process or think you know it all. Whether you focus obsessively on your dream or treat it like a hobby you can pick up and put down whenever the mood takes you. Whether you understand that you're responsible for every element of your life or hide behind excuses, telling yourself that everyone else has it easier than you. All that is *your* decision. Nobody else can make you get out of bed or pick yourself up off the canvas. Nobody else can find your motivation. It has to come from you. That can feel like a frightening thought. And yet it's also exhilarating. You can't change the cards life has dealt you, but you can choose how you play them. Everything is up to you.

## WHY THE FUCK SHOULD I LISTEN TO YOU?

I never thought I'd write a book. It's just not something that people who come from where I grew up do. I don't have any qualifications. I was expelled from school, for fuck's sake. And I know what my reputation is. Some people see me as aggressive, cocky and loud. I know others see me as a bully. There are days when I can see why they might feel that way about me. I sometimes think that some of the silly shit that comes out of my mouth actually guarantees I can't be clever.

But then I remember that I'm really good at figuring my way out of situations in all different walks of life. That's one of the reasons why I decided that I'd take the plunge and become an author. Over the years, I've had approaches from a number of different publishers. They all wanted to make my childhood and all the shit that happens outside the ring a major part of the book. I didn't want to spend 300 pages discussing stuff that happened when I was a kid. Not because I had a bad upbringing – I didn't. I have two very loving parents who have worked very hard their whole lives. Stuff happened in our family, like it does in thousands of others up and down the country, and I've no interest in dragging it up. I don't want to appear as though I'm playing the victim card.

But what did excite me was the opportunity to pass on some of the things that I've learned from my two decades in the ring. I'm not saying I'm anything special. I'm not a role model and I'm never going to say or do the perfect thing on every occasion. But although I'm only thirty-eight, I feel as if I've been through such a lot in life. I've had hard times, I've done bad things that I'm not proud of, but I've always come out the other end.

I had a good career. I was world champion. I had thirty-four professional bouts and won thirty of them. Twenty times, my opponent hit the canvas. Boxing was everything for me and for many years it was the only thing I knew. But since I've retired, my horizons have grown. I've spent time talking to people from different backgrounds, especially those who have seen combat and battled demons like mine.

I began wanting to understand more about myself, particularly the demons that had sat on my shoulder for years. Going on *SAS: Who Dares Wins* brought all that to a head. Days of physical exhaustion and mental torture culminated in me standing face to face with Ant Middleton, the chief instructor, with every single atom in my body urging me to smash him in the face. He'd pushed me to the absolute limit. I remember the moment he braced, preparing himself for the attack that looked inevitable. I could see his jaw clench and his fists tighten. For three or four seconds, the two routes I could take revolved in my brain: *was I going to smack him? Was I going to let it go?* In the end, the reason I pulled my punches was because everybody thought I'd belt him and I was desperate to show people I could control my temper.

My experiences on that show changed me in so many ways. For the first time in my life, I really looked myself in the eye. This book is part of that work.

What I have realised in the months since is that so much of what I did, most of it by instinct or passed down through generations of fighters and trainers, or because I'd taken the time to work it out for myself, isn't just useful in the ring. It can help anyone. Because whether you're a boxer or a soldier or you work in an office, we've all got the same basic equipment and many of the same principles apply. People talk about a boxer having a heart or spirit, but what they really mean by that is their attitude. How much punishment, how much suffering can they take and keep going? How much work are they willing to put into their training? How many sacrifices are they prepared to make outside the ring?

I got to the top of my profession not because I was more talented or physically gifted than other fighters, but because I worked and thought harder than all of them. I'm living proof that you don't need to be born a genius or an athletic freak of nature to achieve your dreams.

Some people were born world champions. They're so obscenely talented that they glide through life. When you look at them, it's as if they've got an aura. I'm not like that. Photographs of me from school show me looking like an absolute fat balloon. Physically, I'm not a lot different now to how I was then. I always found running hard. And circuits were fucking murder. When I was starting out I used to have to psyche myself up to get on the bus that would take me to my Tuesday gym session. I was never the quickest or the strongest. Far from it. And on top of that, my hands are small and vulnerable; they break easily and often. None of that is very useful for a fighter.

What I do have over everybody else is my attitude, my drive. I've never given up or backed down, no matter what I was going through, no matter how hard things were. Most fighters would reach a point in their training when they'd give up. Me? Never. I don't know what it is that's wrong with me. I won't throw in the towel. No matter how tough the problems I faced, I'd try to figure them out – and I'd keep going and going and going until I had. I knew that all the bullshit, all the excuses, all the justifications melt away when you cross the ropes. If you did the work, if you suffered for what you wanted, you'd feel the benefit. If you cut corners, if you went easy on yourself and rested on your laurels, you'd get found out. Painfully. That's what took me from being a clueless kid who'd been expelled from school to champion of the world.

Your ambitions and life circumstances will be different from mine, but I hope that some of the skills and techniques that helped me to achieve my dreams can help you with yours. I've been in some pretty extreme situations, and yet I think so much of what I've been through and learned is applicable to everybody's day-to-day lives. In this book, I'll talk about the importance of hard work and setting the right goals, how you can build your confidence and strengthen your resilience, and why you should never stop learning. I'll explain why you should never let quitting become a habit, the best way to respond to failure and how crucial it is to surround yourself with good people.

None of what I'm going to tell you is really that unusual. I don't have any magic tricks and most of what I say is common sense. But I have lived it all. I know what it's like to be broke, I know what it's like to have people laugh in your face and I've had to pick myself up again after suffering a humiliating defeat. And yet, there was never a point in my two-decade journey when I ever lost faith in myself. Nothing that anybody could ever say or do could shake that belief.

That's why I also know what it's like to win, to achieve all of my dreams. In this book, I want to help you do the same thing.

A ten count. Ten seconds. Count it out loud now to yourself. Ten seconds to find yourself, find who you are and what you can be. I was able to do it and I want you to know that you can, too.

# CHAPTER 1
# THE WEIGH-IN

*It's the second fight of my amateur career, against a kid called Ryan Connolly at the Heatwave Leisure Centre. All this is still so new and thrilling to me. I love the smells, the sounds, the routines that surround a fight. The raw crackle of excitement I feel down my spine when the bell first goes. I cannot believe that I'm allowed to do this.*

*After we have our medical, me and some of the other lads who are fighting tonight go down to put our fight gloves on. A couple of younger kids are hanging around with us. When they try their gloves on, I see that they're briefly overcome with nerves.*

*'Bloody hell,' they say, their voices squeaky with a mix of hormones and anxiety, 'they're thin, aren't they? What happens if I get hit with them?'*

*I can see that I'm different. I exhale with pleasure when I slip them on.*

*'This fuckin' fella's had it when I hit him with these,' I say.*

*The idea that he might hit back barely even occurs to me. Later that evening, I knock Connolly out in twenty-nine seconds. This is the first thing I've ever been really good at. When I go out in the ring, I'm no longer just a tear-arse kid from Wavertree. I'm a fighter.*

Where I come from, nobody gives a shit about anything except boxing and football. Nothing else touches the sides. Football comes first – it runs our city. Next up is boxing, and then after that, quite a long distance after, it's clowns and jokers.

In Liverpool, people grow up wanting to be either a fighter or a footballer. When I was a kid, all I wanted was to play once, just once, even if it was five minutes, for Everton Football Club. In hindsight, there was zero chance of that ever happening, which has been a big disappointment to my wife. I could *play*, I just didn't look as if I could. So nobody ever gave me a fair crack.

What I was definitely good at was fighting. For a long time, though, and I don't really know why, the idea that I might become a professional didn't cross my mind. For me, fighting didn't have much to do with putting on a pair of gloves. It was what you did in the streets around where I grew up in Wavertree. Or at school when somebody picked on my younger brother. (Being one of the biggest, heaviest kids in my year was a definite advantage there.) I've never shied away from a fight. In fact, I've been in that many scraps that I can't even remember the first time I threw a punch, or the first time I took one. If you look at it from one angle, you'd say my life has been a big blur of fighting.

None of that was a surprise. Fighting is in my blood.

Dad was a proper fighting man – one of those fellas who seem to spend their whole life brawling. His dad had been a copper, which meant that my dad would get into brawls the second he walked out of his door. With all that going on, it probably wasn't a shock to anybody that he rebelled by doing some very silly things at a very young age and ended up in prison. But in the years that followed, he put all that behind him and managed to build up a successful security business, which allowed him to combine his love for punching other men very fucking hard with earning an honest living. For a long time, he ran the nightclub doors across Liverpool. He was the prick who was telling my friends' dads: 'You're not getting in.' Sometimes he was the one who was giving them a hiding.

Outside of that, he found time to give boxing a go; although he didn't get very far. He won his first bout but then in the second, he got a couple of jabs to the head he didn't like and lost his rag. As soon as the bell went, he raced back to his corner, picked up a stool and chased his opponent. That was the end of his boxing career. He's a very tough man and even now I wouldn't want to get into a tussle with him. But he never had the discipline you need for boxing. He didn't understand the mindset that you sometimes have to get hit in order to get your shots off. His whole attitude was just bang-bang, good night.

Fighting was a way of making him proud of me. If I'd have come home from school with ten GCSEs, he'd have smiled and given me a tenner. If I'd come home and said,

'Dad, I've just broken another kid's nose in a scrap,' he'd have burst with pride and given me whatever I wanted. I know that sounds mad, but that's just the way our family was. I was no different to any young boy: I wanted to impress my dad.

I've always said he was a fantastic father. Unfortunately, he wasn't a very clever husband. Things went wrong and on the day after Boxing Day 1992, when I'd just turned ten, he left home. His departure made him public enemy number one for everybody else in our house, but I still adored him. I understood that he'd been a fucking idiot and yet he was still my dad. There was never any question that we lacked love – my dad wasn't one of those guys who just disappeared; he was always there for us, always provided – and yet his work – on the doors Friday, Saturday, even Sunday nights – restricted the time he could spend with us. And then he went to jail for the second time, when I was still only fourteen. That felt like another kind of heartbreak.

During all this, my mother was a receptionist at the local sports centre. The break-up hit her really hard. Suddenly, she found she was bringing up four boys almost by herself. She ended up working every hour she possibly could. Mum needed the money, but I think it was also a way for her to take her mind off her situation.

As every year went by, she found it easier to cope, but over that same period I began to drift away. By the time I was in my teens, my friends had become my real family. I had about seven or eight close friends growing up. I've still got the same seven or eight close friends now. Most of us were from broken homes. My mum was out most of the day and night, so my house became the place where we'd all hang out. We didn't have to ask permission to do anything because there was nobody to ask. So we'd all just be in my room, door locked, and there'd be murder going on: shouting, bawling, screaming.

I spent the majority of my time at school either pissing around with my mates or playing football. I was a cheeky kid rather than a nasty one, the kind that had an answer for everything. I had massive respect for some teachers. But not all of them. There was a maths teacher who seemed to like degrading me: he told me I wasn't going to do anything because I was weak-minded and I couldn't stick to a task. My PE teacher knew I had physical ability and yet he also claimed I'd never make anything of myself because of my temper. It's been good to prove those fuckers wrong.

Once I'd given up on the idea of playing for Everton, I was left with a vague plan that I'd get the right quali-fications to stay on in education. I'd always looked up to my brother Westley, the exceptional one out of all of us, the one with real brains who'd gone to university. And I wanted to do the same. Although it's possible I was more interested in getting on the ale and having a laugh rather than actually studying.

As it happened, I never got to find out. One of the teachers at school had a carton of Ribena smashed in her face by a lad who I already didn't like. I said that what he'd done was out of order. That led to some cross words with one of his mates, whom I liked even less. Which led to me smashing his jaw in and knocking out a fair few of his teeth. I belted him so hard and so often that my right hand was swollen for days after. As I was doing this, he was stabbing me in the head with a compass. The net result was that I got expelled and the other kid didn't, which even now doesn't seem that fair.

Actually, it didn't even end there. There was a flurry of phone calls, people ringing me up saying, 'Do you know who the kid's brothers are?' No, I didn't, and nor did I care, but they obviously didn't know who my dad was, either.

There wasn't much about the situation that bothered me. There was a bit of chivalry about what I'd done – that woman should never have got belted off a young boy – but ultimately, it wasn't my fight to fight. I just wanted to scrap. That was always my problem. My fists were quite good at getting me out of trouble, but they were just as capable of dropping me in the shit.

The mad thing is, after the school expelled me, they called to say that they still wanted me to come in and sit my exams. I think what they were trying to say was something along the lines of: *we think you're a good kid and we liked the way you defended one of our teachers, even if in an ideal world you wouldn't have caused so much damage to another pupil's face and body, so for the sake of appearance we're going to punish you.* Madder still, they then invited me back to take sixth-form physical education. Instead of grabbing this lifeline, I was so pig-headed and angry that I told them to fuck off, which to this day is one of the biggest regrets I have.

So that was that. I was fifteen years old without a single qualification to my name and absolutely no idea what to do with my life. I had no job, I was signing on. All I thought was: *What the fuck have I got?* My mates were starting to work out what they were going to do and I was just a bum on the dole.

I had no real belief in myself and I didn't think that I had much chance of making my way out of my circumstances. Growing up where I did, all I thought was: *I'm just another piece-of-shit kid.* We were treated like we were nothing, little cunts who'd achieved nothing and would go on achieving nothing until we died. That sticks with you. I didn't know anyone who'd made it out of our bit of the city. It seemed *impossible* that a kid from Portman Road in Wavertree could ever become a world champion. Nobody else from my neighbourhood had ever become a world champion. As far as I knew, nobody else from round where I grew up had become wealthy or done anything.

Wavertree is the place that defines who I am. It's the place that made me. Without it, I wouldn't exist. And it'll always be special to me, because I have such amazing memories of my life there. There were rough edges, of course, but the people there are like nobody else on the planet: funny, resilient and kind. There was a brilliant sense of community, with everybody looking out for each other. And when I was a kid there were even things to do. You could play football on the streets or in the Aldi car park for hours at a time. We could go to youth centres, where there were pool tables and table tennis, with amazing people who gave up their evenings to look after a load of tear-arse kids. We used to have five-a-side competitions where we'd fight like fuck just to win a carton of juice. Nearly all of those places are gone now, lost to government cuts. It's no surprise that these children, who have nothing to do, are getting involved with guns and knives and other insanity. I was lucky that I grew up in an environment that was tough but not lethal. And yet for all kinds of reasons, our horizons were limited.

When you're a kid, your heroes should be doctors, lawyers and nurses, but nobody like that lived around us. The people we did see, driving around in boss cars, wearing gold chains and Rolexes, were drug dealers. It was much easier for us to idolise them than surgeons, because we knew them. They lived across the street, they had kickabouts (still wearing their Rolexes) with us, slapped us and told us to behave when we got out of line, and kept us away from any really bad trouble. The people doing professional jobs might have only been across the water, but as far as I was concerned, they might as well have lived on Mars. For lads like me, the street corners felt like the only way out. Especially if you had a taste for the nicer things in life. Which, unfortunately, I did.

What stopped me from doing anything more serious than messing around with it all was my dad. It wasn't really anything he said – it was more the example he set. He always had nice things because his security firm was doing well: a BMW sports car, expensive clothes, numerous houses. That showed me that you could get those items by making money the proper way. He chose to stick to the business he'd built, even though the trade he was in meant that he was surrounded by opportunities to start dealing.

If my dad had been earning his money illegally, there's every chance I'd have followed him. So that's why instead of going out on the streets in a big way, I took a job my mum got me as a lifeguard at the Peter Lloyd Leisure Centre. That gave me the chance to look around a bit and try to work out what it was I wanted to do with my life. For a while I considered joining the navy, because I knew it'd remove me from the sorts of temptations that were everywhere in our neighbourhood. I even passed the entrance test. But around the same time, I decided that I was going to try to make a go of a sport that I'd just started taking seriously: boxing.

I actually tried kick-boxing first. Unfortunately, I knocked a couple of people out with punches, so I got disqualified. Instead, when I was fourteen, I began training at the 051 Club gym with Terry Quinn and Noel Quarless, a former pro boxer who was now working the doors with my dad. They taught me the fundamentals of boxing. To begin with, I was only doing it as a hobby, a good way of having a fight without getting nicked. The idea of being a professional, let alone a world champion, didn't really enter my head.

Terry was brilliant – a lovely, lovely man who had a great record in amateur boxing – and he introduced me to proper training. While my dad had shown me the basics of fighting and we'd done some pads in the yard, Terry showed me much more. We did workouts in the sauna, ran up and down the stairs. I learned what it felt like to put your body under extreme amounts of stress. Whatever we did, I'd never shy away from it. I'd be doing exactly the same as the big hard fellas I was training alongside. To begin with I was able to keep up with them, but after a while I started to out-work them.

Those hours spent doing press-ups in the blistering heat of the sauna and killing my legs as I dragged myself up those stairs for what felt like the millionth time in one afternoon were the first indication I had of the hard work that was needed if you wanted to be a decent boxer. Terry was also the first person who spotted I had something. I was there with my dad one day, when he turned to us and said: 'You've got ability. The lad can really box. I know he can. He's got a punch on him.'

That's when my dad took me to my first boxing gym, Kirkdale ABC, which was in an old community centre on Stanley Road. The overpowering memory I have is of sweaty gloves. I did one session, but there was something about the atmosphere that made me feel uncomfortable. I didn't know anybody there and the people weren't anything like me. I couldn't make that connection, so I didn't go back.

I followed that up by going to the famous Rotunda ABC a week later. I did one session there, too. The coach, Jimmy Albertina, asked me if I'd ever boxed before. I said no. He put me on a punching bag. I was moving round the bag like a fucking animal, hosing it with punch after furious punch. Jimmy stopped me and looked me in the eye.

'You've boxed.'

'No,' I said, 'I haven't boxed. I'm telling you, honest to God, I've never had a bout.'

Jimmy wasn't having that. 'The way you move and the way you punch, you've definitely been in a ring before. I don't understand why you're saying you haven't.'

We agreed to disagree and I asked Jimmy the only question that mattered to me: 'All I want to know is: when can I fight?'

Jimmy set me straight. 'Listen, son. You don't tell me when you're going to fight. I tell you. And it's going to be twelve to eighteen months until we put you in the ring.'

As soon as he said that, I walked out and started to talk to Stockbridge ABC. I didn't want to wait. I'm just not somebody who likes to hang around hoping for things to happen; I like to *make* them happen. If you want to get anywhere, you have to create opportunities and take them straight away. More than that, I wanted to test myself. I had to find out whether or not I had the ability to stand there and trade punches. I understood even then that until you've actually put yourself in those situations, you just never know. Not for sure. Within six weeks, I had a match lined up.

Rob Beech was my first amateur opponent. He had a beard on his chin and looked like he had a rug on his chest, whereas I barely had a single hair on my bollocks. My arse was twitching. In the first round he hit me hard, harder than anyone had ever hit me before. Suddenly, I realised that things had got real, very quickly. I remember I could see my dad out of the corner of my eye. That steadied me. I could never spew in front of him. I just wouldn't be able to live with myself if he saw me give up. And then something inside me went: *Right, bite down on your gumshield. Fuck it, let's fight.*

I ended up beating Beech in a third-round stoppage. After that, things suddenly started to move quite quickly. I demolished Ryan Connolly and then found myself in the first round of the Under 10s novice tournament against Ryan Cunliffe from the Wigan ABC at the Montrose Huyton Suite. It was one of those smoke-filled social clubs that you saw everywhere in the amateur game. Kids fighting while old fellas watched, ciggies in hand. Everyone was on the ale and we were just another entertainment. It was all very much, 'Bring out the gladiators.' One night there'd be fighting on the bill, another night it would be an Elvis impersonator.

I went into the match with a bruised rib, although I didn't realise quite how damaged it was. I'd been sparring with an undefeated professional called Gary Lockett who was fighting for the British title and he'd caught me with a left hook on my body, but I thought nothing of it. There was just a really sharp twinge and I said to myself: *that's just what happens when you get hit with a really good body shot.* The thing I really took away was that Gary was astounded by how good I was. I was in a ring with a fighter, a real fighter, and I was holding my own. Terry Quinn's praise had stayed with me, but this was the first time that I realised for myself that maybe I could do something.

The fucked rib didn't do much to affect my confidence. I was 2 and 0. Both knockouts. That rarely happened in the amateur game. Actually, it never happened. Cunliffe came out hard. He jabbed my head and then threw a straight right hand to my body. Oh my fucking God. I went back to the corner: 'I think he's broken my rib.' I remember Mark Kinney, my coach at Stockbridge, and Tosh Fielding, his assistant, were in the corner. They lifted my vest and there was a red patch of blood. Tosh looked horrified.

'Stop it! Stop it! Fucking hell. There's blood under his skin!'

I wasn't willing to give in. 'Don't panic,' I mumbled through my mouthguard. 'I'll get him in the next round.'

Tosh was still a bit stunned. 'No, no, you've got to stop.'

Even then I got tunnel vision when I fought. The only thing that mattered to me was winning, nothing else registered. So I didn't acknowledge what Tosh was saying, I just told him to be quiet. I looked Mark in the eyes and said, 'Just give me another round, I'll get rid of him.'

Mark stared back. 'No problem.'

It didn't last long after that. Cunliffe was out cold and I was up on the ropes screaming at everyone. Right from my first days I was loud and out there. The normal protocol in amateur boxing is that when you win, you nod your head to the judges and that's it. You walk out. It's still got a gentlemanly ethos. Whereas I'd knock people out and then even as their head was slamming down onto the canvas, I'd be jumping up onto the ropes or screaming all round the ring, making sure that everyone in that room knew that 'I'm the best amateur boxer that this country has ever seen.'

I was already thinking like a professional, carrying myself like a professional, even though I was fighting amateurs. Strictly speaking, my style wasn't suitable for the game, but those poor fuckers didn't stand a chance.

Slowly, as I trained, my physique changed. That fat kid who loved playing football became longer and leaner. I was learning more about myself, too.

You can't know if you'll go on to become a world champion. There's too much work, dedication and sacrifice involved. But you can find out quite quickly whether or not you've got the kind of spirit that can at least get you started. The first time you're smashed in the face is, for many, that moment.

Those seconds after being hit are sink or swim. It's your chance to say, 'I've had enough, that's it.' And there'd be no shame in that: that's just the way you're wired; everybody's different. So if at that moment you feel a surge of self-pity or are tempted to quit, then let it go straight away. Find another sport.

If, by contrast, you're the kind of person who says, 'I'll have some more of that,' then you might just be the right person for this game. I loved it. I knew that from the second that Rob Beech's fist had crashed into me. I loved the violence and the pain and the rush of excitement that came with fighting. The first time my nose got burst and filled up with blood, all I thought was: *Right, I'm going to get you.* I'd tasted blood, which freaks most people out, and I thought it was nice. Which is a fucked-up thing in itself.

Boxing gave meaning to my life. It was the first thing I'd ever found that gave purpose to both my body and mind. I don't even remember when the thought first came into my head, but suddenly I found that I'd gone from being a lost fucking bum to a kid with an ambition that not only felt big and mad and intimidating, but also *possible*: I wanted to become world champion. And if I couldn't ever play for Everton, I wanted the next best thing: to win that title at Goodison.

## FIND YOUR GOALS

Boxing gave me everything. It gave me discipline, it gave me hope, a way out. It gave me my dreams, then helped me to fulfil them. That's why it was so hard when it stopped, because suddenly there was this huge hole in my life.

I was lost after I was expelled from school. I had no idea what I wanted to do and no real idea what I was capable of. Boxing changed all that. That burning desire to become world champion meant that for two decades, I had a long-term goal. And no matter what stage of my career I was at, no matter if I'd just lost a fight, that goal never changed. Over time, as my family grew, I realised that I also wanted to be able to ensure that whatever happened to me, Rachael and the boys' future would be secure, so that became another goal. Family security, money and world titles. I stayed focused on those things.

You won't achieve anything if you don't set goals and they're not working towards something that really matters to you. I fought to provide for my family, but it wasn't the money itself that was important to me, it was what it represented: security. Goals provide both the framework and the motivation you need if you want to get anywhere. When I've set myself a goal, I have purpose and a sense that I'm moving forwards. I feel as if I'm in control of my life. I can't find your purpose for you. I can't make you like getting hit and enjoy the taste of blood. But I'm here to say you do need purpose to get anything done. You need to find your equivalent of walking out at Goodison. You need to work out what you're willing to get punched in the face for and keep going. You don't need to have big skyscraping ambitions. Your goal could just be getting to a stage where you can support your family or owning your own business. And your goals don't need to be professional. They could just be about losing weight and getting fitter or becoming a better husband and father.

It's worth devoting effort to thinking hard about what your goals should be. Sometimes you'll know instantly. Other times, it won't be so obvious. Sit down and try to work out what you'd like to change about your circumstances. What are the things that you've always wanted to do but haven't found the space or time in your life to get started on? What about those little voices at the back of your mind that you've always been too busy to listen to? Maybe you've been wanting to start playing five-a-side football again but you know you're short of fitness and the idea of finding a game feels a bit tough, so you keep putting it off. Or it could be that deep down you know that you're not happy with your job and that you want to be doing something completely different.

Don't be stupid with what you ask of yourself. Don't look to achieve the impossible. Nothing demotivates you like failing to reach a goal, however unrealistic, and nothing motivates you more like hitting one. And it has to be something you want, not something other people want for you. My dad's dream was always to have a kid who could fight like fuck. But if boxing hadn't been something I was obsessed by and I just wanted to live out my father's ambitions for him, there's no way in the world I'd have been able to drag myself through those hard times and early mornings. The more passionate you are about something at the beginning, the more likely you are to be doing it still in a year, two years', three years' time. If you can't see that passion lasting more than a couple of months, then ask yourself whether you should consider following a different path.

The reason this chapter is called 'The Weigh-In' is because, at the end of the day, the scales don't lie. You need to look at yourself with the same dispassionate honesty as those scales. What do you want, how can you get there? What are you good at, what are you bad at? What can you do well? What needs work?

Set realistic goals. Achieve them. And once you've achieved them, you have to set more quickly. The moment I tell myself I've done it all, what then? And sometimes, believe me, those goals will scare you. Like writing a book.

## TELL A NEW STORY

When you have a clearly defined ambition, it enables you to look at the world, and yourself, in a different way.

I spent so much of my early life being told I was a waste of space. And there's only so many times you can close your ears before you begin to think: *well, am I?* You end up believing them and it becomes your destiny. *You think I'm filth? Fine, I'll be filth.* Nobody ever encouraged me, nobody ever took the time to point out what I was good at. I had to prove those things to myself.

Boxing offered me a way out of that way of thinking. Once I'd thrown myself behind that dream of becoming world champion, I stopped seeing myself as a failure who was going nowhere and unworthy of anybody's respect. I'd become somebody who was on the road to somewhere. That meant that when I experienced setbacks, I stopped seeing them as failures and started to understand that they were just steps on the path to success. You can't change what happens, but you can change your attitude towards it. And once you realise that, it becomes your greatest power. Everybody has the ability to act as the author of their own story – it's up to you to use it.

What cuts me up is knowing how much potential there is out there for human beings and how much of it goes to waste because people tell others who could accomplish great things that they're worthless. It's not the way it should be but don't let yourself get demoralised by it. Use it as motivation to demonstrate to them that it doesn't matter that they were handed every advantage, you're fucking going to show them what real achievement looks like. And when you make it, it'll feel all the sweeter for it.

## MAKE IT SPECIFIC

I don't think I realised it at the time, but I can see now how that specific, measurable ambition – becoming world champion – was probably more valuable than something vaguer like 'I want to be good at boxing.' Where would I have even started with that?

I don't want to sound too cold or scientific about it. And nor do I want to sound too spiritual, either. But there was definitely something about how specific my dream was – that I wanted to win that belt at Goodison Park – that made it feel personal to me. It also helped me to imagine myself getting there. That image was something I could call upon when I was struggling. No matter how horrible those 5 a.m. runs were – and they were almost always fucking horrible – they were always *for* something.

## LITTLE STEPS

Everyone has to start somewhere. I didn't become a world-class boxer in one leap. I'd have been absolutely annihilated if I'd climbed into the ring against someone like David Haye in my first fight. To get to that point, I had to take a thousand smaller steps.

I know for a fact that if I'd known how much work and sacrifice would be involved in becoming world champion, I'd have got so overwhelmed that I might never have got going. That's why it was so important that I made a commitment, joined a boxing gym and took that first step. It didn't feel significant at the time, but it meant that the next step was easier, and the step after that, and the step after that. You have to find your way in.

The same is true of any project or ambition. You're not going to be able to run a marathon without doing any preparation, but you can start off by going from the couch to a more manageable 5K. That way, suddenly you'll find that the idea of going further isn't so intimidating. You might want to become a barrister, but there's no way you're going to be able to stand there in court in your big fucking wig unless you've got all the qualifications and experience that the job demands. The idea of all the obstacles you're going to have to overcome in the future could become so overwhelming that it paralyses you. Don't let that happen. All you can do is focus on the things you can do now to get you moving in the right direction.

You have to start somewhere and the first step is always the hardest, but once you've made that first small commitment, everything else will follow.

## FIND YOUR MOTIVATION

Nothing's given to you, nothing is easy. Most good things in life come from sacrifice and hard work. In order to reach your goals, you need to find the motivation that will drive you on when times get tough. You need a 'why' as well as a 'what'. There's no point in climbing into the ring and taking punches if you don't know why you're doing it. Otherwise, you're just a fucking madman with a death wish. Once you know why you're opening yourself up to pain and disappointment, then they'll both be easier to bear. I was lucky in many ways, because my workplace gave me a big target to aim for: world champion.

Most boxers come from nothing, like me. They've been starved all their lives, been out on the streets doing nasty things before they got into the ring. They're dealers, pimps, jailbirds. That's why they have that fire in their bellies that makes them want to push and push. There are a very few, like Conor Benn, who have grown up with nice things and gone on to make it. It's rare to come from privilege and be able to go and fight the way he does. But his motivation came in wanting to impress his father.

I didn't come from privilege. The purpose of fighting for me was to escape the place I was born, but in that respect, Conor and I are similar. I loved my dad, but I wanted to show him that I could do stuff he couldn't. Even though he backed me all the way, I still wanted to be better than him or anyone else in my family. I wanted to make my dad proud by becoming a better version of him. And I wanted to give my kids the best life I possibly could. I think all that is perhaps why I was willing to go further than anybody else, because anything was better than the idea of being a failed fighter who'd got stuck in fucking Wavertree.

If your goal is getting a new job, make sure you know what that new job really represents to you, otherwise you're just going to end up chasing an empty shell. Is it because you want a career that challenges you? Or is it just that you want more money to help you lead a better lifestyle?

Once you've identified your motivation, keep it right at the forefront of your mind. Never let it go.

## TRICK YOURSELF

Having a goal isn't enough in itself to drive you on. There were always mornings when I felt that short-term temptation to stay in bed an hour longer rather than go for a run. Or I'd feel that drive to leave the gym early so I could see my kids before they went to bed.

Everyone, no matter how driven and committed they are, has these moments. It can be difficult to think of future benefits when your bed is warm. Your brain is a lazy fucker. It likes doing things that feel good. But it's not very clever at choosing between the different sorts of feeling good. As far as your brain is concerned, it's much less effort to get those nice feelings from playing a game on your phone than it is to get them from finishing the work you need to do for that day. It's quicker and it's easier, which is why you end up playing Angry Birds for eight hours straight rather than finishing that report. If you leave it up to your brain, it'll pick the Mars bar over the kale smoothie every day of the week.

But it's possible to trick your brain into weighing things up differently by emphasising to yourself both the pleasure you'll feel if you achieve your long-term goals and the misery you'll experience if you let them fall by the wayside.

41

One thing that really helped me to get out of bed on those cold winter mornings was to think about how amazing it would be to win a world championship. If I didn't get up, then I'd never get the chance to walk out at Goodison. I also thought about what would happen if I didn't persist. I'd think about how angry and bitter abandoning my dream of becoming world champion would leave me, and the impact that would have on Rachael and the children.

I knew that I'd only be cheating myself and I didn't want to let that become a habit. I'd seen what had happened to some of the other lads who I'd started out training alongside. They'd let go of their motivation. There was never a big moment when they said, 'Fuck this, I don't want to be a boxer any more.' It was more an accumulation of smaller incidents. They'd turn up later and later at the gym and then one day, you'd realise they hadn't turned up at all. The thought of that happening to me killed me. I knew that come the end of the day, I'd already be regretting not having got up. But more than that, I was already afraid of ending up washed-up and bitter, blaming everyone else when deep down, I knew that my failure was my fault and my fault alone.

## THE PLEASURE OF PROVING OTHER PEOPLE WRONG

You're a bullshitter until the moment that you actually achieve something. For a very long time, a lot of people thought I was a bullshitter, which was fair enough. I was actually guilty of the odd white lie when I was a kid, mostly the result of overenthusiasm on my part: 'I know him, he's my cousin' (he wasn't). 'Yeah, I can sort that out for you' (I couldn't). Boxing was different, it meant more. Almost as soon as I'd formulated my ambition, I started telling people about it. Over and over again. I'd tell them that I was going to become world champion at Goodison Park. I'd tell them that I was going to be the best fighter who'd ever come from this city. I had absolutely no right to say any of this. I'd achieved the square root of fuck all.

I'm not one for all that see-believe-achieve shit. What I did realise, however, was that the more I ran my mouth off, the more pressure there'd be on my shoulders to prove that I wasn't actually a bullshitter. In the meantime, I had to live with the constant noise of people criticising me or laughing at me.

But that was the best motivation I could ever have. And that was the mentality I kept with me throughout my career. My whole time in boxing was about proving people wrong.

When people said I was full of shit or when they looked at me and told me to 'Be realistic, you've got no chance,' that would drive me even more. When later on I lost fights and people said, 'You're not going to be able to cut it in the pros,' I didn't stop. 'OK,' I'd tell them, 'we'll see. I'll get there.' Every knock that people gave me only pushed me on further. The more people told me I was chatting shit, the more I wanted to prove them wrong.

When I was a kid starting out, every Boxing Day I met up with my closest mates to have a good bevvy and a good laugh. I remember there was one year when one of my friends' dad's mates was ripping me.

'You're a good lad,' he said, 'but you're not going to make it, are you?'

He made sure all of my mates in the pub could hear him and I knew he wanted to embarrass me. That set me off.

'Listen, lad. I'm going to be rich,' I told him. 'I'm going to be so fucking rich you wouldn't understand. I'm going to own the company.'

I could see he wasn't buying that at all.

'Fuck off,' he said. 'Don't be stupid. You're just an amateur boxer. Don't be ridiculous.'

All I said in reply was, 'You'll see.'

I saw this fella again about four years ago and I said, 'That worked out all right, didn't it, lad?' And he just laughed. He tried to crack on he didn't know what I was on about. But he knew. He 100 per cent knew.

My desire to prove people like him wrong was one of the things that kept me going during the hard times. And gradually, painfully slowly, after years of me forcing this pipedream down so many people's throats, they, too, started to think I could make it happen.

I definitely don't think you should willingly open yourself to as much abuse as I got (and probably deserved), but going public with your plans can end up being really useful. If you announce the night before to anyone – it could be your girlfriend or a mate – that you're going to go to the gym or sign up for that half-marathon, then you'll be putting a subtle amount of pressure on your shoulders. Who wants to look foolish or weak for not keeping their promises? It's a good tool to have up your sleeve ahead of those days when you know you're going to be that bit more vulnerable to temptation. And it's another example of how to trick that lazy brain out of choosing the easiest option.

## YOUR PERFORMANCE IS IMPORTANT – EVERYBODY ELSE'S IS IRRELEVANT

I had days when I looked around the Rotunda and caught sight of the ease with which one of the other lads ran, or the power and grace of a more naturally gifted fighter's left hook, and I'd think: *I'll never be able to do that.* If I wasn't careful, that thought could lead to other ones: *This isn't fair. They were born with so much more than me. What's the point?*

There were days when having that drive and desire to reach their level helped. It also taught me how dangerous it was to spend too much time comparing myself to other people and what they could do. I was determined never to let it become an excuse. Ultimately, the gifts that they were born with were completely irrelevant to me and my goal. The only thing that I could control, and the only thing that was important to me, was *my* progress. All I could do was try to ensure that I left the gym each day in a better position than I'd been in when I walked through its doors. If I could use the idea of keeping up with that guy who was absolutely smashing it in the gym as inspiration, then brilliant, but apart from that, his performance had nothing to do with me or my own progress. So why would I give it a second thought?

Don't judge yourself by other people's standards. It doesn't matter how well other people are doing, how much further than you they're running, how much more than you they're earning. All that counts is your own performance.

## CHANGES

The destination might stay the same, but always be alive to the need to make changes to the route you're taking to get there. What might work for you one month won't necessarily be good the next month. Interrogate what you do and why. For a long while, the part-time jobs I worked were essential in subsidising my boxing, but a point came when they started to act as an impediment.

When you go to make changes, be wary of the temptation of making changes for change's sake. Make sure you're clear about what advantages you're getting out of that switch. You shouldn't see it as a Hail Mary pass to try when you can't think of anything else to do. Later in my career, I ended up changing trainers. I didn't do that just because I wanted to see a fresh face in the gym (although that does have its own value) or because I'd run out of ideas, but because I'd done the research and I knew the exact ways that the new coach could help me to improve.

## SUMMARY

- Find what you're prepared to get punched in the face for. What's your purpose? You need something to fix your eyes on when times get tough.

- Write down your strengths and weaknesses. Be honest. It should feel a bit uncomfortable.

- Set realistic, achievable goals.

- Trick your brain by focusing on the benefits of what you want to do while weighing up the negatives of not achieving your targets. This is how brains work – yours isn't broken.

- Don't listen to the negative voices. In fact, use them as motivation.

- Focus on yourself, not other people. You can't control them. They don't matter.

# CHAPTER 2
# SECONDS IN

*Brooks is a giant. He seems out of place in this tiny social club; like he'd be more comfortable scaring the shit out of villagers as he stomps their houses into matchsticks or rampaging from skyscraper to skyscraper in New York. He's so big that his kit is barely able to contain his body. His shorts, his head guard, even his boots are all bursting at the seams. When he moves across the canvas, I swear I can feel the room shake.*

*Midway into the first round, his big howitzer of a right hand catches me and the lights flash. I fall into the ropes and the referee starts his count. These are both new experiences for me, and I don't like either. I'm annoyed that I've been knocked down, but I'm outraged that the referee has intervened.*

*'What are you counting for?' I'm incandescent. So angry that I'm barely aware of anything except my own sense of injustice. Everything else – the bewildering pain Brooks has caused me, the raucous crowd, even Jimmy's bulky form in my corner – has faded.*

*The referee ignores me and carries on; he's up to five now.*

*By the time he gets to eight, I've had enough. 'You've just counted me to eight for no reason. Move out of the way.'*

*Second round I do him with a right-hander. Boom, kid's out. Game over.*

*I'm fucking high off myself after that. I get back to the corner and start into my familiar braggadocio: 'You've just witnessed the fucking bollocks out there. I am the business. I am better than anyone here.' My words spin out into the smoke-filled room. Everyone is staring at me like I'm a lunatic. Everyone except Jimmy, who gives me a slap on the face and drags me back to the dressing room.*

*'Why was the referee counting me?'*

*'Cos the fucking kid does you. He knocked you back into the ropes. You looked a bit dazed.'*

*'No I wasn't. Don't tell me I was dazed, you big fucking dope.'*

*'I'll tell you, because someone fucking needs to.'*

There are some people who change your life. Jimmy Albertina was the greatest boxing coach I've ever worked with. He was also one of the best men I've ever known.

It was Micky Whitty, an amateur boxer who I knew from security work, who persuaded me to try the Rotunda ABC again. Mick was a good ten years older than me, a feared lad on the street and game as fuck. He told me I should give it a go. We were the same weight, so we could spar together: 'It'll be brilliant. We'll nail each other. We'll bring each other on so much. Albo is the best coach you'll ever meet.'

Yes, I thought to myself, *I'll have a bit of that*.

At Stockbridge ABC I'd been coached by Mark Kinney,

a great guy whom I felt like I was learning a lot from, but he'd just taken a job at Jaguar. He was on a different shift pattern, which meant that two out of three weeks he wouldn't be able to be in the gym. I didn't trust anybody else to coach me, so that was it.

That first day when I went back to the Rotunda it was with my tail between my legs. Almost two years had passed and yet Jimmy looked at me without surprise, like he'd been expecting to see me again.

'All right, lad, you're back.'

I swallowed my pride and asked if they'd let me train. He had a little dig at me and that was it. I was in.

The Rotunda used to be spit and sawdust, a shithole, stinking gym opposite the Easby Estate, which, like any area in Liverpool, had its fair share of lunatics. It was just one compact building. Nothing was new there, not the battered floor nor the ancient gym equipment that seemed as if it had been scavenged rather than bought. I fucking loved it. I loved the infamous gloves room with its rows of Mexico Reyes gloves and stench of decades-old sweat. It was boss. I even loved the matted area in the far left corner where we did the circuits that Jimmy was obsessed by and I hated with a passion.

Nobody cared that the gear was shitty or the area was rough, because the Rotunda ABC was like a factory turning out champions and at the centre of it all was Jimmy. He was small and thickset, a fat little hardcase who might have been a brilliant fighter if he hadn't liked a pint and good scoff so much. What was odd was that he wasn't at all flabby – every part of his body was like rock. His legs, thighs and calves were the biggest I've ever seen. He was like a Scouse Roberto Carlos. And you couldn't miss them, because he was always in cycling shorts. He'd just wobble round the gym in a vest, his big round belly sticking out in front of him, giving out a constant stream of advice. He was so funny, so down-to-earth, and his whole personality permeated right through that gym.

Without Jimmy Albertina, I wouldn't be the man I am today. I've had other great coaches. Terry Quinn taught me how to box. Mark Kinney was a fantastic guy. Noel Quarless helped a lot. All of these men played their part; they all helped me along the way, but it was Jimmy who was the most prevalent person in my life.

Everybody was devoted to him, even those kids who were so out of control even their own parents had given up on them, and they all respected him. They just loved him. In return, he loved us all, looked after us as if we were his own. He was definitely another father figure for me. You could have a laugh with him, but you'd never ever cross him. You'd never answer him back, because you had so much respect for him.

I started working with the likes of Mick Whitty and Paul Ghia. I got to meet Joseph Selkirk, who was a baby of thirteen at the time. I never looked back after that, not once. I just knew that gym was the making of me. It turned out that Jimmy had been watching my first steps in amateur boxing. He'd been there the night I knocked out Ryan Cunliffe when I had a fucked rib. He was there, telling everyone around him: 'Watch this kid, he's got ability.' Then, once I'd turned up at the Rotunda, Jimmy had called Mark Kinney, who'd told him two things. One, that one day I'd be a national champion. Two, that I hated fitness work. 'Anything he does that involves punching or hurting people,' Mark said, 'he does with a smile on his face. But he can't stand doing circuits and he can't stand running.'

Jimmy repeated this conversation to me. The excited glow that had begun to spread in me when he told me about Mark's faith that I could become a champion was quickly stopped when he explained that he'd be giving me twice as many circuits as any other fighter in the gym.

'I'm going to make you run,' he said, 'at the same speed I make the fucking featherweights run.'

'For fuck's sake, Jimmy.'

'You love sparring, you love punching pads and bags, and Mark was right, you love hurting people.'

'I know, yeah, that's what boxing's about.'

'No it's not. It's about being as fit as you can be and the punching will take care of itself. I know what you're good at, Anthony, but I also know what your weaknesses are.'

I'd never had a coach speak to me like that. He saw so clearly that I had to improve my stamina, my sharpness, my explosiveness, my punching power and my basic fitness. I hadn't understood the importance of any of that, but slowly, surely, I realised how right Jimmy was.

I arrived at the Rotunda knowing I was decent and thinking I might have potential, but in truth, I hadn't the first idea what boxing was really about. I'd soon learn. At the Rotunda, they showed me how to train. It was so regimented there and it felt as if you were part of a proper team. When you went in, everyone was working their bollocks off, going right at it. There wasn't even one person slacking. They demanded the best from every single fighter. I remember standing there and feeling that all I wanted in the world was to be part of that. Over and over in my head I was saying: 'This is the place for me. This is the place for me.'

Rotunda ABC had turned out champion after champion – four or five of them every single year. Without fail. New kids, old kids. Most of the lads there had been fighting since they were nine – they were amazing athletes. Things like circuits were easy for them. When we went out for jogs, they all looked as if they could keep on running for ever. For the first time since I'd started boxing, I was really struggling to keep up. Nowadays, some of the people I trained with back then will say, 'I was in the gym with Tony Bellew.' In my head, they're still the stars – as far as I was concerned, I was in the gym with *them*.

The coaches – alongside Jimmy there was Mick McAllister, John Doolan, Michael McNally, George Whittaker, John Wignall and John Warburton – showed me the levels of sacrifice and dedication you needed to get to the top. They focused on strength, stamina and tactics, leaving no stone unturned. But the best thing they helped me with was making me use my feet more in boxing matches. I'd always been able to punch and I always wanted to meet my opponents head-on, but for the first time now I'd use my feet as well as fists as weapons. The coaches at the Rotunda taught me not only how to use my feet to get myself out of trouble, but also how to use them to dictate the range of fights.

That's something I'd keep with me throughout my career. In all the years I've boxed, sparring, pro, amateur, whatever, Oleksandr Usyk is the only fighter with better feet than me. Some of that was my natural talent, but a big chunk of it was owing to the lessons I learned in that funny little gym in the North End of Liverpool.

Jimmy would always be there, chirping away. All I wanted to do was impress him. I was desperate for his approval. My dad would tell me how brilliant I was after each victory. He told me I was going to be a world champion. But that wasn't enough, because of course my dad would say that. But I *needed* to hear those things from Jimmy. I *needed* to hear him say, 'Lad, that was fucking brilliant.' He never once did.

Jimmy wasn't soft. He wasn't a man who'd say nice things for the sake of saying them. And he understood that keeping us motivated wasn't just a question of telling us we were brilliant every second of the day. But Jimmy cared so deeply about us. That's why he could sometimes be harsh.

At the time of writing, I still hold the record for the quickest knockout in the country. It was a novice Under 10s final in 2003 at Knottingley Sports Centre in Leeds against a guy called Ahmed who was 10 and 0. It took six seconds – six seconds and he was stone cold. I hit him so hard on the chin that he fell flat on his face. I knew as soon as my glove slammed into his jaw that he wasn't going to get up.

I felt no pain, like you might expect. First, there was what felt like an electric bolt surging up my arm, right through to the shoulder. Then everything in his body just stopped. No movement, nothing. The referee didn't even bother counting. I walked over to his corner and climbed up onto his section of his ropes. I looked around the hall, made sure everybody was watching, then yelled: 'I'm the best fucking fighter youse lot will ever see.' The *cheek* of me. When I look back, I'm embarrassed.

I swaggered back to my corner, waiting for Jimmy to tell me how brilliant I was. He didn't miss a beat.

'Fucking shit that, lad.'

Then there was me boxing at Everton Park, after I'd been out injured for a spell. I stopped the kid in the first round. I blitzed him and I was shouting to all the people, all of his fans, 'I'm back, I'm fucking back. I've told you I'm back now. Look what I've done to him. I'm back.'

I got back to the corner, and Jimmy grabbed hold of my head guard and said, 'You're back?! Where have you fucking been, you stupid dickhead?'

But behind the scenes, when I was out of earshot, as he sat there chatting to his mates like John Doolan and Mick McAllister, he was saying something different: 'That kid's going to be special.' And what Jimmy actually did for me was far more important than anything he could possibly have said.

Jimmy knew that it didn't matter how good your footwork was or how hard you could punch – people didn't really pay attention until you were put on the right stage. And if he thought you had something about you, he'd put you forwards. Jimmy wasn't willing to waste his time. He only kept fighters at the Rotunda who he thought could cut it. Which is why from time to time a lad would disappear from view. Nobody would ask about them or saying anything; they'd just be gone. If you weren't good enough, you wouldn't get bouts, you wouldn't be entered into competitions. Eventually, you'd get the message. But Jimmy always wanted to work on me. He always wanted me to be out there fighting for Rotunda. That should have told me. It didn't matter how many times he called me a fucking idiot, it was Jimmy Albertina who put me on that stage to shine.

You lose people in life. Jimmy died from a heart attack in 2003. My uncle had passed away from cancer not long before that, but I could process that, because I'd had time to prepare for it. Jimmy going so suddenly felt like the hardest thing I'd ever had to take. I was still so young that I didn't understand the grief that seized me. He'd had a quadruple bypass in the spring of that year and it was fine for a while. I used to go and visit him. On a Friday after the gym, I'd go straight to his and hang out with him before I had to go and work on the doors.

He'd usually be watching television. *Taggart* was his favourite and he'd make a big thing of being annoyed.

'You've come round and disturbed my programme. Bernie, stick that on record, so I can talk to this lad while he's coming.'

Of course, he was delighted that I was there. Part because he liked my company and part because he could plug me for information about the gym he wasn't even supposed to be thinking about while he was recovering.

'Lad, what workout have you done tonight? Tell me exactly what workout you've done and what circuit you've done at the end.'

When I told him, he'd be enraged.

'That cheeky fucker, he's changed my workout. I'll fucking slap him.'

Oh my God! He cared so much, he couldn't ever stop caring.

Losing him was a catastrophe. I remember it was another Rotunda fighter, Paul Smith, who phoned me on a Monday morning.

'Jim is dead.'

'What are you talking about?' I said. 'I was only with him on Friday. What are you on about? You're not making any sense?'

He was crying dead loud down the phone. He said, 'Jimmy. He's dead.'

It felt as if the world was coming down. All I could think was, *oh no, what the fuck*. Selfish shit that I was, this was followed by another thought: *What the fuck am I going to do now for boxing? Is it over?*

We all went to the gym. What else could we have done? Jimmy had all sorts of fellas coming and going in the gym. I think he liked the noise and energy that came with it.

There was this one lad who was always on the rob – books, vitamins, tablets, DVDs . . . there wasn't a WHSmith in a ten-mile radius that was safe from him – and he'd brought Jimmy an Everlast tank top. I was going through this phase of thinking I was a rapper and basketball player, so this vest caught my eye immediately.

'Jimmy, give us that top. You're never going to wear that. It won't fit you. It'll look great on me.'

'No, lad, it'll look great on me with my cycling shorts. Leave it alone.'

I kept pestering him and pestering him. In the end, he said, 'Go on, lad, just take it. Just fuck off and get out my office.'

That day Jimmy died, I drove round to the Rotunda in my mum's car – I didn't even have a driving licence – and sat with Paul, crying in that top, feeling absolutely broken and devastated. It was the first time I'd ever felt grief. The whole gym was there. We were all stunned. It was horrible; it took a really long time to recover. A really, really long time.

The funeral was the biggest I'd ever seen. He'd trained maybe fifty amateur national champions. Any one of them would have carried his coffin when he died. But I was nominated as one of the six men who'd have that honour, which was a huge surprise to me: it was the first time I realised how much Jimmy had thought of me. There were two champions from the past, two from the present and two who he believed would have a brilliant future. I was in that final pair. At the time, all I had to my name was a novice title. Somehow, even after he'd passed away, Jimmy had found a way of making me feel as if I could conquer the world.

After that, the gym was shut for quite a bit. The next time I boxed, it was at the end of the year at the novice Amateur Boxing Association (ABA) championships. I dedicated the title to Jimmy. I cried after I won, because I knew that Jimmy should have been there watching me. Everything I've gone on to achieve in the years since has only been possible because of Jimmy and the impact he had on me. I'm still close with his children; his wife, Bernie, was at my wedding. I still have that Everlast vest. I still think of him every day.

Luckily, I had someone by my side to help me through my sadness. A couple of years before, I'd met a girl called Rachael Roberts. Or to be more accurate, I met her again. It was in the silly hours of the morning and I'd been working at the nightclub in the basement of Club 051. I'd started out there as a glass collector when I was fifteen. That lasted for about three weeks and then I strangled someone.

That night I had been going about my business quietly, when some fella pushed me out of the way. I ignored him and picked up another empty glass. For whatever reason, he carried on giving me hassle, so I got him by the neck and belted him a couple of times. He stopped pushing me after that; largely because it's difficult to push anybody when you're flat on your back.

They moved me to do the security on the DJ box after that. I was given a radio and the instruction that I wasn't to do anything stupid like throw anybody out. I just had to raise the alarm to the boys on the door if I spotted trouble anywhere in the club.

Footballers loved that place. You'd see Paul Ince bowl in and smoke twenty ciggies. They'd all want to get in that DJ box while everyone around them was getting off their cakes. I'd work on the Saturday then head to school the following Monday full of stories. 'You should have seen . . .' Everyone thought I was chatting shit, because I told them all the crazy things I'd seen.

On that particular night, I'd finished working my security shift at the DJ box and was on my way up to do an after-hours club called Sunrise, when a girl stopped me just as I was about to walk in. She was absolutely beautiful. Gorgeous body. Lovely face. Dark hair, dark eyes. Everything you could possibly want.

And then she called me Anthony, which caught me off guard. I thought, *no one calls me Anthony in this area that I know; it's either Bellew or Bomber, or Little Ant.*

'Anthony, Anthony,' she persisted.

I looked and then said, 'All right,' which isn't one of

the all-time great opening lines, but in my defence, it was 4 a.m.

She went, 'It's Rachael.'

All I could say was, 'I don't know a Rachael that looks like that.'

'It's Rachael Roberts, Neil's sister.'

*Fucking hell. Wow, she's grown up*, I thought. *She didn't look like* that *the last time I saw her.*

I'd actually known her since I was eleven and she was ten, when I used to knock around with her brothers, Neil and Ashley. Then they moved house, time flashed on and I didn't see her for years.

I remember saying to her, 'Are you going in?'

I took her and her mate, Rhian, to the front of the queue, got them in for free and then couldn't stop thinking about her. And now here we are, twenty years later.

I'd never trusted women before. I think working in nightclubs – seeing girls sniffing all kinds of drugs, going with all kinds of men, doing absurd things in the toilets – made that hard. But I trusted Rachael from the very first second. I'd known her since she was a kid. I knew her family were good people. I've never really felt as if I've deserved her and I've not always been a perfect husband, but I adored her then and I adore her now. She keeps me in line: when I'm being an idiot, she won't speak to me; she doesn't even want to know me.

More than that, she's been a driving force in my life. I've always wanted to prove to her that I'm worth all the hassle.

Being with her helped to sharpen my ambitions. I realised that by fighting, I could get her everything she'd wanted but couldn't have as a kid. If I hadn't had her by my side over the years, then I know I'd have veered off down the wrong path. It's her and our kids who have kept me on the straight and narrow. Without them, I'd be nowhere.

## SURROUND YOURSELF WITH GOOD PEOPLE

While it's true that the ultimate responsibility for your fate always has to rest on your shoulders, you'll inevitably end up relying on other people at some stage on your journey. Everyone needs a helping hand from time to time. That's why the human beings you surround yourself with are so important. You need to establish as early as you can who genuinely wants the best for you and who's only interested in themselves.

In my time in boxing, I've been lucky to see human beings at their best. The Rotunda was full of people who were desperate for me to become the finest possible version of myself I could be. I was shaped by that scrappy room and the hard, brave, funny men who trained us. Their expertise made me work so much harder than I would have anywhere else. They encouraged me, but they were also unafraid to give me hard lessons when they felt I needed them. The Rotunda coaches are the reason I became an ABA champion and a regular international boxer.

But I've also seen people at their worst and I'm still scarred by some of my experiences. I've learned that you should never be friends with people who are jealous of your success, or who want something from you, or who lie or talk shit about you behind your back. If you feel worse every time you see somebody, you should stop seeing them as soon as you can.

All that is why I believe that when you find good people – whether it's in your personal or professional life – you should do the hard work of treating them well and keeping them close.

## WATCH OUT FOR SHARKS

I wish everybody was good. I wish everybody was more like Jimmy Albertina. But they're not and it's dangerous to pretend otherwise. I went into boxing with that belief and before long, I got done over. That's why I have always kept a very tight circle around me. I've seen too many fighters have the life sucked out of them by the leeches that hang on to them right up until the moment they realise that there's no money left.

Very few people are interested in helping you. There was never a moment when an older fighter turned to me and said, 'Here's the secret. This is what you need to know about the boxing world.' Nobody helps anybody else. There were a couple of occasions when I was younger, before

I'd learned this hard lesson, when I reached out to other fighters. Instead of helping me, they tried to sabotage my career. It was so blatant, as if they weren't even bothered about me finding out.

One time, a little after I'd decided to turn professional, I approached another boxer, who used to be a good friend, and asked him to put in a good word for me with Frank Warren. *No problem*, he told me. I'd done him favours in the past and it seemed like the least he could do. Warren never called, which was odd given that by that time I was a three-time ABA champion, the best prospect in this country; two of those final victories were by knockouts. In one of them, I rendered the other guy unconscious for five minutes – something that hasn't been done before or since – live on television with all the promoters watching.

A year passed. A couple of other promoters approached me to turn pro with them, but the money wasn't right and because Rachael and I had already had Corey by then, I decided to stay as an amateur. Then one day in 2007, I sparred with a guy called John Anthony, a powerful, unbeaten cruiserweight at Dave Coldwell's gym. I was butchering him, smashing him all over the gym. I punched holes in him. Dave turned to me. 'Why don't you go pro?' he asked. I explained what had happened with my friend.

Dave was bewildered by what I told him. Right there and then, in front of me, he called Frank.

'I've found a TV fighter for you.'

I could hear Frank's voice coming faintly over the line.

'What do you mean?'

'I've got this kid in my gym and I've just watched him take my fighter apart. He didn't even break into a sweat.'

'What's his name?'

'Tony Bellew.'

'I've heard of him. I know who he is. Ask him to come to my office on Monday.'

So my dad and I drove up to London. I walked in past the bronze Prince Naseem statue in the hallway, still in a state of shock. It was Frank Warren, a man who created champions like other guys made breakfast. *This was it,* I thought. I told Frank about my previous attempt to contact him. All he told me was that he trusted Dave's judgement.

'If he says you're a TV fighter, then you're a TV fighter.'

He asked me what I'd been offered before. I told him and he promptly doubled it, sweetened by a ten-grand signing-on fee. I was skint, I had a kid and a mortgage and nowhere to go, and it was fucking unbelievable money. There was nothing to think about. All I asked him was how many times a year I could fight: 'As many times as you want.'

A couple of years later, I asked Dean Powell, Frank's right-hand man, why they hadn't signed me first time round.

'We were told you were too fat and lazy to make light heavyweight.'

I'd been done over by that man I'd thought was a friend, who came from the same city as me, who trained in the same amateur gym as me. I should have known – I'd seen him do the same to others.

I don't regret what happened and I don't hold it against him. He was just looking out for himself. If he could keep me out of the limelight, his own chances of making it would have been improved. Maybe not by much. Anyway, I wish him well and hope he's doing OK. It's sad – he was a good fighter.

It was a lesson: never mix friendship and pound notes, ever. Just. Don't. Do. It. As far as I'm concerned, business is business. I've become very cold-hearted like that. It meant that when Riddick Bowe once asked if he could join my training team, I gracefully had to tell him that I was happy with my team. He was the guy I'd grown up idolising – I couldn't risk my judgement being clouded.

I was even more hurt by Frank Warren when it all ended in the way it did. I was fiercely loyal to Frank Warren right until the end. I trusted him – that's why it hurt so much. We were friends, or at least I thought we were. He'd take me up to watch the Arsenal in his box at the Emirates. We talked for hours and hours about boxing. We'd text message each other all the time. So, when everything went wrong between us, it broke my fucking heart. I don't want to go over old ground here and I'm sure he'd tell a different story to me. But what it taught me is that I have to feel like I can trust and rely on everyone in my team completely. If that trust goes, you have to make the change. And for me, that change was Eddie Hearn.

# THE IMPORTANCE OF TRUST

I've never had a contract with Eddie. There's not a single piece of paper that ties us together. But we've had a brilliant relationship because we both trusted each other. When he took me on, he might not have been the best promoter in the world – he certainly didn't have the power he does now – but I could tell he was the most honest. By the same token, I was just a scrappy, promising up-and-comer; he knew I was a risk. He took a chance on me and I've never forgotten that faith. So even later on, when I'd become a box-office star, one of the biggest draws in the country, and was getting solid offers of big money, I told him the same thing: 'I'm going to finish my career with you.'

There were times when I wanted to kill him because he'd thrown me into fights where I was getting tuppence. And there were times when I was phoned by other promoters offering to double my money if I binned off the bout Eddie had arranged for me and fought on their bill instead. I could have fucked Eddie over and taken that cash. But I didn't, because being loyal was important to me.

He stood by me, I stood by him and we stayed loyal to each other. I like to think that that means something. The strength of our relationship has helped to make us money, which is great. But more important than that was the knowledge that whatever happened, I could trust Eddie. When you trust someone, it means that when they tell you they're going to do something, you can be confident that they will. It means that you don't lie awake at night worrying that they might do you over. It means that you know that they'll always have your back.

I want to be able to trust people. And that's why I'll give you the benefit of the doubt. If I get second-hand information that you've been having a bit of a jangle about me, I'm likely to say, 'Oh well, you never know.' It's only when you've nailed me and it can't be anything but that that I just go, *fuck you*. And that's it – you're gone. I'll remove you from my life. You'll never get another chance. No matter how close you are, no matter what we've been through. I won't, can't, ever trust you, and that's it. Someone who's done you over once will probably do it again.

If you can't trust somebody, then you shouldn't keep them around you. If you do, there will always be that shadow lurking in the background. You'll spend your life wondering whether they're lying to you or plotting behind your back. And then at some point down the line – it might be sooner, it might be later, but it will come – they'll turn round and fuck you.

## DO UNTO OTHERS AS YOU WOULD HAVE DONE UNTO YOU

I've always lived by the motto: treat others how you would expect to be treated yourself. I've never done wrong by anybody who didn't have it coming to them.

If you've got good people around you, make sure that they feel trusted and valued. If you're the kind of boss who treats your best employees like shit and constantly ignores their requests for a raise, don't be surprised if they walk out of the door. If you're the sort of friend who walks on by when your mates need you, then you can't expect them to have your back when you're in trouble.

Don't treat relationships like they're transactions. If you enter a friendship thinking to yourself: *What's in it for me?*, I guarantee it won't last. I've seen what boxing looks like when it's every man for themselves, and it's not pretty. That's why I help up-and-coming boxers – I want to give them the sort of nudge in the right direction I wish some-one had offered me when I was in their position. I don't get any money from it, but I do get a buzz out of helping them. When you're lucky, pass it back down. You'll feel much better for it.

## GOOD PEOPLE WILL CHALLENGE YOU

My mates Franny and Gary have been with me since the beginning. They've seen the highs and lows, ups and downs. Gary especially has been a constant presence at my side. He's maybe the person I'm closest to in and around my training camps. During the first phase of my professional career, I was training with Anthony Farnell up in Manchester. I was Commonwealth champion, knocking down every opponent they put me up against, and in my head I was the best prospect in the world.

I liked the situation I had then. I was my own boss there and when I turned up, I was treated like a superstar. I'd bring my friends to watch me train every other day. We'd work out together – they'd tell me how fit I was and I enjoyed helping them to improve. But I wasn't being challenged by anybody. I was the only one who wanted to push themselves – everyone else seemed to be there for a good time. I didn't see that as a problem, but Franny and Gary both thought my focus was slipping.

Eventually, they took me to one side and told me: 'This place is no good for you. You're taking your friends to the gym. It's not a proper job. You're a really good fighter, but you should move gyms. Go back to Liverpool. If you don't make the right decisions, you're going to lose it all for yourself.'

What was clear to them wasn't clear to me. 'No,' I told them, 'I'm going to stay with Farnell. I'm all right. I like going there.'

It was only when we started preparations for my next bout that I had that sick feeling in the pit of my stomach: they were right, I was wrong. The environment in Manchester wasn't professional enough. It was too late by that point – I couldn't change in the midst of the training camp. But I knew it was over.

I got dropped twice in that fight. Not long afterwards, I changed coach and started training in Liverpool, just as Fran and Gary had suggested.

There's a difference between being the sort of person who blows smoke up their mates' arses and somebody who genuinely wants their friends to be the absolute best version of themselves they can be. Your real friends will have difficult conversations with you; they'll tell you when you're out of order. You won't always like what they're telling you, but make sure you listen, because sometimes they'll be right.

## IT'S NOT ALWAYS ENOUGH TO BE NICE

Saying no is hard. When I was a fighter, I always said yes, to almost everything. That's changed as I've got older and realised you can't please everyone, because somebody who lives their life doing that ends up as a clown. If you don't ever say no, no matter how hard it might seem, nobody will ever take you seriously.

I'm soft, I care about people. My missus says it all the time. She reckons that if I got any more laid-back, I'd be asleep. And my kindness gets taken for weakness sometimes. That's happened throughout my life. The problem is, when your kindness gets taken for weakness, people take advantage of you and then you end up doing nasty things to them.

One way of avoiding those situations is to make sure you're consistent in your behaviour. If you set clear boundaries, it makes life more straightforward for you and for everyone around you. It enhances co-operation, and it saves time and hurt feelings. The people I work with know how I'll respond to a given situation. They know what I expect from them and what I expect from myself. For instance, I'm good at making it clear that there's a point beyond which somebody *cannot* push me, partly because I know that when I do overstep the mark, there's no going back.

I'm not suggesting that you should produce a formal list of rules whenever you start a new job or enter a new relationship, but try to do what you can to avoid falling into the grey zones that are so often the places where disagreement and bad feeling grow.

## HARD CONVERSATIONS

You have to be straight with people. You can't duck awkward conversations. I know some fighters who just send their coach a text message saying: 'I'm going to move on. Thank you very much, that's it.' I've always believed in taking the time to sit down with them, no matter how nasty it'll be.

That's not to say I find these sorts of encounters easy. Especially when it's with somebody who means a lot to me. When you work closely with somebody – all those hours in the gym – you do end up caring for them, too. And sometimes I think I'm more aware of others' feelings than my own. I'm very anxious about offending people or making them feel bad about themselves. Twice in my career I've had to sack a coach. And each time I spent the drive on the way to meet them worrying the fuck out of myself. I then had to psyche myself up in my car before I went in to see them. As I sat there in the driver's seat, I told myself that what I was doing was the right thing for me, even if it wasn't going to be that good for them.

In one case, it was just because he wasn't experienced enough at that point in time. But I wasn't experienced enough, either, and at that stage in my career, I needed someone who'd been around a bit more. Almost all coaches I've worked with, perhaps with the exception of Dave Coldwell, are incredibly insecure and insensitive – it seems to go with the territory – so that was something I had to bear in mind. But at the same time, I had to prioritise my own needs over their feelings.

I've definitely had that horrible feeling before of going into a tough conversation really sure of what I wanted to say. But then as soon as I started speaking, I'd look at the other guy's face, see them getting upset or angry and then lose my nerve. To try to avoid this, on these occasions I spent time beforehand thinking about how the coach would feel and what emotions I might feel. I also reminded myself of how bad things would get if I didn't have that conversation, so that I could keep control and avoid getting swayed by sentiment.

My last bit of preparation was to work out what I'd say in advance. I decided that I'd give them a choice: we can either bring somebody else in to give a little help or we can go our separate ways, no hard feelings.

None of this preparation was enough to make the conversations easy or pleasant. But it was so much better that I'd found a way of getting my head in the right space. It also made the exchange more constructive than if I'd just gone in and told them they were shit and didn't want to work with them any more.

Ultimately, you should never forget that you're not responsible for the emotional well-being of others. Be thoughtful, be considerate, treat people respectfully, but remember that if you're not looking out for your own interests, nobody else will. If you do something for the right reasons, in the right way, then you shouldn't have any reason to feel bad.

# SUMMARY

- Surround yourself with people who want to help you become the best version of yourself.

- Treating you well sometimes means telling you things you might not want to hear.

- If someone shows you who they are, believe them.

- Treat people well. It's the right thing to do and it also feels good.

- But never forget that saying no is OK. Treating other people well doesn't mean ignoring yourself.

- Have difficult conversations – your brain won't want to, but trick it to focus on the longer-term benefits and the damage it would cause if you try to duck every confrontation.

# CHAPTER 3
# FAIL TO PREPARE,
# PREPARE TO FAIL

*I know I'm going to beat him. It's too fucking easy. I'm not stupid – I know there's a reason why David Dolan is a super-heavyweight Commonwealth gold medallist. I know he's won the ABAs. I know he's contested close to 100 fights and boxed for England for over six years whereas I've had fewer than 20 bouts. But I'm absolutely flying at the moment. When I sparred with him last month in Crystal Palace, I rocked him all over the place. The way I see it, I'm stronger, faster and more skilful than him. In my head, I'm just thinking:* I'm better than you in every department. I wobbled you with sixteen-ounce gloves. When I hit you with ten-ounce gloves, I'm going to knock you clean out. It's not even going to be hard.

*We touch gloves. Anticipation surges through me. I know I'm seconds away from being able to lose myself in the exhilarating mix of savagery and control only boxing brings me. I'm already looking forward to the moment when I'll catch him hard for the first time.*

*The bell goes and I'm excited by how strong I feel. There's a thrill that comes with being this powerful, this quick. Already I'm beginning to imagine the rush I'll get when the referee counts him out. Most wins have come easily to me so far in my career. I don't see any reason why this will be any different.*

*My body is ready. But I soon discover that my mind is way off. The first round is tight. And then he starts pulling away. After two rounds he's three points ahead. After three his lead is up to five. The fact that I'd knocked the fuck out of him while we were sparring begins to look embarrassingly irrelevant. So what if I'm punching like a professional? This is an amateur bout and his tip-tap style is perfect for it. For every big bump I land on him, he taps me four times. By the end there's a seven-point gap. It's hard to process what's happened. Just minutes ago I was acting as if I'd already won. But I've lost. I've lost badly. And I can't help thinking that I've brought this on myself.*

Sometimes life feels like a hard, vicious struggle. And then, occasionally, you have those spells where everything comes together so perfectly that you almost can't believe the good times will ever come to an end. The loss of Jimmy had knocked me for six, but otherwise I felt like I was flying at the Rotunda.

There was a reason why it was the best gym in the country. It had Joseph Selkirk, Mick Whitty, the Smith brothers, Declan O'Rourke, Joseph McNally, Andy Holligan, kids who'd won gold medals at youth tournaments all over the world. There were twelve to fifteen international boxers in an amateur outfit in Liverpool. That's insane.

I'd walk into that hall full of national champions, a shitty-arse kid from Wavertree, take my headphones off, put my boxing gear on, head straight to the stereo and put my CD on. That's how the other boxers knew that Bomber had arrived. I was different to the rest of them. Not better, but different. For one thing, I was the only South-ender there, everyone else was from the north of Liverpool. On that side of the city, they listened to dance music; that was their culture. I wore gold chains and wanted to listen to rap. Their reaction was always, 'What the fuck's he doing?' And yet nobody ever tried to stop me.

I look back now and I think, *you cheeky bastard*. But that's just the way I was. I wonder if it was a way of laying down a marker – challenging anyone else to make anything of the fact that I was an outsider there.

I'd been a tall, lanky developer when I'd first arrived at the Rotunda, but I was filling out now, growing into my body. I'd also acquired a deep understanding of both my abilities and my limitations. I knew I was never going to be one of those amazing dexterous fighters. That didn't suit either my physique or the portion of talent I'd been blessed with. So I didn't try.

On the other hand, I had crazy power in my punch, my footwork was really good and I could take a lot of punishment. And I had a brilliant boxing IQ. I was able to watch other fighters and very quickly evolve a plan to beat them. Then, once I was in the ring, I could think on my feet, which meant I could adapt my approach according to what the situation demanded. If I needed to pressure a fight, I could; if I needed to go onto the back foot and box, I could; if I needed to fight and make him miss, I could do that. I could fight southpaw; I could punch with either hand. I was never great at any of them, but I was good at all of them. Taken as a package, I knew I was a threat.

This was all allied to a ferocious desire and a deep resilience, and the fact that I was already trying to act and fight like a professional. Once you're being paid to box, there's not so much emphasis on technical ability; a skilful fighter can be overwhelmed by a less talented but hungrier opponent. That suited me down to the ground.

The other boxers all wanted to win matches on points. In all the years I fought as an amateur boxer I barely ever came across an opponent who could punch. There was maybe one, a six foot eight, seventeen-stone bruiser called David Price, where he'd touch me and I'd think, *fuck, I don't want to get hit by him again.* I didn't look so much at the technical aspect: I wanted to hurt people. Skill isn't enough in the professional business. When you're fighting four two-minute rounds then you can get by on pure technical ability. You cannot skill your way through the thirty-six minutes of a pro bout. At some stage you'll have to stand up and say: *Right, I've got to have it here; I've really got to get stuck in.*

I'd be like that all the time, even when I was sparring with my teammates in the gym. I'd dive in, chinning other fighters when we sparred. I was knocking the fuck out of professionals. I knew none of the lads I was fighting was my final destination. I just saw everyone as another obstacle I needed to trample over on my way to achieving my dream. It didn't matter who I was facing or what the stakes were, I'd have chewed my arm off to win. I was still telling anybody who'd listen that I was going to become world champion at Goodison Park. And I was still being called a liar and a maniac and a fucking idiot.

I wasn't bothered. I liked the way that my ambition and the way I carried myself set me apart from all of the other boxers. I was the only one who'd turn up to those tournaments and say 'I'm going to knock him out.' The other ones might have talked about winning, they might even have been very confident of victory, but none of them were boasting about the damage they were going to cause. Nobody else was going round shouting, 'I'm going to chin him – he's got no chance.' I might not have been the most talented amateur boxer out there, yet my approach made me a better prospect for the professional game than anybody I faced.

I had some of my greatest times as an amateur boxer, but it was really just a hurdle I had to leap over. Everything had gone so quickly for me. I had that first bout, won it, then made sure I had another one to check if it was a fluke. I won that. Then I started thinking about entering championships, just to see how I'd get on. I won them, so then I stepped up to the next rank, where I knocked out everyone I faced. Then

I went up to the next level. I wanted to find out how good I really was. Down they all went.

That's when my coaches told me to go to the full senior ABAs. Every single fighter there had fought fifty, maybe sixty amateur bouts. I'd only fought in eleven, and I was fighting at a level ten kilos above the two national titles I'd already won. My coach's line was: *you're just going in for a bit of experience.* My line was: *fuck that, I'm here to win. I'll fuck everyone and you're going to watch.*

No matter how well I was doing, I still had to go out there and work, because I needed money to subsidise my boxing. In those first years after I'd been expelled from school, I had job after job. First working as a lifeguard, then onto the railways, working the doors and a spell doing daytime security and finally in a pillow factory. My mate Chris Walker, who's now a brilliant journalist, got me that job. It was ideal because it was 7 a.m. until 4 p.m. and I had to be at the gym by five, which ruled out a normal nine-to-five.

But stuffing pillows was also hard graft – far harder than you'd think – and long hours. The only things that made it bearable were knowing that the money I was earning was helping me edge closer to my dream and the fact that I could listen to music while I worked.

By 2004, I was living with Rachael at my mum's and my life had started to follow a regular routine: work, bus, boxing. Every night after I'd finished my shift I'd get the 86 bus up to Smithdown Road, then the 27 from Lodge Lane in Toxteth, all the way through Anfield and finally Scottie Road, Kirkdale. You'd meet every kind of reprobate and scumbag you could possibly imagine on these buses. But I'd just keep my headphones on, turning up the music so loud that you couldn't hear anyone else speaking.

Sometimes, if I had the energy, I'd walk from work to the Rotunda. And that was the problem. As the ABAs approached, I noticed that more and more often I'd be fatigued by the end of the day. Duke and Mick McAllister had spotted this, too and asked me what was up.

I said, 'Nothing's up. I came here from work.'

That was fine for the build-up, but they were clear that this couldn't continue once the tournament actually started.

'You're going to have to give up one or the other.'

'What do you mean?'

Duke said, 'You're tired. You're working from seven in the morning until four in the afternoon. Then you come straight here and train like an absolute maniac. And then you're just repeating the same thing Monday to Friday, every day. It can't go on, not if you're serious about this.'

I asked my boss at the pillow factory if I could have a month off, unpaid. For the first two thirds of my training camp for the ABAs I carried on working there, but in the last month I stopped. And that was it. The only work I was doing was the odd weekend on the doors. For the first time, I really felt as if I was a full-time boxer. My initial thought was: *this is sound*. And yet, it was soon followed by another: *I've got to succeed now at this boxing.*

If I won the ABAs, I knew that I'd be able to get one of the scholarships Liverpool City Council were offering to elite athletes, which would put enough money in my pocket to allow me to keep going without having to go back to the pillow factory. A victory would also put me on the radars of all the top promoters, who I knew watched the finals when they were broadcast on television. If I lost, I'd have to think about going down another route. I'd passed the physical to join the fire brigade, so that was an option, but, really, my heart was with boxing. Nothing else had the same pull.

It was yet another reason to push hard. I remember saying to Rachael: 'I know I've done a few fucked-up things, but I've got a plan. I'm going to win the ABAs. I'm going to get National Lottery funding. I'm going to be on the GB squad. I'm going to be the best fighter in this country.' I could tell that this sounded stupid to her. I'd been acting like a typical young lad. Too many late nights, too much nonsense, too much trouble.

Her only response was to say, 'Great, but what's that got to do with me?'

'I need you by my side. I promise you, I'm going to stop fucking about and stop doing the silly shit I'm doing, and everything will work out all right.'

Whether or not she still thought I was talking shit – which she had every right to – she made that choice and stuck by me. It was up to me to do everything I said I would.

I had the hardest fight of my life up to that point on a Friday night at the Everton Park Sports Centre against a lad called Sam Sexton in the ABA quarter-finals. I'd got through the earlier rounds without much difficulty and then been drawn against Sexton, who was a really good fighter. He'd won multiple titles, fought regularly for England, had five times as many fights under his belt as I did and was generally considered to be the overwhelming favourite. Everyone thought I was going to get beaten. Except me, because I was a cocky fucker and wasn't much interested in anybody else's opinion.

The first two or three rounds were an endorsement of the conventional wisdom. Sexton was so tough, so heavy and so good at what he did – far better than anybody else I'd faced in my previous twelve fights. At the end of the first round I was down by one point. I was two down after the second round and by the last round I was five points adrift. I don't know why, but I just couldn't get started. I started asking myself: *Am I good enough? Do I belong at this level?*

When I went back to my corner, my coach, John Warburton, whose nickname was Sore Arse (I've no idea how he got it and was always too afraid to ask), gave me a slap.

'You go out there and you fucking show everybody in here what you're made of.'

It might have been the slap, or it might have been Warburton's short but forceful speech, or it might have been the horrendous fear of losing in front of my friends and my dad. I don't know. But whatever it was clearly had an effect on me. I came out and smashed him all over the place. I wobbled him, landing blow after blow before I caught him so hard with my right hand that I knocked him out on his feet.

The referee started counting him out and just as he reached eight, Sexton seemed to wake up. He grabbed the head guard's strap at the chin and ripped it off. That bought him five minutes to recover, which absolutely enraged me.

'You can't do that,' I protested. Then I started pleading with the referee: 'Let me at him.'

Sexton, who knew exactly what he was doing, just smiled. However, it didn't do him much good in the long run. Having started the last round five behind Sexton, I ended up five points ahead of him.

It felt like such a massive achievement in my fourteenth fight, not only to have beaten someone with Sexton's pedigree, but also to do it over four two-minute rounds. I realised that you don't really learn that much about yourself when you're coasting through fights; you do when you're made to suffer.

And I had suffered. It was the first time I'd had my nose cracked. I'd also smashed my hand, which wasn't ideal with my next fight two weeks away. Even three hours after the fight I had a slow stream of blood coming out of my nose. My hands were shaking and whenever I tried to eat anything, I puked it up almost straight away.

Like a maniac, I turned up to work on the doors later that night with swollen, still quivering hands and a trickle of blood running constantly down my face that I couldn't staunch, whatever I tried. All the other boys on the door looked at me with horror. That was the first time ever that my dad told me to go home. Proud as he was, he was also worried by the sight of his son's black-and-blue features.

For a minute or two, I tried to make my case – I wanted the £100 I'd get paid – but, ultimately, Dad won that argument: 'I own the firm. You'll get paid. Just go home, son, please.' He was backed up by Joey Lynch, who worked with him. Joey's brother, John, had won the ABAs a good few years ago and he always took an interest in me. He knew I was a good kid with a good future, which is why he'd sometimes pay me for staying at home rather than coming in to work. Joey was one of those guys who wanted to give kids every chance of making the best of themselves.

After all that, the rest of the competition felt pretty straightforward. In just my sixteenth amateur bout, I won the heavyweight ABAs, my first televised fight, shown on the BBC. I went in there against the reigning champion, a Royal Marine called Mick O'Connell. Almost everyone had written me off because it was my first year in the competition. Instead, I went in there and absolutely boxed his head off. I schooled him from start to finish, made him look like a novice; I flicked and rocked him and won 12–3. In the process proving *Boxing News*, who'd predicted an O'Connell victory, very wrong. Ha ha.

All of a sudden, I became aware of what I'd achieved. I'd made history in my gym by becoming their first ever heavyweight ABA champion. My family were so proud of me, too. In their eyes I was a superstar, because I'd been on the telly and in the paper. It was exhilarating, addictive. And after that I carried on improving at a drastic pace. The next time I faced Mick O'Connell, I knocked him cold in the second round. I didn't think anybody could stop me.

Then I got jolted. Something that I really needed. David Dolan and his tippy-tappy style had beaten me. Up to that point, I'd been so accustomed to thinking of myself as an inferior boxer that I'd work like a maniac to bridge the difference whenever I came up against someone new. This time, however, I hadn't spent any time thinking about the strengths that had won Dolan that gold medal or about how much more experienced he was than me. I was too busy congratulating myself on how good I'd been when we'd sparred. Normally I'd focus insanely hard before a fight, but this time I was just looking forward to chinning him. Which, of course, was a massive mistake.

I'd got so accustomed just to turning up and smoking my opponents that I'd forgotten that there's no progression, no success, without struggle. I'd forgotten that if I wanted to get to the next level, I'd have to go through some hard times.

I started to shift my priorities. It wasn't enough to fight like a professional in the ring – I had to act like one outside it. Up until then, I might have worked hard in the gym, but I'd always been up for going out on the ale with my mates at the drop of a hat. If I got the call, ten minutes later I'd be there. Now, I'd go three or four months without touching a drop. If I did go out, the timing would be planned with military detail to make sure it never interfered with my training. That fucked off Rachael no end – the sacrifices I was starting to make to help further my ambitions inevitably had an impact on her life. But that became extra motivation: I had to make this work, because I didn't want to put her through that hardship and then have nothing to show for it.

The way to make it work was to give boxing every single ounce of energy I had in my body. I knew that from this point on, I couldn't afford to skip a beat. I couldn't afford to miss a session, I couldn't afford to have a week off here or there. Maybe I was better than any other fighter at this level, but there were so many steps I had to take, so many hurdles I had to leap over. The guys I'd have to beat to achieve my dreams were already way ahead of me.

I swore that whatever happened in my career, however far I got, I'd never let myself get undone by complacency, laziness or a lack of preparation. If I got beaten by a better boxer, fine, I could live with that. If I lost to a bad call by a referee, that would hurt but I'd cope. But if I got a hiding because I was unfit or hadn't got my head right, I knew that I wouldn't be able to forgive myself. Ever.

That attitude drove me on and on, through the last stretch of my amateur career and into the early stages of my time as a pro. Every time I went up a level, I worked even harder. What had started as a hobby was now an obsession.

\*

Even if I was knuckling down, there were lads around me who had different ideas. There's a point early in your career when you're fighting nobodies, when you could, if you wanted to, piss around and still win. I know plenty of men who did. There's one thing that they have in common: they all failed. Frankie Gavin is Britain's only ever amateur world champion. He was training alongside me in Manchester when we'd turned professional. He could have been anything he wanted to be. He had so much more ability than me, it was actually stupid. All he needed to do was take things seriously.

While I was fighting for six grand every blue moon, when he first turned pro he was getting £50,000 for four-round fights. That is *obscene*. That is unheard of. He contested maybe ten bouts, made half a million quid and in all that time didn't face anyone with a winning record. He had an amazing talent but could never take life seriously, so his career just faded.

And then there was Joseph Selkirk. I'd known Joseph for a long time. I'd trained alongside him for the ABAs and he was without doubt the best fighter I've ever seen. That's not hyperbole – he was a simply unbelievable boxer. He had a street fighter's aggression allied to insane levels of skill. His boxing brain was off the chart. Joseph had everything. He trained hard when he was in the gym, but I swear to God, he didn't need to. This fella could have three weeks off, then turn up at the gym, get put in a sparring session and absolutely play with someone.

What he didn't have was the same mentality as I did. He didn't have the same drive. Some days he'd be raring to go, others he couldn't have appeared any less interested. While we were still amateurs and training as a team, you didn't notice it so much. It was only when we turned pro, and suddenly there was a lot more individual responsibility, that it showed.

Joseph was a really nice kid. I loved him. I always have and I always will. In fact, he's like a little brother to me. I'd always tried to look out for him because I didn't feel like he had anyone; he lost his dad in tragic circumstances when he was young. Our bond endured even when someone tried to come between us by telling lies. And because I couldn't bear the idea of him wasting his talent, I took him to training with me when I turned professional. Every day for a whole year, I'd drive the six miles to his house, pick him up, then take him to Manchester.

Some days I'd be waiting outside his house for him to get out of bed. On other days I'd be screaming at him. Occasionally he'd be great, but too often I'd get there and he'd just say, 'I can't be bothered today.' When, later on, I left Manchester and came back to the Rotunda, I brought him with me. For a while he was back on it: the training and coaches were so much better in Liverpool. And yet, gradually, I could see that he just didn't want to do it. There was no money in it for him at that point and I don't think he had the love for the game that I did.

Everyone wants to be rich. Everyone wants to be top of

the bill. But for him, the end goal was just too distant. He wasn't willing to put up with the struggle that's needed to get there. He wanted the nice stuff right there and then.

I care about him and still speak to him now; he was at my wedding, he was at my kids' christenings and he's someone who will always be part of my life. But it kills me that he didn't get where his talent demanded he should have. He had ten times the ability I had. If you'd have been able to stick my mindset on him, he'd have become the greatest fighter this country has ever produced. It's probably too late in the day now – he's into his thirties – and yet, I know he could still come back now and piss the British title, probably the European title, too. If I got him the right world title fight, I'm guessing he'd probably fuck them, as well.

What I knew and Joseph didn't – although I think he does now – was that pissing around wouldn't get you anywhere. If you want the nice things that come with being an elite boxer, you have to do the work that comes with being an elite boxer. And you have to be willing to do it day after day after fucking day. Joseph blew hot and cold, and that was never enough.

## YOU DON'T GET WHAT YOU WISH FOR, YOU GET WHAT YOU WORK FOR

There's nowhere to hide in the ring. Boxing isn't a sport, it's not a business, it's a way of life. You can't fuck about with it. It's not something you can pick up, drop and then go back and pick it up again later on. It's not something that you can half do. You can't cheat your way through it. It'll always find you out. Always. I promise you. So you have to live it. It's got to come before anything. You have to give it everything you've got. It's more important than family, friends, birthdays, Christmases, it doesn't matter. If you don't do it right, it'll get you.

That's why sacrifice, dedication, perseverance are the most important traits to have as a professional fighter. Pure skill and a brilliant boxing IQ clearly give you an advantage, but if your legs are fucked after two rounds, then they very quickly stop being relevant.

I made sure that I worked harder than every single other fighter, because I knew how much ground I had to cover. Lots of people say things like that. I meant it. It's the same ethic that separates Cristiano Ronaldo from all of the others. He's not only fantastically gifted, but he's also fanatically driven, and that's the reason he's able to stay on a plateau with Messi: he works so hard and the others just don't. That's the top and bottom of it.

Hard work will always be rewarded. Hard work is what makes you better at your job, hard work is what makes your relationships better, hard work is how you learn and grow. How long are you willing to suffer for what you want? The ability to keep going when everyone else is done, to keep running, to keep fighting, is earned where nobody sees it. Nobody makes it to the top of their field just because they're lucky or clever or know the right people, although all those things help. The surest foundation of success is hard work. If you want to achieve the goals you've set, whether they're big or small, you're going to have to roll up your sleeves and graft.

## WEAKER TODAY, STRONGER TOMORROW

I like winning. I hate losing. Whatever I'm doing, I've got to feel like I'm winning. Even if it's a shit game that no one else gives a fuck about, I have to win.

That was my mentality when I trained. When I worked hard and felt myself getting better, that was a victory. I might have been feeling exhausted, but I'd know that I'd done more today than I had yesterday. My mentality was: weaker today, stronger tomorrow. With that mindset, I was always winning.

In the gym we'd do something called punch stats, which is where you attach a two-kilo weight to each arm and then throw punches in certain combinations while somebody measured your output and endurance. I'd always beat every single other person. It didn't matter if they were heavyweights, middleweights, even featherweights. I smashed every record, every number, he had. I was like a fucking steam train. I'd just keep chugging and chugging and going and going. Sometimes I'd catch the coach looking at me as if he couldn't believe what he'd just seen.

What I knew and others never understood is that if you want to get to the very top, you can't rely on the gifts you're born with and it isn't enough just to turn in a good performance in the gym once in a blue moon. You have to be on it every day. You have to be willing to go out for those runs early on a November morning when it's pissing down; you have to be willing to carry on in the gym even when your whole body hurts and all you want to do is slump in front of the television and rest.

## DON'T BELIEVE YOUR OWN HYPE

A lot of the lads I came up with were brilliant when they were eighteen, but then just stood still. They were barely any better in their twenties than they had been in their late teens. I think maybe it was because everything had come so easily to them, they'd never had that need I felt to get better all the time. You might be good at something. Great, well done. But there's always room to improve. And it's only by pushing yourself and leaving your comfort zone that you'll ever really progress. A lot of world champions win their belt and then almost instantly forget about all the hard graft they put in to get there. Instead, they relax, which never ends well.

I expect a lot of myself and I'll never settle or rest. I always want to be enhancing something and I never think that I've done enough. Which is tricky, because it means that I'll never be happy. I can't relax, ever, even when I'm playing golf. I might hit three or four good shots on the spin then one slightly bad one. That bad shot will play on my mind. It'll burrow into my brain and sit there, reminding me how shit I am, how I have to work even harder if I want to get better. My mates will point out that I'm just a beginner, and that even professional golfers hit a crap shot now and again. But all I can say is 'Not good enough!' Sometimes I hate being made like this.

But that mindset was also crucial to my success. The second you start thinking you're special is the second that complacency will take hold of you. And that's it, you're on the way down. That's what happened to me against David Dolan: I stopped to admire my own work and ended up getting chinned. From that moment on, my mantra was: don't believe in your own smoke, just keep going.

Don't congratulate yourself on being good at something – find a way of becoming better at it. Don't sit there being smug about all the things you know – remember how much you've still got to learn. Self-improvement should be a lifelong commitment.

## DRESS FOR THE JOB YOU WANT, NOT THE JOB YOU HAVE

One of the reasons I was so excited to be on *SAS: Who Dares Wins* was because I've always admired elite soldiers like Ant

Middleton, Foxy, Ollie and Billy. Being around people who are at the top of their game is exhilarating. You learn so much from both their abilities and their attitude. I don't care whether it's cooking, cleaning or football, if you're in the top echelon of your craft then I think you're fucking great and I'm in awe of you.

My attitude during my career was that if you're always fighting people who are at your level or below, how are you ever going to improve? I always wanted to go up to the next level as quickly as I could, because I knew that just being in the ring with higher-quality fighters would elevate my own performance.

That mindset began when I was a kid studying the great fighters. I was hell-bent on reaching their level. And when I started boxing, that ambition immediately made me stand out from everyone else. It meant I was streets ahead of the people who were just there to look good hitting pads. I was thinking and acting like a professional even when I was an amateur.

At the Rotunda ABC, I was around the likes of Joseph Selkirk, Stephen and Paul Smith, Joseph McNally, Declan O'Rourke, all brilliant boxers. Being in their company drove me on because I fucking hated the idea that I might not be able to keep up. The same was true when I was twenty-one and joined the England boxing team, another group of boxers who were more talented than me.

Most boxers give themselves twenty or twenty-five bouts after they've gone pro before they start competing for a really good title. I just wanted to be pushed so much. I wanted to keep going and going and going, up and up and up, because I knew that my insanely competitive nature meant that I'd force myself to match the level of any fighter.

I barely paid attention to the journeymen I came up against in the early days of my pro career. I knew I couldn't learn anything from them. They were just there to scrap and swing. It was only later, when I got up to European and World level, that I really began to watch again. These guys weren't just stupidly fit, they were clever. Instead of swinging blindly, they'd be trying to manoeuvre you around the ring. Often they were little things, but they were so clever, and completely different to what I'd been exposed to before. Competing against them made me a better fighter.

All that is why I was Commonwealth champion and British champion within thirteen fights. That's why I fought for my first world title in my sixteenth fight. And when I got to that level, I never went back down. I never went for easy fights – I wasn't the sort who chose to fight a fucking crab every six months. I wanted to maintain the calibre of my opponent.

Whatever it is you do, whatever it is you want to achieve, seek out the best in your field. Try to work out what it is they do that sets them apart from the rest and then try to emulate it. This might be challenging, but I guarantee you'll learn a lot. You should never be intimidated by somebody else's abilities or accomplishments. If you learn to regard high-performers as an inspiration rather than a threat, you'll be giving yourself a big advantage.

# WORK SMART

The training at the Rotunda ABC was so good. Far better even than the training I'd receive a bit later on when I started boxing with Great Britain as part of the Olympic programme. It was harder. It was more intense. We trained once a day, but we trained really hard. Whereas in the GB camps we'd have three, four, sometimes even five short sessions in the day and they were shit. They never focused on the things we should have being doing to make us better fighters. Instead of preparing for the kind of thing we'd face once we crossed the ropes, they paid lots of attention to stupid technical things that never actually happened in bouts.

I always bore that in mind in the years that followed, wherever I was training. There would always be a specific aim to the work we did in the gym. It's not enough just to monster yourself. Everything you do should be tailored towards helping you take another step towards that ultimate goal. You can't just work and work and work without a plan. If you turn up at a gym and start randomly working like a beast on every bit of equipment, you can't expect to get any results.

So before you embark on any project, whether that's

a triathlon or switching careers, make sure you take the time to identify areas you need to improve in or the skills you need to acquire. Then work relentlessly until you've overhauled your running style or picked up that essential technical qualification.

Don't fall into the trap of just doing the things that you're already good at. Be honest with yourself about why you're avoiding something. Whether it's leg day at the gym or a task on your to-do list, the thing that you don't want to do is what you almost always *need* to do. Cardio work was torture for me. But I knew it was essential if I wanted to ensure I wasn't immediately gassed in a fight. Don't work at doing what makes you feel good; work on what makes you better.

## WHAT WILL BE, WILL BE

When the fighters I look after tell me they're feeling nervous before a fight, my message to them is: *relax, conserve your energy. What will be, will be. Have you worked as hard as you possibly can in the gym? Have you done all the mental preparation that's required? Have you got a good game plan?* If they say yes, then I tell them they have nothing to be worried about. At the end of the day, if you've done everything right, if you've done the hard yards, you'll climb into that ring and perform. If you've not done it right, if you've cut corners, you'll fall apart.

That's why I was almost never anxious in the dressing room. I'd be excited because I wanted to show everybody what I'd done over the past weeks. For thirty-two out of the thirty-four bouts I fought, it did all come good. Aleksandr Usyk and Adonis Stevenson were just better than me on the night, and I can live with that.

I know that a lot of people suffer from nerves or anxiety ahead of things like job interviews or events when they'll need to speak in public. There are clearly little tricks you can learn to help you cope with those fears. But for me, the surest way to keep calm is to know that I've done everything possible to get ready for that occasion. Anxiety creeps into your mind through the gaps opened up by a failure to prepare properly.

If you're the best man at your mate's wedding, you'll feel a thousand times more afraid if you haven't written or practised your speech in advance. If you're giving a presentation at work and haven't familiarised yourself with the facts and figures you'll be discussing, you'll be far more likely to freeze in front of your colleagues when your boss asks you a question.

Don't leave room for error. When you're on your way to an important meeting, work out your route in advance, give yourself enough time to get there, even if traffic snarls up along the way. When I was still fighting, I used to go out and look at the route from the dressing room to the ring, just to make sure I knew in advance exactly what to expect. It's not rocket science, but you'll be surprised how many people don't even bother to do these simple things.

One last thing to remember: those moments when you feel adrenaline rushing around your veins aren't necessarily something to fear. In the seconds before a fight, every nerve in every limb of my body would be firing. My heart would be beating faster. I'd breathe in short, shallow gasps. At the beginning of my career, I used to see it as anxiety. It was only later that I realised it was my body's way of telling me it was ready. It wasn't crying out for help, it was saying: *let's go, let's go, let's go.* Think about when you went on roller coasters when you were a kid – were you afraid, or were you actually excited?

If you can reframe that feeling as a positive, then what in the past might have hindered you will instead act as a kind of reassurance. You're going into war and your body has got your back.

# SUMMARY

- You get out what you put in. Plan what you want.

- You can't cheat your way to the top. There's no magic trick that will make you a success. You have to work hard. It's as simple as that. The sooner you understand that, the sooner you'll start achieving your goals.

- Complacency is the enemy of success. Never think you've done enough or that you're good enough. There's always room for you to improve. Aim to end every day better than when you started. Endless improvement leads to endless possibility.

- Always try to test yourself. Take yourself out of your comfort zone. You don't improve by competing against people who are on your level. You get better by going up against people who are better than you.

# CHAPTER 4
# LIVE RIGHT, FIGHT STRONG

'Fuck, fuck, fuck.' This was not the plan.

We're in a B&Q car park. It's not long after 7 p.m. A minute ago, everything was almost completely dark. The only light came from the sickly glow cast by a nearby street light. But now everything is bathed in luminous blue.

I hear the thud the police car door makes as it opens then watch in the mirror as the bizzie walks, as if in slow motion, towards our car. It's me and a mate, and somewhere inside the car is a package containing something we really shouldn't have with us. Fuck, fuck, fuck. My breaths are coming in short anxious gasps now. Everything is going really well in my boxing career. People are even starting to recognise me now. But if that bizzie finds the package, and I can't see how he won't, then everything is going to come crumbling down very fucking quickly.

The guy reaches us and puts a heavy hand on the car's roof. Fuck, fuck, fuck. This is not supposed to be happening. I don't know where the idea comes from, but suddenly everything inside me is telling me that my only option is to run the *bizzie over and then get the fuck out of there as quickly as we can.*

*The car is in neutral and my hand hovers over the gearstick, ready to put it in first. I start revving the engine. My mate looks across, his eyes full of panic. He can tell what I'm considering.*

*He implores me, 'Don't do it.'*

*'We're going to get nicked and we're going to go to jail. I can't have that. I can't have that.'*

*He's banging the dashboard and screaming now because he's realised that I'm still thinking about doing something insane.*

*'Don't do it. Don't do it. I'll take the blame; I'll tell them it's all mine.'*

*He leans over and turns the engine off. Immediately, the spell that's been cast over me is broken. As quickly and mysteriously as it had come, that impulse disappears from my brain. It probably doesn't matter whether it was my mate yelling in my face or some deep-seated instinct for self-preservation. The fact is that my hands move away from the gearstick and my body relaxes. The tension in the car slackens and we watch anxiously as the bizzie meticulously searches the car and – in another weird turn of events on this very fucking weird evening – fails to find anything.*

I'm not perfect. My time on this earth has been full of fucking dumb choices. I've done stupid things. I've done dangerous things. So if you think that there's something strange about me sitting here, telling you that you have to live your life right, then it's only because I know how easily everything could have gone very, very wrong. I've made those mistakes and I don't want anyone to have to repeat them.

I sometimes think about the lads I knocked about with when I was a kid. We'd play football at the youth centre, go round to each other's houses. I think about what's happened to me in the decades since and what's happened to them. Most of all, I think about how their fate could have been mine. I wouldn't have needed to take too many more wrong turns or make too many more mistakes.

One of those boys has been done for murder. Another went on to become a gangland assassin with a big number of bodies to his name. He's now doing life. Some have been shot dead. It didn't need to be like that. A couple of them were amazing footballers and fighters who ended up deciding to turn down a different road because they thought there was no hope for them. There were others who never had the same talent but were still more than capable of making something of themselves if they'd been given the opportunity. Instead, they went out on the streets. Rightly or wrongly, they didn't feel as if they had a choice.

Things could have been so different for me. Those margins are so fine. If it hadn't been for boxing and wanting to impress my dad, I know I'd have ended up like them. If I hadn't made it as a fighter, I'd be locked up. No doubt about that at all. My problem is that I've always liked having boss things and I'm willing to do anything to get what I need. It wouldn't have lasted long – I'm no criminal master-mind – but let me tell you, it would have been good while it lasted.

That temptation was always there. I knew so many people who were involved. Boxing entices men to its margins who aren't necessarily fans of the sport itself; they just want the chance to hang round with a fucking hard bastard. While my dad was still on top of his game, he was a brilliant person to have by my side. He was very wise when it came to people, so he'd steer me away from the real villains. But he couldn't be around me all the time.

The biggest problem was that at the beginning of my career, just before I turned professional, we were skint, barely getting by on my GB scholarship. When I look back, all I can think is: *you fucking maniac – what were you thinking?* But I was in a different mindset then. Rachael had had our first son, Corey, and I wanted to be able to provide for him. I'd promised her that after she'd had the baby, she'd never have to work again.

The problem was that there were so many easier ways of making money than boxing. I could make a bit extra doing work with some trusted family members, but I also had friends who were out on the street making proper cash. So, little by little, I found that I was doing unsavoury things to earn money. That's how I ended up in that car. That's how I ended up within seconds of smashing to pieces everything I'd built up to that point.

Everyone has moments in their life when they can see

two very different routes opening up before them. That night was one of them for me.

Afterwards, I thought about how much my dad going away to the big house had hurt me when I was a kid. I couldn't do that to Corey, and I couldn't do that to Rachael.

I knew that whether or not I was struggling to pay the mortgage, I couldn't do anything that would get me into that kind of trouble. If I wanted to make it as a boxer, there were people I couldn't associate with, temptations I had to learn to resist. I couldn't allow anything to distract me from my dream.

It was around this time that my dad was put in a coma for a second time. He got jumped by a group of six or seven men, who left him unconscious for two weeks with a bleed on his brain. At least, that's what I think happened. Some people know everything about those events. I don't: I've never been told the whole story.

Once he was out of hospital, his wife fucked off and suddenly, caring for him became my priority. We'd always been close, now we became inseparable. That was the first test of my new resolve. All I wanted was to track down and break the heads of every single one of the cowards who'd inflicted that on my dad. But I realised that I couldn't, because doing that would have ended up with me in jail; or bleeding into a drain somewhere, all of my limbs broken; or worse. I'd begun to understand that you only get one chance in life. I couldn't fuck mine up.

# BOXING ISN'T A JOB, IT'S A WAY OF LIFE

When I was a professional, boxing was everything to me. Nothing came before it. Nothing. I'd wake up and think about fighting and boxing. As I ate or watched television or went to the shops, I'd be thinking about fighting and boxing. The last thing I'd think about before I went to sleep each night was my next fight.

Everything in my existence was geared towards ensuring that not only was I in brilliant mental and physical shape, but also that I had as few distractions as possible. And this attitude wasn't confined to the weeks leading up to the bouts. I tried to live right all the time. That's why resisting the temptation to go back on the streets was so important. Even if everything had gone well, even if I never got caught or killed, it would still have robbed me of the focus I needed to make the most of my talents.

You don't have to be as obsessive as I was. In fact, I'd actively advise you aren't. But whatever your ambition is, you need to create an environment in which you can perform to the outer limits of your ability. That means eating right and taking exercise, developing good habits and cutting out distractions, whether that's bad company or worries about money. If you live an organised, balanced life, everything else will follow.

# LET THE ANCHOR GO

I'm generally very good at getting rid of stuff that I think could trip me up. No matter how much I love it, I can just walk away. And there's stuff that I've deliberately avoided, because I know it's not for me. I've never taken a drug in my entire life. I gamble about once every decade – and only on things I'm certain of, like boxing. (The exception is Boxing Day, when I see mates and we all drop £100 at the bookies on whatever we want.) It's not that I disapprove of either, everyone makes their own choices, but I've seen what they can do to people and that's something I've never wanted to risk.

I can't tell you how to live. And I can't tell you who you can hang out with or how to spend your money. That's all up to you. I can't make those decisions for you. I *shouldn't* make those decisions for you.

What I will say is that when you're considering doing something or seeing someone, ask yourself one question: Will this help me become the best possible version of myself or will it get in my way? If you think it'll hinder you, then you have to cut it out. That was the decision I had to make all those years ago when I realised that the people I was associating with, and the things I was doing, were putting me in situations that could very easily have undone everything I'd worked so hard for. And I saw the other side of the coin play out, too. A lot of lads who discovered booze, drugs and women when they stepped into adulthood saw their careers fall off the rails. I've always found it useful to imagine I was talking to someone I loved and respected. If I had to tell them what I'd done, would they be proud of me? If the answer's no, then the odds are that it's a bad decision.

Bad habits and bad people are like an anchor tied around your neck. At best they'll hold you back, at worst they'll destroy you by dragging you down to the depths of the ocean. Why take the risk?

## YOU CAN'T UNDO A GOOD CAMP; YOU CAN'T OUTRUN A BAD DIET

A boxer's physique is both his greatest weapon and his greatest weakness. You rely on it utterly and demand so much of it, but it can also betray you. That's perhaps because we have a fucking awful relationship with our bodies. We push them so hard in training that we almost reach breaking point. Then we put them under almost unbearable strain when we try to make weight. And that's all before we get into the ring with a dangerous fucker who's spent the last few months thinking about how he's going to inflict insane amounts of damage upon us. You wouldn't treat your worst enemy the way we treat our bodies. And, if anything, we're even crueller to our minds. It's inhuman to be away from the people you love so much or to subject yourself to that much pressure.

What I mean by this is that being a boxer has taught me a lot about what not to do. I've learned about the importance of balance and becoming comfortable in your own skin. I don't want to go back to the crushing diets, loneliness and punishing exercise regimes that were such a feature of my life in boxing.

I'm not shredded and I don't want to be. Even when I've been at my absolute physical peak, I've never been in danger of being asked to be on the front page of *Men's Fitness*. That's fine with me. When I was a fighter, all the work I did wasn't about looking good, it was about getting into the best shape for the job I needed to do. I still feel the same way: I'm not interested in looking like a Greek god, but I do want to feel fit, lean and positive about myself. What's weird is that I didn't realise how many positive benefits there were to regular exercise until I retired. I'd always had a very functional relationship with exercise. I thought it was what you did to get ready for fights and was looking forward to enjoying getting fat. Except that I didn't enjoy getting fat. I actually started feeling pretty sad. I was used to that flood of endorphins that comes from raising your heart rate and I realised I didn't want to carry spare tyres around my stomach.

Staying fit and healthy is a long-term commitment. It's far better to get into the habit of exercising a moderate amount regularly to maintain your fitness than it is to alternate between sitting like a fat bastard on your sofa one month, then beasting yourself like a maniac in the gym the next. It's not good for you and nor is it sustainable. Eventually, you'll just stop.

That's why I tell the fighters I look after that they need to live in a constant state of readiness. I get angry when they ask me for a twelve-week camp. They shouldn't need twelve weeks to get fit – six weeks should be enough. *You're a professional boxer, do you understand what that means? You need to live a certain lifestyle. You should be in the gym, you tit.* You need to be in the gym all year round, not just the weeks before a fight. You don't go to the gym to get ready for a fight, you go to the gym because you should be constantly trying to improve on your craft as a fighter. If you need to shift ten pounds in six weeks because you've had a good Christmas, that's easy. But two stone is a mountain. You have to be focused, you have to keep that goal in your mind all the time, not just when it suits you.

I had a fighter recently who lied to me about his physical state because he needed a fight to help provide for his kids. He told me he'd been in the gym – he hadn't. He went under the lights on TV, looked dead classy for a few minutes and then by the end of the first round, he was fucked. Now, he's got to work during the day and try to cram his training in his evenings.

The same is true of your diet. Being a boxer can sometimes feel like being a member of a very violent slimming club. We spend our entire careers obsessing over our weights. I wish I could be like my best mate, who's a footballer. He can play every Saturday and then go out every Saturday night. I couldn't do that, because I knew how easily I gained weight. As a result, I've always had to be very careful to put the right things in my body. When I did really struggle to make weight, it wasn't due to the fact that I was fighting at a weight that was lower than I probably should have been or because I'd spent the whole time between fights sinking ales and eating chips. But I watched a lot of other fighters who'd eat like pigs, train badly and then wait until the last week before their match to get fit and lose the necessary pounds. That's insane, and it would have been so easy to avoid.

Frankie Gavin was an amazing fighter. To this day, he's still the only British amateur to win a gold medal at the world championships. We saw a lot of each other when we trained in Manchester and both of us were always fighting to make weight. I had to get down to twelve stone seven, and Frankie, a light welterweight, had to make ten stone. It should have been far easier for him than for me. But he made it hard for himself.

The difference between him and me was that he just couldn't control what went into his mouth after eight o'clock at night. He'd eat a whole bag of Haribo sweets or go to McDonald's and then convince himself that going for a run would make it OK. Of course, it doesn't work like that. He ended up cheating his way through, always convinced he was one step ahead of his body, until eventually it all caught up with him. He didn't realise that living right is about making a series of small sacrifices. And, if you don't, the consequences soon add up.

It's just like with exercise. You could swing between bingeing and then crash dieting, but it's neither healthy nor efficient. Instead, think about what works for you and your lifestyle. What's compatible with your work and family commitments? What do you know that you can realistically keep doing over the long term? Moderation is key.

## HAVE A ROUTINE

When I was in training camps, my day was planned from the minute I woke to the minute I went to sleep. Every second was accounted for. There was barely any time even to think. Clearly, you won't need that level of planning, but you need some.

If you create that framework, everything becomes more straightforward. You don't have to make as many choices, because you already know what you're doing. It makes it easier to both maintain good habits – like exercise and eating right – and drop the bad ones. And it helps you to prioritise: you can determine in advance what your most important tasks are, and then give yourself time and space to achieve them. You're not juggling everything, trying to work out what job to start first. That's why lots of people who don't have a routine will tell you that before the end of the morning, they're already feeling stressed or anxious or overwhelmed.

I still rely on a routine now. It's not as full as it was when I was fighting, but it's still phenomenally important to my ability to stay sane and happy. I need that structure and discipline.

Boxing teaches you about your energy levels and what you need to do to sustain them. Everyone has different peaks and troughs, and everyone has different ways of lifting their spirits and stamina. Try to work out what parts of the day you find yourself at your most alert and energetic. Ask yourself what sorts of exercises and interactions drain you, and which give you that bit of a zip you need.

I build my day around a strong start. Because I'm used to getting all the emotional and physical benefits of training, I still exercise a lot. It helps to clear my head and raise my mood. That exercise could be training hard on my Peloton or just going on a long walk – anything that raises my pulse. My day runs better if I've got up and trained. If I don't, my life doesn't seem to flow right. I can't get started and my productivity falls through the floor.

Those little things might seem insignificant, but they're the foundation of your day and help to get your mindset right. If you begin each morning by procrastinating or mucking about, you'll carry on like that until it's time to go to bed. If, by contrast, you start with purpose and energy, you'll have so much more momentum, which makes it all the easier to resist all those little voices that try to disrupt your progress: 'I haven't slept well,' 'I'll do it later,' 'I just have to do this thing first.'

Along with having a routine, I try to plan my days in advance rather than just winging it. This means that I can get more done, as well as ensuring there's time to relax and exercise. If you're feeling really under the cosh at work, it can massively affect your overall efficiency. This is because you run round in a frenzy, mistaking energy for achievement. You need to work out what matters, what you need to do, and then you need to do it in the right order. What you could do instead is take a moment on your way to the office to list what you want to do most, and in what order. Remind yourself of that list halfway through the day. If you give your day that structure, it'll transform the way you go about things.

Once you have those goals crystallised, you'll be much less vulnerable to distraction, and it's really satisfying to look back and say to yourself: *yep, I got all that done.* Just the act of mentally checking off those items in your head is motivating. By contrast, if you're running around like a blue-arsed fly trying to put fires out the whole time, you generally find that you neither accomplish what you need, nor actually get to rest. When I work with people, the first thing I try to get us to agree on is what we're going to achieve. If they can't explain to me quickly and simply how doing something is eventually going to help us achieve that goal, then they need to rethink it.

# MAKE YOUR ENVIRONMENT RIGHT FOR YOU

When I was in the mindset of being a fighter, I couldn't have nice things. I couldn't be surrounded by softness, because I never feel like I'm making any progress unless I'm also putting myself through pain.

In the days when I was still trying to make light heavyweight and having to get up at half five to run on an empty stomach, I wouldn't brush my teeth because I wanted my breath to taste like shit every step of the way: I wanted to know that I was out there struggling.

And that's why I liked my training camps to be as uncomfortable as possible. I might have been in a dark, cold, gloomy city in the north of England while David Haye was drinking protein shakes on a yacht moored somewhere near Miami. I might have been miles away from my family. But I *wanted* it to be like that. It was perfect for my mindset and my physical approach.

It was me just me, my microwave, my iPad and a double bed in a dingy room in a Holiday Inn Express that cost me £60 a night, breakfast included. Although, come to think of it, I didn't eat much of it beyond the scrambled eggs, because I brought most of my meals with me in Tupperware boxes. I could afford to stay in somewhere more luxurious and I even had the money I'd set aside, yet I chose not to. There was actually a much smarter hotel that found out the rate I was paying and offered me a suite at the same price.

The food was lovely, the room was beautiful, it even had a spa. I stayed one night.

I didn't want any luxuries in camp because I didn't feel as if I deserved them. I hadn't won anything yet. Nice restaurants, nice holidays, whatever: all that could come *after* I had that belt.

I'd be at the gym on Monday and Tuesday, come home Wednesday, then go back there for Thursday and Friday. It was a long fucking slog. If you told fighters now that they'd have to lead the life I did when I was in training camps, they'd just say no.

I had that routine because I knew that that environment brought out the best in me. I'd notice when something was missing, even if nobody else had: it was a bit like hearing a familiar song being played slightly out of tune. All of this was very particular to me – I wouldn't expect anyone to want to do the same. Spend time finding out what you respond to. Do you work best in a room by yourself or surrounded by the chatter of other people? Do you need to listen to music to keep focused or is silence crucial to your productivity? It'll be different for everyone, but creating the right environment is crucial to unlocking your potential.

## REMOVE DISTRACTIONS

There's so much going on in the world, so much shit, that if you can control even small things, it makes a huge difference. For me, creating a mental space that's ordered and calm is as important as having a tidy physical environment.

Although, I probably take it to extremes. I come home every day and put my car keys in the same place. My trainers will always be in exactly the same spot under the stairs. As soon as I arrive at a hotel, whether I'm working or on holiday, no matter how tired I am, I get to my room, unpack my bag and put all of my stuff in the places it needs to be. It's a ball-ache, but it's also essential. It's a massive cliché to say 'tidy desk, tidy mind', but I do genuinely find that when I'm surrounded by mess, it's that bit harder to concentrate. There's always something pulling at the edges of my attention. It's only once I've got everything in order that I can really focus. I've always been that way with lists, too. The way I've always seen it, you can either fill your brain with crap or you can get the crap out of your brain onto a plan or a list and leave space to think about what you actually need to do.

Doing training camps in a different city to the one my family lived in was unbelievably hard, because it shut me away from the people, places and things that I cared for most. But this was why it made such a big difference to my training. I had fewer distractions, so I could focus everything on the task at hand. I wasn't bothered by all those things that were grabbing at the edges of my mind. I didn't have to make difficult decisions about whether or not to interrupt my day to pick up the kids from school or meet a mate for coffee, because I wasn't even faced with those choices any more.

Moving to another city is clearly an extreme solution for most people. However, there's lots about this that you could apply to your own life. Ask yourself what things are distracting you from achieving what you want. This could be small things. If you find that when you work you're constantly derailed by phone calls and emails, why not turn them off, even if just for an hour or two? If you find that you end up lost for hours down social media rabbit holes, then maybe consider downloading an app that can temporarily block them. You don't need to switch them off permanently, just for those stretches of time when you need to be giving everything.

## YOU'VE GOT TO KNOW WHEN TO CHILL

I'd always just keep pushing when I was in camp. There were days when I'd go back to the hotel after having been tanked all over the place in sparring and I'd be so tired, and my body would be in so much shock, that I couldn't sleep. But I found it hard to admit how punishing that pace could be. When I called Rachael in the evening and she said, 'You don't look right, are you OK?' I should have told her that I'd been absolutely mullered in the gym. That I felt like shit, that I was going back to do it all over again in the morning, and that the thought of putting myself through this again was killing me. Instead, I'd lie. 'Yeah, sound, I'm fine.'

Sometimes I'd need saving from myself. I'd go too far and make myself ill. I'd end up with a chest infection, coughing up green phlegm. I finished at least ten camps on antibiotics. It didn't end there. I'd get frantic that I couldn't give in to my illness, so I'd still turn up at the gym. My coach would literally have to push me out of there and force me to stay in a hotel where he could keep an eye on me while I recovered.

All this is a long way of saying that one thing I've learned from pushing myself as hard as I did is that knowing when to stop and how to relax is crucial. You can't give everything during the day if you don't take the time to fill your tank at night. There have been times when I've tried to fit in an extra run or swim in the evening, thinking that it'll help. It never did. I always woke the next morning with heavy legs and I found that it affected everything I did for a long time afterwards.

That's why my performance actually improved when I learned to enjoy my rest days. It didn't matter if I was going out to the cinema, lying on my bed watching television (*Countdown*, *Tipping Point*, *The Chase*, in case you were wondering) or just going to a retail outlet and treating myself to a new T-shirt or pair of training pants. Making that space was useful not just for resting, but because it gave me the opportunity to reflect on what I'd been through. I could ask myself what had worked well and what hadn't. I could also process my personal interactions. If there had been a bit of friction between me and my coach, then I could analyse it: Could I have handled it differently? How could I make it right tomorrow?

And that's also why I'm embarrassed when I hear people boasting about how little sleep they get. For me, it's the same as if I heard somebody boasting about how little time they spend in the gym. When I'm tired, I make shit decisions, I lose my temper too easily and it's harder to find that motivation I need. No car running on empty has ever won a race. You've got to know when to chill.

## FIND THE MUTE BUTTON

Social media has bent the world crazy. I absolutely hate it. I know that it can be a great tool for business, which I've used to my advantage over time, but in general, it's toxic and full of nonsense.

It's not real life, and you should never forget that. Nobody's showing the day-to-day stuff. You don't see anyone admitting that the baby's crying upstairs or posting photos of piles of dirty dishes. Facebook, Instagram, Twitter, they're all dreamworlds.

Of course, the bits of the internet you should really ignore are those people whose entire lives seem to consist of lurking around social media, trying to degrade or pick on people. They're only doing that because, really, they feel bad about themselves. Why else would you spend all day abusing strangers? You're obviously living in your ma's attic or a shed and you're just sitting there trying to provoke a response from somebody you've never met. Fuck me. It's madness.

I find it easy enough to laugh them off ninety per cent of the time. But there's always that 10 per cent who take it upon themselves to go after my wife and family. Sometimes, if they come at me and I'm in the right mood, I might have a pop back. What really gets to them, absolutely *infuriates* them, is money. If somebody thinks that they can get under my skin by telling me that I'm a fucking bum and reminding me – as if I'd forgotten – that I got knocked out by Usyk, I'll point out that I've got so much cash now that I can't even count it.

Instantly, they ping me with twenty messages telling me that I'm a big-headed, money-obsessed prick. 'No,' I'll reply, 'I'm just showing you what this fucking bum has earned. Look at this watch collection – it's worth half a million quid.' I'd never say anything like that in a normal conversation. I'd be fucking embarrassed to. Which I guess tells you everything you need to know about what social media does to you.

In all honesty, the best thing you can do is not engage with these people at all. I don't block anyone any more, because if you do that, then they'll think they've got to you. If you do want to stay online, then try to control as much of the spaces you interact in as you can. On Twitter, I've turned the setting on that ensures that when I send a Tweet out,

I only receive comments from people I follow. And I'm a prolific user of the mute button, which has to be one of the best things ever invented. If I can't see what they're saying, it can't bother me. Even better, you could put the phone down. Go for a run. Breathe in fresh air.

## LOOK AFTER YOUR MONEY AND YOUR MONEY WILL LOOK AFTER YOU

I'm good with numbers and I can count money quickly. That's a legacy from two parts of my old life. The one where I was a trainee accountant for a bit and another that I'd rather not talk about too much. I've had to count obscene amounts of money in an obscenely short amount of time. I've done fifty grand in twenty minutes (although in those days I wasn't alone). Even now, I reckon I could count a hundred grand in under an hour.

It was quite a useful skill when it came to my fighting career. There's an astonishing amount of money in boxing. But so many fighters lose it all. That always played on my mind.

I don't come from a wealthy background. For the majority of my life, I've not had large amounts of cash in my pocket. It wasn't until quite late on in my career – after I'd become world champion in 2016 – that I started earning proper money. Which I think on reflection was a good thing: it's the people who become stunningly rich overnight who can't cope with the insanity that comes with that sort of wealth. Now that I do have a decent bank balance, I've no intention of ever being skint again. It's not nice when you don't know how or if you're going to be able to pay your next mortgage instalment. And it's fucking tough when you can't afford the operation on your hand that you need if you ever want to fight again.

When you're struggling for money, it affects the practical stuff, like not being able to afford food. But it also spills over into every aspect of your life. Worrying about debt or not being able to meet your mortgage payments stops you from sleeping, it damages your relationships with the people you love, it interferes with your brain when you're trying to focus on other things.

Financially speaking, being a professional boxer doesn't mean shit really until you get to the elite level. The vast majority of fighters live month to month, which is why less than one per cent of boxers retire from the game with money in their pockets. There's an uncertain fighting schedule – you never know how many times you're going to get paid in a year, if at all – and there's a lot of people waiting to take their cut as soon as the cheque clears in your account.

You're also at the mercy of your body. If you hurt yourself, you can't fight. And if you can't fight, you can't earn. When you're in a sport where both contestants are trying to destroy each other, there's a reasonable chance that one day something will injure you in such a bad way that your career's going to come to an end. And I knew I had weak hands – even when I was an amateur wearing big pillow gloves, I'd managed to damage them. I was always afraid that my hands might retire me before I got anywhere near a world title.

The first time I really damaged them was in a six-round fight against Phil Goodwin at the Kingsway Leisure Centre, Widnes in December 2008. I snapped the knuckle of my left hand after landing a left hook on his head. It was the first heavy punch of the match and it left my hand feeling like it was on fire.

It was the kind of thing that could have ended everything. So I was lucky that Mike Hayton, the best hand surgeon in the country, worked on it for me. He literally saved my boxing career. I'd never had a general anaesthetic before and I remember saying to the anaesthetist, who had no idea who I was or what I did: 'Listen, I'm not sure if you've ever done this before, but I've never been knocked out, so I don't think this is going to work.'

'Don't worry about it,' he said, 'it's going to work.'

'Listen, mate, I know that, but I get punched in the face, I *can't* be knocked out. So, do you want to put an extra shot in, because I ain't going to sleep off a bit of liquid in a syringe.'

'I tell you what,' he said. 'Count down from ten to one and if after you've got to one, you can tell me what your name is and what operation you're having, I'll give you an extra shot.'

'Mate, that's not going to be a problem.'

'OK,' he said, smiling. 'Lie back and relax.'

He put this fluid in me and I managed to count down to four . . . and that's the last thing I remember. The next thing I knew, I woke with a cast on my hand and I thought, *shit, it's been done, it's happened.* When I woke several hours later, the first thing I saw was my friend Gary sitting there on the end of my bed.

Everything had gone well, but Mike Hayton told me I wouldn't be able to fight until July – seven months is a long time not to be working. I had two kids by this point. I hadn't been getting enough fights with Frank Warren, so I hadn't been able to build up any savings. I had no other sources of income and a mortgage on our terraced house that had seemed reasonable when I took it out but now appeared intimidatingly large.

The six grand that you get paid soon gets whittled down by taxes and fees for your trainer. I had nothing left. I was thinking: *fuck, what am I going to do?* There's no pressure like financial pressure. You haven't got a pot to piss in. January is a long month for boxers anyway – there's no shows, no nothing. There are no fights on the horizon. I couldn't work and I didn't want to go back on the streets – as much as anything because I was beginning to be recognised in public. That financial stress was in my head constantly, like a drum beat. It's the first and last time I've had to borrow money from anybody.

Normally I'd have been in the gym trying to improve

my craft, but because of my hand, I couldn't even do that. All I could manage was jogging. I couldn't punch for three months. Instead, I got steadily fatter and more depressed. Time seemed to slow to a sludgy crawl.

I was allowed to start tapping in March, so I strapped on twenty-ounce gloves covered in extra layers of sponge. I was tapping and tapping and by the end of the month, I was punching, but without much confidence. In April, I started sparring. When I realised that my hand probably wasn't going to fall to pieces, I called Frank Warren and told him to arrange a fight for the next month.

Frank sorted out an eight-rounder against a heavyweight called Mathew Ellis, a bit of a showman who used to arrive in the ring dressed as James Bond – a costume that the ring girls would then rip off. He'd been considered a real prospect once upon a time – a 'great white hope' – and yet now he was a broken man who'd fallen on hard times. He'd gone from everyone raving about him to coming in as a last-minute replacement to fight people two stone lighter than him.

I couldn't afford pity, even if I was worried about the fact that I hadn't hit anybody for months. At the back of my mind was the memory of the way my knuckle had exploded months before. There's a world of a difference between the twenty-ounce gloves you train in and the ten-ounce gloves you fight in. There's no padding, nothing really, in the fighting gloves. When I hit somebody over the head with a left hook, I feel everything.

I was scared, I guess. Scared enough to let it modify my style.

In the fourth round, I caught him with a left hook, hard enough that I saw his legs do a bit of a dance. This was usually the moment when I'd load up, move in and take his chin off. This time, I finished him with a body shot: another thing that boxing teaches you is that a man's torso is a lot softer than their skull. It might have been a departure from my usual game, but it seemed to do the job. After I'd whacked him, he just didn't get up. I think he'd had enough. Afterwards, he tracked me down and gave me what was clearly some advice he'd learned the hard way: 'Don't throw it all away.'

I planned for the future a lot more after that. I worked out that the surest way to avoid finding myself skint again was to invest the money I earned into something that would pay me money, whatever was happening in the ring.

For me, houses were the way. The first was a terrace in Old Swan, Liverpool that I brought off my brother for £93,000 (he had the kecks off me!). I still own that now. To begin with, my goal was to pick up ten terraced houses, which I could pass on to the kids. Even if they were on buy-to-let mortgages, I'd keep chipping away at them so by the time the kids had left school, the mortgages would be paid. I kept chipping away. As time has gone on, I've far surpassed that. I've got over thirty properties now: terraces, shops, a warehouse.

I've worked my bollocks off for that money. I've paid my taxes and amassed a fortune that means I've created great futures for my kids. If I don't want to work, I won't ever need to work again.

We make sure we enjoy our money – there's no point hoarding cash for the sake of it. Don't overindulge, but treat yourself now and again. At the same time, I'm very alert to what I'm spending. You should always live within your means. When you have no money or very little, it's actually weirdly easy to do that. It's only when you've got that bit more coming in that you find that a lot more starts going out. You get nicer things, but you're also at the very edge of what you can afford. You also get accustomed to a certain way of life.

So while I like Rachael and the kids to have nice things, I was never going to be one of those boxers who got rich and just fucking pissed it all up the wall with watches and jewellery, or who was always flying first class to Vegas to drink with their mates. A fast life can soon get out of control.

I also believe that you should always be putting money away for a rainy day. Life throws so many curve balls at you, there's so much that could go wrong, that if you can set something aside to help when times get rough, you'll be doing yourself a huge favour.

All this is a long way of explaining one of the most important things boxing has taught me. We all have such a twisted relationship with money. It's essential for our day-to-day existences and yet it can ruin relationships in the blink of an eye. Having none can be devasting, but having lots of it is no guarantee of happiness, either. What you have to ensure is that money never becomes so important to you that it disrupts the rest of your life.

# SUMMARY

- You only get one shot at life – make sure you give yourself the strongest chance of succeeding.

- At the back of your mind, if there are people or habits that you know are standing in the way of you becoming the best possible version of yourself, then cut them out. Be ruthless.

- Invest time and energy in finding out what sort of environment gets the best out of you.

- Integrate eating well and exercising in your daily life. Look for a diet and an exercise regime that you can sustain over the long term, not just in short bursts. Moderation is key.

- Find a daily routine that works for you.

- Social media can be poison – don't be afraid of using the mute button.

- Money worries can become a huge distraction. Cultivate a reasonable, balanced relationship with money. Don't live beyond your means, but try to enjoy your money, too. If you don't put the effort into saving and managing it, you won't be able to enjoy it. There's no pleasure in spending money if you're too afraid to check your bank balance.

# CHAPTER 5
# ALWAYS START AT THE FEET

*I let the footage spool on for a few seconds. On the little screen in the corner of my room I can see two fighters trading blows, each trying to manoeuvre the other around the ring. I lift the remote up, point, and send everything into reverse. Arms snap back to where they'd started, the men perform funny little skips as they're forced to retreat to their starting positions. I press play again, repeat the process. Then again. Then again.*

*It's 2002, I'm in the first, unsteady, stages of my boxing career and I'm so hungry to learn everything I possibly can about my new craft. I'll never be as quick or as strong as some of the other lads at the Rotunda. I know that. But I also know that my desire to absorb everything I can from the best fighters to ever grace the game will help me narrow that gap. The video I'm watching is from a couple of years ago, Félix Trinidad against Oscar De La Hoya for the WBC welterweight title – just one of the countless tapes that spill out from where they're stored under my bed.*

*I have never seen anybody move like Trinidad: he has so much coiled energy in his feet. He is like a panther getting ready to spring. For the hundredth time tonight I watch Trinidad unleash that beautiful, vicious left hook. There's something hypnotizing about the spectacle. His tendons stretch, his body twists for a moment, then he explodes. I imagine doing the same when I get to the Rotunda, and the excitement begins to build in me. The nerves in the muscles of my left arm twitch, as if they share my impatience to get into the ring.*

*Tomorrow cannot come too soon.*


When I was a kid, there was nobody who loved boxing like I did. I was hungry for every single second of it I could get. Something that was easier said than done back then. Sky Sports covered the big fights, but pretty much the only place you could find coverage of the matches I wanted to watch was on KOTV, which ran on Channel 4 at half two in the morning.

I'd watch documentaries about the great fighters of the past or stay up until four in the morning to see Mike Tyson fight. I'd also buy video cassettes – there was a deal where you'd get three a month for £20 – which would show all the fights from the USA. My dad would fund things like that because it made him proud; it must have felt like a signal I was heading in the right direction. I know that if I'd have asked for the same amount for football subs, he'd have said, 'Behave yourself, lad.' By the age of fifteen, I had 200 stored in a big box under my bed. I kept hold of them for years – something that later on would turn my missus absolutely *mad*.

In fact, I only finally gave them away when I turned professional.

I watched all those videos over and over until some sequences became so blurry and worn out that it looked as if two ghosts were sparring. I can still see those ancient matches now when I close my eyes. So many of these fighters and bouts have been forgotten by the rest of the world – but they're still there in my mind.

If there's anything you want to know about almost any fight that took place in any division from the nineties, through to the millennium and beyond, I'm the person to ask. I know who faced whom, when and where. Fighting styles, records, everything. It just stuck in my mind in a way that nothing else ever would. My memory is shit, except when it comes to boxing.

I remember the first steps of great fighters who went on to become world champion. That's why I know the first person Mike Tyson ever faced – a guy called Hector Mercedes. I knew about Floyd Mayweather before almost anybody else in the country. I saw his bout against Diego Corrales – the only fight where Mayweather came into the match as an underdog. I watched fighters who should have gone on to be amazing, but for whatever reason crashed and burned; and others who fought once, lost and then faded away for ever.

I watched Bernard Hopkins, Joe Frazier, Britain's Johnny Nelson. Most of all, I liked watching Riddick Bowe. I think that was because I could see we had a lot in common. He was naturally a bigger guy, unafraid to raid the fridge. And, like me, he favoured fighting on the inside. Even though the rest of the world was always telling me that I should use my height and reach to keep the other guy away, there was always a moment when I'd think: *fuck that, let's have a fight*. And I'd get up close and dig them in the body. That came from Bowe.

The other person I wanted to emulate was Bernard Hopkins, who was the absolute master at studying, and then destroying, his opponents. By the time he faced Félix Trinidad in 2001 – the first big boxing event after the Twin Towers – the fucker knew every move his opponent would make. Hopkins said that when he fought Trinidad, he didn't need to look at his hands. He watched his opponent's feet and they'd tell him where the next punch was coming from. It blew my mind that Hopkins was able to break down an amazing fighter like that. It also made me realise how much I needed and wanted to learn.

Most of all, it changed the way I watched boxing. Lots of people watch matches and if they see blood and punches, they'll be happy. I loved that, but I was also obsessed with the details. Even before I'd ever set foot in a gym, I'd be alert to certain things: how were their feet moving? How were their hands moving? What did they do with their heads when they got punched?

Everyone else would be saying 'Did you see that cut?' And I'd say to myself: 'What are they watching? They're not seeing what he's just done with his feet, stepping back six inches so that he can then come back from the side and whack him. You were looking at the right hand that landed; I was looking at how he set it up.'

Piece by piece, I started to break down the men I saw on my little television. I'd watch the best fighters to see their strengths and flaws, how they reacted in particular situations, the sorts of mistakes they habitually made. I'd look for signs of what they'd do when they panicked, what they'd do when they got hit with a hard shot. After a while, it got to the point where I could tell within a minute if a fighter was any good.

I'd always start at the feet, because I understood that footwork is the key to almost everything. If you study a boxer's feet closely, you'll see everything. They'll let you know what he's going to do when he's been hurt or is under pressure. They'll let you know what he's doing when he's confident and looking to attack. They'll give an indication of their intentions: how is he trying to manoeuvre you? Is he looking to corner you? Is he trying to set traps?

Then, once I actually started fighting myself, I did everything I could to replicate what I'd seen on my screen. It might be a boxer's movements, or the way he placed punches, or how he used time. When I saw how efficient Lennox Lewis was with his jab, I started to copy it. And it was watching Félix Trinidad who made me change the way I fought.

Félix Trinidad was one of the greatest fighters of his era. I used to idolise watching him throw a left hook; there was something so special about it: a murderous combination of speed and grace. And nobody who was fighting at the same time as him, apart from Mike Tyson, could match it. I watched the way he always kept his right heel just off the floor, like he were a track runner. Other fighters are usually flat-footed the whole time that they're in the ring, but Trinidad gave the impression that he was about to start sprinting at any moment. Before long, I found I was doing the same.

I knew the game inside out. It was the only thing in the world I truly understood. When I watch boxing, my mind ticks and races. It lets me know that I'm not thick. Even now, if you were to give me a fighter, any fighter in the world, even if he's undefeated, and you let me study him over three fights, I'd be able to break him down and tell you how to beat him. I'm not telling you I *would* beat him, but a hundred times out of a hundred, I'd back myself to identify the style that *could* beat him.

It's a hard skill to pass on. Lots of the fighters coming through now aren't willing to put that sort of homework in, and yet that ability to watch and learn and plan was absolutely key to my career. There were very few times when I went into a fight without having a very clear idea of my opponent's specific strengths and weaknesses. In turn, this meant that I also had a very clear idea of how I'd go about beating them. My boxing IQ was one of the things that allowed me to beat fighters who, on paper, should have demolished me. It was also something that helped me to stay calm when everything else around me was threatening to go off the rails.

My September 2012 Alexandra Palace bout against the Colombian Edison Miranda, for the WBC International title, came at a time in my career when I was feeling insane amounts of pressure. There was so much going on in the background that it was sometimes hard to keep my focus on boxing.

Less than a year before, in October 2011, I'd lost for the first time as a professional, against Nathan Cleverly for the WBO light heavyweight title. I actually thought I'd done enough to win, but the judges didn't agree. So that was that. I hated losing, and I hated even more that he ran his mouth off afterwards, claiming that he'd not even had to get out of second gear, that it had been far too easy. In truth, he'd told me immediately afterwards that it was the hardest scrap he'd ever been in. I thought he was a lying scumbag and yet, that couldn't change the fact my record had a blemish on it now. And I was desperate to pick up a win that would help to put me back in contention for another title shot.

Alongside this, I was embroiled in a legal battle with Frank Warren, who didn't make a habit of losing in court. We'd fallen out over a number of things after the Cleverly fight and our relationship never recovered, so I severed ties with him. In response, he sued me, claiming that I was still contracted to his promotional company. What I resented most was that for months, until the claim was resolved, he'd withheld money he owed me and that he knew I was relying on. The sense of betrayal and hurt I felt stayed with me; I was feeling bruised and suddenly unsure if I'd ever be able to trust anybody again.

Although Eddie Hearn had started to represent me, the legal nonsense had made everything far more complicated than it needed to be. I didn't have a contract with Matchroom Sport, so if I fell short the first time I fought with them, it might very well also end up being the last time I fought with them. Everything felt up in the air and uncertain. All this contributed to a situation where winning my next bout felt overwhelmingly important.

I wanted to be able to show Eddie that he'd been right to take me on. I wanted to prove that I was a proper contender who deserved to be given a chance of going up to the next level. And I wanted to show the world that whatever had happened in the courtroom had made no difference to my ability to fight in the ring.

All that gnawed away at me in the weeks after I got matched against Miranda. Sky really liked the fight. We'd been scheduled as chief support to Darren Barker, who was going to fight for the European title, but then Barker picked up an injury, so we ended up top of the bill. This was exciting, but it also meant that there was even more pressure on my shoulders.

Miranda was properly dangerous, with a brutal record of knockouts. He hadn't become a world title contender by accident. The Panther, as he was known, had a reputation for having a massive right hand. He very rarely got stopped and had a respectable record against some of the best fighters in the middleweight and super middleweight divisions.

There was something about his story that made me wary, too. He'd been abandoned by his mother when he was only a month old and everything that followed had been a struggle. He was working full-time as a builder and cattle butcher when he was still just a kid. He'd been homeless and hungry. When somebody has overcome so much, you know that whatever you see on the surface, deep down they must be insanely driven. I could see that he was like me, somebody who'd never give in or give up.

It was a relief to be able to take the time to study him. I watched bout after bout until I felt as if I knew him inside out. Then Mick and I sat down in the gym and talked it through. Once we'd come up with a plan that we thought would manipulate him and punish his flaws, we worked on our game plan day in, day out. We talked right the way through the process, tinkering it as we went along until we were confident it was right.

You clearly can't plan for what will happen at every single moment in a twelve-round bout; there are too many things going on for you to exert that kind of control and as good as I am at reading other fighters, I can't predict the future. You might know what risks the opponent poses, but you can't be certain about how they'll react to particular situations. What you can do is evolve a strategy that allows you to impose yourself on the fight.

It was obvious that Miranda's right hand was as powerful as everyone had told me. There was no doubt that if he caught me right, he'd be very capable of knocking me out. I saw how he'd won fights with vicious punches – he'd broken Arthur Abraham's jaw when they fought. But that was allied to pretty slow footwork. This gave me an opening: I knew that if I could get my shots off, then get out and come away at an angle, I'd be giving myself a good chance.

What nobody had mentioned, and I'm not sure many other fighters had noticed either, was that his body was his weak spot. Other people had hurt him there – Lucian Bute took the wind out of him with a body shot, but I don't think he realised what he'd done, so couldn't take advantage.

Miranda's weakness matched neatly with one of my strengths. I'm a very, very good body puncher, even if I didn't always get credit for it. I'm six foot three, this guy was barely six foot, so I knew if I could keep him at bay with my jab and detonate my right hand on him every time he tried to get close, then I'd be sitting pretty. Most importantly, we were confident that if I just kept digging him down, using my superior footwork, he'd tire quickly. It might take a while, but after eight or nine rounds, he'd be there for the taking.

I went into the fight thinking that he was slow on his feet. Within seconds I found that if anything, I'd been too generous. I couldn't believe that he'd been fighting at world championship level for so many years. That gulf in our quality instantly filled me with confidence: I realised that when I did make the step up to the next level, where I'd be challenging for the biggest titles, I'd be able to compete.

In those first moments of a fight you try to get a feel for your opponent. It's then that you can see how accurate your assessment of them has been. Watching a boxer on-screen is one thing, coming toe-to-toe with them is another. That means that the relentless focus on the other fighter becomes, if anything, more intense when you're actually in the ring.

The first time I hit Miranda in the fight, I touched him at the top of his head. I didn't put much force into the punch. It was just to kid him. I wanted to see how he'd react. Boxers generally fight with one glove up covering their head and another lower down, protecting their body. But if you tap someone's skull, they automatically respond by rushing to cover their head, which leaves a gap for you to exploit lower down, if you're quick enough. As soon as I'd caught Miranda's head, his gloves both leaped up, leaving his torso vulnerable. The better fighters don't fall for those sorts of tricks and traps. That told me something about Miranda. Instantly, I sank one into his body. I could see that when my fist connected, he tightened up and stumbled back half a pace. *Right, you fucker,* I thought, *you've felt that.*

It was too easy, really. I absolutely took this guy apart. He was so ponderous that I'd pop him with a jab, then take a six-inch step out, and he'd be left flailing at empty air. Then

I'd see him pause for a second before lumbering forwards. He couldn't make up the ground, which meant that he was barely able to land a punch. So I just carried on popping him then moving away. The only chance he had was if I stood still. Occasionally, I'd nail him with something quite big in the body, and I'd see him take a big gulp of air and stiffen a bit. That told me my punches were taking their toll.

For most of my career, the ring was a refuge. Once I'd climbed over the ropes, nothing else mattered. It was just a question of getting onto the canvas and fighting. Whatever was going on in my day-to-day life would fall away: the injuries I was carrying, the damage that my opponent had already done, the stuff I was worrying about. Cuts, gashes, pain. I didn't care. All I thought about was winning and fighting. It was the one place where I could escape the rest of the world. That's why I loved it so much.

This night was different. The seal had broken and all the pressure I was feeling outside the ring was flooding in, pressing down on my shoulders. It made me hyper-aware of the danger Miranda posed. He might have been slower than an oil tanker, but I still didn't want to give him even a single chance to smash me with his right hand. My plan was to fight slightly within myself. I wasn't gun-shy, but I was very, very careful.

In the sixth round, I dropped him with another body shot. Normally, this was when I'd move in for the kill.

But instead of putting my foot on the gas, I stayed patient. When I look back at the footage, I'm struck all over again by how cautious I am. Every punch is considered. There are very few moments when we step in and start trading. I think maybe that in that match I feinted more than I hit.

Sky hated that – all they want is drama. Their commentators, who didn't have the first idea about all the things that were pressing in on my mind, tore into me. And yet I couldn't let myself be swayed by the desire to be a showman for the cameras. More than anything there was a part of me that wanted to fight with the same unleashed savagery I'd shown during my time in the amateurs. But I knew I couldn't risk it. If I'd have got knocked out that night, it could have been the end of everything.

I'm sure it was a pretty boring fight to watch. Yet, for me it was one of the most draining experiences of my life. My brain was ticking and ticking and ticking. That's fucking exhausting. It sounds mad to say it, but in some ways that mental exertion was as punishing as any physical assault. I was watching every single move he made, trying to calibrate what risks I could and couldn't take, because I knew that there was no margin for error. And always there was the thought of Frank Warren and everything I'd been through in court. Then there was Eddie Hearn: we had no contract, nothing to tie us. If I lost, he could walk away and nobody would blame him. It didn't matter that the fighting was easy or that I was a far better boxer – all it would take was one lucky punch smashing through my guard and I'd be done.

When, nine rounds in, it was finally all over, I didn't feel elation or excitement; all I felt was relief.

# BE WATCHFUL

The closer you watch the world, the easier you'll find it to achieve your goals. Whatever you do, and whether it's in your professional or personal life, you should cultivate your curiosity. Make it a habit. There were definitely times in my career when I put my head in the sand a bit, because although I sensed something was wrong, I was afraid of confronting it. I was like those people who won't look at their bank balance because they know they're going to be upset by what they see. That's understandable, but it's only ever going to defer that problem.

When you get your head up and start looking around you, you'll find that you're able to spot both obstacles and opportunities earlier than you did before. And the earlier those things come onto your radar, the better you'll be able to create a plan to deal with them.

And if you acquire the habit of watching the world, you'll also have picked up the crucial ability to learn from your own experiences, as well as the skills and wisdom of other people. Lots of people make the mistake of thinking that because they've not had the greatest experience at school, they're not capable of studying. But learning isn't just about academic textbooks and so many of us end up studying without realising it.

I learned so much from obsessively watching the great fighters of the past while sitting in my bedroom. Look outside yourself to see how other people are doing things, because there's always someone you can learn from. Think about how many elite sportspeople borrow from other disciplines to try to get the edge, whether that's footballers doing yoga to extend their careers or rugby players training their peripheral vision. When you're interested in something, try to find out as much about it as you can. Ask people for advice. Don't turn down any chance to increase your knowledge or improve your skills. You'll never become the best version of yourself if you don't give yourself the tools to get there.

## HAVE A PLAN

I had a game plan for every fighter I ever faced. When I stepped into the ring, I always knew exactly what I needed to do and how I was going to do it.

It's so tempting sometimes just to act first and think later. You want to get things done, so why bother with the tedious work of sitting down and planning? But, of course, in real life, just winging it rarely works. In fact, more often than not, it ends up in disaster. You should go into situations with as clear an idea of what you want to achieve, and how you're going to go about it, as possible. Ideally, you'd also know something about the other people involved and how they might react to the situation.

The very act of planning can help to focus your mind. It gives you the opportunity to work out what things are important to you and what's dispensable. And once you know exactly *what* you want, it becomes easier to work out *how* you're going to get it. Going into a negotiation with a vague intention of getting a good deal is only ever going to be half as effective as if you produce a detailed list of priorities in advance.

Planning also helps you to think about what you're about to face in a structured, orderly way. We all have to do things that sometimes we'd prefer not to, but I find that planning can take some of the anxiety out of these situations. It's so much more positive and productive when you're contemplating something that might be hard or unpleasant to think about how you're going to counter it. If I knew that the next guy I was going to fight had a dangerous left hook, just worrying about it wouldn't help. But as soon as I started to think about how I could counter that punch, the problem began to seem manageable. It's not unusual to feel anxious ahead of a job interview. What might help would be to try to think about what questions you'll be asked and what answers you'll give in response.

At a time when everything around me felt really turbulent, the very act of planning for my bout with Miranda brought me a sense of calm. When you're thinking positively about the actions you're going to take in the future, you're exerting a small but significant amount of control over the chaos of life.

## BE ADAPTABLE

I never faced another boxer, with the exception of Oleksandr Usyk, who was as adaptable as I was. None of the rest of them could out-think me. And yet every time I've gone in the ring, my opponent has underestimated me. They'd watch footage of my last fight and come away convinced – usually with good reason – that they were quicker or stronger than I was. I never came across well on camera. I look sluggish and clumsy. But what they missed was that I also had a better brain than they did. That I went into every bout with a plan tailored to exploiting my opponent's weaknesses and masking my own. That I don't think I ever entered the ring with the same mentality as I had the fight before.

Being adaptable, knowing that there wasn't only ever a single way of approaching a situation, was one of the things that allowed me to beat fighters who were, in theory, more talented than me. Someone like Edison Miranda, who moved around the ring clumsily but packed an artillery-like punch, demanded a different strategy to Nathan Cleverly, who didn't have the same capacity to hurt me but was far nimbler on his feet.

It's so easy to believe that what's worked once for you will carry on working indefinitely. Sometimes that's true. More often, it's not. Get as much information as you can about the scenario you're facing. Ask yourself in what ways it's different to other positions you've been in before and in what ways it's similar. Fit the plan to the situation, not the situation to the plan.

## PAY ATTENTION TO OTHER PEOPLE

Watching people is a useful skill and it's one that can be reproduced outside the boxing ring. The ability to observe things closely and draw lessons as a result is something that you can apply in many different areas of your life.

This kind of watchfulness can help you to be a better partner or parent. You don't need to spend hours watching old videos of your kids or wife, like I did with other boxers, but it's not too hard to pay them a bit of close attention. If you make the effort to work out what makes the people around you tick, you can respond to them better, anticipating their emotional needs. If you're the manager of a team, conducting a mental audit of their relative strengths and weaknesses will help you to get the most out of them. Watch people carefully, look out for what they respond to. Some people are motivated by praise, others need a rocket up their arse. So you need to tailor your actions to match what you've observed.

The minute you get out of your own head and try to work out what's going on in someone else's is the minute you'll take a big step forward in your personal relationships.

## KNOW YOURSELF

A lot of people I know who are most unhappy are also those most unwilling to tell the truth about themselves. There are fighters who are riddled with the most extreme bitterness because their careers haven't worked out like they think they should have. They think they deserved more, and they blame everyone and everything for the fact that they're stuck doing nine-to-five jobs. They've never been brave enough to ask whether or not they're living in a shithole because they weren't willing to do the work early doors. They never examined the decisions they took or the mistakes they made. And so they carried on making the same mistakes throughout their career. They'll probably carry on making the same mistakes for the rest of their lives. Do I feel sorry for them? Yes. Do I think the world owes them anything? No.

Pay close attention to what you do and say. What are you good at? Where are your weaknesses? Pay close attention to how others respond to your actions or words. As you do so, try to put yourself in their heads. You might not always like what you see. You might even have moments when you think, *fuck me, I'm horrible,* but that's why it's valuable. If you pretend to yourself that everything's perfect then, you know what, things aren't ever going to get better.

When you watch your own performance more closely, you'll have a much stronger sense of what's effective and what isn't. It's hard work in the short term that might end up saving you a lot of effort further down the line.

# LEARNING IS FOR LIFE

My ability to study my opponents, pick them apart and formulate the plans that would help me to beat them was absolutely central to my rise to the top of boxing. The work I did with my head allowed me to make up the physical gap that separated me and most of the other fighters.

Cultivate the habit of learning as early as you can and then make sure you never stop. Remember that learning isn't just about what you get from books or are told in classrooms. It can also be what you see and hear for yourself. You can learn from watching somebody set a good example. My dad, for instance, showed me the right way to earn money when I was teetering on the edge of going onto the streets. And people can also set a bad example. The fact that my dad lost his shit in a boxing match and that pretty much ended his career was, now I think about it, a very good demonstration of the importance of keeping a lid on your emotions.

# SUMMARY

- Pay attention to the people around you. The more you know about them, the better your relationships will be.

- Be curious about the world and everything in it. Watch others closely to see what you can learn from them.

- Always have a plan. Don't try to blag your way through life. Assess every situation you face and then invest time in coming up with the best plan to deal with it.

- Be adaptable. Remember that every scenario, every person is different. The same approach won't work every time.

- Keep a close eye on yourself. What are you good at? What do you struggle with? How do you come across to other people?

- Never let yourself believe that you know it all. There's always more to learn.

# CHAPTER 6

# THE MOST VICIOUS CREATURE YOU'VE EVER SEEN

James Boyd is a brilliant amateur. He's had over seventy-five contests; he's boxed for England; he's a multiple junior national champion. He's probably the best fighter of his age in the country. Whereas I'm 3 and 0 with a cracked rib that's barely healed after a three-week break from fighting.

None of that bothers me. I don't give any of his medals a second thought. The bell rings and I just steam into him. Feeling good, landing the odd shot, I'm really scrapping, aware that for the first time in my fledgling career, I'm really in a fight. It's close, but second after second I feel I'm getting on top of him. I can feel I've got more power than him. It's just a matter of time before I land the right shot and I beat him.

I get in close and he spits in my face. Something just takes hold of me. I bring my head back and then butt him as hard as I can. I'm still in a red fury when the referee grabs me by the arm and tells me to get out of the ring. I can't understand what's happened. I just *want to keep on fighting. But it's over. My opponent hasn't beaten me – I've beaten myself.*

Boxing exposes your emotions like nothing else. It can tear off layers of skin and leave you raw and vulnerable. It can make you feel invincible. In the ring, I've gone to the outer edges of what it's possible to feel. I know what it's like to stare into the night sky as every single atom in my body screams with joy because I've achieved everything I'd ever dreamed of.

But I've also experienced the horror of defeat and its crushing aftermath: crying alone in a hotel room because it seems that everything is fucked and the world is laughing at me. The feeling that nothing will ever be right again. I've experienced hatred so pure that all I've wanted is to be given the chance to turn another man's face into a mess of pouring blood and jagged bone; and I've felt a surge of tenderness so strong it almost undid me as I stood over the unconscious body of a man whom only seconds before I'd been trying to destroy. I've felt a fierce desire to win that's gnawed at me for days, weeks, months at a time, and I've also heard that soft voice that urges me over and over to quit.

Most of all, I've felt anger. People think that anger is a simple emotion. I'll tell you this: it isn't. Anger is why despite having small, easily broken hands, I was one of the game's most vicious punchers. Anger and a furious desire to prove every fucker in the world wrong is what drove me on. Anger kept me going in the gym when my exhausted muscles were aching and flooded with lactic acid and all I wanted to do was rest. Anger is what made me a world champion.

And yet, it's the thing that could have undone me, too. Finished me well before I ever stepped into a boxing ring.

Anyone who knows me will tell you that I've always been placid and soft. Too placid and too soft, probably. I was the first person to help David Haye up after I'd smashed him through the ropes. My own mother doubted I'd make it as a fighter because she didn't think I was nasty enough. And outside the boxing, I'm soft as shit. Most of the time. But I also have a switch that transforms me from a nice person into the most vicious creature you've ever seen. Cross me and in the blink of an eye I become a fucking animal.

Anger is a part of who I am. Maybe certain events and experiences have increased or changed that rage, but the possibility has always been there. It's something you need, coming from where I do. I grew up thinking that doing bad things to other people was normal. That's what we did. If I ever had to hurt someone, I wouldn't hesitate to use the absolute maximum aggression. If I was in a fight in the street, I'd keeping going and going until the other lad's jaw was smashed in and I'd knocked out all of his teeth. That would affect some people – I didn't give it a thought. I didn't give a shit.

And there have been times in my life when I felt as if I could explode at any moment. All the time, all day long, every day, I have this sense that I could do horrible things. I can't explain it without sounding like a fucking maniac. I just want to be left alone. It often doesn't end well for people who have that in them. The time will come when you take things too far and find yourself facing heavy consequences.

For me, that moment three fights into my career was an important lesson. I'd lost my rag and that had been enough to get me disqualified. I was going to win that fight. No doubt. And my temper had got the better of me. As had Boyd. He was a clever kid and he'd used all of his experience to get a reaction from me.

I didn't dwell on what had happened. I couldn't change it, so overthinking my reactions wouldn't have achieved anything. And nor did I come away thinking that I somehow had to cut away that part of my personality. I just let it ride. I thought it was always going to be a part of me. It's only now, looking back, that I've begun to think, *fucking hell, lad, you were nuts.*

What that incident did do, though, was to make me even more aware than before of who I was, and what my strengths and weaknesses were. I came away thinking: *this is me. For better or worse.* And I had to learn to harness who I was and what I could do. I didn't waste time with recriminations or self-doubt. I just asked myself how I could improve.

I was never going to be able to take that part of me away. For one thing, I realised that it was part of my appeal. The rage is what made people want to see me fight. Which is fucked up if you think about it.

More than that, it's what gave me the edge I needed to become world champion. I'm like many other sportsmen – if you take that element away, I'd have been a very different and probably less successful athlete. Roy Keane or Wayne Rooney were unbelievably gifted football players, but what made them special, what gave them that edge that turned them from being merely very good to being world-class was that viciousness. They both did things that got them into lots of trouble. But they were only in a position to be in that trouble in the first place because of that nasty streak they had.

I probably could have found ways to erase my anger so that it no longer had any place in my existence. I probably could have had it cut out like it were a tumour. Instead, I chose to keep it. I acknowledged its existence and learned to harness it. Because I knew that if I didn't find a way of exerting a measure of control over my rage, then it'd run riot and rule over me.

Boxing gave that rage a home. It meant that the anger that might have destroyed my life could be diverted into a passion that helped me to build an existence for my family that otherwise would never have been possible. If I'd been leading the life my friends had – working Monday to Friday, living for the weekend – rather than dedicating myself to the sport, then I guarantee I'd have hurt somebody really badly and that would have only ended one way: a long spell in jail.

In the time before my boxing career had really got going, I'd had lots of fights and there were close shaves. Me and the Liverpool nightlife was a relationship that would have ended badly. I was arrested twice and on both occasions, the only thing that saved me was that I'd acted in self-defence. I left one guy in hospital after a rugby team attacked us while I was on a GB boxing trip. The last thing I'd seen, before I was taken to spend sixteen hours in a cell, was a man asleep on the floor with blood coming out of his ears.

It hasn't been easy and I've made too many mistakes to mention along the way. However, over time, I was able to evolve ways of managing that element of my personality. It means that I'm so much more in control of what I'm doing now.

I've always been Anthony to the people who are closest to me, who really know me. Other people might have called me Bellew or Bomber. But one of the first steps I took when boxing became really serious for me was to create Tony Bellew. Tony Bellew isn't afraid of anything. He could kill somebody without giving it a second thought. Tony Bellew does exactly what he wants, whenever he wants, to whom he wants. He doesn't give a fuck.

He was fuelled by the memories and emotions I usually kept locked away. The existence of Tony Bellew meant I could channel all of my frustration and hate into an alter ego that I'd step into when I needed him and step out of whenever I returned to my family home.

I'd turn into Tony as soon as I walked through the doors of a boxing gym. I'd become horrible – want to kill the world. When I was Tony, I was vicious and nasty. I'd have mad shit coursing through my mind. Having that ability to turn my anger on and off was central to my success. Without it, I'd never have been able to maintain my equilibrium in the high-stakes, high-pressure world of professional boxing.

It wasn't a perfect tool – I could sometimes lose my shit at the worst possible moment and there were times when I found that while it was easy to switch Tony Bellew on, it could be much harder to turn him off. There was more than one post-match press conference where I'd be sitting there, being asked questions about the fight, and I'd still have that blood lust in me. But most of the time it worked. And it was during the weeks before a fight that being able to become Tony Bellew was most crucial.

The moment I was scheduled to fight someone, I'd slip into street mentality. And that's what I'd keep with me every step of the way. I needed it because that time before a bout is full of overwhelming emotions. Just being in camp makes you nasty. It makes you horrible, it makes you want to kill your opponent. And as week follows week, it only intensifies.

In the first days it's all laughs and smiles. 'All right, lads, what's happening?' I'm back in the mix, I've got my coach with me again, and I'm excited and happy. Come week six, I want to knock him out, as well. Come week seven, I'm not happy. My trips to the camp are more intense and I'm angry all the time. Come week ten, I don't even want to look at anyone. Everything has shrunk to one vicious ambition: I want to annihilate my opponent.

And then come the last two weeks, when your body is flooded with so much testosterone and adrenaline, it feels as if you're existing on a sawed edge. At any single second you could veer wildly from despair to exaltation to the purest, most frightening rage. All of your training, everything you've been doing and thinking about for three months comes down to this short but intense spell.

At that point, you'll have stopped doing any hard work in the gym. You're basically just shaking out the muscles, going through the motions, rehearsing your fight strategy. But if your physical rate is down to a bare minimum, your mental rate is now right up.

This is the moment that you emerge from the seclusion of your camp – for weeks, your world has been reduced to your gym and your hotel room and the short trip that it takes to get between the two places – to find yourself thrust into the spotlight. People are questioning your motives, your aspirations, your expectations. As the days pass, the questions seem to get closer and closer to the rawest, most vulnerable part of you. It's like the journalists are probing for your weakest point. They know that your body is fine – what they want desperately to find out is how you're feeling on the inside. Physically, you know you're in great shape – you feel strong, you can sense the latent power in your arms and legs – emotionally, you're at your fucking wits' end.

When I saw the recent video of Conor Benn breaking down in tears, talking about how he'd had to tear himself away from his family to achieve his dreams and about how wounded he was by all the online abuse he gets, I knew exactly how he felt. I guarantee that ninety-nine per cent of other boxers would, too. They just never talk about it.

You see glimpses of that turbulence we're feeling at the weigh-ins and the press conferences. It's not scripted or put on – well, it might be for Conor McGregor and Floyd Mayweather; they ain't behaving like themselves – and all too easily it can go wrong. How could it not when you've got two men who for almost three months have spent all day, every day thinking about this fucking man who's going to punch their head and then there they are, taunting you. I've butted people, I've pushed them. Other fighters have kissed and slapped their opponent. Spitting, throwing tables. Before you know it, you've done something you regret. All of it is an expression of that pent-up, claustrophobic, confusing mindset. You haven't allowed yourself to step back and analyse the situation from afar. Instead, you get caught up in the hype and allow yourself to explode.

That's why I always tried to stay busy during that horrible last stretch. I did everything I could not to think about my family. I hated having to consider the impact that my obsession was having on them. I didn't like people even talking about them in the final run, because I'd be liable to break down in tears. There's a couple of times I've been so close to cracking like Conor did, and I was only able to hold myself together by closing my eyes and focusing on my opponent.

More than anything, though, it was in the hours before the fight that it was crucial to control my emotions. I needed to find the right balance between calm and the aggression that would always seize me as soon as I reached the arena.

I'm horrible before a fight. I'm *nasty*. At some point, it just happens. It's as if the man I am when I'm around my family and friends recedes and the part of me who's a fighter – Tony Bellew – decides it's time to take over.

I need this savage energy to get me through the fight. I won't punch as hard without it. But I can't spend three hours in this mindset. It's not just that it could all spill over and I'd end up lamping my trainer; although that probably wouldn't be ideal. It's also that it's exhausting being like this. If it went unchecked, I'd have drained myself before I'd even left my dressing room.

What I did instead was to try to break that time before the fight into thirty-minute intervals. The first part was about familiarising myself with my surroundings and making sure I knew in my own mind exactly what was going to happen. See it, look at it, believe it's going to happen. I'd wander around the arena by myself, take a look at the ring, absorb the atmosphere as it began to build.

The next thirty was about complete relaxation. Switching off from everything around me. It didn't matter that I'd be locked in the dressing room, that I was metres away from the ring or that I could hear the crowd. This wasn't the moment to focus on those diversions. It was too soon to be wasting nervous energy on any unnecessary effort. I know lots of other fighters who lose all of their power in the minutes and hours before the fight. Their nerves have drained them before they've even entered the ring.

The thirty to forty minutes it took to have my hands wrapped offered a valuable opportunity to exert some control over my mood. It was a mechanical, almost soothing routine, the same wherever I was fighting. And it was calming to know that Jay Sheldon, the best at that job I've ever encountered, was responsible. I'd always get my left hand wrapped first, because I knew that this would be the first fist that touched my opponent. Sometimes I'd play comedy clips to relax me.

It was also a good way of doing my opponent's nut in. I'd get his entire entourage to watch me and my team pissing ourselves as we watched YouTube on my phone – stupid things like comedy clips or that video of the Man United fan losing it while saying 'give it Giggsy till the end of the season' – while my hands were being wrapped.

Like me, Lennox Lewis used to arrive three hours before his fight began. Unlike me, the first thing he'd do was find the bed he'd had set up at the arena and then sleep for an hour. Or so he claimed. I'm not stupid – there's no way he was stone-cold asleep. But if he'd closed his eyes and rested his body then it amounted to the same thing. And he wasn't stupid, either; he always made sure the cameras came in and showed him sleeping. If your opponent thinks that you're so chilled out that you can take forty winks, that's going to play all kinds of crazy shit with his thoughts.

Then it would change again. The minute the boxing board and the WBC had signed the wrapping off and the other guy's entourage had left the room, I'd say, 'It's time to go to work.'

I'd put my low blow on and instantly the levels in the room would go up. The last sixty minutes was completely different. It was kill or be killed. Simple as that. People might not want to hear that. It's not the kind of aggression that anybody wants to see in their day-to-day lives.

In the final stretch, the twenty minutes before I'm due to fight, I'm pounding the pads with my coach, the music pumping so loud that nobody can hear a thing. I basically think that unless it's rearranging the internal organs of everybody in a fifty-metre radius, it's not loud enough.

Music has been one of the biggest things in my life. When I'm driving my car, you'll hear me from ten miles off. Anywhere I'm going, I've got headphones on. It can trigger me. It can calm me down. It can make me smile. It can make me laugh. It can make me cry. Certain songs remind me of certain things. The lyrics will send me back to particular scenarios in my life, often my childhood. It makes me think of all the stuff I've done and haven't done. There's nothing that playing music can't draw out of me.

Music can take me to the most violent version of me. Music can push Anthony Bellew out of the way and bring out Tony Bellew instead. There was always one song – by Roscoe, from the *Training Day* soundtrack. In it, you hear Denzel Washington talking over a menacing harpsichord loop and a beat that sounds like a pistol going off. Its aggression and message were perfect to take me back to that place I needed to be. It made me think: *How* dare *you do this!* It used to drive me to insane levels of aggression in the dressing room. As soon as it started playing, it made the hairs on the necks of everybody around me stand up. Because they knew I was ready to go and kill someone. That nasty, murderous emotion lasted until I stepped into the ring. And at that moment, it stopped being a street fight and would purely turn into a science.

I was always in control of my emotions when I was in the boxing ring, because I couldn't afford not to be. In the weeks beforehand, that kind of anger was useful. Nothing was ever business – I took it personally every time. But while that pure, untamed aggression is brilliant for the weigh-in and helps to get you through the agonies of the last week, it stops being useful when you get into the ring.

Boxing is violent chess. On the one hand, you have to

keep in your mind the whole time the plan you personally are going to execute. On the other hand, there's your opponent, who's doing everything he can to disrupt your plan and impose his. You've been studying this guy, watching him for months – and that doesn't stop because you're stripped down and in your gloves. You've got to be so switched on. You have to be able to read their face for signs of overconfidence or fear. I'd watch their bodies for those telltale signs that they were tiring. The little involuntary sounds they let out or automatic gestures they made were big fucking clues to me.

*Have I hurt him? Is he ready to go yet? Is his footwork on point? Is he sharp still? Is he just there to be taken?* I know when another boxer is feeling the pace because they'll start trying to navigate around the ring, anxiously trying to avoid touching the ropes because they're tired and they realise that they can't afford to take any body shots. Most of all, you're always trying to anticipate their next move, because if you can spot what they're doing that millisecond earlier, you've given yourself a massive advantage.

I'd say ninety per cent of fighters will look at their opponent's eyes. I never did. Eyes give little glimpses away, but they can also deceive. Someone blinks and you've dodged a punch that never came. I was definitely someone who liked to trick the bollocks off other fighters. Anyone staring into my pupils wouldn't see what I was doing. I'd feint, make little sharp movements. And more than that, I've never been punched in the face by a set of eyes. I'd focus on their gloves and then maybe when I was on the attack, I'd check their feet, see how they were positioned.

You've got all these things to process in your mind at the speed of light, all at the same time. You can't do that if you're seized by bloodlust.

You still need to keep your levels of aggression high; you still need to want to eviscerate your opponent, but you cannot let it get out of control. Everything has to be in the service of the whole reason you're there: winning a boxing match.

Then, when it's all over, that aggression and anger ebbs away. There's no other sport where you go from wanting to destroy someone to feeling a curious sort of love for them in a matter of seconds. That's not every fighter; the game has its fair share of vicious, nasty people. Some of them are born-horrible fuckers. But most of the time, I like to think I did the right thing.

## IF YOU DON'T LEARN TO CONTROL YOUR EMOTIONS, THEY'LL END UP CONTROLLING YOU

Boxing has shown me so much about myself. It highlighted my emotional and mental weaknesses. I wasn't an emotional person before I started fighting. Coming from a broken home knocks that side of you; you don't want to give anything away, especially on the street. I never used to cry about anything. No break-up ever touched me. I was kind and soft, yes, but not emotional. Certainly not around other people. Boxing drew it all out of me. Until I went into the ring, I never knew how fragile I could be. And although I've always known I was a bit nuts – I can accept that because we all have a bit of craziness in us – it was being a fighter that showed me that I'm willing to go further than anyone else. It made me realise that I was willing to die in a boxing ring. I'm not proud of that but at least now I'm aware of it.

You're a human being, not a robot, so you're going to have emotions. Fear, anger, joy, sadness. Our lives are defined by emotion. Everyone will experience them differently. Some people might get easily overwhelmed, others might have a gentle, level temperament that's difficult to stir up. There's never been any point denying that I carry a lot of anger around with me. What I was determined to do was find a way of channelling that emotion so that it worked for me. Because I knew that if I didn't, I'd be at its mercy. The first thing you need to do, as ever, is be brutally honest with yourself. Work out what it is that provokes strong emotions in you. What are the patterns and the triggers?

The most important thing is to realise that not letting your emotions be in charge of you doesn't mean ignoring them completely or denying that you have any. It's about recognising when they're useful to you, when they're not, and behaving accordingly.

# BUILD THE WALL

I'm a different person away from boxing. Anthony Bellew is soft at home. I adore my wife and kids. As much as possible, I've always wanted to protect them from seeing the man I became once I walked into a gym. Having the ability to 'become' Tony Bellew meant that I could establish a wall between boxing and my family life. I wanted to be able to display and use the anger I felt without worrying about what impact me doing so would have on the people I cared most about.

The other side of that coin was that I tried never to let thoughts of my family enter my mind before or during fights. Occasionally, there were flashes when I found myself thinking about Rachael. I'd wonder how she felt about the violence playing out before her. A couple of times when I'd been knocked down, the first thing I thought about was her and how I could reassure her that I was fine. It's not a nice thing to say, but when I was fighting, these human, empathetic emotions were exactly what I wanted to avoid.

My desire to keep those two sides of my life separate almost derailed me on that night in 2016 when I faced Ilunga Makabu. Normally, I wouldn't have wanted Corey (or any of my kids) within a hundred miles of the fight. I don't believe children have any place where people are likely to get seriously hurt. But this was different – I wanted him to see me crowned world champion. So I told Rachael that

I wanted him to be there but that I didn't want to see him. I'd been so emphatic about that. The arrangement was that he and Rachael would be settled somewhere safe, where there was zero chance we'd come into contact.

So when, a bit after seven, it was already starting to get dark and I was making my habitual prematch exploration of the stadium, I wasn't thinking about my family. Part of me had forgotten they were even coming. As Goodison slowly filled up, I walked up the steps towards the hospitality boxes, stopping every so often to turn round and look, trying to remind myself that this was all really happening. It was then, as I reached the top of the stairs and turned round again, that a high little voice from behind me broke into my thoughts. 'Dad! Dad!' I was so far away that I didn't recognise him immediately. I just thought, *that doesn't half sound familiar. It* sounds *like him, but it can't* possibly *be him.*

It was still so early, and I knew Rachael was planning to get her hair done and stuff before bringing Corey here. So it couldn't be him, I told myself. I turned round, convinced I was going to see a kid who just happened to sound like Corey.

Instead, my eyes met my ten-year-old son's and my heart broke. He was gazing back at me like he almost didn't recognise me. It was as if the rage and aggression that was coursing through my body had also taken his father away from him. I'd always seen him as the only innocent part of my life. I'd managed to shield him from so much of what had gone on around him – all the shit, nasty things I'd had to do just to survive. I thought, *you shouldn't be here.* But I couldn't say anything. I just walked away, straight down the stairs. I could feel hot tears rolling down my cheeks as I brushed past the crowd of stewards who'd gathered in the tunnel. On each of their faces there was the same look: *What the fuck is up with him?*

My coach had the same expression on his face when I got back to the dressing room. It's like the horror I felt when I saw my boy was still etched on my face.

'What's going on?'

'I just saw our Corey.'

Seeing Corey let all the anxiety and pressure back in. I knew that I couldn't allow him or any other member of my family to occupy my mind at a moment when I needed to focus only on tearing Ilunga Makabu to pieces. But it was too late. Other thoughts began to flood my brain: *What if something goes wrong? What if I get hurt?* My family were the only weak side of me. Just thinking about them made me vulnerable.

Keeping my worlds apart worked two ways. The boxing ring was also somewhere I could escape to. A lot of fighters over the years have struggled with their mental well-being. Often, it's stuff that's going on in their personal lives. Once I climbed through those ropes, I could shut down from anything that was going on in my life. There was some horrendous stuff – such as the death of my wife's brother – and yet when I was fighting, I felt more peaceful than when I was in the family home.

It's good mental and emotional hygiene to maintain boundaries between the various parts of your life, especially when you have children. I knew that my kids had to have space just to be kids. They didn't need all of my anxiety about fighting Makabu to be hovering over them every time we sat down for dinner. Equally, your job will suffer if you spend half the working day trying to deal with something that's going on in your personal life. If you let one seep into the other, you'll be less efficient and more stressed: there's nothing more draining or confusing than feeling as if your brain is in two places at once.

If you can set boundaries that determine where it is and isn't appropriate to express a particular emotion, then you're already exerting a crucial level of control over it.

## TAKE A MOMENT

I know the temptation of letting your emotions go. It feels so fucking good to give them a good airing. And there's definitely a place for that. If you button everything down, it'll eventually blow up. At the same time, sometimes you have to acknowledge that your emotions can get in the way. That's what happened when I lost it after James Boyd spat at me.

But it could also end up being obstructive even in less pressurised environments. If I was in a bad mood ahead of going to the gym, I could have taken it out on the people around me by being obstructive, snapping at my coach, refusing to take his suggestions on board. That can be satisfying in a weird way, but it's also pointless and negative. Far better to acknowledge that mood for what it is. Once you've identified it, you can try to work out what caused it. Maybe you slept badly or there was traffic on the way in. Once you can name that frustration and realise it's the result of an external event, you can reduce the hold it has over you. If it doesn't, try channelling it into something useful. Try not to get into a place where you end up carrying a negative mood around with you all day.

## SPOT THE SIGNS

My temper is something I clearly cannot hide and that sometimes gets the better of me. All those years ago, Boyd knew it, which is why he spat at me. He'd realised that rage could drive me on, but that it could also sometimes lead me to sabotage myself. I'm never going to be in complete control of my anger. What I have got better at is spotting my early warning signs.

I know what winds me up. If someone unleashes a personal insult on me, I can shrug it off. I've got a pretty thick skin. But there's stuff I'll still draw the line at. I don't like bullies and if someone was to insult my wife in front of me or someone was to in any way threaten my children, I'd lose my shit. I could kill someone, no problem. And I wouldn't think twice about it. That rage is still in me. The difference is that these days it takes an awful lot to get it from me.

Be watchful. If you've got a temper like me, think back to the occasions when you've lost it. Is there a common trigger? Maybe it's when other people try to take advantage of you or the feeling of being stuck in traffic. If so, in future you can try to avoid exposing yourself to those situations. Or if that's unavoidable, it's useful to be at least aware that these events can have such a strong impact on you. It's all about honesty and not making excuses.

As you're doing this, you can also try to think about how your body behaves in the moments before the red mist descends. Do you feel dizzy? Do you grind your teeth or start sweating? Try to make a note of this. If you're aware of what your warning signs are, then when you next experience them, try to pause and assess the situation you're in as objectively as you can.

I have learned to recognise when I'm about to reach level four of my rage. That's when I know that if the situation develops much further, something bad will happen. When I can sense the blood rising, I'll take a moment to assess the situation and ask myself whether or not I'm willing to accept the consequences of absolutely losing my shit. Beforehand, I'd very quickly accelerate from four to five and there wouldn't be much time to think about whether or not what I was about to do was a very good idea. Partly because for a long time I *wanted* the chance to go to level five. This means that if, for example, I get into an argument with another driver and start thinking, *I just can't have people talk down to me and berate me like that cunt has just done. I'll punch your head in, I'll rip your fucking head off,* then it's time for me to take a deep breath before I do something very stupid.

Over the years, I've got better at reading those tense situations that could escalate very quickly in a very nasty direction. I watch the body language of the other guy and in the first five seconds, maybe less, I can sense what's about to happen. I'll notice when their back goes up, the moment their voice rises, the moment their posture changes or they clench their fists.

More generally, though, it's just as important to be able to recognise the signs of anger in somebody else as it is to be able to spot them in yourself. The better you are at it, the better you'll be at making sure anxious moments don't become aggressive ones.

## USE IT OR LOSE IT

Anger can make you braver than you ever imagined you could be. It can allow you to tap into reserves of energy you didn't know you had. And it can boost your resilience in ways you might never have thought possible.

It's only a negative emotion if you let it be. If you can channel it into avenues that help you to achieve positive outcomes, you're far less likely to experience its dark side.

Of course, in order to be able to point your rage in the right direction, you have to acknowledge its existence first. Once you've done that, it becomes an unbelievably powerful tool.

In the weeks before a bout, I'd keep a screenshot of insulting or aggressive things my opponent had said about me saved as the lock screen on my phone. Every time I looked at that image, I felt a surge of controlled rage that drove me on through all the back-breaking sessions in the gym. My desire to prove people wrong by showing them that I could become world champion was another way that I could channel my anger into something positive. It was like a reservoir that I could draw on whenever I thought of quitting.

You're never going to be able to chase that rage away completely, so why not find a way of expressing it in a way that helps you to get closer to your goal?

## CHILL OUT

Everybody goes through extended periods of emotional stress. For me, it was the lead-up to a fight. For other people, it might be exams or waiting to find out if you're going to be made redundant.

In those last weeks before a bout, I'd be thinking constantly about my opponent. I'd be asking myself what he was doing, whether or not he was working harder than me, what sort of mental state he was in, who he was sparring.

I had to learn to deal with that as best as I could, because otherwise, if that was ticking through my head all the time, it'd drain every last drop of the energy I needed for the fight itself.

I'd do whatever I could in that last week to take my mind away from what was coming. The first thing I'd do was reduce my exposure to any information or news about the other boxer that might not motivate me. So, for instance, ahead of my bout with David Haye in 2018, I muted him on Instagram. I didn't need to see what he was doing. (This worked OK until my mates started calling: 'Have you seen David Haye's Instagram? Fucking hell, lad. He's on a yacht! He's training on a yacht! He's sipping his protein shake from a cocktail glass.')

I'd play on my PlayStation, go for walks, go to shops where I'd end up buying some shit that I didn't care about, just for the sake of it. Anything that wasn't boxing. Having a routine was really useful, too: train, eat, eat again, eat again, walk.

This was never enough to eliminate those thoughts entirely, especially for the really high-stakes bouts. With David Haye, he was always there. I don't think ten seconds would go by without the thought of him going through my mind. Even when I tried to focus on nothing or on the PlayStation, he'd creep in somewhere. The only time I could keep it all at bay was when watching films. For two hours I'd be lost in whatever nonsense was unfolding on-screen and I'd be able to forget.

The worst for me was Nathan Cleverly – the only fighter I came up against who I absolutely hated. I genuinely didn't like that boy and in the week before our rematch, I was relentless in trying to get into a mental battle with him. Whatever I felt about him was returned with interest. Perhaps he despised me because he couldn't understand why a genius like him – he had a maths degree – could ever be out-thought by a mindless fat dope like me. Over the course of a week, I out-thought him, I outwitted him, I was cleverer than him. For all his cleverness, he had no banter or street smarts. I also found out what was going on in his personal life and I used it against him. At every press conference, when we came face to face, I'd look into his eyes and whisper these things to him under my breath. Pushing his buttons again and again.

I really got to him and yet what I didn't realise was how much energy I'd expended in the process. In the seconds before the fight began, when I should have been feeling sharp and aggressive, I was numb – completely emotionally drained. I had no snap in me because I'd let the build-up get to me that much. I should have had the power to knock him spark out, but I was too fucked to punch properly and the match degenerated into a dull war of attrition. Because I'd robbed myself of the chance to outbox him, I had to outwork him instead.

Whatever you're going through, remember that thinking about it twenty-four hours a day won't help. Your brain needs space to relax and recover. Find what helps you to escape – even for a limited period. Laugh if you can. Find stuff that amuses you. If you can have a giggle at times of stress and pressure, then believe you me, you can get through anything.

## HOW BAD DO YOU WANT IT?

Everyone has bad days and everyone has days when they need a lift. For me, it could be when I was feeling shit after training or when it was time to get into the zone before a fight. I've always turned to music when I need to raise my spirits or boost my motivation – I listened to Whitney Houston's 'One Moment in Time' about forty times before my first ABA final. The other thing I find works for me is listening to inspirational speeches or moments from films. There's a guy called Eric Thomas, who I think is amazing, particularly a talk he gave called 'How Bad Do You Want It.' But there's also quotes from Muhammad Ali, snatches of dialogue from Will Smith films – stuff that speaks to me. I've compiled them on a motivational playlist that I listen to in training camps or in the build-ups to fights. It might be through my headphones as I travel in or in the dressing room, but it's always been there and it's always done its job.

Just as there will be times when you need to tamp down your emotional responses, sometimes you need to fire them up so that you can enter the headspace you need to confront whatever challenges are before you. Find your equivalent of 'One Moment in Time' or 'How Bad Do You Want It'. It doesn't have to be a song or a motivational track, it could just as easily be a picture or a memory of somebody important. What's crucial is that it's something that has the capacity to enhance your mood.

# SUMMARY

- If you can't control your emotions, then they'll control you. It's as simple as that. Spend time working out which of your emotions affect you most strongly. Be brutally honest with yourself. Pretending that you don't have a problem isn't going to help you in the long run.

- Work out what your triggers are. Are there physical or mental signs that always precede an emotional meltdown? If you can identify these, you can give yourself a chance of avoiding letting things go too far.

- When you've identified that negative emotion, find something positive that you can channel it into. Try to keep this separate from other parts of your life. If you can set boundaries that determine where it is and isn't appropriate to express a particular emotion, then you're already exerting a crucial level of control over it.

- Everybody will go through periods of extended emotional stress, but you can't live in that mindset. Find activities that allow you to escape your stress, even if it's just for an hour at a time.

Nobody ever solved a problem by thinking about it every second of the day.

- Build yourself a toolkit that'll help you to alter your emotions. Find things that can lift you up or calm you down, just as I did with music and inspirational speeches.

# CHAPTER 7

## EVERYBODY HAS A PLAN UNTIL THEY GET PUNCHED IN THE FACE

*The gloves you fight in at amateur level are like pillows. They're stuffed with the same foam that's used in car seats. Professional gloves are the same weight, but they're lined with horsehair. When someone's fist connects with your jaw, you can feel their knuckles.*

*First there is shock, as the concussive force spreads at lightning speed to every part of your cranium. Then there is the kind of pain that will stay with you for days. Then . . . silence. One second you can hear the crowd screaming, your coach shouting instructions. Then the next second: nothing. Your hearing just goes. You can still see the man who has just detonated a punch into your face, you can still think, but it's as if every single sound in the world has been removed. That can last, one, maybe two rounds. Six minutes of awful quiet while the savagery of the fight carries on.*

*I know all of this because of all the times I have crossed the rope and gone toe-to-toe with another man, all the times I have watched blood, my blood, spatter across my chest, all the times I have felt the bones in my hand break into fragments in the fraction of a second that follows the impact of a left hook on somebody else's chin.*

*Every punch I have taken, every cut that has burst open, every rib that has shattered: all of these have helped build my resilience. That is why I know that it does not matter that Roberto Bolonti has turned the two inches that sit above my right eyebrow into a sickening mess of crimson and ivory. I'm still going to win.*

One day when I was a kid taking the number 79 bus home, a lorry smashed into us. I was on a seat that faced the vehicle as it exploded into our view. Seconds later it shattered the windows, covering our faces with glass.

That was the first time I felt what real whiplash was like. It goes right through your entire body. When I woke the next morning, I don't think I'd ever felt so sore. There wasn't a single part of me that wasn't drenched in pain.

I'd feel worse than that, far worse, on the mornings after I'd fought. After I beat Ilunga Makabu, I had a throbbing headache so bad that I couldn't sleep all night. At least the banging had stopped by the next day. It was worse with David Haye. He's got a way of punching you in the back of the head when he gets you in a clinch. It's like he knows how to whack you exactly on the most vulnerable part of your skull. He left me with a head that hurt so bad that it felt as if somebody was conducting a bombing raid behind my eyes. That lasted for four days, which worried me so much that I didn't tell Rachael, I just kept quiet. (Every time he got close during the rematch, I locked and tried to pull his arm out of his socket. He was saying, 'He's going to break my arm.' And I was saying, 'Oh, shut up, you bitch.'

There's no way I was going to risk experiencing that sort of pain in my head again.)

After a really hard fight where you've taken a lot of damage, you might find yourself pissing blood. When it first happened to me early on in my career, while I was in the shower, I was almost pleased. I'd absorbed so much of the mythology around boxing that I liked the fact that this somehow put me on the same level as the iconic fighters. I was less pleased in the aftermath of my first bout with Nathan Cleverly. He'd hit my kidneys with such force that I was pissing blood for a week afterwards. The novelty soon wears off.

I've had my brain shaken so hard that I no longer felt like I was standing up. David Haye once hit me so hard on my forehead that I couldn't believe that I was still on my feet. I couldn't even tell you how many times my nose has been broken. I do know how many times I've fractured or broken my hands: six. I've detached my floating rib and cracked my rib three, maybe four times. There have been gashes in my mouth, a cut in my neck (David Haye, again). My lips have been smashed open too many times to count. Oddly enough, almost the only things that haven't been bruised, broken, cracked or split are my teeth.

All this is a long-winded way of saying that boxers take a lot of punishment. That's common to us all. Even the most talented boxers will end up being given a shellacking from time to time. It could be that they've had a bad day or maybe their opponent just gets lucky and catches them with a fluky left hook. In a sense, none of that matters. The most important thing in the ring isn't *why* something happens to you or even *what* happens to you. It's *how* you respond to the setbacks you'll inevitably encounter during your career. What do you do when you've been knocked to the canvas, your head is spinning and your mouth is filling with blood? Do you meekly wait for the referee to count you out? Do you look up and try to catch your coach's eye for long enough to make sure he knows you want him to throw in the towel? Do you blame bad luck? Do you accept that your opponent is bigger, faster and stronger than you? Or do you fight on, no matter how much pain you're in or how much blood you've shed?

I would never quit. I have never quit. I'd die before I gave up. Nobody ever kept me down on the floor. I've never been left asleep on the canvas. And never once have I chosen to watch from one knee as a referee counted me out. Even when I couldn't get up, I still got up. Even if after I've dragged myself up, I'm walking like a fucking zombie, I'll carry on fighting.

I've had a gash on my face that poured out blood, so deep that it would make most other fighters stop. I carried on for another nine rounds. And won. I've had my right hand explode in my glove and carried on for five more rounds. And won. I've been hit so hard that I've collapsed face first on the floor. I got up and carried on. And won. You don't whinge. You don't complain that you've got a cracked orbital socket. You just fucking fight. Even if someone told me I'd lose my eye, I'd still carry on. Sorry, that's how far I'm willing to go.

That's boxing. That's the mindset you've got to have. You'll not get anywhere without it.

Roberto Bolonti was a short Argentine slugger, just a typical South American. We were matched up in November 2012 for a bout in Nottingham to contest the vacant WBC silver light heavyweight title. It was another step along the road for me, another step closer to being given a shot at a world title.

When I studied him, I saw what I expected from someone with his reputation: he was a rough-and-ready fighter who was tough without having that much skill. He was fast, could hit a little, but I didn't rate his boxing brain. He was rated in the top five of the WBC, which I couldn't believe – I thought he was crap. I watched him and I thought: *I'm going to smoke this fella.* I wasn't worried, even when he was doing all the finger across the throat shit at the weigh-in, pointing at his muscles.

My game plan was simple. I'm six foot three, this guy is five foot eleven. I've got the height and reach on him all day. I knew that if I kept touching him from the outside, he was going to fold in three, maybe four rounds. I'd start slow and then at the right moment, just blast him.

The first round was pretty straightforward. I was on top, controlling every aspect of the fight. When he came out for the second round, he actually caught me with a short left hook, although that didn't change anything. Not long afterwards, I knocked him down onto his arse. That was it – as far as I was concerned, I'd done enough now. As I came out for the third round, I said to Mick, 'He's not seeing the end of this round.'

The bell rang and I hit him hard. One, two and then boom! A left hook. *Fuck off!* The force of my blow sat him down onto the canvas and stranded him there. The poor fucker was clearly in shock, his eyes flitting all over the place as he tried to work out what had just happened to him. I thought to myself, *all right, I'm nearly done now.*

Then I looked over to Mick in the corner, gave him a little nod and went in for the kill. It was then, just as I was about to finish him off, that this cunt closed his eyes completely and swung a wild left hook that caught me just above the right eyebrow on my forehead. Instantly, it felt as if somebody was pouring warm water over me.

Bolonti had opened his eyes now and was staring at me like he couldn't believe his luck. Blood fucking everywhere. The first sign that something was really wrong was that my coach had been replaced in my corner by my cut man, Mick Williamson, who was staring at me as if he'd seen a ghost. His skin had lost all its colour. That's the thing about blood: it's scary when you see it.

I said to Mick, 'It's only a bit of blood.'

He carried on staring at me in horror. Eddie Hearn was in the front row shaking his head like he thought it was all over. Then I turned to Gary.

'What's it like?'

He looked at me and he went, 'It's fine, it's fine. It's only a scratch.'

He was saying this as I felt another splatter of blood on my chest and I thought, *fuck, that must be a bad cut.* Then I just thought, *Gary, you lying bastard.*

In the blink of an eye, everything had changed. One second I'd been just blowing this guy away, the next all I could think was, *fuck me, I'm in trouble.*

Before the fight, I knew that I could smoke him if I could get him to trade, but he'd spent the first three rounds doing everything he could to avoid that. Now, of course, the fucker was absolutely desperate to trade with me and yet I couldn't, because if he touched my cut, the referee would stop the fight. Bolonti was clever – he knew that if the gash had been caused by a head clash, the fight would have been stopped and I'd have been so far ahead on points that I'd have won. But because the cut was caused by a punch, I'd lose if the fight got stopped. Other people might have quit. Other people *definitely* would have quit. There was no fucking way I was going to quit.

By this time, Mick had gathered his composure again. 'Listen, just box this fight,' he said, 'and he can't touch you again. He can't get near you, but this fight could get stopped because of this cut. Just keep him away and box him and box him for nine rounds.'

Thank fuck for Mick Williamson. He's the best at what he does in the world. He'd saved more fighters with cuts than

I can count and had straightened me out numerous times. This, he'd later tell me, was by far the worst cut he'd ever had to deal with in his career. It needed twenty stitches: ten on the inside, ten on the outside. Another stroke of luck was that for some reason, a plastic surgeon was working that night, so he could stitch me up. If someone without that expertise had tried, my eye would probably have been a problem for the rest of my career. But you can't even see it now.

One last piece of luck was the referee, Victor Loughlin, a good man who never panicked. He was well within his rights to stop that fight and I'd have lost.

I said to him, 'Listen, lad, just give me every opportunity to fight. The cut's bad, it's pouring blood. I agree it's got to be stopped, but just let me fight and give me a warning if you're thinking about stopping the fight, because I'll go for him.'

I had to find a way to box through nine rounds – twenty-seven minutes in which I had to make sure he didn't hit the cut. Which was twenty-seven minutes in which the dirty fucker devoted everything he had to trying to get *anything* onto that cut. He was going for it all the time, trying to butt me, using everything he had in his locker to try to get the blood flowing again.

It took four rounds to stop the bleeding. I couldn't even let Bolonti touch me for the first two. As soon as the bell went, Mick would spend a minute squeezing as hard as he could, applying a swab covered in a chemical that would burn all the little molecules inside the cut shut. Then he'd fill it all up with Vaseline. Even after it stopped bleeding, it still looked huge and grotesque, like I had an arsehole on my forehead. And all it needed was for him to catch me there with one punch and the whole thing would open up again.

But he didn't get close. No matter how hard he tried, he didn't lay another glove on me that meant anything. A couple of glancing blows maybe. I just fucking bullied him. I was drawing on skills I'd learned years ago in amateur boxing – relying on my range and footwork to control the fight. By the ninth round, I was exhilarated by it all. Mick had done that good a job that the blood had stopped and I was making a fool of Bolonti. He looked like a novice trying to fight a really good professional.

He'd swing and miss and every time, I'd catch him with a body shot. I'd hear him make the noise that normally would be my sign to jump on him and finish him. That was my only frustration by the end. I couldn't risk it.

Afterwards, during the interviews, one of the security guards told me to look at myself on my iPhone. I caught a glimpse of my eye in a reflection on the black screen of my phone. All it took was one look and my legs went like jelly.

## WINNERS NEVER QUIT, QUITTERS NEVER WIN

A good chin isn't about whether or not you get knocked down. No fighter is invincible. Anybody can get knocked down. Regardless of who you are, how hard you are or what weight you are, if another boxer applies two and a half pounds of pressure to the right point on your chin, your legs shut down and you hit the floor. That's science. That's just a fact. Everyone's button might be in a different place and some people will have a really little button while others a big one, but none of that matters. If you hit me in the right spot I'm going down, and I've got no say in that at all.

What defines a good chin is what happens *after* the fighter gets thrown onto the canvas. The question is: does he get up? I always got up. Every single time in my career that somebody knocked me down, I got straight back up again. As far as I'm concerned, when you get in the ring and you start fighting, you don't stop no matter what. You just don't stop.

A lot of people don't even know the meaning of the words dedication and perseverance. Times are going to be hard. At some point you'll hit a stumbling block. What you need to cultivate is the resilience that means you can just say, 'Fuck it. I'm going to carry on. It's going to hurt, it's going to be horrible, but fucking let's just do it.'

What's the worst that could happen? You might fail. Stick at it, be persistent, try your best. What I would also say is that I'm certain I wouldn't have got up if I thought I was just going to get up to get knocked down again. But I believe I'm getting up there to cause them problems. You knocked me down once, fine. But it's not happening again.

Because I've been honest with myself, I know my

strengths and weaknesses. I've trained hard, I've done my homework and I believe in my abilities. I know that if I break this fight down into pieces and I execute, I'll win. I know this because it's part of my overall goals – I know how each piece fits together into the thing that matters most to me in the world.

More than anything, I feel anger when I see people quit instead. I shouldn't, but I do. I know that they'll regret it, that it'll live with them for the rest of their lives. If I ever quit, it would send me insane. It would finish me. If I knew I'd given up, I wouldn't be able to look myself in the mirror. Here's a fact: if you quit, you can't win. You haven't been beaten by someone – you've beaten yourself. It's a natural law, like gravity.

## THE MORE KNOCKS YOU TAKE, THE EASIER IT GETS

I've found that there's no correlation between talent and resilience. Actually, it's probably often the opposite. The greater the fighter, the lower the amount of punishment they're willing and able to take. They're not used to it and when times get hard, they really struggle. A number of the best fighters of my generation had brilliant careers but they never got to that point where they had to fight on instinct because their senses had been taken away by a cut or a punch that's sent them to the floor.

Whereas fighters like me who have scrapped, who have taken punishment right through our lives, are far better at coping when everything goes to shit. I've never been dropped sparring. Everyone I've gone against I've offered £1,000 on the spot, piled up in a gym bag by the ring, if they could get me to the floor. I've kept that money.

But I've taken some hidings in the gym over the years. I've paid a lot of fighters a lot of money to come in and knock the fuck out of me. David Price absolutely mullered me. Nothing went right for me in that session and he battered me for about six or seven rounds. Most fighters would say, 'I'm having a shit day, I'm getting out.' But it's in me just to take it.

Some fighters will see being knocked about in sparring as a bad thing. For me, it was all a positive. For one thing, I always knew that the most important thing was what happened on the night, under the lights; all this was just a dress rehearsal. More significantly, I knew that every punch I took, every time I took a blow, was something else that would help to prepare me for the shock and violence of actually fighting.

Those hard moments pile up over a lifetime. They mean that when you're really tested, you find that you're ready. You need to think about failure, not ignore it. Don't just practice for a job interview or a presentation that goes perfectly. Think about the one question they could ask that would really trip you up. Then it won't. We've all sat through enough shit best man speeches with pauses for laughter that doesn't come. Hope for the best but prepare for the worst. Luckily for you, this won't involve you paying someone to batter the shit out of you, but it will have the same impact. You don't want to go through life with a glass jaw.

## DRAW ON YOUR PAST

I've never been cut as deep as I was in that fight against Bolonti. But I was able to draw on experiences from my past to help me. It was here that all the years I'd spent studying the masters of their craft came into their own. I'd seen how the best fighters in history responded when they got hurt and knocked down. At that point it hadn't happened to me, but I kept watching fights over and over because I knew that at some point in my career, I'd end up on my arse.

Some of them were clever nuts – they'd just take a second, haul themselves up on one knee by the count of three and then see the rest of the count until it gets to six, breathe and watch the referee count. They'd wait until six or seven to give themselves time to gather their momentum and balance their legs, then they'd leap up all strong again.

All that watching went out of the window when I did get smashed over in the ring. No waiting for me, something in me would always try to get up before the referee got to three. It was like an urgent message in my mind: *I've gotta get up, gotta get up, gotta get up as fast as I can.*

199

Latest it ever took was six, but I'd always be up, wanting to punch the other fighter's face in, showing to the referee I was fit and able to fight. The referee might be a good one who lets stuff flow, they might not. You can't anticipate that and you can't take the risk of them waving the bout off because they think you're fucked, so you've got to be quick.

And there were moments from my own career when I'd been in similarly awkward positions that I could look back on. Back in 2010, when I'd just turned twenty-eight, I went into my first fight with the Jamaican Ovill McKenzie, a 10,000 sell-out for the British Commonwealth Championship, overflowing with confidence. I was the big favourite, 12 and 0, knocking the fuck out of everyone who crossed my path. It was one of the few fights in my career where I hadn't even bothered to do much studying. I'd watched him get knocked out clean by Dean Francis in one round and I'd looked at his record – 18 wins, 9 defeats – and thought, *this fella is just going to get eaten alive. I'm going to smoke him.*

Then this guy, this loser, came out in the first round and before I knew it, he'd banged me on the side of my head and I'd been knocked down on my arse. I got back up on the count of three or four with a pain in my head and an uncomfortable realisation that I was in the ring with a proper rival.

Not that this changed much. In the second round, he hit me right down the pipe on the chin and I dropped flat on my face. That was a heavy, heavy knock-down, the kind that's so hard you don't even know what happened. I heard a loud bang as his glove smashed into me and then it was like an explosion had gone off in my head. My legs went and then all of a sudden, I found myself looking down, with my hands on the floor. A single dazed question swirled through my brain: *What the fuck is going on?*

To this day, I still don't know how I got up, but anyway, on the count of four, there I was. I remember the referee asked if I was OK. I told him I was fine.

Then he said, 'Where are you?'

'I'm in fucking Liverpool,' I told him, just as he'd got to six. 'No fucking way,' I said. 'I'm going to kill him.' I started walking around saying, 'If you don't move out the way, you're fucking dead. I'm going to nail this fella. He's finished.'

The referee stared at me as if he thought I'd gone out of my mind – not the first time in my career that had happened and it certainly wouldn't be the last – and then waved the fight on.

That's when I looked into McKenzie's eyes. The second he returned that glance was the second he lost that fight. His face was a mask of sheer disbelief. He'd hit me with everything he had and still I'd got up. Later on, he'd say he was convinced I was on drugs. He'd started out working as a doorman, he said, and it was only people who were off their tits who could withstand that sort of punishment.

That was it. He fell apart. For the first two rounds he'd been fighting out of his skin. His speed was unbelievable, his power was unbelievable. All it took was planting that seed of doubt in his mindset and it was as if every ounce of his strength and agility had been drained from him.

It was easy after that. I just walked through him and knocked him out in the seventh round. This cunt had knocked me down twice in the first two rounds, he had all the momentum with him, he was fighting levels above what he was normally capable of. This should have been a very fucking good day for him. Instead, he threw it all away because he got spooked. It didn't matter how hard his punches were that night or how quick he could move his feet, he lost his nerve. That moment when he needed his mindset to be resilient, it crumbled.

The specific circumstances of that contest were different to my fight with Bolonti, but the thing that shored up my confidence was knowing that I'd been rocked by an unexpected sequence of events in the ring and come out the other end victorious. The very fact that I'd survived that sort of trouble once meant that I was confident I'd be able to do so again.

# MASTER THE FUNDAMENTALS

In one sense, the Bolonti fight was a step into unknown territory. In another, it was just a reaffirmation of basic principles. I didn't do what I'd planned to do on that particular night, but I still fought in a way I'd practised over and over in the past. When I unleashed a punch combination on another fighter, I never needed to think about what I was doing, because I'd drilled it in me at the gym until it was second nature. It meant that I had space in my head for the stuff that mattered on the night.

Whenever I fought, I was always supremely fit. I might not have looked aesthetically great, but believe you me, I was in unbelievable shape. That's why whenever I got knocked down, I was always up at the count of six or seven at the latest. Other fighters stumbled because their balance is all over the place. I never did. When I got up, my legs were strong beneath me because of all the work I'd put into the camp. That work wasn't sexy – nobody could see it on Instagram – but I knew I could rely on it. Against Bolonti, I had to revert to a fighting style that I'd used in the amateurs. Again, it was an example of me being able to draw on fundamental skills that were ingrained in me through years of practice.

Never forget how important the essential building blocks of your profession are. Often, when things go south, they're the things you'll have to rely on. Whatever your trade, make sure you've mastered the fundamentals. Practise them until you can do them blindfolded. You never know when you might need them.

# ACCEPT CHAOS

Sometimes your carefully laid plans will be exploded by a mistake or an unexpected event. Those things happen – you'd be an idiot if you pretended they didn't. As much as I'd want to dominate another boxer, I couldn't control every single move they made. Bolonti's shut-eyed punch was a fluke. It just happened to be a fluke that reduced my face to a bloodied mess. And nor can you control every aspect of the world. It's too big, too chaotic for that. You can control your reactions to the shocks life throws you and you can also do everything you can to make sure that when you do face those challenges, you're prepared.

Consciously or not, I was preparing myself for the possibility that things would go south. Don't get me wrong, I'd always go into fights thinking I'd win. But you have to find a balance between that belief that you'll prevail and an acknowledgement that times will get tough. If you don't have enough of the latter, you'll find yourself constantly surprised by bad news, which can have a devastating effect on your motivation. People who pretend to themselves that 'everything will be OK, no need to worry' are those who don't take the time to cultivate the discipline needed to confront the brutal realities of life.

So when you think about your goals, devote an equal amount of attention to considering the obstacles you might encounter on the way to achieving them. Think about what could go wrong and how you'll respond. That way, when issues do come up – which I guarantee they will – you'll already be psychologically prepared. You'll be able to put them in perspective: this is just a bump in the road, nothing more.

## ACKNOWLEDGE THE PROBLEM

When I felt blood pouring onto my chest, it would have been madness to pretend everything was OK. Everything was far from fucking OK. Acknowledging that I was in trouble was a start. If I pretended the problem wasn't there, I was never going to be able to solve it. But nor was it a moment to wallow in self-pity. If I convinced myself that the problem was bigger than it really is – perhaps because I want an excuse – then I'd be more likely to be defeated by it. The fact is, while the cut was a setback, it was only that. I was able to put it in perspective and stay calm.

## THE FIRST TIME YOU SPEW IT
## IS THE HARDEST

John 'Duke' Doolan was Jimmy's best friend at the Rotunda. He was never a great boxing coach. He was just a hard fucker who you could always rely on to tell you exactly how he felt. But just as we were preparing for the ABAs, he gave me one of the most important pieces of advice I've ever had. 'I'm not the best boxer,' he told me. 'I'm not going to tell you how to beat fighters. I'm not going to tell you how to do this and that. One thing I'll give you is, don't you ever spew it. The first time you spew it, it's the hardest. After you've spewed it once, you'll spew it again and spew it again. So just do me a favour and don't ever spew it.' That's stuck with me for ever. I never ever spewed it.

Duke had seen something. He always knew I had ability and he knew that I could punch like fuck. He'd also spotted that there were times when I didn't want to work as hard as some of the others or when I was so drained physically that I couldn't, and yet I carried on. For instance, we'd go out on a run or hit the circuits and I wouldn't be able to keep up with the other, more natural athletes. It wasn't laziness, it was because I was the biggest in the gym and my body struggled to match the pace they set.

On some days I'd force myself so hard that I'd be puking at the end of the session. The other lads would be laughing at me, calling me a big girl for being so fucked that I was emptying my guts. Duke was proud, though. 'He's not quitting, that kid.'

And I've never forgotten what Duke told me. What he meant was: if you quit once, you won't be able to stop quitting. It'll become a habit and the thing with habits is that they can be very hard to break. You can't afford to allow even that tiny crack in the wall, because before you know it, the whole house will have fallen to pieces. If there had been a morning when I decided that I couldn't carry on, it wouldn't have been a one-off. It would have been the first in a sequence of mornings when I spewed. That sequence would have ended with me drifting out of the sport.

I've never quit anything I've ever done. No matter how hard it's got, no matter how much I don't want to put my trainers on and get out there. I'm the same now, with my knackered old body and nothing to train for. I'll get on my Peloton and after twenty minutes, I'll just be thinking, *fuck this, I can't be arsed. My knees are killing. My knees are on fire.* But I don't quit, I can't give in. Because I know that if I do, the chances of me getting back on that bike the next morning will already be shrinking fast.

That's the attitude I always had in the ring. Even in fights when I've been getting outboxed or I'm getting outpunched and my face is fucked and my nose has been broken, my hands smashed to pieces, I just can't give in. That's because I've always taken Duke's words to heart: quitting becomes a habit – make sure you never start.

# SUMMARY

- Life will throw all sorts of shit at you. You can't change that, but you can change how you respond to those situations.

- If you pretend that life is always going to be a bed of roses, you're setting yourself up for a big disappointment. Think about what could go wrong. If you can, think about what practical steps you can take if the worst were to happen. But try to prepare yourself mentally, too.

- You build resilience incrementally. It's not something that's handed to you like a new suit off the rack. Get out there. Every knock you take will make you stronger. Every setback you experience will make the next one easier to absorb.

- When you have your fundamentals sorted, it leaves space in your brain to find new solutions to the situation in front of you.

- When your back is against the wall, draw on times in the past when you've overcome obstacles or beaten tough situations. Knowing that you've made it through before will help you to believe you can do so again.

- Never give up. Just. Don't. Do It. If you quit once, you'll never stop.

# CHAPTER 8
# THE NIGHTMARE

30 November 2013, Quebec City, Canada

*This isn't what I'd expected. This isn't what I wanted. I throw a punch at Adonis Stevenson. Any other fighter and I'd have felt a lightning bolt shoot up my arm as my fist connected viciously with his chin. But he's moved so quickly out of my reach that I'm left swiping uselessly at empty space.* What the fuck is this?

*His judgement of distance is incredible, a sickening realisation that hits me harder than his punches. He has an elusive, quicksilver ability to tell exactly when he's two or three inches away from me that cannot be captured in video footage. I'll think I'm safe, then suddenly he appears out of range and catches me with these hard accurate shots. Almost as soon as he's leaned in to smash me with that right hand, he's darted away again. It feels impossible to grasp him. Time after time I've attacked and yet I always struggle to land anything meaningful. It's like fighting a ghost. In the third round he catches me with a straight left on the forehead. There's so much power in his fists. I hear a sickening crack and think he's crushed the bone. I think:* oh my God, he's cracked my fucking skull.

*I just need one chance to land the punch that will destroy him. But my body is empty. I feel as if I've got nothing left. I'm clinging on, to be honest, and every second that goes by drains even more from me. I think about my bravado in the press conference. I'd felt sure of victory then. Now another, far less welcome, outcome seems inevitable. My stomach turns, my mouth dries. I bite down on my guard and try to stop thinking about defeat.*

I'd crippled my body to make weight for the Adonis Stevenson fight. I'd started the camp at fifteen stone six, I needed to get to twelve stone seven. I knew it would be a big ask, but I didn't know how hard it would be. I'd struggled to shed pounds throughout my career and had discovered that losing weight became steadily harder the older I got. There's a photograph of me taken when I was down to thirteen stone three – ten pounds still to lose and there's nothing left of me. I'm a fucking corpse.

I'd felt strong right through camp and then the moment I dipped below 185 pounds, I was fucked, absolutely fucked. I realised then, far too late, that I just couldn't function at any point under thirteen stone three. As I stood on the scales, I thought, *I can't muster anything.* I realised I'd be able to manage two, maybe three minutes of good hard fighting in a thirty-six-minute bout.

That fear was given an extra edge every time I thought about my opponent. He was a vicious hitter: pound for pound, the most dangerous puncher in the world at the time. He was a small fighter, but he had such a long reach. I'd never experienced anything like it.

Stevenson was called Superman. The thing was, he was no hero. There's nothing unusual about a boxer with a past they'd rather not dwell on. But Adonis was fucking nasty. He'd been a violent pimp. He'd beat the prostitutes he controlled or forced them to fight against each other in a gruesome parody of a boxing match, complete with gloves. The women hated him. Two of them had been rendered so desperate by everything he put them through that they actually tried to kill him. When he finally got caught and sent to prison, he'd got into a fight and put another inmate into a coma.

He wasn't the kind of guy you wanted to face when you're drained of all of your power and energy. I knew I'd have to find a way to guide my way through this fight. The problem was, the route didn't seem that clear.

I still had four pounds to lose with an hour before the weigh-in – the only time I'd ever been in that position. The worst of it was that two days before, on the Wednesday, I was bang on the weight. But then I'd eaten two chicken breasts, washed down with 500ml of water, which somehow made me gain five pounds. I got up at 10 a.m. on the morning of the weigh-in, having slept in my tracksuit with the heating on in my room at full blast.

That's how I ended up sitting in a hot bath full of salt. Kerry Kayes, a former bodybuilding champion and the best nutritionist in the world, a guy who'd been with me almost since the beginning, had travelled out to Canada with us.

He said to me, 'Your body is now in a complete state of shock. It won't lose any more weight naturally. You can go on the treadmill for forty minutes and I guarantee you won't lose a single pound. The only way you're going to lose weight now is if you physically draw it out of your body.'

'Great,' I said. 'How can I do that?'

'You have to get in a bath so hot it's going to hurt and it's got to be full of salt.'

We rushed down to the hotel's restaurant, persuaded them to give us a big bag of salt and then sped back up to my room.

Once I'd emptied the salt into the bath, I turned the water on and watched the steam rise as it built up heat. To begin with, I poured ice-cold water on myself. *That hurt,* I thought. Although I soon forget whatever discomfort it had caused. As soon as I stepped into the bath, I felt a pain unlike any I'd ever experienced. There's no agony that compares to feeling your skin burning and knowing that you'll have to endure that experience for another fifteen or twenty minutes.

In a doomed bid to divert my mind, I put Kevin Hart on my iPad and listened to some stand-up. I balanced it precariously on the other end of the bath and during twenty minutes of agony, I alternated between laughing at his jokes and crying at the burning sensation that felt as if it were stripping the skin from every inch of my body. I think it was the closest I've ever come to a mental breakdown. All the while, Fran, who was standing at the foot of the bath, looked on in total shock. My friend Gary, who didn't believe making weight was worth this agony, kept on urging me to get out. But I was already in too far.

It took twenty minutes to force those last four pounds out of my body. For all the good any of this had done me. I hadn't eaten for two days. The last thing that had passed my lips was a single glass of water at 6 p.m. the night before. For almost a week, I'd been draining myself; dragging my energy levels further and further down.

I've never been so convinced that I was dying. One by one, my organs felt like they were shutting down. When you get to that point, it's not just that your tongue is dry and your mouth feels like sandpaper. Although those things were horrible. A moment comes when you can only think about food. Your mind plays tricks. A running tap becomes the source of almost unbearable temptation. You have a paranoid conviction that everybody except you is eating and drinking their fill. It's the kind of mental state that leaves you with scars.

I was fucked.

The weigh-in was nasty, too. All week, Stevenson and his hangers-on had been baiting me, trying to intimidate me. They were just fuckers being cheeky. I wasn't bothered. Instead of dwelling on it, I spent time trying to find out personal information about Stevenson and his team that I could use to my advantage.

When I watch the footage back from the weigh-in, I'm struck by how thin and pale I look, like I need a good meal. Which I did. And then your eyes turn to Stevenson, who was five foot eleven of coiled aggression and strength. He was the kind of fighter who could look dangerous just walking into a room.

When I stared into his eyes as we stood there above the scales and called him a pimp, it was because I wanted to even things up a bit. I saw disbelief on his face and then pure naked rage. It was like he couldn't believe I'd had the nerve to go there. He lost his shit, started getting into my face. I was in my stride by that point, so I started in on his best friend, who followed him around the place like a cheerleader.

'And you can't say anything,' I told him. And then I let him have it using something from his personal life that I knew would mess with his head.

He lost his shit, too. Stevenson came at me and pushed his head in my face. *Fine,* I thought. *If that's the way you want it.* I just pulled my head back and dotted him right on the nose. It might have been the only thing about the fight and the months leading up to it that I actually enjoyed. That was the street in me coming out.

For a few minutes amid all that madness, I felt a sense of exhilaration. I didn't care what happened to Stevenson or whether I'd hurt him. The fracas was over and now the fight was on. I'd made the weight – I was smack bang on twelve stone seven, not an ounce over or under – and I'd seen that I could get to him. I thought, *I'm going to become world champion.* I'd convinced myself that the worst was behind me, so I announced that I'd knock him spark out in three or four rounds. *I'm going to have a good time,* I thought. *This is going to be the one.*

I don't remember much about the fight itself, which is probably for the best, all things considered. All I have is little flashes. Everything else is a blur. There was the brief glimpse I caught of Rachael as I walked to the ring. I hadn't seen her for seven weeks. She had tears in her eyes and it broke my heart in two. I didn't even stop to touch or kiss her. I didn't say anything – I just nodded.

Then there was the sickening understanding that Stevenson possessed an almost supernatural awareness of space. And the dawning realisation that my plan of biding my time and working myself into the fight slowly wasn't working.

The excitement I'd felt at the weigh-in had been replaced by the brutal arithmetic of the situation. I'd dropped so much weight that I knew I couldn't fight for thirty-six minutes. Mick had done a fine job getting me to this point, but now my body had betrayed me. All I had left in me was two minutes of decent work and the conviction that I still had enough to chin him, as long as I got the chance. I'd have to wait for my moment and then knock him out.

But when that moment did come, in the third round,

when I hit him on the side of the head and sent him sprawling on the floor (the referee said he'd slipped – he didn't, I put him down), I couldn't make him pay. That was the end of me. I was on borrowed time after that.

In the sixth round, he caught me with a huge shot that I didn't see coming. There was nothing I could do about it. He hit me so hard I went to sleep on my feet. I went to my corner and bollocked my coach, calling him a fucking idiot because I thought he'd thrown the towel in. He hadn't – it was the referee who'd saved me. In fact, probably saved my life. I was so concussed I had no idea what was going on. The next day, once I could finally bring myself to watch the replay, I had to apologise to him.

Defeat is the loneliest place in the world. You feel as if you've got no one, that you're on your own. I never classed Nathan Cleverly as having beaten me. After that fight, I wasn't really scarred, I thought I'd won. I was more annoyed than anything. In my head I'd been the better fighter on the night. As I saw it, Stevenson was the first genuine loss of my career. I'd given everything and it wasn't enough, which broke my heart. I knew that I had to work to recreate myself and get back into the mix. But knowing that was easy. Doing that was hard.

Once everything was over, I went back to my hotel room. I didn't want to speak to anyone. I didn't see my wife. Nobody. The idea of other people seeing or talking to me seemed impossible. I feared it'd crush whatever was left in me. I lay there in my room and cried myself to sleep. Maybe other things happened, maybe not. I don't remember much from that night.

When I woke the next day, the embarrassment and shame began all over again: you don't want to be seen, so you just try to disappear. As you move around the hotel, you keep your cap on and your head down – you don't want to speak to anyone.

After all the big-up and all the build-up, after all the talk of 'I'm going to do this, I'm going to do that, I'm going to be a world champion,' I'd been stopped on my feet. I was out cold standing up. I never believed that could happen to me. And yet it had. As far as I was concerned, nothing I'd achieved mattered any more. I was a failure.

When you've had a setback, everything can feel like it's falling apart at the seams. It can feel like the world is against you and that you've lost control. Everything is fucked, your dreams are dead and you're never going to get to where you want to go. One of the best things I did after the Adonis Stevenson fight was to start taking positive steps almost immediately.

In the empty days that followed my defeat, I spent a lot of time thinking. That kind of setback makes you question yourself. I went over what had happened again and again. A couple of things were immediately clear: the buck stopped with me. It was nobody else's fault. I was the fighter. It was me who got into the ring. I was the one who'd trained for months on end. I was the one who'd been beaten.

I had to work out where I'd gone wrong. What weaknesses in me or my preparation had the fight exposed? It was a process that demanded complete honesty. Watching the fight back, it was immediately obvious to me that I'd left it too late to go for Stevenson. That had been a massive mistake.

It hadn't just been a question of poor tactics. As broken as I felt, there was still enough of me that believed I was good enough to be a world champion. But I knew I couldn't carry on doing old things the old way and hoping for a new result. I was fooling myself if I thought that fighting at light heavyweight was making the most of my abilities. I wasn't really throwing punches against Stevenson, I was waving my hands at him. It was exciting to think that once I started fighting at my proper weight division, I was going to be so much more powerful and dangerous. At cruiserweight, my punch would regain the ferocity that I'd always been so proud of.

That was the first positive step I could take. I started lifting weights within four days of the fight. You could see the difference almost immediately, as I began to look far bigger and healthier. I was taking on proper nutrition, powerlifting and thriving on the idea that my training would now be about improving as a fighter rather than running endless miles to try to make 175 pounds.

As good as it felt to be back in the gym like this, I also

knew that I was putting off something that I had to do, even if the thought of it alone was killing me. Right through the whole camp I'd had a nagging feeling that something was wrong. That feeling had only grown once we'd reached Canada. But it was only as I sat miserable on the flight home that I could really admit it to myself. I needed a new coach and I needed to find a new way of preparing for fights.

Mick McAllister had been a brilliant coach for me for years. He knew me and my game inside out. In fact, it was Mick who'd been on at me for a long time to go to cruiserweight, because he always thought I'd be better at that level. More than that, he was a huge part of my life. He was one of those men who gave so much passion and energy to the Rotunda without ever asking for a penny in return. It was never about the money with Mick. He'd put years into my career, from the very earliest days, through to the ABA titles and beyond. He'd been there right through, sacrificing time with family and friends in order to help me.

And yet he was sixty years old. I couldn't expect him to be able to do the things physically that he'd been able to pull off a decade before. He was also old-fashioned about quite a lot of things, too. Mick had always been an absolutely amazing amateur coach, but deep down, I didn't believe that he'd be able to give me what I needed to go to the next level of the professional game. I needed new perspectives. I needed someone who could challenge me in fresh ways.

In addition to that, I'd started to think that the way we

were doing camps was wrong. During our preparations for the Adonis Stevenson fight, we'd followed a familiar path. The first section was in Liverpool. I'd be back and forth between the Rotunda and my home, somehow trying to squeeze in what I thought was a normal family life alongside it.

I'd wake up at home and my kids would see me get out of bed, but very soon I'd be in my training gear off to the gym. When I returned, I'd be empty and tired. Whenever the boys tried to speak to me, I'd tell them that I was tired and that they needed to leave me alone. I didn't want to speak – I just wanted to eat my food and then go to bed. This would go on for three months. I was physically present and yet mentally, I was barely there at all. All the same, it was an existence I'd got used to and I couldn't really imagine any other. I was like a fish: I almost didn't realise there was a world outside water.

After that, I lived with McAllister, Fran and Gary in Jersey City for four weeks before we went on to Quebec for the fight. We'd followed that routine two or three times before. The others enjoyed being there and were desperate to help in any way they could, but I realised that wasn't an environment that was right for me. It was good having mates around you on rest days, when we could go on walks or to shopping centres or wherever the fuck. The rest of the time, however, I realised I needed to be on my own so I could focus on the fight. When I'm by myself, then I'm not worried about whether other people are bored or happy. I can give my full attention to the stuff I know is most important at that moment in time. I don't expect anything and nobody expects anything from me. I needed to be lonely when I was in camp to get the best out of myself. That might sound selfish, but it's what I realised I needed.

Dave Coldwell was the obvious person for me to speak to. Dave had so much experience and expertise. He'd learned an incredible amount from working with the great Brendan Ingle and had then gone on to train some of the best fighters around. He was also very definitely based in Sheffield, where his family lived. It's possible that if I'd offered him head-spinning money, he might have dragged his roots up and hauled them over to Merseyside, but him being on the wrong side of the Pennines was what I wanted. There was one other thing. Although Dave had trained world champions before, he'd never made one. I thought the idea that I could be his first would be another incentive – for both of us.

When I called Dave about potentially taking a role, he'd actually taken a step back from training. But he didn't need much persuasion. Mick would be another matter.

To begin with, I tried for a compromise. I took Mick to Long Lane boxing club and I said, 'Mick, we need help. We need to bring someone in. And I think the person we should bring in is Dave Coldwell.'

'What do you mean?' he asked.

'I just think now we're going to move to cruiserweight, he's the ideal person to bring in.'

'No,' he said, 'I'm not answering to no one. I'm the coach.'

'You're going to be the coach. You're going to be in the corner. But bringing him in will be a great addition to me going to cruiserweight and also he can do the physical work.'

'No, absolutely not, no.'

That left me with a tough decision. I knew Dave was the key to me making a success of going to cruiserweight. I had no doubt about that. But there was still a part of me that was saying, 'It's safer to keep things the same. You're comfortable where you are now. Why risk ripping everything up and starting again in a city you barely know?' On top of all this, I knew that Mick would take it hard if I left. I didn't want to leave him, because I felt such a strong sense of gratitude to him for everything he'd done. I had so much love and respect for him; in many ways, he was like a grandfather to me.

I went with Dave. Mick hasn't spoken to me since. We were fifteen years in – he'd coached me ever since I was a kid at the Rotunda. I can understand his hurt, but I hope he knows how much I still adore him. I'll always think the world of Mick and I'll always love his wife, Julie, and his children, Mick and Hayley. I'm so grateful for everything he did for me and although I wish we still had a relationship, I've got to accept that he's made his choice.

As far as I'm concerned, the decision I took had nothing to do with Mick's abilities. It was all about me and what I needed for my family. If I saw the chance to learn something new from another trainer, then I had to take it. A fighter only gets one career, so sometimes they have to do things that can appear selfish. We're not like coaches, who get to work with dozens of boxers. And ultimately, I was the one taking punches. I was the one who was going out there and getting hurt.

I hated having to make that call and yet I knew deep down it was the right thing to do. I wouldn't have become world champion if it hadn't been for Dave Coldwell. In a game in which any fool can claim to be a boxing coach as long as they've paid the fee to get the licence, Dave stands out as a proper teacher. He educates fighters, providing them with skills and techniques they didn't even know they needed. Along with Jimmy Albertina, he's the best thing that ever happened to my career.

It was clear from the very first day that Dave and I were going to work well together, even if his methods and techniques were different to anything I'd experienced before and were at times hard to get my head around. It wasn't so much that he was a better coach than Mick had been. It was more that he offered a completely different approach, which was exactly what I needed at that point in my career.

I started learning new things the second I walked into his gym. Dave added layers to my game. Mick McAllister had been obsessively focused on my feet, which meant that my footwork was brilliant. Dave recognised what I was good at and he wasn't interested in messing about with stuff that didn't need to be fixed. But he was also able to understand where I had room to improve, like my defence and my counter-punching, and then he worked relentlessly to force me to become better.

Dave worked me hard. He didn't just have a deep understanding of my strengths and weaknesses, he also knew how to get the best out of me. He was quicker to praise me than Jimmy had been. At the same time, he was always on at me, challenging me to push myself even harder. He'd say things like, 'How much do you really want it? I always hear you say no one will ever want it more than you, but how much do you *really* want it?' That would always light a fire under my arse. Sometimes we'd clash over something he'd asked me to do and we'd end up not speaking to each other for days. Other times I'd get a cob on but work even harder, just to prove him wrong.

He was just like Jimmy Albertina in that respect: all I ever wanted to do was impress him. And you couldn't buy his respect, you had to earn it. So when he had a little dig at me, my reaction would be: 'I'll show you how much I fucking want it, you twat.' Then I'd go and do extra work in the gym. Sometimes I'd stay in the gym an extra half an hour just to annoy him.

Although my training was going well – I'd easily put on the two stone extra I needed to fight as a cruiserweight – I couldn't ever quite shake off the anxieties that had accumulated after my loss at Stevenson's hands. Defeat hadn't just been a massive blow to my pride, it had also affected my confidence.

I'd never questioned my chin before and yet, as my first fight back approached, I found myself asking: 'Can I still take a shot?' Dave had done so much to rebuild my confidence after my defeat, but when it was time for sparring, Dave had brought in a relatively unknown cruiserweight who turned out to be a bit of a puncher. I was levels above this guy and yet I found myself thinking, *just keep away from me – I don't need to get clocked early.*

I realised that I'd felt the impact of getting stopped by Stevenson much more deeply than I'd first thought. It was sending my mind haywire. I was second-guessing myself, trying to work out how worried and afraid I really was. It was hard to convince myself that I truly was a contender.

And then Eddie Hearn, who I think had lost a bit of faith in me ever becoming world champion, matched me with a bruiser called Valery Brudov, who'd more knockout wins under his belt than I'd had fights. When you come up to a new weight division, you're supposed to be matched up with a nice easy touch – Brudov was anything but.

Right from the earliest seconds, it was clear he was dangerous. He rocked me straight away. He caught me on the top of the head and for a couple of seconds, everything just went. It wasn't enough to knock me down, but that clip was enough to let me know that he was there and that I was in a fight. From that moment on, I was very wary . . . right up until the final round, when I knocked him unconscious with a left hook that threw him flat on his back so hard and so fast that he snapped his ankle in half on the way down.

Even after that victory, the memory of what happened against Adonis Stevenson stayed with me. I was heartbroken and the defeat haunted me for the next five or six fights. It was always on my mind. I was desperate for revenge, but whatever Stevenson said, I knew there was no chance that he'd have fought me at cruiserweight, because we both knew I'd have eaten him alive. It wasn't until I beat Nathan Cleverly in our rematch that I was able to rid myself of the memory. Smashing the great cardio machine to pieces over twelve rounds, outboxing and outworking him every step of the way, helped me to put it all to bed.

After that, I could get on with my career.

## IF YOU WORK HARD, YOU CAN TRANSFORM FAILURE INTO OPPORTUNITY

Defeats or failures are always the end of something. This means that if you look at them in a different way, they can also represent the beginning of something new. I could have looked at that loss and decided the only thing I needed to change was to fight in the right weight class. I could have blamed everything on that. But I learned really important things after I was beaten by Adonis Stevenson. One of them was the freedom to start again. Without that loss, I don't think I'd have made all the changes that ultimately led to me winning the world title. If I hadn't been beaten that night in Quebec, if I hadn't had that bleak period of soul-searching, I wouldn't have hired Dave Coldwell, I wouldn't have moved to Sheffield, I wouldn't have achieved all of my dreams at Goodison Park.

When things are ticking on, when they're OK, it can be dangerous. You get used to thinking that because something is good enough, then there's no need to change it. It gets to the point when the idea of mixing things up can start to feel like it's not worth the effort or you get frightened of doing what, deep down, you probably know needs to be done. To begin with, that defeat felt like it was the end of everything. Instead, it was actually the jolt I needed.

## THAT'S ON ME

When people suffer a setback, they tend to do one of two things. They'll either double down and say, 'Actually, I was doing the right thing before, I just got unlucky. I'll carry on doing the same thing again and again.' Or they can be humble and accept that they need to make changes.

Very few boxers ever shoulder the blame; they're cowards, the lot of them. It's a habit that starts when they're young: amateur fighters lose a fight and then move to another gym because they convince themselves that it was the coach's fault.

227

And that mentality persists right through the career of ninety per cent of fighters. They'll claim they weren't trained right, or they weren't given the right advice or nutrition or whatever the fuck. My view is always, 'Well listen, mate, you knew that before the fucking fight.'

The stuff that Deontay Wilder came out with after he was beaten by Tyson Fury was crazy. He doesn't genuinely believe that Tyson Fury's gloves were fiddled with. He doesn't genuinely believe that Tyson Fury punched him with the wrist part of his glove. That's insane. He *knows* that's insane. But he's got that many yes-men around him telling him what they think he wants to hear that he's actually ended up buying into the hype and the nonsense.

What he should have done instead was sit down and think properly about what really happened and why. It's very hard to be very honest with yourself, because sometimes you're not going to like what you uncover. It's always going to be easier to blame other people. But if you want to get the right results, in any walk of life, you've got to face up to the reality of the situation you're in. When you look in the mirror, you'll know deep down where it went wrong. There's only so many times you can tell yourself the same bullshit before you admit to yourself that, 'Yes, that was my fault. That's on me.'

You have to be brutal. Don't tell yourself comforting fairy tales about why you failed. That's not going to help anyone. Look at it as a sort of audit. Go through what *actually* happened and *why* with the attitude of a forensic accountant.

How did it start? How did it end? When were the mistakes actually made? Defeat is the best teacher. You learn more lessons when you lose than you ever do when you win. Lessons are always there, you just have to be willing to look for them.

That's the process I put myself through after the Stevenson fight. I knew that my approach to making weight had been wrong. I also recognised that I'd chosen to ignore certain things that I knew should have been fixed because I was hoping against hope that they'd resolve themselves on their own. Which, clearly, they didn't. It was fucking difficult. It was also upsetting enough that at one point, I began to cry, but it was also absolutely essential. The end result of me doing that was that I began to put the building blocks in place that would eventually become the foundation of my later success.

Everyone knows how crushing failures or defeats can feel – whatever the circumstances. What you have to try to do is recognise them as a chance to begin again.

## DON'T THROW THE BABY OUT WITH THE BATHWATER

You have to be uncompromising in your search for what went wrong, but don't lose sight of the things that went well, no matter how tempting it might be to want to make a completely fresh start. Dave Coldwell recognised this. He was brilliant at introducing me to new techniques and yet he never tried to interfere with the parts of my game that had taken me to this point. I knew my footwork – my ability to dance while other people my weight only stepped – was a valuable asset, so it would have been foolish to try to reinvent it after one loss. So many boys go from amateur boxing to the professional ranks and forget their footwork along the way, which just turns them into mummies. They end up forgetting about body shots entirely and go 'headhunting' through every fight. I was never interested in limiting myself like that. At the end of the day, it's far better to add to your arsenal of skills than it is to subtract from them.

The other mistake you should be wary of making is over-interpreting a bad day. Sometimes you'll fail to perform not because you've prepared poorly or don't have the necessary skills, but because you woke that morning not feeling 100 per cent or you're distracted by problems elsewhere in your life. Be sure that the change you think you need to implement is necessary. Remember: even legends lose.

## GET BACK ON THE HORSE

Whatever setback you've experienced, you have to accept that it's done, it's over. You can't sit there hoping that the result will be overturned or that some act of God will make everything OK again. Because if you're still holding on to that false hope, you won't be doing the important work of starting again. It's so important that you generate momentum as soon as you can. The longer you leave it, the harder it'll get. If I'd sat around and moped for a few months after the Stevenson loss, I know for a fact that I'd have ended up totally fixated on all the things I couldn't do, rather than reminding myself how good I was and how far I still had to go. That's why I was back in the gym within a week of my loss in Quebec. That's why I was so keen to fight again as quickly as possible.

If you've lost out on getting a job, then instead of dwelling on it or feeling sorry for yourself, get back out there and carry on with your search. It feels good to seize the initiative. My defeats made me a better fighter because they showed me what I could do better. Don't treat a knockback as something closing down. It's just given you the answer to solve the next situation. Before long, you'll find that disappointment is replaced by hope.

# SUMMARY

- Failure is a fact of life. You can't avoid it, so why not try to transform the ruins of your present into the foundations of your future?

- Don't spare yourself in the aftermath of a setback. Find out what went wrong and why. Then commit to doing better next time. Never try to spread responsibility around by blaming others.

- Never forget what got you to this point. Just because you've failed once, it doesn't mean that you're a failure. And you shouldn't jettison everything that made you successful in the first place. Use failure as an opportunity to add to your arsenal, not subtract from it.

- Try to move on as soon as you can. If you spend too much time dwelling on your failure, you'll end up stuck in your past when you could be building your future.

# CHAPTER 9
# BIG MOUTH STRIKES AGAIN

*BJ Flores thinks you can say what you want and avoid the conse-*
*quences. BJ Flores thinks the stuff we've said to each other is just*
*trash talk. BJ Flores is a fucking idiot.*

*I'm different. I might have said stuff for effect before, but this*
*time I mean every word. When I say I'm going to murder him, it's*
*not braggadocio, it's the cold, hard, brutal truth.*

*He's made this chance for himself by stalking me. Fair play. And*
*he's talked shit every time we've come face to face. What he needs*
*to understand is that every time I go into the ring, I'm fighting for*
*my life. It's not a game for me. It's not bright lights and glory; I*
*know there's nothing glamorous about getting your hands, nose or*
*ribs smashed. And yet, if I have to get off the floor a hundred times,*
*I will. I'm dirty, I'm vicious, I don't care how I win.*

*Flores is an Instagram fighter. He exists to throw tough poses in*
*front of the camera. Whereas I've come out to hurt him. I know I*
*look like the sort of traveller who scraps in car parks. Fuck. I don't*
*care. When I hit somebody when I'm wearing ten-ounce gloves,*
*they're going to feel it. You might think I don't really come across*

*like a professional athlete. You might think I'm a bit chunky, a bit flabby. But when I hit you for the first time, you're going to think: What. Was. That?*

*In the first seconds of the fight, Flores still seems confident. It's as if he hasn't listened to a single word of all the warnings I've given him over the last couple of weeks. He still doesn't realise that I was being serious. And for the first couple of rounds, he even holds his own. But by the third round I can see fear in his eyes. He's fought a lot of big punchers, but nobody has ever damaged him like this. Nobody has ever blitzed and bamboozled him.*

*The last few minutes have taught him two big lessons. Number one: I'm the best cruiserweight in the world. Number two: words mean something. If you want to run your mouth off, that's fine, that's the risk you've chosen to take. But you'd better be very fucking ready to back up everything you say.*

The only fight in my whole career that I went into with an agenda was my first defence of the WBC title, against BJ Flores. Except, I wasn't thinking about him – he was just a stepping stone. My focus was almost entirely on David Haye.

Everything had shifted after I'd beaten Makabu. I'd become world champion, the thing I'd dreamed of for so long, and yet here I was, in my shitty hotel room, still doing the same thing as I had when I was a challenger. At night I started thinking: *I've done all the stuff I was supposed to do, why hasn't my life really changed? What am I doing this for? Why am I in Sheffield? Why am I putting my wife and kids through this?*

*Why am I putting myself through this? Why can't I force Dave Coldwell to move to Liverpool?*

It would go over and over and over in my head. I'd achieved all of my goals and dreams. In that respect, I didn't need to fight any more. But we were far from set up and my pride alone couldn't support my family. Fighting could. And if wanted to secure our financial future, a bout with David Haye, one of British boxing's biggest draw at the time, was the obvious answer.

I didn't particularly want to fight Flores. I thought he was a tit then. In fact, I still do now. He's just a pretty boy from Miami who jumps on everybody else's ship and who thinks he's Johnny Big Bollocks. He'd been following me everywhere for what felt like years. Like an absolute knob, he'd turned up at the *Creed* premiere in London with David Haye and was busy chatting shit about how I was just a blown-up light heavyweight. He reckoned I'd never do anything at cruiserweight, could never beat him. Which I thought was an interesting opinion.

It was the fact that he was David Haye's best mate that caught my eye. Eddie had been on at me to fight Flores for a while. I said I would, but only if he could guarantee that Haye would be on ringside commentary. Eddie didn't really understand why I was so keen and I kept my thoughts to myself. But off he went and set it up.

Right through the camp, all the training with Dave Coldwell had been really good, yet I could tell that my mindset wasn't quite right. Usually I'd be spending fight week desperately trying to stop myself from obsessing about the man I was about to go toe-to-toe with. This time round, I realised I was struggling even to focus on Flores. All I could see was David Haye. Which, when I look back on it, was unbelievably stupid of me. Actually, it was worse – it was dangerous.

Nobody had ever knocked BJ Flores out. He'd been in with three world champions previously and had only lost the last one in a split decision, which a lot of people thought should have been given to him. And he had all the motivation in the world: he was that close to achieving his dream in the champion's backyard. But that didn't interest me. When the thought crossed my mind of the fight that was actually coming up, I just said to myself: 'I'm the world champion. I'm going to blast you out in a couple of rounds.' I crashed the weight, picked up an injury to my left hand in my final sparring session and ignored all of it.

I looked shit on the scales when we weighed in, but then so did he. I knew he'd done the weight wrong, trying to shed too many pounds at the last minute, which I knew would leave his body more vulnerable than it would have otherwise. I carried on feeling upbeat. Not quite carefree and yet not too far off it, either. It was only later that night that I suddenly realised that I couldn't afford to lose the fight, because the shame of being defeated on my first defence would be too much. I hated the idea of being remembered as somebody who'd won a title, then spewed it almost straight away, like Tony Tucker, whose reign as world champion lasted a mere sixty-four days.

Even when I got into the ring, even when BJ Flores started eyeballing me, I was only looking at David Haye. Right through the fight, it was David Haye's voice I heard over all the noise in the arena, shouting instructions to his friend from the seat he'd taken in the neutral corner. When BJ Flores looked at me, he saw a championship belt. Whereas I was looking at that tit sitting outside the ring, about to watch his friend get battered, and I saw financial security for my family. David Haye held the keys to my kingdom. It was a calculated risk that I was willing to back up. I knew exactly what I was doing. I went about my business and I made it count.

I turned to David Haye: 'I'm going to fuck you. I'm going to fucking do you in.' All the while, he was sitting there shaking his head in disbelief. It felt like a good idea at the time. I look back now on how I behaved and think, *you absolute tit.* Now that I've got to know him properly, I regret a lot of my behaviour towards Haye – I've changed my opinion of him, he's a sound guy – and yet at the time, all I wanted was to wind him up.

I thought I was levels above Flores. I didn't care about him at all. Before the sound of the first bell had died away, I started taking risks I should never even have been contemplating. I was quicker, stronger and more efficient. I should have been aiming to break him down slowly and yet I got drawn into just trading punches. It was as if I'd forgotten my jab completely. I copped him with a left hook and then he got me with a left hand on the chin. Either of us could have got knocked out. All it needed was for him to catch me on the chin bang on just once and I'd have gone down. I was lucky that the work I'd done with David Coldwell could get me through that fight.

It was a contest in which skill and strategy were less important than aggression and resilience. We were in a brawl and there was no point pretending otherwise. At one point I twatted him one, aimed at the body, but it went so low that I caught him right in the bollocks. It was that kind of fight. He stepped back full of outrage, appealing to the referee, who because he'd been blindsided, hadn't seen anything wrong and just told him to get on with it. Flores was so busy moaning at the referee that he forgot the first rule of boxing: defend yourself at all times. He should have kept his hands up; he didn't and I took advantage of that. Fuck off, I smacked him with another left hook to his chin and boom, he went down.

Almost before Flores had crashed down onto the canvas, I'd walked over to David Haye: 'You're next. You're fucking getting it.' That's why I'd taken those risks: because I wanted him to see me demolish Flores right before his eyes.

I dropped Flores three more times after that. The last time was the only punch in the whole fight that I'd caught him as cleanly as I wanted, but it was enough. Within seconds I was over to Haye again, screaming and spitting through my gumshield. Something happened then. There was a feral chaotic energy in that crowd. It was like they'd smelled blood. And I kicked the inflatable Toblerone that was balanced on the edge of the ring and it had arrowed into his face. 'Fight me. Fight me.' That's when I leaped over the ropes and went for Haye.

I'm not thick. I wasn't going to start a fight while I was wearing boxing gloves and bandaged hands when he'd be there with his bare fists. As if. There was part of me that wanted to give him a belt if I could get close enough, but part of me knew that it would be a very stupid thing to do. I knew damn well that the security guards would get to me before I was anywhere near him. Thank fuck they did.

Red-faced, glistening with sweat, I carried on screaming at Haye, my scratched voice carrying over the roars and shrieks of the crowd. I was hurling threats at him even when I disappeared underneath a mountain of security guys. Haye just stood there, immaculate in his grey suit. For a while he had a complacent smile plastered all over his face, as if he were amused by what he'd seen. But if you watch the footage closely in the minutes that followed, you could see something else beneath his grin: he was rattled.

The whole world could see that I'd laid down a challenge. And now the whole world wanted to see David Haye smash this cocky Scouser prick to bits. He'd gone into that arena to commentate on a fight and he'd come away knowing he'd have to go toe-to-toe with a maniac. Except, of course, that all that craziness had been for show. And I think Haye knew that, which is why he was so unsettled by what he'd witnessed.

It was a weird night. I'd just stopped a man who'd never been stopped, not even by three other world champions. I smashed him inside three rounds. It might have been an ugly fight – one of the worst, and certainly the riskiest, of my career – but it was also a standout result. And yet *nobody*, least of all me, had the slightest bit of interest in that. The 9,000 fans who walked out of the Echo Arena that night didn't waste a word on BJ Flores or my performance. All they were saying was: 'Did you see Bellew attack Haye?'

## YOU MAKE YOUR OWN LUCK

I've got two things going for me: I've always been able to punch like fuck and I'll tell anybody that they're a gobshite. I started out flattening journeymen who couldn't knock the skin off a rice pudding. And as soon as the fight was over, I'd head to the nearest camera and announce that, 'I will fucking baptise anyone.' Those words mattered; they made sure I was on television for my next fight. They forced people to talk about me.

You can't let people be indifferent towards you. Whether they love you or hate you, make them think about you. I understood that from the get-go and as a result, I was a promoter's dream. I always sold the whole show. There are fighters out there who could be megastars: all they need to do is open their mouths. I talk. Sometimes I've ended up making a tit of myself, which is why more than one person has tried to encourage me to curb what I say and let the boxing do the talking. Most of the time, however, it's worked out.

I did all that because I knew, even then, that if you want to move forwards, sometimes you have to give fate a helpful little push. In boxing, there's no such thing as a fluky punch. It doesn't matter if your eyes are closed. If you throw that left hook and it lands, it was *meant* to land. I was always on my toes, looking for new opportunities, because I knew that I couldn't afford to sit around waiting for them to come my way. I used Twitter to make my first world title fight: Nathan Cleverly's opponent Jürgen Brähmer had pulled out, so I created an account and announced that I'd fight him. And that's why I made sure David Haye was ringside commentator for the BJ Flores fight: I wanted Sky cameras to catch me calling him a pussy, because I knew that he'd have to fight me next. The boxing public loves a good rivalry.

I know that a lot of the time it can feel easier to glide through life on autopilot, taking things as they come, but I guarantee that after a while, you'll start to feel frustrated. You'll begin to wonder why it's other people who get what look to you like lucky opportunities. You'll ask yourself why it is that although you feel as if you're working hard all the time, you're not making the kind of progress you'd envisaged. You'll begin to think: *maybe I should have taken a few more risks.*

# BE YOUR OWN CHEERLEADER

Maybe more than any other sport, in boxing you have to open your mouth and sell yourself. If you don't understand that, you won't make it.

I learned about the power of self-promotion at an early age. It was another of the things that came from studying fighters. I looked at the likes of Hector Camacho, Fernando Vargas, Prince Naseem Hamed, James Toney and Roy Jones Jr. and paid attention to how they sold themselves, how they presented themselves to the people who were paying to watch them. As I watched, I tried to take little parts from each of them that I could use for myself.

Mike Tyson didn't say much and when he did, it was something nasty. With him it was very much a case of his actions speaking louder than his words. If you're the sort of person who does the majority of his communication by smashing other boxers' faces in, people will want to see you.

Hector Camacho knocked guys out too, but what really sold him was his braggadocio. To be honest, he couldn't burst an egg, and yet he still found a way of intimidating people. He'd insult you, wear obnoxious clothes, anything to get a rise. Ricardo Mayorga used to smoke cigars and eat pizzas while he stood on the scales during the weigh-in.

Nigel Benn played on his reputation for being vicious and mean and it worked for him. Whereas Chris Eubank dressed himself up in tweeds and ran around lisping 'Hello, sir.' They were all amazing boxers. At the same time, they were amazing showmen. Because they knew that professional boxing is also professional showbusiness. That was where all the feuds and rivalries came from.

*Good,* I thought, *I'll emulate that.*

Everyone in Liverpool is always striving and fighting. It's the only place in the world I know where everyone has the mentality of 'I've got to get on,' which is why it was surprising that as I was coming up as a boxer, there was nobody really flying the flag for the city, nobody really lighting up the game.

Lots of fighters had loads of ability, but none of them really knew how to talk the talk. People like Joe McNally were brilliant in the ring and yet they weren't interested in all the stuff that went on outside. Ultimately, that hurt him. I tried my best for Joe, putting him forwards for Hayemaker and then Frank Warren, but it never happened for him. He had a handful of bouts but if he'd been given the opportunity I still believe he could have been a European champion. All he needed was that one big match that would have showed everybody how good he was. Which is a shame – he would have pissed the British championships. Instead, he lost out to the shitty, political side of the game.

That's not the same as saying he and others like him had bad luck. They just didn't want to do the talking. It didn't matter that they were better boxers than me – I was a better promoter than them. No other amateur was saying or doing the things I was. I was the only fighter who understood what needed to be done and I was the only one who understood that I'd have to accept hate as well as love if I wanted to make it.

It's a sad but true fact that the people who get ahead are those who make others sit up and pay attention. If you don't tell people how hard you're working or what sort of a difference you've made, there's no guarantee that anybody else will notice. If you've done something well at work, celebrate it. Otherwise you might find yourself being passed over in favour of other louder-mouthed colleagues.

## SET YOUR OWN PACE

When I went to the Rotunda that first time and Jimmy told me I wasn't going to box for at least eighteen months, I thought, *fuck this, I'm ready to box now.* I wanted to get out there and test myself in a proper fight, because I knew that doing so would massively accelerate my development. I might have had my tail between my legs ahead of my return to Jimmy's gym almost two years later, but I was also already on my way up. They knew who I was now, they'd seen me render people unconscious, so I wasn't some scraggly kid who'd turned up on their door. I had a record and a medical card with my bouts on it.

Be honest with yourself. If you've still got work to do or things that you need to improve, then cool your jets for a bit. But if you truly do believe you're ready, then don't let other people hold you back. The last thing you want to do is stagnate when you could be greedily hoovering up new experiences and skills.

## TAKE CALCULATED RISKS

So much of boxing is about assessing the ratio of risk and reward. Just getting into the ring against a man who's determined to smash your face in is a risk. At the beginning of your career, when you're fighting journeymen, you don't think so much about losing. It's only when you progress through the ranks and start facing world-class fighters that risk really comes into the equation.

That's when you realise that the odds are no longer stacked in your favour. The 90/10 walkovers become 50/50 battles. You have to start asking yourself whether you really think you can win. You have to assess how many things he can do better than you. How much experience or size or weight am I giving away to him?

When I faced Isaac Chilemba, I knew he'd catch me a lot. I reckoned I'd have to be willing to take four punches clean in the face for every six I landed on him. My bet was that I'd be able to absorb everything he had and then outwork him. It was a calculated gamble, which I wouldn't have made with any other fighter. If I'd tried that approach with David Haye, I'd have been knocked out in the first round.

But it's at that elite level that the rewards can be out of this world. I took a risk by fighting Ilunga Makabu when nobody else would. I fought David Haye even after he threatened to put me into a coma. The risks were evident and yet so were the rewards. That fight not only made me more money than I'd ever even seen in my life, but my victory also elevated me to the top rank of box office fighters.

At some point, if you want to achieve your dreams, you'll have to take risks. That might be remortgaging your home in order to finance a business or swapping a comfortable salary for an uncertain self-employed future.

I threw myself into the BJ Flores fight without really taking my opponent seriously because I was absolutely set on forcing David Haye to take me on. That was a risk and yet I was willing to accept it, because the potential benefits were, for me, worth it. And it was a calculated risk, because although I didn't prepare for Flores as diligently as I might another opponent, I also knew that my performance levels had skyrocketed since becoming world champion. I was fighting out of my skin.

When you're considering doing something that takes you out of your comfort zone, you've got to be upfront about what you stand to lose and what you stand to gain. You also have to have a clear sense of your abilities. I'm not here to say everyone can will themselves into becoming a world champion.

Ultimately, everyone has a very different stomach for risk. I can't tell you how much uncertainty you should expose yourself to – that has to be a personal decision – but I will tell you this: you cannot eliminate all risk from your life. In fact, if you want to get anywhere, at some point you're going to have to embrace it.

## THE HARDER YOU WORK, THE LUCKIER YOU GET

It's no good putting yourself in good positions if you're not in the right mindset to take advantage when you get there. As soon as you get that opening, make sure you commit to it 100 per cent. Try to maximise the chances of converting that opportunity into an achievement.

Ultimately, it all has to be backed up with hard work. You can't wing your way through life, no matter how charming or clever you think you are. If you've made promises, make sure you keep them. If you say you're going to be some-where, make sure you're there. Don't let carelessness be the thing that undermines all the great work you've done.

I was obsessive about getting everything right before I fought. I wanted to square every element away so that I could be confident that I was giving myself the absolute best chance of victory. I knew that I'd created an amazing opportunity for myself by getting to that point, so I couldn't let anything undermine it.

No detail was too small, because those tiny margins

could have been the difference between success and failure. They're the first things that can slip your mind, but very often they'll be the first things to slip you up. That's why I'd turn up at a venue three hours before I actually needed to: I wanted to make sure that whatever happened – traffic, mistakes, cock-ups – I was still going to be there on time. And it would have been no good going into a bout in incredible shape if I was lazy about my kit. So I'd get my hands wrapped a good hour before the action, because there had been times early in my career when my hands felt great for the first five minutes after they'd been wrapped and then I realised they'd gone numb because the blood had stopped. If I'd left that kind of thing to the last minute and hadn't given myself time to fix mistakes, it could have been fatal.

I even took responsibility for the way my low blow was fitted. I'd personally wind the duct tape around my waistband. Then I'd put the low blow on. Only when I was confident it was safe and secure would I then add another layer of duct tape. I'd wrap it round my body once to tighten it, then twist it so the sticky side was facing out before taking it round my body for another layer. Then, when I put my shorts on, they'd stick to the low blow. There was no way they'd move even a millimetre during the whole fight. (This was great for the bout itself, not so great for the moment fifteen minutes before it begins when I remember I need a shit and have try to wipe my arse while wearing my boxing gloves.)

One thing I've found is that coming from where I do,

people tend to make generalisations about me. They're not always favourable. There's not much I can do to change their prejudices, but I can work hard to try to give them as few opportunities as possible to dismiss me out of hand.

So, when I was outside the whole circus of fights and weigh-ins and all that bullshit, I'd be unfailingly polite and respectful. I'll always make sure I say please and thank you. I'll hold the door open for anyone, no matter how old they are. (Obviously, if somebody crosses me, then I chuck those manners out of the window. I'm a polite but very fucking angry driver. I'll wave, let you go, stuff like that, but the minute you've done me, I'll lose my fucking shit straight away.)

Presenting yourself properly is important. In my opinion, everything from your shoes up represents who you are. I can't bear it when somebody turns up wearing rotten trainers. I can't have it. If I walk into a consultation with somebody who I'm meeting for the first time and they're not appropriately dressed, I'm tempted to leave straight away: if they're not taking it seriously, what's the point in being there? I might know fuck-all about what we're discussing, I might not be the brightest there, but I tell you what, I'll look the part.

Recently, I realised that my trainers had dirt on them, so I went into JD Sports, bought another pair and put them straight on. Nobody has any excuse not to be clean and smart. Have a shower, make sure you smell nice. Do that, be on time – *always* be on time – show that you've prepared and you'll gain respect.

# FUCK 'EM

People will tell you you're not good enough. People will tell you that it's not your turn or you don't deserve it. People will tell you it's not your time. People will say that you're not strong or fast enough. People will tell you that you don't want it enough. People will tell you that you're doing it for the wrong reasons. People will tell you that you're aiming too high. People will tell you that the odds are stacked against you. People will tell you a lot of shite. Ignore them.

When people flood you with negativity, there's only one response: fuck 'em. Whenever anybody told me I couldn't do anything, I used what they said as motivation. Always be open to positive criticism, but you should bat everything else away. If they don't like what you're doing, that's their problem, not yours.

# SUMMARY

- Nobody is going to hand you opportunities. Make them for yourself. You only score from the shots you take and good fortune is only ever half the story.

- Don't be afraid of opening your mouth and celebrating your achievements. If *you* don't do that, who else will do it for you?

- Only you will know when you're ready to take the next step, so don't wait for the invitation. If you're happy that you really are in a position to push on, then don't hesitate. Work to your timetable, not other people's.

- When you've made that chance for yourself, make sure you're in the best possible place to seize it. Don't let that opportunity slip away because you haven't prepared properly.

# CHAPTER 10

# NO MATTER WHAT YOU HIT ME WITH, YOU CANNOT HURT ME

*Haye has me backed against the corner. It's the third round of our first match against each other. When he crossed the ropes half an hour ago, he was still convinced that all he needed to do was take his time. And then, blow by blow, he'd take me to pieces. It hasn't worked out like that. I keep evading his grasp, I'm always a half-step ahead of him.*

*He throws a monstrous left hook. It's so quick it's like a whip-lash, and I can see from the way he has put his entire bodyweight into the shot that it's carrying the force of a runaway truck. Haye might already be thirty-six, he might have lost a tiny bit of the aura he had when he was crushing every fighter that crossed his path but he's still possibly the most dangerous puncher in this division. That left hook should settle the fight. It should be the knockout blow that puts me in my place. A full stop at the end of all the vicious words we've hurled at each other over the last few months.*

*Instead he finds himself swiping into empty space. I jerk up, away from his flailing glove, and laugh at him. Three rounds later his Achilles snaps. He should give up. He can barely stand; his balance is fucked; whenever we come together he tumbles to the ground in an ungainly mess of arms and legs. And yet he's still snarling, still trying to damage me. It's like being in the ring with a wounded lion. His face is a mask of hurt and incredulity. Even as I'm smashing him with punch after vicious punch, I don't think he can quite believe what has happened to him.*

*He didn't think this was possible. Nobody thought this was possible. Except me.*

David Haye thought I'd be an easy touch. He was a former undisputed cruiserweight champion of the world, the darling of the British media, and he was up against a live wire Scouse headcase who'd say anything to get attention; a firework who could go off at any minute.

Haye believed I was willing to let myself get smashed to bits in return for a fat cheque. It didn't matter that I was a world champion, fresh from blowing away Haye's friend, BJ Flores, in the first defence of my title; he was convinced our bout was going to be a walk in the park. I'd never seen anyone with that level of arrogance and cockiness – it spilled out of every pore of his body. He sweated conceit.

Even Eddie Hearn didn't think I was going to win that first bout with Haye. In Eddie's opinion, Haye was a proper heavyweight and I wasn't. Like Haye, he thought I was happy to swap a beating for a big wedge of cash.

In one respect, David and Eddie were both right: I *was* fighting for the money. Where they were wrong, very wrong, was that, deep down, I believed that I could and would win. Haye had conveniently forgotten that when I was a boy, fresh off my first ABA title, I'd kicked his arse while we were sparring. I'd been given £100 for the privilege of forcing him down on one knee. This time, I was going to be paid a lot more to do a lot worse.

To this day, I don't think David understands how I beat him. I'm not sure that he can even quite believe that I *did* beat him. He told me this recently, and I said: 'That's your problem right there.' I asked him why he never thought to put a rematch clause in.

'Tone, if somebody had told me you'd beat me, I'd have laughed in their face. You don't understand. As far as I was concerned, it couldn't happen.'

All of that meant that when I leaned in close at the first press conference, so close I could smell his breath, looked him bang in his eyes and said, 'I'm going to smash your fucking face in,' I could see him struggle to process what had just happened. I could tell he was thinking, *the cheeky bastard – he actually thinks he can beat me.* He clenched his jaw. Then I pushed him really hard on his chest. Disbelief was followed quickly by anger. You see so many things when you're in that close. I watched the precise second that Haye lost it and punched me right on the chin. He thought I was going to drop. That was his second surprise.

'What's that, you pussy? Are we punching at press conferences now?' I asked.

'We're punching at press conferences.'

'Good, I know where we stand now. Don't dare come head-to-head with me again.'

The security guards rushed in and the press went crazy. We were surrounded by noise and chaos, and it felt as if there were an explosion of camera flashes, but I was calm. I'd shown Haye that I meant business.

I'm brilliant at all the trash talk and mind games. I know that if I can embroil my opponent in a drawn-out psychological battle, then by the time we're under the lights, I'll already have gained a psychological edge. Some fighters won't play at all, no matter how hard you prod them. Usyk was like that. He acted all soft during the build-up to the fight and made a big thing of not being able to speak English. That was true, but what I realised later, and wished I'd known before, was that the fucker could definitely understand it.

It was different when I fought David Haye the first time round. The psychology of our contest was more important than just about any other element. Over the days that followed our little spat there were more press conferences, more media commitments. I saw them as a game. All I wanted to do was mess around with his mind, keep pissing him off. For him it was mental torture. I kept winding him up, tighter and tighter, playing on that big fucking elephant of an ego he has. I wanted to annoy him so much that he ended up wasting energy on that rather than thinking about the things he should have focused on. Lots of it was stupid. 'David, you've got a hairband on; I can't take you seriously.' But I knew it would get under his skin.

Maybe in the past I'd have got sucked into the drama of it all and ended up doing something stupid. People used to be able to play on my emotional vulnerabilities: I got too attached to people, too involved in situations. But my mentality was changing by then. For most fighters at the very top, whatever they might say, boxing is a business to them. Don't get me wrong, someone like Anthony Joshua is a fighter to his core, but he's been operating at such an elevated level for so long that whatever rough edges he might have had were rubbed off years ago.

Tyson Fury is the same. It's all business to him. He's acting that bravado. For a long time, I was in that minority of boxers who still operated with a street mentality. I saw the same in Dillian Whyte. That time between becoming world champion and fighting Haye was when things shifted and my priorities changed. I wasn't a street kid any more. I couldn't take things personally as I would have once upon a time because that just didn't work in the top echelons. I realised that everything had to be about business first and fighting second.

That meant that I could keep a distance, no matter what David said. I had nothing left to prove. I'd been British, Commonwealth and world champion. I was only fighting now to secure my family's future. He couldn't tick me over. What could he say? That I'd been knocked down? So had he. That I'd lost fights? Yeah, you've lost fights, too, David. I forced him to sit down and think: *How the fuck am I going to get to this fella, because he's getting to me?*

It also meant that when he announced live on TV that he was going to put me in a coma and that the next time my family saw me it would be to visit me in hospital, it didn't affect me as much as he'd obviously hoped it would. I was by myself in my hotel room at the time and to begin with, I was fucking outraged by his words. Nobody had ever gone after me like that. My head was buzzing with thoughts. *Why,* I started asking myself, *would I ever put my kids in this position?*

But then after an hour or so of sitting there thinking about it, I got my head round what he'd done. I began to see it as a source of strength. He wasn't the sort who'd usually talk about personal stuff. In bringing up my family, he'd played his final card. That was the worst he could do or say and it couldn't touch me. I knew then that he was fucked. He'd called me everything, tried to degrade me, and it hadn't worked.

That thought calmed me down. A couple of weeks later, he came to Liverpool and made a fool of himself while wearing a bizarre pair of dark glasses, calling Scousers every name under the sun, bringing up people's mothers. He was fantastic at that press conference.

At one point he shouted, 'Deep in all of your tiny minds, you know this guy is getting drilled to the canvas.' Which, it turned out, was just his warming up. He carried on: 'This right hand is going through your fucking head. All of these fucking retards know it as well.'

I found that hilarious. Mostly because it was more evidence that he'd lost it.

Still, I took Haye's threats seriously. In the days afterwards, I sat Rachael down and said, 'Listen, I could really get hurt in this fight.'

That's why, two weeks beforehand, we walked into Paul Crowley & Co. Solicitors and I drew up a will leaving everything I had to her. We weren't married at the time, so I was worried that if anything were to happen to me, she might end up in trouble. I signed my life over to her and I think that's the moment when, maybe for the first time in my career, she felt genuine fear about what might happen to me. We took the decision that she'd take the kids to Dubai while I was fighting. That was another first.

Whatever she felt, and whatever the rest of the boxing world were saying – mostly that I was going to get eaten alive – I kept my mantra going: 'I'm going to win. Trust me. I know how to beat this guy.' I was determined to try to reassure her as much as I could, so I'd tell her over and over: 'It's going to be fine. Don't worry, don't worry.'

I knew how dangerous he was. As often as I told myself that I was going to beat him, I also knew I might have to get off the floor a couple of times in the process. I knew that whatever happened, I'd find myself in a bad way. And strong as my faith was, it was also a very lonely one. You'd have struggled to find anyone who thought I could win.

But then that was the story of my career. David Haye was a brilliant fighter, far better than I ever was. He was more powerful, more explosive; when his punches land, it feels as if somebody has detonated a bomb inside your head. Everyone knew that. And everyone had also seen our bodies side by side, which was enough for a lot of people to make their minds up. It was Mr Soft against the Black Hulk. Of course he was going to kill me.

They were all missing something, though. Haye thought he would just turn up and box me out of the ring because he'd seen my fight against BJ Flores up close and drawn the wrong conclusions. I looked weak and slow and had allowed Flores to land too many punches. What looking at me didn't tell you was that I was always far harder to hit than you could have guessed, and that my gas tank was bigger than his. It didn't matter that Haye's physique was incredible, with six packs and muscles popping all over the place – I could go longer than him. And it didn't matter how I fought against Flores, I'd be taking a very different approach for Haye. I knew that if I could slowly build into the fight and drag him into the later rounds, then the bout would be there for the taking.

The other thing that they couldn't see was what was going on in our minds. They didn't understand how deeply I'd sunk my claws into Haye's psyche.

He only had five good rounds in him. I could have told you that before a single punch had been thrown. At the end of round five, I knew I had him. I'd made him miss that much that he was gassed.

'Your arse is mine. You're fucked, mate,' I told him.

In the sixth round, the bastard came out and snapped his Achilles heel.

In the build-up, I'd said, over and over, 'You'd better not quit, Dave. This fight is going to get hard, you'd better not quit.'

I swear that is the only reason he carried on. Another fighter, in another bout, against another opponent, would have seen what they'd done to themselves and said: 'That's it.' There'd be no shame in that. He couldn't walk, he couldn't balance himself. His punch was still lethal, but it's difficult to knock me out with a big right hand when you're hobbling.

It still took me another five rounds to get rid of the fucker. That was my fault. I'd been so good at making him throw and miss, but now all I wanted to do was take his chin off his face. That demonstrates what a brave man he really is – one of the most courageous fighters this country has ever seen. Fuck that, he's one of the greatest fighters ever to grace British boxing.

He wasn't fighting a prospect. I was a hard-punching world champion raining blow after blow on his face. And yet he hung on. He still thought he'd get his chance to unleash that devastating right hand.

That first fight earned me three times what I'd earned in my entire career up to that point. I couldn't care less that people were saying I'd only won because of his bust Achilles – I knew the truth. I was already a world champion and now I knew that whatever happened to me, I'd secured my family's financial future. I had what would clearly be a very lucrative rematch on the horizon. Life was good.

Months passed. I began to think about the rematch with Haye. In August 2017, I went out to work as a ringside analyst at the Mayweather vs McGregor fight in Las Vegas. And then, as I sat on the private plane that was bringing me home, I saw my mate Gary's number flashing up on my phone.

'Ashley's gone.'

'What the fuck are you on about? Ashley is on holiday in Mexico. We've just touched down.'

Gary explained that Rachael's brother Ashley had fallen from a balcony. It was an inexplicable, appalling event. It doesn't make sense that a man who, like me, was afraid of heights, would have gone up so high on a forty-foot building. I cannot believe he would have jumped. It's always felt to me like there's an important part of the story missing.

I loved Ashley. I'd grown up with him and only got closer since Rachael and I had been together. I started crying. But even as the tears flowed down my cheeks, there was a part of me that refused to believe what had happened. 'This can't be real. This must be a wind-up.' I stepped off the plane, dazed and devastated but still talking to Gary, and then I got in the car, away from the wind and noise of the runway. I could hear Rachael screaming in the background. I carried on crying all the way home. I didn't know it was possible to cry so much.

I wanted to promise Rachael that everything would be OK and yet I couldn't. Nothing was right, nothing could be right. Those months between August and May were the darkest part of my life. I'd grown up with Ashley, I'd known him since he was a baby, so I was seared with pain. But for Rachael, who was so close to Ashley that they were almost like twins, it was so much worse. The pain and stress she felt was written all over her face. Every time I looked at her, my heart bled again.

Even now, there are days when I come home and I'll look at Rachael and know that all she's thinking about is her brother. That's a heartbreaking place for both of us to be. It's devastating because I can never change what's happened. If I could do something, it'd be the best thing in the world. Knowing I'm powerless to help kills me.

My home was broken, filled with grief. Losing Ashley had torn my family to pieces. Fighting was the space I could escape into where I didn't have to think about any of those other things. I was so selfish. My wife was in tears every day and I just fucked off to Sheffield.

But even then, all I could think about was Ashley. By day, I'd work like a fucking animal in the gym, and that was enough to keep thoughts of what had happened at bay. It was different after dark. I did months of crying, weeping tears of frustration and grief and anger in my hotel room every night before I went to sleep.

A sign of how much the tension and sadness were ripping me up inside was the way that I lost it when David rang to cancel the rematch, which had been planned for December. I was so raw that I needed that fight so much. Then he called to tell me that he had an injury to his bicep and that he was really sorry. I flipped, calling him every name under the sun.

'You're a prick. Do you know what I'm going through in my life? My family is ruined. I'm training to fight you, you gobshite, and you say you've got an injury. Fuck off.' Then I slammed the phone down.

I'm glad now. If we'd fought then, when I was still all over the place, Haye would have beaten me. I'd have done something wild. I know it. I don't know what, or how, but mentally I was in no fit state to be anywhere near a boxing ring. The pressure of fight week would have done me. I'd have attacked him or a security guard or someone who had nothing at all to do with the bout. All that unprocessed, confused sadness and anger would have roared out of me, burning everything it touched. I was all over the place; the cancellation was a blessing.

As the rescheduled rematch approached in May 2018, I felt far more pressure on my shoulders than I had for our first fight. Some of that was because there was now all this history and drama. Haye vs Bellew had become a proper rivalry. It was the sort of grudge match that people couldn't take their eyes off, because they never knew what we might do next.

This time round, Haye was clearly taking me more seriously. He knew how good I was, how clever I could be and how hard I could hit. He was in incredible shape. No injuries, nothing. Even at thirty-seven, it seemed as if physically he'd returned to his absolute peak. The poster boy for British boxing was back. And if I'm going to be honest, I think a lot of fans were keen to find out if what happened last time round had been a fluke. All that translated into incredible box office numbers.

The consensus in the boxing community was that I'd been lucky. It seemed as if every fighter out there was berating me, saying that if Haye had been fit, I wouldn't have been able to live with him, that he'd destroy me in the rematch. They were doing David's talking for him. Especially since everything they said was being echoed by the major boxing journalists.

In response, I ended up heaping even more pressure on my shoulders, because I was so insistent on proving everyone wrong. The world was claiming that I'd only beaten him last time because he was fighting on one leg. *Right,* I thought, *I'll fucking show you.* I told everybody that this time, David would suffer an even more devastating defeat.

When David did surface, he seemed obsessed with retribution. He kept on saying the word 'revenge' like a kind of mantra. The dictionary definition of revenge was stamped all over the posters he'd produced for the rematch. He was absolutely consumed by it.

Luckily, I had a mantra of my own: No matter what you hit me with, you cannot hurt me. The more I repeated that, the more I came to believe it.

Despite all this tension and excitement, the last days before the rematch were much more subdued. Nothing nasty or heavy was said. The final press conference was light-hearted. Making a joke about the fact that I'd called his manager a briefcase wanker, Haye got James Buckley, who played Jay in *The Inbetweeners*, to turn up.

Still, I knew that I had to maintain the psychological assault on Haye that had disturbed him so much the year before. And he seemed equally determined to try to protect himself, however he could. Right the way through the press conference, he'd kept fucking me off, putting headphones on, ignoring what I was saying as I explained repeatedly – so that he and everyone else watching got the point – that in the last match I'd beaten him twice: mentally and physically. It was a bit of pantomime on his part, designed to show that this time he wouldn't let himself get affected by my nonsense.

So, although the little shove I gave him in the final press conference wasn't as charged with aggression and rage as the first time round, it still had a very clear purpose. I wanted him to know that I was prepared mentally. I was telling him: 'Look, I'm here, and if you're not listening to what I'm saying, you'll feel what I'm doing.'

When we sat down for 'The Gloves Are Off' on Sky, I absolutely crucified him. I went for all the things that I knew would lodge in his mind, stuff that would niggle and niggle away at him. 'David, have you had your manicure done? How's your hairband looking?'

He was working so hard to ignore me, just batting away everything I threw at him. He'd take a deep breath and look up at the sky. It was like a game for both of us – one I knew I'd win.

There's no point in just chatting shit for the sake of it. It makes no sense to challenge your opponent's fitness or their jab: you know they're fit, he knows he's fit; they're a professional boxer. You need to make him start questioning himself. Every boxer will have won fights that were close. Fights where they know that they got lucky because they'd caught their opponent at a good time or where the referee's calls were in their favour. I play on all the doubts that lurk in the minds of others and make them explain them to me. 'Why do you think you won that fight? I don't think that you won that fight. Why did your corner throw the towel in against that fighter? I thought you were still fine to fight on.' If you can get to them, you know that whether he wants to or not, he'll start asking himself: *Was I lucky? Did I deserve to win that fight?* When you sow those seeds of doubt, then he's fucked, he's absolutely fucked.

That's exactly what I did against Haye. I knew his career better than he did. I started talking about the 2004 world championships, when he lost to the Cuban gold medallist Odlanier Solís. Haye had hit Solís so hard in the first round that he was knocked out on his feet. But then Solís recovered and battered Haye into submission. Haye had his opponent at his mercy, but he lacked the killer instinct to move in and finish him off.

'You spewed it,' I told him. 'You fucking spewed it.'

Haye just looked at me as if to say: *How do know these things?* I reminded him that he'd quit against Carl Thompson. Everything was precisely calibrated to turn the screw that bit tighter each time.

In the end, he bit. I started on about his defeat against Wladimir Klitschko: 'You quit, you quit, you quit.'

Almost without thinking, he replied, 'I didn't quit.' Then he realised: 'Ah, you nearly got me.' He allowed himself a quick laugh. 'I'm going to stop talking and take another breath.'

I found out later he'd been seeing a mind quack and that they'd talked about the problems he had with me. The coach had warned him against getting into debates with me. And it had almost worked. Instead, I understood, as soon as I walked out of that room, that I'd got to him. And that meant that, once again, I'd beaten him before we'd even stepped into the ring.

As soon as Haye came out for the first round, it was clear he was thinking: *I'm going to box him. I'm going to make a fool of him.* He wanted to punish me in that rematch. He wanted to draw my agony out slowly, painfully.

That didn't happen. The plan was to take the reins early on and then just control the pace right through the fight. If I kept digging and bouncing and bobbing, I knew it would unsettle him. I never lost sight of his strengths, but nor did I forget my own. All of his physical attributes were, in my mind at least, outweighed by my mental ones. My defence was better than his – so was my boxing brain and my ability to navigate my way through a twelve-round fight. I knew that as long as I didn't let him catch me cleanly, the match was mine. He's the heaviest-handed puncher I've ever faced, the strongest man I've ever fought. So I put everything into making sure I stayed just out of his reach. As soon as the first round was over, I knew he'd lost. He knew, too. He couldn't hit me. And he was fucked, absolutely fucked. He'd prepared for the wrong fight. He thought he was turning up to a brawl, but I was playing chess.

Some nights everything clicks for you. This was one of

them. I was fighting on a level that I'd only reached maybe once before in my career. I don't think I've ever been more punch-perfect than I was that night. I didn't put a single foot wrong. Everything went to plan, everything I tried just fell into place. It's so hard to explain adequately how I felt during those moments. I was up against a world-class fighter, a man who throughout his career had devastated his opponents. And while I was surrounded by all the explosive energy and violence you'd expect, I felt calm and composed, flowing easily from one movement to the next.

It's not an out-of-body experience, because you're so in the moment. It's more that your mind and body are working together in complete unity; you can make the world move at a pace of your choosing; you can't believe that any of your punches will ever miss; you can't believe that there's anything the other guy can do that could even touch you.

When you box like that, it's the best feeling in the whole world. Nothing comes close.

I dropped him twice in the third round, then two minutes and fourteen seconds into the fifth I caught him with a beautiful left hook that left him face down on the canvas.

The second that fight ended, my thoughts turned to Ashley. He'd been there at the first fight. I'd left a ringside seat empty for him at the rematch, next to where his brother and dad were. I remember how I looked over at the space where he should have been and broke down into uncontrollable tears.

# CONFIDENCE IS KEY

A boxer's mentality is his strongest weapon. Far more important than his physique. Who can get inside the other boxer's head? Who's better at hiding their vulnerabilities? It doesn't matter how good your footwork is or how much power you pack in your punch. If you can't perform when you get out there under the lights, you'll never be a contender.

So much of the mental side comes down to confidence. In boxing, confidence, and the *appearance* of confidence, are key. You have to believe in yourself and you have to do everything you possibly can to ensure that the rest of the world understands that, too. You have to make them believe that you believe, even if you're wracked by doubt or fear.

Right at the beginning of my career, I'd portray myself as being confident and outgoing. I'd portray myself as being cocky and braggadocious. I always knew I wasn't the greatest athlete, but I'd go on as if I were. I'd talk so much shit. Did I genuinely believe it? No, not really, not at the start. But a point came when I didn't have to fool myself any more. I'd proved to myself so many times that I could overcome any odds to win, that I could beat any fighter who I came up against. It meant I could shut out all the sneering voices.

This was especially important in my two bouts with Haye. I never doubted for a second I'd win and I was determined to show that, because if I'd faltered, even for a second, then the results would have been very different. I couldn't afford to show doubt or weakness to Haye, and nor could I afford to show that sort of vulnerability to myself. With so few people – nobody really – giving me a chance, I had to generate all that momentum on my own.

The way people see you determines to a large extent the way that they treat you. People trust and respect you more if you seem confident. Confident people get better jobs and enjoy better relationships. It probably shouldn't be the case, but that's the way things are. However, if you can learn to carry yourself with the boldness, if not necessarily the brashness, of a boxer, you'll find that many areas of life begin to feel a lot easier to deal with.

## THE BEST LIARS IN THE WORLD

If you want to be able to project confidence, you have to feel it first. That's why boxers are the best liars in the world. We have to be. First, we have to lie to ourselves. Then, we turn round and lie through our teeth to everybody else. There's nobody, going into that first bout after a crushing defeat, who won't have a little voice in their head going: *you lost last time, you're weak, you're finished.* Nobody can know. Nobody. If anyone even senses your anxiety, then you're fucked.

I used to try to kid people into believing I was something that in reality I wasn't. It wasn't quite a lie, but it wasn't the truth, either. After my fourth pro fight, I was completely skint. My left hand had been snapped in half and I didn't have enough money to pay for the operation. I was also beginning to worry I wouldn't be able to cover our mortgage. But the story I was telling people was that I'd had four fights and knocked three fighters out and that I had it all. I was the business, the hottest prospect in UK boxing. I could carry that off when I was out and about. Then the second I walked back through the door of the house I didn't even know I could afford to live in any more, I'd feel appalling levels of stress.

I carried on because I understood the power of that kind of performance. I'd do the same in press conferences. Inside I might have been plagued with doubt, but I'd stride into the room as if I were the most confident man in the world. My message wasn't: *I hope I win.* If you'd seen me, you'd come away with only one impression: *I'm going to smash you to bits.*

There would be times when I'd make weight and although deep down I knew I was fucked – because there's just no way I should be losing ten pounds in three days – I'd sit there at the press conference and announce that

I was in the best shape of my life. Although I'd struggled like fuck to lose the last pounds, having been subsisting on a diet of ice cubes for days, and I felt dead on my feet, I'd never say that. If I did, I'd literally be able to see my opponent expanding as his confidence grew. A minute ago, he'd have been feeling like me. He might have been feeling worse than me. Now, he'd be thinking to himself: *I feel great.*

Instead, I'll tell everyone who will listen that I feel absolutely fantastic. Even as these words come out of my mouth, I know I'm talking shite, that in reality I'm at death's door. My cheekbones are drawn, my forehead will be sunken, my eyebrows sticking out, because I've drained so much fluid from my body. Yet, I'll still be telling myself and the world at large: 'I'm going to do it.' And I'll carry on kidding my bollocks off until I genuinely do believe it.

Your mind is so powerful that it can drown out every single message your poor, damaged body is screaming at you. You project that confidence because you have no choice. And the more you do project that confidence, the more you'll feel it.

The power behind this approach is that it allows you to change your mindset. If you focus on victory more than you do defeat – the things that could go right rather than wrong – then you'll instantly be thinking along more positive lines.

When you're feeling short of confidence, you don't need to bellow about it in a room full of strangers, but it'll help if you spend some time refocusing your mind. Imagine how good it'll feel when you absolutely smash the presentation you're due to give at work. Think about all the times in the past when you've enjoyed success. Reflect on the good qualities you know you possess. Individually, these might not work. Taken together, they supercharge your confidence.

## SHOW, DON'T TELL

There's a feeling that I reckon only boxers know. It's sitting there at the press conferences and weigh-ins before a fight and finding yourself the subject of a scrutiny so intense that you feel as if even your bones are on show to the world. Your opponent, the media and a fucking cartload of other people have an obsessive interest in the exact current condition of both your mind and your body. It begins on the first day that news of the fight breaks; although it's pretty mild then. And then as month follows month, and week follows week, it gets more and more acute. By the time of the match itself, it's almost unbearable.

It's a weird ritual. I sometimes think that somebody watching for the first time would think they were watching two bulls fighting over a female in a nature documentary. It's so choreographed – there are rules and routines – and yet beneath all that it's about rage and power and weakness. Horrible primal emotions.

In your everyday life, people subject you to that scrutiny – that's what human beings do. They'll watch your face as you speak or the way you hold yourself as you enter the room. Most of the time, they won't even know that they're doing this, but unconsciously or not, their brains will be receiving a relentless procession of information. You're always communicating. Whether you're silent and still or jumping around full of energy, you're saying something. You can't change that. What you can try to control is the message you convey.

The difference between boxers and the average person is that we pay specific attention to the way we're perceived. As a result, we make conscious efforts to do as much as we can to control the impression we give out.

I found that the way I stood, the way I held my body, made a difference not just to how I felt, but also to how others perceived me. That was as true when I was a kid wearing a bulletproof vest on the door of a nightclub as it was for those crucial seconds I spent walking from the dressing room to the ring.

Your opponent will be watching you for any sign of weakness. You have to show him that you believe you're invincible. Don't apologise for existing – occupy that space. I project aggression, dominance, presence. It's why when I walk into a room you'll think I'm taller and bigger than I am. It makes me feel more in control of what I'm doing and it determines how people treat me: they'll listen when I speak, they'll probably be nicer, more respectful. Because

I give them the impression of somebody who knows his value, they respond to it. It's not nice, and it's not very polite sometimes, but it's true. If I acted like a loser, they'd treat me like one. It might sound as if this is a very aggressive, confrontational way of living life. Perhaps in some ways it is. But I think it's also a very good way of avoiding those sorts of situations.

I'd learned all that in Wavertree. If you can't fend off the wolves – if you can't show that you're confident and know what you're doing – the people on the streets will eat you alive. That's how they are. You've got to be one of two things in Liverpool. Either you have to know how to handle yourself in a fight or to be able to tell a joke. At some point, you'll need to rely on one of them to get you out of trouble. (To be fair, both of these things are just as likely to get you in trouble if you're not careful.) If you can't do either, then sorry, lad, but you're fucked.

When I was growing up, it was precisely because I carried myself with confidence that I didn't get picked on or pushed around. You're preparing yourself psychologically for those situations and in doing so, you're increasing the chances that you won't have to do anything violent or unpleasant. What I didn't realise until recently is that all the posturing I did in Wavertree has a basis in actual science. Taking a confident stance actually makes you feel confident. Making your mouth into the shape of a smile actually makes you feel happier. Faking it until you're making it actually works.

The confidence you need in boxing is different to other walks of life. In boxing, you need that swagger and arrogance, that willingness to climb on the ropes and scream 'I'm the fucking greatest.' That might not work so well in an office. There's a risk that if you were as brash as I used to be then you could end up alienating others. But a lot of the principles are the same. Body language is so important, so be really attentive to what the signals you give off will communicate to others. If I act stressed or anxious, I'll probably feel stressed and anxious. Everyone around me will pick up on this, probably get stressed themselves and blast those feelings back at me, which will only make me more stressed and anxious. Showing people that you're confident is just as impactful as telling them.

## THE POWER OF EXPERIENCE

Part of confidence is relying on your own reactions; trusting that you'll be able to respond in the right way at the right time. By the time of the David Haye fight, I was so experienced that I was in complete control of everything I was doing and saying. There was nothing that David could say that I hadn't heard before. I was a master of winding people up. He's a clever lad, but he couldn't live with me. No matter what he said, I could bounce back immediately.

The more I went through those high-pressure situations when I needed to project confidence, the better I got at reading the room and calibrating my responses accordingly. Don't be surprised if the first time you try, you end up getting it wrong. Anybody who says it's easy is taking you for a fool. And if you don't quite nail the act first time round, don't be disheartened – keep doing it again and again until you've perfected it.

I know that in the early days, I was much more likely to lose my sense of proportion and end up saying some silly shit. Ahead of my first fight with Nathan Cleverly, I jumped up out of my seat and shouted, 'Get outside, you fucking rat.' It was my first time in the media spotlight and it shows. I wasn't used to being the focus of so much intense attention. So I didn't just overstep the mark, I fucking leaped over it.

The only reason you get better is because you learn your lessons. I went home that day and I knew I'd never make the same mistake again. I also knew that the next time would be easier. Confidence is a skill like any other: the more you practise it, the better you'll get.

## THE IMPORTANCE OF FIRST IMPRESSIONS

Boxers don't get to make the ring walk twice if they fuck it up the first time. And most of the time in life you won't get second chances to make that first impression. A lot of people will have made up their minds about who and what you are before you've even opened your mouth.

I'm mixed-race – my mum is black, my dad is white – but you wouldn't necessarily be able to tell right away. That put me in a strange position, especially in the north of Liverpool, where the Rotunda was. People like me from the south of the city, which was much more diverse, always thought of that area as much whiter.

It made me realise how quick others are to form an opinion based on poisonous old prejudices they'd picked up from their parents and never questioned. For ages, everybody at the Rotunda thought I was white. A couple of times, some horrible shit came out of a fighter's mouth. I'd have my headphones on so I wouldn't hear it, and yet you could lipread easily enough. It wasn't like they were trying to hide it. I wouldn't say anything, I'd just make them pay in the boxing ring. Afterwards they'd be complaining, asking why I was giving out hidings to my teammates.

Nobody ever knew the real answer, not for a long time. I didn't feel like I could open my mouth because I worried what would happen. It wouldn't have got serious: there's no way Jimmy would have let that happen. But there are ways you can make somebody feel uncomfortable, like they don't belong.

I didn't want to risk that so I did what I could to stay away from those people. Ultimately, you just learn to live with it. That's the saddest thing. That's what you do.

People only realised after the first time my mum turned up at the gym and asked if Anthony was there. She was met with blank stares. They just said, 'There's no Anthony here.'

At the time everyone called me 'Bellew'. 'Anthony Bellew,' my mum persisted.

That was when it clicked for Jimmy and the others. It explained the velour tracksuits and loud rap music and the diamonds in my ear. It changed a bit after that, although one thing you learn quickly is that if you scratch the surface, even quite nice people can hold some surprising opinions.

There was one day when a mate who'd just got his first purse after turning pro bought himself a white gold chain. I went back with him to his house and the first thing his mum said was, 'What are you doing with a nigger's chain on?'

My mate looked at me with horror on his face, then started staring at the floor. He didn't say anything to me, what could he say? I just felt painfully uncomfortable. What made it so awkward was that I knew she was a really lovely woman, a brilliant mother.

But that was what she had ingrained in her. That prejudice had been passed on to her by her mum and dad and she'd never thought twice about it since. You see it even now. There are still some people who I look at and think, *You haven't changed your ways. You are exactly the same now.* Education's the only thing that's going to resolve that.

I hate the fact that two decades into the twenty-first century there are still so many people who will judge you on the colour of your skin, not the content of your character. But if I have learned anything from this, it's that when somebody shows you who they are, believe them. They might be racist, or a bully or a liar, it doesn't matter. They've done you a favour by revealing what they're really like. You might be able to change them, more likely you'll find it's too late. All you need to do is steer the fuck away. Your life will be far better for it.

# SUMMARY

- Everyone will have moments when their confidence fails them. Imposter syndrome comes to us all at some point. But you can trick your brain. The more you tell yourself that you're going to win, the more likely you are to enjoy victory.

- People react to the version of you that they see. If you project confidence, you'll feel it yourself and other people will respond positively.

- Don't expect instant results. It took me a while before I could get the hang of all the braggado-cio that goes with big-time fights. But trust that practice will help you to hone your ability to project confidence. You will get there.

- You only get one chance to make a first impression. Don't waste it.

# CHAPTER 11
# AFTERLIFE

Goodison Park, 29 May 2016

*I start talking to myself, 'Three . . .' Then I turn to the referee, who's still counting. 'Move out of the fucking way, I'm going to kill him.'*

*'Four . . . five.'*

*'Get out of the way, let's go.'*

*The ref stares at me. 'You're crazy. Six . . . you're crazy . . . seven.' He grabs my hands, checks to see if I'm OK.*

*I'm lucky that it's Victor Loughlin, the best referee in the country. He's always had perfect timing in fights. He never stops them until the exact right moment. Someone else would have waved the fight off when they saw me roll backwards. Victor lets me get up. He stares at me closely, to check I'm solid on my feet. He knows that the fact that I'm talking to him, even if I'm being a bit of a prick, shows that I know what's going on.*

*'Where are you?'*

*'Goodison Park.'*

*My fitness has saved me. All that work, all that sacrifice, means that my legs are strong. I could fight twenty rounds tonight and still have energy to spare.*

*The bell goes. I'm still in this. There had been a moment earlier on when I thought,* for fuck's sake, he's going to catch me. *But although he knocked me over, I know he cannot finish me. He cannot keep me on the floor. No one, not even Mike Tyson, could keep me on the floor tonight.*

*For the first ten seconds after I get back to my corner, I don't hear a word Dave is saying to me. He's just a small person getting in my face. Then, suddenly, I can make out his penetrating York-shire voice.*

*'You got greedy, you got greedy.'*

*I know that I'm a greedy fat bastard. The last thing in the world I need right now is that little man screaming it at me. I fucking* know *I'm greedy. I've been a big kid all of my life. I start laughing to myself: years ago I'd been a fat boy going nowhere, and now here I am. In a fucking world title fight. It's almost too weird and hilarious to process. Then that's it. Nothing. I don't remember a single moment of the second round.*

*When I stand up for the third round, I've completely forgotten about the preceding minutes. This has happened before. It's the result of the toll that making weight takes on your mind and body. Losing that much of your body mass so quickly, while training like a lunatic, drains your energy and your ability to form and keep memories. Your mind just closes on you. You're fighting on natural instinct. It's like you're in aeroplane mode. The only thing I remembered from my bout against Isaac Chilemba was arriving at the arena; I don't recall a single thing from the fight itself or how*

I got home, or that I went crazy in the dressing room afterwards, smashing it to pieces.

In my head, the clock is still ticking. I can't let this get past six rounds, I can't let this get past six rounds, I've got to get him. I can't let him absorb everything I have, wear me out, then slowly take me apart. I know I've been on the floor and I know that if he drops me heavily again, that could be it. I need to get in and trade with him. I need to draw him in, then counter.

I'm an underrated counter-puncher. It's my strongest weapon. I'm not naturally the strongest or the quickest fighter, but my timing is sweet. More than that, I've worked fanatically, on my fitness and on my game plan. I've studied Makabu so closely that I'm confident I can predict exactly what his next move will be. I'll know before even he does.

The moment I can tempt him into throwing that lazy right-hand jab is the moment I can smash him with my left hook. That's what we've practised over and over during the training camp. All I need is for him to slip once. The minute I feel that his gloves have gone over my shoulder and past my ear, only one thing is coming: a punch that will go right round his body, exploding into his skull from the very edges of his vision. Fuck off, I've kidded you. You're asleep and it's my night.

The third round unfolds. I hurt him numerous times. This is the pivotal moment. The trap I set is perfect. I let him bring me onto the ropes. He thinks he's got me in the corner. What he doesn't realise is that it's a trick. He comes in closer and swings a big left hand, which I block with my right and then I counter.

My right hand was powerful. I'd rendered people unconscious

with it numerous times. But the left hook was the punch I felt most comfortable throwing. I'd perfected it by studying all the great left hookers as a kid: Joe Frazier, Félix Trinidad, Mike Tyson. The short left hook I smash on his temple is the product of all that practice. It doesn't look like a hard punch, but believe you me, it's vicious. His legs shiver, he backs up at the speed of fucking light and I know I've really got him.

I chase after him and get him against the ropes. I hit him with a combination – all the shots are going in. Nothing's really catching. He's blocking most of my punches; only a few are getting through. I continue to chase him, this time to another side of the ropes. I'm on him. He brings his gloves up to his head in a defensive posture. I pull one of them down with my left hand and smash him on the temple with my right. He stumbles and although he's clearly vulnerable, I know he's still dangerous. I can see he wants to knock my head off with the same punch he used in the first round.

Then he throws a right jab. The punch I've been waiting for all night. I see it coming, then slip, moving all of my weight onto my left leg. His glove swings into the space above me where seconds before my body had been. Now. Bang! I move across and unleash my left hook.

A proper punch doesn't just come from your fist and arms. You might be able to hurt somebody that way, but you'll never send them to sleep. If you want that knockout, then the punch has to begin at the bottom of your feet before travelling right through to your hands. My left leg has been loaded with every single volt of power I possess, then I explode. Fuck off!

The second the fabric of my glove kisses his chin, I know he's not *getting up again. To make sure, I hit him with two more to the back of the head as his unconscious frame crumples to the canvas. The referee jumps in. Makabu is asleep on the floor and I look up to the clouds above the stadium and think about Jimmy Albertina. I've done it. I'm still not sure how. But I've done it. I'm world champion.*

*Emotion floods my body and I drop to my knees. There's relief; there's exaltation. I've forgotten about Makabu. Tears roll down my cheeks. I think to myself:* Lad, you've done it. *My whole life has been about reaching this moment.*

*Then Dave is hugging me. Then I have another blackout. I remember almost nothing until the interview. Ten minutes go by where I have no recall of all the people coming up to congratulate me or the crowd going wild.*

*There's one memory that does stay with me. Although only minutes ago I wanted to kill Makabu, now I only have admiration and respect for him. Actually, it's more than that – it's something close to love. I go to him; check he's OK. Because, of course, what's happened to him could easily have happened to me instead.*

Just over two years after my triumph at Goodison, I stepped out onto the canvas for the last time.

I'd known beforehand that I wouldn't be fighting again. For decades I'd asked so much of my body. I'd pushed it and pushed it. My will and determination had extracted more from it than I'd ever thought possible. Now, I was paying the cost. I'd carried major injuries coming into four of my last five fights. Against Usyk, it was a cracked rib that was serious enough to prevent me from sparring in the last two weeks before the fight. Like the others, it was dangerous enough that I probably shouldn't have stepped into the ring, but nobody had ever known about them, because I never wanted it to look as if I were offering up excuses. I fought through pain, I fought full of antibiotics. I knew that if I carried on like this, my body would break down completely. In that respect, retiring wasn't a hard decision. It was time to stop.

It would have been perfect to say farewell to boxing at Goodison. As it was, I prepared for my last fight in a dressing room I didn't like, which in turn was in the Manchester Arena, a venue I'd never been that keen on, either. I'd fought there a number of times, but I could never get on with it in the same way as I did The O2 or the Liverpool Echo. Perhaps it was the memory of the hand I smashed there all those years ago against Hastings Rasani. What made up for that was the fact that the crowd were amazing. The match was a sell-out; it really felt as if they'd all showed up for me – 20,000 Mancs there to see a Scouser get fucked.

I sat there going over my fight plan over and over again, and running through different scenarios in my mind. What if he does this? How will I respond if he does that? How do I adapt to him? There was no space for contemplation of what I'd been through in the last decades, or what I was about to lose. Everything was about this moment. Then Ralph, the man who'd given the final call for every single professional fight of my career, knocked on the door of the dressing room: 'Tone, time to go.'

For the first time ever, I didn't enjoy the walk to the ring. My head was full of an uncomfortable mix of sadness and anger. I was annoyed because I knew that the chance to fight for the undisputed cruiserweight title was coming at the wrong time in my career. I'd had the chance to dive straight into unification fights as soon as I became world champion, but there were other things that needed to be addressed first. Once I had that belt, everything changed. Glory didn't matter so much any more, the next part of my career was going to be all about money. I could have entered the World Super Series and hoovered up all of the other cruiserweight titles, but the two fights with David Haye earned me more than I could have got from every single bout in that tournament put together.

I had a shot at the undisputed cruiserweight title now, it would have been an incredible way to end my years in the ring, but I was facing the best boxer I'd ever come across. I'd spent my entire career being underestimated by other fighters. Now, in my last fight, I realised that I'd underestimated Usyk. I'd studied his footwork beforehand and I knew he was good, but it wasn't until I was in the ring with him that I realised how brilliant he was.

There was something so skilful about the way he positioned and moved his lead foot, fooling me into thinking he was always in range. Which of course he wasn't. What it meant was my mind could never settle or take a break.

Every single second that we were in that ring, he was making me work.

His accuracy was incredible and he also had an amazing ability to adapt and adjust, which meant he was able to frustrate me over and over. There were times when I was trying to force him to stand still while I set a trap for him, only to discover that in fact I'd blundered straight into a trap that he'd set for me. It was crazy.

Still, I felt as if I had the better of him during the opening rounds. And then, from maybe the sixth round, I could feel I was tiring too fast. It was a strange place to be. I knew I was ahead in the fight and yet there was a voice in my head going, 'Lad, you're fucked.'

He never gave me a single moment to rest or recover. I'd be watching him trying to manoeuvre me and thinking, *you sneaky bastard – I can see what you're trying to do.* Except, as I would learn quite soon, it turned out I couldn't.

As the eighth round wore on, I still thought my game plan was working. I was ahead on the cards and there were only four rounds left after this. If I could hang on and avoid being knocked out, I'd win.

The problem was that I was so tired that by this stage, I could barely breathe. When the end came, it came quickly. Usually when I fought, I'd keep my right hand up high to stop me from getting clipped by a punch coming from my blind spot. I still wanted to give myself that defence now, but I no longer had the energy to support my right hand. At the moment that the punch from Usyk hurtled round the side, out of my peripheral vision, my glove was sagging far too low. I'd thought he was looking for a shot down the middle. He'd *convinced* me he was looking for a shot down the middle. I might have been able to stop that. I couldn't do anything about the punch that swung round my glove and slammed into my head.

In truth, he'd finished me long before the eighth round. He'd finished me when he'd dragged out every last piece of energy from my body. I'd come into that fight in good shape – he *made* me tired. He'd drained me physically and mentally because, and it's hard to admit, he has a better boxing brain than me. His fight plan was better than mine and he executed it brilliantly. Although perhaps he's not a fighter who can take you out with one punch, in every other aspect he's perfect, probably the best cruiserweight ever. He grinds you down, makes you pay for every single mistake. There was no shame in losing to someone like him.

I'd been defeated. And then I found I was at peace. In the past I'd felt annihilated by every other loss, every draw. Even those wins that were that bit closer than I'd wanted them to be. Now, I was calm. I'd given everything. I was at my very best but he'd beaten me and that felt fair. Normally, I'd want to get out of the arena as quick as humanly possible. That night was different. I found I was all right. I went to the post-fight press conference – something else I'd never done before after a disappointment – and told everyone there that I'd lost to the best man. I talked about how this was the last time the world would see Tony Bellew. From now on, I was going to go back to Anthony Bellew.

There's a song I was listening to on repeat around then: 'Kill Jay-Z'. In it, Jay-Z lists all of his faults, all the bad things he's done and regrets. It resonated so much with me. I understood that desire to rid yourself of all the stupid shit you carry around on your conscience. I wished I could purge myself. I wished I could take all of it back. I wished I could wipe away all of the Tony shit and just have Anthony left. But you can't. It's all done and you have to learn to accept it.

# YOU CANNOT FIGHT FOR EVER

After the first David Haye fight, Eddie Hearn had phoned me.

'The money's come in. Are you ready for it to drop? When you see your bank balance tomorrow, give me a call. You're a millionaire now, mate, you're a multimillionaire. Pay your tax, pay the VAT, look after it.'

All I could say was, 'Fucking hell.'

My first reaction when I saw the cash was sitting there was: 'Wow.' I had a huge buzz. But this was followed by a very different feeling a couple of minutes later. It didn't give me what I'd always assumed it would. I thought millions would make me happy for ever after and yet all I could think was: *I need another fight.* I saw then that it was never the money I was chasing. It was the brutal, unrepeatable thrill I got from fighting. The money was for my family, the fighting was for me.

The hardest part of retirement has been letting the fight go away, because the desire never goes. I still want, more than anything, that feeling only fighting gives me. I still think I could destroy half the clowns who are out there at the moment. By the standards of the game, I'm not even that old. And my boxing brain is probably more powerful now than it was at any stage in my career. Let me into a ring and I could make a fool of people. Journeymen, really good fighters, I don't care; I'd know how to beat them. I know the little things I'd need to do; I know what buttons to push.

Except they've got the one thing I can never get back, no matter how hard I try: youth. Their bodies can take the gruelling punishment of a twelve-week training camp followed by thirty-six minutes of violence. Mine can't.

Fighting was all I'd known for decades, so retirement felt like losing a piece of myself that I'd never get back. And yet I always came back to my body and my fear of it breaking down. I couldn't get round that. I had to let go.

A lot of people say that the hardest fight of any boxer's career is the one they have to face when they retire and I think there's a lot of truth in that. Change is always tough. It's often forced upon us when we least expect it and when we feel least willing, or able, to embrace it. But it's also an inevitable part of life, something that affects every one of us at one stage or another. When that moment arrives, you

295

have to recognise it for what it is, accept it and move on to something new. Much as you might want to, you cannot fight for ever.

# YOU'VE HAD YOUR TIME, LAD

It's so weird when I go into the arena now. I get all the same cues that used to activate all of my senses: the noises, sights and smells that told me it was time to fight. And I feel sad because I still, to this day, love fighting so much. I miss it more than I can even describe. But there's a voice in me that says: *you've had your time, lad. You've put your family through enough.* Tony Bellew is the part of me that I'm trying to draw away from, even if I'll never let it all go.

I can't stop doing commentary, because it's work, but I have made efforts to make sure that temptation doesn't end up tugging at me too much. I could still go to the gym and box without fighting, but I know that if I did that, it would lead me back into the ring. So I don't. It's a brutal solution and yet it's the only one that works.

And I don't watch my division that much any more – certainly not as much as I used to, probably not as much as I should. I still love boxing and I still love talking about boxing, but I don't ever want to *study* boxing again. I can't afford to immerse myself in the sport like I once would have. That sort of focus would only end up pushing me in a direction I don't want to go any more.

296

When you've put a phase of your life behind you, make the break as complete as you can. There's a reason why lots of recovering alcoholics try to avoid pubs and bars. If you don't put that distance between you and the things you used to do, they'll always be calling to you and you won't be able to make the clean start you need.

## GIVE YOURSELF NEW CHALLENGES

In the beginning, I had doubts about going on *SAS: Who Dares Wins*. Mostly about the 'celebrity' element. Although I'd always embraced my role as a showman, it was only for pragmatic reasons. I did it because I knew that it was important for my career. I wasn't interested in attention for its own sake. Now I look back on it, I wish I could have fought my entire career wearing a mask, with nobody knowing who I was. I just see fame as an intrusion on your privacy.

So I didn't go on because I wanted to get more followers on Twitter or a photospread in *Hello!* magazine. I did it partly because I wanted to be pushed to my limits and find out whether or not I could have been a soldier, and partly because I knew I was in a really dark mental space and I needed something to jolt me out of it.

Before that show I wanted to kill everything. There was so much nastiness in me and for the first time in almost twenty years, I no longer had the outlet that fighting had offered me. The week before I went on that show, I'd literally chased another driver. He'd beeped his horn at me and I just thought, *fuck off*. I was raging, but I might have let it go. Then he stuck his finger up at me.

That pushed me over the edge. I didn't give a fuck that my wife and kids were in the car, and I didn't care that we were in the middle of the city centre. I accelerated and caught up with him at the next set of lights. As soon as I pulled level, I jumped out and started trying to open his car door. All the while I was screaming, 'I'm going to fucking kill you. Get out the car, you shitbag.' He looked up and I could see him shit himself as he realised exactly who I was.

As this was happening, Rachael, who was quite rightly uncomfortable with what her lunatic of a husband was doing, was shouting, 'Get in the car! Stop it.'

Still trying to wrench the door open, I shouted back, 'Fucking shut up! I'm going to kill this cunt.'

Luckily for everybody, the lights changed and he span off. If I'd got him out of the car, I *would* have killed him.

That rage was still swirling around me when I travelled out to the Scottish island of Raasay. Filming was hard. Far harder than you'd think from watching it on screen. You only see maybe a tenth of what the contestants go through; you don't see the butchery and loneliness that goes on. You cannot see the impact of sleep and food deprivation. And all the while the intensity is growing hour after hour after hour.

Ant Middleton just kept on and on at me. Right through

the show, I could sense him trying to find my vulnerable spot and I thought to myself, *it's all well and good poking the lion, but don't poke the lion too much, because you'll get a nasty bite.*

The closest I came to attacking him was the scenario with Nikki Sanderson. He made Nikki Sanderson, who is about five feet tall, pick up all seventeen stone of me. It really infuriated me that he was willing to put a young girl through so much pain. That made me want to belt him. The only reason I didn't was because he kept repeating the same thing over and over: 'Everything I do is for a reason.' And he kept saying it and saying it and I took a deep breath, realised I trusted him, and I thought, *he's using her to get to me. He's trying to break me mentally.*

He didn't break me, as it happened, but he made me open up. I hadn't anticipated that I'd be talking about my personal life, but he made me talk about things that had been going on with me. What had happened ever since Ashley and just how unhappy I was in myself. I'm for ever in his debt for doing that. I have so much respect for him.

I've never watched the show back, so I don't know what other people have seen, but I came home a completely different person.

Ant, who's by far the most positive person I've ever met, made me look at things from a different perspective. My phone became less important and I started spending half the time on it that I had in the past. I switched it off at night. Sometimes I turned it off for a whole weekend.

Instead, I paid more attention to the people around me whom I cared for most.

I also started to question what other people were doing in my life. Everyone who wasn't in my immediate family suddenly seemed less important. And I found that I could see more clearly who was adding to my existence and who was subtracting from it. Those who were hanging around me not for who I was, but for what they thought they could get from me. It's mad to think that such a little episode was able to effect such a change, but it's true.

When you've been immersed in one sort of existence for so long, it's easy to get trapped not only in particular ways of thinking about the world, but also in thinking about yourself. During those transitional phases when you're still trying to find out exactly what it is you want to do next, throw yourself into new, perhaps less friendly spaces. It's often only by leaving our comfort zone that we can learn more about ourselves.

## FIND OUT WHO YOU ARE . . . AGAIN

I used to *love* trouble. I wanted it to come my way. I'd take as much of it as I could.

For a while in the nineties, Society was the hottest night-club in Liverpool. It played the best house music the city had ever seen. Just as importantly, there were three times as many women in there as there were men. You can imagine the mad pressure there was to get in and how fucked off people could get when they found themselves turned away. Dad ran the security, his best friend owned the club and occasionally I'd work the doors there.

One night when it was quieter than usual, I remember talking to a big man called Tony who used to work for my dad. I turned to him and said, 'Tony, this is boring, isn't it? Why can't we have a bit of action, something fucking going on?'

He wasn't having that at all. 'What are you on about, lad?'

'It's just boring. We stand here for three or four hours and nothing happens. Why can't it be like a bank holiday? There's always trouble then. I enjoy that. It's boss.'

'Lad, we don't want trouble. The less there is, the better a job we're doing.'

'But it's boring . . .'

'Ant, you've got nothing to prove here, mate. Honest to God.'

'I know I've got nothing to prove. You've all seen me box. I just want *action*.'

I didn't get it. I couldn't get it. I do now. I'm too scared of what might happen, too aware of what I'm capable of doing.

The last thing in the world I want these days is any trouble. I don't want any drama. I don't want to be around people who cause problems. I just want to have a nice smooth ride and enjoy all the days (and I hope there are a lot of them) I have left. If I died tomorrow, I'd die happy. I've lived a fantastic life. I've been a good example to my kids. I've left them a great head start.

All of that would have been a big surprise to the lunatic I was back then. We had to wear bulletproof vests when we worked, because the club had been shot at multiple times – by lads who couldn't get in, or people from the North End of Liverpool who wanted to cause trouble, or men who had problems with the owners. That life saw my dad get stabbed, run over in the street and put in two comas. And none of it bothered me. Not even the terrible shit my dad went through. The only thought I had in my head then was, *Who am I going to have to do if they get my dad? Who am I going to have to sort out?*

Which all goes to show that we can and do and should change.

We don't always notice even quite significant things because our lives are so full that we rarely have a moment to put our heads up and look at things properly. Retirement gave me a chance to reflect on who I was and how I was living my life.

I realised that I'd got so caught up in my own dream and all the demands that it placed on me, that I never really had time to take in the effect that boxing had on our family.

From leaving school onwards, I sacrificed everything as part of my desire to become world champion. I threw every atom of my body and mind into boxing and in the process, I lost a great deal. I was always thinking about it. I'd be planning my next fight or camp. And even when I was home, I wasn't really *at* home. I was barely present, I didn't care. When I look back now, I realise how selfish I was; at the time, of course I missed them badly, but all I was really thinking about was the fight. I wasn't willing to let anything get between me and becoming world champion.

Knowing that actually affects me more now than it did then. I feel almost a sense of disgust that I could have put fighting before my family. My children didn't ask to be born – I was the one who put them on this planet. They don't care if I'm world champion or not. My eldest lad is fifteen and he's only just beginning to play competitive football now. That's my fault. I should have been there to take him to games.

It was change that gave me the space to interrogate and reorder my priorities. What seemed essential to me ten years, five years, even two years ago, is now less significant. As time has gone on, I've lost touch with lots of the people who were important to me through my career. We've all changed. I'm never going to stop being grateful to my team, I'm proud of what we achieved together and know that although I was the only person actually going into the ring, I never felt I was alone. But I've realised that, for me, the be-all and end-all is everything that happens within the four walls of my home. What's important is what I create out of these kids and what I pass on to them.

Change can be bewildering. It can feel as if it's shaking everything in your life. But when it does happen, you should see it as a welcome chance to work out what's most important to you. You might end up surprising yourself.

## KEEP SETTING GOALS

Once I'd retired, I realised I'd become what I wanted to be, I'd earned what I ever wanted to earn and I'd got everything out of the sport I'd ever wanted. What was I supposed to do with my life?

I don't know if I'll ever again be gripped by a relationship as obsessive as the one I had with boxing. But I know I still have to keep setting myself goals. Even if it's little things, like golf (which I'm spending a lot more time, and far too much money, on) or just trying to make my relationship better with my wife and kids. I'm also involved in charity schemes. One that I'm particularly passionate about at the moment is called Weapons Down Gloves Up. When I was growing up, there were shootings in my area, but only serious people could get hold of guns, so deaths were few and far between. Now, however, it feels as if stabbings are becoming an epidemic. So I want to do what I can to encourage kids to think twice about doing something very stupid.

At home I want to bring up my boys to understand how lucky they are. I want to do everything I can to be happy and healthy and to maintain great relationships with my whole family. Most importantly of all, I want to do everything I can to support them in their dreams.

None of these activities will ever take over my life like boxing did, but until I do find that big new passion, they all help to give meaning and structure to it. I still get the sense that I'm learning new things, taking little steps forwards.

This book, the process of writing it, of taking myself out of my comfort zone, of trusting other people, in a world I know nothing about, has been one of those steps. Thank you for taking it with me.

# SUMMARY

- Change, like failure, is a fact of life. Don't fight it – use it as another chance to grow.

- Don't look back. If you're going to make the most of change, you cannot be clinging to the past.

- When one phase of your life ends, it can be difficult to work out what to do next. Don't put too much pressure on yourself. Throw yourself into new experiences. Embrace new challenges. Learn new things.

- We can become so focused on putting one foot in front of the other that we rarely look around and ask ourselves whether we're on the right path. Change gives you this opportunity to reassess your life: make sure you take it.

- Whatever happens, no matter how much your life changes, keep setting goals.

# ACKNOWLEDGEMENTS

Rachael. I said it at the beginning of this book and I'll say it at the end: it's all because of you.

Dad, all I ever wanted to do was impress you.

My boys. One day I hope you read this and understand that you were all the motivation I needed thoughout all the pain and the sacrifices.

Gary Dilsey and Fran Perry. You always believed I'd get there. I've spent many months with both of you living in apartments across the world. I hope I represented DoorSec as well as you'd hoped.

To my past coaches at Rotunda ABC. My goals wouldn't have been possible without you. That gym changed my life.

To Mick McAllister. You are a good man and a great coach. A student of the game. I'll never hear a bad word said against you and I'm so grateful for what you did for me.

To the man who changed me as a professional fighter, Dave Coldwell. You are an amazing teacher and people don't give you enough credit. I wouldn't have become world champion without you.

To Eddie Hearn. Thank you for your honesty and keeping your word. Even though I should have got a bit more on a couple of occasions (ha ha), you and your dad genuinely made me believe in boxing again after I'd been scarred. You both helped save boxing in this country.

To Albo. Jimmy, you are the greatest. I miss you and I love you. Bernie is doing great and your boys Mikey and James are both Rotunda ABC through and through. I know you'll be very proud of them.

I'll give the last word to Ashley Roberts. Your sister, your mum, your dad, Colin, Sarah, Neil, Budgie, we all miss you dearly, lad. We will never forget you and I believe you're up there now smiling at your football team and laughing at mine. You were the gentle giant with a heart of gold. I'll see you again, lad x.